'The handbook is a timely, one-stop resource that covers some of the most important aspects of EU-Africa relations. Contributions are historically grounded and theoretically sound, and they point to a glaring, albeit underappreciated, fact, which is that EU-Africa relations are a significant dimension of global politics, both historically and in contemporary times, and are bound to shape the future in dynamic ways.'

Amy Niang, *University of the Witwatersrand, South Africa*

'This is an essential and comprehensive guide on the current state of debates in Africa-EU relations. It is timely, as the EU and the AU are reorganising the relationship, and will be highly interesting to scholars and practitioners.'

Christine Hackenesch, *German Development Institute, Germany*

'Against the backdrop of deep structural changes impacting the EU and Africa, this handbook provides a much-needed reference for navigating through the meanders of EU-Africa relations and making sense of this unique and troubled partnership. The collection of essays included in this impressive volume provides a well-crafted and intellectually engaging mix of theoretical, empirical and policy analyses that will appeal to all students and professionals of EU-Africa relations. A noteworthy contribution to the field.'

Jack R. Mangala, *Grand Valley State University, USA*

'This handbook is a timely addition to the study of EU-Africa relations and is set to be a standard reference for scholars and practitioners alike. Drawing together contributions from a wide range of experts, this volume uniquely blends historical contexts, contemporary dynamics and future-oriented insights in providing comprehensive and critical analysis of the theoretic perspectives, themes, issues and practices central to EU-Africa relations.'

Faith Mabera, *Institute for Global Dialogue, South Africa*

'At a time when other actors and processes are shaking up the historical connections between the EU and Africa, this timely collection provides excellent insights into these enduring, if strained, relationships.'

Ian Taylor, *University of St Andrews, UK*

'This is a timely and pioneering volume on the relationship between the European Union and Africa, and an essential guide to understanding the evolving interaction and collaboration between the two continents. The contributions boldly interrogate and navigate through the asymmetrical relationship that has historically existed between Europe and Africa. This seminal book outlines practical modalities of how to consolidate and strengthen the partnership between the two continents, as a basis for addressing persistent global challenges.'

Tim Murithi, *University of the Free State, South Africa*

'Africa matters in a world in which multilateralism is in decline; not only does the continent have more than a quarter of the world's states, but it is also home to novel technologies and energetic networks. This timely volume captures the dynamics of Africa in 2020 and the new generation of analysts and approaches – African agency advancing development alternatives via multifaceted interregional relations with an EU in flux.'

Timothy M. Shaw, *University of Massachusetts Boston, USA*

'As the European Union and Africa are redefining their relationship in a fast-changing world, this excellent edition of chapters could not be more timely. Thanks to the contributors' depth of expertise, the handbook offers an invaluable assessment of the intricacies of this relationship.'

Jean-Marc Trouille, *University of Bradford, UK*

The Routledge Handbook of EU-Africa Relations

This handbook provides a comprehensive overview of the changing dynamics in the relationship between the African continent and the EU, provided by leading experts in the field.

Structured into five parts, the handbook provides an incisive look at the past, present and potential futures of EU-Africa relations. The cutting-edge chapters cover themes like multilateralism, development assistance, institutions, gender equality and science and technology, among others. Thoroughly researched, this book provides original reflections from a diversity of conceptual and theoretical perspectives, from experts in Africa, Europe and beyond. The handbook thus offers rich and comprehensive analyses of contemporary global politics as manifested in Africa and Europe.

The Routledge Handbook of EU-Africa Relations will be an essential reference for scholars, students, researchers, policymakers and practitioners interested and working in a range of fields within the (sub)disciplines of African and EU studies, European politics and international studies.

The Routledge Handbook of EU-Africa Relations is part of the mini-series Europe in the World Handbooks examining EU-regional relations and established by Professor Wei Shen.

Toni Haastrup is Senior Lecturer in International Politics at the University of Stirling in Scotland, United Kingdom.

Luís Mah is Lecturer in Development Studies at ISEG (Lisbon School of Economics and Management), Universidade de Lisboa, Portugal; and an Associate at CEsA (Centre for African and Development Studies) at ISEG. He is also a Policy and Advocacy Officer for ACEP (Association for the Cooperation of the People), a Portuguese development NGO.

Niall Duggan is Lecturer in the Department of Government and Politics at University College Cork, Ireland.

Routledge International Handbooks
Europe in the World Handbooks *(sub-series)*
Series Editor: *Wei Shen, Deakin University, Australia, and EU-Asia Centre, ESSCA School of Management, France*

THE ROUTLEDGE HANDBOOK OF EU-AFRICA RELATIONS
Edited by Toni Haastrup, Luís Mah and Niall Duggan

The Routledge Handbook of EU-Africa Relations

This handbook provides a comprehensive overview of the changing dynamics in the relationship between the African continent and the EU, provided by leading experts in the field.

Structured into five parts, the handbook provides an incisive look at the past, present and potential futures of EU-Africa relations. The cutting-edge chapters cover themes like multilateralism, development assistance, institutions, gender equality and science and technology, among others. Thoroughly researched, this book provides original reflections from a diversity of conceptual and theoretical perspectives, from experts in Africa, Europe and beyond. The handbook thus offers rich and comprehensive analyses of contemporary global politics as manifested in Africa and Europe.

The Routledge Handbook of EU-Africa Relations will be an essential reference for scholars, students, researchers, policymakers and practitioners interested and working in a range of fields within the (sub)disciplines of African and EU studies, European politics and international studies.

The Routledge Handbook of EU-Africa Relations is part of the mini-series Europe in the World Handbooks examining EU-regional relations and established by Professor Wei Shen.

Toni Haastrup is Senior Lecturer in International Politics at the University of Stirling in Scotland, United Kingdom.

Luís Mah is Lecturer in Development Studies at ISEG (Lisbon School of Economics and Management), Universidade de Lisboa, Portugal; and an Associate at CEsA (Centre for African and Development Studies) at ISEG. He is also a Policy and Advocacy Officer for ACEP (Association for the Cooperation of the People), a Portuguese development NGO.

Niall Duggan is Lecturer in the Department of Government and Politics at University College Cork, Ireland.

Routledge International Handbooks
Europe in the World Handbooks *(sub-series)*
Series Editor: *Wei Shen, Deakin University, Australia, and EU-Asia Centre, ESSCA School of Management, France*

THE ROUTLEDGE HANDBOOK OF EU-AFRICA RELATIONS
Edited by Toni Haastrup, Luís Mah and Niall Duggan

The Routledge Handbook of EU-Africa Relations

Edited by Toni Haastrup, Luís Mah and Niall Duggan

LONDON AND NEW YORK

First published 2021
by Routledge
2 Park Square, Milton Park, Abingdon, Oxon OX14 4RN

and by Routledge
52 Vanderbilt Avenue, New York, NY 10017

Routledge is an imprint of the Taylor & Francis Group, an informa business

© 2021 selection and editorial matter, Toni Haastrup, Luís Mah and Niall Duggan; individual chapters, the contributors

The right of Toni Haastrup, Luís Mah and Niall Duggan to be identified as the authors of the editorial material, and of the authors for their individual chapters, has been asserted in accordance with sections 77 and 78 of the Copyright, Designs and Patents Act 1988.

All rights reserved. No part of this book may be reprinted or reproduced or utilised in any form or by any electronic, mechanical, or other means, now known or hereafter invented, including photocopying and recording, or in any information storage or retrieval system, without permission in writing from the publishers.

Trademark notice: Product or corporate names may be trademarks or registered trademarks, and are used only for identification and explanation without intent to infringe.

British Library Cataloguing-in-Publication Data
A catalogue record for this book is available from the British Library

Library of Congress Cataloging-in-Publication Data
Names: Haastrup, Toni, 1983– editor. | Mah, Luís, editor. | Duggan, Niall, editor.
Title: The Routledge handbook of EU-Africa relations/edited by Toni Haastrup,
Luís Mah and Niall Duggan.
Other titles: Handbook of EU-Africa relations
Description: Abingdon, Oxon; New York, NY: Routledge, 2021. |
Series: Routledge international handbooks | Includes bibliographical references and index.
Identifiers: LCCN 2020033007 (print) | LCCN 2020033008 (ebook) |
ISBN 9781138047303 (hardback) | ISBN 9781315170916 (ebook)
Subjects: LCSH: European Union countries–Foreign relations–Africa. |
Africa–Foreign relations–European Union countries. |
European Union countries–Foreign economic relations–Africa. |
Africa–Foreign economic relations–European Union countries. |
Economic development–Africa–International cooperation.
Classification: LCC JZ1570.A56 R68 2021 (print) |
LCC JZ1570.A56 (ebook) | DDC 341.242/2096–dc23
LC record available at https://lccn.loc.gov/2020033007
LC ebook record available at https://lccn.loc.gov/2020033008

ISBN: 978-1-138-04730-3 (hbk)
ISBN: 978-1-315-17091-6 (ebk)

Typeset in Bembo
by Newgen Publishing UK

To our mothers

Contents

List of figures	xiii
List of tables	xiv
List of contributors	xv
Preface	xxiii
Abbreviations	xxv

    Introduction   1
    Niall Duggan, Toni Haastrup and Luís Mah

PART I
Theorising Africa-EU relations through history   7

    Introduction to Part I   9
    Toni Haastrup

1 International Relations theory: Comparative reflections on EU–Africa relations   14
    Olukayode A. Faleye

2 Regionalism and interregionalism in EU-Africa relations   26
    Frank Mattheis

3 Applying postcolonial approaches to studies of Africa-EU relations   38
    Rahel Weldeab Sebhatu

PART II
Evolving governance in EU-Africa relations   51

    Introduction to Part II   53
    Mary Farrell

Contents

4 From the Treaty of Rome to Cotonou: Continuity and change in the governance of EU-Africa relations — 59
António Raimundo

5 Foreign policy and EU-Africa relations: From the European Security Strategy to the EU Global Strategy — 70
Lesley Masters and Chris Landsberg

6 European External Action Service — 80
Nele Marianne Ewers-Peters

7 European Neighbourhood Policy in the South Mediterranean — 90
Anthony Costello

8 The evolution of the Joint Africa-EU Strategy (2007–2020) — 105
Fergus Kell and Alex Vines

9 The African Union as an interlocutor in European Union-Africa relations? — 121
John Akokpari and Primrose Z.J. Bimha

PART III
Issues in EU-Africa relations — 131

Introduction to Part III — 133
Nicoletta Pirozzi and Bernardo Venturi

10 EU development cooperation with Africa: The Holy Grail of coordination — 144
Sarah Delputte and Jan Orbie

11 Democracy and human rights promotion — 159
Edalina Rodrigues Sanches

12 Peace and security in the context of EU-Africa relations — 175
Ueli Staeger and Tshepo T. Gwatiwa

13 Regional integration — 188
Giulia Piccolino

14 Interregionalism and bilateralism in the context of EU-Africa relations — 202
Andrzej Polus

15 Trade and the Economic Partnership Agreements in EU-Africa relations — 211
Victor Adetula and Chike Osegbue

16 Africa-Europe science, technology and innovation cooperation: Trends, challenges and opportunities 224
John Ouma-Mugabe and Petronella Chaminuka

PART IV
External actors in Africa's international politics and the Africa-European Union relationship 233

Introduction to Part IV 235
Andrew Cottey

17 Inter-organisational cooperation in flux? Impact of resources and state interests in the cooperation between the European Union, United Nations and African Union 241
Norman Sempijja

18 The China effect: African agency, derivative power and renegotiation of EU-Africa relations 256
Obert Hodzi

19 EU-Brazil-Africa triangular cooperation in the 21st century: Unfinished business 266
Carolina Pavese and Guilherme Ziebell de Oliveira

20 Toward a post-Westphalian turn in Africa-EU studies? Non-state actors and sustainable development 282
Mark Langan and Sophia Price

PART V
Opportunities to cooperate on new global challenges 293

Introduction to Part V 295
Asteris Huliaras and Sophia Kalantzakos

21 Migration and the Mediterranean Sea: A maritime bridge between the EU and Africa 301
Ana Paula Moreira Rodriguez Leite, Thauan Santos and Daniele Dionísio da Silva

22 Environment and climate change in the context of EU-Africa relations 314
Simon Lightfoot

23 The role of civil society in EU-Africa relations 324
Uzoamaka Madu

Contents

24 Agriculture and land in EU–Africa relations   336
    Edward Lahiff

25 Gendering cooperation   349
    Laura Davis

    Conclusion   358
    Luís Mah, Toni Haastrup and Niall Duggan

Index   363

Figures

10.1	The evolving meaning of EU coordination	145
11.1	Major aid uses by individual Development Assistance Committee donors (% of total bilateral commitments)	165
11.2	Percentage of EU development aid (gross disbursements) for good governance, as received by various sectors (2007–2016)	166
11.3	Freedom in Africa (1973–2017)	167
11.4	Overview of selected human rights in Africa (1981–2011)	168
15.1	EU trade with Africa (2007–2016) (€ billion)	216
15.2	EU trade with Africa, by product group (Standard International Trade Classification section) (2016) (€ billion)	217
19.1	ABC expenditures on cooperation projects with Africa (USD) (2000–2014)	269
19.2	Brazil-Africa bilateral trade (USD million) (2002–2014)	271
21.1	Mediterranean routes to the EU	303
21.2	Maritime jurisdictions in the Mediterranean Sea	310

Tables

11.1	Promotion of human rights and democracy: Key agreements and funding instruments	163
11.2	Net disbursements of ODA to sub-Saharan Africa, by donor	164
11.3	Determinants of democracy	171
12.1	Overlap of EU, AU and UN peacekeeping missions in Africa, since 1990	180
12.2	Deployment of military, police and civilian personnel in peace and security in Africa (2018)	181
13.1	Financial allocations to regional programmes under the 8th, 9th, 10th and 11th EDF (€ million)	192
13.2	Financial allocations to regional programmes under the 11th EDF (2014–2020) (€ million)	193
14.1	Selected EU Member States' embassies (with the exclusion of consulates) in Africa	206
15.1	Trends in EU–Africa trade (1980–2001)	214
19.1	EU-Brazil Strategic Partnership and triangular cooperation with Africa	275
21.1	Irregular arrivals by sea, by route (2015–2019) and by main origins, main destinations and sex (2018)	304

Contributors

Victor Adetula is Head of Research at the Nordic Africa Institute, Sweden, and Professor of International Relations and Development Studies at the University of Jos (Nigeria).

John Akokpari is an Associate Professor/Senior Lecturer in the Department of Political Studies, University of Cape Town, South Africa. He has a PhD from Dalhousie University, Canada (1996), and his research interests include globalisation and Africa, Africa's international relations, international migration and democratisation in Africa.

Primrose Z.J. Bimha is an International Relations scholar who is currently studying towards a PhD at the University of Cape Town, South Africa. Her research interests include foreign policy analysis, strategic cooperation, migration studies and gender justice. She previously served as Policy Research Officer in the Zimbabwe Ministry of Foreign Affairs and International Trade and has taught courses on Global Governance and Development.

Petronella Chaminuka is the Principal Economist at the Agricultural Research Council (ARC) in South Africa. She heads the Economic Analysis Unit, which is responsible for integrating socioeconomics in ARC research programmes and evaluating the impact of ARC research and development programmes to guide investment decisions. Petronella holds a PhD in Environmental Economics from Wageningen University in the Netherlands and an MSc in Agricultural Economics from the University of Zimbabwe. She has more than 20 years' international experience working as a lecturer, researcher and facilitator in rural development processes. Her research interests are in agricultural and food policy analysis, food security and livelihoods analysis, HIV/AIDS and gender-integrated planning. With extensive experience working in multidisciplinary teams, she has participated in many international collaborative projects focusing on capacity development and research. Petronella participated in WP5 of the ProIntensAfrica project and several workshops of the CAASTNet Plus projects.

Anthony Costello is a Lecturer in Politics and International Relations in the School of Humanities at Liverpool Hope University. His research interests lie in national preference formation and intergovernmental preference bargaining in EU negotiations. As per the scope of his research, he has a special interest in economic governance and EU foreign policy decision-making. In addition to his research on EU decision-making, he has conducted research on the EU's democratic deficit in the face of the Future of Europe Debate. He is currently the convener of the PSAI Participatory and Deliberative Democracy Specialist Group.

List of contributors

Andrew Cottey is EU Jean Monnet Chair in European Political Integration and Senior Lecturer in the Department of Government and Politics, University College Cork, Ireland. His publications include *Security in 21st Century Europe* (Palgrave Macmillan, 2nd edition, 2013), *Understanding Chinese Politics: An Introduction to Government in the People's Republic of China* (co-authored with Neil Collins, Manchester University Press, 2012) and *Reshaping Defence Diplomacy: New Roles for Military Cooperation and Assistance* (co-authored with Anthony Forster, Oxford University Press/IISS, 2004), as well as articles in journals such as *JCMS: Journal of Common Market Studies*, *International Affairs*, *Armed Forces & Society*, *European Security*, *Contemporary Security Policy* and *European Foreign Affairs Review*.

Laura Davis is Senior Associate leading the European Peacebuilding Liaison Office's work on Gender, Peace and Security. She is also a Senior Consultant on gender and political economy analysis and transitional justice. She is now based in the Middle East after a decade working in and on central Africa. Laura holds a Master's in Modern History from the University of Oxford, United Kingdom, and a PhD in Political Science from the University of Ghent, Belgium. Her book *EU Foreign Policy, Transitional Justice and Mediation* (Routledge, 2014) is the first scholarly analysis of this subject, and she publishes extensively on transitional justice, mediation and women's empowerment.

Sarah Delputte is a Post-doctoral Assistant at the Centre for EU Studies and Lecturer in the Department of Political Science at Ghent University, Belgium. In her teaching and research she takes a critical approach to EU development policy and the interlinkages with other external policy fields, as well as EU interregional relations with Africa, the Caribbean and the Pacific. She also co-supervises several PhD projects relating to these topics. She has extensive field research experience in sub-Saharan Africa. Her research has been published in various edited volumes and international journals. She is a co-convener of the European Association of Development Research and Training Institutes working group on the European Union as a Development Actor.

Daniele Dionísio da Silva is a Professor in the Institute of International Relations and Defense (IRID) at the Federal University of Rio de Janeiro (UFRJ), Brazil. She holds a PhD (2015) and a Master's in Comparative History (2011) from UFRJ. She is Vice-coordinator of the Laboratory of Studies of Security and Defense at the IRID and Researcher at the Laboratory of Simulations and Scenarios at the Brazilian Navy War College. Her studies focus on international relations, security and national defence, military technical cooperation, public policy and maritime studies.

Niall Duggan is a Lecturer in the Department of Government and Politics at University College Cork, Ireland, where he teaches on International Relations, International Political Economy and Asia Studies. His main research focuses are emerging economies in global governance and international relations (IR) of the Global South, with a special focus on Sino-African and Sino-EU-African relations. The theoretical focus of his research is non-Western IR theory, the development of role theory and the role of ideas in IR.

Nele Marianne Ewers-Peters is a Postdoctoral Fellow in the School of Advanced International Studies at Johns Hopkins University, United States, and a Research Fellow at the Global Europe Centre at the University of Kent, United Kingdom. She previously taught at the University of Kent and University College London. Her research focuses on the relationship between security organisations, including the African Union, the European Union and the North Atlantic Treaty Organization and the study of the contemporary European security architecture.

Olukayode A. Faleye is a Lecturer in the Department of History and International Studies at the Edo University Iyamho, Nigeria. He holds a Bachelor's degree in History and a Master's in African Studies. He holds a PhD in History and International Studies from the University of Ilorin, Nigeria.

Mary Farrell is Professor in International Relations in the School of Government at the University of Plymouth, United Kingdom. Her research interests include the political and policy processes in global governance, the interface between regional and global governance, the United Nations in global politics and policy, European Union external relations and Africa in the international system. She has published widely on the European Union at the United Nations, EU-Africa relations and comparative regionalism.

Tshepo T. Gwatiwa is a Lecturer in the Department of International Relations at the University of the Witwatersrand in Johannesburg, South Africa. He is also a Research Associate at the African Centre for the Study of the United States at University of the Witwatersrand. He is joint editor of *Expanding US Military Command in Africa: Elites, Networks and Strategy* (Routledge, forthcoming). His publications have appeared in *Intelligence and National Security* and *Review of African Political Economy*.

Toni Haastrup is a Senior Lecturer in International Politics at the University of Stirling in Scotland. She is also joint Editor in Chief of *JCMS: Journal of Common Market Studies*. Her research focuses on regionalisms including Africa-EU relations, the security practices of regional organisations and intersectional feminist international studies, with a particular focus on the Women, Peace and Security agenda. She has published widely on these themes.

Obert Hodzi is a Lecturer in Politics at the University of Liverpool, United Kingdom. His research focuses on the politics of human rights and development and non-Western emerging powers in global governance, with empirical expertise in China and Africa. He holds a PhD in Political Science from Lingnan University, Hong Kong.

Asteris Huliaras is Professor in Comparative Politics and International Relations in the Department of Political Science and International Relations at the University of the Peloponnese, Greece, where he holds a Jean Monnet Chair on EU relations with Less Developed Countries. His articles on Africa's international relations have appeared – among others – in *African Affairs*, *Commonwealth and Comparative Politics*, *Conflict, Security & Development*, *Geopolitics*, *Global Society*, *The Hague Journal of Diplomacy*, *JCMS: Journal of Common Market Studies*, *Journal of Contemporary African Studies*, *The Journal of Modern African Studies*, *The Journal of North African Studies*, *Middle East Policy*, *Orbis*, *The Round Table: The Commonwealth Journal of International Affairs* and *Survival: Global Politics and Strategy*.

Sophia Kalantzakos is Global Distinguished Professor in Environmental Studies and Public Policy at New York University/NYU Abu Dhabi. During 2019–2020 she was a Fung Fellow at Princeton's Institute for International and Regional Studies, working on China's Belt and Road Initiative in the Horn of Africa. In the 2020–2021 academic year she will be Senior Fellow at the Rogers/Research Institute for the History of Science and Technology at Caltech and the

List of contributors

Huntington. Her most recent books include *China and the Geopolitics of Rare Earths* (Oxford University Press, 2018) and *The EU, US, and China Tackling Climate Change: Polices and Alliances for the Anthropocene* (Routledge, 2017).

Fergus Kell is Projects Assistant with the Chatham House Africa Programme, where he provides logistical and research support to the programme's project-based activities. He holds an MPhil in International Relations and Politics from the University of Cambridge, United Kingdom.

Edward Lahiff is a Lecturer in International Development at University College Cork, Ireland. He spent ten years in southern Africa working with rural non-governmental organisations and at the University of the Western Cape, South Africa. His current research focuses on links between small-scale farming and nutrition in Ethiopia and the experience of rural-urban migrants in Vietnam. Dr Lahiff has published widely on food, agriculture and land reform in Africa

Chris Landsberg is Professor and Chair of African Diplomacy and Foreign Policy at the University of Johannesburg (UJ), South Africa, and Senior Associate at the UJ School of Leadership. He is the former Head of Politics and International Relations at UJ. He studied as a Rhodes Scholar at Oxford and was formerly Hamburg Fellow at Stanford University in the United States. Previously he was Director of the Centre for Policy Studies in Johannesburg and Co-founder and Co-director of the Centre for Africa's International Relations at the University of the Witwatersrand in South Africa.

Mark Langan is a Senior Lecturer in International Politics at Newcastle University. He is author of *Neo-colonialism and the Poverty of 'Development' in Africa* (Palgrave Macmillan, 2018).

Simon Lightfoot is Professor of Politics at the University of Leeds, United Kingdom. He is co-convenor of the European Union as a Development Actor working group for the European Association of Development Research and Training Institutes.

Uzoamaka Madu is a Public Affairs and Communications Consultant based in Brussels, Belgium, specialising in Africa-Europe relations. She supports African and international organisations to raise their profile, tell their stories and be heard in order to shape the EU policy decisions that affect them. She has more than eight years of experience in strategic communications and public affairs in the European Union and international landscape in various sectors such as healthcare, agriculture, digital and trade. She has worked in a number of leading EU consultancies, supporting her clients to navigate through the EU decision-making process and speak to policymakers and the public to further their organisational goals. Uzoamaka is also an experienced moderator and public speaker, having spoken at several high-level conferences, including the London School of Economics and Political Science's Africa Summit, the World Trade Organization's Aid for Trade Review, the European Commission's European Development Days and the EU-Africa Business Summit. She has also provided commentary for BBC News, *African Business* magazine, Forbes Africa, Ventures Africa and *International Politics & Society*. She is the creator of What's in it for Africa – an online platform dedicated to commentary and analysis of the Africa-Europe relationship, with a distinct focus on the African viewpoint.

Luís Mah is a Lecturer in Development Studies at ISEG (Lisbon School of Economics & Management), Universidade de Lisboa, Portugal. He is also an associate at CEsA (Centre for

Africa and Development Studies) at ISEG and has been working as global development advocate and policy officer for non-governmental organisations for more than a decade. His current research focuses on the role of multilateral and bilateral development finance institutions and the business sector in addressing the Sustainable Development Goals.

Lesley Masters is Programme Lead and a Lecturer on International Relations and Diplomacy at the University of Derby, United Kingdom, and a Senior Research Associate as well as SARChI Chair in African Diplomacy and Foreign Policy at the University of Johannesburg, South Africa. She has also held the position of Senior Researcher and Lecturer at the University of Johannesburg. Prior to this, Lesley was a Senior Researcher at the Institute for Global Dialogue based in Pretoria, South Africa, responsible for the management of projects on foreign policy and diplomacy. She received her PhD in International Relations from the University of Leicester, United Kingdom. Her research continues to focus on South Africa's foreign policy, global governance and international diplomacy.

Frank Mattheis is a Researcher at the Institute for European Studies at the Université libre de Bruxelles, Belgium, as well as an Associate Research Fellow at the United Nations University Institute on Comparative Regional Integration Studies and the University of Pretoria, South Africa. He is trained in Global Studies and holds an MA from the Universities of Leipzig, Germany, and Vienna, Austria, and a DPhil from the University of Leipzig. His research deals with processes of region-making and unmaking, comparative regionalism and interregionalism.

Ana Paula Moreira Rodriguez Leite is a Researcher and Pós-doctorate at the COPPEAD Institute, Federal University of Rio de Janeiro (UFRJ), Brazil. She holds a master's degree and PhD in Comparative History from UFRJ. She is a Researcher for the Pró-Defesa IV project funded by the Ministry of Defense of Brazil and CAPES (Coordenação de Aperfeiçoamento de Pessoal de Nível Superior).

Jan Orbie is an Associate Professor in the Department of Political Science and member of the Centre for EU Studies at Ghent University, Belgium. His research focuses on EU external relations, in particular the external trade, social, development, humanitarian aid and democracy promotion policies of the European Union. He has recently published papers and op-eds on EU fair trade policy and European aid policy from a post-development perspective. He has co-edited special issues on pluralism in EU trade politics (*Journal of Contemporary European Research*, 2013), the EU trade-development nexus (*Contemporary Politics*, 2014), EU democracy promotion (*European Foreign Affairs Review*, 2011; *Cambridge Review of International Affairs*, 2015), the Europeanisation of development (*European Politics and Society*, 2016), labour rights in EU trade policies (*Politics and Governance*, 2017) and politicisation of European development policy (*JCMS: Journal of Common Market Studies*, forthcoming).

Chike Osegbue is a Teacher and Researcher in the Department of Political Science, Chukwuemeka Odumegwu Ojukwu University, Igbariam Campus, Nigeria.

John Ouma-Mugabe is a Professor of Science and Innovation Policy at the Graduate School of Technology Management, University of Pretoria, South Africa, and founding Director of the Foundation for Innovation and Technology-Africa, Pretoria. He is former Executive Director of the African Centre for Technology Studies in Nairobi, Kenya, and Director of the Office of Science and Technology of the New Partnership for Africa's Development, Midrand, South Africa.

List of contributors

Carolina Pavese holds a PhD in International Relations from the London School of Economics, United Kingdom. She is an Assistant Professor at ESPM (Escola Superior de Propaganda e Marketing), São Paulo, Brasil. She previously taught on International Relations at the Pontifical Catholic University of Minas Gerais. Dr Pavese's areas of expertise include EU-Brazil relations, multilateralism, international organisations and gender studies.

Giulia Piccolino is a Lecturer in Politics and International Relations in the School of Social Sciences and Humanities at Loughborough University, United Kingdom. She collaborated on the project on The EU, Regional Conflicts and the Promotion of Regional Cooperation, funded by Compagnia di San Paolo through the Europe and Global Challenges programme. She is currently involved in two research projects, one on the consequences of rebel governance in Côte d'Ivoire and one on territorial planning for state-building in post-conflict Colombia.

Nicoletta Pirozzi is Head of the Programme on the European Union and the Institutional Relations Manager at the Istituto Affari Internazionali (IAI), Italy. She works mainly on EU governance, policy and institutional developments in Common Foreign Security Policy/Common Security and Defence Policy, civilian crisis management and EU relations with the United Nations and the African Union. She is the Scientific Coordinator of the Horizon 2020 project EU IDEA – Integration and Differentiation for Effectiveness and Accountability. From 2013 to 2019, she was an Adjunct Professor at Roma Tre University. In 2018, she was an Associate Analyst at the EU Institute for Security Studies in Paris and a Marshall Memorial Fellow. In 2012, she served as Seconded National Expert at the European External Action Service. She is author and editor of a number of publications and an active member of various research associations and institutions. She is also a member of IAI's Steering Committee and Executive Committee and of the Scientific Board of the online journal *AffarInternazionali*.

Andrzej Polus is a Professor in the Institute of International Studies, University of Wroclaw, Poland. His research work focuses on the political economy of hydrocarbons management and the current political situation in sub-Saharan Africa. He has participated – as principal investigator or co-investigator – in 14 research projects devoted to development studies, and he has conducted field research in Botswana, Ghana, Namibia, South Africa, Tanzania, Uganda, Zambia and Zimbabwe.

Sophia Price is Head of Politics and International Relations at Leeds Beckett University, United Kingdom. Her research focuses on feminist political economy and EU-Africa development cooperation relations.

António Raimundo is a Postdoctoral Research Fellow at the University of Minho and an Associate Fellow at ISCTE-University Institute of Lisbon, Portugal. Previously he was an Invited Assistant Professor in International Relations at ISCTE. He holds a PhD in International Relations from the London School of Economics and Political Science. His research and publications have covered topics such as Europe-Africa relations, EU foreign policy, Europeanisation of foreign policy and Portuguese foreign policy.

Edalina Rodrigues Sanches is an Assistant Professor in African Studies and a Researcher at the Centre for International Studies, ISCTE – University Institute of Lisbon. Her research interests comprise democratization, elections, political parties and party systems, with a focus on Africa. She has published in journals such as African Affairs, Journal of Contemporary Africa, Parliamentary

Affairs and Electoral Studies and her latest book is Party Systems in Young Democracies: Varieties of institutionalization in Sub-Saharan Africa *(Routledge, 2018)*.

Thauan Santos is an Assistant Professor at the Graduate Programme in Maritime Studies at the Brazilian Naval War College, Coordinator of the Economy of the Sea Group and a Researcher at the Latin American Council of Social Sciences.

Norman Sempijja is a Senior Lecturer in the School of Law at the University of Navarra in Spain. He has a PhD in International Politics from Kingston University in the United Kingdom, a Master's in Diplomatic Studies from Keele University in the United Kingdom and a BA Social Sciences from Makerere University in Uganda. His research interests are in international security, inter-organisational cooperation, peacekeeping and peacebuilding. His key areas for study include, but are not limited to, Africa, the European Union and the Middle East.

Ueli Staeger is a PhD candidate in International Relations/Political Science at the Graduate Institute of International and Development Studies, Geneva, Switzerland. He is working on a dissertation on the financing and reforms of the African Union. His publications have appeared in *JCMS: Journal of Common Market Studies*, *International Spectator* and *West European Politics*.

Bernardo Venturi is a Senior Fellow at the Istituto Affari Internazionali (IAI), Italy, where he focuses on Africa, civilian crisis management, the European Union's Common Foreign Security Policy/Common Security and Defence Policy, peacebuilding and development. He holds a PhD from the University of Bologna and has 14 years of experience in different think tanks, universities and non-governmental organisations working on research, monitoring and evaluation, teaching, project management and advocacy. He is also Co-Founder and Co-Director of the Agency for Peacebuilding, and he lectures for several international universities and training centres. At IAI, he currently works on different Africa-EU initiatives, contributes to the activities of the European Think Tank Group and leads the research project on Governance and security in the Sahel: Tackling mobility, demography and climate change.

Alex Vines has led the Africa Programme at Chatham House in the United Kingdom since 2002 and became Managing Director for Ethics, Risk and Resilience in 2019. Previously, he has held roles at Chatham House as Director for Regional Studies and International Security and Director for Area Studies and International Law. He chaired the UN Panel of Experts on Côte d'Ivoire from 2005 to 2007 and was a member of the UN Panel of Experts on Liberia from 2001 to 2003. He was also a member of the Commonwealth Observer Group to Mozambique in 2019 (and Ghana in 2016) and a UN election officer in Mozambique (1994) and Angola (1992). He worked at Human Rights Watch as a senior researcher on its Africa, Arms, and Business and Human Rights programmes, and he has served as a consultant, including for the UN Office on Drugs and Crime, the Japan International Cooperation Agency, the UK Department for International Development, the United States Agency for International Development, the European Union and the Economic Community of West African States. He is an Assistant Professor at Coventry University and sits on the editorial and advisory boards for the *South African Journal of International Affairs*, *Africa Review* (journal of the African Studies Association of India) and the *Journal of Southern African Studies*. He is also a director of EG Justice – a non-governmental organisation focused on Equatorial Guinea – and is on the advisory board of the John & Elnora Ferguson Centre for African Studies at the University of Bradford. Alex

List of contributors

was awarded an OBE in 2008 in recognition of his work including founding and developing Chatham House's Africa programme. He holds a PhD from Coventry University.

Rahel Weldeab Sebhatu is a PhD candidate in Global Politics in the Department of Global Political Studies at Malmö University, Sweden. She received her master's degree at Lund University's Graduate School in Global Studies (major: Political Science). Her research interests include international relations, Africa-EU relations, postcolonial feminism, postcolonial theory, decoloniality, negotiation theory, diplomacy, critical security studies, (youth participation in) peacebuilding, pan-Africanism, transnational activism and resistance.

Guilherme Ziebell de Oliveira holds a PhD in Political Science from the Federal University of Rio Grande do Sul (UFRGS) in Brazil, where he is currently a Lecturer. He previously taught at the Pontifical Catholic University of Minas Gerais. He also holds a double BA in International Relations and Economics from UFRGS and was an exchange student at the University of Toulouse II-Le Mirail (2011). His main research interests are the Global South, African studies and international political economy.

Preface

When the series editor Professor Wei Shen invited us to edit this handbook, he had a clear vision – that the collection would reflect our current epoch. This handbook was therefore not going to be about the European Union's (EU's) policy towards Africa. Like Professor Wei Shen – who we must thank for his reviews and suggestions – we were very clear that the existing canon that constituted 'EU-Africa' relations was overtly Eurocentric. This Eurocentrism is not just a moral failing for knowledge but constitutes a major blind spot in that it has failed to fully explore and account for the complex relations between the African continent and the EU. In particular, much of the scholarship of the relationship continues to place the EU materially and normatively in a hegemonic position over Africa. In this handbook, we seek to move away from a lens that looks at the EU's policies in Africa to one that attempts to articulate African agency.

But how do we account for Africa's relationship with Europe (and the EU) to meet our aims when the current narrative of this entanglement shapes much of how we live in Africa and Europe today? Africans and Europeans live with the legacy (and others may argue, present influence) of European colonial rule in Africa every day. For years, challenges by African diaspora to statues of slave traders and the colonial administrators across European capitals have been ignored, much like the negative implications of the militarised interventions in the Sahel and Horn of Africa by Europeans. Africans have never been further from and yet so close to Europe. For much of Africa, the status quo persists, perhaps due to the elite institutionalisation of the relationship.

But Africans, as a diaspora on and off the continent are pushing back. We see this through demands for European museums to return looted art and through the transnational demand of the Black Lives Matters movement. By reflecting on these challenges to the status quo and being motivated not simply by looking at EU policies in Africa but at the relationship holistically, we can know, for example, that the triumphal arch in Brussels Parc du Cinquantenaire is both a beautiful and a grotesque reminder of the relationship between Africa and Europe. Indeed, without Africa or, more precisely, the wealth of Congolese rubber plantations, Brussels, the heart of the EU, would likely not exist. In 2020, we must reckon with these truths of Africa-Europe relations.

Our first meeting as the editors of this handbook was in 2017. We met in Lisbon, the capital city of a country that once counted as a part of its empire Cape Verde, Guinea-Bissau, São Tomé and Príncipe, Angola and Mozambique. As in Brussels, it is difficult to unsee the impact of colonialism on its streets, society and economy. We would say the same for London and Paris, yet it might be surprising to think this was also a characteristic of Lagos or Johannesburg.

These complexities formed a part of our initial discussion as we sought to write a proposal that reflected the multiple layers of African-European relations and how these layers have

Preface

different implications based on global positionalities. Even the title of the book itself confronted us with a challenge. We were very clear that the 'EU-Africa relations' descriptor of the relationship between African countries and the EU itself reflected a means through which hegemonic power relations are institutionalised; in the end, a preference for alphabetic ordering proved challenging. Yet, for the book we committed to ensuring diversity by way of scholar location, gender and discipline. Life has happened since we started, so we likely didn't always get it right. In terms of the focus of each chapter, again, we tried to select topics which would reflect the complex nature of the relationship between Africa and the EU. In particular we have tried to explore areas where challenges often have their root cause in both continents and solutions require actions and cooperation by both African and European actors on a partnership basis – migration, climate change and trade, among others. We also wanted to focus on topics which would move the relationship between Africa and the EU beyond that of the narratives defined by the foreign policy of the former colonial powers such as France, the United Kingdom and Germany or by the major African powers like Nigeria, South Africa and Egypt. This resulted in a greater focus on civil society and institutions, a broader understanding of development cooperation as well as explorations of democracy and human rights promotion and new normative frameworks like the women, peace and security agenda.

Helped by the very useful feedback given to us by the blind reviewers – for which we are grateful – we have tried to strike a balance with regards to themes at a time of rapid change within Africa and Europe and between the two regions. For example, we invited the first set of contributors during the slow exit of the United Kingdom from the EU. This period has also coincided with the move to renegotiate the relationship between African countries and the EU as both actors contend with increased militarisation of EU engagements in Africa as a deterrence to irregular migration. As is often the case with any project of this size, to paraphrase Robert Burns, *the best-laid plans of mice and men often go awry*. Authors and editors during this time had to overcome many challenges and inconveniences, including major health issues, relocation, restriction on academic freedom, budget cuts, strikes, the death of loved ones; yet we have also celebrated important happy moments, including marriages, engagements, promotion and the arrival of new loved ones. Since we started work on this handbook, life has happened – and intensely. With the arrival of COVID-19, the handbook was finally completed in the middle of global pandemic. Authors and editors battled with remote working, poor internet connections and welcome and unwelcome contributions by their pets and children to online meetings.

As the editors, we are indebted to the authors, our co-producers of this knowledge, for making the handbook what it is and especially for their patience and understanding – this was not the end to the journey that we envisioned, but we are grateful. We thank Richard Milner for his assistance in formatting and proofing the text – this support was instrumental to us in the last stages. This handbook would also never have overcome the highs and lows without the helpful encouragement and endless patience of our publishers at Routledge, Sophie Iddamalgoda and Andrew Taylor, who guided us throughout the process. To them, our endless appreciation.

Niall Duggan, Cork, Ireland
Toni Haastrup, Stirling, Scotland
Luís Mah, Lisbon, Portugal

Abbreviations

AAMS	Associated African and Malagasy States
AASM	Associated African States and Madagascar
ACP	African, Caribbean and Pacific
AEEP	Africa-EU Energy Partnership
AEF	Afrique Equatoriale Française
AfCFTA	African Continental Free Trade Area
AGN	African Group of Negotiators
AMCEN	African Ministerial Conference on the Environment
AMCOST	African Ministerial Council on Science and Technology
AMISOM	AU Mission in Somalia
AMU	Arab Maghreb Union
AOF	Afrique Occidentale Française
APF	African Peace Facility
APSA	African Peace and Security Architecture
A-SA	Africa-South America
AU	African Union
BMZ	Federal Ministry of Economic Cooperation and Development (Germany)
BNDES	Brazilian National Bank for Economic and Social Development
BRICS	Brazil, Russia, India, China and South Africa
CARIFORUM	Caribbean Forum
CEAO	Communauté Economique de l'Afrique de l'Ouest
CEEC	Central and Eastern European country
CEMAC	Communauté Économique et Monétaire de l'Afrique Centrale
CEN–SAD	Community of Sahel–Saharan States
CFSP	Common Foreign and Security Policy
CMPD	Crisis Management and Planning Directorate
COMESA	Common Market for Eastern and Southern Africa
COSATU	Congress of South African Trade Unions
CPCC	Civilian Planning and Conduct Capability
CPLP	Community of Portuguese Language Countries

Abbreviations

CSDP	Common Security and Defence Policy
CSO	civil society organisation
DAC	Development Assistance Committee
DCI	Development Cooperation Instrument
DG	Directorate-General
DG DEVCO	Directorate-General for International Cooperation and Development
DGHR	democratic governance and human rights
EAC	East African Community
EACSO	East African Common Services Organization
EC	European Commission
ECCAS	Economic Community of Central African States
ECOSOCC	Economic, Social and Cultural Council
ECOWAS	Economic Community of West African States
ECOWAS-CET	ECOWAS Common External Tariff
EDCTP	European and Developing Countries Clinical Trials Partnership
EDF	European Development Fund
EEAS	European External Action Service
EEC	European Economic Community
EEZ	Exclusive Economic Zone
EIB	European Investment Bank
EIDHR	European Instrument for Democracy and Human Rights
EJN	Economic Justice Network
ENI	European Neighbourhood Instrument
ENP	European Neighbourhood Policy
EPA	Economic Partnership Agreement
ESC	Economic and Social Committee
ESS	European Security Strategy
EU	European Union
EUCAP	European Union Capacity Building Mission
EUD	European Union Delegation
EUGS	European Union Global Strategy
EUNAVFOR	European Union Naval Force
EUROMED	Euro-Mediterranean Partnership
EUSR	European Union Special Representative
EUTM	European Union Training Mission
FAO	Food and Agriculture Organization
FOCAC	Forum on China-Africa Cooperation
FNSSA	Food and Nutrition Security and Sustainable Agriculture
FP	Framework Programme
FTA	free trade agreement

GATT	General Agreement on Tariffs and Trade
GDP	gross domestic product
GGWSSI	Great Green Wall of the Sahara and the Sahel Initiative
HDI	Human Development Index
HR	High Representative of the Union for Foreign Affairs and Security Policy
ICC	International Criminal Court
IcSP	Instrument contributing to Stability and Peace
IGAD	Intergovernmental Authority on Development
IIAG	Ibrahim Index of African Governance
IMF	International Monetary Fund
IPE	International Political Economy (Studies)
IR	International Relations (Studies)
ISIE	Independent High Authority for Elections (Tunisia)
JAES	Joint Africa-EU Strategy
JAP	joint action plan
JEG	Joint Expert Group
JTF	Joint Task Force
LDC	least developed country
LGBT	lesbian, gay, bisexual and transgender
MD	Managing Directorate
MDG	Millennium Development Goal
MPCC	Military Planning and Conduct Capability
NAFSN	New Alliance for Food Security and Nutrition in Africa
NAP	National Action Plan
NATO	North Atlantic Treaty Organization
NEPAD	New Partnership for Africa's Development
NGO	non-governmental organisation
NIEO	New International Economic Order
OAU	Organization of African Unity
ODA	official development aid
OECD	Organisation for Economic Co-operation and Development
PALOP	Portuguese-speaking African Countries
PC	political conditionality
PSD	private sector development
PSO	Peace Support Operation
R&D	research and development
RAP	Regional Action Plan
REC	Regional Economic Community
SADC	Southern African Development Community
SDG	Sustainable Development Goal
SHIBRIG	Standby Forces High Readiness Brigade
SME	small and medium-sized enterprise

Abbreviations

SSR	Security Sector Reform
STI	science, technology and innovation
TDCA	Trade Development and Co-operation Agreement
UfM	Union for the Mediterranean
UN	United Nations
UNCLOS	United Nations Convention on the Law of the Sea
UNDP	United Nations Deleopment Programme
UNECA	United Nations Economic Commission for Africa
UNFCCC	United Nations Framework Convention on Climate Change
UNSCR	United Nations Security Council Resolution
WAEMU	West African Economic and Monetary Union
WPS	Women, Peace and Security
WTO	World Trade Organization
ZOPACAS	South Atlantic Peace and Cooperation Zone

Introduction

Niall Duggan, Toni Haastrup and Luís Mah

Since 2000, relations between the European Union (EU) and African countries and regional organisations, otherwise known as EU-Africa relations, have been undergoing a dynamic institutional and organizational re-ordering. The establishment of periodic EU-Africa/Africa-EU/AU-EU Summits (2000, 2007, 2010, 2014 and 2017) created the basis for a region-to-region forum bringing together African and European leaders. Further, the launch of the 2007 Joint Africa-EU Strategy (JAES) political framework provided the opportunity to change the power asymmetries between Africa and Europe into one in which Africa's agency is better realized. This framework, ostensibly informed by shared values and common interests, thus inferring equality between partners, has not met its potential. At the same time, the debate on the future of the existing Africa-EU relationship is in flux. Despite the JAES which emphasised the equality of region-to-region collaboration, the basis of Africa-EU relationship remains the Cotonou Partnership Agreement. This relationship however also includes EU engagements with Caribbean and Pacific countries (forming the so-called ACP Group[1]). The co-existence of the Cotonou Partnership Agreement which had exclusively set the terms of the post-colonial approach to development, economic and trade and relations between the EU and its member states' former colonies sits uneasily alongside aspirations for a more equal relationship. The EU-ACP arrangement has been criticised for failing to help African states achieve their development goals and for acting as a barrier to the African integration project. Moreover, the dynamic of the African countries and the EU within this relationship ensures that African partners are not treated as equals to their European counterparts. Despite these critiques, the EU continues to reify the transregional Cotonou Partnership Agreement, which formally expired on 29 February 2020. Although negotiations have been ongoing to seek a replacement to this specific arrangement, disagreements and the articulation of regional agency in Africa, primarily through the African Union (AU) has contributed to the delays in renewal. The 2020 COVID-19 has not helped and consequently the proposal for a new solution on the basis of EU-ACP relations has been delayed in the first instance until 2021.

The tensions between the aspirations of the JAES and the persistence of the EU-ACP relations have come about as a result of the EU claiming to want to further solidify its relationship with African actors through greater levels of cooperation. Discursively, the EU emphasises equality and partnership as the basis for deeper cooperation, the same framing for the JAES.

Further commitment to the direction of such a relationship has been articulated in the 2016 EU Global Strategy (see also Masters and Landsberg, this volume), the 2017 European External Investment Plan (European Commission, 2016) and the 2018 Africa-Europe Alliance for Sustainable Development and Jobs (European Commission, 2018) proposed by former president of the European Commission Jean Claude Junker and most recently with the 2020 EU-Africa Strategy (European Commission, 2020). This is a logical step from the EU's perspective having gone itself through an organizational and institutional transformation since the 2009 Treaty of Lisbon. This Treaty created new institutions and legal instruments to strengthen the EU's external action: the new post of High Representative (HR) for Foreign Affairs and Security (FASP) (who is simultaneously vice-president of the European Commission) and the European External Action Service (EEAS). The Treaty thus sought to institutionalize the EU's external relations actions and capabilities. These new EU institutions and legal instruments have created a new dynamic in Africa's relationship with the EU (Haastrup, 2013; Helly 2013; Mangala 2013b). However, in many ways, these new tools have been used to reinforce the role of the EU as a normative power in EU-Africa relations, propagating the unequal relationship between the EU and Africa (Bossuyt, Orbie and Drieghe, 2020; Luciano, 2020; Staeger, 2016).

Changes have also been abounding on the African side since 2000. In 2000, African leaders re-committed to a new regional institution, the African Union (AU) to replace its lackluster predecessor Organization for African Unity (OAU) created in 1963. In light of the changes happening at the African and European levels, the Cairo Declaration and Action plan of 2000 was the first signal towards a new interregional relationship that set out a clear political dialogue between Africa and Europe within a framework of inter-regionalism (Haastrup, 2013: 4). The creation of the AU provided the EU with a new interlocutor committed to the ideal of intensified regional integration, a uniquely shared aspiration with the EU. Launched in 2002, the AU draws on some of the EU's organogram including a Commission. However, the AU lacks the same delegated authority that is present within the EU, remains strictly inter-governmental for the most part and with limited capacity is comparison to the EU (see also Haastrup, 2013; Farrell, 2013; Murithi, 2005; Akokpari, Ndinga-Muvumba, Murithi, 2008). Since its inception and especially since 2015, the AU has made major strides to position itself as the main continental/regional interlocutor on behalf of Africa and Africans, and thus a major global actor. In addition to spearheading innovative moves within the global governance architecture, for example, the development of a women's mediator network (FemWise) alongside other regional women's mediator networks, there was a lot of emphasis on regional economic integration.

By 2017, the economy of the AU, collectively, making it larger than the economies of Italy and Spain (Eurostat 2019). But it was also very fragmented with many barriers to intracontinental trade. Following years of negotiation and a lot of labour on the part of the AU institutions, African leaders consented to the created of the African Continental Free Trade Area (AfCFTA) under the aegis of the AU. AfCFTA is the largest free trade area since the creation of the World Trade Organization in 1995. AfCFTA created a single continental market for goods and services, lowering tariffs on at least 90 percent of products traded across AU member with plans to reduce tariffs to a maximum of 3 percent by 2035 (Luke and Macleod 2019, Obeng-Odoom 2020).

The changing dynamics between and within the two regions have developed alongside global transformations with the rising role of (re-)emerging economies led by Brazil, India, Russia and the People's Republic of China (Carmody, 2013; van der Merwe, Taylor and Arkhangelskaya, 2016). This has helped foster a growing South-South cooperation with African leaders, who are now more confident and ready to assert their views on global affairs as their countries become more integrated in the world economy, diversify their international alliances and affirm their development policy choices (Modi, 2011; Gürcan, 2019). This new posture impacts the relational patterns of Africa with its most important trade and aid partner – the EU. External actors' increased activity on the continent and the possible re-emergence of the United Kingdom as a competitor in Africa (Mold, 2018; Price, 2019) has forced the EU to re-evaluate its approach towards Africa.

The new European Commission led by Ursula von der Leyen has made clear that the EU is pivoting to Africa directed by geopolitics. This pivot was backed up most recently by the 10th AUC-EC Commission-to-Commission meeting, which took place in early 2020. It was held at the AU's headquarters in Addis Ababa and was attended by 22 EU commissioners – the largest delegation ever to be sent outside the EU (European Commission 2020). This was highly symbolic and intended to signal the seriousness with which the EU now looked to its African partners in forging ahead with a reinvigorated rule based multilateral order. The message from the EU delegation was that 2020 would be a pivotal year for Africa-EU relations, as the EU recommits to moving away from the asymmetric relationship of old, not just because it is right but because it can no longer afford not to. But the extent to which the new geopolitical orientation which prioritises interests is compatible with the partnership aspiration ought to be questioned. We already see that on issues like migration, the Africa and the EU are not on the same page. Moreover, as the world grapples with the economic and social implications of the COVID-19 pandemic, the more likely tendency is that countries including EU member states are more inclined to be more inward looking and consequently this may have negative implications for the EU's external relations including those in Africa.

It is the changing dynamics and uncertainties about the future of the relationship between Africa and the EU that motivates this handbook. Specifically, the rising agency of African actors is likely to pay a significant role particularly in reshaping the current asymmetry that exists in the relationship. Moreover, this handbook is an opportunity to reframe and contribute to the discourse of the erstwhile EU-Africa relations in a way that genuinely acknowledges this agency and the transformation to Africa-EU relations. The handbook takes stock of the relationship between African and European actors, institutions and policies in historic context, with the view to make better sense of contemporary practices and inform future cooperation. Four pivotal questions have guided this book:

1. How can we critically analyse and understand Africa-EU relations?
2. What are the institutions, rules, norms, narratives, or practices that shape actors' behaviour within this relationship?
3. What are the main issues and institutions influencing the dynamic workings of Africa-EU relations?
4. What are the new opportunities for Africa and the EU to cooperate in tackling global challenges?

The contributors to this volume come at these questions from a diversity of perspectives. Some of these also contribute to the discourses around decolonizing knowledge by acknowledging the epistemic eurocentrism of Africa-EU relations. At the same time, the handbook shows how existing knowledge becomes embedded. For example, though as the editors acknowledge the capabilities that have emerged as a result of Africa agency and consequently a discursive shift to 'Africa-EU relations', many scholars within this handbook have stuck to the better-known EU-Africa relations, even while they do contribute to challenging the existing canon. We, nevertheless, believe that by engaging a diversity of scholars including African scholars outside of the 'usual suspects', we too contribute to disrupting the hegemonic knowledge around the relationship, enriching the scholarship, and bring new perspectives with implications for its future.

This book is structured into five main sections, excluding the introduction and conclusion. Each section is inclusive of an introduction which provides broad strokes of the issues assessed by introducing each chapter and appraising and reflecting on the findings.

The first section, *Theorising EU-Africa Relations Through History* offers two main perspectives on Africa-EU relations. One states the relationship within broader International Relations theory and discourse, while the second considers the value of post-colonial theory. These perspectives contribute a pluralistic understanding of Africa-EU relations drawing attention to the issues underpinning this relationship that are then explored in the rest of the Handbook. The second section which focuses on *Governing Africa-EU Relations* elaborates on the ways the relationship EU-Africa relations are framed within a set of institutions, rules, narratives and practices to shape concrete policy outcomes. The third section examines *Issues in Africa-EU Relations* and offers overviews of key policy priorities structuring Africa-EU relations. In section four, the handbook calls attention to *The Role of Other Actors in Africa-EU Relations*. Here, the chapters examine the implications of other actors like China, Brazil or non-state organisations like the United Nations on Africa-EU relations as well as in specific policy concerns. The fifth and final section is forward looking and titled accordingly in *Opportunities to Cooperate on New Global Challenges*. The chapters explore the ways in which the EU and African countries and institutions work together on issues that transcend their borders such as climate change, migration, gender discrimination, agriculture and land access.

While these chapters reflect a range of concerns in which Africa-EU relations are implicated, they are by no means exhaustive. For example, emerging in Africa-EU relations is the role of youth in governance. In policy terms, the EU has often couched concerns about youth with respect to the "demographic challenge" where Africa's majority youth population is seen as a problem for Europe particularly with regards to migration. At the same time, discourses in Africa around youth focuses on the possibilities of a dividend, a positive for growth and well-being on the continent and potentially for Europe's ageing population. Undoubtedly, this will remain a concern within Africa-EU relations in the short to medium term and will certainly be a feature of the 2020 Africa-EU Summit.

Another concern this book does not delve into is around digitisation. One of the things that the 2020 COVID-19 pandemic has highlighted in both Africa and Europe is the necessity and opportunities of digitisation – harnessing the power of digital technology – for keeping the partnership going when physical travel is not possible. But beyond the immediacy of virtual networking, both the African and European sides have declared the need for a digital partnership that helps to innovate, contributes to economic growth, facilitates trade and engenders connectivity. Africa, compared to Europe, is in a more disadvantage position but as of 2019 the continent recorded the world's fastest growth in internet access (Friends of Europe, 2019). These two examples reinforce, at the very least, that Africa and the EU will remain entangled for a while yet; not just because of their histories but their futures too. This Handbook too is an affirmation of this reality.

Note

1 The ACP Group is now called Organisation of African, Caribbean and Pacific States, following a name change in 2020. The original name is used throughout this volume, reflecting the nomenclature during the events discussed in the individual chapters.

Bibliography

Akokpari John, Angela Ndinga-Muvumba, Timothy Murithi (2008) *The African Union and Its Institutions*. Johannesburg: Jacana Media.

Austen, Ralph. (1987) *African Economic History: Internal Development and External Dependency*. Portsmouth, NH: Heinemann.

Bossuyt, Fabienne Jan Orbie & Lotte Drieghe (2020) EU external policy coherence in the trade-foreign policy nexus: foreign policy through trade or strictly business? *Journal of International Relations and Development* 23, pp 45–66.

Carbone Maurizio, (2013) EU-Africa Relations in the Twenty first century: evolution and explanations. In Carbone Maurizio, (ed) The European Union in Africa incoherent policies asymmetrical partnership declining relevance. Manchester: Manchester University Press, pp 3–24.

Carmody Padraig (2013) *The Rise of the BRICS in Africa The Geopolitics of South-South Relations*. London: Zed Books.

Council of the European Union (2007) *2007 The Africa-EU Strategic Partnership A Joint Africa-EU Strategy*. www.consilium.europa.eu/uedocs/cms_data/docs/pressdata/en/er/97496.pdf (accessed 25 May 2020).

Eurostat (2019), The European Union and the African Union A Statistical Portrait, https://ec.europa.eu/eurostat/documents/3217494/9767596/KS-FQ-19-001-EN-N.pdf/376dc292-0d2d-4c66-9a36-5bc63c87466c (accessed 02/07/2020)

European Commission (2020), *Towards a comprehensive strategy with Africa*, Joint Communication to the European Parliament and the Council, Join (2020) 4 final https://ec.europa.eu/international-partnerships/system/files/communication-eu-africa-strategy-join-2020-4-final_en.pdf (accessed 22 June 2020).

European Commission (2020) *10th African Union Commission-European Commission meeting-Joint Communiqué* https://ec.europa.eu/commission/presscorner/detail/en/STATEMENT_20_365 (accessed 24 June 2020).

European Commission (2018), Communication on a new Africa – Europe Alliance for Sustainable Investment and Jobs: Taking our partnership for investment and jobs to the next level, COM (2018) 643 final https://ec.europa.eu/commission/sites/beta-political/files/soteu2018-africa-europe-jobs-alliance-communication-643_en.pdf (accessed 25 June 2020).

European Commission (2016), *Strengthening European Investments for jobs and growth: Towards a second phase of the European Fund for Strategic Investments and a New European External Investment Plan*, COM (2016) 581 final https://eur-lex.europa.eu/legal-content/EN/TXT/PDF/?uri=CELEX:52016DC0581&from=en (accessed 28 June 2020).

Farrell M (2013) African regionalism: external influences and continental shaping forces in Africa incoherent policies asymmetrical partnership declining relevance? In Carbone M, (ed) *The European Union in Africa incoherent policies asymmetrical partnership declining relevance?* Manchester: Manchester University Press, pp. 98–120.

Friends of Europe (2019). *Africa's digital revolution: towards an EU-Africa digital partnership*. www.friendsofeurope.org/events/africas-digital-revolution-towards-an-eu-africa-digital-partnership/ (accessed 30 June 2020)

Getz, T.R. (2013) *Cosmopolitan Africa, c. 1700–1875. African World Histories*. Oxford: Oxford University Press.

Goodwin, S. (2009) *Africa in Europe: Antiquity into the Age of Global Exploration*. Vol. 1. Lanham, MD: Lexington Books.

Gürcan, Efe Can (2019) *Multipolarization, South-South Cooperation and the Rise Post-Hegemonic Governance*. London: Routledge.

Haastrup T (2013) *Charting Transformation through Security: Contemporary EU-Africa Relations*. London: Palgrave MacMillan.

Haastrup T (2013) EU as Mentor? Promoting Regionalism as External Relations Practice in EU–Africa Relations. *Journal of European Integration*, 35 (7), 785–800.

Hansen P and Jonsson S (2014) *Eurafrica: The Untold History of European Integration and Colonialism*. London: Bloomsbury Academic.

Helly D (2013), 'The EU and Africa since the Lisbon Summit of 2007: Continental drift or widening cracks?' *South African Journal of International Affairs*, 20, 137–157.

Luciano BT. (2020) A Clash between Creature and Creator? Contemporary Relations between the Pan-African Parliament and the European Parliament. *JCMS: Journal of Common Market Studies* 54.

Luke D and Macleod, J (2019) *Inclusive Trade in Africa. The African Continental Free Trade Area in Comparative Perspective*. London: Routledge

Mah Luis (2015) Reshaping European Union development policy: collective choices and the new global order. *Revista Brasileira de Política Internacional* 58 (2), 44–64.

Mangala J. (2013a) Africa-EU Strategic Partnership: Historical Background, Institutional Architecture, and Theoretical Frameworks. In: Mangala J. (eds*) Africa and the European Union*. New York: Palgrave Macmillan.

Mangala J. (2013b) Five Years after Lisbon: Lessons Learned and the Way Forward. In: Mangala J. (eds) *Africa and the European Union*. New York: Palgrave Macmillan.

Modi R. (eds) (2011) *South-South Cooperation Africa on the Centre Stage*. London: Palgrave Macmillan.

Mold, A. (2018) The Consequences of Brexit for Africa: The Case of the East African Community. *Journal of African Trade* 5, 1–17.

Murithi, T (2005) *The African Union Pan-Africanism, Peacebuilding and Development*. London: Routledge.

Obeng-Odoom Franklin (2020) The African Continental Free Trade Area, *American Journal of Economics and Sociology* 79 (1), 167–197.

Price, Sophia (2019) The Impact of Brexit on EU Development Policy. *Politics and Governance,* 7 (3), 72–82.

Staeger Ueli. (2016) Africa-EU Relations and Normative Power Europe: A Decolonial Pan-African Critique. *JCMS: Journal of Common Market Studies* 54 (4), 981–998.

The European External Action Service (2016) *Shared Vision, Common Action: A Stronger Europe A Global Strategy for the European Union's Foreign And ecurity Policy* http://eeas.europa.eu/archives/docs/top_stories/pdf/eugs_review_web.pdf (accessed 25 May 2020).

Van der Merwe, J., Taylor, I and Arkhangelskaya A (2016) *Emerging Powers in Africa a New Wave in the Relationship?* London: Palgrave Macmillan.

Part I
Theorising Africa-EU relations through history

Introduction to Part I

Toni Haastrup

Studying Africa-European Union (EU) relations as 'EU-Africa Relations' is now an established subfield, particularly within studies on EU foreign policy. This particular framing of how we know, theoretically, this relationship is important since it in part animates this handbook. Because the relationship engages two partners external to each other, the study of Africa-EU relations mainly sits within International Relations (IR).

While recent years has seen the expansion in practice of Africa-EU relations outside of its traditional focus on development assistance and trade to new areas of cooperation such as science and technology and gender equality, among others, the former continue to dominate how we understand the relationship. As the bulk of this literature invariably shows, there persists an asymmetry of power between the two regions, with the EU dominating. The reality of power imbalances explains, in part, why perspectives in IR continue to have relevance. Importantly though, it is not enough to simply locate this scholarship; we have to understand its implications for how we know Africa-EU relations.

Here, I reflect on IR's entry point, highlighting (as articulated by Faleye in Chapter 1 of this volume) the ways in which IR theorising can undermine African agency. Yet, the emergence of regionalism, and especially comparative regionalism as a subfield, has allowed for a more robust engagement with Africa's own integration processes. While this provides an opening to take Africa seriously, the dominance of the EU as the core model for regional integration and its power vis-à-vis its African counterparts mean that comparative regionalism does not necessarily seek to excavate the ways in which African agency are manifested. A move away from IR to International Studies, however, allows for the consideration of Africa (as a continent and with respect to individual states) as constitutive of the 'international' or the 'global'. It is worth acknowledging that knowledge creation and the practices of Africa-EU relations, including those that have privileged the European side, are co-constitutive. Thus, theoretical approaches that allow us to reflect on this co-constitutiveness are especially important to this moment in Africa-EU relations. Here is where Weldeab Sebhatu's account (Chapter 3) of postcolonial approaches to Africa-EU relations challenge the existing blind spot in theorising.

This chapter is a reflection on the whole of the relationship in three parts. First, it contextualises how Africa-EU relations has been theorised. In the subsequent section, I advocate for a broader emphasis on International Studies and show how this has helped us conceptualise African agency. Yet, the sustainability of this focus is only possible when we pay attention to the co-constitutive nature of knowledge and practice in Africa-EU relations. To this end, postcolonial (and decolonial) approaches come in useful to lay out, theoretically, the implications of the existing blind spots in how we understand the dominant relationships within Africa-EU relations. Finally, I contend that Africa-EU relations can no longer afford the privileging of European perspectives in theorising the relationship as a result of the current realties of our current age.

Contextualising the theorising on Africa-EU relations

Until about a two decades ago, the literature that examined the relationship between Africa and the EU did not see Africa on its own terms. The implication of this was that the majority of theorising also started outside of Africa. This literature ensured that the EU's relationship with the group of African, Caribbean and Pacific (ACP) countries was the main conduit for understanding the relationship. The focus of this relationship was on economic development assistance, poverty reduction and trade, and ultimately the EU had the most power. Moreover, by focusing on these aspects of the relationship, these literatures also missed the development of new African institutions created to articulate African agency and represent African interests in the various practices of international politics.

The evolvement of policy areas apart from development and the economy has, of course, pushed research to consider new ways of knowing. Pursuit of these studies has revealed some of the blind spots in traditional IR theorising. For example, Haastrup's (2013b) study on security drew on new institutionalism to illustrate the impact of the past on Africa-EU relations but also to underscore African agency. Despite these innovations, these works remain situated within the EU foreign policy subfield of IR and consequently only offer limited challenge to the hegemonic processes of knowledge production.

To be sure, and as Faleye shows, the grand IR theories are not entirely useless for understanding elements of the relationship between the two continents. However, as Söderbaum and Stålgren (2010) note, the implication of drawing on these traditional approaches is that the EU is really the focus of inquiry. The EU's role as an actor is 'implicitly or explicitly framed within rather conventional statecentric notions about world politics' (ibid.: 2). Framing the EU's role as an international actor through state-centric lenses is, however, limited. When the emphasis is on the EU, Africa, whether through its states or institutions, can only play one role: as receivers of international relations practices rather than active participants. Of the main IR approaches, constructivism perhaps offers the more generous reading of the relationship, since it goes beyond a focus on power and state-centrism to potentially acknowledge the changes in the relationship.

In their constructivist analysis of EU activities in international politics, Bretherton and Vogler (2007) account for the possibility of third parties' impact on the EU's foreign policy practices. This is important in the context of Africa-EU relations, as it suggests the capacity of African actors 'to behave actively and deliberately in relation to other actors in the international system' (Sjöstedt, 1977: 16). In other words, Africa and Africans have the capacity to exercise agency. Yet, this trait is often reserved for the EU, not African states or equivalent organisations like the African Union (AU). Beyond the grand IR theories, many of the new analytical frameworks only reinforce the EU perspective. These literatures focus on the internal dimensions of the EU's international identity as the path to determining its relationship with other actors, including African ones. Consequently, the dominance of IR largely obscures African actorness and the possibilities of its agency.

In recent years, the literature has caught up such that African perspectives can inform some theorising of Africa-EU relations. The development of comparative regionalism, especially, has facilitated this attention to the African side of the story (see Fawcett and Gandois, 2010; Haastrup, 2013a; Shaw, 2015; Börzel and Risse, 2016). In his contribution (Chapter 2), Mattheis rightly argues that the diversity of regionalisms in Africa itself demands that we pay attention to Africa when we think about regionalisms. Yet, the dominant literature still tends to locate Europe as the originator of regionalism. Indeed, Mattheis notes an inherent Eurocentrism has often characterised theorising regionalism.

The normative turn in regionalism and the empirical changes in regionalism in the Global South (especially Africa and Latin America) have created the space for Africa's visibility in regional integration discourses. In particular, the creation and capacities of institutions like the AU and the more recent African Continental Free Trade Area (AfCFTA) have demonstrated Africa's regionalism apart from Europe and European parameters. This is reflected in the tensions that have emerged as African countries attempt to negotiate new terms within the EU-ACP relationship that is the bulk of Africa-EU interregionalism. Yet, the aspirations of the AU and AfCFTA have existed since at least 1963 when the Organisation of African Unity was formally established. So why has Africa not received as much treatment in the literature? Further, what implications does this have for the practice of so-called 'EU-Africa' relations? While comparative regionalism provides an opening, African agency is at best an unintended consequence. So, these questions remain.

Their implications for the absences in knowledge and practice are increasingly being examined by those who seek to understand African agency through Africa's international relations (Beswick and Hammerstad, 2013; Tieku, 2013; Bah, 2017). These newer inquiries are in fact not new; rather, they continue the work that African scholars have been doing, only bringing them to wider attention. In this sense, they deal with what might be termed International Studies (as opposed to IR), drawing on multidisciplinary knowledge and centring the African experience.

African agency in theory or a brave new world for Africa-EU relations?

Shifts in Africa-EU relations have implications for political outcomes due to the changes in the characteristics of the political context. We see this especially in the aftermath of the agreed Joint Africa-EU Strategy which seemed to shine a light on the capabilities of African actors to underscore African regionalism. At the same time, the broadening of the ambit of African and European actors, including the interregionalisation of new policy areas, demand close attention. As Bah (2017) notes, the creation of an organisation like the AU pushes back against the hegemonies of actors like the EU while articulating alternatives that reflect Africans within a pluralistic global order.

So how do we understand African agency? There is no definitive answer to this question. It is a question that scholars of Africa's relationship with the EU are increasingly drawn to asking, though they certainly did not originate it. For instance, Murray-Evans argues for African agency as 'influence or resistance' (2015: 1847). This notion of African agency is to an extent tied to a universalist understanding of agency. This is captured by Hay's definition of agency: 'the ability or capacity of an actor to act consciously and, in so doing, to attempt to realise his or her intentions' (2002: 94). To accept this definition is also to accept a definition of agency that situates Africa (as a whole continent of 55 states) as playing to the rules of an often-hostile international system. This understanding, however, limits the possibilities for a holistic engagement of African capabilities and experiences.

Importantly, however, these sorts of limitations of understanding show why the move away from traditional IR is essential. Thomas Kwasi Tieku, for his part, defines African agency as 'the autonomy of African citizens, through their lawful representatives (governments), have to define, act, own, control and lead on issues that affect them' (2013: 514), whereas Brown and Harman, refer to African agency as taking 'African politics, actions, preferences, strategies and purposes seriously, to move past the tired tropes of an Africa that is victimised, chaotic, violent and poor' (2013: 1–2). In this framing, Africa is constitutive of the international or global, rather than relying on the international to define it.

African agency vis-à-vis the EU must thus integrate the socio-historical dimension not just descriptively but as fundamental to mythologising the relationship. The postcolonial nature of the relationship is ontological, just as it is epistemological and methodological. In a manner, this is the insight that postcolonial/decolonial theorising brings to the theorising of Africa-EU relations.

In her contribution, Weldeab Sebhatu argues for the utility of postcolonial theory in understanding Africa-EU relations broadly and in explaining the lack of attention to African agency and its implications in existing studies. Where constructivism via International Relations is arguably quite malleable in how it may be able to give Africa more space our understanding of Africa-EU relations, postcolonial theory unabashedly seeks to challenge the Eurocentrism of both 'EU-Africa' knowledge production and the practices of 'EU-Africa' relations. It is a critical theoretical tradition that sits within a broader international study whose genealogy extends to before the discipline of IR and fuses normative, material and practical accounts of the relationship. In applying a postcolonial lens to Africa-EU relations, the roles of the EU is also recast in ways that had not been previously excavated.

In their book, *Eurafrica*, Hansen and Jonsson (2014) also draw on postcolonial theory to show how the postcolonialism re-narrates European integration as dependent on the colonisation and then the exploitation of Africa. Importantly, they contend that the architecture of European integration has rested on the manner of this relationship, thus articulating 'dependency' in this relationship quite differently to received knowledge. This perspective on Africa-EU relations, in decentring Europe and questioning the motivations and justification of European engagement with Africa, allows for a more nuanced accounting of interregionalism that upsets prevailing arrangements of power. Postcolonial theory thus shines a light on the blind spots of the nexus between theory and practice.

Conclusion

In this first section of the handbook, three scholars seek to articulate different perspectives on how particular theoretical approaches have been and can be used to understand Africa-EU relations. While this chapter has tried to introduce the relationship between the different theoretical traditions and African agency with Africa-EU relations, it is important that attempts at articulating agency not simply be a theoretical exercise.

As the three contributions show, Africa-EU relations are often co-constituted by their practice. This is manifested in the policy arena, though dominated by development assistance, trade agreements and increasingly security engagements. The new instruments of regionalism in Africa and extended capabilities in Europe facilitate this practice of interregionalism. Yet, the theories presented in the three contributions also reveal that the EU's continued dominance in the relationship has the tendency to obscure African agency.

Africa-EU relations are now at a critical juncture. The quest for African agency does not seek to idealise it in relation to the EU, however. In other words, to seek African agency is no guarantee to a progressive outcome. True agency accounts for the complexities of the relationship, reflected in the different chapters in the handbook (see also Haastrup, forthcoming). Yet, the new instruments of regionalism in Africa do have important implications for its position in the international system and vis-à-vis the EU that can no longer be ignored. There is already pushback against what is considered the modus operandi of the EU's approach to the continent. This defines the manifestation of agency. Nowhere is this more evident as the EU seeks to renegotiate its flagship Cotonou Agreement. While the EU continues to push for continued engagement within the ACP arrangement, the AU seeks more continent-to-continent engagement, partly to ensure the success of the AfCFTA. For the EU, there is a rhetorical commitment to 'partnership' with its African counterparts. The extent to which this is possible remains to be seen. What is clear from theorising the relationship is that it can no longer be based on decisions originating in Brussels or European capitals and must look also to Addis Ababa and other African capitals.

Bibliography

Bah, A.B. (2017) African agency in new humanitarianism and responsible governance. In A.B. Bah (ed.), *International Security and Peacebuilding: Africa, the Middle East, and Europe*, Bloomington: University of Indiana Press, pp. 148–169.

Beswick, D. and Hammerstad, A. (2013) African agency in a changing security environment: Sources, opportunities and challenges. *Conflict, Security & Development*, 13 (5), 471–486.

Börzel, T. and Risse, T. (eds) (2016) *The Oxford Handbook of Comparative Regionalism* Oxford: Oxford University Press.

Bretherton, C. and Vogler, J. (2006) *The European Union as a Global Actor*, 2nd ed. Abingdon: Routledge.

Brown, W. and Harman, S. (eds) (2013) *African Agency in International Politics*. Abingdon: Routledge.

Fawcett, L. and Gandois, H. (2010) Regionalism in Africa and the Middle East: Implications for EU studies. *Journal of European Integration*, 32 (6), 617–636.

Haastrup, T. (2013a) EU as mentor? Promoting regionalism as external relations practice in EU-Africa relations. *Journal of European Integration*, 35 (7), 785–800.

Haastrup, T. (2013b) *Charting Transformation through Security: Contemporary EU- Africa Relations*. London: Palgrave Macmillan.

Haastrup, T. (forthcoming) Critical perspectives on Africa's relationship with the European Union. In D. Bigo, T. Diez, E. Fanoulis, B. Rosamond and Y.A. Stivachtis (eds), *The Routledge Handbook of Critical European Studies*. Routledge.

Hansen, P. and Jonsson, S. (2014) *Eurafrica*. London: Bloomsbury.

Hay, C. (2002). *Political Analysis: A Critical Introduction*. London: Red Globe Press.

Murray-Evans, P. (2015) Regionalism and African agency: Negotiating an Economic Partnership Agreement between the European Union and SADC-Minus. *Third World Quarterly*, 36 (10), 1845–1865.

Shaw, T. (2015). African agency? Africa, South Africa and the BRICS. *International Politics*, 52 (2), 255–268.

Sjöstedt, G. (1977). *The External Role of the European Community*. Farnborough: Saxon House.

Söderbaum, F. and Stålgren, P. (2010) The European Union and the Global South. In F. Söderbaum and P. Stålgren (eds), *The European Union and the Global South*. Boulder, CO: Lynne Reiner, pp. 1–15.

Tieku, T.K. (2013) Exercising African agency in Burundi via multilateral channels: Opportunities and challenges. *Conflict, Security & Development*, 13 (5), 513–535.

1

International Relations theory
Comparative reflections on EU-Africa relations

Olukayode A. Faleye

The subjectivity of International Relations (IR) theory has led to the emergence of theoretical multiplicity, which has found expression in the endurance of hegemonic and pluralistic perceptions of global relations. As observed by Crawford (2000: 1), 'no intellectual field today suffers more from the ambiguity of its subject matter, or the contestability of its theories, than International Relations'. Whereas the study of European experience in IR is well documented, African Studies within IR theory is a recent development (Murphy, 2001). Consequently, the African experience is often perceived in IR theory through the lenses of European reality. The marginalisation of the African agency in IR theory has been traced to the artificial invention of the African states. Consequently, the distinctiveness of African history challenges the Eurocentric notion of the 'universality' of IR concepts such as the state, sovereignty, power and nationalism (Grovogui, 2001; Malaquias, 2001; Dunn and Shaw, 2001; Bilgin, 2008; Tickner and Waever, 2009; Cornelissen et al., 2012; Faleye 2014). However, the African experience cannot be isolated from the global reality of human existence.

In this light, Harman and Brown (2013) note the inversion of Africa from the 'margins' to the 'centre' of the emerging international order in the face of the Chinese ascension in the 21st century. However, as this paper shows, beyond the rise of China and South-South cooperation, the endured marginalisation of the African agency in IR theory through hegemonic theoretical expositions emanate from intellectual imperialism. As observed by Englebert and Dunn (2013: 1), the peculiarity of African history 'serves as a reminder of the universality of human experiences and of the sometimes hidden relevance of even the most marginal of regions to our own concerns, wherever we may be'. Whereas the study of EU-Africa relations abounds in the literature, the synthetic analysis of this theoretical multiplexity is yet to be documented. Thus, this chapter examines the history of EU-Africa relations based on a comparative analysis of IR theories of realism, liberalism and constructivism.

Structural pattern

The dynamism of IR is inherently linked with the multiplex contribution of IR theory to the understanding of global relations. However, these counter-theories arouse scepticism about the empirical relevance of these seemingly 'philosophical' assumptions. Understanding the applicability of these theoretical cacophonies is vital in the face of globalisation, regionalism and growing interregional dependence. In explaining these realities, the contributions of the major theoretical divide of hegemonic and pluralist approaches are reappraised in a holistic framework. The focus here is EU-Africa relations.

Thus, the operationalisation of the international system is decoded by the macro perspectives of the IR theories of realism, liberalism and constructivism. Embedded in this framework is the perception of a realist world of 'anarchy' lacking central government and where 'national interest' is predominant (Gilpin, 2001; Waltz, 2001). On the other hand, the international system is seen as constituting an interdependent world where institutions regulate interstate cooperation rather than the brutal force of 'self-help' (Keohane and Nye, 1977; Keohane, 1984, 1989). The 'international' is perceived as being governed by social norms and rules that evolved through interstate socialisation. This is presumed to create symbolic identities for harmony or crisis (Wendt, 1992, 1994; Vendulka et al., 1998; Reus-Smit, 2013). These comparative theoretical approaches bring to the fore the multiplex nature of global existence.

Realism and international anarchy: The case of EU-Africa relations

Realist theory in international relations provides a deep insight into the place of national interest in interstate relations. As observed by the realists, the absence of global government necessitates survivalist strategies among competing states in the international system. In this vein, despite the existence of global organisations and international law, national interest as shaped by materialism has continued to influence interstate diplomacy overtime (Gilpin, 2001). The conflict of interest between states has been attributed to the selfish nature of man, and all other factors are secondary (Waltz, 2001). Hence, international politics is characterised by the law of the jungle in which the strongest (great powers) dominate in a world of anarchy. In this respect, regional integration in Europe under different umbrellas – from the European Economic Community to the EU – was a historical process informed by the anarchist nature of the distribution of power in the international system. It appears the EU is a regional necessity born out of the changed global power configuration following the collapse of the Union of Soviet Socialist Republics and the end of the Cold War in the early 1990s. As noted by Hill et al. (2017: 4), 'the EU can be seen as one of the world's two economic "superpowers", and a significant influence in the realms of international diplomacy, "soft diplomacy" and a broader world order'.

In this vein, EU external relations are inherently automated in the interest of Europe. This suggests that EU's clamour for more presence in Africa can only be understood through the optic of global imperialism. This perceptiveness has often been tested in the laboratory of Afro-European history. Trans-Atlantic trade and European colonialism are landmarks in this regard. The two different but related events were forged by European imperialism that evolved from interregional cooperation. Considering this background, the incursion of European powers in Africa suggests a political power play and the quest for resource accumulation. As noted by Rodney (1972), colonialism in Africa left the continent without the tools, skills and political capital required to mobilise its resources for developmental purposes. Consequently, the continent has been perpetuated into a state of underdevelopment in a world policed and structured by the imperialistic countries of the Western world. The positioning of Africa for failure within the social sciences exemplify the realist's hegemonic thought that thrives on the caricature stratification of actors into a constructed centre and periphery of a glocalising world. Acquiescing to this monolithic theoretical assumption in EU foreign policy formulation is to relegate Africa to the dark ages of development within the EU-Africa strategic partnership framework. While there is no doubt about the unique nature and challenges of the African state, its attested dysfunctionality is an antithesis to the Eurocentric construction of the 'international'. Moreover, the challenges of Africa and its structural confusion that produces underdevelopment exemplify the crisis of the state (Ake, 2013). More than the plundering of colonisation, this is a crisis emanating from the endurance of the Eurocentric social science theories in public policy. As Ake puts it:

> Western social science scholarship on developing countries is imperialism in the sense that … it foists, or at any rate attempts to foist on the developing countries, capitalist values, capitalist institutions, and capitalist development … it focuses social science analysis on the question of how to make the developing countries more like the West; and … it propagates mystifications, and modes of thought and action which serve the interests of capitalism and imperialism. … Every prognostication indicates that Western social science continues to play a major role in keeping us subordinate and underdeveloped; it continues to inhibit our understanding of the problems of our world, to feed us noxious values and false hopes, to make us pursue policies which undermine our competitive strength and guarantee our permanent underdevelopment and dependence. It is becoming increasingly clear that we cannot overcome our underdevelopment and dependence unless we try to understand the imperialist character of Western social science and to exorcise the attitudes of mind which it indicates.
>
> *(1979: i–ii)*

Indeed, Africa's challenges with territoriality, statehood, border, and sovereignty, among others could be resolved if contextual social theories are applied in public policy. For instance, economic and political regionalisation promises a resolution to the issues of state territoriality in Africa (Faleye, 2016, 2019). Of course, African regional cohesion is of vital importance to equitable EU-Africa relations. However, the driving machinery of governance in Africa is the selective state-centric theories of Western social science. Hence, the proposed weaknesses, peripherality and dysfunctionality of the African states as mirrored by the realists attest to the mass failure of Western epistemologies in Africa. In this light, it is no longer news that the political arbiters that evolved from the marriage of colonialism and nationalism in postcolonial Africa marshalled the dysfunctional state-centric theories, such as realism, in the consolidation of state capture.

The internal challenges of the African states were reflected in the making of the Cotonou Agreement of 2000 as amended in 2005, which laid emphasis on poverty eradication, antiterrorism and arms race as well as the recognition of emerging powers of non-state character. This showcases the recognition of the African economic decline and state-centric political instability since independence (Babarinde and Faber, 2004; Banthia, 2007). Moreover, it affirms the contemporary reality of growing terrorist movements and the emerging influence of alternative forms of power in the region. The Cotonou Agreement led to the partitioning of the African, Caribbean and Pacific (ACP) nations[1] into regional developmental blocks (based on ACP states that are low-development countries ACP states that are not low-development countries) (Holland, 2002, 2003; Babarinde and Faber, 2004). This was, as the realists would put it, an indication of the EU's strategy to divide and rule (Dur and De Bievre, 2007).

The Cotonou framework emphasises the Economic Partnership Agreements (EPAs) aimed at establishing a common market between the EU and regional blocks in Africa. The Cairo EU-Africa Summit of 2000, which emphasised regional integration, economic globalisation, democracy and refugee rights and safety, led to the Lisbon summit of 2007, characterised by the Joint Africa-EU Strategy framework of fostering human security, democratic governance, interregional trade, environmental protection, migration and infrastructure development. This has metamorphosed into different action plans since 2008 (Africa-EU Partnership, 2014; Gudz, 2015). However, these appear to be agreements between two unequal partners (coloniser/

colonised; industrial/agrarian). Consequently, it could be argued that the agenda tilts against the African interest. As noted by Eyinla (2004), the outcome of the 2000 Africa-EU Summit in Cairo reflects the prioritisation of European unity, peace and security over the African quest for development aid policy. This is perhaps informed by the fragile nature of the African states and the likelihood of their posing security threats across the Mediterranean Sea. Hence, the realist asks the question: what benefit would the EU and Africa derive from these interregional frameworks for cooperation?

For analytical purposes, the EPA framework is reviewed from the realist perspective. The EPAs evolved from the 2000 Cotonou Agreement with a focus on fostering an open market between the EU on one side and ACP countries on the other. The EU supplies a large part of the equipment that contributes to economic growth and development in the West African region and is the main export market for its agricultural and fisheries products. The agreement was one of the first to technically integrate West Africa's bifurcated regional blocks of the Economic Community of West African States (ECOWAS) and the West African Monetary and Economic Union (Union Economique et Monétaire Ouest Africaine, UEMOA) into a collaborative framework with an external actor – a phenomenon the EU sees as maturity of regional integration in West Africa (European Commission, 2017). It is against this background that the EU perceives itself and West Africa as equal partners in progress. The EPAs are expected to 'increase exports to the EU, stimulate investment and contribute to developing productive capacity, with a positive effect on employment. … For the EU, it opens new business opportunities and increases legal certainty for European investors in the region' (European Commission, 2017: 1). The EU argument has been a point of contention for realists, who perceive a free trade agreement between industrial Europe and agrarian Africa as a neocolonial mechanism to perpetuate African underdevelopment. Indeed, it has been noted that the EU's developmental framework for cooperation with African countries legitimises 'world market expansion' in Europe's advantage (Price and Nunn, 2016). As Gilpin puts it, 'although nations want to take advantage of foreign markets, they are frequently unwilling to open their own economies' (2001: 196). How do we explain this phenomenon from the realist point of view if not to say that the disparities in regional economic and political structures automatically create a partnership of two unequals between the EU and Africa?

The structural disparities between the EU and Africa are often defined by the nature of the state. In this vein, the coloniality of the imperial structures in postcolonial Africa exemplifies the absence of the state in the European notion (Bates, 1981; Englebert and Dunn, 2013; Faleye, 2019). In essence, if IR theory as seen by the realists is dependent on the Eurocentric statist framework, the existence of distinct 'Afrocentric states' invalidates its universal assumptions. Hence, the African experience showcases the existence of different types and functionalities of states in diverse ecologies as determined by the distinctive as well as interlocked histories of the world. This unveils the futility of an absolute value, whether in the evolution of social structure or in the development of knowledge. The perception of the core or periphery spaces within the international system is a subjective phantom in the face of glocalisation. Indeed, the perceived deviance of the African agency within the international system symbolises an important frontier of knowledge with reflections on the region's socio-spatial genome and the trail of its engagement with the wider world.

Liberalism and EU-Africa interregional dependence

Liberalism sees interregional cooperation as a product of globalisation born out of the rationality of state survival in the international system. As observed by Robert Keohane, 'the future of the fragile global ecology itself depend[s] on the ability of human beings to cope successfully with economic interdependence' (1989: 21). In this respect, the anarchical challenges of international relations are expected to be resolved through the rational harmonisation of interests by former intergovernmental organisations engineered by states in the global space (Keohane and Nye, 1977; Keohane, 1984, 1989). Thus, state policy is a product of ongoing glocal interactions of politics. The liberals posit that these interactions are often partial, as they are born out of social pressures mounted within and outside the state, thereby defining state preferences in policy and practice. Thus, liberals offer a framework on 'how institutions transform interests' based on a process of interaction of actors in the international system (Wendt, 1992: 394).

Moravcsik (1997) notes that the importance of a state in the international system is determined by the nature of its interests, which define its preferences. The bias of liberalism as regards a state's rationality defines its uniqueness. It is on this basis that liberals define global cooperation or discord through states' preferential harmony and conflicts, which are often influenced by pressure groups made up of state and non-state actors. This phenomenon is perceived as ideationally and materially driven. The anarchical nature of the global system stimulates the rise of national interests that are often regulated by international institutions built on the multipolar nature of actors and power blocs at local and global levels. The peculiar nature of national histories is reflected in the distinctiveness of states' foreign policies and diplomatic practices. However, the convergence of local and international interests in state policy preferences informs the nature of interregional cooperation (Moravcsik, 1997). Thus, the liberals perceive regional integration in Europe as a product of societal necessity to promote peace, security and progress in the face of the growing interconnectivity of global resources. In this respect, the externalisation of the EU's intra-regional attachment to Africa symbolises the EU's commitment to defend its interest in Africa through soft power diplomacy enshrined in the principle of peaceful coexistence of nations through global cooperation.

The role of international organisations such as the EU, ECOWAS, and the African Union (AU) in defusing aggressive anarchist movements in the international system is important in this regard. This informs Gruhn's (1993: 19–20) observation that the prospect of EU-Africa relations lies with the development of 'paralleled' strong regional institutions in Africa; in this vein, these would 'become the conduits for demilitarising corrupt and dysfunctional states in cooperation with the international system'. The EU seems to have played some role in this by promoting interstate institutionalism, democratic governance and international institutions through conditional aids, thereby demonstrating its capacity as a senior partner in its relations with Africa (Scheipers and Sicurelli, 2008; Börzel and Hackenesch, 2013).

While the state-rationality discourse appears to apply technically in the case of Europe, the distinctiveness of the sociopolitical architecture of regions (in this case the EU and Africa) suggests otherwise. How rational is the state in Africa? The implantation of democracy in African states gained momentum since the close of the 20th century; however, this has not guaranteed development in the region. Indeed, the democratic transition engineered through electoral malpractices and 'godfatherism' in Africa legitimises the state in the interest of the political elites. As noted by the late Nigerian Afro-beat musician Fela Anikulapo Kuti, democracy manifests in Africa as 'demo-crazy'. It is against this background that liberal democracy catalyses unequal development, fierce power struggle and marginalisation of the majority of Africans by few privileged Africans.

The asymmetric capitalist structure often propels violent conflicts, insurgencies and wars in Africa (Ake, 1995; Amin, 1996; Nkiwane, 2000). In this vein, the African political landscape operates in an atmosphere of patronage and clientelism. This neo-patrimonial rentier order based on the privatisation and appropriation of state resources operates in a distinct manner that differs from the European terrain (Lewis, 1994; Yates, 1996; Englebert, 2000; Van de Walle, 2001). The neo-patrimonial order endures, as illustrated by recent studies in African political economy, development and policy studies (Chasukwa, 2019; Faleye, 2019; Madonsela, 2019; Titeca and Thamani, 2018; Titeca and Edmond, 2019). This is a system traceable to the colonial hybridisation of traditional and formal authority between the grassroots and the colonial capital. However, the decolonisation process that followed World War II, with an attendant admixture of private and public interests in the state bureaucratic system, failed to institute an '"autonomous" legal-rational' bureaucracy in the region (Erdmann and Engel, 2006: 19).

In a system where state policies hitherto seen as state 'interests' operate as an appendage of the elitist's empire, socio-economic disparities in the region translate to interstate elitist competition, which ultimately weakens regional institutionalism. This reality manifests in the reluctance of state actors in West Africa to commit themselves to regional (internal and external) tariff plans, which ordinarily would have harmonised the region's economy as the first step towards formal regionalism. The cases in point include the harmonisation of the ECOWAS Common External Tariff (ECOWAS-CET) and the EPA. Indeed, it has been observed that the productivity of free trade is driven by the nature of public institutions (that are often malfunctioning in Africa) (Bormann et al., 2005; Bormann and Busse, 2007). This explains the EU frustration with Africa's lack of developmental progress in the 1990s despite its heavy financial aid investment in the continent since the 1950s (European Commission, 1996). Thus, the liberals perceive interregional cooperation based on macroeconomic-cum-political institutionalisation as a panacea for African stunted development. However, the weakened nature of African states as agents of progressive change in the region questions Africa's ability to nurse a functional regional institution and legitimately negotiate with the EU on behalf of its people. Whereas public policy is driven by rational bureaucracy in Europe, the reverse is the case in Africa, where state rationality often lies in private interests.

EU-Africa relations in constructivist perspective

The constructivist approach emphasises the social construction of IR. As noted by Reus-Smit (2013: 217), 'constructivism is characterised by an emphasis on the importance of normative as well as material structures, on the role of identity in shaping political action and on the mutually constitutive relationship between agents and structures'. The constructivist shows that society is the product of the people. In doing so, the constructivist showcases how social interactions structure state behaviour through the dialogue between people and societal norms. The operationalisation of social norms constitutes societal practices. The engagement of individuals and groups with such practices defines their level of agency in societal transformation. Societal transformation has occurred due to the attainment of goals by this agency. These goals reflect people's needs and wishes in light of their material circumstances, as defined by human agency. Thus, social norms represent the agents' practices emanating from their agenda, that creates the pathway for the emergence of institutions (Kubálková et al., 1998). These institutions often restructure in the quest for legitimacy and effectiveness as a response to internal and external stimuli. In sum, the constructivist sees anarchy as an international structure governed by dynamic social norms constructed historically in the global space of socialisation. This historical reconstruction embodies the activities of diverse agencies of state and non-state characters, cascading at local and international levels. These dynamics manifest in state character, decisions and purpose.

Wendt (1992) uncovers the central role of state actors in this respect and how national identities and interests are made by social forces rather than human nature and domestic politics.

Self-help, as perceived in realism, is an institution born out of the state's interpretation of the international society. As Wendt (1992: 406) puts it: 'It is through reciprocal interaction, in other words, that we create and instantiate the relatively enduring social structures in terms of which we define our identities and interests'. Hence, a world of anarchy is created among competitive institutions – where actors act dangerously – rather than in cooperative ones – where interests are re-formed in a mutually benevolent manner in a space of choice and consequences. While the state-centric constructivism as propounded by Wendt is delimited by the peculiar nature of rational-legal bureaucracy in Africa, the state remains a dominant unit of analysis in IR. The state-centric constructivists appear to have nurtured the fear of IR disciplinary drift into Sociology (Brown, 2006).

However, beyond the realist and liberal schools of thought, constructivism seems to provide potential answers to the inherent challenges facing IR theory in comprehending the African experience (Price and Reus-Smit, 1998: 266). As observed by Rosenberg (2016), the disciplinary crisis of IR arises due to its subservient position as an extension of Political Science – a situation he describes as IR 'in the prison of Political Science'. Thus, redefining IR, Rosenberg argues that the word 'international' refers to multiple forms of human experience across deferred 'interacting societies' (2016: 21) – a disciplinary peculiarity. Considering the pluralist nature of the world, Rosenberg redefines the 'international' concept to encapsulate the socioeconomic, as well as political relations between structured human groupings with distinct nationality or institutions with central political authority (be it ethnic, tribal or artificial states). In this light, 'the state is only one of multiple units of analysis [characterized by] informal and formal networks of groups of individuals and organizations linked to each other and to the global economy and polity' (Pomerantz, 2008).

In explaining EU-Africa relations, it is vital to adopt a holistic constructivist framework that emphasises the normative structures at local and international levels where the state becomes a nominal unit of analysis in global relations. Using this framework, social relations hinge on the historical experience and its attendant symbolic codes. This creates the logical basis for understanding the dynamic transition of the state's identity in response to the convergence of domestic and external stimuli (Koslowski and Kratochwil, 1995; Reus-Smit, 2013; Hurd, 2008). EU-Libya relations in the post-Gaddafi era provide a striking example in this respect. For instance, the influx of African refugees into Europe en route to the Libyan maritime coast has led to calls to militarise national borders (Broeders and Hampshire, 2013). According to the EU, the objective of tougher border control is 'to manage the crossing of the external borders efficiently and address migratory challenges and potential future threats at those borders, thereby … addressing serious crime with a cross-border dimension and ensuring a high level of internal security within the Union' (European Commission, 2016: 1).

This approach to the refugee crisis has led to increased fatalities among African migrants taking more dangerous routes to avoid EU border police (Rooney, 2013). The outsourcing of the EU's external border control to buffer zones in Libya and Niger showcases an emerging tripartite alliance between a state-centric regional institution, state actors and non-state actors in Europe and Africa. It has been argued that the externalisation of the border as a 'remote control' strategy may automatically hinder immigration into Europe (Ruhrmann and FitzGerald, 2017: 4). However, the outcome of this strategy as seen in the alleged rape, torture, enslavement and assault of African migrants across the Sahel-Sahara appears to reveal the genuine 'identity' of actors as either a friend or foe. This would impact EU-African relations in the long run. As observed by Wendt (1992: 398), identities often reflect institutional roles as well as 'social definition of the actor grounded in the theories which actors collectively hold about themselves and one another and which constitute the structure of the social world'.

The pattern of EU-Africa relations feeds on the perception of the duo as constructed by historical realities. What is the EU's perception of African identity? And how does Africa see the EU? To answer these questions, it is important to unveil the nexus between EU and African identities in historical perspective. First, to conceptualise 'Africa' as a unitary identity would be a blunder. In Africa, the ethnic groups that constitute states and the states that make up regional institutions, such as ECOWAS and the Common Market for Eastern and Southern Africa, differ in historical experience. For instance, in West Africa, despite the shared history of colonialism and its attendant divisiveness, European imperialism tends to harmonise the distinctive precolonial primordial affinities along francophone and anglophone identities. This phenomenon, facilitated through the French policy of assimilation and the contrasting British system of indirect rule, created a historical landmark in the region's pattern of identity formation (Miles, 1994). In West Africa, it is the francophone and anglophone countries' perception of France and the United Kingdom (and, by extension, the EU), as well as the African view of the EU, that defines their relationships. These different colonial orientations have led to the bifurcation of the region's political and economic architecture along francophone and anglophone lines. Whereas France maintains political ties (such as defence pacts) with its ex-colonies in West Africa, such treaties were rejected by Nigeria in 1963 as they were seen as part of Britain's neo-colonial strategy.

Economically, France supervises a monetary union in francophone African countries through the machination of CFA franc (Fielding and Shields, 2003; Masson and Pattillo, 2001). Contrarily, ex-British colonies in West Africa have adopted their own national monetary units. It can be inferred that the francophone African countries seem to have shared a common 'macro identity', embedded in the French colonial policy of assimilation. The anglophone countries have maintained, to a great extent, their hybridised precolonial and colonial identities. The ensued interstate economic disparities and the elitist exploitative strategies challenge formal regionalism and encourage transborder informality in West Africa (Faleye, 2014, 2016). This phenomenon calls for the formalisation of informal regionalism as a natural pathway for an effective integration movement in sub-Saharan Africa (Meagher, 1994, 2011, 2014). The scenario has metamorphosed into intra-regional division on integrative policy frameworks like the ECOWAS-CET and the EPAs. This conflict of interests in regional macro-identity formation moulded by historically constructed norms has continued to mar interregional relations between the EU and Africa (Price and Nunn, 2016). This suggests that in spite of the successful social codification of neo-liberalism as an international norm in Europe and elsewhere in the world, this phenomenon fails in Africa.

The constructivist provides an open-ended framework for EU-Africa relations due to its nondeterministic position that affirms interregional socialisation as the bases of international relations. The socially constructed cohesive relations between France and its former colonies in West Africa provide a good example. Hence, international relations appear to be driven by 'intersubjective understandings and expectations' of states as regards the conceptions of self and other – a raw material for foreign policy formulation in tandem with relational identities (Wendt, 1992: 397). Thus, the future seems to lie in the unification of African geopolitical blocs. For instance, this would entail a systematic unification of ECOWAS and UEMOA in West Africa as well as other regional blocs under the AU. This appears to be the first step towards EU-Africa interregional cooperation. As observed by Haastrup (2013), the EU is technically a mentor in this regard (though its model is being undermined by Brexit (Haastrup and Ansorg, 2016)). In line with this paradigm, the EU as a senior partner may woo African geopolitical blocs into a mutually profitable relationship by formulating and implementing a fair, friendly and progressive policy framework of interregional cooperation.

Conclusion

This chapter examines the historical pattern and prospects of EU-Africa interactions in the context of realist, liberal and constructivist traditions of IR. It unveils a perspective in the literature bordering on the realist orientation of structural global power politics. As this chapter has shown, the state-centric approach undermines the role of social forces in the EU-Africa interregional intercourse. Moreover, all the macro-theoretical expositions of realism, liberalism and constructivism contribute partially to our understanding of EU-Africa relations. The multiplex nature of the contributions reveals the pluralist and dynamic nature of the global system. While constructivism promises a more holistic framework for these historical realities, the eclectic theoretical approach adopted in this paper reveals the shared history, space and problems of two distinct regions that could be reconstructed for harmony or discord.

Note

1 In 2020, the ACP Group became the Organisation of African, Caribbean and Pacific States.

Bibliography

Africa-EU Partnership (2014) Action Plan 2014–2017: Priorities for Future Cooperation in the Area of Migration and Mobility in the Framework of the Africa-EU Strategic Partnership. www.africa-eu-partnership.org/en/documents/action-plan-2014-2017-priorities-future-cooperation-area-migration-and-mobility-framework

Ake, C.E. (1979) *Social Science as Imperialism: The Theory of Political Development*. Ibadan: Ibadan University Press.

Ake, C.E. (1995) The new world order: A view from Africa. In H.H. Holm and G. Sorenson (eds), *Whose World Order? Uneven Globalization and the End of the Cold War*. Boulder: Westview Press (pp. 19–42).

Ake, C.E. (2013) The present crisis in Africa: Is it economic crisis or crisis of the state? In J.O. Ihonvbere (ed), *The Political Economy of Crisis and Underdevelopment in Africa: Selected Works of Claude Eleme Ake, 1939–1996*. Ota & Waterloo: Third World Publishers (pp. 19–27).

Amin, S. (1996) On the origins of economic catastrophe in Africa. In S.C. Chew and R.A. Denemark (eds), *The Underdevelopment of Development: Essays in Honor of Andre Gunder Frank*. Thousand Oaks: Sage (pp. 200–216).

Babarinde, O. and Faber, G. (2004) From Lomé to Cotonou: Business as usual? *European Foreign Affairs Review*, 9 (1), 27–47.

Banthia, A. (2007) Success or failure? An evaluation of fifty years (1957–2007) of European Union development policy in Africa, Caribbean, and the Pacific. *Political Perspectives*, 2 (1), 1–36.

Bates, R. (1981) *Markets and States in Tropical Africa: The Political Basis of Agricultural Policies*. Berkeley: University of California Press.

Bilgin, P. (2008) Thinking past 'Western' IR. *Third World Quarterly*, 29 (1), 5–23.

Bormann, A. and Busse, M. (2007) The institutional challenge of the ACP/EU. *Journal of World Affairs*, 9 (2), 161–175.

Bormann, A., Busse, M. and Neuhaus, S. (2005) EU/ACP Economic Partnership Agreements: Impact, options and prerequisites. *Intereconomics*, 40 (3), 169–176.

Börzel, T.A. and Hackenesch, C. (2013) Small carrots, few sticks: EU good governance promotion in sub-Saharan Africa. *Cambridge Review of International Affairs*, 26 (3), 536–555.

Broeders, D. and Hampshire, J. (2013) Dreaming of seamless borders: ICTs and the pre-emptive governance of mobility in Europe. *Journal of Ethnic & Migration Studies*, 39 (8), 1201–1218.

Brown, W. (2006) Africa and International Relations: A comment on IR theory, anarchy and statehood. *Review of International Studies*, 32 (1), 119–143.

Chasukwa, M. (2019) Multiple faces of democrats: Satisfaction with democracy and support for democracy in Malawi. *Insight on Africa*, 11 (1), 18–37.

Cornelissen, S., Cheru, F. and Shaw, T.M. (eds) (2012) *Africa and International Relations in the 21st century*. London: Palgrave.

Crawford, R.M.A. (2000) *Idealism and Realism in International Relations: Beyond the Discipline*. London and New York: Routledge.

Dunn, C.K. and Shaw, T.M. (eds.) (2001) *Africa's Challenge to International Relations Theory*. Basingstoke: Palgrave Macmillan.

Dur, A. and De Bievre, D. (2007) Inclusion without influence? NGOs in European Economic Partnership Agreements. *Development Policy Review*, 25 (4), 403–416.

Englebert, P. (2000) Pre-colonial institutions, post-colonial States, and economic development in tropical Africa. *Political Research Quarterly*, 53 (1), 7–36.

Englebert, P. and Dunn, K.C. (2013) *Inside African Politics*. Boulder: Lynne Rienner Publishers.

Erdmann, G. and Engel, U. (2006) *Neopatrimonialism Revisited – Beyond a Catch-All Concept*. GIGA Working Paper No 16. Hamburg: German Institute of Global and Area Studies.

European Commission (1996) Green Paper on Relations between the European Union and the ACP Countries on the Eve of the 21st century. Challenges and Options for a New Partnership. 20 November. https://op.europa.eu/en/publication-detail/-/publication/fd0026af-3614-4e2d-9330-73b2078bb9b1/language-en/format-PDFA1B

European Commission (2016) Regulation (EU) 2016/1624 of the European Parliament and of the Council of 14 September 2016 on the European Border and Coast Guard and amending Regulation (EU) 2016/399 of the European Parliament and of the Council and repealing Regulation (EC) No 863/2007 of the European Parliament and of the Council, Council Regulation (EC) No 2007/2004 and Council Decision 2005/267/EC. http://frontex.europa.eu/assets/Legal_basis/European_Border_and_Coast_Guard.pdf

European Commission (2017) Economic Partnership Agreement with West Africa – Facts and figures. http://trade.ec.europa.eu/doclib/docs/2014/july/tradoc_152694.pdf

Eyinla, B.M. (2004) Beyond Cairo: Emerging pattern of Euro-African relationship. *Africa*, 59 (2), 159–178.

Faleye, O.A. (2014) Africa and international relations theory: Acquiescence and responses. *Journal of Globalization Studies*, 5 (2), 81–90.

Faleye, O.A. (2016) Regional integration from 'below' in West Africa: A study of transboundary town-twinning of Idiroko (Nigeria) and Igolo (Benin). *Regions & Cohesion*, 6 (3), 1–18.

Faleye, O.A. (2019) Border securitisation and politics of state policy in Nigeria, 2014–2017. *Insight on Africa*, 11 (1), 78–93.

Fielding, D. and Shields, K. (2003) *Economic Integration in West Africa: Does the CFA Make a Difference?* Discussion Papers in Economics 03/8, Department of Economics, University of Leicester. www.le.ac.uk/economics/research/discussion/papers2003.html

Gilpin, R. (2001) *Global Political Economy: Understanding the International Economic Order*. Princeton and Oxford: Princeton University Press.

Grovogui, S.N. (2001) Sovereignty in Africa: Quasi-statehood and other myths in international theory. In C.K. Dunn and T.M. Shaw (eds), *Africa's Challenge to International Relations Theory*. Basingstoke: Palgrave Macmillan (pp. 29–45).

Gruhn, I. (1993) *The Evolution of African-European Relations*. Washington: European Community Studies Association.

Gudz, N. (2015) The European Union in Africa: Incoherent policies, asymmetrical partnership, declining relevance? *West European Politics*, 38 (3), 742–743.

Haastrup, T. (2013) EU as mentor? Promoting regionalism as external relations practice in EU-Africa relations. *Journal of European Integration*, 35 (7), 785–800.

Haastrup, T. and Ansorg, N. (2016) Brexit will blow a hole in EU-Africa relations. *The Conversation*, 29 September. http://theconversation.com/brexit-will-blow-a-hole-in-eu-africa-relations-65925

Harman, S. and Brown, W. (2013) In from the margins? The changing place of Africa in international relations. *International Affairs*, 89 (1), 69–87.

Hill, C., Smith, M. and Vanhoonacker, S. (2017) *International Relations and the European Union*, 3rd ed. Oxford: Oxford University Press.

Holland, M. (2002) *The European Union and the Third World*. Hampshire: Palgrave.

Holland, M. (2003) 20/20 vision? The EU's Cotonou Partnership Agreement. *The Brown Journal of World Affairs*, 9 (2), 161–175.

Hurd, I. (2008) Constructivism. In C. Reus-Smit and D. Snidal (eds), *The Oxford Handbook of International Relations*. Oxford: Oxford University Press (pp. 298–316).

Keohane, R. (1984) *After Hegemony*. New Jersey: Princeton University Press.

Keohane, R. (1989) *International Institutions and State Power*. London: Westview Press.

Keohane, R. and Nye, S.J. (1977) *Power and Interdependence: World Politics in Transition*. Canada: Little, Brown and Company.

Koslowski, R. and Kratochwil, F. (1995) Understanding change in international politics: The Soviet empire's demise and the international system. In R.N. Lebow and T. Risse-Kappen (eds), *International Relations Theory and the End of the Cold War*. New York: Columbia University Press (pp. 127–166).

Kubálková, V., Onuf, N. and Kowert, P. (eds) (1998) *International Relations in a Constructed World*. Armonk, NY: M.E. Sharpe.

Lewis, P.M. (1994) Economic statism, private capital, and the dilemmas of accumulation in Nigeria. *World Development*, 22 (3), 437–451.

Madonsela, S. (2019) Critical reflections on state capture in South Africa. *Insight on Africa*, 11 (1), 113–130.

Malaquias, A. (2001) Reformulating international relations theory: African insights and challenges. In C.K. Dunn and T.M. Shaw (eds), *Africa's Challenge to International Relations Theory*. Basingstoke: Palgrave Macmillan (pp. 11–28).

Masson, P. and Pattillo, C. (2001) *Monetary Union in West Africa: An Agency of Restraint for Fiscal Policies?* Washington, DC: International Monetary Fund.

Meagher, K. (1994) Regional complementarities or policy disparities? Cross-border trade and food security among Nigeria and her Sahelian and coastal neighbours. In G.A. Obiozor, A.O. Olukoshi and C.I. Obi (eds), *West African Regional Economic Integration: Nigerian Policy Perspectives for the 1990s* (pp. 63–78). Lagos: Nigerian Institute of International Affairs.

Meagher, K. (2011) Informal economies and urban governance in Nigeria: Popular empowerment or political exclusion? *African Studies Review*, 54 (2), 47–72.

Meagher, K. (2014) Disempowerment from below: Informal enterprise networks and the limits of political voice in Nigeria. *Oxford Development Studies*, 42 (3), 419–438.

Miles, F.S.W. (1994) *Hausaland Divided: Colonialism and Independence in Nigeria and Niger*. New York: Cornell University Press.

Moravcsik, A. (1997) Taking preferences seriously: A liberal theory of international politics. *International Organization*, 51 (4), 513–553.

Murphy, C. (2001) Foreword. In C.K. Dunn and M.T. Shaw (eds), *Africa's Challenge to International Relations Theory*. Basingstoke: Palgrave (pp. ix–x).

Nkiwane, T.C. (2000) The end of history? African challenge to liberalism in international relations. In C.K. Dunn and T.M. Shaw (eds), *Africa's Challenge to International Relations Theory*. Basingstoke: Palgrave Macmillan (pp. 103–111).

Pomerantz, P. (2008) International relations and global studies: The past of the future? *Global-e*, 29 August. http://global-ejournal.org/2008/08/ 29/international-relations-and-global-studies-the-past-of-the-future/

Price, R. and Reus-Smit, C. (1998) Dangerous liaisons? Critical international theory and constructivism. *European Journal of International Relations*, 4 (3), 259–294.

Price, S. and Nunn, A. (2016) Managing neo-liberalisation through the sustainable development agenda: The EU-ACP trade relationship and world market expansion. *Third World Thematics: A TWQ Journal*, 1 (4), 454–469.

Reus-Smit, C. (2013) Constructivism. In S. Burchill, A. Linklater, R. Devetak, J. Donnelly, T. Nardin, M. Paterson, C. Reus-Smit and J. True. *Theories of International Relations*, 5th ed. Basingstoke: Palgrave (pp. 217–239).

Rodney, W. (1972) *How Europe Underdeveloped Africa*. London: Bogle-L'Ouverture.

Rooney, C. (2013) Exploiting a tragedy: The securitization of EU borders in the wake of Lampedusa. Border Criminologies blog. http://bordercriminologies.law.ox.ac.uk/exploiting-a-tragedy

Rosenberg, J. (2016) International relations in the prison of Political Science. *International Relations*, 30 (2), 127–153. http://sro.sussex.ac.uk/60241/

Ruhrmann, H. and FitzGerald, D. (2017) *The Externalization of Europe's Borders in the Refugee Crisis, 2015–2016*. Working Paper No 194. Center for Comparative Immigration Studies, University of California-San Diego. https://escholarship.org/uc/item/2bb8x619

Scheipers, S. and Sicurelli, D. (2008) Empowering Africa: Normative power in EU-Africa relations. *Journal of European Public Policy*, 15 (4), 607–623.

Tickner, A.B. and Waever, O. (eds) (2009) *International Relations Scholarship around the World*. London: Routledge.

Titeca, K. and Edmond, P. (2019) The political economy of oil in the Democratic Republic of Congo (DRC): Corruption and regime control. *The Extractive Industries and Society*, 6 (2), 542–551.

Titeca, K. and Thamani, J. (2018) *Congo's Elections and its Political Landscape: Some Key-Insights*. Analysis and Policy Brief No 33. Institute of Development Policy, University of Antwerp.

Van de Walle, N. (2001) *African Economies and the Politics of Permanent Crisis, 1979–1999*. Cambridge: Cambridge University Press.

Vendulka, K., Onuf, N. and Kowert, P. (eds) (1998) *International Relations in a Constructed World*. New York and London: M.E. Sharpe.

Waltz, K.N. (2001) *Man, the State and War: A Theoretical Analysis*. New York: Columbia University Press.

Wendt, A. (1992) Anarchy is what states make of it: The social construction of power politics. *International Organization*, 46 (2), 391–425.

Wendt, A. (1994) Collective identity formation and the international state. *The American Political Science Review*, 88 (2), 384–396.

Yates, D.A. (1996) The *R*entier *S*tate in Africa: Oil *R*ent *D*ependency and *N*eocolonialism in the Republic of Gabon. Trenton, NJ, and Asmara, Eritrea: Africa World Press.

2
Regionalism and interregionalism in EU-Africa relations

Frank Mattheis

From European to regional integration

Regionalism and interregionalism are defining vectors of relations between Africa and the European Union (EU). The EU constitutes the most well studied instance of a regionalism in the sense of being a political project with the intention to produce a region that transcends nation state boundaries. The African side is the region with the most regional organisations in the world and thus offers a large diversity in terms of regionalism, including a continental organisation (the African Union, AU), a postcolonial group (the African, Caribbean and Pacific Group of States – ACP)[1] and a multitude of regional organisations covering parts of Africa (e.g. the Southern African Development Community) (Mattheis, 2018). The linkages between the EU and the various African entities consequently constitute one of the densest webs of interregionalism, understood as relations between two distinct regional organisations within an institutional framework (Mattheis and Litsegård, 2018; Baert et al., 2014).

Numerous theoretical explanations for regionalism and interregionalism have been produced over the past 70 years. Early regional integration theories, such as the functionalist, federalist or intergovernmentalist schools of thought, were chiefly concerned with explaining the European integration process (Jørgensen et al., 2006; Diez and Wiener, 2018), which complicated the application to other world regions. For instance, neofunctionalism proposed that the concept spill over to explain how integration in one sector could lead to increasing demand for integration in another sector. This concept was based on a strong link between economic interdependence and institutional capacity (Keohane and Nye, 1975). However, regional organisations emerged in many parts of Africa at the time despite a lack of significant economic interdependence. And although neorealists and intergovernmentalists were not by principle attached to Europe as a case, their point of departure in terms of nation states and bureaucracies made their theories biased towards Europe. Within the field of integration studies, research on the economic and political regional processes in Africa remained either isolated empirical work or constituted the transfer of theories devised for the European case (cf. Hazlewood, 1967; Wallerstein, 1967; Robson, 1968).

The theoretical and empirical Eurocentrism, which made it difficult to incorporate African regionalisms in theory-building, remained a relevant bias in the second wave of theorising in the 1990s and 2000s. Neorealists, constructivists and liberal intergovernmentalists have disagreed on whether the driving force of regionalism is power, identity or institutionalisation, but the struggle to decontextualise concepts from the EU and recontextualise them elsewhere remained (Malamud and Schmitter, 2006). Concepts such as supranationalism often served as benchmarks on an archetypical EU, while fundamental categories for understanding regionalism, such as sovereignty, deviated substantially (Engel and Olsen, 2004; Söderbaum, 2015). After a series of debates around whether or not to separate the discipline of EU studies from regionalism studies (Postel-Vinay, 2007), considerable efforts were made to consider the EU as a case of regionalism that is in many regards deviant, but remains a comparable case nonetheless (Breslin et al., 2002; Bilgin, 2017). In recent years, attempts to position the European experience within a broader context of regionalism, rather than treating it as a unique phenomenon, have gained further momentum through the more common use of comparison and quantitative methods (Warleigh-Lack et al., 2011; Börzel and Risse, 2016). In addition, a normative turn has facilitated more plurality in regionalism studies (Acharya, 2012). With reference to the European integration process, regional integration has often been understood as being a positive development associated with the provision of regional public goods or the response to regional challenges. The literature on sovereignty-boosting regionalism and on authoritarian regionalism demonstrates that it is equally important to capture detrimental effects of regionalism – whether intended or unintended.

In sum, the study of regional integration has originated around the European integration process, and although the EU remains the most studied case to date, its uniqueness is increasingly being challenged. Applying the insights and concepts gained from studying the EU to other parts of the world has been a standard procedure to investigate regionalism. However, relying on a singular manifestation of region-building does not necessarily capture the idiosyncrasies and universalities of regionalism in Africa and elsewhere (Engel et al., 2016). The remainder of this chapter is divided into three parts. The next section highlights the contribution of Latin American thinking to African regionalism. Then follows an account of African regionalism in a context of interregionalism with Europe. The last section uses the case of EU-Africa relations to illustrate and expand conceptual approaches to interregionalism.

Beyond a Eurocentrist reading of African regionalism

Theories of regional integration have predominantly been the dominion of European and North American scholars reflecting on the European integration process after World War II. Consequently, African regionalism has often been explained and evaluated through that specific lens (Fawcett and Gandois, 2010). Yet, despite having been considered marginal, contributions from other world regions, in particular from Latin America, to integration theory in general and African regionalism in particular are relevant. A key contribution has stemmed from dependency theory, a current that emerged in the 1960s in Latin America. The theory spelled out an alternative economic thinking to modernisation theory and the associated capitalist model of development (Frank, 1967). The basis for the dependency school was to depart from an understanding of Latin America, which, though politically sovereign, was still occupying a subordinated position in a global economy into which it had been forcefully incorporated in the colonial period. Instead of changing the economic model along with political liberation, Latin America still provided natural resources to the economic centre at volatile and decreasing prices. This assessment tied in with another Latin American intellectual contribution, namely the explanation of a widening gap between industrial countries and Latin America through a structurally engrained continuous deterioration of the terms of trade (Prebisch, 1950).

This theory not only flourished among scholars but also became an influential paradigm for the setting up of regional organisation in Latin America. Raul Prebisch, as head of the United

Nations Economic Commission for Latin America, spearheaded the concept of industrialisation by import substitution (Cardoso, 1971). This economic policy took into account the limited market size and economic power of individual countries and thus proposed regional integration as a way to industrialise internally and shield off the economies externally vis-à-vis industrial countries. Although the basic capitalist paradigm of economic development was not put into question, a rather radical rebalancing of the global economic system was envisaged.

The theorising fell on fertile ground in African countries that gained their political independence during that period (Nkrumah, 1965). The amalgamation of capitalism and imperialism resonated with an African interpretation of socialism that envisaged industrial development disrupting an oppressive division of labour with the former colonies. The concept of neocolonialism was used to understand how external domination continued despite formally declared independence, and economic asymmetries and exploitation figured as central explanations (Rodney, 1974). In addition to European powers and the United States, this understanding also targeted the white minority rule in several southern African countries, such as apartheid South Africa. Although the neocolonial angle focused on exogenous causes and thus underplayed the deficiencies of the first postcolonial sovereign governments, it also provided a rationale for regional integration, even if plans for regional industrialisation were torn apart by the nationalist behaviour of the new leaders trying to consolidate their power.

By making the question of economic development contingent on breaking neocolonial relations, the dependency school added a new angle to integration theory. Whereas European theories had posited an antagonism between integration and nationalism, for developing countries integration was understood to be primarily in opposition to dependency. Integration thus represented an economic unification of development countries that cut their ties with neocolonial powers (Amin, 1978). The creation of regional organisations entailed an exclusive delineation, limiting membership to developing countries, and constituted a direct emancipatory reaction to the global economic system (Prebisch, 1950).

Dependency theory did thus offer a clear purpose and objective for regional organisations, which was taken up in Latin American and African regional projects during the 1960s and 1970s. In Africa, several subcontinental organisations emerged in this vein as inward-looking centralised institutions; for instance, the East African Community (EAC). Simultaneously, on a continental level, the Organization of African Unity (OAU) was launched in 1963 as an alliance of states that had recently reached political independence as well as liberation movements still under way (van Walraven, 1999). However, the regional and continental integration projects did not sustain the initial momentum. The organisations were either dismantled amidst nationalist fragmentation or entered prolonged periods of stagnation. Despite the initial failures, the underlying paradigms of pan-Africanism and the dependency school did not vanish. In 1980, the OAU proposed a continental economic community based on the creation and eventual convergence of regional pillars, the so-called Regional Economic Communities (RECs). Although the economic achievements have since lagged far behind the reiterated ambitions, the idea of a developmental regionalism has never been entirely abandoned and resurfaces regularly, in particular concerning the AU's self-positioning in strategic planning such as Agenda 2063 or the ongoing ambition to implement an African Continental Free Trade Area (AfCFTA) (Luke and MacLeod, 2019).

Postcolonial regionalism in Africa and the role of interregionalism with Europe

The founding period of contemporary regional integration can be dated to the 1950s for Europe and the 1960s for Africa. The paradigms of regional integration were able to unfold in a context where the preceding regimes of territorial separation – colonialism in Africa and nationalism in Europe – had collapsed. In Africa, the retreat of European colonial rule enabled an anti-imperial reading of pan-Africanism to emerge as an orientation for political reorganisation. Echoing the values of self-determination and racial equality proclaimed by the United Nations, pan-Africanism embodied the ambitions towards a postcolonial and unified continent (Hill and Pirio, 1987). However, as most African colonies gained political independence by transforming into sovereign nation states, fragmentation emerged between these newly created entities. Although the anti-colonial struggle relied on solidarity across colonial borders, most of the latter were taken over for the demarcation of nation states. Political power was forged on a national basis, and a territorial reorganisation of the continent according to pan-African logics thus represented a threat to many of the new governments (Cooper, 2008). Consequently, the first postcolonial regional organisations were short-lived, whether they represented colonial continuity, such as French Equatorial Africa, or postcolonial ambitions, such as the EAC. In addition, divisive lines between North and sub-Saharan Africa, and between francophone and anglophone states, remained in place and contributed to regional orientations cutting across the African continent, from the United Arab Republic to the Commonwealth.

In 1963, the OAU was created by the governments of the independent African states at the time with a view to incorporating the remaining colonies on the continent once they had been liberated. This institution constituted the least common denominator between African leaders committed to pan-Africanism and those concerned with the reinforcement of individual nation states (Welz, 2012). The modus operandi was dominated by summits of heads of state and consensus building. Non-interference in internal affairs and the freezing of colonial borders were upheld as red lines and undermined ambitious attempts to forge continental integration. The OAU intended to bridge across the existing dividing lines between North and sub-Saharan Africa as well as francophone and anglophone Africa. As decision-making required consensus between heads of state, nationalism retained an advantage over attempts at continental unity. Regionalism was subdued to the creation of national sovereignties.

Numerous regional and continental organisations have been created, resurrected or reformed since the 1960s. Given the initial goals of enhancing economic independence from the former colonial centres through protected industrialisation, Europe initially did not appear as a reference point for pan-African integration. However, it played a central role for the regionalisms that directly followed in the footsteps of colonisation, in particular the ACP Group and the regional monetary arrangements underpinning the opaque 'Françafrique' (Bovcon, 2013). The presence of the European institutions in pan-African regionalism at large became significant in the course of the 1980s, when the economic paradigm on the African side shifted towards liberalisation and regional organisations gained a visible profile as development aid receivers. Regional organisations not only offered to be partners in a wide range of policy fields, from conflict management to economic harmonisation, but by making the EU their main interlocutor, the modalities of European integration itself became a reference point. Today, there is hardly an institutional instance of African regionalism that does not rely on some vector of Europe-Africa relations. From the African Standby Force to the African Tax Administration Forum, African regionalism would look rather different without interregionalism. At the same time, political and intellectual movements that identify with the anti-imperial legacy of pan-Africanism remain relevant, and through their vision of strategic autonomy, they continue to posit the relations with Europe as a central point of regional thinking. But although regionalism in Africa is closely associated with a pan-Africanist emancipatory paradigm, regionalism also continues to exist in the shape of imperial or colonial legacy. Most notable are the South African Customs Union, which ensures financial hegemony of South Africa vis-à-vis its neighbours, and the CFA franc zone, which binds the currency of francophone countries in West and Central Africa to France and the EU (Bach, 2015).

Moreover, the interregionalism with Europe mirrors the topographic ambiguities of demarcating Africa as a region. The EU plays a pivotal role in the prevalence of competition between a continental Africa (as advocated in the Joint Africa-EU Strategy and the AU-EU summits) and a sub-Saharan Africa (as pursued in the ACP Group). Although the EU is not in a position any more to unilaterally dictate a spatial format, it provides visibility, resources and legitimacy and can thus increase or decrease the actorness of selected regionalisms (Adebajo and Whiteman, 2012). However, such processes require a favourable context with committed counterparts, as the failed attempt of the Euro-Mediterranean Partnership showed. Furthermore, EU-Africa interregionalism diverges over how to handle the many entanglements between the supposedly neatly separated entities of Africa and Europe. European overseas territories coexist in Africa alongside independent states, whereas Europe is home to significant African diasporas.

Despite Europe and Africa being the two continents on the globe where regionalism has become most strongly engrained and despite their strong interregional linkages binding their pathways, pronounced unique characteristics between the two continue to exist.

Regionalism in Africa oscillates between pan-African ideals of uniting the continent in an anti-colonial legacy and close ties with the EU as the main partner. The combination of an uncontested exclusionary regional paradigm and the strong presence of an external actor has produced a series of ambiguities that fall out of line with conventional integration theories. Centralised bureaucratic institutions have been designed, but delegation of power has been minimal. Regionalist colonial and imperial legacies coexist with pan-African institutions without causing direct conflict. Rather than obtaining their legitimacy and resources from one source, regional organisations are indebted to two principals: member states and external actors. By contrast, European regionalism has given way to a sophisticated institutionalisation with supranational elements, and the EU has established itself as the dominant and uncontested regional actor of integration. The EU also stands out due to its significant role for other regional organisations, with the interregionalism towards Africa being a prime example.

EU-Africa relations through the lens of interregionalism

This section examines relations between the EU and the ACP Group to illustrate central elements of the concept of interregionalism and to explore its limits by highlighting discrepancies.

Fluid regional delineations

In its narrow interpretation, the concept of interregionalism presumes the existence of at least two regionalisms. The approach of juxtaposing two regionalisms poses the question of what fundamentals the regions are based on. Social constructivists, political geographers and scholars of the New Regionalism Approach have underlined that territorial contingency might be a relevant element in the production of regions but does not constitute a determining one. Regions can be held together by social, economic, cultural or political references, allowing for territorial incongruences. The ACP Group illustrates that a region can be widely spread out in topographic terms, as evidenced in its 78 members from three disconnected continents. To hold the group together, other strong commonalities, such as shared interests and relations with the former colonial powers, exist (Hurt, 2003). The current framework of the EU-ACP Group interregionalism, the Cotonou Agreement, has further demonstrated the dynamic and fluid delineation of both regionalism and interregionalism. The delineation of the ACP Group illustrates well the difficulties of aligning spatial, institutional and functional formats within a fixed regional set-up.

On the EU side, through the Eastern enlargement based on the acquis communautaire, the agreement came to apply far beyond the original group of European countries negotiating it. Cotonou has thus covered changing geographies of Europe during its lifetime, in tandem with the evolution of the EU. On the ACP side, the group's expansion to Timor Leste has been less impactful but also entailed a fluid geography. In addition, some ACP Group members have not adhered to the Cotonou process, which means that countries such as Cuba or Sudan are formally part of the ACP Group but do not take part in the main raison d'être, namely the governance of relations with the EU.

Interregionalism and asymmetry

In its pure form, interregionalism is set to occur between two formal regional organisations (Mattheis and Wunderlich, 2017). The underlying assumption is that both sides constitute institutions that are similar enough to act on par with one another. However, the EU-ACP interregionalism shows that disparities between the two parties can be considerable in terms of resources, power and colonial continuities (Kotsopoulos and Mattheis, 2018). As a consequence, the central topics of the interregionalist framework reflect the interest of the stronger party, whereas the weaker party struggles to set the agenda. The framework thus entails a clear unidirectional set-up (Taylor, 2016). The main themes reflect European key global interests, such as peace, migration management, development and environment, all of which are primarily to be addressed in the ACP Group rather than in the EU (ACP Group, 2018). This also applies to the new umbrella framework currently under negotiation; this contains six priorities, five of which are to be achieved in the ACP Group, while only migration is framed with goals on both sides. Objectives such as building peaceful societies and combatting terrorism are generally not understood to be relevant for Europe – either because they are not considered as issues within Europe or because a contribution from the ACP Group is not envisaged. The ACP Group in general is not expected to play any role in European integration, whereas the reverse is explicitly foreseen.

The lack of reciprocity underlines that asymmetric interregionalism occurs under the guiding question of what the EU – in cooperation with the ACP Group – can achieve in Africa, the Caribbean and the Pacific. The question of what can be jointly achieved or what can be achieved in Europe is generally not addressed, except in certain areas such as migration, where the EU has put the enforceability of returning ACP citizens on the agenda. The EC not only acts as the main penholder in devising proposals for a new framework; it also conducts evaluation to prioritise specific scenarios, thus making the policies more prescriptive and less shared. The unilateral bias is facilitated by the ACP Group's positions being channelled via the ACP Secretariat – an entity composed of ACP Group members but funded by the EU. Finally, the ACP Group also illustrates how the underlying but often misguiding conception of interregionalism occurring between two regional entities that meet on par is being practiced (Delputte and Williams, 2016). Despite the evident disproportion between the ACP Group and the EU, much emphasis is put on the appearance and performance of symmetry. For instance, the ACP-EU Joint Parliamentary Assembly is constituted of 78 Members of the European Parliament and 78 parliamentarians from countries in the Afican, Caribbean and Pacific region. In sum, the EU-ACP Group relationship illustrates well that interregionalism does not necessarily occur between equals but more importantly how asymmetry can be structured and formalised within interregionalism.

Regional cohesion

Since the concept of interregionalism relies on the notion of pre-existing regionalisms, internal divisions fade into the background. However, regions are not monolithic, and internal divisions have an important impact on interregionalism, as the post-Cotonou negotiations show (Carbone, 2013). Divisions between the former colonial powers and the East European members impact the negotiations between the EU and the ACP Group as much as the differences among African, Caribbean and Pacific countries. On the European side, the institutional ACP Group process initially only concerned the six founding members, who were predominantly former or current colonial powers. This balance was maintained in the 2000 Cotonou Agreement, as 10 of the 15 members that constituted the EU at that time had previously been colonial powers in the African, Caribbean and Pacific region.

However, the majority has switched since, as of 2020, only 9 out of 27 EU member states having been colonial powers in the African, Caribbean and Pacific region. This trend is set to continue given the list of EU candidate countries for future enlargement. Consequently, the negotiations towards a post-Cotonou agreement are the first that involve the latest 13 member states that joined the EU. As these members do not identify with a colonial past in the African, Caribbean and Pacific region, their diplomatic, military and aid presences are at very low levels, comparatively. The recent nature of their involvement also entails a more transactional approach to this interregionalism as well as divergence over the budgeting of development aid (Council of the European Union, 2018a). The Visegrád countries, for instance, primarily associate the relationship with African, Caribbean and Pacific countries with their interests in the field of migration. In this context, the financial cost of the aid payments to the African, Caribbean and Pacific countries are also questioned (Barbière, 2018). The bulk of countries, however, have not developed a specific interest or position vis-à-vis the African, Caribbean and Pacific region, and they focus on underlying issues, such as funding, or align with traditionally leading countries, like France, in exchange for diplomatic gains, such as recognition or status. However – and this adds to the asymmetry discussed above – while the post-Cotonou framework foresees three separate geographic pillars inside the ACP Group, no such differentiation is envisaged on the EU side. Significant differences in member state interests are subdued to group cohesion, preventing the creation of pillars that distinguish between EU members according to their priorities.

Interregionalism and institutionalisation

Although the ACP Group–EU relationship qualifies as interregionalism and thus shares numerous basic characteristics with other cases, there are several elements of institutional formality that set it apart. Most interregionalisms rely on a light institutional framework with informal and non-binding characteristics. More often than not, irregular summits with heads of state produce joint declarations that face substantial hurdles in implementation. By contrast, the EU–ACP Group relationship contains significant legally binding agreements with the possibility of sanctions and a dispute settlement mechanism (Del Biondo, 2011). Due to the power asymmetry discussed above, the application of sanctions is not unbiased and has a unilateral inclination in practice.

Furthermore, the EU–ACP Group relationship is not only limited to high-level meetings such as summits of heads of state or ephemeral negotiating groups. The institutional architecture of EU–ACP Group relations is formalised and sophisticated, spread over multiple policy areas and layers of governance, including parliamentarians, ambassadors and ministers. Public consultations are also held. In addition, typically, interregionalisms do not have their own resources. The host of a summit offers to shoulder the bulk of expenses; there is no central budget. However, EU–ACP

Group relations are able to rely on a separate budget that spans over several years and enables a long-term approach.

The ACP Group also illustrates the formalisation of institutions in (inter)regionalism. Compared to most other cases, the arrangement ranks rather high with respect to formalisation, with a centralised secretariat that manages both regionalism and interregionalism, a multilayered actor structure and several organs. At the same time, institutionalisation also creates backlash, as the expansion creates competition with other entities. On the European side, the European External Action Service competes in the policy area of EU-Africa relations, and on the African side, this is the case for the AU and the affiliated RECs. In addition, the European side covers the bulk of the costs of the ACP Group, which generates attempts, in particular by member states that have other priorities, to divert funding.

Overall, the institutionalisation of the EU-ACP Group relationship is remarkably advanced and habitual, compared to most other interregionalisms (Smith, 2004). As a consequence, this relationship is more resilient and more difficult to dismantle. Other interregionalisms wax and wane, as casual neglect often suffices to stall them. While in the Cotonou framework the sheer size of membership (over half the members of the United Nations) and the vast number of policy fields complicate far-reaching integration, there is also a strong reluctance to abandon the sophistication that has been accomplished. Thus, the EU-ACP Group relationship illustrates the resilience of institutionalised interregionalism. Despite compartmentalisation into regions, the umbrella of the ACP Group is being maintained (Council of the European Union, 2018b). On the side of the ACP Group and many of its members, reluctance to dismantle the group is also connected to its privileged access to the EU and the dedicated financial endowment provided by the EU. Aside from the advantage of being a long-standing framework with financial stability, it also provides a platform to streamline EU objectives on a comprehensive level.

The ongoing fragmentation of the ACP Group is not merely an institutional dismantling but also entails reinforcement of institutional regionalism in other forms. The AU, the Caribbean Community and the Pacific Islands Forum consider themselves to be regional representatives, though their incongruence with the ACP Group's subgroups causes new friction lines. The conundrum of mismatched overlaps is set to repeat itself, as the three regional organisations have more members than the ACP Group's subgroups, some of which would be challenging to include. However, either the entire regional organisation needs to opt in to the post-Cotonou umbrella or an internal fragmentation will occur, thus perpetuating the deconstruction and reconstruction of regionalism.

The interregionalism-regionalism nexus

Research on regionalism and on interregionalism have often been linked, and this has extended to studying the mutual impact between interregionalism and regionalism (cf. Mattheis and Wunderlich, 2017). Generally, they are considered to be mutually reinforcing: potent regional organisations generate more interregionalism, and interregionalism is capable of increasing the actorness of regional organisations. The relationship between the EU and the ACP Group confirms that interregionalism and regionalism are closely interwoven (Haastrup, 2013). This occurs in complex ways and entails unintended consequences (Lopez Lucia and Mattheis, 2021). For instance, interregionalism established the format of Economic Partnership Agreements (EPAs) to advance economic regionalism across the ACP.

The EPAs involved the EU concluding separate trade agreements with individual regions within the ACP Group. In principle, the regions were supposed to be represented by existing regional organisations, but the unintended consequences have been a fragmentation of those formats according to diverging interests and the establishment of new regional groups sharing trade interests (Keijzer and Bartels, 2017). In a landscape of overlapping regionalism, such as in Africa and Europe, interregionalism inevitably affects other regionalisms, even if they are not a direct party to interregionalism (Kotsopoulos and Mattheis, 2018). As a result, the Cotonou interregionalism has fostered regional integration in Africa in the sense of reconfiguring regional groups, but to a significant extent this has not happened in the expected frame of the RECs.

Conversely, the increasing profile of the AU as a regional actor – partly due to the interregional support of the EU – has emboldened it to challenge the ACP Group as key interlocutor for EU-Africa relations. The interregionalism-regionalism nexus can also be discerned with respect to regional parliaments in Africa, such as the Pan-African Parliament, an assembly of national members of parliament from the continent. The EU, in particular the European Parliament, has emphasised the need for a significant participation of this body in the ACP Group, thus augmenting its position within African regionalism itself. This points to a multilayered form of interregionalism, where different actors within one regionalism engage with different partners and according to different agendas. For instance, the European Parliament has forged a common position with the ACP Group through the ACP-EU Joint Parliamentary Assembly to safeguard budgetary privileges, thus being at odds with the European Commission within its own regionalism. Such coalitions and oppositions generally emerge on specific issues but are reflective of the structural nature through which interregionalism transcends regionalism.

From interregionalism to interregionalisms

From a conceptual point of view, interregionalism is considered as a process that, while dynamic in its arrangement, is not predetermined to arrive at a specific end state. In principle, interregionalism entails a continuous entanglement between two regions, but this can be sustained by regular summits as much as by far-reaching legal agreements. Interregionalism is thus a self-sufficient process, and the end of this process is either envisaged as a separation of the two regions or as a rapprochement that intensifies to the point of becoming one single regionalism. The EU-ACP Group relationship has shown trends of both dissolution – as it has become fragmented in the EPA process – and shared region-building – as the framework foresees common positions in global institutions – thus contributing to the actorness of interregionalism. Beyond this bifurcation, the EU-ACP Group relationship illustrates a third pathway: a reconfiguration of interregionalism that does not centralise, but rather undergoes amorphic transformations.

Since its inception as a group of European colonies, the ACP Group has constantly expanded in membership, thus reducing the odds of a strong common denominator. Breaking points within the group have been formally articulated with the EPA negotiations. In the absence of an overarching ACP Group position on trade, the negotiations foresaw different conditions for agreements for seven regional groups of countries. Not only did the ACP Group suffer a blow by giving up group cohesion in the policy domain of trade, but also the regrouping in Africa ended in an impasse, as the initial attempts to base the groups on existing regional organisations exhibited substantial incongruences between trade interests and membership in existing regional organisations. The creation of truncated regional groups or ad hoc groups only offered temporary solutions and contributed further to the sprawling overlapping regionalism. One way out of this deadlock has been for the EU to envisage trade negotiations with Africa to the AfCFTA, which is being created under the auspices of the AU. This offers the advantage of engaging with an institutionalising economic integration project, even though its delineation undermines the shape of the ACP Group. Similarly, the policy area of migration, which was foreseen as an area of cooperation in the Cotonou Agreement, is mainly addressed at a bi-continental scale, as promoted by the Valetta Summit on Migration.

The continentalisation of EU-Africa relations has been accompanied by the devising of separate frameworks for each region of the ACP Group (i.e. for Africa, for the Caribbean and for the Pacific) (European Commission, 2017). Each of the regions is assigned different topics according to the priorities of the EU; for instance, peace and security in Africa or biodiversity in the Pacific. This procedure echoes a topographical interpretation of regionalism with expectations of neighbouring countries sharing the same expectations towards interregionalism. The EU has therefore diluted the idea of a unified agreement for the ACP Group – however, without completely disconnecting them. With the proposed umbrella framework, the EU-ACP Group relationship challenges conventional understandings of interregionalism (Council of the European Union, 2018b). Rather than covering two regionalisms, the relationship is becoming a multiregional structure centred on the European hub and with weaker, but still relevant, linkages between the spokes. Moving towards a regional delineation under an ACP Group umbrella entails an expectation of priorities and positions being clearer within coherent topographical limits and existing institutional bureaucracies to forge a common position inside the region. This expectation previously failed to materialise during the delineation of EPAs, but it is maintained in an attempt to precisely re-delineate the problematic junctures between the EPA groups in Africa (Kononenko, 2018). Although far from being free of ambiguities, inconsistencies and contradictions, the reconfiguration process illustrates that one outcome of interregionalism can be the multiplication of interregionalism, as different interests and priorities emerge between regional subgroups and undermine the cohesion of the original regionalism (European Parliament, 2018).

The planned establishment of a lighter ACP Group umbrella framework that allows for differentiated and tailored regional agreements offers the opportunity to review the dividing line between the ACP Group and other developing countries. The umbrella framework positions itself as a structure to embody all of the EU's development aid, except for the relations with strategic partners or potential accession countries (Pichon, 2018). Regions that are hitherto excluded from the ACP Group, such as North Africa, Central America or the EU overseas territories, would be integrated. The larger the framework becomes, the more it would lose its regional characteristics; but at the same time the framework would serve as a basic and uniform blueprint for the bulk of EU-related interregionalism. The ACP Group umbrella could thus be likened to the relationship between the AU and the RECs – a set of distinct regionalisms joined through their link with an overarching regionalism.

Note

1 In 2020, the ACP Group became the Organisation of African, Caribbean and Pacific States (OACPS).

Bibliography

Acharya, A. (2012) Comparative regionalism: A field whose time has come? *The International Spectator*, 47 (1), 3–15.

ACP Group (2018) ACP Negotiating Mandate for a Post-Cotonou Partnership Agreement with the European Union. ACP/00/011/18. 30 May, Lomé.

Adebajo, A. and Whiteman, K. (2012) *The EU and Africa: From Eurafrique to Afro-Europa*. London: Hurst.

Amin, S. (1978) Propositions pour une association monétaire des états de l'Afrique de l'Ouest (CEAO et CEDEAO). *Cahiers économiques et sociaux*, 16 (2), 201–212.

Bach, D. (2015) *Regionalism in Africa: Genealogies, Institutions and Trans-state Networks*. London: Routledge.

Baert, F., Scaramagli, T. and Söderbaum, F. (eds) (2014) *Intersecting Interregionalism*. Berlin: Springer.

Barbière, C. (2018) MEPs condemn Hungary's post-Cotonou agreement blockade. *Euractiv*, updated 18 June. www.euractiv.com/section/africa/news/meps-condemn-hungarys-post-cotonou-agreement-blockade (retrieved 21 November 2019).

Bilgin, P. (2017) A global international relations take on the 'immigrant crisis'. *TRAFO – Blog for Transregional Research*, 10 January. https://trafo.hypotheses.org/5699 (retrieved 21 November 2019).

Börzel, T.A. and Risse, T. (eds) (2016). *The Oxford Handbook of Comparative Regionalism*. Oxford: Oxford University Press.

Bovcon, M. (2013) Françafrique and regime theory. *European Journal of International Relations*, 19 (1), 5–26.

Breslin, S., Higgot, R. and Rosamond, B. (2002) Regions in comparative perspective. In S. Breslin, C.W. Hughes, N. Phillips and B. Rosamond (eds), *New Regionalism in the Global Political Economy: Theories and Cases*. London: Routledge (pp. 1–19).

Carbone, M. (ed.) (2013) *The European Union in Africa: Incoherent Policies, Asymmetrical Partnership, Declining Relevance?* Oxford: Oxford University Press.

Cardoso, F. (1971) *Dependencia y desarrollo en América Latina: ensayo de interpretación sociológica*. México: Siglo Veintiuno.

Cooper, F. (2008) Possibility and constraint: African independence in historical perspective. *The Journal of African History*, 49 (2), 167–196.

Council of the European Union (2018a) Multiannual Financial Framework (2021–2027): State of Play. 11871/18. 10 September, Brussels.

Council of the European Union (2018b) Negotiating Directives for a Partnership Agreement between the European Union and its Member States of the One Part, and with Countries of the African, Caribbean and Pacific Group of States of the Other Part. 8094/18 ADD 1. 21 June, Brussels.

Del Biondo, K. (2011) EU aid conditionality in ACP countries: Explaining inconsistency in EU sanctions practice. *Journal of Contemporary European Research*, 7 (3), 380–395.

Delputte, S. and Williams, Y. (2016) Equal partnership between unequal regions? Assessing deliberative parliamentary debate in ACP-EU relations. *Third World Thematics: A TWQ Journal*, 1 (4), 490–507.

Diez, T. and Wiener, A. (2018) *Introducing the Mosaic of Integration Theory*. KFG Working Paper 88. Berlin: Freie Universität Berlin.

Engel, U. and Olsen, G.R. (eds) (2004) *Africa and the North: Between Globalization and Marginalization*. London: Routledge.

Engel, U., Zinecker, H., Mattheis, F., Dietze, A. and Plötze, T. (eds) (2016) *The New Politics of Regionalism: Perspectives from Africa, Latin America and Asia-Pacific*. London: Routledge.

European Commission (2017) Recommendation for a Council Decision Authorising the Opening of Negotiations on a Partnership Agreement between the European Union and Countries of the African, Caribbean and Pacific Group of States. COM(2017) 763. 12 December, Strasburg.

European Parliament (2018) Resolution on the Upcoming Negotiations for a New Partnership Agreement between the European Union and the African, Caribbean and Pacific Group of States. 2018/2634(RSP). 22 June.

Fawcett, L. and Gandois, H. (2010) Regionalism in Africa and the Middle East: Implications for EU studies. *European Integration*, 32 (6), 617–636.

Frank, A.G. (1967) *Capitalism and Underdevelopment in Latin America: Historical Studies of Chile and Brazil*. New York and London: Monthly Review Press.

Haastrup, T. (2013) EU as mentor? Promoting regionalism as external relations practice in EU–Africa relations. *Journal of European Integration*, 35 (7), 785–800.

Hazlewood, A. (ed.) (1967) *African Integration and Disintegration: Case Studies in Economic and Political Union*. Oxford: Oxford University Press.

Hill, R.A. and Pirio, G.A. (1987) Africa for the Africans: The Garvey movement in South Africa, 1920–1940. In S. Marks and S. Trapido (eds), *The Politics of Race, Class and Nationalism in Twentieth Century South Africa*. Harlow, UK: Longman (pp. 209–253).

Hurt, S.R. (2003) Co-operation and coercion? The Cotonou Agreement between the European Union and ACP states and the end of the Lomé Convention. *Third World Quarterly*, 24 (1), 161–176.

Jørgensen, K.E., Pollack, M. and Rosamond, B. (eds) (2006) *Handbook of European Union Politics*. Thousand Oaks, CA: Sage.

Keijzer, N. and Bartels, L. (2017) *Assessing the Legal and Political Implications of the Post-Cotonou Negotiations for the Economic Partnership Agreements*. Discussion Paper 4/2017. Bonn: Deutsches Institut für Entwicklungspolitik.

Keohane, R. and Nye, J. (1975) International interdependence and integration. In F. Greenstein and N. Polsby (eds), *Handbook of Political Science*. Andover, MA: Addison-Wesley (pp. 363–414).

Kononenko, V. (2018) *A Renewed Partnership with the Countries of Africa, the Caribbean and the Pacific*. Briefing. European Parliamentary Research Service. Brussels: European Union.

Kotsopoulos, J. and Mattheis, F. (2018) A contextualisation of EU–Africa relations: Trends and drivers from a reciprocal perspective. *South African Journal of International Affairs*, 25 (4), 445–460.

Lopez Lucia, E. and Mattheis, F. (eds) (2021) *The Unintended Consequences of Interregionalism: Effects on Regional Actors, Societies and Structures*. London: Routledge.

Luke, D. and MacLeod, J. (eds) (2019) *Inclusive Trade in Africa: The African Continental Free Trade Area in Comparative Perspective*. London: Routledge.

Malamud, A. and Schmitter, P.C. (2006) La experiencia de integración europea y el potencial de integración del Mercosur. *Desarrollo Económico*, 46 (181), 3–31.

Mattheis, F. (2018) African regionalism. In A. Paasi, J. Harrison and M. Jones (eds), *Handbook on the Geographies of Regions and Territories*. Cheltenham, and Northampton, MA: Edward Edgar (pp. 457–467).

Mattheis, F. and Litsegård, A. (eds) (2018) *Interregionalism Across the Atlantic Space*. Berlin: Springer International Publishing.

Mattheis, F. and Wunderlich, U. (2017) Regional actorness and interregional relations: ASEAN, the EU and Mercosur. *Journal of European Integration*, 39 (6), 723–738.

Nkrumah, K. (1965) *Neo-colonialism: The Last Stage of Imperialism*. New York: International Publishers.

Pichon, E. (2018) *Le futur partenariat de l'UE avec les pays d'Afrique, des Caraïbes et du Pacifique («post-Cotonou»)*. Briefing. European Parliamentary Research Service. Brussels: European Union.

Postel-Vinay, K. (2007) The historicity of the international region: Revisiting the 'Europe and the rest' divide. *Geopolitics*, 12 (4), 555–569.

Prebisch, R. (1950) *The Economic Development of Latin America and its Principal Problems*. Lake Success, NY: United Nations Department of Economic Affairs.

Robson, P. (1968) *Economic Integration in Africa*. London: Allen Unwin.

Rodney, W. (1974) *How Europe Underdeveloped Africa*. Washington: Howard University Press.

Smith, K.E. (2004) The ACP in the European Union's network of regional relationships: Still unique or just one in the crowd? In K. Arts and A. Dickson (eds), *EU Development Cooperation*. Manchester: Manchester University Press (pp. 60–79).

Söderbaum, F. (2015) *Rethinking Regionalism*. London: Macmillan.

Taylor, I. (2016) Bait and switch: The European Union's incoherency towards Africa. *Insight on Africa*, 8 (2), 96–111.

van Walraven, K. (1999) *Dreams of Power: The Role of the Organization of African Unity in the Politics of Africa 1963–1993*. Farnham: Ashgate.

Wallerstein, I. (1967) *Africa: The Politics of Unity*. London: Random House.

Warleigh-Lack, A., Rosamond, B. and Robinson, N. (eds) (2011) *New Regionalism and the European Union: Dialogues, Comparisons and New Research Directions*. London: Routledge.

Welz, M. (2012) *Integrating Africa: Decolonization's Legacies, Sovereignty and the African Union*. London: Routledge.

3

Applying postcolonial approaches to studies of Africa-EU relations

Rahel Weldeab Sebhatu

To say that Africa/African Union (AU) and European Union (EU) relations are postcolonial in nature should be stating the obvious, and yet studies that discuss and analyse Africa-EU relations from a postcolonial perspective or through postcolonial approaches are hard to come by. This chapter outlines the importance of postcolonial approaches for the study of Africa-EU relations. It contextualises such approaches in negotiation practices and outcomes of the EU proposed Economic Partnership Agreements (EPAs). Though academic literature on Africa-EU relations tends to define such relations as being asymmetrical, the politics around the negotiations of the EPAs through postcolonial lenses reveals contestations around the assumptions of such asymmetries. In particular, the dominant narratives of asymmetry locate African states as being in a weaker position, thus silencing the articulations of African agency. Yet in undertaking a postcolonial account and paying attention to resistance towards the EU's imposed EPAs – through diplomacy by state actors and the actions of civil society – this chapter is able to highlight African agency in the context of Africa-EU relations.

Theoretical and epistemological standpoints in the way Africa-EU relations have been studied vary. Positivist approaches tend to focus on 'the asymmetries of material power to explain bargaining outcomes almost exclusively in terms of power imbalances' (Hurt et al., 2013: 68), while constructivist approaches document how prevailing discourses are tools for dominant states to achieve policy goals and how weak actors mitigate material power asymmetries by making use of rhetorical action (ibid.). Constructivist accounts have shown that there is a weak correlation between the outcomes of EPA negotiations and market dependency on the African, Caribbean and Pacific (ACP) countries, thus rendering materialist explanations inadequate (Heron and Murray-Evans, 2017: 358). Postcolonial approaches go a bit further than constructivist ones, as they seek to deconstruct and decentre Eurocentric perceptions through postcolonial theory and perspectives. Consequently, and in the context of Africa-EU relations, postcolonial approaches can be used to demystify and demythologise African agency. Here, to demythologise means to reframe and add to existing mainstream arguments so as to rectify Eurocentric bias in mainstream knowledge production on Africa-EU relations (Rutazibwa, 2014: 296).

Africa-EU relations are complex in their scope and history. Kotsopoulos and Mattheis (2018) discuss seven trends and drivers of Africa-EU relations, namely elements of colonial legacy, partnership, asymmetry, market liberalisation, politicisation, regional actorness and the changing global order. They also make it clear that 'the full context of Europe-Africa relations requires going beyond these compartmentalisations' and that 'many elements are intertwined' (ibid.: 456). The areas of cooperation between African states and the EU – such as trade, development and political engagement – are in themselves intertwined, as all such pillars of engagement are outlined in major policy documents, including the Cotonou Agreement and the Joint Africa-EU Strategy. Such complex relations have been analysed through mainstream theories in the disciplines of Economics, Political Science and International Relations (IR), but without serious consideration of how such relations are informed and shaped by colonial legacies. This chapter argues for a research strategy that gets to the core of these relations: coloniality.

Coloniality refers to the deep structures that not only justified colonialism in the eyes of the coloniser, but also produced the hierarchies that made modernity possible. In other words, coloniality and modernity are constitutive of each other (see Quijano, 2007), and this is easily revealed through colonial legacies. Postcolonial theories and approaches to the study of Africa-EU relations allows for a deeper understanding of the dynamics of Africa-EU relations from a historical and global perspective, an alternative to mainstream accounts that gloss over the impact of colonialism as historical, therefore missing its constitution with modernity.

Postcolonial approaches present 'a kind of radical intellectual practice that challenges the dominant ways of producing knowledge about the so-called developing or Third World' (Chandra, 2013: 491). The desire to challenge knowledge produced about the Third World might not appeal to some researchers, but postcolonial approaches – at the very least – allow for more nuanced and rigorous scholarship that interrogates and deconstructs myths about issues around international relations and global politics. By myths, I mean any floating signifier – like *asymmetry* between African states and the EU – 'whose terms are external to what is representable in the objective spatiality constituted by the given structure' (Laclau, 1990: 61); that is, postcolonial subjectivity (and its silencing) within structures of a postcolonial world order. By interrogating myths, scholars can and will be in a better position to develop more grounded theories – theories that cannot be easily debunked or provincialised as is the case with many Eurocentric studies.

The application of postcolonial approaches to Africa-EU relations is rare even as some take into consideration the postcolonial nature of contemporary relations between Europe and its former colonies. Postcolonial IR scholars have, however, diligently theorised on how postcolonial approaches can inform research design and analyses in contemporary international politics (see Sabaratnam, 2011, 2013; Chandra, 2013; Fisher Onar and Nicolaïdis, 2013), thus providing theoretical and conceptual frameworks to analyse Africa-EU relations.

Recent scholarship in postcolonial international relations argues for postcolonial approaches against the backdrop of mainstream approaches being Eurocentric but presented as universally applicable. Many scholars of Africa-EU studies have adopted postcolonial perspectives in their research. However, research that studies Africa-EU relations through mainstream theories in IR have, for the most part, focused on the descriptive postcolonial space. It is through positivist and realist accounts of Africa-EU relations that coloniality has been, and continues to be, reproduced. This is problematic because it tends to silence agency on the part of African actors. It may be argued that such misrecognition of agency can lead to miscommunication and negotiation deadlock between African and European actors.

Throughout this chapter, references to and examples of the politics around EPA negotiations – launched in 2000 and which were supposed to be finalised by 2007 in order to meet a World Trade Organization (WTO)-mandated deadline – are analysed through postcolonial approaches with the aim of contextualising the reasons as to why negotiations did not lead to the signing of EPAs by the 2007 deadline. Accordingly, after discussing what postcolonial approaches are, this chapter discusses how to consider and analyse colonial legacy by decentring

Europe, how to analyse partnership from a postcolonial perspective, how to contextualise market liberalisation in a changing world order within a context of a postcolonial global economy, as well as how regional actorness should be analysed through the politicisation and rearticulation of subjectivity.

What are postcolonial approaches?

Postcolonialism as a critical theory and as a field of study emerged through theories around the psychological effects of colonialism (Fanon, 1967); colonial violence and resistance (Fanon, 1963); cultural representation (Said, 1978); epistemic violence, especially towards subalterns (Spivak, 1999); and cultural difference, hybridity, ambivalence and mimicry (Bhabha, 1994). Although postcolonial theory emerged, for the most part, out of the humanities, such canonical theorisation established the foundation from which postcolonial and non-Western theories in IR emerged (cf. Chowdhry and Nair, 2002; Gruffydd Jones, 2006; Shilliam, 2010; Jabri, 2013). The term 'postcolonial' is broadly used to define the situation of formally colonised countries and peoples, including in regard to their place in the global political economy. Postcoloniality refers to 'transcending an imperialist past not just coming after' (De Alva, 1995, cited in Fisher Onar and Nicolaïdis, 2013: 293–294), something that has yet to happen in Africa and in Europe. The 'post' in 'postcolonial' may be used to describe the situation of African countries after their political decolonisation from European colonisation; however, many scholars have made grounded claims that the structures of colonialism are still present in today's postcolonial world, and Africa is no exception. Consequently, 'coloniality is constitutive of modernity and should not be thought of separately' (Maldonado-Torres, 2007, cited in Capan, 2016: 3). Postcolonial theory is therefore a critical theory that acknowledges colonial legacies. It provides approaches and an analytical lens to studying coloniality in contemporary times, when Europe does not directly occupy African lands yet still produces the knowledge that informs foreign policies that effect formally colonised lands and peoples.

Coloniality is constitutive of modernity, and both are legitimised through Eurocentrism. Eurocentrism can be defined as 'the sensibility that Europe is historically, economically, culturally and politically distinctive in ways that significantly determine the overall character of world politics' (Sabaratnam, 2013: 261). Postcolonial approaches, through an understanding that colonial legacies continue to provide the foundation for knowledge production that reproduces coloniality through Eurocentrism, seek to contest and disrupt colonial epistemologies by critiquing and provincialising Eurocentric theories and analyses. Besides provincialising Eurocentric approaches and world views around modernity, postcolonial approaches have a normative aim to 'search for emancipatory alternatives in the realms of knowledge and praxis' (Chandra, 2013: 481). Emancipatory alternatives are provided through research strategies that seek to decolonise[1] mainstream ones. Meera Sabaratnam (2011) writes about six decolonising strategies for the study of world politics, all of which will be discussed in this chapter: pointing out discursive orientalisms; deconstructing historical myths of European development; challenging Eurocentric historiographies; rearticulating subaltern subjectivities; diversifying political subjecthoods; and reimagining the social-psychological subject of world politics. Sabaratnam (2013), after outlining avatars of Eurocentrism within critical debates on liberal peace, also offers three intellectual strategies for decolonising critique: recovering historical political presence; moving from debates on (alien) 'culture' to alienation; and decolonising political economy. Making similar arguments, Uday Chandra (2013) makes the case for a postcolonial approach to the study of politics by highlighting three approaches: critiquing existing Eurocentric theories of comparative politics; using a bottom-up ethnographic and historical understanding of politics as they pertain to particular contexts; and re-evaluating key political concepts in light of different non-Western experiences. Like the trends and drivers of Africa-EU relations, these postcolonial approaches and strategies are intertwined, and to research Africa-EU relations through postcolonial approaches requires going beyond such compartmentalisations. It is for this reason that this chapter discusses these strategies under the themes of analysing colonial legacies through decentring Europe, partnership from a postcolonial perspective, market liberalisation within a context of a postcolonial global economy and regional actorness through the politicisation and rearticulation of subjectivity.

While postcolonial approaches to the study of Africa-EU relations are rare, not all studies employ theoretical and methodological frameworks that may be Eurocentric. Many studies have taken into consideration the postcolonial nature of Africa-EU relations through theories around global political economy that decentre Eurocentric perspectives and take African agency seriously (cf. Langan, 2016, 2018; Murray-Evans, 2019). Consequently, and as a 'mission' of postcolonial approaches for knowledge production, one is required to recognise that it is important to challenge Eurocentric views through a process of decentring. Decentring may be best described as 'interrogating, disturbing, engaging, reframing, challenging, mocking, or even undoing mainstream, privileged ways of viewing the world' (Nayak and Selbin, 2010: 8). When it comes to studying Europe's relations with the non-European developing/Third World, decentring is 'necessary both to make sense of our multipolar order and to reconstitute European agency in a non-European world' (Fisher Onar and Nicolaïdis, 2013: 283). Accordingly, postcolonial approaches are used not just to analyse African agency, but European agency as well. The negotiations around the EPAs provide an interesting event that – through decentring – allows for a rigorous analysis of both African and European agency.

With the domination of Eurocentrism in positivist accounts and analyses of Africa-EU relations, it has become 'commonsensical' to evaluate them as being asymmetrical, because the EU is purported to have more material resources than ACP states and their respective regional bodies. However, as the 2007 deadline for the signing of regional EPAs came and passed, literature on the negotiation processes between the EU and African regional bodies could not ignore the fact that negotiations were not being driven by material asymmetries. Even when mainstream positive approaches did consider the agency of the 'weak', they did so in terms of 'rational actions around calculations of economic interests, where weak actors influence outcomes by reducing power asymmetries through collective action strategies based on shared economic interests' (Hurt et al., 2013: 68, citing Drahos, 2003, Narlikar, 2004, Steinberg, 2002, and Zartman, 1971). Decentring the EU and dominant discourses about its power can and should be used as a tool to unravel the puzzle around how supposedly weak states can prove to be a challenge to the EU, especially when it comes to the EPA negotiations. The aim of such an approach should not be to argue for/about power on the part of African states, but to take African agency seriously and to rigorously analyse the material and structural reasons as to how African negotiating power is discursively constructed as being weak.

Negotiations for EPAs with the ACP Group[2] started in 2002, but then devolved to negotiations at the regional level in 2004 (Meyn, 2008: 518), with the aim of replacing the economic and trade component[3] of the Cotonou Agreement by 2007. This deadline was set in relation to the end of a waiver period set by the WTO for the EU to rectify its preference agreements with the ACP. Instead of considering alternatives to the contentious EPAs (see Stevens, 2015), the EU chose to use a coercive approach in their negotiations. The fact that the EU had to resort to such an approach is a sign that EU and ACP countries define what their partnership entails in different and often conflicting ways. As Meyn reminds us:

EPAs embody a changing EU attitude and mark a new era in post-colonial history and relations between the EU and ACP countries. Contrary to the Commission's analysis, however, this changing relationship has not been marked by a 'partnership of equals' but by the EU's coercive power and its increasing neglect of ACP development concerns.

(2008: 526)

Despite EU attempts to use coercive power to get Africa's Regional Economic Communities (RECs) to sign EPAs by 2007, the protracted negotiation processes and amendments made to the original proposal after 2007 demonstrates an event that contests the common myth that African states have little bargaining power when it comes to the EU. The bargaining power around the EPAs might not be comparable to that during the Lomé negotiations, when 'the bargaining power of Africa had reached unprecedented levels' (Kotsopoulos and Mattheis, 2018: 455); however, African agency had not completely succumbed under the circumstances. There is a deafening silence around African agency in literature on diplomacy and negotiation theory. The reasons for this can be understood by taking into consideration the colonial legacies that prevail in the knowledge produced on Africa and how it consequently reproduces coloniality through articulations of power between Africa and the EU.

Colonial legacy, historical amnesia and decentring Europe

Colonial legacy refers to the sociopolitical remnants of governance structures, trade, economy and law established through and during colonisation that have remained even after the political decolonisation of former colonies and which are reproduced at a global level. Today's state borders on the African continent are a representation of colonial legacies, as it is only the northern border of South Sudan – which gained its independence in 2011 from Sudan – that has not been drawn out by European colonisers. It was not just the colonial borders that remained after African countries gained independence (through peaceful means or through armed liberation struggle); many governance structures, laws, education systems, financial structures, markets, etc. established during colonisation still remain today. Colonial legacy not only shapes many structures within African states, but also reproduces discourses on Africa in postcolonial times and influences the nature of relations between Africa and Europe today. Moreover, colonial legacy frames not just the discourses around Africa-EU relations, but also the self-positioning and perception of African states within the EU and vice versa (Kotsopoulos and Mattheis, 2018). Remnants of colonialism make up colonial legacy, whereas the deep structures that maintain colonial legacies and their discursive power is known as coloniality.

The very constitution of the EU was also a product of colonial legacy. The pursuits of European colonisers stretched throughout the world, but unlike the Americas and Asia, Africa held a special place in the efforts to construct European economic integration. During colonisation, Africa's economies were oriented towards the needs of European capital rather than that of local populations (Kotsopoulos and Mattheis, 2018: 448). The central objective of Europe's integration – vis-à-vis the Treaty of Rome and the establishment of the European Economic Community (EEC – today's EU) in 1957 – was dictated through a collective agreement among European countries that they needed Africa in order to restore Europe's productive power in the aftermath of World War II. This was also a time when former African colonies were starting to become independent states. The geopolitical constellation that went by the name Eurafrica (Hansen and Jonsson, 2018: 40) appears repeatedly throughout EEC discourse on European integration until the mid-1960s, but then disappears under the different guise of development, aid and diplomatic counselling (ibid.: 44; also see Hansen and Jonsson, 2014). This 'disappearing act' of Africa's place in the very construction of a European community is representative of the larger historical amnesia that continues to reproduce Africa's 'underdevelopment' from an ahistorical perspective. This historical amnesia is co-constitutive of how the EU imagines itself as a global actor and power; 'by forgetting [its] colonial past and successfully entrenching the myth of its own "virgin birth"' (Nicolaïdis, 2008, cited in Fisher Onar and Nicolaïdis, 2013: 292), the EU has been able to legitimise its own trajectory towards modernity while negotiating with 'underdeveloped' African countries as a self-described model and an 'ethical intervener' (Rutazibwa, 2010). The myth of the EU's 'virgin birth' and its trajectory to becoming modern cannot and should not be understood as being separate or exclusive from its colonial past. European countries were able to generate wealth, industrialisation and development through the exploitation of the resources and people of their former colonies. Accordingly, when discussing Europe's power and self-imaginary, a postcolonial approach deconstructs this fundamental historical myth of Europe(an) development. The discourse that Europe 'was technologically advanced, economically developed, that it advanced the problems of international coexistence through the institutionalisation of state sovereignty, that it was the origin of enlightened and universalist ethical and political thought' has been used to legitimise the forms of authority and control (Sabaratnam, 2011: 787–788) over the meanings and terms of Africa-EU partnership by placing one continent in a dominant/superior position over the other.

Myths about Europe's development are sustained through Eurocentric histographies, and postcolonial approaches have and will continue to challenge this. The alternative, as Sabaratnam reminds us, is 'to think in terms of "multiple modernities" occurring in the context of "connected histories" to avoid analysis that only refracts understanding of social relations through a truncated telling of the European experience of industrialisation' (2011: 789). The de-silencing of the fact that the European Community was born out of the desire 'to manage collectively a colonial world that was escaping its member States individually and above all the African continent' (Fisher Onar and Nicolaïdis, 2013: 293) must be part of the decentring agenda that postcolonial approaches are ultimately a part of. To decentre Europe in this context means to interrogate discourses that proclaim that Africa has needed Europe more than Europe has needed Africa. Accordingly, if Africa-EU scholars are to displace the errors that are produced by an ahistorical reading of the formation of the EEC – an error that silences the fact that Africa's incorporation into the European enterprise was a central objective which aimed to exploit the continent's resources (ibid.) – they must employ the strategy of recovering the historical political presence (Sabaratnam, 2013) of which Africa-EU trade agreements and negotiations are constituted. An appreciation of the historical political presence of Africa in the constitution of Europe would draw out the 'longstanding connections of mutual constitution between different societies that are so often buried by intervention discourses' (ibid. 2013: 271); that is, the mutual constitution of Europe and Africa in a postcolonial world. It is also through recovering this historical political presence in the mutual constitution of Europe and Africa that we can re-evaluate *partnership* in light of African experiences.

The meaning of partnership: Paternalism and the ontological Other

With the Lomé Convention negotiations in 1973, ACP states surprised the EEC when they decided to negotiate as a bloc (i.e. ACP postcolonial states together) rather than as regional groupings (i.e. African, Caribbean and Pacific states as three separate regions) (Hall and Blake, 1979, cited in Flint, 2009: 81). This, in turn, created an unprecedented level of bargaining power for the ACP. Lomé I[4] was the accord that came closest to presenting Africa and Europe as partners, as there was 'little or no conditionality and ACP members were free to formulate their own economic policies without undue outside interference' (ibid.: 81–82). Here, agency is represented by the bargaining power brought by the collective voice of the ACP, that, in turn, became conducive to a partnership of equals, though neoliberal conditionalities do not dictate such partnership. However, the debt crisis of the 1980s, the end of the Cold War and the collapse of world commodity prices led to the erosion of the ACP's bargaining power (ibid.: 82), and consequently partnership as defined under the Lomé Convention was eroded. The essence of this partnership would be replaced with economic conditions that mimicked those of the Bretton Woods institutions and a neoliberal discourse that would be used to promote neoliberal reforms to alleviate poverty. Africa would be reinstated into imperial discourse as 'the white man's burden'.

The partnership that existed during the Lomé I accord did not erode solely because of material asymmetries between Africa and Europe. Rather, the coloniality of power that positions African states in a postcolonial global economy had already set the stage for the erosion of the Africa-Europe partnership. According to the European Commission, EPAs 'are trade and development agreements negotiated between the EU and ACP *partners* engaged in regional economic integration processes' (2019b, emphasis mine), and yet various RECs and African states have contended that EPAs risk further fragmenting regional economic integration while strengthening dependency on Europe (Khumalo and Mulleta, 2010: 211). Instead of viewing the original EPA proposals as a deal that would strengthen economic and trade partnerships between the EU and Africa, most ACP countries – especially African states – viewed EPAs as a drawback of the trade agreement outlined within the Cotonou Agreement. The Cotonou Agreement was already considered a disappointment compared to its predecessor, the Lomé Convention, which established privileged and non-reciprocal access for ACP exports to EU markets from 1975 to 2000 (Flint, 2009: 79). The EPAs, in turn, would be viewed as the full implementation of a neo-colonialist regimen.

Partnership between the EU and the ACP is a central claim of the Cotonou Agreement, along with poverty reduction (Hurt, 2003: 173); however, the meaning of partnership between African states and the EU is 'subject to diverging interpretations of what concessions and commitments are required' (Kotsopoulos and Mattheis, 2018: 451). Whereas many ACP states view partnership as cooperation sans paternalistic interventions, the EU has used the term to emphasise commitment to and ownership of Africa's development by African states. As Whitfield and Fraser (2010: 342–343) explain, proposing ownership on the part of those who receive aid is to 'end conditionality and encourage recipients to identify their own priorities', while on the part of donors (i.e. the EU and its member states), it is 'frequently used to refer to the *commitment* of recipients', and the failure to meet development goals is diagnosed as a lack of 'ownership of neoliberal reform/development policies' which are, in one way or other, set by the very conditions imposed by the EU.

The partnership ethos of the Lomé Convention was already waning with the Cotonou Agreement's neoliberal economic conditionalities (Flint, 2009: 82) and a noticeable shift in language emphasising a 'pro-poor' development policy (ibid.: 84). Although changes in the global political and economic order were taking place during this shift, the change of language did not appear out of nowhere. Rather, it is part of a broader discourse, the genealogy of which can be easily traced to colonialism (see Gruffydd Jones, 2013: 49–50). Although explicitly racist vocabulary no longer taints North-South trade and development policies, discourses on development – especially (but not exclusively) in regard to Africa – still reproduce Africa and Africans in paternalistic ways reminiscent of the discourses produced to justify colonisation's brutality. In other words, the shift in language still produces the coloniality that shapes Africa-EU relations. A postcolonial approach towards such paternalistic representations would be to point out ontologies of otherness. As discussed earlier, colonial legacies and historical amnesia about how Europe became modern silence the fact that the two regions mutually constitute each other. This is made possible through Othering; what Africa is to Europe is Europe's Other.

Discourses that position Africa (underdeveloped, weak) as Europe's (modern, developed, strong) 'Other' have been sustained mainly through culturalist Eurocentrism. As Sabaratnam reminds us, there is a need to re-politicise such culturalist notion by focusing on the 'alienating' character of it; 'that is, its displacements, violence, silencing, humiliations and dispossessions' (Sabaratnam, 2013: 272). The differences that may lead to tensions or deadlock in negotiations do not occur because of cultural differences between the EU and Africa, but because of colonial difference. It is this colonial difference that informs and affects the ways in which African and European 'partners' view each other. Africa-EU relations, as they stand today and as was witnessed during EPA negotiations, are framed 'in terms of the persistence of the imperial structure of the discourse [read: coloniality] that produces the relationships' (Doty, 1996, cited in Sabaratnam, 2011: 786). To analyse Africa-EU relations in isolation of the formation of African states after the colonial period is to do so in a Eurocentric, ahistorical manner characteristic of Eurocentric histographies. Such histographies are marred by the epistemic violence that is reproduced through the asymmetry discourse and which is the probable cause of tensions within diplomatic negotiations.

Power asymmetry between African states and the EU – the former discursively constructed as being 'weak' and the latter as 'strong' – is *the* dominant discourse as far as mainstream studies on Africa-EU relations are concerned. A postcolonial approach to asymmetry discourse is not concerned with arguing against the fact that economic disparities exist between Africa and Europe. It is, rather, concerned with contextualising why and how such disparities exist in the first place (i.e. the structural and material reasons that can be traced to coloniality). Moreover, a postcolonial approach would recognise the epistemic violence behind this discourse, including from an historical perspective, and how such an epistemology silences African agency. In other words, acknowledging the epistemic violence behind asymmetry discourse would be to recognise the power and functionality of the latter (i.e. coloniality) with the aim of not reproducing it as a sort of self-fulfilling prophecy. It would also recognise how the discourse effects the way in which African and European actors perceive each other. If such agency had not been silenced in the first place, it would not have been a puzzle as to why African states contested the terms on which the EU negotiated the EPAs.

Market liberalisation and a changing world order in a postcolonial global economy

Since the 1990s, Africa-EU relations have been based on neoliberal principles, with the EU considering trade and market liberalisation as central to poverty reduction while African leaders have also equated it with development (Kotsopoulos and Mattheis, 2018). Such principles, of course, were reproduced in the EPA negotiations, but as has been observed, many African states believed that the liberalisation promoted through the EPAs was a threat to the trade liberalisation African states sought through their RECs. So, if market liberalisation has been a central issue for interregionalism for both the African RECs and the EU, then why has it produced friction (ibid.) during the EPA negotiations?

As moral norms of pro-poor development are not seen as being moral in terms of their outcomes and impact on the lives of vulnerable ACP citizens, these same norms have been used to rationalise asymmetric economic ties (Langan, 2012: 243). In order to analyse political economy from a perspective that takes into consideration the impact on the lives of vulnerable ACP citizens in a postcolonial global economy, one is required to think of political economy in a way that seeks to decolonise mainstream assumptions that market liberalisation enables development. Sabaratnam (2013: 273–274) offers two ways that one can begin to do this: engage with those targeted by the intervention to interpret its material effects; and analyse such narratives in a way that 'politicizes the various forms of entitlement, dispossession and accumulation that characterizes the rationales for intervention and its distributive effects'. This also speaks to what Chandra proposes as a postcolonial approach to politics; that is, 'to offer alternatives to mainstream political science theories via in-depth, bottom-up empirical understandings of politics in postcolonial settings' (2013: 490). Sabaratnam presents these intellectual strategies within the context of liberal Peace Studies, and Chandra through Political Science, but these strategies can be applied when analysing trade agreements between Africa and the EU. To politicise EPAs in this way becomes possible especially because the EU presented and rationalised reciprocity of trade through market liberalisation as being pro-poor, thus rationalising it as a necessary intervention for development even though there is very little evidence that allowing EU products to enter African markets unabated would result in economic growth or development. As Sabaratnam rightfully reminds us, however, entangling the politicisation of entitlement, dispossession and accumulation with the language of 'development' should be avoided, because such language is fundamentally colonial and depoliticises poverty and economic policy (Escobar, 1995; Ferguson, 1990, cited in Sabaratnam, 2013: 274). Instead, one should 'begin to challenge the historical terms on which this dysfunctional political economy is made thinkable' (ibid.); that is, through coloniality.

Besides African states, civil society organisations (CSOs) – both in Africa and in Europe – challenged the EPAs' purported pro-poor agenda by pointing out how trade liberalisation would negatively affect Africa's local economies. Del Felice's study on the STOP EPAs campaign explains how CSOs and their transnational activism contributed to shaping the discursive and politicisation processes of the negotiations by 'both reproducing and challenging underlying assumptions of trade and development policies, fostering the inclusion of more voices and issues in debates, and shaping subjects' identities' (2014: 145). As positivist traditions in IR tend to focus almost exclusively on state actors, the agency of CSOs, especially on the African continent, would be entirely missed if one would ignore (rather than engage) with those targeted by the interventions. This is also why postcolonial approaches seek to understand how postcolonial subjects politicise things in ways that rearticulate their subjectivity as agents for change.

Politicisation and regional actorness: Rearticulating subjectivity

In regard to politicisation in Africa-EU relations, Kotsopoulous and Mattheis (2018) refer to two meanings, namely as a means for the EU to impose conditionality for cooperation and as the establishment of tools that supposedly permit the EU and the ACP countries to move beyond aid and trade; both are used to prioritise political dialogue around good governance for human rights and democracy. Inquisition of the EU in the internal affairs of African states, of course, has been controversial and met with resistance throughout the decades of Africa's relations with Europe. This has created tension in terms of development cooperation and trade. When it comes to trade relations and the EPA negotiations, a postcolonial approach would pay serious attention to the ways in which both African and European actors (states and CSOs) use their agency to politicise and depoliticise aspects of the EPAs through their regional bodies.

Regional actorness refers to the ways in which regional institutions demonstrate agency and power on a collective level. The EU, as a collective of European member states, practises agency and gains power through the coherence of its policies and actions, which are conducted under 'one European voice'. African countries – through the AU and/or RECs (African Union, n.d.) – have also used a collective voice to enhance their negotiating power with the EU. But even when African regional institutions use collective voice to amplify their agency, mainstream IR literature on Africa-EU relations is predisposed by coloniality. A Eurocentric perspective sees regional actorness in terms of a dichotomy of modern/underdeveloped institutions and sees Europe's institutions as superior to those of its ontological 'Other' (i.e. Africa). Through Eurocentric comparative analyses of African and European institutions, the nuances of African agency are overlooked.

The perception that the evolvement of the Organization for African Unity (OAU) into the AU in 2002 mimicked the emergence of the EU from its predecessor, the EEC, is problematic (see Haastrup, 2013). What has been erased and silenced through this interpretation is the fact that the OAU emerged as a Pan-African response to (neo)colonialism. Haastrup rightfully reminds us that 'the diffusion literature on the "EU as a Model" narrative erroneously prioritises the EU quest for self-replication' by overlooking 'Africa's motives for regional integration' and that scholars should look beyond such Eurocentric perspectives (ibid.: 797–798). A postcolonial approach to analysing Africa-EU relations would recognise that the ways in which the RECs contested the original prospectus of the EPAs is co-constitutive of the response against neocolonialism through African regionalism.

With a mandate to liberalise trade among the ACP countries, the EU chose to negotiate EPAs at a regional level because the WTO allowed for agreements between regional blocs, and not for non-reciprocal agreements (Flint, 2009: 85). According to Hurt (2003: 173), the EU initially suggested splitting the ACP Group into six regions, four of which were in Africa (i.e. West Africa, Central Africa, East Africa and the Southern African Development Community (SADC)), with only the SADC corresponding to the existing RECs across the continent. The AU recognises eight RECs, and many African states are members of multiple RECs. Eventually, due to the incompatibility of negotiating EPAs in regions that are not coherent with the already established RECs, the EU negotiated with seven regional bodies: the Economic Community of West African States, the SADC, the Eastern and Southern Africa Community, the East African Community, the Economic and Monetary Community of Central Africa,[5] the Caribbean Forum (CARIFORUM) and the Pacific region. Out of these seven regional bodies, the negotiation with CARIFORUM was the only one that concluded with a full EPA by the 2007 deadline (Khumalo and Mulleta, 2010: 210), an EPA which produced an outcome resembling the original prospectus (Heron and Murray-Evans, 2017: 357).[6]

The EU's initial approach to negotiating the EPAs with regions not correlated with the already established RECs is a typical example of how a misrecognition of regional actorness could lead to a misarticulation of African subjectivity. It is also important to recognise that African states did not negotiate their regional stances in a homogenous manner, as different states and regions would have been affected by the initial EPA prospectus in different ways (see Vickers, 2011; Olomola, 2014). A postcolonial approach to analysing regional actorness would take into consideration the international environment, prioritising knowledge of the local environment and local ownership (Haastrup, 2013: 798). To do this would mean diversifying, rearticulating and reimagining the subjectivity of African actors – both in government and in the African citizenry – in ways that render them 'more than principally the instruments of history or social forces' (Sabaratnam, 2011: 790).

Conclusion

Employing postcolonial approaches when studying Africa-EU relations (and IR in general) would, in significant ways, revamp the field. Such revamping is necessary both in regard to recognising and acknowledging African agency and in rearticulating European agency in a changing world order, one that may be described as a postcolonial world order. As has been argued in this chapter, postcolonial approaches could lead to more rigorous research and to an understanding and rearticulation of how partnership between the two continents should be; that is, a partnership that respects the challenges of development and cooperation marred by colonial legacies. Trade and cooperation between Africa and the EU would hopefully be built around a more rigorous understanding of the negative effects of market liberalisation on African local economies. Moreover, relations can be strengthened if Europe comes to accept the diverse subjectivities that African actors already possess. Ultimately, postcolonial approaches could lead to the development of more coherent policies that do not just propagate falsehoods but which are shaped with the aim of bringing about emancipatory alternatives for both Africa and Europe.

Notes

1. There are distinctions between postcolonial theories and decolonial theories, and robust academic discussions around the decolonial option (see Mignolo and Escobar, 2013). It is outside the scope of this chapter to get into a deep discussion about decolonial options. However, when applying postcolonial approaches in research, decolonising research strategies allow for the utility of postcolonial theories.
2. The ACP Group was renamed in 2020 and is now the Organisation of African, Caribbean and Pacific States.
3. There are three components (or pillars) that make up the Cotonou Agreement: development cooperation, political cooperation and economic and trade cooperation (see European Commission, 2019a).
4. Note that the Lomé Convention was renegotiated and renewed in 1982 (Lomé II), in 1985 (Lomé III) and in 1989 (Lomé IV).
5. The Economic and Monetary Community of Central Africa is also known as CEMAC – in French: Communauté Économique et Monétaire de l'Afrique Centrale.
6. It should be noted that progress in terms of the implementation of the EPA for member states of CARIFORUM has been impeded for several reasons, including widespread doubts about neoliberalism – doubts which were fuelled by the global economic crisis of 2008 (Khumalo and Mulleta, 2010: 210). See Girvan (2010) for a thorough critique on how the initialed EPA for the CARIFORUM institutionalised the relationship of asymmetric power between Caribbean states and the EU based on principles of neoliberal globalisation.

Bibliography

African Union (n.d.) Regional Economic Communities (RECs). https://au.int/en/organs/recs (retrieved 27 December 2019).
Bhabha, H.K. (1994) *The Location of Culture*. Abingdon and New York: Routledge.
Capan, Z.G. (2016) Decolonising international relations? *Third World Quarterly*, 38 (1), 1–15.
Chandra, U. (2013) The case for a postcolonial approach to the study of politics. *New Political Science*, 35 (3), 479–491.
Chowdhry, G. and Nair, S. (eds) (2002) *Power, Postcolonialism and International Relations: Reading Race, Gender and Class*. London and New York: Routledge.
Del Felice, C. (2014) Power in discursive practices: The case of the STOP EPAs campaign. *European Journal of International Relations*, 20 (1), 145–167.
Escobar, A. (1995) *Encountering Development: The Making and Unmaking of the Third World*. Princeton, NJ: Princeton University Press.
European Commission (2019a) ACP – The Cotonou Agreement. https://ec.europa.eu/europeaid/regions/african-caribbean-and-pacific-acp-region/cotonou-agreement_en (retrieved 1 September 2019).
European Commission (2019b) Economic partnerships. https://ec.europa.eu/trade/policy/countries-and-regions/development/economic-partnerships/ (retrieved 8 October 2019).
Fanon, F. (1963) *The Wretched of the Earth*. New York: Grove Press.
Fanon, F. (1967) *Black Skin, White Masks*. London: Pluto.

Fisher Onar, N. and Nicolaïdis, K. (2013) The decentring agenda: Europe as a post-colonial power. *Cooperation and Conflict*, 48 (2), 283–303.

Flint, A. (2009) The end of a 'special relationship'? The new EU-ACP Economic Partnership Agreements. *Review of African Political Economy*, 36 (119), 79–92.

Girvan, N. (2010) Technification, sweetification, treatyfication. *Interventions*, 12 (1), 100–111.

Gruffydd Jones, B. (2006) *Decolonizing International Relations*. Plymouth: Rowman & Littlefield Publishers.

Gruffydd Jones, B. (2013) 'Good governance' and 'state failure': Genealogies of imperial discourse. *Cambridge Review of International Affairs*, 26 (1), 49–70.

Haastrup, T. (2013) EU as mentor? Promoting regionalism as external relations practice in EU-Africa relations. *Journal of European Integration*, 35 (7), 785–800.

Hansen, P. and Jonsson, S. (2014) *Eurafrica: The Untold History of European Integration and Colonialism*. London and New York: Bloomsbury Academic.

Hansen, P. and Jonsson, S. (2018) European integration as a colonial project. In O.U. Rutazibwa and R. Shilliam (eds), *Routledge Handbook of Postcolonial Politics*. Abingdon and New York: Routledge (pp. 32–47).

Heron, T. and Murray-Evans, P. (2017) Limits to market power: Strategic discourse and institutional path dependence in the European Union–African, Caribbean and Pacific Economic Partnership Agreements. *European Journal of International Relations*, 23 (2), 341–364.

Hurt, S.R. (2003) Co-operation and coercion? The Cotonou Agreement between the European Union and ACP states and the end of the Lomé Convention. *Third World Quarterly*, 24 (1), 161–176.

Hurt, S.R., Lorenz-Carl, U. and Lee, D. (2013) The argumentative dimension to the EU-Africa EPAs. *International Negotiation*, 18 (1), 67–87.

Jabri, V. (2013) *The Postcolonial Subject: Claiming Politics/Governing Others in Late Modernity*. Abingdon and New York: Routledge.

Khumalo, N. and Mulleta, F. (2010) Economic Partnership Agreements: African-EU negotiations continue. *South African Journal of International Affairs*, 17 (2), 209–220.

Kotsopoulos, J. and Mattheis, F. (2018) A contextualisation of EU–Africa relations: Trends and drivers from a reciprocal perspective. *South African Journal of International Affairs*, 25 (4), 445–460.

Laclau, E. (1990) *New Reflections on the Revolution of Our Time*. London and New York: Verso.

Langan, M. (2012) Normative power Europe and the moral economy of Africa-EU ties: A conceptual reorientation of 'normative power'. *New Political Economy*, 17 (3), 243–270.

Langan, M. (2016) *The Moral Economy of EU Association with Africa*. Abingdon and New York: Routledge.

Langan, M. (2018) *Neo-colonialism and the Poverty of 'Development' in Africa*. New york: Palgrave MacMillan.

Meyn, M. (2008) Economic Partnership Agreements: A 'historic step' towards a 'partnership of equals'? *Development Policy Review*, 26 (5), 515–528.

Mignolo, W.D. and Escobar, A. (eds) (2013) *Globalization and the Decolonial Option*. Abingdon: Routledge.

Murray-Evans, P. (2019) *Power in North-South Trade Negotiations: Making the European Union's Economic Partnership Agreements*. London and New York: Routledge.

Nayak, M. and Selbin, E. (2010) *Decentering International Relations*. London and New York: Zed Books.

Olomola, A.S. (2014) EU-Africa Economic Partnership Agreements: Risks, rewards and requisites for agricultural trade and African development. In T. Moyo (ed.), *Trade and Industrial Development in Africa: Rethinking Strategy and Policy*. Dakar: Council for the Development of Social Science Research in Africa (pp. 123–158).

Quijano, A. (2007) Coloniality and modernity/rationality. *Cultural Studies*, 21 (2–3), 168–178.

Rutazibwa, O.U. (2010) The problematics of the EU's ethical (self)image in Africa: The EU as an 'ethical intervener' and the 2007 Joint Africa–EU Strategy. *Journal of Contemporary European Studies*, 18 (2), 209–228.

Rutazibwa, O.U. (2014) Studying Agaciro: Moving beyond Wilsonian interventionist knowledge production on Rwanda. *Journal of Intervention and Statebuilding*, 8 (4), 291–302.

Sabaratnam, M. (2011) IR in dialogue … but can we change the subjects? A typology of decolonising strategies for the study of world politics. *Millennium: Journal of International Studies*, 39 (3), 781–803.

Sabaratnam, M. (2013) Avatars of Eurocentrism in the critique of the liberal peace. *Security Dialogue*, 44 (3), 259–278.

Said, E. (1978) *Orientalism*. New York and London: Penguin Books.

Shilliam, R. (ed.) (2010) *International Relations and Non-Western Thought: Imperialism, Colonialism and Investigations of Global Modernity*. London: Routledge.

Spivak, G.C. (1999) *A Critique of Postcolonial Reason: Toward a History of the Vanishing Present*. Cambridge, MA, and London: Harvard University Press.

Stevens, C. (2015) Economic Partnership Agreements and Africa: Losing friends and failing to influence. In M. Carbone (ed.), *The European Union in Africa: Incoherent Policies, Asymmetrical Partnership, Declining Relevance?* Manchester: Manchester University Press (pp. 164–188).

Vickers, B. (2011) Between a rock and a hard place: Small states in the EU-SADC EPA negotiations. *Round Table*, 100 (413), 183–197.

Whitfield, L. and Fraser, A. (2010) Negotiating aid: The structural conditions shaping the negotiating strategies of African governments. *International Negotiation*, 15 (3), 341–366.

Part II
Evolving governance in EU-Africa relations

Introduction to Part II

Mary Farrell

Part II of this volume addresses the formal governance processes underpinning cooperation between the European Union (EU) and Africa. As the chapters indicate, there have been significant changes to the formal structures and policies as well as the actors, particularly since the start of the millennium and as relations between the two regions moved onto a more formal basis. Governance is not government, but rather a distinct set of regulatory processes adopted to address common interests, which raises questions around who has authority and how decisions are implemented. In Part II, the governance analytical framework takes account of the actors, institutions, rules and norms, and policies that have emerged in EU-Africa relations. There are also normative elements of governance that frame policies and practice internally and in the EU's external relations, including democracy promotion, respect for human rights, and the rule of law.[1]

As the chapters indicate, there is a distinctly political nature to the evolving governance in EU-Africa relations that affects what policies are selected and how these are implemented by both regions. The interests of the states and non-state actors as well as the interests of the supranational institutions have undoubtedly converged to shape the governance structure over time. However, more actors and a greater diversity of interests as well as different opportunity structures in both the EU and Africa can impact the strategic calculations of all actors, with implications for future choices on governance arrangements.

From the Treaty of Rome to Cotonou

Intercontinental governance presents many challenges beyond what might be expected in the context of interstate cooperation. A sovereign state establishes diplomatic relations with other states on a bilateral basis, based upon diverse motives and different national interests, political priorities and historical ties. There are also the changing strategic interests of the participant states in the context of dynamic regional and global developments. The presumption of national interest is widely accepted in the academic International Relations literature and, although littered with ambiguity and a tendency towards oversimplicity, the notion provides some common ground in analysing and understanding the motivation of the individual state in international relations and the respective foreign policies that shape agreements and commitments entered into by national leaders at different times. Inevitably, a collective interregional agreement among multiple state actors will reflect many layers of engagement that require diverse responses at the governance and policy levels.

The chapters in Part II describe the evolving nature of governance that has shaped relations between Europe and Africa from the Treaty of Rome through to the Joint Africa-EU Strategy (JAES) adopted at the Lisbon Summit of 2007. Although the relations between Europe/EU and Africa were given little attention by the six member states in the European Community's founding treaty, some of these countries had colonial or commercial relations with the continent that were based on historical ties and exploitative commercial relations of unequal exchanges. From the start, the internal organisation of the European Community was based upon an institutional governance structure finely tuned to reflect the national interests of the member states and the authority of the supranational institutions. The successive EU treaties instigated the institutional reforms and deeper integration accompanied the balance between intergovernmentalism and supranationalism.

In Chapter 4, António Raimundo notes that the institutional frameworks have historical roots, evolving over time through the interaction of different actors and shaping policy outcomes. The European countries brought their distinct individual historical experiences and political priorities to Africa-EU cooperation. Initially, France was motivated by moral responsibility and solidarity towards Africa, in contrast to the different perspectives of Germany and Netherlands which from the beginning focused on trade and economic relations. As decolonisation gathered pace there was a rethink of old ties, and the subsequent Yaoundé and Lomé agreements showed how interests and values on both sides changed to reflect a new political climate facing actors in the two regions. Trade reciprocity was a nod in the direction of the General Agreement on Tariffs and Trade system, and although the Yaoundé text declared the principles of political equality, it would eventually be viewed as clientelist and donor influenced.

However, this agreement did establish a multilateral institutional framework with a region-to-region format that would continue for the next half-century, adapting as necessary to internal pressures arising from the changing priorities of the partnership and to the pressures from external forces. But, as Raimundo points out, the institutionalised partnership between Africa and Europe inevitably had its critics. Although the Lomé agreements were regarded initially at least as moving towards interdependence and partnership, these arrangements came under criticism with the economic crisis of the 1980s and the perceived dependence on the West due to the economic and political conditions attached to the agreements. Raimundo details the sometimes difficult institutionalised cooperation between the European and African countries. While the partnership continued, it did so on the basis of gradual changes to the governance framework, additional member states on both sides, new objectives emphasising poverty reduction, sustainable development and the gradual integration of the African, Caribbean and Pacific countries into the world economy. By 2000, the shared agenda included issues around peace and security, migration and governance. However, the inclusion of political conditionality and the 'essential elements' of cooperation, notably human rights, democratic principles, the rule of law and good governance, demonstrate the widening political agenda that was increasingly underpinning Africa-EU cooperation.

The Cotonou Agreement was subject to periodic reviews that extended the agenda to include new priorities – regional integration, climate change, state fragilities and aid effectiveness. Since 2000, the areas of disagreement between Africa and the EU covered themes such as migration, human rights, sexual discrimination and the International Criminal Court (ICC). While the ICC may prove ultimately less contentious given the generally mixed political support among the international community, it seems likely that both Africa and the EU will continue to disagree over these issues where each region has its respective material interests underpinned by distinct normative standards that do not necessarily overlap. Raimundo's case is that each region is already working with alternative partners, in a world very different from that in which Africa–EU cooperation emerged and where new priorities point towards more strategic cooperation agreements and fewer (or different) ties with traditional partners.

Foreign policy

Foreign policy is long regarded as an important instrument in the policy toolbox of the sovereign state. There remains a core element in the national policy portfolio that reflects the consistent nature of the state's internal political strategy and its relations with neighbouring countries. Nonetheless, state interests can change over time and foreign policy priorities will shift to reflect new realities in the national and international domains. Foreign policy in regional organisations like the EU and the African Union (AU) is both complex in formulation and more challenging to implement. In Chapter 5, Masters and Landsberg offer an insightful commentary on how these two regions address the issues that the academic and policy literature generally associate with the nation state.

EU foreign policy is the outcome of internal negotiations among the member states and reflective of the community's normative principles (democracy, rule of law, respect for human rights, fundamental freedoms) as well as strategic interests of the member states in the community. The EU has emerged as an actor (in its own right) in certain global policy arenas, notably the United Nations negotiations on development, peace and security, and climate change. The European capacity to speak internationally with one voice emerged gradually as the institutional framework took shape and the opportunities to test this system became more plentiful post 2000. At this stage, the EU looked to consolidate new relations with the African continent, taking a continent-to-continent approach based upon the principles of co-ownership, joint action, co-management and co-responsibility.

In their chapter, Masters and Landsberg examine JAES initiatives, highlighting the possibility for cooperation between two regional partners with historical ties. However, it is the common interests and differing aspirations that ultimately determine or limit the scope of cooperation. The authors suggest that the AU is focused on the continent, seeking to establish trade, foster development and maintain peace and security, while the EU has global ambitions to be a normative global player. While norms matter in the AU agenda, the organisation is far less institutionalised, and there is significant variation among the member states in their adherence to regional norms and institutions.

More broadly, the record of interregional cooperation instigated by the EU underlines the political and policy challenges when there are differing views that are already multilayered through multiple state membership and multidimensional policy diversity. The EU and the AU both emphasise multilateralism, but in the global arena of the United Nations, it is the member states that are the main actors.

European External Action Service

States implement foreign policy through the network of embassies around the world, deploying ambassadors who represent their respective governments views and priorities in diverse international diplomatic forums. Diplomacy has a long tradition with well-established rules and practices that have become institutionalised for the global diplomatic community and where the rules of engagement offer a degree of familiarity to participants who have progressed through national foreign service career structures. In this environment, whether the national interest is stable or changing incrementally, foreign policy actors will play a critical role in shaping priorities and processes within the national context.

EU foreign policy is also implemented through the global network of delegations under the authority of the European External Action Service (EEAS). This entity was established to provide some coherence to the diverse elements that made up EU foreign policy, which include the policies of the individual member states, the European Commission's external policies and the EU as international actor in Common Foreign and Security Policy and Common Security and Defence Policy. Presided over by a High Representative for Foreign Affairs and Security Policy, the EEAS bureaucracy is Brussels-based and supported by staff from the European Commission and the European Council as well as a global network of EU delegations around the world.

The EEAS organisational structure is hierarchical, with five regional area departments that reflect the global orientation. Thematically, the emphasis on crisis management and development sets the direction of diplomatic relations and, organisationally, the EEAS has bilateral relations with African partners at many levels and through multiple instruments. As a unique diplomatic channel focused on external representation, the broad scope of EEAS responsibilities means that it engages with many EU institutions as well as coordinating with the member states to formulate common positions on external policy.

Nele Marianne Ewers-Peters, in Chapter 6, brings out the complexity of this EU organisation and highlights the extremely ambitious scope of the external relations agenda.

European Neighbourhood Policy

In Chapter 7, Anthony Costello reviews the operational features of European Neighbourhood Policy (ENP) and the normative principles that underpinned this particular policy. From the 1990s, the EU engaged in diplomatic programmes intended to build and sustain good relations with near neighbours through initiatives such as the Barcelona Process, the Euro-Mediterranean Partnership and the Union for the Mediterranean. The ENP emerged out of these initiatives, more ambitious in its objectives and in strategic orientation.

Introduced in 2004, the ENP involved cooperation and partnership agreements on economic and cultural relations with 16 neighbouring countries that were not potential accession states.[2] The policy was distinct from the EU's enlargement strategy and was driven in large part by economic and security considerations following the Arab Spring and the migration crisis. The ENP arose from concerns about a potential spillover of political and economic security risks from the eastern and southern neighbourhoods, and the policy objectives were intended to share the benefits of the 2004 enlargement but without any intention to offer membership. The two subsequent revisions of the ENP, in 2011 and 2015, offered some modifications to the scope and strategy, but it retained the essential emphasis on fostering good relations with the neighbours.

The European Commission approach to programming was technocratic, and this was reflected in the ENP Action Plans, but there was also a strong normative dimension to be seen in the requirements on good governance, rule of law, recognition of human rights, gender equality and the emphasis on neoliberal principles in a market economy. The level of policy detail is also seen in the requirements on labour rights, product standards, structural reforms, assistance for sustainable development, support to combat terrorism and weapons of mass destruction.

The ENP appeared to be another one of the grand strategies favoured by the EU, with its thematic focus and policy areas resonant with the instruments, tools and norms to be found in other programmes. The 16 countries targeted were not exactly next-door 'neighbours'; rather, they were spread out over a large geographic area covering North Africa, the Middle East, Eastern Europe and Central Asia. These countries have significant differences in terms of population, economy, political system, ethnicity, culture and identity. But they all have coastlines to the south and east of EU borders along the Mediterranean Sea and the Black Sea.

Viewed against the varied and diverse economic and political backgrounds of the countries targeted by the ENP, the policy can be considered as ambitious in scope and substance. However, it also attracted wide criticism from the countries that the policy was directed towards, and many of the programme elements were received with scepticism as to the political or economic benefits. Although the EU favoured conditionality clauses in many agreements with third countries and/or regions, the use of such clauses was criticised by the ENP states, since EU accession was not on offer in return for political and economic transformation even in the long term.

Similarly, the ENP countries considered that the joint ownership principle, where the EU would not impose values and conditions on individual states, was not applied in practice. Instead, the neighbour countries were obliged to accept action plans and targets that were imposed with little consultation or democratic input and which carried financial penalties for inadequate results. Subsequent programmes in 2011 and 2015 focused on sectoral transformation, civil society and socio-economic areas with initiatives to foster education and training as well as financial support to small and medium-sized enterprises.

The evolution of the Joint Africa-EU Strategy 2007–2019

The JAES emerged with the idea of taking relations between Europe and Africa forward based on equality between the two parties, focusing on shared ownership and people-centred partnerships. In a sense these principles were not new, but on the African side there was a desire for a partnership of equals to replace the donor-recipient relationship that had characterised previous cooperation programmes. The Cotonou Agreement of 2000 did cover development cooperation as well as the regional Economic Partnership Agreements, but these excluded some key African countries.[3] Historically, as previous discussion suggests, many of the EU's programmes adopted distinct strategies and actions for North Africa and sub-Saharan Africa, in part due to the historical evolution of policy and the piecemeal approach of the European states.

From 2000, continental integration came more into focus, as Fergus Kell and Alex Vines note in Chapter 8, although even then the regional and national levels of authority and policymaking were generally more active in practice. The JAES priorities picked up on themes resonant with historical concerns as well as the emerging priorities of global development policy and the Millennium Development Goals. Peace and security, governance and human rights, and trade and regional integration were undoubtedly priorities for continental Africa and perhaps more for some countries than others in the two continents. In any event, the JAES was ambitious in both scale and scope, and the European Commission brought all the tried and trusted bureaucratic tools into play to activate the strategy, including regular summit meetings, road maps and interregional collaboration. However, substantive progress in meeting the priorities was slowed by the limited financial resources provided for the strategy and, inevitably, by the external shock of the 2015 migration crisis. Britain, as a member state of the EU with historical ties to Africa, had a strong interest in advancing the European initiatives towards Africa, particularly relating to trade and development. How this relationship between Britain and individual African countries as well as the regional groupings plays out post-Brexit is not clear; however, it is likely that new strategic priorities will create new economic and trade relations for all sides. Kell and Vines suggest an increased role for the private sector in development initiatives and, for politicians in Europe and Africa alike, more focus on migration, mobility and employment.

In Chapter 9, John Akokpari and Primrose Z.J. Bimha examine the capacity of the AU to act and speak for the collective interests of the continent in EU-Africa relations. The ambition of the AU was for an integrated political continent driven by citizens and member states, with a focus on continental growth and development, and with the potential to be a dynamic force in the global arena. The chapter presents a convincing narrative of the individual state and regional community relationships with the AU, highlighting the way in which individual African countries and the regional economic communities have taken opposite positions to the AU (which itself lacks authority to sanction individual states). As the authors note, the AU is weakened in the context of an environment where the sovereign state matters, and the solidarity of the continental community in EU-Africa relations is by no means confirmed. At the international/global level, African states often adopt individual national positions on issues such as global peace and security, human rights, the ICC and other institutions of global governance.

In 2020, the European Commission introduced a new strategy of engagement and cooperation with Africa that built on common interests while reflecting a clear acknowledgement of the continent's transformative agenda under the AU's Agenda 2063, the African Continental Free Trade Area, the African Visa-Free Area, the African Single Digital Market and the Single African Air Transport Market. The European Commission sees the continental integration resulting from these initiatives as an opportunity for Europe and proposed five partnerships in this new strategy, covering green transition and energy, digital transformation, sustainable growth and jobs, peace and governance, and migration and mobility.[4] While it will be some time before the impact of this latest European strategy for Africa can be seen, it is evident that the proposed strategy covers some long-standing concerns for the EU around migration and security, while also seeing the mutual benefits from the green agenda and digital transformation.

Africa is changing rapidly economically, and the continent has a population of over one billion people, with a large young population and a growing middle class. While the continent has exhibited steady economic growth in recent years, there is a need for jobs, energy and infrastructure. Against the background of a changing and dynamic continent, the EU has to forge a new relationship based on equality and reciprocity and where conditionality is unlikely to be the currency of exchange and engagement. There are other influential actors in Africa, including states and non-state actors such as big business and multinational corporations that can exercise pressure and persuasion on governments and public institutions in individual states. External state actors have an increasing presence across the continent – notably China, which has different interests and priorities to those of the EU and a different approach to cooperation with a state or a regional grouping of states.

Notes

1. Given the nature of the EU as a political community of sovereign states, the normative dimension has become increasingly important for reaching consensus and decision-making. Norms are wide-ranging and include sustainable peace, respect for human rights, rule of law, good governance, sustainable development, consensual democracy, equality and social solidarity.
2. The ENP states included Algeria, Morocco, Egypt, Israel, Jordan, Lebanon, Libya, the Palestinian Autonomy, Syria, Tunisia, Armenia, Azerbaijan, Belarus, Georgia, Moldova and Ukraine.
3. These were Algeria, Egypt, Libya, Morocco and Tunisia.
4. Joint Communication to the European Parliament and the Council, Towards a comprehensive Strategy with Africa. JOIN (2020) 4 final. Brussels, 9 March 2020.

4

From the Treaty of Rome to Cotonou

Continuity and change in the governance of EU-Africa relations

António Raimundo

Introduction

Relations between the European Union (EU) and Africa have been governed by a series of institutional arrangements, which have been important in shaping the interregional relationship. In the 1950s, the founding texts of the EU already included provisions for an 'association' with countries in Africa that had 'special relations' with some of the European member states. Subsequently, new mechanisms were devised to manage those relations, reflecting developments of a different nature in Europe, Africa and the wider world. This chapter provides a long-term and comprehensive assessment of the institutional frameworks governing EU-Africa relations, from the 1950s Rome Treaty to the 2000s Cotonou Agreement. It takes stock of how the set of institutions, rules, narratives and practices that govern those relations have evolved historically, examining their origins, nature and effects. In that endeavour the analysis considers how key actors dynamically interacted within these institutional frameworks and their main contexts to shape concrete policy outcomes. The primary goal was tracing major patterns of continuity and change. Since EU-Africa relations have been organised over time by several distinct policy frameworks (some reviewed in other parts of this volume), the geographical scope of this chapter regarding the African side is circumscribed to the sub-Saharan subregion, which for most of the period analysed here structured the main of its relationship with Europe as part of the broader Africa, Caribbean and Pacific (ACP) Group.[1] The remainder of this chapter considers what have been the principal arrangements governing those delineated relations: the Rome Treaty (1957–1963), the Yaoundé conventions (1963–1975), the Lomé conventions (1975–2000) and the Cotonou Agreement (2000–2020).

Rome Treaty arrangements: A unilateral associationism (1957–1963)

The origins of the formal relationship between the EU and Africa date back to the very creation of the European Economic Community (EEC) by the 1957 Treaty of Rome. Despite their relative decline and the strong decolonisation pressure of the post-World War II context, some of the European founding member states still had colonial ties when the Rome Treaty was negotiated (Mayall, 2005). This was especially the case for France, which among the Six founders had kept the widest colonial interests and presence, mainly in Africa. These links were perceived as important for economic and politico-diplomatic reasons, buttressing the country's status and influence in the world. Moreover, the ideology of associationism, defending the complementarity between metropoles and colonies as well as the mutual benefits deriving from their economic and political 'cooperation', remained very influential on French soil. Not unrelated to this vision of Eurafrique, notions of solidarity and moral responsibility towards Africa were equally very common among some European political parties and wider public opinions (Grilli, 1993: 1–4). As the process of European economic integration had important external implications, France sought to protect its privileged relations with its dependencies. Paris wanted to prevent the creation of the EEC as a customs union affecting its colonial trade arrangements. It also hoped to share the burden of its aid, which was seen as useful for countering separatist and pro-communist impulses in Africa. The other member states were reluctant to follow France's associationist plans. Strong opposition came from West Germany and the Netherlands, which had a more open and globalist outlook while at the same time being fearful of neocolonial accusations and unwilling to shoulder the costs of joint aid. Faced with France's firm insistence, these objections were ultimately overridden by the priority given to European reconciliation and reconstruction, as well as through some concessions (Lister, 1988: 1–18; Twitchett, 1978: 1–15).

The Rome Treaty provided for an association between the EEC and the colonies and overseas territories of Belgium, Italy, France and the Netherlands, with the stated purpose to 'promote the economic and social development' of these dependencies and to 'establish close economic relations between them and the Community as a whole'. This association system was based on three main elements: trade, financial aid and formal relations. Its reciprocal trade preferences meant that the privileged access existing between metropoles and colonies was maintained, but also extended to all other members of the association. Aid was allocated through the specifically established European Development Fund (EDF), with contributions from all Six member states and administered by the European Commission. Even if relatively small, EDF was disbursed in the form of grants and supplemented the bilateral aid from the EEC countries. Moreover, the association was given a legally based nature and celebrated for a (renewable) period of five years. This institutionalisation of the relationship between the EEC and the associates suited France's position particularly well, since it contributed to preserving the country's 'special relations' in Africa while lightening some of its burden in a potentially enduring way. Simultaneously, this Europeanisation of colonial bilateral ties meant that these became interlinked with a wider system of governance, involving a multitude of actors with different perspectives and requiring compromises (Grilli, 1993: 8–14; Lister, 1988: 19–20; Twitchett, 1978: 17–31).

The association had a unilateral nature, since it was defined solely by the EEC and imposed on the associates. As dependencies at the time, the associated countries had no choice over whether to join the association and were not involved in its implementation in any meaningful way. Moreover, despite the declared intention to be mutually beneficial, the association's emphasis on economic development (contrasting with its silence on political aspects) did nothing to dispel the perception of a 'collective colonialism' that could render independence in Africa more difficult (Lister, 1988: 13–14, 18). Part of this discontent was related to the exclusive features of the association. Its preferential trade discriminated against third parties, which posed a question of legality under the liberal principles of the General Agreement on Tariffs and Trade (GATT) and raised criticism particularly among non-associated developing countries with competing exports to European markets. These discriminatory features were tolerated by the United States due to the association's peripheral economic and political importance as well as Washington's Cold War strategy of containment. European post-imperial relations were broadly perceived as maintaining Western influence in the Third World (Grilli, 1993: 11–13; Mayall, 2005: 296–297). In just a few years the majority of the associates became independent, and most favoured the preservation of close links with the EEC. This preference reflected the conservatism and Europe-oriented feelings among many leaders in francophone Africa, who wanted to avoid the uncertainties of independence by maintaining the support from the EEC. Although the association's economic results were not impressive, such multilateral support was seen as less overtly involved with politics and as having less colonial overtones than direct cooperation with ex-metropoles. In retrospect, the fact that associationist ties managed to survive decolonisation further underlines the significance of the Rome Treaty arrangements (Lister, 1988: 10, 20–31; Twitchett, 1978: 33).

Yaoundé: A negotiated and contractual associationism (1963–1975)

The wave of decolonisation that swept across the African continent in the early 1960s created an urgent need to rethink the nature of the association. Such reassessment led to the 1963 Yaoundé Convention of Association between the EEC and a group of 18 countries, essentially former French colonies in Africa, known as the Associated African and Malagasy States (AAMS).[2] This move coincided with a period marked by increased attempts at foreign policy cooperation among Western European countries, partly spurred by the ambiguous French Gaullist vision of Europe as a 'third way', independent of the superpowers. Simultaneously, with the setting up of its agricultural and commercial policies over the 1960s, the EEC was taking steps towards becoming a more cohesive and visible external actor. On the African side, despite the spread of Pan-Africanist ideas, the continent was mostly divided among different blocs of countries. Efforts such as the establishing of the Organization of African Unity in 1963 proved largely unable to displace the much more significant links between African states and their external sponsors. Moreover, preference was given to more national political and economic strategies in Africa (Clapham, 1996: 106–113). Modernisation Theory ideas, favouring market-centred notions of development, also formed part of the contextual factors that inspired the Yaoundé system (Holland and Doidge, 2012: 23–24). In many ways a continuation of previous institutional arrangements, Yaoundé introduced some changes that triggered new dynamics in Europe-Africa relations.

One key innovation of Yaoundé was its recognition of the political equality of the newly independent associates. The convention's preamble expressed the desire to maintain the association on the basis of 'complete equality and friendly relations'. This formal parity was particularly cherished by AAMS leaders, keen to ascertain their freshly won national sovereignty and on the defensive due to the criticisms of Eurafricanism by anti-imperialist and Pan-Africanist movements (Grilli, 1993: 18). Unlike the Rome Treaty arrangements, Yaoundé was freely negotiated, given contractual status and subject to ratification by all parties. This novelty did not prevent EEC member states from controlling the negotiations, the end results of which essentially reflected a compromise among their differences, facilitated by the European Commission. Even so, during the discussions the AAMS tried to exert some pressure by appealing to the honour and moral integrity of the Six (Lister, 1988: 36–37; Twitchett, 1978: 80–82). To facilitate the processes of negotiation and implementation of the agreement, joint institutions were also created in which the two sides were represented on an equal footing. Again, this departure was not without important limits, as such institutional structure mirrored that of the EEC and decision-making power rested mainly with the European side. Simultaneously, it was a symbol of parity between the two parties as well as a useful framework to promote dialogue and mutual awareness (Twitchett, 1978: 109–113, 139–140).

The Yaoundé system also displayed much continuity with previous arrangements in its economic provisions. Crucially, it preserved preferential reciprocal trade relations between the EEC and the AAMS. However, instead of aiming at a sort of wide Eurafrican trading area, as under the Rome Treaty, Yaoundé provided for bilateral free trade areas between the EEC and each of the associated countries. Moreover, the associates were free to organise their commercial relations, both with each other and with third countries. These changes were partly an adaptation to the new independent status reached by the associates. But equally they were an attempt to make Yaoundé conform more with GATT rules and an answer to the criticisms of neocolonialism and divisiveness levelled in particular by some African Commonwealth countries (Grilli, 1993: 19–20; Twitchett, 1978: 121–125). Following the failure of the British EEC application, several of these anglophone African states ended up signing their own association agreements with the EEC, even if with less far-reaching features than Yaoundé (Twitchett, 1978: 90–93, 145–146). Also, the requirement of trade reciprocity was often criticised as being ungenerous from the European side, but it was supported by the AAMS as a token of their legal parity with the EEC. In part to compensate for the lower level of trade preferences granted, Yaoundé increased the volume of aid channelled through the EDF (Lister, 1988: 40–55; Twitchett, 1978: 97–109, 124–137).

As was the case under the Rome Treaty, the main achievements of the Yaoundé system were chiefly political. Contrasting with its limited economic results in general, Yaoundé was able to preserve the Eurafrican association by adapting it to the postcolonial era (Lister, 1988: 55; Twitchett, 1978: 137–140). From a unilateral form of associationism, the relationship evolved into a negotiated one, more attentive to norms of sovereign statehood and legal equality. Although patently short of overcoming significant power imbalances and enduring forms of dependence, Yaoundé's innovations created precedents, laying the ground on which future agreements between Europe and Africa have since been built. Yaoundé was distinct in providing for a common contractual basis for interactions between countries located on the two sides of the North–South divide. It established a multilateral institutional framework with a level of stability, favouring the development of a complex relationship between the two parties along a region-to-region format (Holland, 2002: 28). Despite the signs of greater openness and less exclusiveness, Yaoundé remained narrowly focused on francophone Africa and a very special relationship linking the associates in an alliance with Europe and the West, not with the socialist or developing world (Lister, 1988: 45). Simultaneously, such asymmetrical entente, rooted to a large extent in colonial legacies, was not immune to an important degree of paternalism, mainly of French inspiration. Indeed, despite the efforts towards greater parity, Yaoundé inaugurated a pattern of interactions based to a large extent on a clientelist paradigm, with many reverberations in subsequent arrangements.

Lomé: The rise and erosion of a unique 'partnership' (1975–2000)

The first EEC enlargement, from the original Six to the Nine, in 1973 opened the door to a reformulation of the Europe-Africa relationship. Britain was interested in protecting its Commonwealth ties, which went well beyond the African continent and were marked by a more liberal disposition than was the case in francophone contexts. EEC countries such as the Netherlands and West Germany used the prospect of British membership as an opportunity to press for a more open and broader system than Yaoundé. In that endeavour they gathered the support of the European Commission, which was eager to expand its bureaucratic tasks in this domain at a time when the EEC members had made new efforts to advance their international profile (Holland, 2002: 32–33). At first, the extension of Yaoundé was met with hesitation by AAMS and Commonwealth countries in general. However, the dissatisfaction generated by the gradual erosion of trading preferences, the lack of options and the desire to obtain whichever benefits were made available, together with weaker divisions in Africa and a sense of Third Worldist solidarity, contributed to allay qualms and encouraged some convergence. As a result, these countries decided to emphasise their shared interests in order to jointly negotiate with the EEC, later forming what became known as the ACP Group (Lister, 1988: 61–70; Ravenhill, 1985: 77–85).

Although the EEC was initially seeking a mere extension of Yaoundé, broader international developments forced the Europeans to be more accommodating towards the ACP. The 1973 oil crisis raised concerns in the industrialised world about raw material supplies and stimulated the developing countries' willingness to use their 'commodity power' to push for their cherished New International Economic Order (NIEO). European states felt particularly vulnerable due to their high dependency on imported oil and other commodities. This atmosphere of uncertainty reinforced the EEC's interest in having good economic and political relations with Africa, while strengthening the ACP position in negotiations with the EEC (Brown, 2002: 46–52; Grilli, 1993: 25–27). In 1975, the Nine EEC members and 46 ACP countries, comprising virtually all of sub-Saharan Africa as well as some small states in the Caribbean and the Pacific, signed the first Lomé Convention.[3] The new convention committed its signatories to 'establish, on the basis of complete equality between partners, close and continuing co-operation, in a spirit of international solidarity' and create 'a new model for relations between developed and developing States'. In fact, both sides were interested in stressing Lomé's novelty and difference vis-à-vis past narratives and practices. Thus, the rhetoric of an 'equal' partnership replaced the use of the term 'association', and greater visibility was given to notions of North-South solidarity as well as political 'neutrality' (Lister, 1988: 58–59; Twitchett, 1978: 149).

In terms of substance, some of the main innovations of Lomé I were the abandonment of trade reciprocity and the introduction of STABEX. Non-reciprocal concessions meant that ACP countries were merely obliged to treat EEC exports at least as favourably as exports from other developed states. In turn, STABEX was a compensatory scheme, financed totally by the EEC, providing an element of security to ACP export earnings, even if with some restrictions. The amount of aid was increased in nominal terms in comparison with Yaoundé II, and the ACP countries were involved in its administration, though final decisions remained with the EEC. This financial assistance was presented as more 'generous' than other aid programmes, as well as 'non-political' – that is, allocated regardless of the politics of the recipient countries (Brown, 2002: 58–62; Grilli, 1993: 27–34; Lister, 1988: 76–95). Rather than being neutral, Lomé was in reality politically discreet, as it sought to distance itself from colonialism and superpower rivalries, claiming a sort of 'middle way' while being closer to the United States (Lister, 1988: 189–192). Part of these new measures echoed NIEO demands for special treatment and greater assistance to developing countries, which had been influenced in some measure by Dependency theory ideas favouring protectionist and state-led development strategies (Holland and Doidge, 2012: 24–25).

On balance, Lomé I included elements of both change and continuity with past institutional arrangements. While representing more of a negotiated scheme, taking on board some of the ACP concerns, its fundamental elements were still set by the European side. Indeed, despite an expanded geographical scope that went beyond former imperial areas, the new convention remained greatly based on the historical legacies of some EEC members and with a strong focus on Africa. Simultaneously, this larger and more diverse framework brought with it new challenges in terms of intra- and inter-group relations. The overall significance of Lomé I was the object of a lively debate. While more positive perspectives looked at it as an important step away from colonialism towards increased interdependence (Gruhn, 1976), more critical viewpoints emphasised the continuities with past patterns of engagement, describing Lomé as a neocolonial device (Galtung, 1976) or as a form of 'collective clientelism' (Ravenhill, 1985: 22). Regardless of which interpretation might appear more accurate, Lomé did privilege the ACP Group over other EEC developing partners, granting the ACP countries more than they managed to achieve elsewhere (Brown, 2002: 27; Mayall, 2005: 298). Furthermore, it proved to be a resilient framework, remaining the main institutional mechanism structuring the EEC/EU-Africa relationship for 25 years.

Despite this longevity, following an initial phase, the Lomé system started to stagnate. The Lomé Convention was renegotiated four times and continually attracted new members.[4] However, throughout the framework's duration no major new measures were introduced, and its results ended up generating disappointment. This gradual loss of impetus reflected the weakened ACP position and the evolution of EEC/EU priorities. From the late 1970s, the economic deterioration and deepening debt, especially among African countries, increased their dependency on the West and diminished the efficacy of moral arguments depicting them as 'victims'. Also with the worsening of the global economic situation and the growing influence of neoliberal views, European attitudes towards the relationship became in general less enthusiastic and more demanding (Grilli, 1993: 36–40). The late 1980s and 1990s saw increased pressures for economic and political liberalisation globally. The rise of the Washington Consensus led to the application of structural adjustment programmes in most African countries. Simultaneously, the GATT Uruguay Round threatened ACP preferences while the Cold War's end diminished the strategic relevance of the Third World, leading to drastic cuts and political conditionalities in Western aid. At European level, steps towards greater economic integration through the Single Market programme raised fears of an introspective 'fortress Europe'. Moreover, the Southern and Northern enlargements brought in new member states with few interests in ACP countries. Whereas the fall of the Berlin Wall triggered new political ambitions in Brussels, the foreign priorities of the newly born EU centred on its 'near abroad'. These trends were necessarily reflected in Lomé's renegotiations.

Unlike its predecessors, Lomé IV was signed for ten years, with a mid-term review after five years. This extended duration was meant to provide extra stability, but it was also indicative of a certain 'Lomé fatigue'. For the first time, explicit economic and political conditions were introduced in the convention. A significant proportion of EDF aid was directed towards structural adjustment support, which led to a reduction of funds targeting long-term development. Moreover, Lomé IV included a human rights clause stipulating that development 'entails respect for and promotion of all human rights'. In the following years, several African countries saw their aid suspended for political reasons, a move condemned by the ACP countries (Brown, 2002: 73–114; Lister, 1997: 108–131). The Lomé IV mid-term review expanded political conditionality and EU control over aid resources. Respect for human rights, democratic principles and the rule of law were made 'essential elements', and a 'suspension clause' was inserted, stating expressly that non-observance of these conditions could lead to sanctions. Apart from that, EU development objectives were explicitly included in the convention, hence increasing the European influence over Lomé's policies. Moreover, the mid-term revision introduced phased programming that allocated funds in two tranches, with the second one subject to a successful review of progress. This more flexible and performance-based system was criticised by the ACP countries for reinforcing the possibility of conditionalities and undermining Lomé's founding principles (Brown, 2002: 115–138).

Overall, the evolution of the Lomé framework shows a gradual shift from an emphasis on equality, solidarity and neutrality to a greater accent on European objectives, efficiency and conditionality. This trend towards less generous and more conditional and politicised terms meant that the initial rhetoric of an equal partnership and new model for North–South cooperation lost further ground. It also implied that the relationship became less unique and special, with the ACP Group moving down in the EU 'pyramid of privilege', overtaken by Eastern European and Mediterranean countries in the second half of the 1990s. By that phase, against Lomé's poor development results in general and the liberalising pressures stemming from the newly created World Trade Organization (WTO), increasing doubts were being raised about the adequacy of such a system of cooperation and its future (Crawford, 1996; Holland and Doidge, 2012: 65–66).

Cotonou: A failed attempt to revitalise the EU-ACP 'partnership'? (2000–2020)

The expiry of the Lomé Convention at the turn of the century offered the opportunity for an overhaul of EU-Africa arrangements. Although the view about the need to reform was widely shared, the ACP side was less keen than the EU in general on far-reaching changes. Reflecting their own weaknesses, the ACP countries were mainly interested in preserving the benefits of Lomé and their identity as a group. In Europe, a main divide was initially visible between those who wanted to retain special ties and those who instead wished to 'normalise' relations with their developing counterparts (Carbone, 2013: 744). For the more revisionist, in particular, a key argument for change was the need to conform to WTO rules. The preservation of trade preferences for the ACP countries required securing special waivers, that were depicted by some as increasingly unworkable. The final compromise among those different European views represented an intermediary position, which largely defined the outcome of the subsequent negotiations to replace Lomé. Following lengthy and intense discussions, the Cotonou Partnership Agreement was signed in 2000 by the then 15 EU member states and 77 ACP countries (Babarinde and Faber, 2005). Among the latter was South Africa, which had joined Lomé in 1997 as a qualified member only.[5] While building on the experience of previous arrangements, the new EU-ACP agreement introduced several changes to the Lomé acquis. Cotonou was signed for a 20-year period, with provisions for review every five years. Its main stated goals were 'reducing and eventually eradicating poverty consistent with the objectives of sustainable development and the gradual integration of the ACP countries into the world economy'. This new focus on poverty, linked to other dimensions, reflected changing European priorities and broader international debates emphasising holistic development approaches (Holland and Doidge, 2012: 26–27, 71).

Despite the expressed commitment to poverty reduction, the initial EDF allocation for Cotonou represented no increase in real terms. Seeking to promote greater efficiency, Cotonou simplified its management procedures and financial instruments, dropping the old STABEX and SYSMIN mechanisms to the disappointment of the ACP countries. More explicit criteria for the allocation of resources were also introduced, based on recipient needs as well as performance. A new programming system, comprising jointly designed plans but with financing decisions reserved for the EU, became the tool to target interventions to specific countries and make regular adjustments. Yet some of the main innovations brought about by the Cotonou Agreement were arguably in the domain of trade. The existing non-reciprocal trade regime applied to the whole ACP Group was to be replaced by reciprocal free trade agreements, the so-called Economic Partnership Agreements (EPAs), to be concluded with six regions (four in Africa, one in the Caribbean and one in the Pacific) by the end of 2007, in order to comply with WTO rules. This gradual trade liberalisation along regional lines was based on the understanding that regional integration would facilitate a smoother integration of the ACP countries into the global economy. Notwithstanding the introduction of a liberalisation principle, Cotonou provided for the preservation of non-reciprocal trade for all least developed countries. Such economic differentiation represented a further departure from the uniform regime of Lomé, that acknowledged ACP diversity but also had divisive implications (Carbone, 2017: 300).

Cotonou also reinforced the political dimension of the EU-ACP relationship. Political dialogue became a more central feature and was turned into a third 'pillar' of cooperation, alongside the traditional aid and trade dimensions. Seeking 'to exchange information, to foster mutual understanding, and to facilitate the establishment of agreed priorities and shared agendas', dialogue was expanded to new issues such as peace and security, migration and governance. Although the idea of partnership was given great prominence, political conditionality continued and was even extended to new aspects. During the negotiations, the EU had tried to include good governance as another of the 'essential elements', but this proved highly controversial. Eventually, good governance was added as a 'fundamental element', implying that 'serious cases of corruption' could still lead to sanctions as a 'measure of last resort'. Simultaneously, the 'consultation procedure' was strengthened, including the possibility of external arbitration. Moreover, in contrast to the essentially government-to-government approach of Lomé, Cotonou gave a new emphasis to the involvement of non-state actors. This innovation was viewed by EU representatives as important in building democracy within ACP states, but was resented by ACP governments as interference (Bretherton and Vogler, 2006: 122).

According to Carbone (2017: 300–301), the Cotonou Agreement represented a 'fundamental break' with the past. While preserving the partnership model and the twin pillars of aid and trade, it promoted a new type of cooperation combining trade liberalisation and politicisation. Yet this contractual and comprehensive nature, linking different dimensions in novel ways, was unparalleled at the time, making of Cotonou a 'unique agreement' just like the Lomé Convention had been (Holland and Doidge, 2012: 78). Subsequently, the first review of Cotonou in 2005 introduced some amendments, mainly to the political pillar. Reflecting the post-9/11 context and the EU's global ambitions, the revised agreement gave a new emphasis to security aspects (Hadfield, 2007). New clauses were included on terrorism, mercenary activities, the International Criminal Court (ICC) and weapons of mass destruction, which was added as a new 'essential element'. Concurrently, the review clarified the modalities for political dialogue and the consultation procedure. These changes were described as an attempt to rebalance an ineffective and unfairly weighted process that favoured the EU (Holland and Doidge, 2012: 80; Mackie, 2008: 148). In the domain of aid, apart from an expressed commitment to the United Nations Millennium Development Goals, the review introduced more flexibility into the aid disbursement process, increasing the EU's powers over its use.

The second review of Cotonou in 2010 emphasised issues such as regional integration, climate change, state fragility and aid effectiveness while giving more attention to cooperation in international fora and the role of ACP national parliaments. Greater significance was accorded to the continental dimension of Africa, recognising the African Union as a key interlocutor in peace and security matters. Moreover, seeking to put political dialogue on a more equal footing, the review stipulated that 'the principles underlying essential and fundamental elements' should apply equally to both the ACP and the EU. The two sides, however, disagreed on aspects related to sexual discrimination, illegal migration and the ICC (Bartelt, 2012). These amendments and disagreements echoed in part the interregional relationship's changing environment, one in which the relevance of the EU-ACP framework was starting to be challenged. The EU's eastern enlargements brought in a wide range of new member states devoid of affinity with Europe's postcolonial legacies and more oriented towards other geographies. Moreover, the ACP as a group was given a less prominent place in the new institutional arrangements of the Lisbon Treaty, whose ambitions to foster the EU's external role were hindered by the subsequent economic and political crises in Europe. On the ACP side, this period was marked by rapid economic growth (especially in Africa), increased heterogeneity among its members, the reinforcement of subregional dynamics and enduring difficulties to act as a collective group. Simultaneously, the emergence of new global players and different forms of cooperation in the South provided new options to ACP countries, beyond old partners such as the EU.

Against this backdrop, the final review of Cotonou in 2015 was called off. Instead, the EU launched a public consultation on the future of the ACP-EU cooperation post 2020 and an evaluation of the first 15 years of Cotonou. The EU's self-assessment pointed to progress on aspects such as poverty reduction, trade flows, peace and security, while recognising weaknesses in relation to political dialogue, human rights, migration and involvement of non-state actors. Limitations were also admitted in relation to dealing with the growing heterogeneity and regionalisation trends in ACP countries, the agreement's institutional set-up and cooperation in multilateral fora. Independent evaluations also emphasised difficulties such as the limited ownership of aid, the mainly rhetorical commitment to human rights and politicisation/securitisation of the relationship, as well as the tensions generated by the controversial EPA negotiations (Carbone, 2013: 746–749). Besides these implementation gaps and controversies, the emphasis on subregional dynamics and the emergence of parallel policy frameworks (such as the separate strategies for Africa, the Caribbean and the Pacific) led to a gradual and relative dilution of the EU-ACP 'partnership'. As the trade and political pillars of Cotonou were largely 'regionalised', EU-ACP cooperation was de facto reduced to a mostly development tool. Thus, over time the Cotonou Agreement lost momentum and was not able to revitalise the EU-ACP relationship (Bossuyt et al., 2016). Such evolution did not imply a loss of importance of EU-Africa relations, but the latter's governance became more separated from the ACP framework (Adebajo and Whiteman, 2012).

Conclusion

The long-term evolution of the EU-Africa relations governance system considered in this chapter displays, unsurprisingly, many changes, but also important continuities. From the 1950s Rome Treaty to the early 21st-century Cotonou Agreement, the institutional frameworks governing such relations widened in terms of membership, increasing their geographical reach and heterogeneity. While the initial arrangements only involved the Six West European founding members and a small number of essentially francophone territories in Africa, the Lomé Convention significantly expanded such spatial scope and diversity by bringing in the more liberal outlook of Britain and its ex-colonies in Africa, the Caribbean and the Pacific. The trend continued under Cotonou, leading to a framework of more than 100 members and increased heterogeneity, especially within the EU due to the accession of a large number of Eastern and Central European states with no significant ties to Africa, but also within the ACP Group owing in particular to the distinct economic performance of its members. This evolution entailed scale advantages as well as additional coordination challenges. In general, the interests and perspectives of the EU side predominated. The key role of France and Britain, the balance between 'regionalist/globalist' and 'traditionalist/revisionist' viewpoints and the European Commission's contribution are some central intra-EU aspects which this chapter could not cover in depth. Similarly, the francophone/anglophone divide, the growing effect of subregional dynamics and the greater room for manoeuvre in recent times due to the rise of alternative partners represented major determinants internal to the African/ACP side. Ultimately, despite their gradual opening, the frameworks governing EU-Africa relations continued to express a regional preference and exclusive features.

European contextual factors too played a central part in moulding the EU-Africa governance evolution. Among the most important factors were post-war decline and retreat, the endurance of Eurafrican norms as well as the deepening and widening of the EU. The successive waves of EU enlargement, in particular, had an important impact, as they brought in new member states that changed the EU's politics and policies, including towards Africa. This was especially the case with the so-called British and Eastern enlargements. On the African side, postcolonial legacies and the role of Pan-Africanist ideas, together with the ups and downs of the continent's economic situation, also helped shape developments. To be sure, these endogenous circumstances were not unrelated to wide and powerful global processes, such as the Cold War, GATT/WTO liberalisation rounds, the spread of Modernisation, Dependency and Neoliberal ideas, the post-9/11 security atmosphere, the emergence of BRICS (Brazil, Russia, India, China and South Africa) as well as United Nations development initiatives. Yet this interplay between endogenous and exogenous dynamics has not always received adequate attention in the Europe-Africa relations literature (Farrell, 2015). For instance, the attachment of some African ruling elites to their ex-metropoles and the reliance on the EU that many passages of this chapter alluded to can be better understood when the international relations of African countries are related to their specific national and regional contexts. Thus, there is much to be gained in this area from linking different levels of analysis and bringing together the insights from different bodies of literature, disciplines and traditions.

Over time, the nature of EU-Africa governance arrangements evolved from 'associationism' to 'partnership'. Based on ideas of 'complementarity' and 'friendship' between Europe and Africa, the initial steps given by the Rome Treaty and Yaoundé sought in a bold and narrow way to help preserve economic and political ties. In a period of superpower competition and European weakness, this Eurafrican association emphasised economic dimensions and used 'soft' tools, such as preferential trade, development aid and legal-institutional mechanisms. Reflecting the colonial legacies of some of its members, this original institutionalisation implied a degree of multilateralisation of such 'special' links. Moreover, despite its limited economic results, it crucially defined the template for subsequent arrangements, along a donor-recipient pattern. Lomé tried to move the relationship towards a more balanced and solidary 'partnership of equals' that could represent a new model for North-South relations. While it managed to introduce some innovative and more generous practices that contributed to Lomé's distinctiveness and uniqueness in the world, the relationship remained asymmetric. Besides, the Lomé system soon stagnated and evolved towards a more EU-centred arrangement, particularly with the introduction of conditionalities. This greater post-Cold War interference and poor development results fed disappointment. Cotonou represented an attempt to revitalise the 'partnership' by following a holistic approach combining development goals and political dialogue on an increasingly diversified range of issues. However, its differentiated trade liberalisation and politicisation did not work to stop the partnership's erosion and relative marginalisation. Still, some features of the EU-ACP framework continued to be valued, such as its contractual nature, comprehensive scope and joint institutions. Overall, this evolution of EU-Africa arrangements reveals an incremental process of institutionalisation that appears to have been driven by the sort of path dependencies, calculations, cultural norms and discursive structures that New Institutionalist insights would help illuminate.

Notes

1. The ACP Group is now known as the Organisation of African, Caribbean and Pacific States, following a change of name in 2020.
2. Signed for a five-year period, the Yaoundé Convention was revised in 1969 (Yaoundé II) without major changes and for a similar duration of time.

3   The ACP signatories comprised 37 African countries (most anglophone and francophone states in sub-Saharan Africa as well as a few countries with no colonial ties to the Nine), six from the Caribbean and three from the Pacific. The Asian ex-colonies of Britain (some with large or diversified economies) were excluded from Lomé.
4   The convention was renewed in 1979 (Lomé II), 1984 (Lomé III), 1989 (Lomé IV) and 1995 (Lomé IV bis) between the EEC/EU and 58, 65, 68 and 70 ACP members, respectively. Lomé II and III were very similar to the original convention.
5   Full Lomé membership was denied to South Africa on the basis that its economy was superior to most ACP countries.

Bibliography

Adebajo, A. and Whiteman, K. (eds) (2012) *The EU and Africa: From Eurafrique to Afro-Europa*. London: C. Hurst & Co.
Babarinde, O. and Faber, G. (eds) (2005) *The European Union and the Developing Countries: The Cotonou Agreement*. Leiden: Martinus Nijhoff Publishers.
Bartelt, S. (2012). ACP-EU development cooperation at a crossroads? One year after the second revision of the Cotonou Agreement. *European Foreign Affairs Review*, 17 (1), 1–25.
Bossuyt, J., Keijzer, N., Medinilla, A. and De Tollenaere, M. (2016) *The Future of ACP-EU Relations: A Political Economy Analysis*. ECDPM Policy Management Report 21. Maastricht: ECDPM.
Bretherton, C. and Vogler, J. (2006) *The European Union as a Global Actor*, 2nd ed. London and New York: Routledge.
Brown, W. (2002) *The European Union and Africa: The Restructuring of North-South Relations*. London: Tauris.
Carbone, M. (2013) Rethinking ACP-EU relations after Cotonou: Tensions, contradictions, prospects. *Journal of International Development*, 25 (5), 742–756.
Carbone, M. (2017) The European Union and international development. In C. Hill, M. Smith and S. Vanhoonacker (eds), *International Relations and the European Union*, 3rd ed. Oxford: Oxford University Press (pp. 292–315).
Clapham, C.S. (1996) *Africa and the International System: The Politics of State Survival*. Cambridge: Cambridge University Press.
Crawford, G. (1996) Whither Lomé? The mid-term review and the decline of partnership. *The Journal of Modern African Studies*, 34 (3), 503–518.
Farrell, M. (2015) Europe-Africa relations over time: History, geo-politics and new political challenges. In K.E. Jørgensen, A. Kalland Aarstad, E. Drieskens, K. Laatikainen and B. Tonra (eds), *The SAGE Handbook of European Foreign Policy*. Los Angeles: SAGE (pp. 779–792).
Galtung, J. (1976) The Lomé Convention and neo-capitalism. *The African Review*, 6 (1), 33–42.
Grilli, E.R. (1993) *The European Community and the Developing Countries*. Cambridge: Cambridge University Press.
Gruhn, I.V. (1976) The Lomé Convention: Inching towards interdependence. *International Organization*, 30 (2), 241–262.
Hadfield, A. (2007) Janus advances? An analysis of EC development policy and the 2005 Amended Cotonou Partnership Agreement. *European Foreign Affairs Review*, 12 (1), 39–67.
Holland, M. (2002) *The European Union and the Third World*. Basingstoke: Palgrave.
Holland, M. and Doidge, M. (2012) *Development Policy of the European Union*. New York: Palgrave Macmillan.
Lister, M. (1988) *The European Community and the Developing World: The Role of the Lomé Convention*. Aldershot: Avebury.
Lister, M. (1997) *The European Union and the South: Relations with Developing Countries*. London: Routledge.
Mackie, J. (2008) Continuity and change in international co-operation: The ACP-EU Cotonou Partnership Agreement and its first revision. *Perspectives on European Politics and Society*, 9 (2), 143–156.
Mayall, J. (2005) The shadow of empire: The EU and the former colonial world. In C. Hill and M. Smith (eds), *International Relations and the European Union*. Oxford and New York: Oxford University Press (pp. 292–316).
Ravenhill, J. (1985) *Collective Clientelism: The Lomé Conventions and North-South Relations*. New York: Columbia University Press.
Twitchett, C.C. (1978) *Europe and Africa: From Association to Partnership*. Farnborough: Saxon House.

5

Foreign policy and EU-Africa relations

From the European Security Strategy to the EU Global Strategy

Lesley Masters and Chris Landsberg

Introduction

A state's foreign policy is the framework guiding its external relations. It is also a reflection of the state's history, socio-economic conditions, culture, politics and perceived role identity as it engages other actors in the international milieu (Holsti, 1970). As argued in Wallace (1991: 65), foreign policy is 'about national identity itself: about the sources of national pride, the characteristics which distinguish a country from its neighbours, the core elements of sovereignty it seeks to defend, the values it stands for and seeks to promote abroad'. While foreign policy analysis has been typically state-centric in its approach, it is not, however, just individual states that engage in international relations. Intergovernmental organisations in their varied forms, from the supranational entity of the European Union (EU) to regional bodies such as the African Union (AU), assume a role as active participants on the world stage.

While at different stages in their foreign policy development, the EU and AU have policy frameworks outlining their ambitions, aims and priorities. There is considerable analysis on what Carlsnaes (2013: 303) calls the 'Innenpolitik' (domestic factors) when it comes to understanding EU foreign policy; less so for the AU's emerging position. This chapter, however, focuses on understanding the systemic factors that shape state behaviour, particularly how the development and implementation of the EU's foreign policy has shaped relations with Africa. Adopting a longitudinal approach, the analysis traces the challenges of implementation, from the EU's Common Foreign and Security Policy (CFSP, 1993) to the EU Global Strategy for the European Union's Foreign and Security Policy (EUGS, 2016). The analysis highlights that it is the gaps between the EU's foreign policy principles and its implementation in practice that have undermined EU-Africa relations.

Foreign policy in defining an international role

Broad definitions of foreign policy analysis indicate that it is aimed at building an understanding of the policy approach states adopt in dealing with their external environment. This understanding, however, limits analysis to the state, disregarding the growing international role of other actors (non-state and even sub-national actors) as they build their strategies and goals to engage the international milieu. Neack et al.'s definition is more appropriate for this analysis as it expands foreign policy analysis beyond the state-centric approach, pointing out that it is 'a diverse set of activities, dedicated to understanding and explaining the foreign policy process and behaviors of actors in world politics' (Neack et al., 1995: 1). This definition highlights two streams of analysis that have been adopted. The first is the focus on the foreign policy process, assessing elements such as decision-making, psychology and the impact of bureaucratic wrangling in defining policy positions. The second includes studies that consider the behaviour of actors in the implementation of foreign policy in practice. While there has been a move towards positivism in the explanations of how foreign policy is made, there remains a need for in-depth studies assessing how the foreign policy framework shapes the role of actors in the international milieu.

Linking these two streams of analysis, the constructivist approach to foreign policy highlights the role that shared norms play in shaping foreign policy as well as the subsequent actions of actors. In other words, the socially constructed identity of the actor 'not only define state preferences but have also been used by decision makers to justify and to pursue particular forms of foreign policy' (Carlsnaes, 2013: 314). The usefulness of the concept 'identity' is, however, the subject of debate. In addressing diverging positions, Chafetz et al. (1998) set out to demonstrate the role played by identity in explaining behaviour in international relations. Its value, they argue, is that is creates distinction between one actor and another. Identities then provide a framework for understanding actor relations, although recognition needs to be given to their dynamic nature, where interaction may lead to subsequent adaptation and change. This means that an actor may have multiple identities depending on whether negotiations are multilateral or bilateral, who they negotiate with and the issue under debate (ibid.).

Hill (2003: 290) argues that the development of foreign policy by intergovernmental organisations such as the EU adds a new layer of international activity but does not replace the central position of a state's own foreign policy. What is significant, however, is that organisations such as the EU and the AU are developing greater political capacity as actors on the international stage. For the EU, foreign policy has been central in defining and consolidating its 'actorness'. As Romaniuk argues, the EU has sought to establish 'itself as a genuine and viable player using both elements of force and diplomacy in a manner that inexorably define it as a strategic actor on a global scale' (2011: 5). For Mälksoo, anyone would be 'hard-pressed to find another international actor so obsessed about its global outreach, security identity, and international credibility as the EU' (2016: 374). As international actors, the EU and the AU have played a part in multilateral negotiations in the United Nations (UN) Framework Convention on Climate Change, negotiating peacekeeping and security in countries such as the Democratic Republic of the Congo and as participants in the negotiations on the Sustainable Development Goals (SDGs) (Masters, 2017, 2012). Acting bilaterally, the EU has signed ten strategic country partnerships, while the AU maintains diplomatic representation in the United States and the EU. As international agents, these organisations have become greater than the sum of their parts (member states), as they consolidate an identity as actors on the world stage. This identity has drawn on a shared understanding of the rationale and values of the organisation in its external conduct between the respective member states, as well as through international recognition from other actors on the world stage.

EU foreign policy: From normative Europe to principled pragmatism

The EUGS (introduced in June 2016) builds on decades of international relations following from the signing of the Treaty of Rome (1957) and the establishment of the initial European

Economic Community (EEC). With the formalisation of the EU (1992), it sought to expand the existing international focus on trade and economic agreements to furthering relations with its neighbours on questions of peace and security. The result was the CFSP (1993) and the European Security and Defence Policy (ESDP, 2000). These policies provided the framework for the EU's external relations in terms of safeguarding common values and interests, ensuring the security of its member states, promoting international cooperation as well as promoting the norms of the consolidation of democracy 'the rule of law, respect for human rights and fundamental freedoms' (Bindi, 2010: 27; Carbone, 2010: 246).

The growing emphasis on the pursuit of these normative elements, and the use of multilateralism in achieving them, exemplified the EU's self-perceived international role during the latter part of the 1990s and into the early 2000s. The perception of 'normative power Europe' that emerged from Brussels linked the EU's identity to the pursuit of peace, democracy, human rights and the respect for international law in its external relations. As Newman argues,

> These cosmopolitan values not only constitute the European identity, but in theory they contribute to a worldview that guides Europe's interaction with external partners, for example in promoting and supporting democracy, human rights and good governance. They also represent a standard of practice to aspire to for those who wish to do business with Europe.
>
> *(2018: 202)*

This normative approach was again present in the European Security Strategy (ESS, 2003), which reflected a 'coming of age' for the EU as an international actor, as it expanded its role in conflict resolution in Afghanistan, East Timor and the Democratic Republic of the Congo. Mälksoo argues that the ESS 'showcases the EU's explicitly transformative zeal, putting an emphasis on spreading good governance, especially rule of law and protecting human rights as well as democracy promotion more generally' (2016: 378). The ESS also reflected the EU's ambition to pursue a role as a 'global power' through participation in multilateral forums, either as a member or an observer, in order to develop 'a stronger international society, well-functioning international institutions and a rule-based international order' (EU, 2003: 9). The challenge was the lack of clear policy objectives, means and instruments to achieve these foreign policy aims. This resulted in further discussion on the need to update the ESS, where the focus shifted to the creation of a 'grand strategy' to ensure a strategic approach (Howorth, 2010: 463).

The EUGS reflects the impact of changing international and domestic dynamics on the EU. With shifts in geopolitics, the socio-economic impacts of the 2007/08 financial crisis lingering, the decision by the United Kingdom to leave the EU and a rise in nationalist sentiment across the region, the principles of the GS highlight the importance of unity, engagement, responsibility and partnership (EU, 2016: 16–18). The policy emphasises a 'whole of EU' approach, with 'global' referring to the focus on a broad range of thematic areas rather than geographic ones (Tocci, 2016: 464). The priorities include security and defence, counterterrorism, cybersecurity, energy security and strategic communications (EU, 2016: 18–23).

While the GS contains the normative elements that underpin the EU's foreign policy identity, there is also evidence of a shift in emphasis as to how these should be pursued in practice. For instance, this includes recognition by the EU of its international responsibility, but with the addition of the call for *shared* responsibility. This shared responsibility, or 'co-responsibility', is set out as the guiding principle in the organisation's pursuit of a 'rules-based global order' and one which will underpin 'revamping our external partnerships' with states, intergovernmental organisations, regional groupings, civil society and the private sector (EU, 2016: 18, 8). It calls for inclusive resolutions and comprehensive agreements 'rooted in broad, deep and durable regional and international partnerships' (EU, 2016: 29). This is an indication that the EU's external relations are under review and that the GS places a new emphasis on selectivity in working with core partners, like-minded countries and regional groupings (EU, 2016: 18). Mälksoo argues that the EU's geographic focus is now clearly on Europe, while engagement outside of its immediate neighbourhood is more 'targeted' (2016: 381). Drawing on input from across the member states on foreign policy, the GS sets out to address growing international concern on the ability of the EU to reconcile foreign policy principles with practice through the inclusion of 'principled pragmatism'. This is cited as a guiding principle of the EU's international relations, linking interests and values in the foreign policy approach towards peace and security, prosperity, democracy and rules-based global order (EU, 2016: 16).

As Cross argues,

> the EU's approach to its foreign policy is made up of both *realistic assessment* and *idealistic aspiration* (or together, *principled pragmatism*). This renewed narrative gets to the heart of the EU's recent struggles in communicating its own identity, capabilities, and goals to the outside world.
>
> *(2016: 403, emphasis in the original)*

Diverging principles and practice: Impact on EU-Africa relations

The divergence between foreign policy principles and what happens in practice has seen a widening gap in EU-Africa relations, in what was already a lukewarm relationship. Initial relations between the then newly emerging EEC and Africa on trade and aid were set out in the Yaoundé Convention, which highlighted the hierarchical structure between participants. The subsequent Lomé Convention (1975–2000) aimed at shifting relations towards partnership between the EEC/EU and the African, Caribbean and Pacific (ACP) Group[1] with the idea of 'contractual right to aid' replacing the position of 'aid dependent on performance' (Carbone, 2010: 240). Despite these principles, conditionalities crept into the programmes and were later imposed by the negotiated Cotonou Agreement (2000), with Economic Partnership Agreements being negotiated to replace the preferential trade system. For developing countries, this reflected little of the normative values espoused by the EU. These relations supported perceptions that 'EU delegations often imposed their priorities; in some instances, ACP officials even saw the programming process as a serious challenge to their sovereignty' (Carbone, 2010: 243).

The expanding foreign policy priorities of the EU (through the CFSP, the ESDP and the ESS) included among its initiatives the short-lived African Strategy (introduced in October 2005).[2] Driven by the EU, the African Strategy presented a 'whole of Africa' approach to 'improve coordination, coherence and consistency of the Union's policies and instruments aimed at a particular region' and to 'give the EU a **comprehensive, integrated and long-term framework** for its relations with the African continent' (Commission of the European Communities, 2005: 2, emphasis in the original). However, following criticism on the lack of consultation with stakeholders (Carbone, 2010: 248) and in an effort to present a more engaged approach away from reasserting the hierarchy of the trade-aid relations, the EU's Africa Strategy was replaced two months later with EU and Africa: Towards a Strategic Partnership (Council of the European Union, 2005). The move towards a strategic partnership included the EU's continued commitment to a normative foreign policy identity, working with Africa on peace and security, human rights and governance, development assistance, sustainable economic growth, regional integration and trade, and supporting investment in people. Yet it also includes the more pragmatic recognition that it is in the EU's interest to have 'a peaceful, prosperous and democratic Africa' and states that the EU's 'strategy is intended to help Africa achieve this' (Council of the European Union, 2005: 5).

The challenge was that in practice the change from the Africa Strategy to the Strategic Partnership did little in terms of 'present[ing] any new thinking on EU-Africa relations as it brought together already existing commitments' (Carbone, 2013: 7). In addition, the Strategic Partnership demonstrated the gap between principles and practice in the EU's promotion of the 'one continent' approach (Council of the European Union, 2005: 1).[3] Not only did this raise questions on the wisdom and efficacy of dealing with Africa 'as one', as this discounts the diverse nature of Africa's 55 states and the myriad integration and developmental efforts that have taken place across the continent since decolonisation began (Olivier, 2006), but the approach was also challenged for its contradictions where the EU continued to maintain relations through the different groupings of the ACP, relations with North Africa through the European Neighbourhood Policy and South Africa through the Trade, Development and Cooperation Agreement and the Strategic Partnership.

The shortfalls of the Strategic Partnership prompted the launch of the Joint EU-Africa Strategy (JAES) (Council of the European Union, 2007). This bought together 80 heads of state and government from Africa and Europe, who agreed to pursue common interests and strategic objectives together to transcend the traditional donor-recipient focus as a partnership of equals. Reflecting the EU foreign policy identity the JAES brings to the fore the normative emphasis on values and objectives underpinning the relationship (respect for human rights, freedom, equality, solidarity, justice, the rule of law and democracy). Arguably, this suggests that both Europe and Africa share similar ideals about regionalisation, with both trying to promote their international agendas through the instrumentality of soft power, multilateralism and rules-based international interaction.

That Africa shared these perspectives was already apparent in the Africa-EU Summit in Cairo, which coincided with the emergence of the so-called 'new' Africans, spearheaded by Thabo Mbeki, Olusegun Obasanjo, Abul Aziz Bouteflika, Meles Zenawi and Joachim Chisano. Their vision of African agency was based on ownership and a genuine partnership. These new Africans, or what Gilbert Khadiagala (2015: 9) calls the 'renaissance coalition', viewed Africa with a sense of renewed confidence, as a continent increasingly independent economically. This was supported by the growing interest of the emerging powers (China, India and Brazil) looking to engage Africa. As the EU set out,

> Africa is now at the heart of international politics, but what is genuinely new is that Africa ... is emerging, not as a development issue, but as a political actor in its own right. It is becoming increasingly clear that Africa matters – as a political voice, as an economic force and as huge source of human, cultural, natural and scientific potential.
>
> *(European Commission, 2007)*

Increasingly, the argument was that Brussels did not want to lose out in a 'new scramble' for Africa (The Economist, 2004). To an extent, the JAES reflects the ambition of the EU to become a 'privileged partner' of Africa and to 'make the most of its relations with Africa'. Nevertheless, when it came to implementation of the JAES, as has been shown over and over again, the gap between the two 'partners' in terms of foreign policy is apparent. While the EU placed an 'emphasis on political issues, notably democracy and peace and security, African representatives concentrated on economic aspects, notably trade and aid' (Carbone, 2010: 247). Despite the normative emphasis on paper, in practice JAES was seen as a vehicle 'for up-scaling European commitment to economic and political advancement in a strong, united African ally, in exchange for African positions that are more sympathetic to European needs and expectations bilaterally and globally' (Bello, 2010: 2).

While the logic of multilateralism underscores the JAES, it represents a bilateral approach to foreign policy relations between the AU and the EU. The JAES also builds on the existing complicated, if not cumbersome, diplomatic/bureaucratic architecture put in place over time, reflecting the scope, regularity and continuation of interaction. In its interactions, the EU continues to 'take Africa as one' working by way of annual College-to-College meetings between the European Commission and the Commission of the AU, as well as the Brussels-based Africa Working Group.

Since the agreement on the JAES there has been little progress in moving EU-Africa relations forward. The result is that the JAES has not met its strategic partnership ambitions. High-level political meetings are sites of contention, and a number have failed to take place. N'Guettia Kouassi, Director of Economic Affairs at the Commission of the AU, has gone as far as arguing that the 'unilateral changes in the governance structures imposed by the EU to reflect the development of its own internal institutional apparatus, without prior consultation with African counterparts, have left the AU-EU cooperation looking tired and outdated' (2017: 5).

Finding a common ground? The AU, the EU and multilateralism in international norm-setting

Analysis points to a number of externalities that challenge EU-AU relations, including economic strain, conflict in the Middle East, changes in political leadership and the threats posed by terrorism (Mackie et al., 2017: 1). It is the EUGS and the AU's Agenda 2063 (AU, 2015) that provide the frameworks guiding these organisations as they travers these challenges. For the EU, the EUGS presents a continued emphasis on deepening relations with regions through 'invest[ing] in regional orders, and in cooperation among and within regions' (EU, 2016: 4). However, as Mackie et al. argue, the 'fact that the [EUGS] does not mention the ACP configuration provides something of a reality check on the ACP-EU partnership's prominence' (2017: 6). Nevertheless, as former EU President José Manuel Barroso notes, 'The EU has multilateralism in its DNA' (2010). The AU too points to the importance of participation, particularly in multilateral forums, in achieving normative and pragmatic priorities including peace and stability, food security, economic integration, developing Africa's human capacity, the empowerment of women and youth, resource mobilisation, effective communication and building institutional capacity (AU, 2015).

The foreign policy identity of both these organisations is tied to their systemic context. Both the EU and the AU favour a comprehensive multilateral system through which they can exercise influence in bringing about effective, worldwide, rules-based international dispensation to deal with major world and regional issues. The distinction between the two approaches is that the AU is less revisionist than the EU about a global application of multilateralism, engaging primarily on continental issues and North-South inequities, while the EU aspires to emerge as a normative global player, based on the conviction that the future of its own integration model and the well-being of its citizens are dependent on the evolution of a world governed by norms and rules. African multilateralism, in turn, is more inward-looking – building trade relations and with a developmental and peace and security focus, concentrating more specifically on greater equity between North and South, the resolution of continental developmental issues and peace and security problems by influencing the international agenda. Having been at the receiving end of external exploitation for centuries and still struggling for its place in a competitive world, multilateral engagement gives Africa some leverage to escape the shackles of the past and assert itself in multilateral organisations of a new global order which is more equal, more democratic and more accommodating towards the problems of the developing world. The ability to 'speak with one voice' in these multilateral contexts is seen as important leverage in international forums such as the UN's General Assembly and its Specialised Agencies, affecting decisions on peace and security and the structuring or restructuring of the system of global governance.

Although the AU borrowed heavily from the EU's architecture in its own construction, the two entities have followed different paths as they developed. As such, their structure and the manner in which they exercise and promote multilateralism is different in many respects. The AU's experience in multilateralism is far less institutionalised than that of the EU. The AU also faces something of an 'accession' crisis in the sense that member states typically fail to adhere to the norms and values, or to respect the institutions, of the AU. While the EU aims to 'act globally to address the root causes of conflict and poverty, and to champion the indivisibility and universality of human rights' (European Union, 2016), there is less agreement between AU member states on how best to engage globally on aid/development partnerships, how conflict and peacekeeping should be managed and how they should they approach human rights (particularly when it comes to lesbian, gay, bisexual and transgender (LGBT) rights). The EU on the other hand has a much tighter accession regime that its members adhere to. Notwithstanding the prevalence of 'strong man' politics and an overreliance on personal diplomacy in Africa, multilateralism is also the 'DNA' of African politics, and the continent boasts a long, albeit chequered, track record in this regard.

As 'champions of multilateralism', both organisations look to the UN as central to global governance (despite differences of opinion on how it should be reformed). The EU looks 'for a strong UN as the bedrock of the multilateral rules-based order' and aims to 'develop globally coordinated responses with international and regional organisations, states and non-state actors' (European Union, 2016), while the AU notes that 'we are part of the global drive through the United Nations and other multilateral organisations to find multilateral approaches to humanity's most pressing concerns' (AU, 2015: 14). The UN is, however, facing challenges from an increasingly unilateral United States (already reducing its contribution to peacekeeping initiatives), and neither the AU nor the EU have full membership. The international system continues to be underpinned by Westphalian thinking, meaning that the political influence of both the EU and the AU is restricted in determining the global agenda. In this respect, despite the pursuit of agency, both organisations suffer from a 'deficit of recognition' when it comes to the system of global governance.

In line with expanding participation, there has been growing rhetoric from both the EU and the AU on the importance of inclusivity. The EUGS points to a 'networks' approach as part of understanding 'complex interdependence'. There are numerous networks already in place between the member states of the EU and the AU, with representatives from civil society, the private sector, youth organisations and research organisations included in the side events of the EU-Africa summits since 2010. In practice, translating an emphasis on participation into an effective partnership between the EU and the AU still has some way to go, as is evident by the growing pressure from 'below'. There have been a number of protests by citizens in Europe – unhappy with the lack of recognition and inclusive democratic practices at the level of state and regional organisation, particularly following the United Kingdom's referendum decision to leave the EU – and in Africa – around the perceived distance between the people and governance structures. Despite advancing the norms of democracy, participation and inclusivity within foreign policy positions, perception from within the domestic constituencies is that the EU and the AU remain overly bureaucratic, technocratic, top-down and out of touch with the grassroots.

How this is addressed in practice will shape the perceived legitimacy for these organisations internationally.

Multilateralism in international affairs is dynamic. As the AU's international role grows, there has been a shift in focus from intra-continental engagement and North-South (neocolonial) relations to the potential offered by South-South cooperation. This has seen Africa turning to the 'new' development assistance partners such as India, China, Brazil and the BRICS New Development Bank. While the European Consensus on Development is under review, the role of development-assistance remains an area of contention. This has created an obstacle in managing EU-AU relations on where EU member states continue to jealously guard their individual development assistance approaches. The more pragmatic approach the EU has taken towards development assistance as a tool in its foreign policy has not gone unnoticed, not least the EU's use of Official Development Assistance in the EU-Turkey refugee deal and the diversion of Official Development Assistance contributions to managing the refugee crisis within the EU (Mackie et al., 2017: 3). The EU's use of the Regional and National Indicative Programmes has also served to complicate relations between the two regions. As N'Guettia Kouassi points out, the slow rate of disbursement of funds has resulted in 'a whole series of unused envelopes [which] are permanently "recycled", giving the impression of a continuously renewed European commitment to Africa' (2017: 5). The result is that EU-AU relations are driven by an acute awareness of an existential complex interdependence on both sides, with the EU more sensitive than vulnerable and Africa more vulnerable than sensitive.

Internationally, there continues to be polarisation between the two organisations on the multilateral platform of the International Criminal Court (ICC), with African states looking to withdraw from an institution they see as fundamentally biased, as well as disagreement on migration and human rights (LGBT rights in particular). Despite these challenges, there are a number of opportunities for furthering EU-AU relations. EU-AU relations bring together over 80 states, and building leverage in multilateral institutions has paid off in getting traction in the negotiations on climate change and the SDGs. The EUGS points to a conscious effort to position the EU as an environmentally conscious, or 'green', actor. Africa too is looking to expand and develop its trade, industrialisation and agricultural processes. Partnership in the green economy, the blue economy and capacity building (infrastructure and developing skills) are areas where both benefit and where there has been expanding engagement at the level of civil society and the private sector. The challenge is that relations remain primarily transactional – highlighting the hierarchy and differentiation between the two actors. This was evident in the acrimony caused in the dispute between the EU and the AU on the payment of peacekeepers in Somalia (Williams, 2017).

Conclusion

The EU's foreign policy identity has emphasised its role as normative actor in international relations, building on its soft power credentials, through its support of the ICC and its commitment to environmental negotiations and climate change commitments (Kyoto Protocol). For its part, the AU's emerging foreign policy approach has both normative and pragmatic elements, including peacebuilding, prosperity, political and economic integration underpinned by Pan-Africanism. The challenge has been in the perceived discrepancies between stated foreign policy norms and values and how foreign policy plays out in practice.

When it comes to EU-AU relations, the foreign policy position of the EU has, in the main, downplayed any notion of inequality or asymmetry, being well aware that it could be a stumbling block and a source for African hesitation, even reluctance, to engage in partnership. The EU is also well aware of a persistent residue of historical scepticism on the part of Africa and that its real intentions, especially as a postcolonial power, are being second-guessed by the latter. This has dampened the deepening of relations. While the two regions' foreign policy approaches both stress similar principles and interests, engagement between the regions has been consumed by political mistrust. While both the EU and the AU give emphasis to multilateralism in advancing foreign policy norms and principles, in practice their approaches on issues such as aid and the ICC diverge, leaving considerable work to be done in the efforts to deepen EU-AU relations.

Notes

1. The ACP Group became the Organisation of African, Caribbean and Pacific States in 2020.
2. Formally, this is the EU Strategy for Africa: Towards a Euro-African Pact to Accelerate Africa's Development (Commission of the European Communities, 2005). Prior to Morocco's return to membership of the AU in 2017, after 33 years absence, the EU preferred to use the reference 'Africa' rather than 'AU'. It is also its stated preference as per the Joint African-EU Strategy to deal with Africa 'as one'. In this chapter, the term 'Africa' also refers to the collective entity as represented by the AU.
3. As a rule, statements, communiques, etc. on EU-Africa relations emanate exclusively from the European Commission. It is assumed that these reflect a consensus, as no evidence exists about them being challenged or contradicted. This, of course, may give a one-sided, asymmetrical view of the true state of the relationship.

Bibliography

African Union (2000) Constitutive Act of the African Union. www.achpr.org/instruments/au-constitutive-act/ (retrieved 25 January 2018).
African Union (2015) Agenda 2063: The Africa We Want. https://au.int/sites/default/files/pages/3657-file-agenda2063_popular_version_en.pdf (retrieved 11 January 2018).
Barroso, J.M. (2010) Europe's rising global role. *The Guardian*. www.theguardian.com/commentisfree/2010/jan/03/europe-global-role (retrieved 15 January 2018).
Bello, O. (2010) *The EU-Africa Partnership: At a Strategic Crossroads*. Policy Brief No 47. Madrid: FRIDE.
Bindi, F. (2010) European Union foreign policy: A historical overview. In F. Bindi (ed.), *The Foreign Policy of the European Union: Assessing Europe's Role in the World*. Washington DC: Brookings Institution (pp. 13–40).
Carbone, M. (2010) The EU in Africa: Increasing coherence, decreasing partnership. In F. Bindi (ed.), *The Foreign Policy of the European Union: Assessing Europe's Role in the World*. Washington DC: Brookings Institution (pp. 239–252).
Carbone, M. (2013) EU-Africa relations in the twenty-first century: Evolution and explanations. In M. Carbone (ed.), *The European Union in Africa: Incoherent Policies, Asymmetrical Partnership, Declining Relevance?* Manchester: Manchester University Press (pp. 3–21).
Carlsnaes, W. (2013) Foreign policy. In W. Carlsnaes, T. Risse and B.A. Simmons (eds), *Handbook of International Relations*. London: SAGE Publications (pp. 298–325).
Chafetz, G., Spirtas, M. and Frankel, B. (1998) Introduction: Tracing the influence of identity on foreign policy. *Security Studies*, 8 (2–3), 7–22.
Commission of the European Communities (2005) Communication from the Commission to the Council, the European Parliament and the European Economic and Social Committee: EU Strategy for Africa: Towards a Euro-African Pact to Accelerate Africa's Development {Sec (2005) 1255}. COM(2005) 489 final. Brussels, 12 October.
Council of the European Union (2005) The EU and Africa: Towards a Strategic Partnership. C/05/367. Brussels, 19 December, 15961/05 (Presse 367).
Council of the European Union (2007) The Africa-EU Strategic Partnership: A Joint Africa-EU Strategy. Lisbon, 9 December. 16344/07 (Presse 291). www.concilium.europa.eu/Newsroom 16344/07
Cross, M.K.D. (2016) The EU Global Strategy and diplomacy. *Contemporary Security Policy*, 37 (3), 402–413.

European Commission (2007) Communication from the Commission to the European Parliament: From Cairo to Lisbon, the EU-Africa Strategic Partnership. Brussels, 27 June.

European Commission (2017) Joint Communication to the European Parliament and the Council for a renewed impetus of the Africa-EU Partnership. Brussels, 4 May. http://eur-lex.europa.eu/legal-content/EN/TXT/?uri=CELEX%3A52017JC0017 (retrieved 26 January 2018).

European Commission (2018) State of the Union 2018: Towards a New 'Africa-Europe Alliance' to Deepen Economic Relations and Boost Investment and Jobs. Press release, 12 September, Brussels. http://europa.eu/rapid/press-release_IP-18-5702_en.htm (retrieved 29 November 2018).

European Union (2003) A secure Europe in a Better World: European Security Strategy. 15895/03. Brussels, 8 December.

European Union (2007) *The Africa-EU Strategic Partnership: A Joint Africa-EU Strategy*. 16344/07 (Presse 291). Lisbon, 9 December.

European Union (2016) *Shared Vision, Common Action: A Stronger Europe. A Global Strategy for the European Union's Foreign and Security Policy*. Brussels: European Union. https://eeas.europa.eu/archives/docs/top_stories/pdf/eugs_review_web.pdf (retrieved 11 January 2017).

Holsti, K.J. (1970) National role conceptions in the study of foreign policy. *International Studies Quarterly*, 14 (3), 233–309.

Khadiagala, G.M. (2015) *Silencing the Guns: Strengthening governance to prevent, manage and resolve conflicts in Africa*. New York: International Peace Institute. www.ipinst.org/wp-content/uploads/2015/05/IPI_Rpt-Silencing_the_Guns-Strengthening_Governance_Africa.pdf

Hill, C. (2003) *The Changing Politics of Foreign Policy*. Houndmills: Palgrave MacMillan.

Howorth, J. (2010) The EU as global actor: Grand Strategy for a Global Grand Bargain. *Journal of Common Market Studies*, 48 (3), 455–474.

Mackie, J., Deneckere, M. and Galeazzi, G. (2017) *Challenges for Africa-EU Relations in 2017: Matching Means and Priorities*. ECDPM Challenges Paper, Issue 8.

Mälksoo, M. (2016) From the ESS to the EU Global Strategy: External policy, internal purpose. *Contemporary Security Policy*, 37 (3), 374–388.

Masters, L. (2012) Sustaining the African common position on climate change: International organisations, Africa and COP17. *South African Journal of International Affairs*, 18 (2), 257–269.

Masters, L. (2017) Negotiating the North-South divide in the post-2015 development agenda: What role for South Africa. In S. Zondi and P. Mthembu (eds), From MDGs to Sustainable Development Goals: The Travails of International Development. Pretoria: Institute for Global Dialogue (pp. 146–165).

Neack, L., Hey, J.A.K. and Haney, P.J. (1995) *Foreign Policy Analysis: Continuity and Change in its Second Generation*. Englewood Cliffs, NJ: Prentice Hall.

Newman, E. (2018) The EU Global Strategy in a transitional international order. *Global Society*, 32 (2), 198–209.

N'Guettia Kouassi, R. (2017) Ensuring a more effective and beneficial cooperation. *Great Insights Magazine*, 6 (5), 4–9.

Olivier, G. (2006) *South Africa and the European Union: Self-Interest, Ideology and Altruism*. Pretoria: Protea Book House.

Romaniuk, S.N. (2011) The entire world's a stage: The EU's strategic presence in the contemporary international arena. *Romanian Journal of European Affairs*, 11 (2), 5–30.

The Economist (2004) China's business links with Africa: A new scramble. 25 November. www.economist.com/node/3436400#print (retrieved 26 January 2018).

Tocci, N. (2016) The making of the EU Global Strategy. *Contemporary Security Policy*, 37 (3), 461–472.

Wallace, W. (1991) Foreign policy and national identity in the United Kingdom. *International Affairs*, 67 (1), 65–80.

Williams, P.D. (2017) Paying for AMISOM: Are politics and bureaucracy undermining the AU's largest peace operation? IPI Global Observatory. https://theglobalobservatory.org/2017/01/amisom-african-union-peacekeeping-financing/ (retrieved 29 November 2018).

6

European External Action Service

Nele Marianne Ewers-Peters

Introduction

The foreign policy of the European Union (EU) is complex and multidimensional in nature. It takes a distinct form, composed of three key features: member states' national foreign policies; the European Commission's external policies; and the development of the EU's profile as an international actor in the form of Common Foreign and Security Policy (CFSP) and Common Security and Defence Policy (CSDP). The creation of the European External Action Service (EEAS) was an innovation needed to channel these features into a single outlook to allow the EU to act as a unified actor in its external relations and to engage with its network of partners worldwide. In the EU's foreign policies, relations with Africa take a special position because of the historical links, economic relations and political exchanges between the two regions. Because of its expertise, resources and extensive global network of delegations, the EEAS presents itself as a key institutional development to manage the EU's external relations with Africa. In fact, with its establishment, the EU has finally created a body that allows it to be a truly global actor and one that can act coherently and with a single voice.

The Lisbon Treaty authorised the creation of the EEAS in 2010, a unique body of the EU's external relations, including a diplomatic service. Among the responsibilities of the EEAS are the external representation of the Union and its member states and the assumption of diplomatic tasks. This pivotal institutional development and the combination of all areas of the EU's external relations, including foreign policy, international trade and development cooperation, allows the Union to exercise a 'one voice' foreign policy. With the EEAS, the EU has made a major advancement in its external relations and facilitates regular and streamlined diplomatic interactions with key partners, which is evident in the relationship between the EU and its southern partners. While the Service faces institutional challenges, it needs to shape its own profile and to enhance its position vis-à-vis partners in the EU's external relations and foreign policy (Furness, 2013; Henökl, 2014; Tannous, 2013).

This chapter emphasises the role of the EEAS in the relations between Africa and the EU by reflecting on its establishment, newly assumed responsibilities and engagement with African partners. In what follows, this chapter first introduces the EEAS and outlines its objectives, responsibilities and institutional structures. It then turns to the Service's interactions with the

African partners, highlighting its contributions to EU-Africa relations and giving an outline of the challenges and limitations of the EEAS. Finally, the chapter concludes with an outlook for the EU's external relations and the role of the EEAS in interactions with Africa.

Understanding the EEAS in the EU's external relations

By introducing the EEAS, the Lisbon Treaty introduced new organisational structures and institutional reforms to the EU, particularly its foreign and security affairs, to enhance the Union's global profile. The EEAS was officially established through the Decision of the Council of the EU of 26 July 2010 (Council of the European Union, 2010), and formally launched on 1 January 2011. The objective of creating this new body was to give the EU a single voice, which had been a central issue ever since the start of European integration (Dialer and Austermann, 2014). The organisational development of the EEAS and tasking it with certain duties and responsibilities has not been controversial among the EU member states. It was perceived as an improvement to the EU's external voice and international positioning. As a 'hybrid service', it combines diplomacy, defence and development (Onestini, 2015). The question of the Service's institutional affiliation has been of greater debate, however, as reflected by controversies among member states and EU institutions. Since its introduction, it has assumed several roles and responsibilities and undergone institutional modifications to adjust to the structural and political demands within the EU.

The institutional design of the EEAS is unique and fits into the sui generis nature of the EU, since it combines the bureaucratic body in the headquarters located in Brussels, the High Representative for Foreign Affairs and Security Policy (HR) and the EU Delegations (EUDs) on the ground. It has therefore been described as an 'organisational hybrid' as well as an autonomous body (Duke, 2011; Henökl, 2014: 382; Onestini, 2015). The EEAS combines members of staff from the European Commission and the Council of the European Union's Secretariat as well as national diplomats seconded from member states. This has created significant diversity among staff, which allows swifter synchronisations with member states' diplomatic services and enhanced inter-institutional cooperation and cohesion within the EU institutions. For example, staff from different directorate-generals (DGs), such as the DG for International Cooperation and Development (DEVCO) and DG Trade, work closely together with member states' embassies and diplomats – a process that aims to improve the effectiveness and efficiency of the EU's external policies.

The EEAS follows a hierarchical structure which is headed by the HR and supported by the Secretary-General and Deputy Secretary-General. The Service is organised in five regional departments – Africa, Americas, Asia and Pacific, Europe and Central Asia, and Middle East and North Africa – and one thematic department with a global outreach dealing with human rights, global and multilateral issues, as well as one bureaucratic department charged with the budget and administration and the unit of the EU Military Staff. There are four additional units that are responsible for issues specifically allocated to the EU's CFSP and CSDP, including the Crisis Management and Planning Directorate (CMPD), Military Planning and Conduct Capability (MPCC), Civilian Planning and Conduct Capability (CPCC) and the Situation Centre. These play a crucial part in coordinating the EU's multiple crisis management and development instruments. In the conduct of CSDP missions and operations, the EEAS and its units act as essential coordinators of the EU's multiple instruments and efforts.

As the head of the EEAS, the HR is the chief of the EU's foreign policy and external relations. This position is not comparable to a national minister of foreign affairs due to its intergovernmental nature, as the HR cannot exert control over the EU's foreign policy; yet it allows the EU to move closer to speaking with a single voice. Prior to the Lisbon Treaty, the HR was solely responsible for the external representation of the EU's interests and positions. With the institutional reforms, the main responsibilities of the HR include external representation of the EU, chairing the Foreign Affairs Council and maintaining political dialogue with the EU's partners (EU, 2012). The HR is in charge of coordinating the activities of the European Council and Council of Ministers in alignment with the Commission. Yet, this has resulted in a complex distribution of power and competencies among this body and the EU institutions. Additionally, the HR acts as Vice-President of the Commission, making it a double-hatted position, in which it is tasked with the external projection and the internal workings of the EU on the basis of its embeddedness in the Commission. As the EU's key external representative, the HR also hosts meetings with Commissioners of the African Union (AU) (e.g. as part of the task force on migration) and interacts directly with representatives of the AU to maintain good relations between the two organisations and their member states. Concerning its role within the EEAS, the HR facilitates the coordination of policies and leads the Service's bureaucratic apparatus, while the management of the EEAS is outsourced to the Executive Secretary-General. The HR plays an overarching role in which it connects the Commission's internal policies with the EEAS' global outreach and external relations.

During negotiations over the creation of the EEAS, there was little contestation, though member states left its tasks and the division of labour concerning other institutions vague and open to interpretation. Overall, the EEAS serves four main purposes in the execution of the EU's external relations and foreign policy. First, as the prime diplomatic service of the EU, it functions similarly to national embassies, though without the same legal status. It is responsible for the Union's external representation and relations with third countries and international actors and further represents the interests of the EU in its entirety. In this position, it is tasked to 'strengthen the diplomatic toolkit of the European Union' (Maurer and Morgenstern-Pomorski, 2018: 306). Second, the Service collaborated and coordinates efforts with member states' diplomatic services to ensure synchronisation of their foreign policies. It gathers and shares information with member states' embassies and with the EU institutions to draft policies and to engage with local actors. For example, in the Democratic Republic of the Congo it acts through the delegation in Kinshasa as a coordination hub and linkage point between those member states with local embassies and representations in the country and local authorities (Hanses and Spence, 2015). In this position, it also organises the meetings between the EU and its partners, such as for the EU-Africa Summits and bilateral meetings between the Union and third countries. Because of its regular interactions with partners, the EEAS has therefore been characterised as the 'channel for negotiations and dialogue' (Henökl, 2014: 385). Third, the EEAS supports the work of the HR and assists the President of the European Council and the President of the Commission in their functions of external representation. The EEAS does not have any power on its own, since it lacks fundamental autonomous decision-making powers (Furness, 2013; Vanhoonacker and Pomorska, 2013), but it is able to exert some influence through the activities of the HR. Fourth, the EU's civilian missions and military operations under the CSDP framework are planned and managed under the aegis of the EEAS. The EU Military Staff and the EU Special Representatives (EUSRs) (e.g. for the Sahel), which are heavily involved in crisis management activities under CSDP, are also both situated within the Service. Yet, the EEAS is not the only player in this realm, since member states retain influence on the design and conduct of military and civilian operations (Weston and Mérand, 2015).

In addition to the EEAS headquarters in Brussels, the Service employs over 140 EUDs worldwide, which facilitate the Union's external representation, and seven EUSRs to promote the EU's interests in crisis regions. There are 52 EUDs located on the African continent, including the EU liaison office to the AU (EEAS, 2019). With the creation of the EUDs, the EEAS gained a vital player for external relations and representation abroad as well as a coordination hub for the different foreign policy instruments on the ground. Originally rooted in the former European Commission Delegations, the EUDs transformed with the enforcement of the Lisbon Treaty to gain a greater scope of responsibility and a distinguished institutional character. Whereas the European Commission Delegations were the external representations of the Commission, the EUDs represent the interests of the EU in its entirety (EU, 2012). The staffing of delegations reflects the hybrid nature, and while the majority of them are composed of staff from the Commission, about one-third of staff are employed by the EEAS, including national diplomats. Each delegation is led by a Head of Delegation, a national diplomat at ambassador level, and is composed of administrative staff, seconded personnel from Brussels and the EU member states as well as local staff. The main responsibilities of the delegations include the coordination and synchronisation of member states' foreign policies, cooperation with their diplomatic services, consular protection of and support for EU citizens, gathering information on the ground about partner countries' developments and polices, external representation of the EU and support of the EEAS' work in the field as well as the implementation of the EU's development policy abroad (Helly et al., 2014).

A unique player in the field: The EEAS in EU-Africa relations

In EU-Africa relations, the EU's institutions and administrative bodies are mostly involved in three distinct areas. These are development, trade, and foreign and security policy. While the EEAS is primarily responsible for the EU's foreign and security policy, it is essential to work in close cooperation and coordination with other institutions to ensure coherence of the EU's external actions. Its hybrid structure and the conflation of expertise in diplomacy, defence and development, make the EEAS a unique actor that facilitates bilateral relations with African partners via its multiple instruments and channels of interaction.

As the main point of contact for cooperation between the EU and its African partners, the EEAS primarily acts as a bureaucratic body since it cannot be considered as a 'fully-fledged institution' (Pierre Vimont, cited in Hadfield and Fiott, 2013: 172). It is primarily tasked with managing bilateral relations with African countries and multilateral relationships with the AU and the Economic Community of West African States (ECOWAS). It does so, however, in coordination and accordance with the Commission, the Council Secretariat and the EU member states as well as in close cooperation with the HR and the delegations on the ground. The establishment of the EEAS as the main diplomatic service and the transformation of the EUDs helped the EU to create a unique administration for its foreign policy and external representation. The network of EUDs and the cooperation with member states' embassies and consulates has been perceived as especially positive (Maurer and Morgenstern-Pomorski, 2018). The key advantage of the EUDs is that they allow the EU and its member states to project a single voice and united foreign policy to their partners in Africa, which further strengthens the capabilities and significance of CFSP, CSDP and the range of EU external action instruments. Both the EEAS and the EUDs contribute to a more coherent foreign policy approach and help to create a linkage between the EU's various efforts and instruments. For example, the EUD in the Democratic Republic of the Congo is the key contact point for local authorities as well as for the CMPD to plan missions and operations, whereby it acts as an interlocutor for information sharing, communication and exchanges. The organisational restructuring under the Lisbon Treaty therefore 'brought the EU Delegation and the two CSDP missions under the common roof of the EEAS'; these were previously accountable to two different actors, the European Council and the Commission (Hanses and Spence, 2015: 318).

Within the EEAS, the division of labour is more clearly defined, and specific portfolios are allocated to regional divisions. The main responsibility for EU-Africa relations is located in the Managing Directorate (MD) Africa and MD Middle East and North Africa. Occasionally, MD Global and Multilateral Affairs also get involved for interactions with regional organisations such as the AU and ECOWAS. MD Africa is organised in five subdivisions that work on regional issues, which include the Horn of Africa and East Africa, Central Africa, South Africa and Indian Ocean, West Africa and Pan-African Affairs. There are frequent exchanges between the regional subdivisions and the subdivision on Pan-African Affairs to ensure consistency across policies and strategies. Hence, coordination and inter-institutional cooperation among MDs and with DGs of the Commission and EU institutions are essential to maintaining coherence across policies and forms of external representation.

Desk officers in these subdivisions manage specific portfolios of the EU's relationships with individual African counties. This means that there is at least one desk officer for each state in Africa. Their responsibilities include regular communication and interactions with the respective EUDs and maintaining information flows about events in the partner countries to local partners and the EU institutions. Concerning exchanges with national governments of African partner countries, the Delegation is the main contact point, while the EEAS desk officers only interact directly with governments and national partners during overseas missions to the respective countries. The EEAS as a whole, with its subdivisions and the desk officers at the headquarters in Brussels, craft and draft the EU's foreign policy strategies and approaches to African partner countries, which include political dialogue and financial assistance (Helly, 2013). These desk officers mainly act as key linkages to the EU while the EUDs serve as 'the hub of European diplomatic cooperation abroad in third countries' (Maurer and Morgenstern-Pomorski, 2018: 310). For example, during the Arab Spring and the ensuing crises in Libya and Egypt in 2011–2012, the newly established EU Delegation to Libya was a vital source of local information for the EU to respond to the conflict and to assist the capability assessment team. Similarly, the HR and the EEAS with its staff at the EU Delegation facilitated the EU's involvement in Egypt, as they were heavily involved in diplomatic and political dialogue when meeting with relevant parties (e.g. the Muslim Brotherhood) (Hadfield and Fiott, 2013), thus supporting a democratic transition alongside promoting human rights and trade.

Some of these subdivisions and country profiles receive higher levels of attention during times of regional conflict and crisis (e.g. the Horn of Africa and Central Africa as well as MD Northern Africa and Middle East) because of the EU's civilian and military operations in these regions. In these circumstances, desk officers for the specific portfolios concerning countries in crisis support the EU Military Staff as well as local actors, such as the AU and ECOWAS, in planning civilian and military operations. Since the specific instruments – including diplomacy, crisis management and planning capabilities, like the MPCC and CPCC – are located in the realm of the EEAS, it is the key actor alongside the EU member states in engaging in international and regional conflicts and crises that threaten the EU's security and interests. Staff from the EEAS and EU Military Staff craft the EU's Concept of Operations and Operation Plan for its own civilian and military operations, and they sometimes also support local actors such as the AU in drafting these documents. For such situations, the EEAS Crisis Response System has been created, which facilitates the mobilisation of EU crisis management instruments to ensure a united and comprehensive approach.

The EEAS therefore plays a crucial role in the EU's involvement in African states in times of conflicts and crises. Under CSDP, the EU is currently conducting ten civilian missions, of which four are located on the African continent: EU Border Assistance Mission in Libya; EU Capacity Building Mission (EUCAP) Sahel Niger; EUCAP Sahel Mali; and EUCAP Somalia. It is also deploying troops to five military operations in the area: EU Training Mission (EUTM) Mali, EUTM RCA in the Central African Republic, EUTM Somalia, and the two naval operations – EU Naval Force (EUNAVFOR) MED Irini, previously EUNAVFOR MED Sophia, in the Mediterranean Sea and EUNAVFOR Atalanta in the Horn of Africa and the Gulf of Aden (EEAS, 2020). In these engagements, the EEAS not only plays a fundamental role in planning and conduct, but is also a crucial actor in crisis management, with the help of its diplomatic toolkit and the pursuit of a comprehensive approach. The Service assumes key responsibilities due to the inclusion of relevant bodies such as the Crisis Response System, CMPD and a variety of military and civilian instruments. However, not all crisis management tools under CSDP have been fully integrated into the EEAS, since member states keep control of security and defence. This affects the Service's ability to effectively plan, coordinate and conduct missions in Africa, which require a comprehensive approach based on the wider toolbox (Weston and Mérand, 2015).

For example, quickly after its creation, the EEAS identified two key geographical areas important for European interests and foreign policy: the Horn of Africa and the Sahel. Concurrently, Sudan and South Sudan became a hotspot for simmering conflict following the independence referendum in South Sudan in 2011. Subsequently, in 2012, the EU transformed its office in the capital, Juba, into a fully fledged EU Delegation to South Sudan, and this came to play a crucial role in the engagement in the 2013 civil war (EEAS, 2020; Furness and Olsen, 2016). The delegation established itself as the main provider for information and the platform for exchanges between all EU actors involved. Moreover, the local Head of Delegation in South Sudan chaired the meetings of the Heads of Mission, in which the delegation coordinated activities, including the implementation of the Comprehensive Peace Agreement, with the support of the EEAS and the Commission's Single Development Strategy. In addition, the EU has launched several initiatives and projects in South Sudan, such as education programmes and infrastructure projects to support the country's development. This case demonstrates the crucial role of the EEAS through its delegations on the ground as well as the significance of its collaboration with other EU institutions, particularly the Commission, which has not always been easy.

Inter-institutional contestation and division of labour

Because of the hybrid character and institutional design of the EEAS, it assumes several positions and tasks in the EU's interactions with Africa. While focusing on the Union's external representation, it is also responsible for maintaining internal cohesion among the EU institutions – specifically with DG DEVCO, DG Trade, the Council and even the European Parliament – and for coordinating member states' foreign policies. For example, the hybrid organisational structure contributes to the diversity of staff with different backgrounds that allow for combining activities relating to diplomacy, defence and development. Furthermore, desk officers in the EEAS, particularly those tasked with portfolios of countries on the African continent that receive aid programmes and/or host CSDP missions and operations, are in constant exchange with desk officers from DG DEVCO and DG Trade and with the delegations to agree on common approaches (Weston and Mérand, 2015). This has led to a blurred division of labour in the EU's external relations and increased contestation among these multiple actors. Since its establishment, the EEAS has had to adapt its structures and procedures to gain more autonomous capabilities in its interactions and exchanges with third counties and international actors. It has therefore taken a more adaptive and flexible role in the relations with African states and the AU.

One of its crucial tasks is to act as 'the overall coordinator of the EU's external relations agenda' (Hadfield and Fiott, 2013: 170). The EEAS seeks to connect the EU institutions and member states to third actors and strategic partners worldwide, whereby it supports the Union to become a truly global actor.

The EU's foreign policy and external representation has long suffered from a lack of coherence, clear leadership and visible actions. The EEAS' establishment and the transformed role of the HR sought to meet the increasing demands and pressures to make EU foreign policy more effective, consistent and coherent. With the plurality among its staff members, its headquarters and the boots on the ground through the delegations, the Service is supposed to create synergies between the EU and its member states as well as among the institutions in Brussels (Duke, 2011). Its hybrid character and the staffing from the Commission, Council Secretariat and member states was geared towards the improvement of inter-institutional cooperation and coordination between these actors. What has become evident, however, is that the EEAS faces multiple challenges and obstacles which inhibit its ability to ensure consistency and coherence.

As one of its key responsibilities, the EEAS seeks to embody the EU's single voice in foreign policy and external affairs. While the Union has lacked clear leadership in this field, a new administrative body with the institutionally transformed role of the HR would help to achieve a security actorness status that would allow it to play a more important role in global affairs. The EU's organisational set-up tells a different story, however. Instead of providing a clearer role specification for external representation, the enforcement of the Lisbon Treaty brought forward even greater confusion about who does what. Accordingly, three actors are charged with external relations: the HR, the President of the European Commission and the President of the European Council (EU, 2012). Within the Commission, the three DGs that work on related issues are DG DEVCO, DG Trade and DG for Neighbourhood and Enlargement Negotiations (NEAR). The multitude of actors responsible for the EU's foreign policy and the plurality of staff members of the EEAS have triggered sources for tensions and obstacles, which have direct consequences for the EU's relations with African states and multilateral actors in the region.

First, an inter-institutional contestation has emerged over leadership in EU foreign policy. While the HR officially carries the title of the *representative* of the EU's foreign and security policy, with the support from the EEAS as the administrative body to manage its work and activities, both the President of the Commission and the President of the Council also claim to be the external representatives of the EU's interests, which have triggered tensions (Duke, 2011). This has left many cooperation partners in African countries in confusion even though each African state is generally assigned a desk officer in the EEAS. The vague provisions in the Lisbon Treaty thus still fail to clarify previous confusion in third countries, which is hampering the EEAS' effectiveness.

Second, and linked to the previous issue, the EEAS suffers from an overflow of agents who seek to influence the Service's work. Operating under the command of the Commission, Council Secretariat and member states as well as being under the scrutiny of the European Parliament triggers internal and inter-institutional conflict over the EU's foreign policy approach. When interacting with African partners, particularly during crises that demand a comprehensive approach and the use of the EU's wider toolbox, delays in responses and incoherent approaches have been noticed. For example, as the crisis in Mali emerged, France was at the forefront while the EEAS, local EUD and the Commission chose their own paths of engagement. Similarly, EU member states are sometimes driven by their national interests and consequently not very transparent about their bilateral relations with African states and multilateral actors. This is particularly the case for former colonial powers that maintain close relations with their former colonies, such as France, Portugal and the United Kingdom (Furness and Olsen, 2016; Gibert and Nivet, 2013).

Such behaviour not only negatively impacts the ability of the EEAS to create coherence in EU foreign policy, but also hampers its effectiveness in crisis management and its engagement with partner countries.

Third, the effectiveness, levels of activity and credibility of EUDs are highly dependent on the contribution and input of the Head of Delegation, including their personality and experience as a national diplomat, and the delegation staff on the ground. Recognition of the added value of having to deal with only one European diplomat has spread among African partners. In this context, Maurer and Morgenstern-Pomorski find that 'host governments use the EU convening power often strategically: they look for it, if it is in their interest to have the EU support, they avoid it when the EU message might not be to their liking' (2018: 311). Moreover, a lack of trust and suspicion as well as diverging objectives of the relationships between the host governments in Africa and the EUDs still persist. Again, this particularly applies to those African states that heavily advocate local ownership and which have been under the aegis of former colonial powers.

Lastly, the inter-institutional contestation between DG DEVCO and the EEAS has become evident in the interactions with African countries. General divergences have been noticed over time between the EU's security policy agenda, which is located within the EEAS but also set by the Council, and the development cooperation agenda outlined by DG DEVCO. These divisions frequently lead to turf battles over competencies and policies in which both actors seek to exert influence. Among the sensitive issues are the budgeting of their projects and the diffused division of labour over areas in which both claim responsibility. For example, with the creation of the EEAS, development policy was added to the EU's overall toolbox for its external relations, which usually falls under the realm of DG DEVCO and DG Trade instead of CFSP. This clash has been evident in the EU's humanitarian assistance and disaster response and in the pursuit of a comprehensive approach. Humanitarian assistance, again, is located within DG DEVCO and focuses on the EU's long-term efforts to promote development and humanitarian well-being in several African countries and regions, including the Democratic Republic of the Congo, the Central African Republic and the Horn of Africa (Somalia, Ethiopia, Kenya). Emergency and disaster responses often take place in the same regions and countries but are managed by the EEAS. Similarly, the EU and the AU have agreed to cooperate on peace and security issues. The EU seeks to enhance the link between development cooperation, governance and conflict prevention, which are all issue areas spread across the responsibilities of both the EEAS and DG DEVCO that have been criticised for the lack of achievement. Clashes over agendas and policy objectives therefore hamper the coherence and effectiveness of the EU's external actions. This triggers discontentment in partners, as they perceive that this approach is focused too much on the EU itself, rather than on the needs of African countries (Miyandazi et al., 2018).

The clash between the EEAS' work under the EU's foreign and security policy and DG DEVCO's development cooperation policies are further illustrated by the budgeting issue and authority over the instruments for external assistance. As most EU institutions bargain over their share of the overall budget, both the EEAS and DG DEVCO take this even further, since they enter into contestations over projects and initiatives which fall into their overlapping responsibilities. This also means that they compete to gain their share of the EU's external assistance budget. Yet, the Commission retains a higher financial stake, since the funds allocated within the Development Cooperation Instrument are over eight times higher than those for CFSP (European Commission, 2019). Moreover, in the early stages of the Service, former HR Catherine Ashton drafted a plan to move the external assistance instruments to the EEAS, which was heavily criticised and opposed by the Commission as it feared losing fundamental competencies within the EU's development policy (Tannous, 2013). Due to the initial divisions between the EEAS and the Commission, they signed an inter-service agreement in 2011 which outlines the provisions for coordination and cooperation among the two actors to ensure coherence in their approaches to crisis management and development. Closer collaboration and the arrangement concerning division of labour have proven essential for the EU's relations with Africa. For instance, the EU is able to pursue its comprehensive approach in Somalia and the Horn of Africa because of the improved working relations and division of labour between the Commission, the EEAS and the EUDs on the ground. Similarly, in the Sahel region, there are frequent exchanges and a clear strategy executed by all actors involved – DG DEVCO, the EEAS in the Brussels headquarters, the local delegations in Chad and Mauretania as well as the EUSR for the Sahel (Venturi, 2017).

Conclusion

This chapter provided an overview of the EEAS as a unique actor for the EU's external relations and foreign policy towards its partners in Africa and beyond. With the establishment of the EEAS and the transformation of both the role of the HR and the EUDs, the Union created a unique player to represent its interests and objectives worldwide. This administrative body has the ability to directly engage with national governments and local partners through its delegations on the ground, which have proven to be crucial sources of information and key linkages to the EEAS' projects and initiatives. Through desk officers' management of relations, the Service maintains a profound overview of its exchanges with African partners, in which it has moved from a one-size-fits-all approach towards individual engagements based on regional and country portfolios. More importantly, the HR and the delegations play strategic roles in communicating the EU's foreign policy interests and preferences through direct interactions and exchanges on the ground. The EU has a track record of crisis management operations and civilian missions under CFSP and CSDP on the African continent. The EEAS is a relevant actor in these situations, as it manages crisis response and deployment of troops, through which it has made distinct contributions to the EU's engagement and relations with several African countries, particularly in the Horn of Africa and the Sahel region.

One can conclude that the EEAS has made a novel contribution due to its hybrid institutional design, global network and direct linkages to African partners. It has become evident, however, that the EEAS still faces internal challenges and contestation with other EU institutions, especially DG DEVCO, over certain external action competencies. Much of the efficiency and success of the EEAS in its interactions and exchanges depends on the delegations on the ground – their credibility and acceptance as actors by local governments and partners. The Service has shown that it is able to engage specifically in crisis situations. Yet, the EU's comprehensive approach to regional crises on the African continent requires smooth cooperation among the EEAS, the Commission and the EU member states, and this suggests that the EEAS still needs to sharpen its role as policy coordinator.

Bibliography

Council of the European Union (2010) Council Decision of 26 July 2010 Establishing the Organisation and Functioning of the European External Action Service (2010/427/EU). *Official Journal of the European Union*, 201/30.

Dialer, D. and Austermann, F. (2014) Giving the EU one voice abroad: The European Union delegations. In D. Dialer, H. Neisser and A. Opitz (eds) *The EU's External Action Service: Potentials for a One Voice Foreign Policy*. Innsbruck: Innsbruck University Press (pp. 97–118).

Duke, S. (2011) Learning to cooperate after Lisbon: Inter-institutional dimensions of the EEAS. *Cuadernos Europeos de Deusto*, 44, 43–61.

European Commission (2019) EU funding programmes 2014–2020. Heading 4: Global Europe [online]. https://ec.europa.eu/info/about-european-commission/eu-budget/spending/topic/funding-programmes-2014-2020/heading-4-global-europe_en (retrieved on 29 March 2019).

European External Action Service (2019) EU in the world – EU delegations [online]. https://eeas.europa.eu/headquarters/headquarters-homepage/area/geo_en (retrieved on 27 March 2019).

European External Action Service (2020) Military and civilian missions and operations [online]. https://eeas.europa.eu/topics/military-and-civilian-missions-and-operations/430/military-and-civilian-missions-and-operations_en (retrieved on 12 May 2020).

European Union (2012) Treaty on European Union (Consolidated Version). *Official Journal of the European Union*, C326/30.

Furness, M. (2013) Who controls the European External Action Service? Agent autonomy in EU external policy. *European Foreign Affairs Review*, 18 (1), 103–126.

Furness, M. and Olsen, G.R. (2016) Europeanisation and the EU's comprehensive approach to crisis management in Africa. *European Politics and Society*, 17 (1), 105–119.

Gibert, M.V. and Nivet, B. (2013) Dissonant paths to partnership and convergence: EU-Africa relations between experimentation and resistance. *African Security*, 6 (3–4), 191–210.

Hadfield, A. and Fiott, D. (2013) Europe and the rest of the world. *Journal of Common Market Studies*, 51 (S1), 168–182.

Hanses, B. and Spence, D. (2015) The EEAS and bilateral relations: The case of the EU Delegation in the Democratic Republic of Congo. In D. Spence and J. Bátora (eds), *The External Action Service: European Diplomacy Post-Westphalia*. Basingstoke: Palgrave Macmillan (pp. 306–322).

Helly, D. (2013) The EU and Africa since the Lisbon Summit of 2007: Continental drift or widening cracks? *South African Journal of International Affairs*, 20 (1), 137–157.

Helly, D., Herrero, A., Knoll, A., Galeazzi, G. and Sherriff, A. (2014) *A Closer Look into the EU's External Action Frontline: Framing the Challenges Ahead for EU Delegations*. European Centre for Development Policy Management, Briefing Note No. 62. Maastricht: ECDPM.

Henökl, T. (2014) The European External Action Service: Torn apart between several principals or acting as a smart 'double-agent'? *Journal of Contemporary European Research*, 10 (4), 381–401.

Maurer, H. and Morgenstern-Pomorski, J.-H. (2018) The quest for throughput legitimacy: The EEAS, EU delegations and the contested structures of European diplomacy. *Global Affairs*, 4 (2–3), 305–316.

Miyandazi, L., Apiko, P., Abderrahim, T. and Aggad-Clerx, F. (2018) AU–EU relations: Challenges in forging and implementing a joint agenda. *South African Journal of International Affairs*, 25 (4), 461–480.

Onestini, C. (2015) A hybrid service: Organising efficient EU foreign policy. In D. Spence and J. Bátora (eds), *The External Action Service: European Diplomacy Post-Westphalia*. Basingstoke: Palgrave Macmillan (pp. 65–86).

Tannous, I. (2013) The programming of EU's external assistance and development aid and the fragile balance of power between EEAS and DG DEVCO. *European Foreign Affairs Review*, 18 (3), 329–354.

Vanhoonacker, S. and Pomorska, K. (2013) The European External Action Service and agenda-setting in European foreign policy. *Journal of European Public Policy*, 20 (9), 1316–1331.

Venturi, B. (2017) *The EU and the Sahel: A Laboratory of the Experimentation for the Security-Migration-Development Nexus*. IAI Working Papers, 17 (38).

Weston, A. and Mérand, F. (2015) The EEAS and crisis management: The organisational challenges of a comprehensive approach. In D. Spence and J. Bátora (eds), *The External Action Service: European Diplomacy Post-Westphalia*. Basingstoke: Palgrave Macmillan (pp. 323–340).

7
European Neighbourhood Policy in the South Mediterranean

Anthony Costello

Introduction

The European Union (EU) is one of the most influential and identifiable foreign policy actors in contemporary world affairs. Through its Common Foreign and Security Policy (CFSP), its presence abroad, particularly in foreign conflict zones, is traditionally based on a humanitarian approach and is marked by military passivism as well as constructivist approaches to conflict resolution.[1] However, the EU's foreign policy actions are not limited to mere troop deployment in conflict zones with the intention of 'keeping the peace'. EU foreign policy is more complex and extensive. In the 'new world order', global interdependence brings with it the potential contagion of globally sourced risk. Economic and political openness or exposure to the wider world enhances both state and regional vulnerability. The EU – as a complex multi-governmental organisation consisting of 28 member states[2] bound by a single market – engages in multiple bilateral and multilateral agreements with international partners around the world, not solely to address destabilising conditions abroad through a sense of duty or responsibility, but to enhance its own security and ensure its own stability. This is particularly evident today in its relationship with its nearest neighbours through the European Neighbourhood Policy (ENP).

Constituting part of the EU's foreign policy framework, the ENP has aimed to mitigate risk-causing factors that could likely undermine and challenge the integrity and security of Europe's internal economic and political framework. In response to the EU's fifth and largest enlargement process in 2004, the ENP was established as a means to contain potential inward contagion of external threat by aiming to transform risk-causing factors and structures abroad through various mechanisms that would extend integrational opportunities to non-EU member states to the east and south of the EU's so-called external borders. By fostering enhanced diplomatic relations with neighbouring states and extending economic opportunities to their societies, the EU could bring neighbours closer to Europe without them constituting part *of* Europe. In turn, Europe could mitigate foreign-sourced risk and enhance security for the Union.

Since its inception in 2004, the ENP has undergone revisions in 2011 and 2015 by EU leaders and neighbours in response to a series of unprecedented destabilising political developments across the eastern and southern parts of the neighbourhood – not least the Arab Spring and the associated migration crisis. In recent years, the neighbourhood has perceptively become more threatening to Europe, and in turn Europe's response has changed. Over time, the ENP has become a more developed foreign policy framework on paper, complimenting such bilateral arrangements as the Euro-Mediterranean Partnership (EUROMED) and, later, the Union for the Mediterranean (UfM). But in the process of its revision and development, it's underlying rationale has been criticised and its ability to foster successful transformation in parts of its neighbourhood, particularly in the southern region, has been brought into question (Ghazaryan, 2016; Gillespie, 2013). The EU has remained committed to the region, and whilst there is still much to be desired in terms of wholesome transformation, small yet important moves toward change have already begun. This is noticeable in Morocco, but also in more vulnerable North African states such as Tunisia and, to a lesser degree, Algeria.

This chapter explores the development of the ENP with a particular focus on the EU's South Mediterranean neighbourhood. The chapter explores the origins and development of the ENP between 2004 and 2015 in response to a changing external environment along the EU's southern 'border'. Taking Algeria and Tunisia as cases for analysis, the chapter evaluates the quality of social, economic and political transformation in these countries in light of their relationship with the ENP, in the hope of better understanding how the ENP may be impacting states in the North African region.

In close proximity: Developing the ENP

> The idea that post-modern Europe remains vulnerable to threats emanating from its 'modern' neighbourhood represents the security logic on which the ENP is founded.
>
> *(Cebeci, 2017: 59)*

The EU's 2004 enlargement extended membership to ten new member states. As the Union's largest accession process to date, the accession of eight Eastern European States (plus the Mediterranean states of Malta and Cyprus) shifted the EU's external borders farther toward the east – bringing it closer in line with Russia's sphere of influence.[3] Europe was now in close proximity with some of Eastern Europe's most politically volatile states, such as Belarus, Moldova and Ukraine. The eastern enlargement assumed greater complexity within the neighbourhood and enhanced the potential for external political and economic risks for the Union. Although the accession of Cyprus to the Union in 2004 appeared to bring Europe's so-called external border closer to Syria, Israel, Palestine and Lebanon, as an integrated community, Europe's external borders have been traditionally in close geographical proximity with the Middle East, and with North Africa since the accession of Greece to the European Economic Community in 1981, followed by Spain and Portugal in 1986. Europe's preparations for risk mitigation from the South Mediterranean long proceeds the creation of the ENP in 2004. In 1995, EU foreign ministers and their counterparts from North Africa, the Middle East and Balkans initiated the Barcelona Process (1995), which later gave way to EUROMED. At the time, EUROMED was the most dynamic response by EU member states toward the Southern Neighbourhood, later only 'supplemented' by the ENP in 2004 (Smith, 2005: 759). EUROMED eventually gave way to the UfM in 2008. Today the UfM remains a fundamental bilateral and multilateral framework in its own right, yet it mirrors many of the principles, and even compliments many of the objectives, of the ENP. However, like the ENP, it is also subject to many similar criticisms (Ghazaryan, 2016: 19; Kausch and Youngs, 2009).

The ENP formally came into existence in 2004 following the European Neighbourhood Strategy paper (European Commission, 2004) which built on the normative architecture of the European Commission's 2003 Wider Europe – Neighbourhood document.[4] Not long after its inception, stagnant political and economic transformation in the southern neighbourhood throughout the 2000s brought into question the effectiveness of the ENP in the North African region (see Kausch and Youngs, 2009). Across North Africa, the years following the new millennium saw a continuation in dictatorships, electoral malpractice, weak democratic institutions (and structures), deficiencies in political checks and balances, an absence in the rule of law, ongoing suppression of civil liberties and political rights, gender inequality, ethnic and tribal conflict, socio-economic inequality and high unemployment and poverty rates.

It was suggested that the ENP's ability to foster effective transformation in North African partner states was waning and that this had something to do with the fundamental nature of the EU's motivations and methods; not least associated with the EU's policy of 'conditionality' directed toward its neighbours, which had seemingly effected its legitimacy (see Haukkala, 2008; Telò and Ponjeart, 2013). Economic incentives effectively became the 'carrots' encouraging neighbours to adapt to EU political and economic standards and norms, and as these standards and norms are adequately met by neighbours, the EU's security is expected to improve (see Ghazaryan, 2016: 11; Haukkala, 2008; Smith, 2005). The EU's method of conditionality which encourages neighbours to adhere to, and implement, EU values and norms in return for arguably vague and unclear economic incentives has led to the EU being criticised for being a 'normative hegemon' using its 'normative clout' to achieve self-serving security objectives and for turning neighbours – particularly in the South Mediterranean – into securitised 'EU subjects' through domestic impacts (see Haukkala, 2008; Schimmelfennig, cited in Gstöhl, 2017: 9). Neighbours are said to be influenced by EU policy but limited in their ability to actually influence the ENP in turn. Thus, they are seen as policy-takers as opposed to policy-shapers and/or makers (see Barbé and Johansson-Nogués, 2008). Apart from its top-down strategy to foster change, the ENP was criticised for its vagueness in establishing expected time frames and quality of outcomes as well as not offering 'bigger carrots' to neighbours for altering their states and societal norms to satisfy EU security objectives (see Gillespie, 2013: 130; Smith, 2005: 764). The ENP did not (and still does not) offer neighbours full membership to the EU, and this has impacted on its ability to foster aspirations of change. Moreover, this weakens its legitimacy as a framework across the neighbourhood. 'It is clear that ENP conditionality is not as strong as enlargement-related conditionality' (Gänzle, 2009: 1729).

Since 2004, in response to increasingly uncertain conditions across the EU's neighbourhood, the ENP has come to prove itself as a 'living document', and as expected, the changing nature of threat within the neighbourhood required a revision in strategic response and objectives. With the unprecedented onset of the Arab Spring in 2010 (later contributing to an unmanageable migration crisis), the ENP found a new impetus for revision and allowed the EU an opportunity to acknowledge and attempt to rectify some of its original failings through a new and improved response (Ghazaryan, 2016). ENP failures have been attributed to lack of transparency and clarity regarding expectations for southern partners, lack of consistency in its objectives, its questionable procedure of 'conditionality' as an incentive to encourage (or even coerce) democratic change, its inability to offer EU membership as a long-term objective to southern partners (small carrots) and its poor efforts to facilitate democratic change beyond mere financial support. Titled A New Response to a Changing Neighbourhood (European Commission, 2011b), the revised ENP in 2011 built on an earlier communication titled A Partnership for Democracy and shared Prosperity with the Southern Mediterranean (European Commission, 2011a). However, it has come to be criticised as being anything but a label (see Ghazaryan, 2016: 29), and although it has changed and evolved (in parts) to securitise and mitigate new threat particularly associated with the Arab Spring and migration crisis, the revised ENP leaves room for further criticism, not least with regards to its persistent adherence to conditionality as a measure to foster transition abroad.

Although maintaining the principle of conditionality for its neighbours, the document approaches (in particular) the Southern Neighbourhood via an accentuated procedure of so-called 'differentiation' which would help determine resource allocation for fostering 'change for opportunity' to those neighbours expressing greater interest/willingness and capabilities to transform. Arguably sensible in approach, especially to the neorealist scholar, this strategy also brings risks. Not only might it create divisions and contrasting gains between different states in the same region; it also has the potential to hinder the true economic potential of regionalism in the Southern Mediterranean – something which is an important facet of the ENP.

The revised ENP documents in 2011 and 2015 are optimistic in vision and particularly more 'southern focused' in their efforts. However, developments in North Africa since the Arab Spring may deem them perhaps slightly too enthusiastic in their foresight. The 2011 document suggested that the Arab Spring represented a 'profound transformation' for the region (European Commission, 2011a). It is from this supposed transformation that the opportunity to revive the EU's response and actions in the region could be realised. Although its optimism is to be commended, recent history shows us that large-scale transformation in North Africa is far from profound. Transformation across the region appears to be differentiated, conditional, slow and incremental due to persistent sociopolitical, socio-economic and cultural complexities in North African states. Given that economic incentives (driven by conditionality) alone cannot be expected to foster change under such circumstances, the 2004 ENP (in particular) may be criticised for its disregard toward these complex conditions.

Consistency and change: The ENP from 2004 to 2015

> Recent events throughout the Southern Mediterranean have made the case for this review even more compelling. The EU needs to rise to the historical challenges in our neighbourhood.
> *(European Commission, 2011b: 1)*

Cognisant of the potential spillover of political and economic security risk from and beyond the EU's eastern (and southern) neighbourhood, the 2004 ENP contained three core objectives: to share the benefits of the 2004 enlargement in the wider neighbourhood; to prevent new dividing lines between *ins* and *outs*; and to offer neighbours a chance to participate in political, economic and cultural cooperation (European Commission, 2004). The 2004 ENP was explicit in the fact that sharing benefits and preventing dividing lines was not a path to European membership.

> Since this policy was launched, the EU has emphasised that it offers a means to reinforce relations between the EU and partner countries, which is distinct from the possibilities available to European countries under Article 49 of the Treaty on European Union.
> *(European Commission, 2004: 3)*

Oxymoronically, in making such an explicit statement, the EU was in fact fostering dividing lines before the ENP was even implemented. The ENP aimed to bring its neighbours closer to the EU – without being part of the EU – through a clear set of priorities mediated via action plans. Core to the action plans are a required move toward the rule of law and good governance, recognition and respect for human rights (particularly minority rights), gender equality, good neighbourly relations, the implementation of liberal and neoliberal market principles, as well as labour rights and good working conditions, enhanced standards for good and services (including agricultural products), promotion of structural reforms such as welfare state reform, assistance to foster sustainable development, assistance in combatting terrorism and combatting the proliferation of weapons of mass destruction, encouraging an abidance to international law and facilitating conflict resolution. In addition to its core objectives and principles, the action plans would also provide cooperation on justice and home affairs, the fostering of political dialogue and reform, the offering of a *prospective* stake in the EU's internal market through cooperation in energy, transport and environmental policies as well as research and innovation and the information society (European Commission, 2004). Action plans would effectively become the means by which neighbours could be qualitatively assessed in terms of their progress over time, which in turn would help the EU to determine the degree of assistance provided through established frameworks. The implementation of action plans would allow the EU to measure if its normative values are being adequately adopted by partners; in turn it could then make judgements on resource allocation and extended economic opportunities. Achieving the expectations inherent in the action plans required 'joint ownership' between EU and neighbourhood partners. The 2004 ENP declared that the EU would not impose values and conditions on neighbours and that for success to be met, neighbours would have to be truly willing to accept the action plans and recognise the potential benefits of their implementation. Albeit a reasonable point on paper, the imposition of financial restrictions or penalties for poor progress could open this statement up to much criticism. After all, the 2004 ENP states that actions plans would entail 'deliverables' of importance to the EU (and neighbouring partners).

Within the revisions to the ENP in 2011 and 2015, respectively, the EU recognised that conditionality alone was not wielding adequate results and that greater emphasis on differentiation (in addition to conditionality) was needed so that the EU could focus its normative efforts in those countries who are willing to advance further in their transitions – that is, a principle of 'more for more'. Although the principle of differentiation is often attributed to the revised ENP in 2011, it was actually a component of the 2004 ENP. 'The Action Plans will draw on a common set of principles but will be differentiated, reflecting the existing state of relations with each country, its needs and capacities, as well as common interests' (European Commission, 2004: 3). Recognising previous failures linked to its top-down approach toward fostering change through normative guidelines, as well as financial assistance and conditionality procedures, the revised ENP documents now placed renewed focused on expanding support for bottom-up structures by fostering transformation through the empowerment of civil society, namely through the Civil Society Neighbourhood Facility. This was deemed essential in the aftermath of the Arab Spring amidst several North African Arab societies seeking to navigate their way toward democratic transition whilst remaining ever vulnerable to both domestic and neighbouring destabilising forces vying for influence in their political domains. The 2011 revision called for further funding for humanitarian aid in Tunisia, Libya and Egypt to support democracy building 'from below' as well as funding for the promotion of 'appropriate legal frameworks' for holding elections (particularly in Tunisia). Media freedom, human rights, better use of the CFSP in combatting conflict and supporting conflict resolution and the creation of inter-parliamentary cooperation were all key in the revised document in 2011. In addition to strong emphasis on democracy building from below, the documents placed even greater emphasis on promoting socio-economic change through training, education and enhanced lending by the European Investment Bank (EIB) for small to medium-sized enterprises to promote job creation and unlock economic freedoms and empowerment for citizens.[5] In line with a principle of 'mutual accountability', it planned assessment processes to measure progress across the Southern Neighbourhood, and from these assessments, better 'strategy' for resource allocation could be determined.

In the midst of the migration crisis following the 2010 Arab Spring, the 2015 revision called for an address toward irregular migration flows from North Africa, as well as more effective border management, cooperation of security surveillance and helping aid effective societal transition as a means to inhibit the motivation behind emigration. Keeping in line with EU values, the promotion of market liberalisation and the economic potential of the individual was regarded as essential to compliment the changing political and social realities of citizens in burgeoning democracies. Although offering a change in scope and strategy, the 2004, 2011 and 2015 ENP documents remain generally consistent. Where changes are identified, these focus on providing a clearer portrayal of the EU's mechanisms for assistance and better outlines of various instruments for change. Given that the revised ENP maintains the principle of conditionality (with differentiation), this naturally opens contemporary ENP strategy up to scrutiny. After all, the conditionality procedure is a product of the EU's combined normative and rationalist motivations in its neighbourhood, and it has been regarded as inhibiting wholesome progress in the North African region in the past. However, although conditionality may be a hindrance to fully achieving democratisation and economic liberalisation in North Africa, one cannot fully deduce that the ENP has not been of some benefit to transformation and change (Barbé and Johansson-Nogués, 2008). As Thulmets and Del Sarto state, rationalist and constructivist (norm-based) values can, and do, complement one another in security seeking (see Gstöhl and Schunz, 2017). Barbé and Johansson-Nogués argue that ENP is both 'self-serving' and 'other-serving' in its execution and, therefore, works in such a manner that even if altruistic intentions are mere instruments toward self-serving ends, those ends cannot be achieved or sustained without positive transformation that wields positive sociopolitical responses (legitimacy) abroad (see Browne, cited in Barbé and Johansson-Nogués, 2008). Therefore, despite its motivations and the potential hindrance posed by conditionality, the ENP may still be considered a policy with potential for positive transformation abroad. Given that the ENP is not a prerequisite to EU membership (see Smith, 2005), the fact that partner states have still signed up to its principles suggests that there is a willingness to adapt to normative ideals, at least to some degree. 'Normative power rests not (only) on coercion, but is crucially dependent on the perceived legitimacy of the Union's actions in the eyes of its partners' (Haukkala, 2008: 1603). Although transformation in the southern neighbourhood may be slow and incremental and not necessarily to the satisfaction of EU member states, North African societies have nevertheless, to a certain degree, experienced positive transformations since the ENP was established in 2004 – albeit in a differentiated manner.

The ENP in North Africa: Algeria and Tunisia

> The EU cannot alone solve the many challenges of the region, and there are limits to its leverage, but the new ENP will play its part in helping to create the conditions for positive development.
>
> *(European Commission, 2015b: 2)*

The European Commission has committed to conducting ongoing report processes to trace the ENP's transformational efforts in the South Mediterranean after the 2011 and 2015 revisions, especially in the face of a migration crisis stemming largely from key North African ports. EU support for multilateral 'transition' and 'modernisation' in its southern neighbourhood is facilitated through diplomatic, institutional and financial frameworks and programmes, both through the ENP and the work of the UfM. With the revised ENP, an emphasis on people-to-people programmes and agencies was central to the success of meeting the objectives of action plans so that broader prospective economic and political opportunities could open up to partners. Building cultural, educational and societal links is expected to build the necessary social and cultural conditions toward sustaining meaningful transition and democratisation – thus bringing neighbours closer in line with EU values and norms. Educational opportunities and opportunities for cultural transaction are achieved through programmes such as Erasmus Mundus and Tempus, as well as the encouragement of youth political participation through the YOUTH Programme Med Culture and EUROMED audio-visual programmes. Economic transition is fostered though financing from various mechanisms, such as the European Neighbourhood Instrument (ENI),[6] the EIB and the Facility for Euro-Mediterranean Partnership. Humanitarian aid would be offered by the EU (in part) via the EU INTEREG fund. In addition, societal and socio-economic transition is further encouraged through important programmes such as the European Instrument for Democracy and Human Rights (EIDHR), the European Endowment for Democracy, the Euro-Arab Judicial Training Network as well as the MEDA financial instrument, which traditionally funds the Euro-Mediterranean partnership as encompassed by UfM.

Evaluation of the ENP's efforts in the Southern Mediterranean region is better understood through examination of European Commission reports. In particular, the Commission's 2015 report on the implementation of the ENP (see European Commission, 2015a) provides useful insight into the EU's efforts in the South Mediterranean in the period 2014 to 2020. The report shows that financial assistance to the region was multifaceted in its attempt to foster wholesome transformation. It included the following.

- A €11 million counterterrorism and capacity building project with Southern Mediterranean states was prepared under the ENI.
- The EU worked with southern partners through the Euro-Arab Judicial Training Network as a means to support governments working on developing judicial reform (good governance, rule of law and judicial independence).
- In the fight against corruption, the EU worked with partners via the EIDHR. A €6 million grant was contributed by the European Commission via the European Development Days.
- The EU, in association with the Organisation for Economic Co-operation and Development, continued to collaborate via a €12 million interregional programme under the SIGMA initiative, which provides assistance to parliaments' administrative services to tackle corruption, engage integrity measures and assist ministries with public finance management.
- A grant of €11 million was awarded through the Civil Society Facility at regional and national levels in partner states to encourage democratic transition from the grassroots level of society.
- The European Commission agreed to a grant of €7 million to the Ann Lindh Foundation between 2015 and 2017 in support of its efforts in fostering intercultural dialogue, exchange and partnership in the South Mediterranean region. Funding also continued through the EIDHR to help finance civil society organisations, promote their efforts and empower society from the grassroots level.
- The EIB external lending mandate allocated €9.6 billion to the Southern Mediterranean region for the 2014–2020 period for reconstruction, development and institution building. The European Commission also contributed €265.3 million to the Neighbourhood Investment Facility for these purposes.
- The EU approved a €300 million Macro-Financial Assistance programme for Tunisia, with additional dialogues held for Algeria regarding the programme.

- The Mediterranean Cross-border Cooperation programme was allocated €200 million for surveillance and migration management.
- The European Neighbourhood Programme for Agriculture and Rural Development received a contribution of €63 million to empower agricultural workers and local economies.

The EU has clearly committed itself to aiding North African states and societies toward achieving multidimensional development, and although the underlying motivations and methods of the ENP may very well be criticised for inhibiting regional democratisation at rate that would satisfy the EU, its financial assistance in North Africa should not go under-recognised. It still remains difficult to fully deduce if there is an exact correlation between the efforts of ENP and transformation in North African states. After all, while the ENP provides a framework providing guidelines and assistance, the rate and quality of transition is fundamentally the responsibility of the sovereign ENP partner states, and finances alone cannot be responsible for fostering change. Although it is difficult to definitively deduce that any change in the North African partner states as a direct result of ENP efforts, there is no doubt that since the ENP was established and partnership associations have commenced, North African states have experienced some degree of gradual and incremental changes in certain dimensions of their societies and their functionings. However, much is still desired.

Relative financial contributions

Although Morocco may be said to be on its way to becoming North Africa's success story given its ENP 'advanced' status since 2008, this chapter instead focuses on the rate and quality of transition in Tunisia and Algeria, relatively more vulnerable states due to their geopolitical positioning in the region. As origin points for migrant departures for Europe, political, social and economic transition in these countries is of great importance to the EU to help stem migration flows and mitigate potential associated risks (terrorism, rising population rates, resource dependence, etc.) for the Union.

Tunisia has enjoyed privileged partnership with the EU via the ENP since 2012. This is clear from the level of financial assistance that it receives relative to its North African counterparts, such as Algeria. A similar point is made by Govantes (2018) regarding Morocco. It is necessary to note that the level of aid and financing offered to Tunisia may not necessarily be as a result of its 'model student' status within the ENP in terms of societal transformation, but is perhaps due to the EU's strategic interests pertaining to securitisation of migration flows and the associated risks (potential terrorism, Islamic extremism, economically motivated migrants, etc.). Tunisia is associated with being a key point of departure for migrants trying to access European soil, particularly through southern Italy. Consequently, Italy was the largest bilateral contributor toward Tunisia between 2014 and 2016, with contributions amounting to €880 million for the three-year period (Cohen-Hadria et al., 2018). It is a fair point given the sheer degree of financing that Tunisia receives compared to Algeria. Whilst the quality and rate of transformation in Tunisia outweighs that of Algeria, Tunisia has a considerable way to go before it meets EU expectations in the fields of democracy, good governance and economic liberalisation – so the relative degree of its financing is of interest to observers.

Between 2014 and 2017, Tunisia received €2.4 billion in grants from the EU; €800 million of which was for macroeconomic assistance. Tunisia was also said to receive between €504 million and €616 million from the ENI for the 2017–2020 period. However, it has been suggested that between 2018 and 2020 alone, Tunisia received €800 million on top of the €300 million it received in 2017 from the ENI (Cohen-Hadria et al., 2018). Tunisia also received €50 million from the ENI 'umbrella fund' in 2014 for making adequate progress in ENP action plans. This increased to €95 million in 2017. It is also the first Arab country fully associated with the EU's Horizon 2020 programme (see European Commission, 2019b). In contrast, between 2018 and 2020 Algeria was to benefit from between €108 million and €132 million from the ENI (European Commission, 2019a). Whilst Algeria received €200 million between 2011 and 2016, Tunisia received €1,350 million for the same period. Thus, it is clear to see that Tunisia receives substantially more than its Algerian counterpart, likely due to its geopolitical positioning in the North African territory, its apparent willingness to transition and its gradual efforts toward actual transition. In turn, these sums no doubt influence the relative quality and rate of its transitional efforts. In spite of relative or absolute financing via the ENP, North African countries (especially Tunisia and Algeria) are still far from adequately meeting ENP goals.

Internal progress among ENP partners

In 2019, Tunisia's growth rate averaged 2.7% of GDP. The country still experiences high macro-economic imbalances (IMF, 2019b) and has an unemployment rate of circa 15% and an equivalent poverty rate. With a lower growth rate of 2.3% of GDP in 2019 (IMF, 2019a), Algeria too experiences economic imbalances and has an unemployment rate of circa 10% (United Nations Development Programme, 2018). Despite a circa 15% poverty rate in Tunisia, life expectancy at birth is improving, with an average of 75.7 years as of 2016. As of 2017, average life expectancy at birth in Algeria is 76 years. The rate of secondary education in Algeria remains low at around 37.7% of the population over the age of 25 years, compared to 51.8% in Tunisia (ibid.). According to both the World Bank and Freedom House, Tunisia is gradually transitioning toward democracy. The Bertelsmann Transformation Index deems Tunisia a 'defective (or flawed) democracy' (see BertelsmannStiftung, 2018), and an examination of its path to transition indicates that it is slowly moving toward meeting core ENP objectives – at least in the political sphere. However, economic liberalisation is still very much inadequate in the country – which sows seeds for concern given that ENP goals promote economic liberalisation as a core facet for true democratisation to be enabled and promoted. Algeria on the other hand is deemed a 'moderate autocracy', making very little progress politically and economically.

Tunisia

The Freedom House report on Tunisia (Freedom House, 2019b) classifies the country as 'Free' with an 'aggregate freedom rate' of 70/100 and partial freedom in terms of the internet and the press. Although Tunisia has claim to the origins of the Arab Spring (see Ghanem, 2016) and continues to experience relatively slow economic progress, it has made some notable, though minor, leaps in terms of transformation. Tunisia has scored high in terms of its electoral process. Following the establishment of its new constitution in 2014, Tunisian elections for head of state and the legislature were considered 'competitive and credible' with opposition parties deemed to have adequate opportunities to increase support, compete, gain power and challenge executive forces. As of 2017, legislation requires there to be an equal number of men and women at the top of candidate lists, as well as at least one candidate with a disability and three people under the age of 35 on each list. 'For the 2018 municipal elections, 50 percent of candidates were under the age of 35 and nearly half were women. Women ultimately won 48 percent of the seats' (Freedom House, 2019b). Initially, Tunisia's Independent High Authority for Elections (ISIE) was praised by Tunisian and international observers for its impartiality. However, since 2017, the ISIE has come under criticism following the resignation of its President Chafik Sarsar due to his reservations about the true independence of the authority. Party affiliation, campaigning and organisation are relatively free in Tunisia, and sociopolitical pluralism is slowly improving. However, ambiguous campaign financing laws are still observed to be potential threats to campaign competition and outcomes. Whilst Tunisian citizens are generally free to develop political values and principles without direct interference from formal institutions and organisations, voter attitudes and behaviour are deemed to be swayed by domestic oligarchies with significant networking capital in economic policymaking. The imposing role of the state in market economics goes some way to influencing economic values amongst the public. One may argue that this can influence geopolitical/geo-economic attitudes and interests among citizens and may even influence cultural values, principles and expectations. In terms of corruption and transparency, progress in Tunisia is gradually improving but is far from adequate. In September 2017, controversial legislation was implemented offering amnesty to senior public officials who engaged in economic crimes during the Ben Ali regime. However, in July 2018, new legislation to tackle corruption was implemented. This promoted greater transparency among senior public officials, as it required them to declare their assets. Large financial penalties or imprisonment now apply those not compliant with the law.

In terms of political rights and civil liberties, Tunisia rates 32/40 for political rights and 38/60 for civil liberties. Whilst freedom of religion and faith is constitutionally protected, Islam and Islamic practices take precedence in the state and command social respect and adherence. Due to the role of Islam in state and society, discrimination is widespread, especially toward those who live/wish to live lifestyles which diverge from (or contradict) established religious and cultural values and norms, such as the LGBT community, who have few rights and little sympathy within the state. In addition, the societal role and status of women is only marginally changing. In terms of the information society, 2016 figures show that 55.5% of the population were users of the internet. Based on 2017 statistics, there was apparently no limitations/blocking of social media apps or political/social content, although social media is actively monitored. For example, many Facebook users, social media influencers and bloggers have been accused and arrested for political defamation of leading politicians and the military on social media platforms (Freedom House, 2017, 2019a; Human Rights Watch, 2019). Despite such occurrences, Tunisia's Freedom on the Net score (where 100 represents 'least free') has improved, with a score of 38 in 2017 as opposed to 81 in 2011 (the period of the Arab Spring).

Whilst academic freedom is constitutionally protected, censorship still applies to some aspects of academic research. And discussion of various social issues that may contradict cultural and religious values remain fundamentally taboo and challenged. Whilst freedom of association, protest and development of non-governmental organisations (NGOs) and trade unions are legally protected, efforts have been taken by officials in recent years to reduce the strength of such organisations and of organised behaviour in the public sphere as a means to disempower critics of the establishment. Since the State of Emergency implemented in 2015, officials have continued to dampen public protests and organisations and impose house arrest for those suspected of being 'threats to national security'. This has caused social stigma, economic hardship, food insecurity and lack of access to education/pursuit of study for those accused and their wider family units (Human Rights Watch, 2019). In terms of economic liberties, some concerns still persist regarding private economic and property rights in Tunisia. Corruption (and oligarchical behaviours) are impediments to the liberation of economic and private property rights in the state.

Algeria

Algeria is classified by Freedom House as a 'Not Free State' and has an aggregate freedom rate of 34/100 (Freedom House, 2019a). Algeria's electoral process is far less progressive than Tunisia's (ibid.). In April 2019, President Abdelaziz Boutefika resigned from office following anti-corruption protests after 20 years in power. Winning 81.5% of the vote in the 2014 presidential elections, Boutefika came under considerable scrutiny from critics who argued that electoral manipulation was the source of the victory. Like the 2014 presidential elections, the 2017 national assembly elections were scrutinised for lack of transparency and unfair and questionable voting practices. In addition to fraudulent electoral behaviour, the independence of Algeria's High Independent Commission for Electoral Oversight has been brought into question by observers. Electoral turnout for national assembly elections is consistently low, meaning that opportunities for opposition parties to hold government to account is weakened. In addition, the Interior Ministry reserves the power to approve political parties before they may run for election, thus the governing party effectively has direct influence over party political culture in the state. With such influence, the government could strategically act in such a way that party political opponents can be regulated, thus further empowering those already in power. Therefore, in Algeria democratic checks and balances remain significantly weak with a great deal of political power residing with the executive and relatively unchallenged. In addition to this, judicial independence in Algeria remains low. As the assembly has little influence to hold the executive to account, this has resulted in low voter turnout and has dissuaded public participation in Algerian politics. This has harmed opportunity for the growth of pluralism and democratisation. In 2017, Algeria was classified 115th of 180 countries deemed perceptively corrupt (European Commission, 2018).

Algeria rates at 10/40 for political rights and 24/60 for civil liberties. Although, Algerian authorities have been strengthening their promotion of participatory democracy at the local level and paving the way for enhanced pluralism (European Commission, 2018), the state goes to great efforts to preserve the 'unity' of peoplehood in accordance with strict and homogenous religious (Islamic) values and social codes. Like Tunisia, although women's rights (particularly regarding marriage) and general political participation is rising, rights and opportunities for political participation of other minorities is relatively low. Religious freedom outside the established Sunni Islamic faith is relatively limited, and religious persecution of minorities such as Christians is a regular occurrence. Due to ethnic, cultural and religious conditions, political space for LGBT citizens in Algeria is extremely restricted. In addition, only 42.9% of the Algerian population use the internet (United Nations Development Programme, 2018); still, media and social media censorship in Algeria remains high, with websites being monitored and even blocked in accordance with 'public decency' laws. Like Tunisia, there have been incidents of journalists and bloggers being detained on the grounds of political defamation, accused of 'undermining national unity' (Freedom House, 2019a). Censorship is also applied in some cases of academic research and academic publishing. Like Tunisia, the development of social organisations, trade unions and NGOs is strictly monitored, and there is active legislation in Algeria to curtail the establishment of NGOs. Freedom of assembly is highly monitored and regulated, and public protests are often subject to dismantling by officials. The political influence of government and economic corruption places restrictions on the extension of private economic liberties such as property ownership and business development.

Conditionality or culture?

Tunisia's relationship with the EU via the ENP's 'more for more' principle and associated agreements is evidently more advanced than Algeria's at present. However, there is only a minimal contrast in the rate of transition between Tunisia and Algeria. This may suggest that the ENP's differentiated approach (associated with the principle of conditionality) has only marginal impact on the rate of transition between states in North Africa. However, whilst structural change in such states is extremely slow, this does not mean that the ENP's differentiated approach or conditionality principle are solely responsible for the unwholesome transition in North African States. Regardless of how much money is invested into North Africa, from a qualitative perspective the rates of development in countries such as Tunisia and Algeria do not yet reflect the expectations underlying the ENP. Considering the wider discourse in the field, perhaps the restrictive and coercive nature of the principle of conditionality is indeed a partial cause of this. However, North African countries like Tunisia and Algeria still signed up to the ENP and its associated agreements and remain committed toward internal developments despite the so-called flaws and limitations associated with the principle of conditionality. Thus, it may be suggested that progress and development is likely influenced by persistent complex social and cultural conditions as well as path-dependent institutionalisms which have defined the functioning of North African societies for decades. There is no doubt that large-scale efforts are being made on the part of the EU, but results are only marginal and data suggests that in many cases political participation, pluralism and democracy seem to be hindered by national authorities (in part) on the grounds of religious and cultural values, whilst economic liberalisation is inhibited by ongoing elite corruption. And despite the apparent desire and willingness to positively transform in line with EU-prescribed goals, perhaps scholars and EU leaders – in all their efforts to foster political, economic and social progress in the neighbourhood – need to be more cognisant of role that culture and religion play in impacting interpretations of society, politics, economy and the rule of law in the region.

Conclusion

Scholarship surrounding the ENP remains rather critical of its underlying motivations and the methods which define the policy in action. The ENP is criticised for being an instrument to securitise external threat by coercing neighbours to adapt to European values of democracy through economic incentives and punishing neighbours when they do not live up to expectations. The ever persistent principle of conditionality within the ENP is regarded as a leading factor in hindering wholesome transformation in the EU's neighbourhood – particularly in the Southern Mediterranean region such as North Africa. One could make the argument that if the carrots (i.e. EU membership prospects) were more attractive, then wholesome change would be better incentivised in North African societies. However, it is difficult to see how this type of rationale could foster wholesome transition in neighbouring states, for it assumes that economic incentives trump the long-established role of cultural values in designing North African societies.

It is evident that the ENP is attractive in terms of what it can offer. This is clearly demonstrated by the fact that several North African states have signed up to the policy and have committed themselves to transition, albeit slowly and incrementally. However, transition has been only marginal despite the extensive structural assistance in North African ENP partner states – Algeria and Tunisia being examples of this. From an examination of the current state of politics and society in the ENP partner states of Algeria and Tunisia, it is clear that the motivations for change exist, but actual change is excruciatingly slow. The data presented in this chapter indicate that political and social transition is hindered by persistent cultural and religious values, which seem to determine approaches to governance, policy and law in North African states. Thus, whilst it may be suggested by theorists that an enlargement of the carrots would promote further incentive toward change, one could argue that this may not be the case and that if the EU leaders wish to see better results from the ENP, especially in North African states, the policy cannot be exercised in a way that suggests economics alone 'will set neighbours free'. In addition, the ENP cannot continue to provide objectives for change which fit the narrative of western-style narratives alone. If the ENP is to be successful, especially in North African states, it may need to be more inclusive and regarding of unique cultural conditions and variations in interpretations of society beyond its borders. Instead of encouraging neighbours to somewhat replace their values with western-style interpretations of governance and democracy, perhaps more success will be met through better incorporation and amalgamation of 'other values' in ENP overall objectives.

Notes

1. Although the EU – via the CFSP – is regarded as a humanitarian force in foreign conflict zones, individual EU member states have acted in a differentiated fashion toward foreign conflicts as per their foreign policy autonomy (e.g. the military approaches of the United Kingdom and France to the wars in Iraq and Afghanistan). Such actions have led to the EU and its member states being criticised for inconsistencies.
2. As of the United Kingdom's exit from the EU in 2020, the EU has 27 member states.
3. Although commonly known as the EU's 'Eastern' enlargement, the 2004 enlargement also included the accession of Malta and Cyprus. With the addition of Cyprus, Europe now neighboured Syria, Israel and Palestine, and Lebanon. Turkey had already been in close proximity with Europe since the Greek accession in 1981.
4. Although it implemented objectives for the EU's southern neighbours, its focus was on the eastern dimension of the neighbourhood due to the EU's enhanced exposure to risks stemming from political and economic volatility experienced in many post-soviet eastern European states.
5. The Erasmus Mundus, EUROMED Youth, Tempus and Vocational Educational Training programmes were essential to enable upskilling and educational development. These programmes would also open up opportunities for North Africans to engage in cultural transactionalism with western partners. This would likely facilitate the transportation of western values and norms, as well as educational standards, into the neighbourhood states.
6. The ENI is the chief financial mechanism under the ENP. It has a total budget of €15.4 billion for the period 2014 to 2020. It represents 24% of European External Action Service expenditure (European External Action Service, 2019).

Bibliography

Barbé, E. and Johansson-Nogués, E. (2008) The EU as a modest 'force for good': The European Neighbourhood Policy. *International Affairs*, 84 (1), 81–96.

BertelsmannStiftung (2018) Bertelsmann Transformation Index. www.bti-project.org/en/home/ (retrieved 26 April 2019).

Cebeci, M. (2017) Deconstructing the 'ideal power Europe' meta-narrative in the European Neighbourhood Policy. In D. Bouris and T. Schumacher (eds), *The Revised European Neighbourhood Policy: Continuity and Change in EU Foreign Policy*. London: Palgrave MacMillan (pp. 57–76).

Cohen-Hadria, E., Abderrahim, T., Cherif, Y., Colombo, S., Ghanmi, E., Kausch, K., Meddeb, H., Van der Loo, G. and Zardo, F. (2018) The EU-Tunisia Privileged Partnership – What Next? EUROMESCO Joint Policy Study 10. Barcelona: European Institute of the Mediterranean. www.euromesco.net/wp-content/uploads/2018/04/EuroMeSCo-Joint-Policy-Study_EU-Tunisia-Partnership.pdf (retrieved 16 April 2019).

European Commission (2003) Communication from the Commission to the Council and the European Parliament. Wider Europe – Neighbourhood: A New Framework for Relations with our Eastern and Southern Neighbours. COM(2003) 104 final. Brussels, 11 March. http://eeas.europa.eu/archives/docs/enp/pdf/pdf/com03_104_en.pdf

European Commission (2004) Communication from the Commission. European Neighbourhood Policy Strategy Paper. COM(2004) 373 final. Brussels, 12 May. https://ec.europa.eu/neighbourhood-enlargement/sites/near/files/2004_communication_from_the_commission_-_european_neighbourhood_policy_-_strategy_paper.pdf

European Commission (2011a) A Partnership for Democracy and Shared Prosperity with the Southern Mediterranean. Joint Communication to the European Council, European Parliament, the Council, the European Economic and Social Committee and the Committee of the Regions. COM(2011) 200 final. Brussels, 8 March. https://ec.europa.eu/research/iscp/pdf/policy/com_2011_200_en.pdf

European Commission (2011b) A New Response to a Changing Neighbourhood: A Review of European Neighbourhood Policy. Joint Communication by the High Representative of the Union for Foreign Affairs and Security Policy and the European Commission. COM(2011) 303 final. Brussels, 5 May. https://library.euneighbours.eu/content/new-response-changing-neighbourhood-review-european-neighbourhood-policy

European Commission (2015a) Implementation of the European Neighbourhood Policy Partnership for Democracy and Shared Prosperity with the Southern Mediterranean Partners Report. Joint Staff Working Document. Brussels, 25 March. SWD(2015) 75 final. https://publications.europa.eu/en/publication-detail/-/publication/bc0fa7d2-d2df-11e4-9de8-01aa75ed71a1 (retrieved 15 April 2019).

European Commission (2015b) Joint Communication to the European Council, European Parliament, the Council, the European Economic and Social Committee and the Committee of the Regions. Review of the European Neighbourhood Policy. JOIN(2015) 50 final. Brussels, 18 November. http://eeas.europa.eu/archives/docs/enp/documents/2015/151118_joint-communication_review-of-the-enp_en.pdf (retrieved 16 April 2019).

European Commission (2018) Document de travail conjoint des services. Rapport sur l'état des relations UE-Algérie dans le cadre de la PEV rénovée. SWD(2018) 102 final. Brussels, 6 April. https://eeas.europa.eu/sites/eeas/files/rapport_sur_l27etat_des_relations_ue-algerie_2018.pdf (retrieved 29 April 2019).

European Commission (2019a) Algeria. European Neighbourhood Policy and Enlargement Negotiations. https://ec.europa.eu/neighbourhood-enlargement/neighbourhood/countries/algeria_en (retrieved 23 April 2019).

European Commission (2019b) Tunisia. European Neighbourhood Policy and Enlargement Negotiations. https://ec.europa.eu/neighbourhood-enlargement/neighbourhood/countries/tunisia_en (retrieved 23 April 2019).

European External Action Service (2019) Financing the ENP. The European External Action Service, 18 August. https://eeas.europa.eu/headquarters/headquarters-homepage_en/8410/Financing%20the%20ENP (retrieved 18 April 2019).

Freedom House (2017) Tunisia. Freedom on the Net 2017. https://freedomhouse.org/report/freedom-net/2017/tunisia (retrieved 11 April 2019).

Freedom House (2019a) Algeria. Freedom in the World. https://freedomhouse.org/report/freedom-world/2019/algeria (retrieved 11 April 2019).

Freedom House (2019b) Tunisia. Freedom in the World. https://freedomhouse.org/report/freedom-world/2019/tunisia (retrieved 11 April 2019).

Gänzle, S. (2009) EU governance and the European Neighbourhood Policy: A framework for analysis. *Europe-Asia Studies*, 61 (10), 1715–1734.

Ghanem, H. (2016) *The Arab Spring Five Years Later: Toward Greater Inclusiveness*. Washington, DC: Brookings Institution Press.

Ghazaryan, N. (2016) The fluid concept of 'EU values' in the neighbourhood: A change of paradigm from East to South? In S. Poli (ed.), The European Neighbourhood Policy: Values and Principles. Abingdon: Routledge (pp. 11–33).

Gillespie, R. (2013) The European Neighbourhood Policy and the challenge if the Mediterranean Southern rim. In M. Telò and F. Ponjaert (eds), *The EU's Foreign Policy: What Kind of Power and Diplomatic Action?* Farnham: Ashgate (pp. 121–134).

Govantes, B. (2018) Is Morocco EU's model student at ENP? An analysis of democracy and human rights progress [online]. *British Journal of Middle-Eastern Studies*. DOI: https://doi.org/10.1080/13530194.2018.1549979

Gstöhl, S. (2017) Theoretical approaches to European Neighbourhood Policy. In S. Gstöhl and S. Schunz (eds), *Theorising the European Neighbourhood Policy*. Abingdon: Routledge (pp. 3–22).

Gstöhl, S. and Schunz, S. (2017) *Theorising the European Neighbourhood Policy*. Abingdon: Routledge.

Haukkala, H. (2008) The European Union as regional normative hegemon: The case of the European Neighbourhood Policy. *Europe-Asia Studies*, 60 (9), 1601–1622.

Human Rights Watch (2019) Tunisia: Events of 2017. World Report 2018. www.hrw.org/world-report/2018/country-chapters/tunisia (retrieved 23 April 2019).

International Monetary Fund (2019a) Algeria [online]. www.imf.org/en/Countries/DZA (retrieved 24 April 2019).
International Monetary Fund (2019b) Tunisia [online]. www.imf.org/en/Countries/TUN (retrieved 24 April 2019).
Kausch, K. and Youngs, R. (2009) The end of the 'Euro-Mediterranean Vision'. *International Affairs*, 85 (5), 963–975.
Telò, M. and Ponjaert, F. (2013) *The EU's Foreign Policy: What Kind of Power and Diplomatic Action?* The Globalisation, Europe, Multilateralism Series. Farnham: Ashgate.
United Nations Development Programme (2018) Human Development Reports [online]. http://hdr.undp.org/en/home (retrieved 26 April 2019).

8

The evolution of the Joint Africa-EU Strategy (2007–2020)

Fergus Kell and Alex Vines

Introduction

The overarching political framework for relations between Africa and the European Union (EU) is the Joint Africa-EU Strategy (JAES), formally adopted at the Lisbon Summit in 2007 by representatives of 53 African and 27 European states. As a long-term continent-to-continent strategy, the JAES seeks to define a partnership of equals through which consensus on priorities is jointly identified and ownership of initiatives to address these can be shared. Since its inception, however, the JAES has been adapted in response to rapidly changing policy contexts, both institutionally and externally, as reforms of the African Union (AU) have emerged alongside new EU global and bilateral strategies while external developments in the spheres of migration and security have intensified EU focus on an Africa partnership. Pre-existing EU partnerships with North Africa and sub-Saharan Africa under the European Neighbourhood Policy (ENP) and Cotonou Agreement, respectively, alongside new bilateral agreements with individual states, including South Africa and Nigeria, additionally present significant sources of both opportunity and tension for the continental agenda.

This chapter examines the evolution of Africa-EU relations as shaped by the development and implementation of the JAES. It analyses the diverse range of sectoral objectives, financial instruments and multiple overlapping geographical strategies the agreement incorporates, from the background to the 2007 Lisbon Summit through to subsequent high-level Africa-EU summits in Tripoli in 2010 and in Brussels in 2014 and the AU-EU Summit in Abidjan in 2017.[1] Although overly ambitious and slow to adapt to the realities of continental partnership, the JAES has achieved modest results, particularly in the domain of peace and security. Its future direction will now be largely determined by the intersection of two concurrent processes: on one hand, the progress of negotiations on the Africa pillar of the successor to the Cotonou Agreement; and on the other, the proposed creation of a new strategic framework for Africa-EU relations, which is still uncertain in institutional and financial terms.

Background to the JAES

Relations between Europe and sub-Saharan Africa in the second half of the 20th century stemmed primarily from the latter's membership of a union of African, Caribbean and Pacific

(ACP) states (the ACP Group²) under the Yaoundé conventions of the 1960s and the four Lomé conventions covering 1975–2000. The relations they oversaw were predominately oriented around economic cooperation and centred on non-reciprocal trade preferences for ACP exports. At the turn of the millennium, as an intensified global drive for long-term poverty reduction was expressed via the UN's Millennium Development Goals (MDGs), the new Cotonou Agreement adopted for the period 2000–2020 sought to outline a more extensive scope for ACP-EU relations, with development cooperation at its core (European Commission, 2014b). Among its most notable initiatives was the replacement of non-reciprocal trade arrangements with regional Economic Partnership Agreements (EPAs) that divided sub-Saharan Africa into West, East, Central and Southern regions. Cotonou's initial funding cycle between 2000 and 2007 totalled €15.2 billion, financed primarily through the European Development Fund (EDF) (D'Alfonso, 2014).

Although it commands the largest EU external action instrument in both financial and geographic terms (European Commission, 2018e), the Cotonou Agreement does not cover several North African states (Algeria, Egypt, Libya, Morocco and Tunisia) who are non-members of the ACP, nor South Africa, which has a special arrangement with the EU and is not a party to the same preferential trade agreements under Cotonou. Prior to the adoption of the JAES in 2007, therefore, relations between these countries and the EU were variously framed by agreements emphasising a shared proximity to the Mediterranean. In 1995, the Barcelona Declaration by 15 EU and 12 Mediterranean countries – among them Algeria, Egypt, Morocco and Tunisia – formalised the Euro-Mediterranean Partnership to guide cooperation on economic, political and cultural issues. The partnership saw the admission of Libya with 'observer' status in 1999 (Joffé, 2012), but with the successful accession of Eastern European states into the EU, it became effectively overwritten in 2004 by a broader ENP and was eventually incorporated within a new Union for the Mediterranean in 2008.

Ahead of the 2007 Lisbon Summit, the experience of the Cotonou Agreement and concurrent Mediterranean initiatives showed that EU approaches to both sub-Saharan and North Africa were distinct, albeit similarly structured: in neither case were African states the collective focus of a formal EU partnership agreement. Nonetheless, the intention to institutionalise a continental agenda had already become clear at the turn of the millennium, as a summit in Cairo in 2000 brought together African and EU heads of state 'under the Aegis of the OAU and EU' (European Commission, 2000) – a title crafted to enable Morocco to attend as a non-member of the Organization of African Unity. An increasing appetite for African continental integration in subsequent years, heralded by the advent of a New Partnership for Africa's Development and the newly constituted AU, placed further emphasis on the joint commitment made in Cairo to enhance intercontinental links. On the EU side, this agenda was pursued with the launch of a Strategy for Africa in 2005 (European Commission, 2005), which explicitly acknowledged that 'for too long the EU's relations with Africa have been too fragmented, both in policy formulation and implementation' (see Whiteman, 2012). More than seven years after the first Africa-EU summit, therefore, expectations for tangible progress at the second summit, in Lisbon, were high.

The JAES and its early implementation (2007–2013)

The Lisbon Summit occurred as a result of Portugal's Prime Minister José Sócrates holding the presidency of the EU Council for the latter half of 2007. The Portuguese, with discrete backing from the Germans and support from Finland, Slovenia and Sweden, had always been major backers of the idea of a second summit. However, high-profile tensions in the build-up focused on the invitation of Zimbabwe's President Robert Mugabe despite an EU travel ban and other sanctions against his government. This issue, which had led to the cancellation of a prospective Africa-EU summit in 2003 after African states disputed the EU's refusal to invite Mugabe, flared up again as UK Prime Minister Gordon Brown threatened to boycott the 2007 meeting (Mail & Guardian, 2007).

Despite these misgivings, the jointly agreed strategy that resulted from the summit did create momentum by seeking to place an intercontinental approach, ostensibly led by the AU and EU institutions, at the core of Africa-EU relations. Alongside this came a commitment to enhanced and more frequent dialogue in future through summits at regular three-year intervals, as well as action plans on specific policy objectives for the inter-summit periods. Equally as important as the new geographic status of the strategy – as a continent-to-continent agreement – were the more relational aspects it conveyed. The language used in the Lisbon Declaration (Council of the European Union, 2007a) and in the original JAES (Council of the European Union, 2007b) highlighted a desire to overcome the traditional donor-recipient relationship of previous decades and replace it with a 'partnership of equals' built on jointly identified values and goals. Similarly prominent within the agreement is the notion of shared ownership, whereby the future direction taken by the partnership, rather than simply its founding values, is the responsibility of both parties. Finally, underlying these commitments is a pledge to promote a 'people-centred partnership' in which civil society organisations and local stakeholders are engaged in Africa-EU dialogue and play an active part in processes resulting from it. The priorities of the JAES at its inception were codified under four Strategic Framework features:

- Peace and security: Promoting a safer world;
- Governance and human rights: Upholding our values and principles;
- Trade and regional integration: Raising potential and using opportunities; and
- Key development issues: Accelerating progress towards the MDGs.

In identifying these broad objectives, particularly within the economic realm, the JAES inevitably duplicated many of the commitments made under the Cotonou Agreement and the ENP for sub-Saharan and North African states, respectively (Adebajo and Whiteman, 2012). Nonetheless, the prominent inclusion of a priority area on peace and security did add a new dimension to formal Africa-EU relations. Moreover, it is critical to note that the JAES also explicitly called for 'the progressive establishment of a Pan-African financial support programme' to support continental initiatives. While the JAES detailed ambitious goals under each of its four strategic framework headings, the impetus for specific policy initiatives would be further defined by cyclical devices and involve a multitude of financial instruments. The first of these, the EU-Africa Action Plan (2008–2010), outlined eight priority partnering areas for the time frame (Africa-EU Partnership, 2007). It began with a partnership on Peace and security that called for enhanced dialogue, predictable funding for African-led Peace Support Operations (PSOs) and the operationalisation of the African Peace and Security Architecture (APSA). The second partnership pertained to Governance and human rights; and the third to Trade and regional integration. The fourth partnership focused solely on enhancing partnership on the MDGs, and the fifth and sixth dealt with cooperation on Energy and Climate change, respectively. The final two partnerships encompassed a range of clustered issues in Migration, mobility and employment, and Science, information society and space.

This proliferation of strategic and financial objectives is undoubtedly a testament to the momentum generated by the Lisbon Summit as well as the long and genuinely shared exercise of consultation and drafting that preceded it. However, progress on implementation largely failed to match this aspiration for change – partly due to a lack of high-level political traction on both sides to push forward with the complex and challenging partnership, as well as a growing disengagement from EU member states. The follow-up summit in Tripoli in 2010 was characterised by 'a much more cautious note and realistic mood, with less high-level representation' (Helly, 2013). Although the 2010 summit introduced the theme of Investment, economic growth and job creation, it served primarily to reaffirm the initial eight priority areas and retained these largely intact for the Second Action Plan (2011–2013) (Africa-EU Partnership, 2010). In addition to this limited and uneven progress on specific sectoral objectives, the extent to which policies have reflected a truly continental partnership of equals is open to question.

Alternative channels: Economic partnership and instruments

Despite the JAES arising in part from the EU's acknowledgement that its approach to Africa had become overly fragmented, substantial elements of this fragmentation appeared to persist both in policy approaches and in financing instruments after 2007. The North African states involved with the Euro-Mediterranean Partnership, for instance, became involved with a new EU initiative – the Union for the Mediterranean – in July 2008, just seven months after they adopted the JAES. This Union became incorporated within the ENP and also fell under its new financing mechanism, the European Neighbourhood and Partnership Instrument, established in January 2007 with a budget of €11.2 billion for the period 2007–2013 (European Commission, 2014c). When contemplating this series of overlapping agreements, it is dubious whether the JAES – a strategy without any distinct financial instrument until 2014 – could truly claim to have decisively addressed fragmentation in the EU approach to North African states. Tunisia, one of the EU's largest trading partners on the African continent, is a clear example in this respect: in addition to its continental position, the various locations it is grouped within by the EU 'include North Africa, the Maghreb sub-region (itself undefined), and the southern shoreline of the Mediterranean Sea' (Powel and Sadiki, 2010: 84).

With respect to sub-Saharan Africa, the Cotonou Agreement, having been revised at its midway point in 2010, acknowledged the AU as a 'partner of the EU-ACP relationship' (European Commission, 2014b). Any notion of strategic convergence this implied, however, could be challenged by consideration of the financial division of labour between Cotonou and the JAES. The former, funded through the EDF, attracted a total of nearly €22 billion for the 2008–2013 period (European Commission, 2006), whereas the latter still lacked any distinct financial instrument over this time frame – its creation having been opposed by a large majority of EU states. This apparent financial disconnect between initiatives was further compounded by a series of bilateral partnerships between the EU and individual African countries.

South Africa, the EU's largest trading partner in Africa, was not a signatory to the trading relationship under Cotonou and instead adopted its own Trade, Development and Co-operation Agreement (TDCA) in 1999 as the legal basis for relations with the EU. Although the TDCA concluded in 2016 when South Africa entered into an EPA as part of the Southern African Development Community, this still did not leave the JAES as the principal framework for EU-South Africa strategic relations. Rather, since May 2007, when a Joint Action Plan was signed in Brussels, South Africa has a bilateral Strategic Partnership with the EU, one of only ten such EU country-level agreements worldwide and the only one on the African continent (European External Action Service, 2018a). Not only has this agreement been pursued through more regular summits than those of the JAES – the seventh EU-South Africa summit took place in Brussels in November 2018 – but since 2014 it has been subject, as an 'exceptional case', to direct EU financial support under the EU's new Development Cooperation Instrument (DCI) of €241 million in 2014–2020 (European Commission, 2015b). This notion of exceptionality, moreover, is equally applicable to the EU-South Africa partnership while it was covered by the TDCA, under which financial support – totalling €980 million between 2007 and 2013 (Bertelsmann-Scott, 2012) – came directly from the EU budget rather than the separate EDF mechanism used for Cotonou (D'Alfonso, 2014).

Another of Africa's major economies, Nigeria, has also enjoyed a distinct political dialogue with the EU. Discussions culminated in the launch of a Nigeria-EU Joint Way Forward in 2009; an initiative designed to take 'political dialogue and cooperation to a new level' and supported by periodic ministerial meetings (European External Action Service, 2009). Angola would also sign a similar Joint Way Forward with the EU in 2012. Although a signatory to the Cotonou Agreement, Nigeria shared with South Africa a reluctance to commit to the trade arrangements it entailed. To date, the country has not agreed to the EU's regional EPA with West Africa despite its prominent position within the Economic Community of West African States – a situation that surely factors into the EU's decision to pursue a bilateral dialogue. Insofar as the Nigeria-EU partnership is a response to the faltering EPAs, therefore, it also appears to be symptomatic of the shortcomings of the JAES as a continent-to-continent strategy. As one commentator puts it, the experience of the EPA negotiations have 'definitely widened the cracks within African regional organisations and thereby contradicted decade-long processes of institution-building efforts as well as the very rationale of the 2007 Joint Africa-Europe Strategy' (Helly, 2013).

A third variety of bilateral EU agreement is found in the EU-Cape Verde Special Partnership agreed in Brussels in October 2007 (European Commission, 2007). Cape Verde is also a member of the Cotonou Agreement, but through this Special Partnership has sought enhanced dialogue and policy convergence with the EU on issues deemed to relate to the archipelago's specific set of circumstances. The Special Partnership operates separately to Cotonou, but is nonetheless still financed by the EDF, to the tune of €51 million between 2008 and 2013 (European Commission, 2018d). In addition to these relationships with individual sub-Saharan states, the EU has also adopted specific regional approaches for the Horn of Africa, the Gulf of Guinea and the Sahel. These originated in 2011 with the creation of a Strategic Framework for the Horn of Africa and a Strategy for Security and Development in the Sahel (Council of the European Union, n.d.). Both are primarily oriented around broad regional challenges of development, governance and security, but acknowledge possible implications of these challenges for European citizens by connecting them to extremism and arms trafficking (Council of the European Union, 2011). An additional regional strategy for the Gulf of Guinea emerged in March 2014, focused on coastal criminal activities such as piracy and trafficking. The range of experiences of these states and regions with respect to EU strategies and financial instruments, as well as the ongoing tensions surrounding EPA negotiations, has undoubtedly raised questions over the ability of the JAES to foster continental solidarity within the realm of economic cooperation and trade. For a strategy born out of a desire to address the fragmentation of the past, by 2013 a case could certainly be made that continent-to-continent relations had splintered even further (Rodt and Okeke, 2013).

Peace and security

As identified above, the inclusion of peace and security at the forefront of the JAES strategic priority areas marked a point of departure from Cotonou's primarily economic focus. Consequently, the JAES has been characterised as lying at the intersection between development (as the dominant frame for Africa-EU relations previously) and security (Haastrup, 2013). It was this domain, therefore, that perhaps presented the clearest opportunity for the new strategy to distance itself from previous agreements in practice (Vines, 2013).

Progress towards the three objectives set at the Lisbon Summit – to enhance dialogue, provide predictable support for African-led PSOs and operationalise APSA – materialised to varying degrees. On the first, annual joint meetings of the EU Political and Security Committee and the AU Peace and Security Council have taken place alternatively in Brussels and Addis Ababa since October 2008 (Pirozzi et al., 2017), suggesting that the relationship between the two continental bodies on security matters has become increasingly institutionalised. Nevertheless, the extent to which such meetings have reflected formal instances of planning and coordination, rather than being simply forums for mutual consultation, is debatable (ibid.). Second, although not solely attributable to the JAES, strides have also been made in terms of support for African-led PSOs. These have largely relied upon an EU funding mechanism created in 2004, the African Peace Facility (APF), which is financed through the EDF and hence has its legal basis in the Cotonou Agreement. Yet as the EU has been keen to emphasise, the APF originated in response to a request from AU leaders at a summit in 2003 – and the continental institution has remained central to the execution of many of the 14 PSOs supported by the APF in subsequent years. In sectoral terms, the APF is one of the largest EU financial commitments for Africa, with €2.3 billion having been contracted since its inception – of which over €2.1 billion has gone directly to PSOs (European Commission, 2018c). Of these, the African Union Mission in Somalia has been the largest recipient by far of APF funding – receiving more than €1.5 billion since 2007 – while the APF has also supported regional coalitions such as the G5 Sahel (in which the AU's role has been less clear). One initiative that has emerged under the JAES, however, is the APF's Early Response Mechanism (ERM), established in 2009 as a source of modest but quickly available funds to react to emerging situations in Africa. It has proven to be a useful and widely utilised tool, funding 35 initiatives between 2010 and 2017 (at a total cost of €30 million), of which 25 were implemented directly by the AU Commission and the remainder by regional institutions (European Commission, 2018c). With funds available in as little as ten days, the ERM has proved popular with the AU for reducing the administrative burden (International Crisis Group, 2017) and hence also provides a key example of a truly close channel between the two continental institutions. Although uneven, the role of the AU in PSOs and initiatives such as the ERM has enabled it to position itself as an essential player in the security realm (Tardy, 2016).

On the third objective, progress towards implementing APSA – which includes the creation of an African Standby Force (ASF) – has been marked by repeated postponements to the original target of full operation by mid-2010. The APF-funded training cycle Amani Africa II between 2011 and 2016 saw the ASF carry out a field exercise in South Africa in late 2015, but a subsequent monitoring report concluded that its operational capacities for rapid deployment were still not fully developed (Styan, 2017). While progress in the domain of peace and security under the JAES has been sufficient to classify it as the most advanced link between the two continents, the delays and uncertainty that have plagued APSA continue to invite concern for the strategy's claims of a 'partnership of equals' (African Union, 2013). Accordingly, the following sections examine whether more recent institutional and external developments present a genuine opportunity to address these issues.

The Brussels Summit and Roadmap (2014–2017)

Discussions on the AU side ahead of the Africa-EU summit in Brussels in 2014 focused on the adoption of a new long-term strategy for the organisation, to be known as Agenda 2063 (Council of the European Union, 2014a). At the core of this agenda is an intensified drive for

African continental integration, expressed through flagship policy objectives such as the creation of an African Continental Free Trade Area (CFTA). By October 2013, the inaugural meeting of the Continental Task Force – a new AU body tasked with implementing the CFTA – had taken place. This theme would carry over into the Africa-EU summit in Brussels the following April, where leaders in attendance acknowledged these emerging trends and – despite largely reaffirming the JAES in positive terms – pledged to give 'new momentum' to the partnership (Council of the European Union, 2014a: 1).

Changes were indeed evident in the wake of the Brussels Summit. A new Roadmap 2014–2017 for the JAES called for a 'results-oriented approach' (Council of the European Union, 2014b). With this apparent focus on results came also a streamlined set of five priority areas, compared to the eight under the preceding two action plans. The Roadmap proposed a focus on:

- Peace and security;
- Democracy, good governance and human rights;
- Human development;
- Sustainable and inclusive development and growth and continental integration; and
- Global and emerging issues.

In addition to these refinements, a notable development in terms of financing would also emerge in the wake of the Brussels Summit. The EU's new Pan-African Programme, launched in July 2014, marked the first ever instrument in development and cooperation covering the African continent as a whole (European Commission, 2018a). It was funded through the DCI for a total of €845 million for the 2014–2020 period, with €415 million to cover the period until the next Africa-EU summit in 2017 (European Commission, 2014a). Of this initial figure, moreover, over half was allocated to the fourth priority area of the Roadmap – and therefore also to continental integration efforts such as the CFTA.

The internal strategic momentum generated by the summit in 2014 was, however, perhaps overtaken by the reaction to exogenous developments of migration in the year that followed. More than a million refugees and migrants from Africa and the Middle East crossed into Europe by sea in 2015, with nearly 4,000 believed to have drowned while attempting the journey (Clayton and Holland, 2015). The crisis led EU and African leaders to call a conference in Valletta in November that year, insisting that an approach to tackle root causes of irregular migration was essential (European Council, 2018). Towards this end, the Valletta Summit resulted in the launch of another new financing instrument, the EU Emergency Trust Fund for Africa (EUTFA). The EUTFA was launched with an initial EU contribution of €1.8 billion, with the funds helping to implement policies across the Sahel, Horn of Africa and North Africa regions (Hauck et al., 2015). Earlier in 2015, moreover, the EU had launched regional action plans covering the period 2015–2020 for its existing strategies on the Sahel and the Horn of Africa. Of these, the Horn of Africa strategy explicitly refers to the EUTFA as key to its implementation, with both strategies incorporating a far greater emphasis on migration and forced displacement than at their inception (Council of the European Union, 2015). Yet the approach emerging from the Valletta Summit arguably contradicted the EU's principles on aid provision, by directing assistance to African countries that lie on major migration routes, and led to a perception among African partners that the EUTFA is an externally imposed agenda over which they have minimal say (Parshotam, 2017). Despite the efforts made at Brussels to generate a fresh iteration of the JAES, therefore, the subsequent priority given to migration issues would largely overshadow this process.

Institutional change

Since 2014, moreover, Africa-EU relations have been subject not only to post-Brussels strategic refinements and the external shock of Europe's migration crisis, but also to a succession of intra-institutional developments. A framework for the AU's Agenda 2063 was finally agreed at a summit in January 2015 along with a backdated ten-year implementation plan for 2014–2023. Its flagship programmes include establishing the CFTA, creating an African Passport to enable free movement of citizens across the continent and the ambitious aim to 'Silence the Guns by 2020' – representing an end to all wars, civil conflict and gender-based violence (African Union Commission, 2015). Simultaneously, the AU put forward a Declaration of Self-Reliance that set a medium-term target for member states to fund 100% of the AU's operating budget, 75% of the programme budget and 25% of PSOs (Assembly of the African Union, 2015). This would advance further in July 2016 during an AU summit in Kigali, when members adopted a Decision on the Financing of the Union to fund these efforts by instituting a 0.2% levy on imported goods (Assembly of the African Union, 2016). Such commitment undoubtedly reflects an effort to shift the funding basis of EU-Africa engagements towards a more equitable partnership, as well as an acknowledgement that the AU has been heavily dependent on the EU in this respect since the inception of the JAES. With this financial asymmetry widely recognised as a signal that the partnership of equals envisaged at the Lisbon Summit has not materialised (Pirozzi and Godsäter, 2015), increased African contributions could well help the AU to exert more strategic influence over the common agenda in the long term. Within three years of its adoption, 16 African countries had implemented the levy, with funds contributing to the AU Peace Fund, a special endowment for PSOs worth $115 million and aiming to be operationalised in 2021 with a target of $400 million (Apiko and Miyandazi, 2019).

Developments in Europe over the same period equally have significant implications for the JAES; the United Kingdom leaving the EU after its 2016 referendum result, for instance, inevitably affects the financial and strategic outlook for partnership with Africa (International Crisis Group, 2017). In addition, with the launch of a new Global Strategy in 2016, the EU made clear its belief that internal security increasingly must be obtained through external stability – an approach that in the words of then High Representative Federica Mogherini, 'focuses on military capabilities and anti-terrorism as much as on job opportunities, inclusive societies and human rights' (European External Action Service, 2016). A November 2015 joint communication on the ENP had already called for a regional step up in partnership on counterterrorism and security sector reform initiatives, following the terror attacks in Paris the same month (European Commission, 2015a) – but the Global Strategy explicitly extends such concerns beyond North Africa and highlights their interconnection with the rest of the African continent.

2017 Abidjan Summit: Refined strategy, reinvigorated partnership

By early 2017, therefore, it was undeniable that the operating context for the JAES had changed considerably since the initiation of the Roadmap in 2014 – whether related to exogenously generated circumstances such as the migration crisis or new institutional dynamics and priorities within the AU and EU. In a joint communication released in May, the European Commission adopted conclusions on the need to provide a 'renewed impetus' for the AU-EU partnership, reflecting on Africa's increasing strategic importance for security and prosperity in Europe and proposing a revitalised programme based around the guidance of Agenda 2063 and the Global

Strategy. It notes the scale of demographic changes in Africa – with the continent projected to have a predominately youthful population of 2.4 billion by 2050 – and connects these to economic and political challenges, particularly surrounding the need to create more and better jobs for young people (European Commission, 2017). As such, the joint communication, not unlike the JAES as a whole, can be seen to be 'anchored to an African vision, but mainly linked to the EU's strategic interests' (Pirozzi et al., 2017: 4).

The areas highlighted by the joint communication would be repeated at the Abidjan Summit in November, as made immediately apparent by its theme: Investing in Youth for Accelerated Inclusive Growth and Sustainable Development. Although the summit's declaration reaffirmed that the JAES agreed ten years earlier remains the overarching framework for partnership, it equally called for a 'paradigm shift' in the approach, expressed through a further streamlined set of strategic priority areas:

- Investing in people – education, science, technology and skills development;
- Strengthening resilience, peace, security and governance;
- Migration and mobility; and
- Mobilising investments for African structural sustainable transformation.

These priority areas represent a shift from previous summits not only in plain numerical terms, but equally as a reflection of areas of both tension and opportunity in recent years. This is particularly clear when considering that migration, mobility and employment were crammed into just one of eight priority areas in the first two action plans, but are central to at least two of these four priorities formed at Abidjan. Although its inclusion reflects a positive step for cooperative efforts, migration still remains a potentially destabilising issue for the partnership, fuelled by diverging viewpoints and a perception on the African side that the EU has pursued a one-way dialogue via a securitisation of the agenda (Pirozzi et al., 2017). Enhanced inter-summit dialogue, particularly around the status of the EUTFA, will be essential to preventing disagreement on the issue from defining the partnership.

Also apparent from the summit was a shift towards an increased role for the private sector in development initiatives. Towards this end, discussions welcomed efforts under another new EU instrument – the European Fund for Sustainable Development – to establish an External Investment Plan (EIP), which focuses primarily upon the African continent (European Commission, n.d.). Under the EIP, €4.1 billion has been committed for investment in Africa, but this is expected to ultimately leverage more than €44 billion in investments by diminishing risks for foreign investors. Such efforts reflect the EU perception of Africa's growing youth population not simply as a source of fragility with respect to migration, but as a significant opportunity for economic growth in innovative and underdeveloped sectors – with the private sector now stated as the key to unlocking these.

To return to the overarching vision of a continental partnership under the JAES, it is worth highlighting again that the Abidjan Summit oversaw a change in name from the Africa-EU to the African Union–European Union Summit following Morocco's readmission to the AU in January 2017. This provided an opportunity to encourage a more cohesive partnership in the context of the AU's emerging reforms and increasing ambition for greater strategic influence. The position of the CFTA within the JAES is symbolic in this regard: as an AU-led initiative, it has decisively overtaken the EPAs as the flagship programme for continental economic integration. EU rhetoric – pushed by the Directorate-General for Trade in particular – has subsequently begun to present the EPAs in an instrumental sense in terms of what they can contribute as building blocks for the CFTA as opposed to individually (Chatham House, 2018). Given that the two processes appear largely incompatible, however, such statements are perhaps better interpreted as a retrospective attempt to soften the failures of the EPAs in light of a superior, African-led initiative. Nonetheless, the renewed Pan-African Programme for 2018–2020 retains a predominant focus on supporting the CFTA in addition to continental governance initiatives (European Commission, 2018b). Progress in this respect, however, should be tempered by an awareness that the Pan-African Programme is modest in size compared to other EU financial instruments operating in Africa and remains largely disconnected from them – a situation that has fostered 'silo thinking and turf wars among institutions in Brussels' (Pirozzi et al., 2017: 14). Seen in this light, therefore, the Abidjan summit amounts to a largely familiar story for the JAES: strategic restructuring and streamlining in line with EU priorities, but limited commitment to creating continental instruments with which to pursue these.

Looking ahead: Post-Cotonou negotiations and the future of the JAES

Conspicuous in its absence from the agenda at Abidjan was discussion of the future of the JAES after the initial expiry of the Cotonou Agreement in February 2020, despite the clear opportunities presented at such a critical juncture to decisively address fragmentation within the continental partnership. On this basis, the EU acknowledged as early as 2016 that Cotonou had been unable to address the importance of the AU as a continental organisation, noting that this 'should be reflected in any future partnership decision making and institutional set-up' (European Commission, 2016: 6). Such indications would be reflected formally in June 2018 with the release of the EU's post-Cotonou negotiating mandate, which called to adapt the relationship with the ACP by establishing an 'umbrella' agreement and three regional partnerships with Africa, the Pacific and the Caribbean, respectively. The Africa pillar, moreover, proposed to include the 'involvement or accession' of North African countries as well as promising a 'prominent role' for regional organisations including the AU (Council of the European Union, 2018: 82) – thereby opening up the EU-ACP partnership to greater integration with the JAES, albeit with considerable ambiguity on how exactly to do so. Over the same period, the EU released a proposal for its next long-term budget, covering 2021–2027, outlining a 30% increase for external action that would see the EDF incorporated within the central budget as part of a general reduction and simplification of its financial instruments (European External Action Service, 2018c).

Prompted by the EU's ambiguous offer of inclusion within this African 'pillar', the post-Cotonou conversation on the African side has been marked by tension between the AU and ACP over the terms of a restructured agreement, as well as the balance of their respective roles in negotiating it. A first major public step was taken in March 2018 with the AU's adoption of an African Common Position at its summit in Kigali, recommending that a new agreement with the EU should revolve around continent-to-continent partnership and be oriented towards the goals of Agenda 2063 (African Union, 2018a). It stated that the agreement should be separated from the ACP context, although it would preserve existing bilateral agreements with the EU held by North Africa and individual countries such as South Africa. In May 2018, however, this common position was refused the floor at a meeting of the ACP council of ministers in Lomé, and a separate ACP negotiating mandate was released instead, calling to retain the EU and ACP as the sole parties to the agreement (Carbone, 2018). Confusion over this apparent U-turn would be stoked at the AU's next summit at Nouakchott in July, with a declaration encouraging the postponement of post-Cotonou negotiations pending further consolidation of the African Common Position (African Union, 2018b). Regardless, official political negotiations for a new ACP-EU partnership were launched on the margins of the UN General Assembly in

New York in September 2018; these were expected to concentrate first on the establishment of the 'umbrella' or common foundation before moving to talks on the specific regional pillars.

The African Common Position that arose in March 2018 was a reflection of a view held by many within AU circles that the ACP relationship is an outdated mechanism for EU cooperation based on the delivery of aid, one that has 'contributed to fragmenting Africa, weakening and slowing down the pace of integration' (Carbone, 2018). From this perspective, the core continental priorities for the AU under the JAES – revolving around the four key pillars of peace and security, trade and the CFTA, climate change and migration – cannot be adequately subsumed under the EU-ACP relationship and need to be the starting point of a wholly reconfigured arrangement after 2020. Such division is mirrored on the European side: the EU's Directorate-General for International Cooperation and Development (DG DEVCO) has been inclined to see the ACP as the more convenient interlocutor for financial and aid support, while the European External Action Service has pushed for the prioritisation of a more strategic AU relationship. Yet with the beginning of negotiations in New York realistically marking an end to calls for the ACP's effective disbandment, the AU changed course: the declaration from its final 2018 summit in Addis Ababa in November endorsed the ACP negotiating mandate and offered its technical support to the process, while also calling to strengthen the post-2020 AU-EU partnership under a two-track process (African Union, 2018c). Critically, this would be mutually reinforced at the first EU-AU Ministerial Meeting in Brussels in January 2019, from which a delayed joint communique eventually committed both continental institutions to pursue the establishment of an enhanced partnership, backed by 'appropriate instruments' (Council of the European Union, 2019: 5).

EU-ACP consultations on the regional pillars for Cotonou's successor duly proceeded through the early months of 2019. Yet little evidence of a firm agreement on either the foundation agreement or pillars had emerged by the time of a joint EU-ACP ministerial summit in May, with key issues such as development financing and an updated approach to migration still unresolved. Speculation mounted that a year-long delay to the post-Cotonou framework was imminent, and discussions at the summit itself would indeed pave the way for the necessary legal measures for an extension to take place (Fox, 2019). On the AU side, however, the initial impetus for a unified African continental approach to effectively overwrite the ACP's role in EU partnership continued to dissipate, as Egyptian President Abdel Fattah el-Sisi succeeded Rwanda's Paul Kagame as AU chairperson in February 2019. Regardless of the EU's vague original proposal for their inclusion in its post-Cotonou negotiating directives, North African countries continued to express little interest in engaging under the EU-ACP banner, and they also retained doubts over a new continent-to-continent agreement (De Groof et al., 2019). Delays to negotiations therefore represented a tactical move from the AU side, both in waiting for greater clarity from the EU and for el-Sisi's term to run its course. They were further prompted by changes of personnel in Brussels with the appointment of a new Commission and Directors-General. In standing at this crossroads amidst the dying throes of an EU administration, very little appetite was present among African partners to finalise a post-Cotonou deal.

The arrival of the new European Commission in December 2019 – heralded as the 'geopolitical Commission' by incoming president Ursula Von der Leyen (2019: 7) – saw a resurfacing of expectations for its relationship with Africa. Early signs pointed to renewed EU emphasis in this respect, including the appointment of Jutta Urpilainen to the new role of Commissioner for International Partnerships (replacing the previous development commissioner title) and a trip to Addis Ababa marking the first foreign visit of the new term of office, alongside repeated promises to develop a new 'comprehensive strategy for Africa' (Kell and Kurtagic, 2019). A formal extension of the Cotonou Agreement until December 2020 soon followed, with Urpilainen keen to push through negotiations before turning focus to the continental level and a scheduled sixth

EU-AU summit in Brussels in October. In March 2020, the Commission released a joint communication: Towards a Comprehensive Strategy with Africa (European Commission, 2020). The document outlines five core partnerships for a new strategy: green transition and energy access; digital transformation; sustainable growth and jobs; peace and governance; and migration and mobility (ibid.). If its aim was indeed to pursue a less paternalistic tone than previously (Byiers, 2020), then by this metric it succeeds: avoiding the tired promise of a 'partnership of equals' and appealing to 'respective interests', not simply mutual ones. However, while pursuing a less overbearing approach and capturing relevant interests is commendable in itself, the document contains virtually no discussion of the precise instruments and financing mechanisms by which the final strategy might be implemented. Moreover, shortly after its release, the road to finalising an agreement at the sixth AU-EU summit became increasingly bumpy: punctuated by further delays and revisions to 2021–2027 EU budget and stunned by the shockwave of the COVID-19 pandemic. Though a new long-term budget was eventually agreed in July 2020, a significant proportion of increases to proposed external action spending were cut or dropped – including the geographic allocation for sub-Saharan Africa, which will now remain broadly constant with 2014–2020 levels. By September, ongoing disruption due to COVID-19 had forced the postponement of the AU-EU summit until 2021 despite proposals that it might go ahead in a virtual format, while post-Cotonou negotiations were also faced with a further extension into 2021.

This uncertain global context, however, reveals precisely why a more cohesive framework for Africa-EU relations is desperately required. Major reconstructive efforts on both continents in the coming years will ultimately be served best by an approach that eschews fragmentation and bureaucracy – while in turn, newly introduced cooperative mechanisms may be consolidated under broader circumstances of upheaval. For example, in light of the pandemic's emergence, the new EU High Representative for Foreign Affairs, Josep Borrell, suggested that Africa can offer a strategic alternative to China for the diversification and shortening of key supply chains to Europe (Borrell, 2020). Thus, although the opportunity presented by Cotonou's initial expiry has been squandered, the extended delay period into 2021 still presents a vital second chance to reset relations, with incentives on both sides. For a strengthened and modern partnership to emerge in the post-Cotonou context, African member states must recognise that their own rhetoric regarding an equal partnership is at odds with a simple reversion to the familiar North-South development cooperation model of the ACP; while the EU, with the onus on DG DEVCO in particular, must look to present greater clarity of intention and unity beyond the outdated ACP framework and previous convoluted proposals for a 'hybrid' solution (Medinilla and Bossuyt, 2019).

Conclusion

At its adoption in Lisbon in 2007, the JAES was envisaged as the spine of a continental partnership of equals between Africa and Europe, built around co-ownership of a broad agenda to overwrite the donor-recipient dynamic of the past. While its original objectives remain valid, changing realities on both sides have buffeted the strategy ever since its inception – from the new institutional initiatives of Agenda 2063 and the EU's Global Strategy to external developments such as the migration crisis. Despite recent updates working to streamline priority areas and integrate a greater focus on the contentious topics of demographic change and migration, the overall trajectory of the JAES has been hindered by fragmentation and overambition, illustrated by a highly uneven record of delivery on key objectives.

The sphere of peace and security reflects perhaps the most advanced link facilitated by the partnership, as the APF has helped the AU become an essential player on the African continent even while delays continue for the operationalisation of APSA and the ASF. This area of cooperation looks likely to remain at the centre of any future partnership, in light of increased African contributions via the new Peace Fund and following the EU's proposal to implement a new instrument, the European Peace Facility, from 2021 onwards. Worth €8 billion, the European Peace Facility replaces and expands the APF mechanism, providing more predictable funding and increased support for capacity building initiatives (European External Action Service, 2018b).

On trade and economic issues, the partnership has been plagued by setbacks, but African ownership of the CFTA is providing much-needed impetus to the integration agenda, surpassing the protracted EPA negotiations. Although the more recent mobilisation of the European EIP shows some awareness of Africa's stark demographic realities and an attempt to move away from 'traditional' donor-recipient relations, the financial relationship overall remains highly imbalanced at the continental level, as well as divided across different regional groupings within Africa. The outgoing President of the European Commission, Jean-Claude Juncker, touched upon the promise of an EU-Africa free trade agreement during his final State of the Union address in September 2018 (European Commission, 2018f), but as post-Cotonou negotiations fluctuate, it remains unclear what continent-to-continent instruments such an initiative would be built upon.

Overall, the notions of equality and shared ownership so central to the JAES at its inception have remained more of a vision than a reality, with much of the continental relationship still heavily reliant on EU-donated money. On key issues such as migration, the EU has continued to set or initiate the agenda and often fails to regularly consult its African partners – an issue exacerbated by its proliferation of bilateral strategies with individual African states and use of multiple financing instruments. Negotiations on a successor to the Cotonou Agreement and a new comprehensive strategy continue to offer an unprecedented opportunity for a genuine reset of relations, but these have been repeatedly obstructed by disunity and confusion on both sides. Until such fragmentation is decisively addressed, the continent-to-continent partnership of equals envisaged for the JAES more than a decade ago will remain far from fruition.

Notes

1. The summit was rebranded after Morocco rejoined the AU in 2017.
2. The ACP Group is now known as the Organisation of African, Caribbean and Pacific States, following a name change in 2020.

Bibliography

Adebajo, A. and Whiteman, K. (eds) (2012) *The EU and Africa: From Eurafrique to Afro-Europa*. London: Hurst & Company.

Africa-EU Partnership (2007) First Action Plan (2008–2010) for the implementation of the Africa-EU Strategic Partnership. Accra, 31 October. www.africa-eu-partnership.org//sites/default/files/documents/jaes_action_plan_2008-2010.pdf

Africa-EU Partnership (2010) Joint Africa EU Strategy: Action Plan 2011–2013 [online]. www.africa-eu-partnership.org//sites/default/files/documents/03-jeas_action_plan_en.pdf

African Union (2013) 50th Anniversary Solemn Declaration. Addis Ababa, 26 May. https://au.int/sites/default/files/newsevents/workingdocuments/29149-wd-50_declaration_en.pdf

African Union (2018a) Decision on a New Agreement on Post-Cotonou Cooperation with the European Union. Assembly/AU/Dec.694(XXXI). Nouakchott, 1–2 July. https://au.int/sites/default/files/decisions/34634-assembly_au_dec_690_-_712_xxxi_e.pdf

African Union (2018b) Decision on Post-Cotonou Negotiations. Addis Ababa, 17–18 November. https://au.int/sites/default/files/decisions/35378-ext_assembly_dec._1-4xi_e.pdf

African Union (2018c) Decision on the African Common Position for Negotiations for a New Cooperation Agreement with the European Union. Ext/EX.CL/Dec.1(XVIII). Kigali, 19 March. https://au.int/sites/default/files/decisions/34054-ext_ex_cl_dec_1-2xviii_e26_march.pdf

African Union Commission (2015) Agenda 2063: First Ten-year Implementation Plan 2014–2023 [online]. www.un.org/en/africa/osaa/pdf/au/agenda2063-first10yearimplementation.pdf

Apiko, P. and Miyandazi, L. (2019) *Self-financing the African Union: One Levy, Multiple Reforms*. Discussion Paper no. 258. The European Centre for Development Policy Management. Maastricht: ECDPM. https://ecdpm.org/wp-content/uploads/Self-Financing-African-Union-Levy-Reforms-ECDPM-Discussion-Paper-258.pdf (retrieved 18 September 2019).

Assembly of the African Union (2015) Declaration on Self-Reliance. Decl.5 (XXV). www.un.org/en/africa/osaa/pdf/au/adoption_first10yrplan_2015.pdf

Assembly off the African Union (2016) Decision on the Outcome of the Retreat of the Assembly of the African Union. Dec.605 (XXVII). https://au.int/sites/default/files/pages/31955-file assembly_au_dec_605_financing_the_au.pdf

Bertelsmann-Scott, T. (2012) South Africa and the EU: Where lies the strategic partnership? In A. Adebajo and K. Whiteman (eds), *The EU and Africa: From Eurafrique to Afro-Europa*. London: Hurst & Company (pp. 121–136).

Borrell, J. (2020) *The Post-coronavirus World is Already Here*. ECFR Policy Brief, 30 April. www.ecfr.eu/publications/summary/the_post_coronavirus_world_is_already_here

Byiers, B. (2020) The EU and Africa: Should, would, could ... but how? ECDPM blog, 16 March. https://ecdpm.org/talking-points/eu-and-africa-should-would-could-but-how/

Carbone, M. (2018) Caught between the ACP and the AU: Africa's relations with the European Union in a post-Cotonou Agreement context. *South African Journal of International Affairs*, 25 (4), 481–496.

Chatham House (2018) Redefining partnership: The EU-Africa relationship beyond the Cotonou Partnership Agreement [online]. 26 March. www.chathamhouse.org/event/redefining-partnership-eu-africa-relationship-beyond-cotonou-partnership-agreement

Clayton, J. and Holland, H. (2015) Over one million sea arrivals reach Europe in 2015. UNHCR, 30 December. www.unhcr.org/uk/news/latest/2015/12/5683d0b56/million-sea-arrivals-reach-europe-2015.html

Council of the European Union (n.d.) EU-Africa relations [online]. www.consilium.europa.eu/en/policies/eu-africa/

Council of the European Union (2007a) Lisbon Declaration – EU Africa Summit. 16343/07 (Presse 290). Lisbon, 9 December.

Council of the European Union (2007b) The Africa-EU Strategic Partnership: A Joint Africa-EU Strategy. 16344/07 (Presse 291). Lisbon, 9 December.

Council of the European Union (2011) Council Conclusions on the Horn of Africa. 16858/11. Brussels, 14 November. http://register.consilium.europa.eu/doc/srv?l=EN&f=ST%2016858%202011%20INIT

Council of the European Union (2014a) Fourth EU-Africa Summit Declaration. Brussels, 3 April. www.consilium.europa.eu/media/23894/142096.pdf

Council of the European Union (2014b) Fourth EU-Africa Summit: Roadmap 2014–2017. Brussels, 3 April. www.consilium.europa.eu/media/21520/142094.pdf

Council of the European Union (2015) Council Conclusions on the EU Horn of Africa Regional Action Plan 2015–2020. Press Release, 26 October. www.consilium.europa.eu/en/press/press-releases/2015/10/26/fac-conclusions-horn-africa/

Council of the European Union (2018) Negotiating Directives for a Partnership Agreement between the European Union and its Member States of the One Part, and with Countries of the African, Caribbean and Pacific Group of States of the Other Part. Brussels, 21 June. https://data.consilium.europa.eu/doc/document/ST-8094-2018-ADD-1/en/pdf

Council of the European Union (2019) Joint Communique, EU-AU Ministers of Foreign Affairs Meeting. Brussels, 21–22 January. www.consilium.europa.eu/media/37940/190122-eu-au-joint-communique-en.pdf (retrieved 18 September 2019).

D'Alfonso, A. (2014) *European Development Fund: Joint Development Cooperation and the EU budget*. European Parliamentary Research Service. Brussels: European Union. www.europarl.europa.eu/EPRS/EPRS-IDA-542140-European-Development-Fund-FINAL.pdf

De Groof, E., Bossuyt, J., Abderrahim, T. and Djinnit, D. (2019) *Looking North and Moving South: Little Enthusiasm for a Continent-to-Continent Approach*. European Centre for Development Policy Management, Discussion Paper 238. Maastricht: ECDPM. https://ecdpm.org/wp-content/uploads/DP238-North-Africa-double-pursuit-Part-1-looking-north-moving-south-continent-to-continent-ECDPM-January-2019.pdf

European Commission (2018a) Pan-African Programme [online]. International Cooperation and Development. https://ec.europa.eu/europeaid/regions/africa/continental-cooperation/pan-african-programme_en

European Commission (2018b) Pan-African Programme 2014–2020: Multi-annual Indicative Programme (MIP) 2018–2020. 22 May. https://ec.europa.eu/europeaid/sites/devco/files/mip-pan-african-programme-2018-2020-annex_en.pdf

European Commission (2018c) *African Peace Facility Annual Report 2017*. Luxembourg: Publications Office of the European Union.

European Commission (2018d) Cape Verde [online]. International Cooperation and Development. https://ec.europa.eu/europeaid/countries/cape-verde_en

European Commission (2018e) External action financing instruments [online]. International Cooperation and Development. https://ec.europa.eu/europeaid/funding/about-funding-and-procedures/where-does-money-come/external-action-financing-instruments_en

European Commission (2018f) State of the Union 2018: The Hour of European *Sovereignty*. 12 September. https://ec.europa.eu/commission/sites/beta-political/files/soteu2018-speech_en_0.pdf

European Commission (n.d.) EU External Investment Plan [online]. https://ec.europa.eu/europeaid/sites/devco/files/factsheet-eip-20171120_en.pdf

European Commission (2000) Africa-Europe Summit under the Aegis of the OAU and the EU. Cairo Declaration. Conseil/00/901, Cairo, 3–4 April.

European Commission (2005) EU Strategy for Africa: Towards a Euro-African Pact to Accelerate Africa's Development. COM(2005) 489 final. Brussels, 12 October.

European Commission (2006) Internal Agreement 10th EDF. *Official Journal of the European Union*, L 247/32, 9 September.

European Commission (2007) Communication from the Commission to the Council and the European Parliament on the Future of Relations between the European Union and the Republic of Cape Verde. COM(2007) 641 final. Brussels, 24 October.

European Commission (2014a) Pan-African Programme 2014–2020: Multiannual Indicative Programme 2014–2017 [online]. https://ec.europa.eu/europeaid/sites/devco/files/mip-pan-african-programme-2014-2017_en.pdf

European Commission (2014b) *The Cotonou Agreement*. Luxembourg: Publications Office of the European Union.

European Commission (2014c) *European Neighbourhood and Partnership Instrument: 2007–2013 Overview of Activities and Results*. Brussels: European Commission and EuropeAid.

European Commission (2015a) Joint Communication to the European Parliament, the Council, the European Economic and Social Committee and the Committee of the Regions: Review of the European Neighbourhood Policy. JOIN(2015) 50 final. Brussels, 18 November.

European Commission (2015b) *Multi-annual Indicative Programme for South Africa 2014–2020*. 22 January. https://ec.europa.eu/europeaid/sites/devco/files/mip-south-africa-edf11-2014_en.pdf

European Commission (2016) Joint Communication to the European Parliament and the Council: A Renewed Partnership with the Countries of Africa, the Caribbean and the Pacific. JOIN(2016) 52 final. Strasbourg, 22 November. https://ec.europa.eu/europeaid/sites/devco/files/joint-communication-renewed-partnership-acp-20161122_en.pdf

European Commission (2017) Joint Communication to the European Parliament and the Council for a Renewed Impetus of the Africa-EU Partnership. JOIN(2017) 17 final, Brussels, 4 May.

European Commission (2020) Joint Communication to the European Parliament and the Council: Towards a Comprehensive Strategy with Africa. JOIN(2020) 4 final. Brussels, 9 March. https://ec.europa.eu/international-partnerships/system/files/communication-eu-africa-strategy-join-2020-4-final_en.pdf

European Council (2018) Valetta Summit on Migration, 11–12 November 2015 [online]. www.consilium.europa.eu/en/meetings/international-summit/2015/11/11-12/

European External Action Service (2009) Nigeria-EU joint way forward [online]. https://eeas.europa.eu/sites/eeas/files/the_nigeria-eu_joint_way_forward_en_0.pdf

European External Action Service (2016) *A Global Strategy for the European Union's Foreign and Security Policy*. Brussels: European Union. https://eeas.europa.eu/archives/docs/top_stories/pdf/eugs_review_web.pdf

European External Action Service (2018a) Factsheet: EU-South Africa Strategic Partners. Brussels, 14 November. https://cdn1-eeas.fpfis.tech.ec.europa.eu/cdn/farfuture/p5oxrc0oLR_zXdb0_fSpSEKAe9PHRvUhQ115Z-ifTL4/mtime:1542185382/sites/eeas/files/eu-south_africa_factsheet.pdf

European External Action Service (2018b) European Peace Facility – An EU off-budget fund to build peace and strengthen international security. Brussels, 13 June. https://eeas.europa.eu/headquarters/headquarters-homepage/46285/european-peace-facility-eu-budget-fund-build-peace-and-strengthen-international-security_en

European External Action Service (2018c) EU to boost investment in global role with 30% budget increase for external action [online]. 14 June. https://eeas.europa.eu/topics/humanitarian-emergency-response/46545/eu-boost-investment-global-role-30-budget-increase-external-action_en

Fox, B. (2019) EU-ACP Cotonou successor faces one year delay. *EURACTIV.com*, 17 May. www.euractiv.com/section/development-policy/news/eu-acp-cotonou-successor-faces-one-year-delay/

Haastrup, T. (2013) *Charting Transformation through Security: Contemporary EU-Africa Relations*. Basingstoke: Palgrave Macmillan.

Hauck, V., Knoll, A. and Cangas, A.H. (2015) *EU Trust Funds: Shaping More Comprehensive External Action*. European Centre for Development Policy Management, Briefing Note 81. Maastricht: ECDPM.

Helly, D. (2013) The EU and Africa since the Lisbon summit of 2007: Continental drift or widening cracks? *South African Journal of International Affairs*, 20 (1), 137–157.

International Crisis Group (2017) *Time to Reset African Union-European Union Relations*. Africa Report No. 255. Brussels: International Crisis Group. www.crisisgroup.org/africa/255-time-reset-african-union-european-union-relations

Joffé, G. (2012) The EU, the Maghreb and the Mediterranean. In A. Adebajo and K. Whiteman (eds), *The EU and Africa: From Eurafrique to Afro-Europa*. London: Hurst & Company (pp. 137–152).

Kell, F. and Kurtagic, D. (2019) Can the New European Commission deliver on its promises to Africa? [online]. Chatham House, Expert Comment, 4 December. www.chathamhouse.org/expert/comment/can-new-european-commission-deliver-its-promises-africa#

Mail & Guardian (2007) Brown opts out of EU-Africa summit over Mugabe. 27 November. https://mg.co.za/article/2007-11-27-brown-opts-out-of-euafrica-summit-over-mugabe

Medinilla, A. and Bossuyt, J. (2019) *Africa-EU Relations and Post-Cotonou: African Collective Action or Further Fragmentation of Partnerships?* European Centre for Development Policy Management, Briefing Note 110. Maastricht: ECDPM. https://ecdpm.org/wp-content/uploads/BN-110-Africa-EU-relations-post-CotonouAfrica-EU-relations-and-post-Cotonou-african-collective-action-fragmentation-partnerships-ECDPM-March-2019.pdf

Parshotam, A. (2017) *Valetta 2015 to Abidjan 2017: Recent Trends in AU-EU Migration Relations*. South African Institute of International Affairs, Policy Briefing 168. SAIIA.

Pirozzi, N. and Godsäter, A. (2015) *The EU and Africa: Regionalism and Interregionalism Beyond Institutions*. Atlantic Future Working Paper No. 26. Barcelona: Barcelona Centre for International Affairs. http://iaitestnew.asw.bz/sites/default/files/af_wp_26.pdf

Pirozzi, N., Sartori, N. and Venturi, B. (2017) *The Joint Africa-EU Strategy*. Brussels: Policy Department, European Parliament Directorate-General for External Policies.

Powel, B. and Sadiki, L. (2010) *Europe and Tunisia: Democratization via Association*. London: Routledge.

Rodt, A.P. and Okeke, J.M. (2013) AU-EU 'strategic partnership': Strengthening policy convergence and regime efficacy in the African peace and security complex? *African Security*, 6, (3–4), 211–233.

Styan, D. (2017) Europe's multiple security strategies towards Africa. In S. Economides and J. Sperling (eds), *EU Security Strategies: Extending the EU System of Security Governance*. Abingdon: Routledge (pp. 100–120).

Tardy, T. (2016) *The EU and Africa: A Changing Security Partnership*. Paris: EU Institute for Security Studies.

Vines, A. (2013) A decade of African Peace and Security Architecture. *International Affairs*, 89 (1), 89–109.

Von der Leyen, U. (2019) Speech in the European Parliament Plenary Session. Strasbourg, 27 November. https://ec.europa.eu/info/sites/info/files/president-elect-speech-original_1.pdf

Whiteman, K. (2012) The rise and fall of Eurafrique: From the Berlin Conference of 1884–1885 to the Tripoli EU-Africa Summit of 2010. In A. Adebajo and K. Whiteman (eds), *The EU and Africa: From Eurafrique to Afro-Europa*. London: Hurst & Company (pp. 23–44).

9

The African Union as an interlocutor in European Union-Africa relations?

John Akokpari and Primrose Z.J. Bimha

Introduction

The transformation of the Organization of African Unity (OAU) to the African Union (AU) in 2002 excited both hope and euphoria, given the many failures of the former. In retrospect, the OAU was a loose alliance of states with the objective of ridding the continent of the remaining vestiges of colonisation and apartheid; promoting unity, solidarity and territorial integrity of the continent; fostering adherence to the principles of sovereignty and non-interference; and coordinating and intensifying cooperation among African states for development (African Union, 2019a; Welz, 2013; Organization of African Unity, 1963). The AU was inaugurated in July 2002 with the aim of promoting an 'integrated, prosperous, peaceful Africa, driven by its own citizens and representing the member states collectively, as a dynamic force in the global arena' (African Union, 2019a). The replacement of the OAU with the AU was informed by the realisation among African leaders of the need to refocus attention towards collectively driving the continent's growth and economic development (African Union, 2019a; Gruzd and Turianskyi, 2015: 8). Importantly, there was heightened expectation that the AU would perform an interlocutory role for the continent, serving as Africa's spokesperson and chief negotiator. The European Union (EU) has remained one of the key external actors with whom Africa maintains relations. While most of the 28 members of the EU[1] maintain bilateral relations with African states, Brussels has remained the key interlocutor in Europe's external engagements with Africa. Through the EU, Europe speaks with a common voice on relations with Africa. It does this by crafting broader policy frameworks and contexts which shape and inform EU member states' relations with Africa. Can this be said of the AU?

This chapter examines the extent to which the AU serves as an interlocutor of the continent in its relations with the EU. It argues that while theoretically the AU is the key spokesperson and negotiator in Africa's dealings with the EU, this is hardly the case in practice. On the contrary, there have been occasions when regions or individual African states have assumed contradictory, often directly oppositional, postures to the official stance of the AU. Lacking effective instruments of compulsion, the AU has failed to reprimand such 'errant' states. Indeed, for much of the time, the AU had remained at the background, leaving individual states and regions to directly negotiate trade deals with the EU. The chapter is arranged as follows: the next section provides some brief overview of EU-Africa relations, while the subsequent sections underscore the limits of the AU's interlocutory role in Africa's relations with the EU. The conclusion summarises the key arguments in the chapter.

EU-Africa relations in historical perspective

To understand the emergence of the AU as an interlocutor and the manner in which it can take on this role, it makes sense to provide a specific but brief EU-Africa relations context. Since Africa's independence decade of the 1960s, the continent's relations with Europe have been crafted within institutionalised frameworks from the Yaoundé agreements to the Lomé conventions. The current framework agreement governing EU-Africa economic relations, the 2000 Cotonou Agreement, was due to expire in 2020. There were three palpable, yet important, features characterising these institutionalised agreements. First, within each of these agreements, Africa was lumped together with Caribbean and Pacific countries, as these were largely former European colonies. Some critical observers argue that these new framework agreements were another way of re-establishing Europe's dominance and the asymmetrical relations with Africa (Williams, 2015). Europe lumps African states with the Pacific and Caribbean countries possibly because they share common characteristics – poverty, fledgling economies and general underdevelopment. Accordingly, the agreements were known to be defining relations between Europe on the one hand with African, Caribbean and Pacific (ACP) states on the other. For the purpose of this chapter, however, emphasis is placed exclusively on EU-Africa relations.

In addition to perceived commonalities, the second feature of these agreements was that each specified the nature and scope of the relationship between the EU and Africa. In matters of trade, for example, the commodities that were involved, the percentage reduction of import duties and the tax exemptions that were to be enjoyed by both parties are all clearly stipulated when negotiations are concluded. Thus, the official formalisation and signing of the agreements did not grant a blanket and unregulated access of Africa to the EU market. Typically, the agreement offered incentives and rewards in the form of 'most favoured nation' status, by which the EU confers special privileges on African states in terms of access to the EU market. By virtue of Africa's exports being primarily agriculture commodities, which do not find a market on the continent, accessing the EU market was an important route for gaining valuable export revenue. The inability of African states to trade among themselves is partly due to what Callaghy (1994) referred to over two decades ago as the 'fallacy of agricultural composition'; that is, African states produce similar agricultural products, as a result of which they have difficulty trading in these commodities among themselves. For example, the main exports of the East African countries of Kenya, Tanzania, Uganda, Ethiopia and Rwanda are coffee and tea. In West Africa, cocoa remains the primary agricultural export of Togo, Ivory Coast and Ghana, until 2011 when oil became Ghana's leading foreign exchange earner. In the Economic Community of Central African States, the export of crude oil is the main source of foreign income. The fact that these countries produce similar commodities limits intra-regional trade. Consequently, intra-African trade remained at a dismal 19.6% in 2016, up from a paltry 10.3% in 2008. The 2016 figure is significantly pale in comparison to Europe, Asia and North America, with intra-regional trade of 59%, 51% and 37%, respectively (World Trade Organization, 2018).

Thirdly, in all these agreements, whether the Yaoundé and Lomé conventions under the OAU or the Cotonou Agreement (which was initiated under the OAU but concluded under the AU), the African continental body did not sign on behalf of states. Neither did regional bodies sign for individual states, although much of the Economic Partnership Agreements (EPAs) were negotiated on a regional basis. Rather, it was individual states that signed the agreement, albeit reluctantly, after coming under EU pressure and threats of being denied access to the EU market. In the Yaoundé, Lomé and Cotonou agreements, therefore, the continental body merely accepted the offers in principle, leaving the actual signing and commitments to the discretion of individual states. The process of merely agreeing to the said conventions and leaving the details and signing to individual states significantly questions the interlocutory authority of the AU in Africa's relations with the EU.

In an effort to champion a common Africa-EU policy framework, the Joint Africa-EU Strategy (JAES) was launched at the Africa-EU Summit in Lisbon in 2007. The intention was to dilute the criticisms against the EU's EPAs, which were to govern trade and development negotiations under the EU-ACP Group[2] framework. The JAES stipulated that Africa and Europe would collectively champion the principles of democratic governance and respect for human rights, equality, global development goals, as well as peace and security (African Union, 2007). However, the JAES was subsumed under the EU-ACP framework, which emphasised similar values. This was despite the fact that the JAES sought to break donor-recipient dynamics by opposing EU-induced fragmented EPAs, which were not based on the AU's Regional Economic Community (REC) structures (Carbone, 2018: 488). The AU-EU partnership is largely based on the realisation that global challenges and globalisation have made states increasingly interdependent (African Union, 2007). Despite the negative implications of European imperialism, which led to the oppression of African nations, dispossession and continued patterns of asymmetry, the AU and EU cannot afford to be enemies in the contemporary global order. Accordingly, anti-west sentiments pronounced by some African states and governments, as well as rhetoric about threats of neo- or re-colonialism have not completely deterred prospects for further Africa-EU partnerships. The forces of globalisation and the inevitable interdependence of states in the international system will continue to influence AU-EU relations. The prospects for the renewal of the Cotonou Agreement, together with the strong emphasis on the JAES could provide an opportunity to address overlaps and rethink relations between the EU and Africa more generally.

Why the interlocutory role of the AU is limited or almost non-existent

As noted already, one of objectives of the AU was to provide a voice for the continent in its engagements with external actors. This is consistent with the AU's objective 'to promote and defend African common positions on issues of interest to the continent and its peoples' (African Union, 2019a). Although unstated, the expectation was for the AU to negotiate on behalf of the continent on critical matters at international fora, especially on matters such as trade, the continent's growing indebtedness and debt remission, as well as the receipt of official development assistance (ODA). Often regions and sometimes states have openly defied the AU on its positions on critical international issues. In its relations with the EU, the defiant positions of states have been palpable, especially regarding the conclusion of the (in)famous EPAs, which were a central component in the Cotonou Agreement.

A key offshoot of the Cotonou Agreement, EPAs were crafted by the EU to regulate trade relations between Brussels and the 77 ACP countries. The EPAs demand that African countries liberalise 80% of their markets and agree for the EU to use the continent as a market for its industrial and agricultural goods, including wheat, rice, vegetable oil, poultry and milk powder, among others. In return, Africa would access the European market to sell its largely primary agricultural commodities. For Africa, largely as a result of the fallacy of agricultural composition, EPAs were, theoretically speaking, a welcoming agreement. By 2016, the EU market was taking 85% of Africa's total agricultural exports as well as accounting for 75% of sub-Saharan Africa's trade (Taylor, 2016: 96; Kotsopoulos and Mattheis, 2018). In addition to providing markets, relations with the EU have enabled Africa to receive Brussel's ODA through the EU Delegation to the AU. Between January 2007 and December 2011, the EU Delegation facilitated a support programme for Africa valued at €55 million (Akokpari, 2017: 63). A further €40 million of EU financial assistance went to support agriculture, the environment and initiatives to combat the impact of climate change over four years (European Union, 2019). Other EU aid went into promoting science and technology (€14 million) and infrastructure (€10 million) (Akokpari, 2017: 63). The assistance to various sectors fell under what the EU referred to as the African Union Support Programme, aimed at strengthening AU-EU partnership, as well as to enhance the capacity of the AU Commission to serve as a vehicle for accelerating the integration process in Africa. Since 2011 over 60% of the AU's operating budget has been financed by the EU, China and the United States (European Union, 2019). Africa's benefits from the EU cannot therefore be overemphasised.

Despite these advantages, and in spite of the tacit acceptance of EPAs by the AU as a continental institution, the negotiations were met with open opposition from most African states. African opposition to EPAs intensified when the EU set a deadline of October 2014 by which all countries were to sign the agreement. Nigeria, the biggest economy in West Africa, led opposition against EPAs in the region. A meeting of the Economic Community of West African States (ECOWAS) finance and trade ministers in Dakar, Senegal, in February 2014, to formulate a common subregional position on EPAs ended inconclusively. While Ghana and Ivory Coast, leading cocoa producers, were inclined to sign, having already acceded to their interim EPAs in December 2007 and November 2008, respectively, Nigeria argued that EPAs would undermine industrialisation and compromise African jobs. A subsequent meeting in Ivory Coast two months later in April 2014 also failed to agree on a common ECOWAS stance on EPAs because of divisions among countries. Similarly, in East Africa, Kenya, the biggest economy in the region, kicked against EPAs; while in the Southern African Development Community (SADC), Botswana, Namibia and Swaziland became the fiercest critics of the agreements. In central Africa, Cameroon led opposition to EPAs. Thus, across the continent, opposition to EPAs was high although the AU was tacitly in support of them. Indeed, not even an AU-organised continental meeting in Addis Ababa later in 2014 was able to garner a common continental stance or support for EPAs, highlighting the limits of the AU's interlocutory authority.

Yet, the AU became decidedly feeble and an ineffective interlocutor because of some of the regional organisational policies introduced by EPAs. Following the recommendations of the 1991 Abuja Treaty, the AU recognised eight RECs in Africa. These RECs were the Arab Maghreb Union, the Common Market for Eastern and Southern Africa (COMESA), the Community of Sahel-Saharan States, the East African Community, the Economic Community of Central African States, the ECOWAS, the Intergovernmental Authority on Development and the SADC. The main objective of the AU was to use these RECs as a stepping stone to the eventual creation of a wider African Economic Community (African Union, 2019b). In addition to these recognised RECs, there are other subregional formations, such as the West African Economic and Monetary Union and the Manor River Union within ECOWAS and the Southern Africa Custom Union within SADC, to name just two. Paradoxically, the existence of these RECs only served to complicate and, in fact, impede efforts towards rapid regional integration in Africa, as most states hold multiple and overlapping memberships. The many RECs with overlapping memberships are perceived as wasting effort and resources. Having multiple groups adds to the work of harmonisation and coordination and complicates the eventual fusion of RECs into the AU (cited in Lwanda, 2013: 184). In addition to complicating coordination and harmonisation, multiple memberships impose additional costs in the form of fees and loyalties. This has served as a disincentive for states to remain in these RECs. Namibia, for example, withdrew from COMESA in 2005 because of what it considered the high cost of membership.

As Africa grappled with the challenges of states maintaining multiple membership in RECs, EPAs came to compound this already disconcerting situation. For purposes of negotiating EPAs, the EU reconfigured most of the existing RECs. Some memberships in the five geographical regions within Africa recognised by the AU – North, South, East, West and Central – were altered. For example, some five members of SADC, including Malawi, Mauritius, Seychelles, Zambia and Zimbabwe, were included in the EPA groupings of Eastern and Southern Africa, while Mauritania, a North African country, was included in the West Africa EPA group (Akokpari, 2017). In addition to creating a complex and intertwined web of RECs and undermining regional integration in Africa, the redivision of Africa into EPA groups further deprived regions of the critical cohesion required to present a common voice. The unnatural redivision of Africa was reminiscent of the old and familiar 'divide and conquer' policy used by western colonialists to both dominate and control the continent. The fact that the AU was fully aware of this disturbing development and yet watched helplessly was not only an indictment on the continental body but also a clear testimony of its waned prowess as an interlocutor in Africa-EU relations.

Worse yet, the truncated interlocutory role of the AU manifested in the region's rejection of the AU position, even on the security policy of the continent, showed the lack of interlocutory authority. In 2011, conflict broke out because of the dispute over the 2010 national elections in Ivory Coast. Laurent Gbagbo, the incumbent, who lost the election to Alassane Ouattara, his bitterest rival, refused to cede power. ECOWAS maintained that Gbagbo had lost and therefore had to hand over power to his victorious rival. However, the AU envoy who visited Ivory Coast, former South African President Thabo Mbeki, indicated that the results were inconclusive. Typical of his approach to conflict resolution, Mbeki recommended the formation of a unity government that would include both government and opposition representatives (Akokpari, 2008). Although details of Mbeki's proposed unity government plan were never revealed, it was clear that Gbagbo was going to remain leader, with Ouattara as Prime Minister, something similar to what was experimented after the election violence in Kenya and Zimbabwe in 2007 and 2008, respectively. After weeks and months of violence, Gbagbo was eventually arrested on 11 April 2011, with the assistance of French forces, and handed over to the International Criminal Court (ICC) as the conflict spawned growing numbers of refugees and internally displaced persons. Here, again, was a case of the AU not only being challenged, but also having its authority successfully defied.

Similarly, as the popular revolt against Muamar Gaddafi intensified in 2011, the UN Security Council sought to pass a resolution which would help weaken the ability of Libya's military to crash the uprising. Resolution 1973, which was eventually adopted on 17 March 2011, established a no-fly zone with the ostensible objective of protecting civilians, but in reality to provide both context and pretext to deploy the firepower of the North Atlantic Treaty Organization, of which the EU is more or less part, to topple Gaddafi's government. A few days from the vote on the adoption of Resolution 1973, the AU took a collective decision not to be part of the resolution, but rather to support the organisation's roadmap to peace for Libya. The AU roadmap included facilitating dialogue between government and protestors. The agenda also called on Gaddafi to make significant political concessions, including being excluded from the governance of the 'new' Libya. Surprisingly, the three African states then serving as non-permanent members of the Security Council – Gabon, Nigeria and South Africa – all voted in favour of the resolution in open defiance of the AU decision. It was even more surprising that Nigeria and South Africa, the two big brothers of the continent, who were crucial for maintaining the integrity and autonomy of the AU, became part of the defiance. Less surprising though was that the AU neither reprimanded nor chastised the deviant African states. It was as though the AU had become, to borrow Thomas Hobbes' most quoted phrase, 'a Leviathan but with the feet of clay' (2004: xxiii). Importantly, such defiance underscored the diminished interlocutory power of the AU.

Until recently, Africa remained a theatre of human rights abuses and undemocratic governance. Thus, in its dealings with the continent, the EU has insisted on respect for human rights and adherence to basic democratic principles as conditions for aid and investments (European Commission, 2019). In response, the Constitutive Act of the African Union, adopted in 2000 (African Union, 2000), and the subsequent Protocol on Amendments to the Constitutive Act of the African Union, adopted in 2003 (African Union, 2003), articulated commitment to the promotion of democratic principles and institutions, popular participation and good governance, as well as the promotion and protection of peoples' rights (African Union, 2019a). The AU as a lead continental institution was to ensure adherence to these values by states. However, in spite of the entrenchment of democracy-inducing provisions in the AU Constitutive Act, misgovernance and grotesque human rights abuses are rife in Africa. According to the Mo Ibrahim Foundation, in 2017 African states' average score on the Ibrahim Index of African Governance (IIAG) was 49.9% (Mo Ibrahim Foundation, 2018). Thirty-four states had improved, 18 had deteriorated, there was no change in 1 state, and indices were not available for another (ibid.). The IIAG relied on indicators such as: safety and rule of law; participation and human rights; sustainable economic opportunity; and human development. The statistics suggest that African states are still far from attaining the AU's good governance goals. Countries such as Swaziland, Zimbabwe, Sudan and Cameroon continue to make international headlines as epicentres of human rights abuses in Africa. Other countries, such as Rwanda and Uganda, often trumpeted as doing well economically, have been harassing and jailing opposition elements. By failing to stimulate principles of democratic governance or openly denounce the undemocratic actions of such democracy-threatening states, the AU maintains a slothful posture which is a further indication of weakness in its interlocutory capacity.

Africa's relations with the ICC provided a test of the interlocutory authority of the AU. Led by Kenya, Uganda, South Africa, Gambia and Burundi, amongst others, the AU passed a resolution on 1 February 2017 urging all African states to withdraw from the ICC. The anti-ICC countries alleged that the Court was biased and targeted only African leaders. This was in spite of the alleged perpetrators being reported to the ICC by their own citizens. In retrospect, the ICC was designed to prosecute individuals for crimes against humanity, genocide and war crimes. It was the lack of effective national and regional judicial systems to prosecute heads of state, warlords and that necessitated the referral of such cases to the ICC (Vilmer, 2016). For example, warrants of arrest for former Sudanese president Omar Al Bashir, former Democratic Republic of Congo Vice-President Jean-Pierre Bemba and current President of Kenya Uhuru Kenyatta are examples of cases that would not have been heard at REC or AU levels. Though the proposed resolution was framed as an 'all-Africa' approach, it was not supported by many. For example, it was fiercely opposed by Nigeria and Senegal. Despite threats of withdrawal by several states, Burundi is the only AU member state that has so far completely pulled out. President Pierre Nkurunziza's quest for lifetime presidency enforced by intimidation of civilians is definitely a major reason for this drastic decision. Pretoria rescinded its decision to withdraw after Cyril Ramaphosa took over from Jacob Zuma. Gambia did the same after Yahya Jammeh ceded power to Adama Barrow. The anti-ICC debate has, relatively speaking, waned. All EU member states are signatories to the ICC, and they remain the Court's strongest supporters (Coalition for the International Criminal Court, 2019). The same cannot be said of the AU. Only 34 of 55

AU member states are signatories, and there is no common stance regarding the institution. This typifies yet another example of the AU's debilitated interlocutory authority.

A further area revealing the truncated interlocutory capacity of the AU is in championing a clear campaign for the recognition of minority rights. The rights of lesbian, gay, bisexual and transgender (LGBT) persons remain heavily contested by most governments on the continent. While positive legislative acknowledgements of LGBT communities have been passed in South Africa, and more recently in Botswana and Angola, many counties remain opposed to the recognition of LGBT rights. Uganda has tough anti-homosexuality laws, making the practice punishable by long prison terms. Similar anti-homosexual regulations exist in Nigeria and other countries where, though no formal anti-gay/lesbian legislation exists yet, such practices are abhorred in the mainstream culture. There, LGBT practices are considered un-African and unnatural (Dlamini, 2006; Wahab, 2016). At the Nouakchott Summit of the AU Executive Council in 2018, most member states officially denounced LGBT rights, referring to African values and traditions. Anti-LGBT countries argue further that the practice is a western importation that is incompatible with African traditions (Institute for Security Studies, 2018). Constitutions typically enumerate the rights of individuals in a state. However, some African states have often contradicted themselves by, on the one hand, affirming the African Charter on Human and Peoples' Rights – which caters for the rights of all people (Gruzd and Turianskyi, 2015: 5) – and, on the other hand, refusing to accept LGBT rights.

The backgrounding of LGBT rights corresponds with social denouncement(s) of their identities, especially homosexuality (Dlamini, 2006; Wahab, 2016). Besides South Africa, where such rights are explicitly enshrined in law, most African states are either against or choose not to recognise LGBT rights (Wahab, 2016; Institute for Security Studies, 2018). According to the Institute for Security Studies, 32 of the 71 countries worldwide which criminalise homosexual relations are in Africa (ibid.). Attacks on LGBT persons, though not widespread, occur in all these countries, as well as in perceived LGBT-friendly countries such as South Africa. Most African leaders are not convinced that there is a need to interpret broad human rights principles as inclusive of LGBT rights. Accordingly, there is no explicit mention of these rights in the laws of these countries. The EU has established guidelines on lesbian, gay, bisexual, transgender and intersex people, with the aim of protecting same-sex relations and combatting discriminatory laws and policies against LGBT communities (European Union, 2018). The EU has increasingly placed emphasis on LGBT rights being recognised and codified in text as a condition for aid, but the prospects of the AU successfully leading a campaign for the protection of the rights of these minority communities remain minimal. The AU is also far from declaring an official African stance on LGBT rights, thus underscoring the limits of its interlocutory role.

Why the AU shows a weakened capacity to lead

Chutel (2019) contends that the OAU's founding principles of protecting the sovereignty of African states while building a united Africa are preventing the AU from pushing the continent into the 21st century. Since the AU originated from an intergovernmental organisation which sought to eradicate colonialism and shield the continent from neocolonialism, it did not have strong economic ambitions similar to those of the EU at its inception. The EU's predecessor, the European Economic Community (EEC), which was created in 1958, was aimed at 'increasing economic cooperation between Belgium, Germany, France, Italy, Luxembourg and the Netherlands in the aftermath of the Second World War' (European Union, 2019). The disparity between the organisations in terms of their initial numbers – 6 for the EEC and 36 for the OAU, and 27 for the EU and 55 for the AU at present – could also be a factor which ensures greater cooperation for EU member states but undermines prospects for the same amongst AU states. Welz (2013: 5) posits that the most profound problems impeding cooperation on the continent are political, cultural and social heterogeneity, as well as lack of commitment (some member states do not actively participate, thus undermining the institution's capacity). Given that the AU is younger than the EU, and considering the comparative advantage and leverage gained by the European bloc over the years, it would be unfair to compare the two. Nonetheless, the EU's higher levels of cooperation and coordination of efforts are traits which AU member states should aspire to, as this is to their own advantage.

Solidarity is a key ingredient in integration; it is the glue that holds together regional and continental institutions. Without it, partnerships are bound to be fragile. However, solidarity is neither a given, nor can it be permanent, despite shared histories, challenges and development needs. The international system is bound by the independence of sovereign states which cannot fully trust each other (Waltz, 2010; Mearsheimer, 1995). Both the AU and the EU highlight the importance of solidarity, especially through commitment to issues of common interest. Therefore, it can be said that, in theory, both the AU and the EU are defined as interlocutors in their respective regions' international relations. However, the disjuncture between theory and practice has become palpable in the case of the AU. Whilst the EU serves as a global model and an interlocutor for Europe both in theory and practice, the AU enjoys this status only in theory, never in practice.

Conclusion

This chapter demonstrated why the AU's interlocutory role is limited. Firstly, since the 1960s, the decade of independence, the AU has failed to forge a common African approach to EU-Africa relations, thus undermining its capacity to push for the JAES. It is expected that prevailing conditions will persist in the post-Cotonou phase after 2020. Secondly, divided opinion over EPAs on their utility for different regions on the continent further stifles prospects for cooperation with the EU. Thus the practice of signing agreements by individual member states is certain to persist in the future, as the AU shows a truncated ability to exercise an effective interlocutory role. Thirdly, on matters of peacemaking, peacebuilding and general conflict resolution, the weakness of the AU to lead and get the continent behind it became palpable. The Libyan crisis provided a clear example of this. Similarly, the growing polarisation among African states on LGBT rights along with the seeming inability of the AU to not only champion a clear position but also rally African states behind that particular stance demonstrate the limits of the interlocutory authority of the continental body. And the failure of the AU to remain firm on its commitments in the protection of human rights and the promotion of the security of Africans has not helped its cause. The decision to pass a resolution, albeit non-binding, for African states to pull out of the ICC, knowing that African leaders were sent to the Hague by their own citizens, underscores the pliability of the AU. The continental body imparted a major contradiction in advocating human rights while in the same breath creating conditions for impunity. While the EU speaks with a common voice in its relations with Africa, the AU appears to lack the capacity to be the voice of Africa in its relations with the EU. Herein lies the limited, almost non-existent, interlocutory authority of the AU.

Notes

1 With the exit from the EU of the United Kingdom in 2020, there are now 27 member states.
2 The ACP changed its name in 2020 to the Organisation of African, Caribbean and Pacific States.

Bibliography

African Union (2000) Constitutive Act of the African Union [online]. https://au.int/sites/default/files/pages/34873-file-constitutiveact_en.pdf

African Union (2003) Protocol on Amendments to the Constitutive Act of the African Union [online]. https://au.int/sites/default/files/treaties/35423-treaty-0025_-_protocol_on_the_amendments_to_the_constitutive_act_of_the_african_union_e.pdf (retrieved 10 October 2019).

African Union (2007) The Africa-EU Strategic Partnership: A Joint Africa-EU Strategy [online]. www.africa-eu-partnership.org//sites/default/files/documents/eas2007_joint_strategy_en.pdf (retrieved 10 October 2019).

African Union (2019a) About the African Union [online]. https://au.int/en/overview (retrieved 10 October 2019).

African Union (2019b) Regional Economic Communities (RECs) [online]. https://au.int/en/organs/recs (retrieved 10 October 2019).

Akokpari, J. (2008) You don't belong here: Citizenship and Africa's conflicts – reflections on Ivory Coast. In A. Nhema and P. Zeleza (eds), *Roots of African Conflicts: The Causes and Costs*. Oxford: James Currey (pp. 88–105).

Akokpari, J. (2017) The EU and Africa: The political economy of an asymmetrical partnership. In A. Montoute and K. Virk (eds), *The ACP Group and the EU Development Partnership: Beyond the North-South Debate*. Cham: Palgrave Macmillan (pp. 55–78).

Callaghy, T.M. (1994). Civil society, democratisation and economic change: A dissenting opinion about resurgent societies. In J. Harbeson, D. Rothchild and N. Chazan (eds), *Civil Society and the State in Africa*. Boulder, CO: Lynne Rienner (pp. 231–254).

Carbone, M. (2018). Caught between the ACP and the AU: Africa's relations with the European Union in a post-Cotonou Agreement context. *South African Journal of International Affairs*, 25 (4), 481–496.

Chutel, L. (2019) The African Union has a brilliant plan for Africa, if it could get it right [online]. Quartz Africa, 16 February. https://qz.com/africa/1551786/the-african-union-has-a-brilliant-plan-for-africa-if-it-could-get-it-right/#:~:text=The%20African%20Union%20has%20a,it%20could%20get%20it%20right&text=The%20AU%20was%20founded%20as,while%20building%20a%20unified%20Africa.

Coalition for the International Criminal Court (2019) European Union [online]. www.coalitionfortheicc.org/state-support/regional-organization/eu (retrieved 10 October 2019).

Dlamini, B. (2006) Homosexuality in the African context. *Agenda*, 20 (67): 128–136.

European Commission (2019) EU position in world trade [online]. https://ec.europa.eu/trade/policy/eu-position-in-world-trade/ (retrieved 10 October 2019).

European Union (2018) EU Annual Report on Human Rights and Democracy in the World 2018 [online]. https://eeas.europa.eu/regions/north-america/62179/human-rights-and-democracy-world-eu-annual-report-2018-adopted_en (retrieved 10 October 2019).

European Union (2019) Delegation of the European Union to the African Union [online]. http://eeas.europa.eu/delegations/african_union/eu_african_union/development_cooperation/index_en.htm (retrieved 8 October 2019).

Gruzd, S. and Turianskyi, Y. (eds) (2015) *African Accountability: What Works and What Doesn't*. South African Institute of International Affairs.

Hobbes, T. (2004) *Leviathan*. New York: Barnes and Noble Books.

Institute for Security Studies (2018) Although homophobia is a phenomenon that occurs globally, the idea that homosexuality is 'un-African' persists [online]. Peace and Security Council Report, 20 August. https://issafrica.org/pscreport/psc-insights/the-african-union-and-the-question-of-lesbian-gay-bisexual-and-transgender-lgbt-rights

Kotsopoulos, J. and Mattheis, F. (2018) A contextualisation of EU–Africa relations: Trends and drivers from a reciprocal perspective. *South African Journal of International Affairs*, 25 (4), 445–460.

Lwanda, G. (2013) Southern African Customs Union (SACU): A viable building block for the African economic community. *African Journal of Political Science and International Relations*, 7 (4), 182–189.

Mearsheimer, J.J. (1995) The false promise of international institutions. *International Security*, 19 (3), 5–25.

Mo Ibrahim Foundation (2018) 2018 Ibrahim Index of African Governance: Index report [online]. www.tralac.org/documents/resources/africa/2363-2018-ibrahim-index-of-african-governance-index-report/file.html (retrieved 10 October 2019).

Organization of African Unity (1963) OAU Charter [online]. https://au.int/sites/default/files/treaties/7759-file-oau_charter_1963.pdf (retrieved 1 October 2019).

Taylor, I. (2016) Bait and switch: The European Union's incoherence towards Africa. *Insight on Africa*, 8 (2), 96–111.

Vilmer, J.J. (2016) The African Union and the ICC: Counteracting the crisis. *International Affairs*, 92 (6), 1319–1342.

Wahab, A. (2016) Homosexuality/homophobia is un-African? Un-mapping transnational discourses in the context of Uganda's Anti-Homosexuality Bill/Act. *Journal of homosexuality*, 63 (5), 685–718.

Waltz, K.N. (2010) *Theory of International Politics*. Illinois: Waveland Press.

Welz, M. (2013) *Integrating Africa: Decolonization's Legacies, Sovereignty and the African Union*. New York: Routledge.

Williams, Y. (2015) The EU as a foreign policy actor: Shifting between hegemony and dominance. *Caribbean Journal of International Relations & Diplomacy*, 3 (1), 7–33.

World Trade Organization (2018) *World Trade Statistical Review 2018*. Geneva: World Trade Organization. www.wto.org/english/res_e/statis_e/wts2018_e/wts2018_e.pdf (retrieved 12 April 2019).

Part III
Issues in EU-Africa relations

Introduction to Part III

Nicoletta Pirozzi and Bernardo Venturi

Introduction

Part III of this volume collects a series of analyses on key issues in European Union (EU)-Africa relations: development cooperation, democracy and human rights promotion, peace and security, regional integration, patterns of bilateralism and interregionalism, and trade and the Economic Partnership Agreements (EPAs). All these issues have shaped the cooperation between Europe and Africa, with different degrees of prioritisation, while their conceptualisation and practical implementation have changed over time in connection with the evolving realities within and outside the two continents. Development cooperation has traditionally occupied a central role in the EU-Africa relationship. However, as described in Chapter 10, by Sarah Delputte and Jan Orbie, the EU's focus has progressively shifted from aid effectiveness to external action impact, while its coordination approach to development cooperation has remained too technocratic, thus overlooking its political implications and the diversity of views within and outside the EU. Human rights and democracy became significant elements of the EU-Africa agenda after the end of the Cold War and since then have shifted to an equation of political conditionality. In her contribution (Chapter 11), *Edalina Rodrigues Sanches* tests the influence of foreign aid in this sector and how this interacts with political institutions, shedding light on the importance of domestic and international driving forces of democracy and human rights in Africa. Peace and security has been gradually added to postcolonial European policy in Africa, while the institutionalisation of EU-Africa security relations is a more recent phenomenon. In Chapter 12, Ueli Staeger and Tshepo Gwatiwa explain how the EU-Africa security relations are now dominated by the 'security-development nexus' mantra, with the issue of African agency coming increasingly to the fore. The assumption of a positive effect of regional integration is a landmark of the EU's relations with Africa and other developing regions. It seems that a potential chapter 13 is missing Giulia Piccolino (Chapter 14) analyses model-setting mechanisms of diffusion of regional integration in the EU's relationships with Africa and focuses on development aid, trade and political dialogue as tools for promoting regionalism. She proposes an assessment of bilateral and interregional dynamics in EU-Africa relations and concludes that despite the narrative on 'Africa rising' and 'partnership among equals', EU-Africa relations remain asymmetric and the EU and its member states continue to impose forms and formats of relations on its African peers. Victor Adetula and Chike Osegbue (Chapter 15) investigate Africa's trade relationship with the EU, with specific attention to the EPAs, claiming that they represent the most visible expression of the unequal partnership. Finally, John Ouma-Mugabe (Chapter 16) discusses the trends of science, technology and innovation in Africa-Europe cooperation. He argues that the two continents have intesified their cooperation in various areas of science and technological development through joint programmes and networks. However, this cooperation should move beyond the established research and development or science initiatives towards more equitable sustainable partnerships in product and process development. The analyses and reflections offered by these chapters stimulate further analyses and reflections on the evolution – in terms of content and approach – of the EU-Africa agenda. On this basis, it is possible to derive some indications on the possible and desirable future issues in EU-Africa relations and the connected changes needed in the research agenda.

Issues in EU-Africa relations: A historical overview

Starting with the immediate postcolonial period, relations between the European Community/ the EU and Africa were traditionally dominated by trade and development cooperation. Today, the EU is still the principal partner of Africa for trading, development and humanitarian assistance. However, key sectors of cooperation became increasingly important in the last 15 years, ranging from security and governance to regional integration, from energy to climate change and from migration to science and technology. This shift in EU-Africa relations has been reflected in a series of landmark steps: the first EU-Africa Summit held in Cairo in 2000, the 2005 EU Strategy for Africa, the new Joint Africa-EU Strategy (JAES) adopted in December 2007 and related implementation documents, including the First Action Plan (2008–2010), the Second Action Plan (2011–2013) and the Roadmap (2014–2017), and up to the 2017 Abidjan Joint Declaration (African Union-European Union, 2017).

The JAES and its two action plans took stock of this evolution and identified eight priorities for cooperation, the first of which was peace and security (African Union-European Union, 2007).[1] The Roadmap 2014–2017 has reduced the number to five: peace and security; democracy, good governance and human rights; human development; sustainable and inclusive development and growth and continental integration; and global and emerging issues. In its introduction, the Roadmap claims a focus on priority areas where cooperation between the two continents is essential and has high potential in the framework of the Joint Strategy and where substantial added value can be expected (African Union-European Union, 2014). These statements reveal the intention to invest political and financial resources on actions that fall within the scope of the strategy as a specific instrument for regional, continental and global partnership, distinct from other frameworks of cooperation.

The EU's promotion of African regional integration, despite significant limitations and inconsistencies, stretches back to the colonial time, as underlined in Piccolino's chapter in this section. However, it became a more conscious and central objective of EU's relations with sub-Saharan Africa starting in the 1990s in connection with the enlargement of the EU's scope and toolbox – not only aid, but also trade and political dialogue. However, as Piccolino concludes, the internal legitimacy crisis affecting the EU is impacting also on its external projection and has triggered a more critical attitude towards its model of integration by African partners, which might be pushed to find alternative solutions for their own continental and regional integration.

At the 5th AU-EU Summit in Abidjan, EU and African leaders adopted a joint declaration outlining new priorities for the Africa-EU partnership in four strategic areas from 2018 onwards: investing in people – education, science, technology and skills development;

strengthening resilience, peace, security and governance; migration and mobility; and mobilising investments for African structural sustainable transformation (African Union-European Union, 2017). The changing priorities included in the basket of the EU-Africa partnership follow the developments of the rapidly evolving political context at the global level and within Europe and Africa. At the same time, they mirror the new strategic vision of the parties that emerged in two landmark documents adopted by the African Union (AU) and the EU, respectively: Agenda 2063, adopted in 2013, which outlines the socio-economic transformation of the African continent over the next 50 years; and the 2016 EU Global Strategy (EUGS) (European External Action Service, 2016), which set the future foreign and security policy agenda of the EU. This is clear, for example, in the extended attention devoted to migration and mobility issues, but also in the change of language from 'democracy and human rights' to 'resilience and governance'.

In parallel with the broadening range of issues addressed in the EU-Africa relationship, its political dimension has been significantly strengthened. The political dialogue at continental level between Europe and Africa has been conducted mainly through the subsequent Africa-EU Summits in Cairo (2000), Lisbon (2007), Tripoli (2010), Brussels (2014) and Abidjan (2017). An ongoing Africa-EU dialogue takes place between summits in various institutional frameworks, at different levels and on different issue areas, including, for example, thematic ministerial-level meetings on foreign policy, migration and agriculture; annual joint meetings between the EU Political and Security Committee and the AU Peace and Security Council with a focus on peace and security and recently focused on counterterrorism, radicalisation and violent extremism, and migration; annual College-to-College meetings between the European Commission and the AU Commission and contacts and meetings between ad hoc delegations from the European Parliament and the Pan-African Parliament to address specific topics. In addition, high-level dialogues and expert level meetings ensure the implementation of the partnership in many sectors, ranging from infrastructure to science, technology and innovation. In fact, this dialogue has been instrumental in fostering mutual understanding and exchange of information between the parties on issues of mutual concern, but ensuring unity of intent on common challenges is still an unaccomplished objective. Moreover, technical expert structures are still affected by a number of shortfalls, mainly due to insufficient communication and coordination.

Lately, the tendency to securitisation and externalisation of the migration agenda has further reinforced the African perception of a one-way dialogue, ultimately aimed at imposing the EU's agenda on its counterpart. This asymmetrical relationship still based on a 'logic of coloniality' is also detected by Staeger and Gwatiwa in the EU's intent to 'modernise African security' and 'in the notion of security-development nexus' as defined by the EUGS and operationalised through the African Peace Facility instrument. The authors correctly claim that the EU has failed to reflect context and local needs in the development of its African security agenda, pursuing unrealistic long-term goals instead and risking running short on tactical, short-term security goals. If the EU wants to remain a relevant partner in African security matters, it has to find a new balance in agenda setting and create space for 'African agency' within its security system.

Political conditionality: A shrinking space for democracy and human rights

The EU is often labelled as a 'normative power' (Manners, 2002), and one of the crucial characteristics of EU external action can be identified in the promotion of basic principles such as democracy and human rights. However, is this normative power a distinct feature of the EU compared to the other main global actors or is it mainly a self-representation? The literature on this issue presents different positions (but often little evidence and systematic analysis), with many authors critical or sceptical about the definition of the EU as a normative power (Crawford, 2013). This is due to the vagueness of the concept (Sjursen, 2006) or linked to the questionable assumption that foreign policy could be only value driven (Youngs, 2004; Hackenesch and Castillejo, 2016).

Certainly, human rights and democracy are widely present in the EU's strategic documents, but this can only confirm the self-perception argument and how the EU would like to represent itself in the public arena. Instead, its political will to act as a normative power can be assessed by considering if these areas are supported financially, if they are promoted through specific policies, if conditionality is effectively and coherently applied and, finally, if they have an impact. Our overall assessment is that the idea that human rights and democracy should conditionate EU development cooperation and trade agreements has been losing momentum in recent years, as discussed below. In this section of the handbook, Rodrigues Sanches presents two generations of political conditionality since the 1990s. The first generation, at the end of the last century, was focused on democracy, and the EU used the Lomé IV suspension clause (suspension of development cooperation with countries perceived to have violated the principles of human rights, respect for the rule of law and democratic principles) several times. Indeed, Lomé IV (1989) represented a peak in conditionality related to human rights. At the beginning of the new millennium, the second generation of political conditionality focused more on governance issues, and the Cotonou Agreement (2000–2020) follows this trend. Except for the emphasis on the support to the International Criminal Court (Scheipers and Sicurelli, 2008), the first two decades of the 2000s show a decreasing political will on the part of the EU to tie its foreign projection in Africa to principles and values.

The JAES, for instance, shows little to no attention on democratic governance and human rights (DGHR) at the political level (Crawford, 2013). While the EU supports specific initiatives related to DGHR – such as Strengthening the African Human Rights System (European Commission, 2015a), adopted in 2015 under the Pan-African Programme – as a cross-cutting issue and conditionality for other programmes, the EU has toned down its approach on human rights, at least since 2014 (Pirozzi et al., 2017). Progressively, human rights are also slowly less central in public documents and narratives. For instance, in the EU's Joint Communication for a Renewed Impetus for the Africa-EU Partnership, the human rights dimension almost disappears, mentioned only with reference to 'encouraging the ratification and implementation of international and AU's own human rights instruments at national level' (European Commission/High Representative of the European Union, 2017: 10). Responsibilities for this trend are shared between the two continents. Part of the African leadership has tried to hijack human rights and democracy in Africa-EU relations. For instance, in 2008 the Egypt of Mubarak, a regime with a long track record of human rights violations, chaired the Africa Implementation Team on DGHR. More recently, Egypt also limited the active participation of civil societies organisations in the JAES framework.

We can define the current phase as a third generation in EU conditionality. Two main observable features characterise this period. Firstly, there is an emphasis on good governance, but mainly subordinated to state-building and formal institutional building with little connection to democracy and human rights support (Crawford, 2013). This means that governance expenditure is oriented to strengthening government capacities, often not considering whether the governments are democratic or supporting of human rights. Secondly, conditionality appears anchored to short-term European interests more than to principles and values. For instance, this can be seen in several African countries where the EU linked conditionality to development cooperation as a means to stem migration and border control in programmes like the EU Emergency Trust Fund for Africa (European Commission, 2015b) and in different bilateral cooperation frameworks in the Sahel.

This third generation has its political and theoretical vulnerability in the 'principled pragmatism' – the combination of realistic assessment of the strategic environment and of idealistic aspiration to advance a better world – enounced by the EUGS. Realist self-interests predominate as an underlying consolidated policy in the EU external action. Human rights and democratic values are practically absent in the reality of its implementation. In sum, this third phase completed a process starting from a chasm between rhetoric and reality on human rights and democracy and leading to a kind of principled pragmatism perspective dominated by EU short-term interests. While the EU declares human rights and democratic principles to be strategic areas, both the EU and African partners are not interested in prioritising, or even acting, in these areas. Sadly, or ironically, as Crawford (2013) states, these areas are an element of partnership in Africa-EU relations in that neither partner is interested in pushing for their promotion.

This trend can be reversed in the future if some political shifts take place. Firstly, a joint work on how the respect of human rights – in all its four generations, from civil rights to sustainable environment – and the promotion of some forms of democracy can be of mutual interest for prosperous growth and healthy institutions in Africa and in the EU. Africa still has several authoritarian and illiberal states. At the same time, the EU experiences increasing trends towards authoritarian and populist leadership. The EU could apply at home the measures suggested abroad and focus on all the transnational and interrelated issues, from trafficking to corruptions, connected to human rights. This approach can also contribute to avoiding double standards and member state fragmentation. The EU should also be aware that conditionality has a minimal impact in a context where African countries have more options in global partnerships. This approach requires deeper analysis of African societies so as to better identify where the triggers of change are in place.

Development cooperation and trade policy between coordination and coherence

In the realm of development cooperation, the EU has made great efforts to improve its aid impact, effectiveness and coordination among member states and beyond. In the first two decades of the new Millennium, coordination represents the 'holy grail' for EU development, as presented by Delputte and Orbie in their chapter. In particular, during the first decade, coordination was mainly considered through the lens of aid effectiveness: we should not forget that at the end of the 1990s, the EU's role in development aid had a bad reputation (Short, 2000). Then, the second decade has shown the progressive inclusion of development cooperation as part of a joined-up EU external foreign projection strengthened by the EUGS. Donor coordination is certainly one of the two pillars, together with recipient ownership (OECD-DAC, 2005) of development aid, in the new century, and the EU incorporated these two tied principles in the Consensus on Development (European Commission, 2005) and in the New Consensus (Council of the European Union, 2017). However, this connection has created a contradiction. For the EU, better internal coordination (e.g. between EU institutions and member states) could mean less space for negotiating with the receiving partners and, consequently, less local ownership (Carbone, 2013). Ownership also remains jeopardised, at best, due to other reasons. Firstly, in many countries the practical implementation of the ownership principle by the local partners is often evaluated more on the basis of their 'commitment to policies' than on their 'control over policies' (Carbone, 2013: 124). Also, the EU bureaucracy is still a challenge for many African partners.

Development being both a technical and a political matter, its inclusion in the framework of EU external action might be taken for granted. The EUGS makes clear that development policy should align with the EU's strategic priorities. As Delputte and Orbie properly highlight, 'its dominant rationale has seen a transformation from ensuring aid effectiveness towards ensuring external action impact'. As a consequence, development has conspicuously become an instrument to contribute to security and migration agendas. For this reason, Delputte and Orbie's proposal to 'support flexible and variable geometry in the cooperation between small groups of donors' is far from being a grand strategy, but stands as a concrete way to keep development cooperation focused on poverty eradication (and not subordinated to other European needs), to make steps forward in coordination and to apply the EU motto 'united in diversity' in its external action. Overall, it acknowledges that coordination is a political process and that it has political consequences, not only bureaucratic and technical effects.

Shifting aid from poverty eradication toward other priorities truly represents a risk for the present and future EU role in development cooperation. From a micro-analysis perspective, it could appear as part of the dynamics of the integrated approach, as a small risk to be managed rather than as a fire alarm, as it is presented by non-governmental organisations. EU civil servants are often reluctant to engage in discussions related to the developing trends of securitisation or externalisation of halting migration. The mantra 'the EU remains the largest donor to the African continent' is often repeated in Brussels. Yet the risk is to bypass the 'leave no one behind' commitment. For instance, the amount of EU aid reaching the least developed countries is not meeting the United Nations target of spending 0.15% to 0.20% of gross national income (European Commission, 2018). According to European Commission data, hosting and assisting refugees in donor countries is the fourth voice in EU foreign aid. Turkey, for instance, is by far the main recipient country due to the high number of refugees and the risk that they head to EU countries. However, if the main objective of development cooperation is poverty eradication, a large part of development resources should be devoted to fragile countries and areas of extreme poverty.

Against this backdrop, governance seems to represent the new hut to cover resources diverted from poverty eradication. Additionally, governance is often connected to human rights, as in the case of the Sahel (Venturi, 2019). As a consequence, it can be perceived by the African partners mainly as a way for the EU to pursue its agenda and as conditionality on reforms and good governance (Carbone, 2013).

Even though national interest is gaining legitimacy as a dominant starting position for international cooperation, the EU can still escape the idealistic-realistic dualism. Brussels can improve European development by encouraging a principled aid approach (ODI, 2019) at the national level: targeting it to the countries that need it most, supporting global cooperation and adopting a public-spirited focus in aid allocations. This approach could be a starting point to 'foster more profound political discussions on global justice in North-South relations', as is hoped by Delputte and Orbie, and can also inspire trade policies. In fact, concerning trade, the EU can learn from the failure of the EPAs and engage with a more nuanced approach when it comes to the African Continental Free Trade Area (AfCFTA). The chapter by Adetula and Osegbue argues properly on how the Cotonou Agreement aligned the trade relations under the EU-ACP framework with the World Trade Organization rules. However, reciprocal and hasty trade liberalisation, combined with market deregulation, could create more inequalities and social problems in the weakest economies. The authors also underline that there is little evidence that the EU-Africa trade relations have resulted in increased capacity for African countries in the global market.

In addition, emerging global trends can affect this approach. Firstly, and notably, African countries and regional organisations have a growing number of relevant partners globally and the EU is only one of them. This trend is clearly providing more alternatives for African countries. The EU will benefit from negotiating fair and balanced agreements, accepting it is just one of the

African continent's trade partners – perhaps while aiming to remain the largest trading partner for African countries. Secondly, in the last two decades the global order has become more illiberal than ever before: this is reflected in a decline in multilateralism and of the architecture of international regulations and global governance. In this changing scenario, unlimited and fast trade liberalisations are inconsistent with development policies and should make space for new approaches.

The EU appears committed to multilateralism, but its ways of dealing with trade and African regional organisations need to be updated. Firstly, as presented by Adetula and Osegbue, the idea that the EU can help Africa to 'to play a full part in international trade' seems entirely out of date. It is now evident that EPAs have created tensions among African regions and new barriers to intra-regional trade. The launch of the AfCFTA generates an opportunity for the EU to support the AU to establish this trade area through new perspectives in the continent-to-continent relations and to avoid fuelling interregional rivalries. Overall, the main challenge for the EU on development cooperation and trade will be represented by the coherency of its policies and programmes. If the EU is to overcome the Eurafrica approach and turn the New Consensus from a policy statement to a reality on the ground, it should work not only on technical consistency but also on making its policies coherent with the principles mentioned in the document. For instance, the massive liberal approach of the EPAs is clearly not consistent with human and sustainable development. This process is long and complex, and it will be possible only through an enhanced political dialogue on all levels and nuanced political economy analysis on the ground.

Bilateralism and interregionalism in EU-Africa relations: An issue-based assessment

The progressive institutionalisation of the EU-Africa partnership has not reduced the complexity of the relationship, which seems to cover almost the full spectrum of possible definitions of interregionalism systematised by Francis Baert et al. (2014), including forms of pure interregionalism, quasi-interregionalism and trans-regionalism. Forms of pure interregionalism – which develop between two clearly identifiable regional organisations within an institutional framework – can be clearly observed at continent-to-continent level between the EU and the AU and in relation to all the issues included in the JAES and its implementation documents, from trade to development cooperation and peacekeeping. These forms also developed between the EU and African regional organisations, which constitute a distinctive feature of African regionalism. The EU's relations with the Economic Community of West African States (ECOWAS) date back to the 1970s: they have traditionally focused on economic integration and trade, with the objective of supporting the establishment of a common market and the creation of a customs union, but the EU's funds increasingly targeted regional security, stability and peacebuilding (Pirozzi and Litsegård, 2017). The support for regionalism towards a customs and monetary union is the priority in the EU's relations with the Southern African Development Community, while in the case of the East Africa Community economic integration is accompanied by a focus on political cooperation, natural resources and the environment (ibid.).

In line with the objective contained in the JAES of developing a 'people-centred partnership' that is 'co-owned by European and African non-institutional actors', European and African partners have strived to create forms of trans-regionalism – that is, transnational (non-state) relations, including transnational networks of corporate production or of non-governmental organisations. However, attempts like the Africa-EU Civil Society Forum, created in 2010 as 'a permanent platform for information, participation and mobilisation of a broad spectrum of civil society actors', have not enabled these actors to play effective and predictable roles in the partnership (Pirozzi et al., 2017). Although civil society networks have managed to impact on issues related to climate change and environment, they remain marginal in other sectors such as peace and security.

Interregional patterns in EU-Africa relations have also taken the form of cooperation between a regional organisation on one side and a country on the other –so-called quasi-interregionalism. One notable example is the EU-South Africa relationship in the field of trade, regulated since 1999 by a Trade, Development and Cooperation Agreement. Since 2007, the EU and South Africa have entered into a Strategic Partnership, which is developed through regular summits and ministerial meetings. Another example is the cooperation between France and ECOWAS specifically in the field of security.

Bilateral dynamics between European governments and African states are still dominating the EU's agenda in Africa and EU-Africa relations. Here it is still important to make a distinction between 'old' EU members, with a colonial past and vested interests in the African continent, which usually have a defined foreign policy line towards Africa and know how to translate it into EU interest, and the Central and Eastern European states, which do not have mid- and long-term strategies and rely on EU institutions for policy setting. These dynamics, Andrzej Polus (Chapter 14) says, can be clearly observed both in relation to trade – dominated by seven EU countries, namely France, Germany, the Netherlands, Belgium, Spain, Italy and Portugal – and diplomatic relations in Africa – with numbers of bilateral embassies in the African continent ranging from 47 French embassies and 1 Slovenian Embassy. In addition, Nordic countries have developed their own agenda on Africa, specifically centred on democracy, gender, environment and human rights, which has been progressively Europeanised in its preferences and principles since the 1990s.

The coexistence of different forms of interregional and bilateral relations has created a complex framework of cooperation between Europe and Africa, which has exposed the EU to accusations of incoherence and lack of accountability and has increased the risk of fragmentation and ineffectiveness in policy implementation. The intersection and overlapping of differentiated patterns of cooperation also makes it difficult to streamline EU-Africa dialogue and policies on issues of common concern, bilaterally and in international fora. This difficulty seems to suggest the need for a reassessment of the cooperation scheme towards an enhanced coordination of EU and national initiatives and the rationalisation of the connected instruments across different policy sectors, as suggested by the leitmotif of the joined-up Union in the EUGS. However, this aim cannot be accomplished without an increased buy-in of those European national governments that are still sidelined in the development of the EU-Africa partnership, in terms of both political and financial capital. The contribution of civil society should also be further encouraged, with a view to ensuring accountability but also to inject fresh ideas in the implementation of the current policies and to include new sectors of cooperation.

Setting the agenda for the future of EU-Africa relations

The analyses contained in Part III of this volume outline the possible and desirable trends in the agenda setting of future EU-Africa relations and the related research priorities. Peace and security are likely to remain a priority in EU-Africa cooperation, due to the many common security challenges affecting the two continents and the increasing attention devoted by the EU to the nexus between internal and external security. However, the EU's approach heavily based on the security-development nexus should be revised, both to attenuate the tendency to divert resources originally allocated to development cooperation and poverty reduction to issues such as border control and maritime security and to target security initiatives based on immediate needs of African institutions and governments. These needs include developing capabilities for conflict prevention and conflict resolution, as well as predictable funding for African peace and security interventions.

The promotion of democracy and human rights has been progressively toned down in EU-Africa relations, also due to growing divergences between the parties and a more pragmatic EU approach to the human rights dimension, including conditionality. For the future, the vision of democratic governance in the EU-Africa partnership should be enlarged so as to promote initiatives to build accountable and inclusive political systems in Africa, beyond electoral processes. At the same time, the respect of human rights should be prioritised, especially in the management of the migration issue and as a shelter against its excessive securitisation at the expense of humanitarian considerations. Setting the post-Cotonou agenda, with a view to rationalising the current relationship and identifying further opportunities to build synergies between the EU-ACP and EU-Africa partnerships, is also a key issue to be addressed by EU and Africa. The EU-ACP was created in a different historic framework, and an exclusive agreement with each region can be a forward-looking outcome for future cooperation. In addition, greater emphasis should be paid to the 2030 Development Agenda and to the transition from Millennium Development Goals to the Sustainable Development Goals. A joint effort should be undertaken – led at the institutional level but involving businesses, civil society, research and academia – to decline the Sustainable Development Goals at the local level (both African and European) and to define major points of contact/cooperation and key actions. This would be instrumental in restoring the link between the allocation of development funds and long-term development goals, not diverting aid from the pivotal objective of eradicating poverty and respecting the principle of joint planning with local partners.

Finally, additional efforts should be devoted to rethinking the promotion of regional integration in Africa and reorganising interregional and bilateral EU-Africa relations. Rejecting the paradigmatic approach that tends to judge the achievements of other integration projects on the basis of the European example is a precondition for a more candid assessment of African regionalism and the delineation of a more context-sensitive agenda. At the same time, the EU and Africa should find innovative ways to integrate alternative forms of interregionalism, including quasi-interregionalism and transregionalism, in the framework of the institutionalised EU-Africa partnership. This also deserves increased attention for future research.

The future of EU-Africa relations will also depend on how the two continents face other new and old issues: climate change, sustainable energy, natural resources and education. Climate change and sustainable energy represent sectors where Africa and Europe can cooperate and work together on common challenges. However, the Partnership on Climate Change, launched by the JAES, came to a deadlock after early enthusiasm (Sicurelli, 2013). In contrast, the Abidjan Declaration dedicated significant space and allocated resources to 'climate change mitigation and adaptation, disaster risk management and reduction, as well as in the sustainable management of natural resources and ecosystems', and its implementation can be pivotal for the partnership (African Union-European Union, 2017). The EU support to an AU-led project like the Great Green Wall Initiative, aimed at halting desertification in the Sahel, represents another example where there have been effects on issues from migration to food security.

A clear and effective pan-African regulatory framework for the management of natural resources is still missing, as well as economic financial agreements between EU members states and African states, both in term of pricing and for the transformation of raw materials in Africa that might guarantee sufficient levels of investment along with more control on the behaviour of the actors involved (Pirozzi et al., 2017). Finally, 'investing in people – education, science, technology and skills development' represents the first of the four key priorities defined by the Abidjan Declaration (African Union-European Union, 2017) where recognition of qualifications is a key prerequisite. Mobility policies are of key importance to let both African and European students and scholars work in, and establish concrete collaborations and build bridges with, the other continent.

Note

1 The eight areas of cooperation were: peace and security; democratic governance and human rights; trade, regional integration and infrastructure; Millennium Development Goals; climate change; energy; migration, mobility and employment; and science, information society and space.

Bibliography

African Union-European Union (2007) The Africa-EU Strategic Partnership, A Joint Africa-EU Strategy. 2nd EU-Africa Summit, Lisbon, 2–3 April. www.africa-eu-partnership.org/sites/default/files/documents/eas2007_joint_strategy_en.pdf

African Union-European Union (2014) Roadmap 2014–2017. 4th EU-Africa Summit, Brussels, 2–3 April. www.africa-eu-partnership.org/sites/default/files/documents/2014_04_01_4th_eu-africa_summit_roadmap_en.pdf

African Union-European Union (2017) Investing in Youth for Accelerated Inclusive Growth and Sustainable Development. Declaration. 5th AU-EU Summit, Abidjan, 29–30 November. www.africa-eu-partnership.org/sites/default/files/documents/final_declaration_au_eu_summit.pdf

Baert, F., Scaramagli, T. and Söderbaum, F. (eds) (2014) *Intersecting Interregionalism: Regions, Global Governance and the EU*. Dordrecht: Springer.

Carbone, M. (ed.) (2013) *The European Union in Africa*: Incoherent Policies, Asymmetrical Partnership, Declining Relevance? Manchester and New York: Manchester University Press.

Council of the European Union (2017) The New European Consensus on Development: Our World, Our Dignity, Our Future. 9459/17. Brussels, 19 May.

Crawford, G. (2013) EU human rights and democracy promotion in Africa: Normative power or realist interests? In M. Carbone (ed.), *The European Union in Africa*: Incoherent Policies, Asymmetrical Partnership, Declining Relevance? Manchester and New York: Manchester University Press (pp. 142–165).

European Commission (2005) European Consensus on Development [online]. http://ec.europa.eu/development/body/development_policy_statement/docs/edp_summary_en.pdf

European Commission (2015a) Action Document for 'Strengthening the African Human Rights System', Annex 2 [online]. https://ec.europa.eu/europeaid/sites/devco/files/annex-2-human-rights_en_0.pdf

European Commission (2015b) A European Union Emergency Trust Fund for Africa. European Commission Fact Sheet. http://europa.eu/rapid/press-release_MEMO-15-6056_en.htm

European Commission (2018) *Investing in Sustainable Development: The European Union's Contribution*. Staff Working Document. Brussels: European Commission. https://ec.europa.eu/europeaid/file/57734/download_en?token=2tdP3V0G

European Commission/High Representative of the EU (2017) Joint Communication for a Renewed Impetus for the Africa-EU Partnership. JOIN(2017) 17 final. Brussels, 4 May. https://eeas.europa.eu/sites/eeas/files/http_eur-lex.europa.pdf

European External Action Service (2016) *Shared Vision, Common Action: A Stronger Europe. A Global Strategy for the European Union's Foreign and Security Policy*. Brussels: European Union.

Hackenesch, C. and Castillejo, C. (2016) *The European Union's Global Strategy: Making Support for Democracy and Human Rights a Key Priority*. Bonn: European Think Tanks Group.

Manners, I. (2002) Normative power Europe: A contradiction in terms? *Journal of Common Market Studies*, 40 (2), 235–258.

ODI (2019) The Principled Aid Index: Understanding Donor Motivations. Policy Briefing. London: ODI. www.odi.org/sites/odi.org.uk/files/resource-documents/12635.pdf

OECD-DAC (2005) *Paris Declaration on Aid effectiveness*. Paris: OECD-DAC.

Pirozzi, N. and Litsegård, A. (2017) The EU and Africa: Regionalism and interregionalism beyond institutions. In F. Mattheis and A. Litsegård (eds), *Interregionalism across the Atlantic Space*. Cham: Springer (pp. 75–93).

Pirozzi, N., Sartori N. and Venturi, B. (2017) *The Joint Africa–EU Strategy*. Brussels: European Parliament. www.europarl.europa.eu/RegData/etudes/STUD/2017/603849/EXPO_STU(2017)603849_EN.pdf

Scheipers, S. and Sicurelli, D. (2008) Empowering Africa: Normative power in EU-Africa relations. *Journal of European Public Policy*, 15 (4), 607–623.

Short, C. (2000) Aid that doesn't help. *Financial Times*, 23 June.

Sicurelli, D. (2013) Africa-EU Partnership on Climate Change and the Environment. In J. Mangala (ed.), *Africa and the European Union. A Strategic Partnership*. New York: Palgrave Macmillian (pp. 149–169).

Sjursen, H. (2006) The EU as a 'normative' power: How can this be? *Journal of European Public Policy*, 13 (2), 235–251.

Venturi, B. (2019) *An EU integrated approach in the Sahel: The role for governance*. IAI Papers, 19 (3). www.iai.it/sites/default/files/iaip1903.pdf

Youngs, R. (2004) Normative dynamics and strategic interests in the EU's external identity. *Journal of Common Market Studies*, 42 (2), 415–435.

10
EU development cooperation with Africa
The Holy Grail of coordination

Sarah Delputte and Jan Orbie[1]

Introduction

Coordination has become the Holy Grail of European Union (EU) development policy towards Africa. Since the turn of the millennium, observers have referred to a 'new season' (Carbone, 2011: 157) or a 'metamorphosis' (Bué, 2010: 43) of European development policy, during which the EU has increasingly attempted to coordinate member states' aims, approaches and activities towards developing countries (Orbie, 2012). Although the EU's 'federalising' role in development cooperation between the institutions and the member states has always been controversial (Carbone, 2007; Grilli, 1993; Holland and Doidge, 2012), the search for more and better coordination has become a key characteristic of EU–Africa relations since the early 2000s. This chapter aims to provide an overview, explanation and critical assessment of what we call the EU's coordination fetish. In doing so, we refer to the major policy documents on EU development and discuss the state of the art of academic literature.

First, we outline the major milestones and some operational initiatives on coordination in EU development policy. In doing so, we recognise that definitions of coordination abound (see Bigsten, 2006; De Renzio et al., 2004; Faust and Messner, 2007; Kjellman et al., 2003; Penh et al., 2004; United Nations Development Programme, 1994; World Bank, 1999), and as a result, coordination can even be considered an 'empty signifier' representing an infinite number of interpretations. While the notion of coordination may seemingly have lost its prominent status, we argue that such an assessment is mainly due to a reorientation of the concept in itself, linking aid coordination to strengthening the EU's external action impact, rather than a sign of the EU abandoning coordination as the Holy Grail of development policy. Moreover, as we indicate, some of the most promising coordination initiatives that were launched in the so-called 'new era' have only recently started to be fully implemented. Furthermore, in line with this handbook's pluralist perspective, we provide various theoretical explanations as to why the EU has focused so strongly on coordination and how we can understand the shift from aid effectiveness to external action impact.

EU development cooperation with Africa

Second, we provide a critical perspective on the EU's coordination imperative. More specifically, our criticism is twofold. On the one hand, we argue that the EU's coordination approach is too technocratic. EU coordination constitutes yet another example of an EU development policy instrument which is defined and elaborated in a predominantly technical and depoliticised manner, hiding the political dynamics that are part of any coordination effort and which include divergent interests, ideas and visions. On the other hand, the EU's approach to coordination focuses too exclusively on the EU level, which is almost blindly considered to be the optimal scale for making progress on aid effectiveness. Moreover, in aspiring to too much power by aiming to play a more central role in coordinating development policies, the EU also increases the risks that its activities will be hijacked by other agendas.

In the concluding section, we argue that in being obsessed with its own international role, the EU has overlooked a diversity of views and approaches that exist within and outside Europe. We put forward a different notion of coordination, whereby the EU would adopt a more modest but potentially vital facilitator role, fostering best practices and more fundamental discussions of foreign aid.

The EU's coordination 'Holy Grail'

Coordination for what?

While coordination has been omnipresent in EU development policy since the 2000s, in this section we distinguish between the first decade of the new millennium, when it was mainly understood in terms of aid effectiveness, and the second decade, when coordination to increase the EU's impact in its external action became the leading rationale (see Figure 10.1).

After several rather unsuccessful initiatives by the European Commission to forge more EU coordination in the 1970s and 1980s and then the inclusion of EU development policy in the Treaty of Maastricht (1993), the 2000 Development Policy Statement symbolises the first expression of the 'European doctrine' for development built on the idea of coordination. The first test in this regard was the United Nations (UN) Conference on Financing for Development in Monterrey, where the EU was able to arrive at a common position and speak with one voice (Carbone, 2007; Orbie, 2003). These events can be considered as early precursors to the developments that occurred from 2005 onwards. In that year, the first European Consensus in

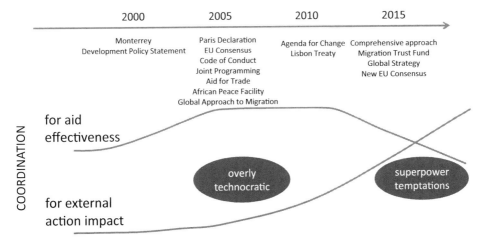

Figure 10.1 The evolving meaning of EU coordination

145

50 years of development cooperation was adopted, which revised the 2000 Development Policy Statement and turned it into a political declaration which applied not only to the EU but also to the member states. These ambitions to foster internal EU coordination coincided with developments at the international level and especially with the 2005 High Level Forum on Aid Effectiveness in Paris. The Consensus comprised a common framework of objectives, values and principles that the EU should support and promote as a global player. In subsequent years, the Consensus served as the main framework for numerous policy initiatives to improve aid effectiveness. While it would go beyond the scope of this chapter to discuss them all, as EU coordination incorporates many different interpretations, a division of labour and joint programming are the most elaborated and operationalised policy ideas in the EU's coordination doctrine.

In 2006, the Commission presented a package of measures to improve aid effectiveness and translate the European vision of coordination into practical policies. Central in this policy package was the introduction of joint programming as a strategy to reduce transaction costs and avoid duplication amongst EU donors. The main objective of joint programming is to incorporate bilateral country programming by the EU member states and institutions into a single EU country strategy which aligns with the partner country's national development plan. One year later, the Code of Conduct on Complementarity and the Division of Labour in Development Policy (European Commission, 2007) between member states and the Commission was adopted. The Code of Conduct laid down operational but voluntary principles for cross-country and in-country complementarity among EU donors. In essence, through the Code of Conduct, EU donors committed to focus on a maximum of three sectors per country (in-country complementarity) in areas where they can bring added value, with a maximum of five EU donors per sector (cross-sector complementarity). Furthermore, the EU member states agreed to concentrate on a limited number of priority countries while ensuring adequate funding for aid orphans and fragile states (cross-country complementarity). To implement the Code of Conduct, in 2008 the EU launched the Fast Track Initiative on Division of Labour and Complementarity in 30 partner countries. In 2009, the Council endorsed the Operational Framework on Aid Effectiveness, establishing a set of joint practical measures aimed at rapidly advancing implementation of the existing commitments.

With the Treaty of Lisbon (2009) and the creation of the EEAS, the EU aimed to achieve more coherence and coordination in its external policies. In the field of development cooperation, the Treaty did not alter the shared competence between the member states and the EU institutions, but reiterated the legal obligation of coordination (see Article 210). In the years after the adoption of the Lisbon Treaty, we can distinguish a slow shift towards a more realist vision of development cooperation in which self-interest takes a more prominent place and development aid is increasingly used as an instrument of the European Foreign (and Security) Policy (Orbie et al., 2016). Accordingly, it is in this period that the EU increasingly framed its coordination imperative in terms of 'integrated external action', thereby slowly stepping away from aid effectiveness as the dominant rationale.

This shift towards more 'superpower temptations' (Orbie, 2012) was already visible in the Agenda for Change, which the Commission published in 2011 with the aim of modernising the EU's development policy. The document puts the focus on economic growth and the mutual interests related to development, such as security and migration. In the area of coordination, the Agenda reiterates the importance of 'working together better' through joint multiannual programming and implementing the Code of Conduct on Division of Labour. However, the shift was even more visible from the adoption of the Joint Communication on the EU's comprehensive approach to external conflict and crises in 2013. In this document, the High Representative of the Union for Foreign Affairs and Security Policy (HR)/Vice-President and the Commission laid the foundations of a joined-up policy to more effectively respond to the causes and manifestations of instability, especially in fragile situations, thereby putting forward the need for comprehensive and coordinated EU responses to address (sustainable) development, peace and security. The EU Global Strategy on Foreign and Security Policy (2016) builds on the same ideas and introduces the concept of an 'integrated approach to conflicts and crises'. It explicitly links the need for more EU coordination and 'unity' to realising the EU's own interests 'in a more complex world of global power shifts and power diffusion' (European Union, 2016: 8): 'our shared interests can only be served by standing and acting together' (ibid: 16). It thus envisages that 'development policy will become more flexible and aligned with our strategic priorities' (ibid: 48).

More recently, the adoption of the international 2030 Agenda and the Sustainable Development Goals (SDGs) spurred the EU in 2017 to 'renew' its Consensus on Development. The New European Consensus on Development links the EU's vision of development explicitly to the objectives of the Global Strategy, in line with the tendency towards a more integrated approach in its external action. The coordination objective is still reiterated in the introduction and the first sections of the Consensus, inter alia under the heading 'Stronger and more effective EU action in a changing world', where EU coordination is discursively linked to the broader concept of 'external action'. However, in the second half of the document, a separate section on 'working better together' shows that the technocratic character of EU coordination remains relevant as well. In this section, it is emphasised that joint programming remains key in the EU's approach to coordination, as its implementation has only recently fully taken off. Additionally, 'joint implementation' appears in the Consensus as a catch-all term for 'more coherent, effective and coordinated EU support based on shared objectives in selected sectors or on specific cross-sectoral themes and tailored to the country contexts', a move which has been welcomed by European development practitioners as an opportunity to enhance the work together (Practitioners Network for European Development Cooperation, 2016).

From this overview, it becomes clear that coordination has been functioning as the Holy Grail for the EU's development efforts in the past decades, although its dominant rationale has seen a transformation from ensuring aid effectiveness towards ensuring external action impact. In the next section, we discuss how we can explain this persistent coordination imperative as well as the shift in its interpretation.

Different explanations

Why has the EU focused so strongly on coordination in its development policies with Africa? This section aims to provide a framework to answer this question and also addresses the secondary question of why the coordination agenda has shifted from aid effectiveness to external action impact. In line with this handbook's pluralistic ambitions, we make a pragmatic distinction between 'ideas', 'institutions' and 'interests', which then allows us to show how the interaction between the three 'i's as viewed from various theoretical perspectives. From an ideational perspective, in the early 2000s a European and international consensus emerged that donor coordination was necessary in order to guarantee aid effectiveness. This resulted in the Organisation for Economic Co-operation and Development (OECD) High Level Forums on Aid Effectiveness in Rome (2003) and Paris (2005). The EU played a proactive role in the construction of the 'Paris consensus' (Carbone, 2007), encouraged by like-minded left-wing policymakers (Development Ministers Claire Short and Eveline Herfkens in the United Kingdom and the Netherlands, respectively; Development Commissioner Poul Nielson from Denmark). Ideational factors also shed light on why coordination at EU level has been so much emphasised, namely the idea of a

'European family' of donors that share common values by virtue of their membership of the EU as a model of regional cooperation (Delputte, 2013). This should be seen against the EU's aspired identity as a leading and moral actor towards the developing world and a normative power in world politics (Manners, 2002; Orbie, 2003; Langan, 2012), which had come to dominate EU discourse in the early 2000s. However, towards the end of the decade, the EU's thinking gradually shifted from more idealist towards more realist views on international politics and development (Orbie et al., 2016). Resonating with this changing ideational context, the idea behind coordination became less framed as 'being better' and more as 'being stronger', less about 'their development' and more about 'our interests'. At the same time, however, it can be questioned whether the EU has a distinctive vision on development or whether it should not rather be seen as a 'norm-taker' from other donors (Farrell, 2008). Lacking a clear and distinct vision on how development should be done – except for signing up to the Millennium Development Goals and more recently the SDGs agreed at UN level – one strategy of the EU has been to highlight procedural and institutional dimensions of development and most prominently the need for coordination.

Institutional factors further explain the pursuit of coordination at EU level. Regional coordination constitutes the raison d'être of the EU and its institutions, or its DNA, as is often stressed in EU public discourse. This 'coordination reflex' also explains why the European Commission has been at the forefront of European coordination initiatives on development (Carbone, 2017). Confronted with loss of responsibilities towards the Directorate-General (DG) for Trade and the DG for External Relations on the one hand and difficulties in performing as a separate aid donor on the other, the coordination agenda provided a new opportunity for the Commission's DG for International Cooperation and Development (DEVCO) to raise its profile and enhance its sphere of action. However, it has been difficult for DG DEVCO to assert itself within turf battles with the EU institutions. With the Treaty of Lisbon (2009), the EU aimed to improve coherence and coordination in its external policies. The creation of the European External Action Service (EEAS) in 2010, led by the HR, heralded an important shift in the institutional architecture of EU development cooperation. The EEAS and DG DEVCO became co-responsible for the programming of development aid, as this should enable the integration of development goals into EU foreign policy and thus allow for more holistic approaches (Kostanyan, 2014; Van Seters and Klaver, 2011; Furness, 2013). Moreover, the former Commission Delegations had turned into EU Delegations which represent the Union instead of the Commission and operate under the authority of the HR. Hitherto primarily occupied with aid and trade matters, they were now given additional political tasks.

This ties in with interest-related explanations. In addition to development-oriented member states' interest in uploading their agendas to the EU level and DG Development's interest in expanding its bureaucratic scope, the EU as a whole has an interest in coordinating in order to strengthen its collective power (Carbone, 2017). The logic behind this is quite simply that more coordination allows the EU to speak with one voice, which in turn strengthens the EU's leverage towards third countries (Buse, 1999). While this leverage was originally seen in terms of advocating for the EU's development principles among other donors, international institutions and partner country governments, it has increasingly been seen to strengthen the EU's overall foreign policy clout (e.g. trade, security and migration interests) and 'superpower status' (Orbie, 2012). In other words, we notice a shift from enlightened self-interest, or 'milieu goals', towards realistic self-interest, or 'possession goals'. Throughout the process, EU development policy and in particular its budgetary resources become increasingly instrumentalised for non-development purposes.

The interaction between these three 'i's explains why coordination has taken such a central place in European development initiatives towards Africa. Depending on one's theoretical perspective, the way in which they interact differs. Schematically, this leads to five theoretical perspectives. Institutionalist perspectives take the ideational consensus on the need for coordination for granted and engage in technocratic analyses of how this could be improved (e.g. improving administrative procedures in terms of planning cycles and financial management (see Carlsson et al., 2009; O'Riordan et al., 2011; Schulz, 2007); this perspective characterises early academic and policy-oriented research.

Political economy accounts proceed from similar assumptions but then examine how institutional incentives (e.g. annual performance assessments in human resource management) can solve collective action problems between member states and create win-win situations through European coordination (de Renzio et al., 2004; Hout, 2012; Hopwood, 2009; Faust and Messner, 2007; Klingebiel et al., 2017). These studies usually take a rational choice perspective. For example, EU coordination, and especially division of labour, has been used by individual EU donors to disguise domestic political motivations. The exit of Dutch development cooperation from Zambia and Burkina Faso in 2013 is an example of a decision which was officially justified by aid effectiveness arguments, whereas observers pointed to the instrumentalisation of division of labour to justify official development assistance (ODA) budget cuts (Delputte, 2013; de Kemp et al., 2016).

Constructivists highlight how ideational factors redefine interests and thereby contribute to overcoming collective action problems and cementing European coordination (e.g. Orbie et al., 2017). For instance, in the early 2000s the EU's desire to position itself as a good international actor fostered EU coordination on development budgets and the 0.7% target even when going against member states' rational interests (Orbie, 2003). Neorealist analyses would contend that member states will only coordinate when this serves their economic and geopolitical interests; for example, by strengthening the EU's power vis-à-vis third country governments and other donors such as China (Holden, 2012). From this perspective, the aid effectiveness agenda constitutes the ideological legitimation, and the EU institutions are the policy vehicle for the advancement of these interests. For instance, the establishment of the EU Emergency Trust Fund for Africa by the EU and most member states constitutes a previously unseen case of efficiency and budgetary commitment in development policy (yet see below for critical notes).

Critical studies also take power and interests seriously. However, these notions are examined in a less reductionist way, through a problematisation of what constitutes 'interests' and a more holistic view of how interests relate to hegemonic discourses within an institutional setting. Their main concern lies less with those who hold power (i.e. western donors) and more with those who lose (i.e. developing countries and their populations). Specifically, the European coordination drive could be seen as an effort to revive the EU as a superpower (Orbie, 2012), as a soft imperial (Hettne and Söderbaum, 2005), a neoliberal (Hurt, 2012), a neo-imperial (Bachman, 2013) or a neocolonial (Langan, 2018) power and/or to legitimise the EU as a morally superior actor (see postcolonial studies such as Rutazibwa, 2010), much at the expense of the so-called 'partner' countries, which lose influence towards donors and remain trapped within a dependency relationship.

While most studies combine diverse theoretical approaches, existing research on European (and international) donor coordination largely falls within the institutionalist and political economy perspectives. Some authors have been informed by constructivist insights. However, neorealist or critical scholars have rarely engaged with the topic of European coordination, presumably because this falls outside their comfort zone. Nevertheless, drawing on related studies of development, as well as on insights from existing studies, a number of critical remarks can be made. This is done in the next sections, which examine the EU's overly technocratic approach to coordination and its almost exclusive focus on the EU level.

Critical perspectives

Existing academic studies usually highlight the constraints in EU coordination, with particular emphasis on obstacles since the end of the 2000s (Carbone, 2017). Instead, we argue that there has been a considerable drive towards coordination of EU policies towards the Global South, although the meaning of coordination has evolved over time (see Figure 10.1), and that this can be problematic for at least two reasons.

An overly technocratic approach

A first major critique of the EU's coordination 'fetish' suggests that it is too technocratic. EU coordination constitutes yet another example of an EU development policy instrument which is defined and elaborated in a predominantly technical and depoliticised manner, hiding the power dynamics that are part of any coordination effort and the variety of ideas on aid and development within and outside the EU. This criticism is not only directed at the EU, but also applies to the aid effectiveness paradigm of the Paris Declaration in general, which put the norm of donor coordination at the very heart of the international development agenda. Critics (Armon, 2007; Burrall et al., 2006; Wilks, 2010) have emphasised that the Paris Declaration is mainly limited to technocratic approaches of efficiency in aid management and delivery, focusing on mechanisms and neglecting the political aspects of development assistance. The Declaration put forward a rather narrow and technocratic interpretation of donor coordination, which can be seen from the definition of 'harmonisation': 'donor countries coordinate, simplify procedures and share information to avoid duplication' (OECD-DAC, 2005). This narrow perspective is also reflected in the indicators to monitor progress on harmonisation (Wathne and Hedger, 2009). It is claimed that as a result, the Declaration risked reinforcing 'micro-management' and the need for quick results (Booth, 2008; Odén and Wohlgemuth, 2011).

In contrast to what EU policies seem to assume, coordination is never a neutral practice. Coordination is inherently a political process, which implies power struggles around ideas and interests, both at the donor level and between donor and partner countries. Although it has been argued that the EU's approach to donor coordination is slightly more political (Orbie et al., 2016), the formulation, operationalisation and implementation of the EU's coordination initiatives still suggest a predominantly bureaucratic approach to donor coordination (see Figure 10.1). The political dimension of coordination is being neglected or even covered up, as if coordination could be achieved through a number of institutional fixes. This is very much in line with the institutionalist perspectives on coordination already discussed. While political economy approaches have also addressed the political dimension of European coordination, they remain largely focused on institutional dynamics. Instead, there is a need for critical analyses that problematise more fundamentally how the coordination agenda indirectly (and unintentionally) reinforces power asymmetries and hegemonic ideas in favour of the EU. Such inquiries would do more justice to the diversity in approaches within the EU and the broader development landscape, thereby explicitly including marginalised ideas and engaging with alternative pathways for better development outcomes. These analyses would reveal at least three fundamentally political issues with the EU coordination fetish.

First, EU coordination initiatives seem blind to the power asymmetry between donors and partner countries in aid coordination processes. Coordination is often donor-driven or even a donors-only process with little to no involvement of the partner country government; this applies especially in developing countries with weaker institutional capacity or less commitment to taking the lead in coordinating the donor community. However, it has been considered fundamental for the realisation of more effective aid that aid coordination processes are recipient-led instead of donor-driven (Hopwood, 2009). Some observers have pointed out perverse effects of the EU's coordination fetish, resulting in less room for partner country ownership (Carbone, 2008). EU coordination is often perceived as inward-looking, top-down and guided by a one-size-fits-all approach which bypasses government leadership (Delputte, 2013). Coordination may even be purposely used as an instrument to maintain or strengthen EU leverage in a developing country, resulting in donors ganging up (Delputte, 2013) or acting as a bloc (Orbie et al., 2017). With the recent (discursive) shift to promoting coordination for the sake of the EU's own external action impact, EU coordination becomes even less aligned to the partner countries' development strategies. As a result, there is less scope for a proper engagement with the partner countries, which undoubtedly reinforces western approaches to doing development and silences potentially challenging ideas.

Second, and in line with constructivist perspectives, there is also much diversity on development thinking within the EU, inspired by different world views, which becomes obscured through the EU's coordination fetish. For example, Nordic countries' development policies have typically been inspired by 'international solidarism' and 'multilateralism' (Olsen, 2011) as well as by 'non-material more altruistic motivations' as they consider development cooperation a 'moral duty' (Carbone, 2007). On the other hand, donors such as the United Kingdom, France, Germany and southern member states are considered to be driven by a more realistic world view which translates into the influence of self-interest in their development policies (ibid.). Different traditions also translate into different ideas about 'doing development', as witnessed by the varying degrees of adherence to the aid effectiveness agenda in general ('well-performing' Nordic Plus versus 'underperforming' southern member states), different sector-specific approaches (e.g. various European views on health assistance; see Steurs et al., 2018) and the different composition of EU donors' aid portfolios (project support and technical assistance versus programme support and budget support; see Koch and Molenaers, 2016), as well as in the use of these modalities (technocratic versus political conditionalities). When it comes to coordination, according to Stern, 'the extent to which donors are willing to harmonise among themselves will depend on the extent that they share development objectives which are not overshadowed by other commercial or political objectives incompatible with development needs' (2008: 46). EU coordination thus depends on the degree to which EU donors agree on its functionality and its potential outcomes in terms of aid and development effectiveness. For example, there is no consensus that coordination at the EU level adds value to what is already being done within the wider donor community (Hoebink, 2004). Our research has even pointed to the existence of a paradox between EU donors' support for EU integration and their support for aid coordination in general, with Nordic Plus donors being more supportive of harmonised aid modalities in general, albeit in a non-EU framework (Delputte, 2013). Instead of cherishing different donor identities within the EU as part of a pluralist engagement with the Global South, several accounts indicate that EU coordination does indeed aim to construct a common European identity, which may conflict with other identities, either national (such as the United Kingdom as a respected influential and responsible donor on its own) or competing collective (the Like-Minded Countries or Nordic Plus donors) (Delputte and Orbie, 2014; Delputte and Söderbaum, 2012; Elgström and Delputte, 2015).

Third, the obsession with coordination and the bureaucratic procedures for its implementation, as well as the current dominant discourse of coordination to strengthen the EU's external action impact, obstructs substantive discussions on what constitutes 'development' and how relations between the 'North' and 'South' should be structured. The EU's development rhetoric, as expressed in the major milestone documents outlined in the previous section, involves the promotion of a range of fundamental principles such as inclusion, equality and equity, or social justice, but refrains from elaborating a vision of or recognising the existence of diverse interpretations of these fundamental concepts. This is in contrast to the attention that has been paid to operationalising its coordination approach to joint programming or division of labour. Even in the run-up to the New European Consensus, such fundamental discussions were absent. In that sense, the EU's coordination fetish risks excluding any thinking outside its own preconceptions and any questioning of its own assumptions about aid and development, thereby neglecting how underdevelopment, inequality and lack of equity are linked to unjust global processes rooted in deeper power imbalances. The lack of a genuine exchange of substantive ideas within and outside its borders raises doubts about whether the EU is able to transcend its rhetoric and contribute to transforming global processes into a more just and fairer world.

In conclusion, both in policy and in the academic literature, far less attention has been paid to uncovering these different power dynamics behind the often apolitically portrayed policies and forms of governance. In refraining from recognising the existence of different interests, the EU also seems to cover up the diversity in approaches and ideas. As we have shown, the recent discursive shift towards EU coordination in terms of ensuring external action impact, which suggests a more political framing, merely perpetuates – and even risks further restricting – the potential of this diversity.

An excessive focus on the EU level

Our second major criticism of the EU's fetish with coordination is that the focus lies almost exclusively at the EU level and is preoccupied, specifically, with how the EU could play a larger role in coordinating member states' development policies. This criticism that the EU aspires to too much power may sound paradoxical, as it is often and rightly stressed that the EU has only limited power in development policy. Development policy is a shared competence with the EU member states, which jealously guard their national prerogatives in dealing with the Global South (Carbone, 2007; Lundsgaarde, 2012; Van Reisen, 1999; Holland and Doidge, 2012; Söderbaum, 2010). However, we take issue with the argument that this calls for more EU coordination.

What makes the EU coordination mantra problematic is that the EU is implicitly or explicitly considered to be the optimal scale for making progress on aid effectiveness. If coordination is really about avoiding duplication and fragmentation, it seems logical to involve *all* relevant donors even if they are not EU member states. Donor-wide and partner country-led coordination is the best guarantee of aid effectiveness and is, therefore, in the interests of the recipient countries – hence the Paris Agenda and its emphasis on international donor coordination. EU coordination, by definition, does not involve OECD donors such as the United States, Canada, Australia, New Zealand, Japan and Korea, international institutions such as the World Bank and UN agencies, and new donors such as South Africa, Brazil and China, all of which play an important role in certain countries and/or sectors.

Against this criticism, it could, and has been, argued that EU-level coordination is a stepping stone towards multilateral coordination. For instance, the Code of Conduct states that

> the EU should act as a driving force for complementarity and division of labour within the international harmonization and alignment process, and that the EU should follow

an inclusive approach that is open to all donors, and whenever possible build on existing processes.

(European Commission, 2007: 6)

The EU has indeed envisaged a leadership role for itself in international development and argued that its initiatives can be emulated at the multilateral level. Most notably, it has proactively contributed to the Paris Agenda and successfully uploaded its principles on complementarity and division of labour to the Accra conference (Schulz, 2009).

Nonetheless, this stepping stone view should be analysed critically. First, research on EU coordination within the UN Human Rights Council (Smith, 2006) and other international fora (da Conceiçao-Heldt and Meunier, 2014) has shown that internal cohesiveness and speaking with one voice does not always lead to external effectiveness. For instance, the energy required to reach internal agreement within the EU can restrict its capacity to engage in external negotiations. Since EU member states are reluctant to cede power in development policy and hold diverse preferences on how development should be done (see above), coordination is bound to be difficult and time-consuming. As mentioned earlier, intra-EU coordination then leaves less room for donor-wide coordination and for negotiations with the partner country.

Second, and more fundamentally, the stepping stone conception of how coordination should be organised is arguably too static and too linear. Given that development policy is inevitably characterised by heterogeneous preferences – donors' views differ depending on domestic politics, institutional requirements, the sector concerned, the partner country context or even individual factors – it cannot be realistically expected to have efficient and ambitious coordination at any level, whether it be the EU or a donor-wide platform. Promising coordination initiatives typically emerge bottom-up from a limited number of like-minded countries whose preferences in a specific (sub)sector and/or in a specific country have converged. Some EU member states have more in common with non-EU countries and international organisations. For instance, the 'Nordics' or 'Nordic Plus' countries tend to differ more from other EU member states than from non-EU countries such as Norway, Switzerland and Canada (Selbervik and Nygaard, 2006; Elgström and Delputte, 2015). While information exchange can be useful and organised at any level, and the EU could facilitate successful coordination between groups of EU and non-EU donors, more ambitious practices of coordination should not be confined within the straitjacket of the EU or multilateral platforms. Instead of the stepping stone metaphor, which conceives of the EU and the multilateral as the two major stones that should be bridged, it may be more promising to envisage coordination as many piles of pebbles of diverse shapes, whose workings should be facilitated without being coerced into a fixed level.

An additional argument against EU-wide coordination is that when the EU acts as a bloc towards developing countries, this can provoke resistance, as it brings up vivid memories of colonial times when Europe imposed its will and local agency was seriously constrained (Carbone, 2008). Criticism of neocolonialism veiled with moral rhetoric has been regularly voiced, for instance when the EU has been negotiating Economic Partnership Agreements or imposing human rights conditionality. This criticism should be taken seriously by the EU, as it has already been shown that intra-EU coordination negatively impacts on partner governments' ownership (ibid.). Instead, a more pluralist approach would allow for negotiations of a higher deliberative quality, involving the discussion of different perspectives on a more equal basis (Delputte and Williams, 2016).

Moreover, if the EU were to play a more central role in coordinating development policies, there is a greater risk that its activities would be hijacked by other agendas. We have already witnessed this in those domains where EU development policy has significant power, namely when it comes to budget that has been instrumentalised for purposes other than poverty reduction. First, the Aid for Trade commitments, which were crucial for the continuation of the European Commission's DG Trade strategy with the World Trade Organization (Hong Kong Summit) and with the African, Caribbean and Pacific countries (via Economic Partnership Agreements) in the mid-2000s, have mostly been financed through existing development budgets (Holden, 2014). Second, the involvement in the African Peace Facility since 2004, financed by the European Development Fund (EDF), has supported the EU's emerging security and defence policy agenda (Keukeleire and Raube, 2013; Del Biondo et al., 2012). Third, climate financing commitments, which were important for the EU to buttress its alleged leadership role in fighting climate change, have led the EU to convert ODA budgets into climate-related assistance, as exemplified by the Global Climate Change Alliance, which has supported programmes tackling climate change since 2008, financed by the EDF and the Development Cooperation Instrument (Brown et al., 2010). Fourth, the EU's attempts to address increasing migration flows have involved the further externalisation of migration policy through the Global Approach to Migration and Mobility (2005) and more recently the establishment of the EU Emergency Trust Fund for Africa (2016), which again is financed with development money (Langan, 2018). Fifth, since 2010 the EU has spent more development aid in its European, North African and Middle Eastern neighbourhood countries than in sub-Saharan Africa (Orbie et al., 2016). If coordination initiatives were more dispersed at multilateral and mini-lateral levels, there would perhaps be fewer chances of their becoming contaminated by non-development agendas that serve the EU's and its member states' more direct political interests.

Last but not least, indications of effective and practical impact of EU coordination are hard to find. In the field, EU initiatives for coordination have often followed pre-existing coordination schemes. Ironically, then, the EU risks duplicating coordination instead of providing real added value (Delputte, 2013). Even joint programming, the flagship of EU development coordination, has yielded limited results so far. In light of initial experiences, the literature is rather critical about joint programming (Carbone, 2017; Orbie et al., 2017). The claim that joint programming paves the way for joint implementation has only materialised in a small number of countries (i.e. Kenya and Cambodia). Where joint programming appears relatively successful, it often builds on pre-existing collaborations between donors. This shows that EU-designed grand schemes for development coordination may not be the most efficient way forward. Instead of taking the long and difficult road from joint programming through joint strategies to joint implementation, a bottom-up focus on coordination initiatives that already exist between a limited number of donors (whether EU members or not) seems a more promising avenue. The EU could facilitate such mini-lateral initiatives instead of wanting to play a central role.

Conclusion

Coordination has been the Holy Grail of EU development policy towards Africa since the start of the new millennium. Building on the existing literature and insights from our own research, this chapter has provided an overview, explanation and critical assessment of the centrality of coordination in the realm of EU development. Our two major critiques of the overly technocratic and EU-focused nature of the coordination both imply that the EU has paid insufficient attention to diversity in development policy. The EU has been mainly (and increasingly) obsessed with its own international role, thereby overlooking a diversity of views and approaches within and outside Europe. While the principle of coordinating European development policies can hardly be contested as such, the way in which this has been done effectively marginalises those who are supposed to be these policies' main beneficiaries. On the one hand, the coordination agenda has focused so much on procedures and technicalities that fundamental political questions of power inequality and visions of development have been overlooked. On the other hand, the coordination agenda has become more and more exposed to superpower temptations. Under the banner of the need for a coherent, integrated and comprehensive approach, original development purposes have become effectively subordinated to trade, security and migration agendas.

Building on these insights, we propose a third notion of coordination that fully embraces the politics and diversity of international development. It concerns a more modest but potentially vital facilitator role whereby the EU does not claim a central role but fosters best practices and discussions of foreign aid. Recognising the diversity of views on development policy, the EU could facilitate (e.g. in terms of budget, expertise, political support) existing and relatively successful coordination practices that have emerged bottom-up (Delputte, 2013). Instead of engaging in grand top-down schemes such as joint programming or Trust Funds, the EU should support flexible and variable geometry in the cooperation between small groups of donors (Orbie et al., 2018). More fundamentally, the EU could foster more profound political discussions on global justice in North-South relations which also dare to question the idea of 'development' and the EU's own ethical stance towards the Global South (cf. Eriksen, 2016). Again, this requires a reflexive position whereby the EU critically examines its approach to development and provides space for debates on a diversity of views. In playing this facilitator role, the EU would become a more 'political' and more 'comprehensive' actor in development, but in a different way than we have seen in recent years.

Note

1   Both authors have contributed equally to the different sections of the article.

Bibliography

Armon, J. (2007) Aid, politics and development: A donor perspective. *Development Policy Review*, 25 (5), 653–656.

Bachman, V. (2013) The EU as a geopolitical and development actor: Views from East Africa [online]. *L'Espace Politique*, 19/2013-1. https://espacepolitique.revues.org/2561, 22.03.2018.

Bigsten, A. (2006) Coordination et utilisations des aides. *Revue d'économie du développement*, 20 (2), 77–103.

Booth, D. (2008) *Aid Effectiveness after Accra: How to Reform the 'Paris Agenda'?* ODI Briefing Paper 39. London: ODI.

Brown, J., Bird, N. and Schalatek, L. (2010) *Climate Finance Additionality: Emerging Definitions and their Implications*. Climate Finance Policy Brief 2. London: ODI.

Bué, C. (2010) *La politique de développement de l'Union européenne: construction et projection de l'Europe par le Sud, 1957–2010*. Doctoral dissertation, Paris, Institut d'études politiques.

Burrall, S., Maxwell, S. and Rocha Menocal, A. (2006) *Reforming the International Aid Architecture: Options and Ways Forward*. ODI Working Paper 278. London: ODI.

Buse, K. (1999) Keeping a tight grip on the reins: Donor control over aid coordination and management in Bangladesh. *Health Policy and Planning*, 14 (3), 219–228.

Carbone, M. (2007) *The European Union and International Development: The Politics of Foreign Aid*. London: Routledge.

Carbone, M. (2008) Better aid, less ownership: Multi-annual programming and the EU's development strategies in Africa. *Journal of International Development*, 20 (2), 218–229.

Carbone, M. (2011) Development policy: The EU as a multilateral and bilateral donor. In J.U. Wunderlich and D. Bailey (eds), *The European Union and Global Governance: A Handbook*. London: Routledge (pp. 157–165).

Carbone, M. (2017) Make Europe happen on the ground? Enabling and constraining factors for European Union aid coordination in Africa. *Development Policy Review*, 35, 531–548.

Carlsson, B., Schubert, C. and Robinson, S. (2009) *Aid Effectiveness Agenda: Benefits of a European Approach*. Brussels: European Commission.

da Conceição-Heldt, E. and Meunier, S. (2014) Speaking with a single voice: Internal cohesiveness and external effectiveness of the EU in global governance. *Journal of European Public Policy*, 21 (7), 961–979.

de Kemp, A., van der Linde, M. and Ouédraogo, I. (2016) *Impact of Ending Aid: Burkina Faso Country Study*. The Netherlands: Ministry of Foreign Affairs.

De Renzio, P., Booth, D., Rogerson, A. and Curran, Z. (2004) *Incentives for Harmonisation in Aid Agencies: A Report to the DAC Task Team on Harmonisation and Alignment*. London: ODI.

Del Biondo, K., Oltsch, S. and Orbie, J. (2012) Security and development in EU external relations: Converging, but in which direction? In S. Biscop and R. Whitman (eds), *The Routledge Handbook of European Security*. London: Routledge (pp. 126–141).

Delputte, S. (2013) *The European Union as an Emerging Coordinator in Development Cooperation: An Analysis of EU Coordination in Tanzania, Zambia, Burkina Faso and Senegal*. Doctoral dissertation, Ghent University. https://biblio.ugent.be/publication/3262275

Delputte, S. and Orbie, J. (2014) The EU and donor coordination on the ground: Perspectives from Tanzania and Zambia. *The European Journal of Development Research*, 26 (5), 676–691.

Delputte, S. and Söderbaum, F. (2012) European aid coordination in Africa: Is the Commission calling the tune? In S. Gänzle, D. Makhan and S. Grimm (eds), *The European Union and Global Development: An 'Enlightened Superpower' in the Making?* Hampshire: Palgrave (pp. 37–56).

Delputte, S. and Williams, Y. (2016) Equal partnership between unequal regions? Assessing deliberative parliamentary debate in ACP-EU relations. *Third World Thematics*, 1 (4), 490–507.

Elgström, O. and Delputte, S. (2015) An end to Nordic exceptionalism? Europeanisation and Nordic development policies. *European Politics and Society*, 17 (1), 28–41.

Eriksen, E.O. (2016) *Three Conceptions of Global Political Justice*. GLOBUS Research Paper 1/2016. Oslo: Arena Centre for European Studies.

European Commission (2007) Code of Conduct on Complementarity and the Division of Labour in Development Policy. COM(2007) 72 final. Brussels, 28 February.

European Union (2016) *Shared Vision, Common Action: A Stronger Europe. A Global Strategy for the European Union's Foreign And Security Policy*. Brussels: European Union.

Farrell, M. (2008) Internationalising EU development policy. *Perspectives on European Politics and Society*, 9 (2), 225–240.

Faust, J. and Messner, D. (2007) *Organizational Challenges for an Effective Aid Architecture – Traditional Deficits, the Paris Agenda and Beyond*. Discussion Paper 20/2007. Bonn: DIE/GDI.

Furness, M. (2013) Who controls the European External Action Service? Agent autonomy in EU external policy. *European Foreign Affairs Review*, 18 (1), 103–125.

Grilli, E. (1993) *The European Community and the Developing Countries*. Cambridge: Cambridge University Press.

Hettne, B. and Söderbaum, F. (2005) Civilian power or soft imperialism: The EU as a global actor and the role of interregionalism. *European Foreign Affairs Review*, 10 (4), 535–552.

Hoebink, P. (2004) *The Treaty of Maastricht and Europe's Development Co-operation*. Brussels: European Union.

Holden, P. (2012) Looking after the 'European' interest? Neoclassical realism and the European Union's engagement with sub-Saharan Africa. In A. Toje and B. Kunz (eds), *Neoclassical Realism in European Politics*. Manchester: Manchester University Press (pp. 161–181).

Holden, P. (2014) Tensions in the discourse and practice of the European Union's Aid for Trade. *Contemporary Politics*, 20 (1), 90–102.

Holland, M. and Doidge, M. (2012) *Development Policy of the European Union*. Basingstoke: Palgrave Macmillan.

Hopwood, I. (2009) Donor policies in practice: The challenges of poverty reduction and aid effectiveness. In R. Joseph and A. Gillies (eds), *Smart Aid for African Development*. London: Lynne Rienner Publishers (pp. 103–120).

Hout, W. (2012) The anti-politics of development: Donor agencies and the political economy of governance. *Third World Quarterly*, 33 (3), 405–422.

Hurt, S.R. (2012) The EU–SADC Economic Partnership Agreement negotiations: 'Locking in' the neoliberal development model in Southern Africa? *Third World Quarterly*, 33 (3), 495–510.

Keukeleire, S. and Raube, K. (2013) The security–development nexus and securitization in the EU's policies towards developing countries. *Cambridge Review of International Affairs*, 26 (3), 556–572.

Kjellman, K.E., Harpviken, K.B., Millard, A.S. and Strand, A. (2003) Acting as one? Co-ordinating responses to the landmine problem. *Third World Quarterly*, 24 (5), 855–871.

Klingebiel, S., Negre, M. and Morazán, P. (2017) Costs, benefits and the political economy of aid coordination: The case of the European Union. *European Journal of Development Research*, 29 (1), 144–159.

Koch, S. and Molenaers, N. (2016) The Europeanisation of budget support: Do government capacity and autonomy matter? *European Politics and Society*, 17 (1), 90–104.

Kostanyan, H. (2014) The rationales behind the European External Action Service: The principal-agent model and power delegation. *Journal Of Contemporary European Research*, 10 (2), 166–183.

Langan, M. (2012) Normative power Europe and the moral economy of Africa–EU ties: A conceptual reorientation of 'normative power'. *New Political Economy*, 17 (3), 243–270.

Langan, M. (2018) Security, development, and neo-colonialism. In *Neo-Colonialism and the Poverty of 'Development' in Africa*. Basingstoke: Palgrave Macmillan (pp. 149–175).

Lundsgaarde, E. (2012) The future of European development aid. *Futures*, 44 (7), 704–710.

Manners, I. (2002) Normative power Europe: A contradiction in terms? *Journal of Common Market Studies*, 40 (2), 235–258.

O'Riordan, A., Benfield, A. and de Witte, E. (2011) *Joint Multi-Annual Programming. Study on European Union Donor Capacity to Synchronise Country Programming (and joint programming) at the Country Level*. Brussels: European Commission.

Odén, B. and Wohlgemuth, L. (2011) *Where is the Paris Agenda Heading? Changing Relations in Tanzania, Zambia and Mozambique*. ECPDM Briefing Note 21. Brussels: ECDPM.

OECD-DAC (2005) *Paris Declaration on Aid Effectiveness*. Paris: OECD-DAC.

Olsen, G.R. (2011) Scandinavian Africa policies: Value-based foreign policies between British affinity, French national interests and EU norms. In T. Chafer and G. Cummings (eds), *From Rivalry to Partnership. New Approaches to the Challenges of Africa*. Farnham: Ashgate (pp. 91–105).

Orbie, J. (2003) EU development policy integration and the Monterrey process: A leading and benevolent identity. *European Foreign Affairs Review*, 8, 395–415.

Orbie, J. (2012) The EU's role in development: A full-fledged development actor or eclipsed by superpower temptations? In S. Gänzle, S. Grimm and D. Makhan (eds), *The European Union and Global Development*. London: Palgrave Macmillan (pp. 17–36).

Orbie, J., Bossuyt, F., DeVille, F. and Delputte, S. (2016) Van moreel voorbeeld naar bedreigde wereldmacht: de paradoxen van het Europese externe beleid in een globaliserende wereld. In J. Carlier, E. Vanhaute and C. Parker (eds), *De hermaakbare wereld? Essays over Globalisering*. Lannoo: Academia Press (pp. 91–107).

Orbie, J., Delputte, S., Bossuyt, F., Debusscher, P., Biondo, K.D., Reynaert, V. and Verschaeve, J. (2017) The normative distinctiveness of the European Union in international development: Stepping out of the shadow of the World Bank? *Development Policy Review*, 35 (4), 493–511.

Orbie, J., Delputte, S. and Verschaeve, J. (2018) *Variable Geometry in Development Policy: Towards a Facilitator Role for the EU*. European Union Studies Association. www.eustudies.org/eusa-forum/eusa-interest-section-essays/13/download

Penh, B., Medina, S. and Behrend, L. (2004) *Donor Coordination: Strategies and Perspectives*. Washington: USAID Development Information Services.

Practitioners Network for European Development Cooperation (2016) Declaration on Joint Implementation [online]. www.fiiapp.org/wp-content/uploads/2016/11/FINAL-Declaration-08112016.pdf

Rutazibwa, O. (2010) The problematics of the EU's ethical (self)image in Africa: The EU as an 'ethical intervener' and the 2007 joint Africa-EU strategy. *Journal of Contemporary European Studies*, 18 (2), 209–228.

Schulz, N.-S. (2007) *Division of Labour among European Donors: Allotting the Pie or Committing to Effectiveness*. Development in Context, 9. Madrid: FRIDE.

Schulz, N.-S. (2009) *International Division of Labour: A Test Case for the Partnership Paradigm*. Working Paper 79. Madrid: FRIDE.

Selbervik, H. and Nygaard, K. (2006) *Nordic Exceptionalism in Development Assistance? Aid Policies and the Major Donors: The Nordic Countries*. CMI Report, R 2006: 8. Bergen: Chr. Michelsen Institute.

Smith, K.E. (2006) Speaking with one voice? European Union co-ordination on human rights issues at the United Nations. *JCMS: Journal of Common Market Studies*, 44 (1), 113–137.

Söderbaum, F. (2010) *European Union Development Cooperation in Africa: Is the Commission 'Just another Donor'*. Paper presented at the Book Workshop: The European Union and Global Development.

Stern, E. (2008) *Thematic Study on the Paris Declaration, Aid Effectiveness and Development Effectiveness*. Copenhagen: Ministry of Foreign Affairs of Denmark.

Steurs, L., Van de Pas, R., Delputte, S. and Orbie, J. (2018) The global health policies of the EU and its member states: A common vision? *International Journal of Health Policy and Management*, 7 (5), 433–442.

United Nations Development Programme (1994) *Aid Coordination and Management by Government: A Role for UNDP*. UNDP Policy Division.

Van Reisen, M. (1999) *EU 'Global Player': The North-South Policy of the European Union*. Utrecht: International Books.

Van Seters, J. and Klaver, H. (2011) *EU Development Cooperation after the Lisbon Treaty*. Brussels: ECDPM.

Wathne, C. and Hedger, E. (2009) *Aid Effectiveness through the Recipient Lens*. ODI Briefing Paper 55. London: ODI.

Wilks, A. (2010) *Aid and Development Effectiveness: Towards Human Rights, Social Justice and Democracy*. Quezon City: IBON Books.

World Bank (1999) *The Drive to Partnership: Aid Coordination and the World Bank*. Washington: World Bank.

11
Democracy and human rights promotion

Edalina Rodrigues Sanches

Introduction

Research on political change in Africa suggests that it has powerful domestic sources (Bratton and van de Walle, 1997). In the late 1980s, set against a backdrop of severe economic and political crisis, incumbent authoritarian parties in Africa faced intense and persistent popular protests to change the outgoing regimes and to recognise fundamental political rights and civil liberties as law, including freedom of association and expression, freedom to strike, access to free and independent media and free political opposition. But international factors were also influential. The collapse of the Soviet Union and the end of the Cold War meant a breach in the established alliances and the withdrawal of much of the international support that authoritarian regimes in Africa enjoyed (Chabal, 1998). The 1990s also witnessed an uprising of democracy and human rights within the EU policy agenda (Crawford, 2005; 1997; Olsen, 1998; Börzel and Risse, 2004; Molenaers et al., 2015; Brown, 2005; Wetzel, 2011; Hurt, 2004; Williams, 2004; Mangala, 2013a, 2013b). In addition, political conditionally emerged more systematically in donors' official discourses and cooperation instruments, entailing a stronger connection between aid flows and recipients' domestic political performance in terms of respect for human rights, democracy, rule of law and good governance. However, any understanding of the primacy given to these issues must encompass a time-based perspective as well as an empirical assessment of the extent to which aid has effectively helped democracy and human rights prosper. To this end, this chapter is organised as follows. The next section provides a historical background of the main EU-Africa agreements and funding instruments, seeking to locate the points of departure in terms of human rights and democracy promotion policies. Then, a longitudinal overview of key indicators of democracy and human rights is presented (covering most of the period between 1973 and 2017). Finally, a statistical analysis is performed to test the individual and joint effects of aid and domestic political institutions on democracy. The concluding section presents new avenues to explore in future studies.

EU democracy and human rights promotion: A historical perspective

Following the Cold War, democracy and human rights gained momentum in EU-Africa relations and dialogues, and political conditionality emerged more systematically within the EU's external relations. However, a historical perspective allows us to demarcate different periods and important shifts in the salience and priority given to these issues within the EU's broad agenda for development and cooperation (Crawford, 2005, 1997; Olsen, 1998; Börzel and Risse, 2004; Molenaers et al., 2015; Brown, 2005; Wetzel, 2011; Hurt, 2004; Williams, 2004; Mangala, 2013a, 2013b).

According to Williams (2004), the first period (1950s to 1960s) was the 'formative period', during which many African countries achieved independence and the European Community was established by the 1957 Treaty of Rome. The treaty furthermore expressed the European Community's desire to promote trade agreements, economic and social development, and prosperity in colonies and overseas countries with historical ties to European Community member states, and it foresaw the creation of the European Development Fund (EDF) for this purpose (Williams, 2004; Panagariya, 2002). This culminated in the Yaoundé I (1963–1969) and Yaoundé II (1969–1975) agreements between the European Community and African, Caribbean and Pacific (ACP) Group.[1] The agreements retained the original focus on economic relations, and at this point, non-conditionality of development aid was seen as a form of compensation for colonial injustice (Mangala, 2013b). The second period (1970s to 1991) was marked by the European Community's institutional development and the quest for affirming its identity and normative power, with the promotion of democracy and human rights coming across more explicitly in EU development policies (Scheipers and Sicurelli, 2008; Sicurelli, 2010; Del Biondo, 2015). The Lomé agreements signed between the European Community and ACP countries – Lomé I–III (1975–1989) and Lomé IV (1990) – signalled an important shift in the relevance given to democracy and human rights issues. Contrary to its predecessors, Lomé III placed a stronger emphasis on human rights as a definitive aspect of European identity, thereby marking an important normative shift that would infuse the design of future agreements (Mangala, 2013a: 70). Provisions for democracy, human rights and rule of law were included for the first time under Lomé IV, but – at least rhetorically – these issues seemed to have lost salience (Mangala, 2013a: 70). Additionally, there was no link to specific sanctions, in the sense that punitive measures were mentioned but not specified (Börzel and Risse, 2004: 4).

The third period (1991 onwards) witnessed a reformulation of EU development policies resulting from three broad factors: 'the deepening of EU's integration, the end of the Cold War, and EU's willingness to expand its development cooperation beyond traditional ACP states' (Mangala, 2013a: 73). Inside the EU, two documents signalled the paradigm shift. The first was the EU Council of Ministers Resolution of November 1991 on 'Human Rights, Democracy and Development', which made 'promotion of human rights and democracy both an objective and a condition of development cooperation' to be 'applied to both Community aid programmes, administered by the European Commission, and those of the member states' (Crawford, 2005: 574). The second was the Treaty on the European Union (the Maastricht Treaty), which came into force in November 1993. It established the protection and promotion of human rights as a defining principle of the EU identity, which was to be pursued in all activities and levels of cooperation. In terms of external relations, the Common Foreign and Security Policy expressed the EU's commitment with democracy, rule of law and respect for human rights and fundamental freedoms (Crawford, 2005: 574).

In the mid-term review of Lomé IV bis, the EU strengthened the political dimension of the agreement to more effectively bind development policy to human rights and democracy (Mangala, 2013a: 72). This marked the beginning of both economic and political conditionality in EU development policy. Economic conditionality – in which governments adjust economic policies as a condition for aid – has been in place in Africa since the late 1980s via International Monetary Fund and World Bank adjustment programmes and EU aid policies (Flint, 2009: 82).

On the other hand, political conditionality (PC) – that is, 'the allocation and use of financial resources to sanction or reward recipients in order to promote democratic governance and human rights'[2] (Molenaers et al., 2015: 2) – emerged as the most effective tool for engaging recipient countries to work to achieve higher standards in terms of human rights, democracy, rule of law and good governance. In the past, ACP countries had successfully prevented the EU from introducing clauses on democracy and human rights (Börzel and Risse, 2004: 4), and the European Community/EU itself seemed less committed to these principles (Hurt, 2004; Crawford, 2005; Brown, 2005); however, this is no longer the case.

The literature identifies two generations of political conditionality since the end of the Cold War, marking a shift from a more punitive to a more pragmatic and selective approach (Del Biondo, 2015; Molenaers et al., 2015). The first generation was propelled by the span of the wave of democratisation around the globe. Political conditionality was mainly reactive and punitive in character, in that donors resorted to sanction mechanisms such as threats to suspend or reduce aid in cases of human rights violations and democratic backslides (Stokke, 1995, Molenaers et al., 2015: 2). During the 1990s, the EU invoked the Lomé IV suspension clause (Article 366a) several times against countries like Nigeria, Rwanda, Burundi, Niger and Sierra Leone (Holland, 2002: 134). For instance, in 1999, the EU consulted Niger, Comoros and Guinea-Bissau under Lomé Article 366a; coups d'état in the former two and an outbreak of violence in the latter led the EU to apply pressure for the restoration of democracy and rule of law as a condition for the normalisation of bilateral relations.

The outcomes of the first generation of conditionality were mixed at best, with several authors highlighting problems both on the donors' and on the recipients' sides (Crawford, 1997, 2005, 2002; Brown, 2005). In an exercise to assess the effectiveness and consistency of donors'[3] sanctions during the 1990s, Crawford (1997) arrives at interesting results. First, aid sanctions only resulted in a minority of cases, thus revealing the weakness of the measures implemented and the strength of the recipients. Second, the application of sanctions was largely inconsistent, with instances where conditionality was not applied or was applied in accordance to donors' economic and political interests.

The second generation of political conditionality emerged in the new millennium following a turn towards governance issues (Molenaers et al., 2015: 3). The new paradigm entailed that aid allocation was going to be more selective: recipients needed to meet political conditions first. Moreover, aid prescriptions sought to make conditionality more effective. For example, the European Commission Governance Incentive Tranche (launched in 2007) and the Good Governance Contracts (2011) emphasised the need for recipient countries to implement political reforms. In addition, EU member states discussed ways to make the EDF more selective regarding democratic governance and human rights (Molenaers et al., 2015: 2).

The Cotonou Agreement (2000–2020) epitomised an example of second-generation conditionality. It encompassed two innovations over Lomé IV. A first innovation was 'the ending of the nonreciprocal duty free access concession that ACP enjoyed' and a second was the 'imposition of democracy, good governance, and human rights on ACP states as conditions for gaining access to the EU's financial aid largesse' (Babarinde and Wright, 2013: 97–98). Besides the emphasis on political dialogue, it established an enforcement mechanism that included the use of both positive and negative measures in cases of human rights violations. In the latter case in particular, the agreement stated that sanctions must be placed as a last resort (Mangala, 2013a: 73). The Cotonou Agreement was revised in 2005 and 2010. The 2005 revision recognised the jurisdiction of the International Criminal Court (ICC), which prompted Sudan and Equatorial Guinea to refuse to sign or ratify the revision.[4] The 2010 revision coincided with the entry into force of the Lisbon Treaty (2009), which introduced a restructuring of the EU's external relations. The EU felt the need to address the regional dimension of development in order to strengthen relations with the African Union (AU) as a key interlocutor for peace and security in Africa (Bartelt, 2012).

The most recent framework for EU-Africa cooperation is the Joint Africa-EU Strategy (JAES), which complements and overarches all other existing activities and levels of cooperation. The JAES was launched at the Africa-EU Summit in Lisbon in 2007, which brought together the leaders of 27 European and 54 African states, as well as the presidents of continental institutions.[5]

One of the cooperation partnerships established under the JAES is the Partnership on Democratic Governance and Human Rights. Its first Action Plan (2007–2010) underscored the shared Africa-EU belief that 'democratic governance and human rights are key for sustainable development' (Mangala, 2013a: 77). The first priority action aimed for the two regions to move beyond the traditional donor-recipient relationship via the development of joint positions and common interests. The second priority action was to promote the African Peer Review Mechanism and support the African Charter on Democracy, Elections and Governance. This required setting up instruments for a more efficient African Governance Architecture and the institutionalisation of political dialogue under an African Governance Platform, which represents two particularities not found in any of the other JAES thematic partnerships (Mangala, 2013a: 77). The third priority action was to strengthen cooperation in the area of cultural goods,

> which included a key demand from African states – the return of illegally acquired cultural goods – and a long standing issue that speaks to a colonial past that saw the looting of African cultural treasuries now on display in Western cities' museums and other private collections.
>
> *(Mangala, 2013a: 77–78)*

In terms of conditionality, the approach taken seemed to be more pragmatic and less punitive. As stated in the JAES,

> the EU will work toward a limitation of conditionalities and further move towards result-oriented aid, with a clear link with [Millennium Development Goal] indicators and performance. In this context, Africa and the EU will also improve and expand their cooperation in the field of statistics so that policies and decisions are made on the basis of clear evidence.

Plus, some aspects, such as human rights conditionality and the ICC, are judged more pragmatically 'with a view to give the AU full responsibility for implementation' (Pirozzi et al., 2017: 34). At the 28th African Union Summit in Addis Ababa (22–31 January 2017), heads of state and government adopted a strategy for withdrawing the ICC over the Court's alleged institutional bias against Africa and its leaders.[6] Countries like South Africa, Gambia and Burundi have publicity announced their intention to leave the ICC Yet only the latter left.

The promotion of democracy and human rights has been pursued through various financial instruments (see Table 11.1). The most substantial resource for sub-Saharan African countries is the EDF, which was established in 1959. Other instruments include the European Neighbourhood Instrument for North Africa, the Development Cooperation Instrument (DCI), the European Instrument for Democracy and Human Rights (EIDHR), the EU regulation (no 235/2014) that establishes a financing instrument for democracy and human rights worldwide and the Trust Fund for Africa,[7] which also supports improvements in overall governance by promoting conflict prevention, addressing human rights abuses and enforcing the rule of law. EU member states' own aid programs are also bound to democracy and human rights through their EU obligations

Table 11.1 Promotion of human rights and democracy: Key agreements and funding instruments

	1959–1989	Pre 1989	1990s		2000	
Agreements	Yaoundé I (1963–1969) and Yaoundé II (1969–1975)	Lomé I–III (1975–1989)	Lomé IV (1990)	Lomé IV bis (1995)	Cotonou (2000–2020)	JAES (2007)
Human rights and democracy	Withdrawal of human rights aspects from development policy	Reference to human dignity and economic, social and cultural rights in Lomé III (but not in Lomé I and II)	Provisions on democracy, human rights and rule of law	Provisions on democracy, human rights, rule of law and good governance	Provisions on democracy, human rights, rule of law and good governance	Provisions on peace and security, democracy, good governance, human rights and human development
Political conditionality	No PC	No PC	1st generation PC	1st generation PC: • Suspension clause for democracy, human rights and rule of law violations • Political dialogue	2nd generation PC: • Suspension clause for democracy, human rights, rule of law and good governance violations (corruption) • Political dialogue	2nd generation PC: • Strengthening of political dialogue • Pragmatic approach
Main funding instruments	EDF (1959–)				EDF (1959–); EIDHR* (2000–2006); EIDHR (2007–2013); DCI**; Regulation (EU) No 235/2014; Trust Fund for Africa	

Notes: * European Initiative for Democracy and Human Rights. ** Through the thematic line 'Global Public Goods and Challenges and Civil Society and Local Authorities'.

Source: Author's compilation on the basis of selected contributions (Börzel and Risse, 2004; Crawford, 1997; Panagariya, 2002; Molenaers et al., 2015; Mangala, 2013a; Williams, 2004)

Table 11.2 Net disbursements of ODA to sub-Saharan Africa, by donor

	USD million at 2015 prices and exchange rates						
	2000–2001ª	2005–2006ª	2012	2013	2014	2015	2016
Australia	59	64	269	240	136	91	69
Austria	202	340	148	71	53	47	53
Belgium	333	707	665	474	427	403	434
Canada	287	805	1,369	1,144	982	944	942
Czech Republic	1	5	6	5	5	5	6
Denmark	645	666	645	542	498	382	439
Finland	103	163	238	249	275	213	159
France	1,615	4,059	2,681	1,820	1,596	1,645	1,449
Germany	1,033	2,834	2,060	1,400	1,507	1,872	2,256
Greece	3	11	5	1	2	1	0
Hungary		5	1	1	0	1	3
Iceland	6	7	11	16	14	13	13
Ireland	174	327	313	301	298	272	251
Italy	361	979	91	97	137	196	294
Japan	758	1,644	1,138	1,664	1,070	1,419	993
Korea	9	38	238	250	298	341	394
Luxembourg	70	106	91	99	107	121	118
Netherlands	1,057	1,287	612	697	622	618	632
New Zealand	11	18	6	4	10	8	8
Norway	515	716	616	676	635	614	615
Poland	1	47	2	37	34	43	82
Portugal	182	124	258	212	167	94	63
Slovak Republic		21	2	2	2	2	2
Slovenia			1	1	0	0	0
Spain	144	408	218	313	100	32	112
Sweden	501	818	828	859	817	803	799
Switzerland	278	403	434	453	509	550	507
United Kingdom	1,560	4,534	3,164	3,599	3,670	3,805	3,732
United States	1,669	5,681	9,001	9,575	9,564	9,413	9,780
DAC (total)	11,577	26,815	25,109	24,800	23,535	23,948	24,204
Multilateral Agencies (total)	7,070	10,992	15,924	16,840	16,337	17,993	17,368
Other countries (total)	230	174	362	314	278	773	493
Total	18,877	37,982	41,395	41,954	40,150	42,714	42,065

Notes: ª average values.

Source: OECD statistics on resource flows to developing countries: www.oecd.org/dac/financing-sustainable-development/development-finance-data/statisticsonresourceflowstodevelopingcountries.htm

(Crawford, 2005: 576–577). Table 11.2 presents the Net official development assistance (ODA) to sub-Saharan Africa. The longitudinal trend is upward (with the exceptions of 2014 and 2016), and the largest contributors are members of the Development Assistance Committee (DAC). On average, their contributions amount to 60% of the overall aid flows. Given that the DAC is mostly composed of EU members (23 out of 29), the EU remains Africa biggest donor. However, only a small share of aid is dedicated to human rights issues, despite the increase verified since

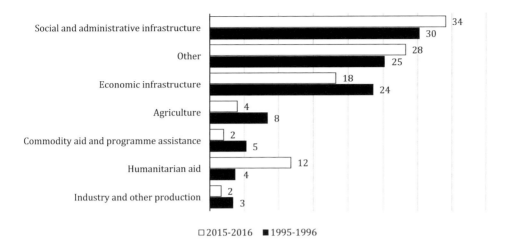

Figure 11.1 Major aid uses by individual Development Assistance Committee donors (% of total bilateral commitments)

Source: OECD – Statistics on resource flows to developing countries: www.oecd.org/dac/financing-sustainable-development/development-finance-data/statisticsonresourceflowstodevelopingcountries.htm

1995–1996 (Figure 11.1). This suggests that donors' emphasis on democracy and human rights has not been supported by actual aid flows (Brown, 2005: 193).

Looking more specifically at the share of aid dedicated to good governance and civil society through the EU's various instruments allows us to complement this depiction (Figure 11.2). During the 2007–2016 period, 37% of the total EU development aid was allocated to supporting democratic institutions and principles (participation, civil society, elections, human rights, women's equality, free media, legislatures and political parties), while 63% was aimed at improving the effectiveness of government institutions in areas such as public policy and public administration management, legal and judicial reform, management of public finances, the fight against corruption and decentralisation (Zamfir, 2018).

In terms of regional distribution, most of the recipients of the largest amounts of EU governance aid are mainly located in the Western Balkans and the EU's eastern and southern regions. Among the recipients not located close to the EU, some – namely Afghanistan, the Democratic Republic of the Congo, Iraq and Mali – have been affected by major episodes of political conflict, while others – Côte d'Ivoire and Nigeria, for example – still have fragile political systems despite significant democratic improvements (Zamfir, 2018: 8). Additionally, the EU has sent electoral observation missions and has provided electoral support to partner countries, overseeing over 170 elections to date, 87 of which were in sub-Saharan and North African countries.[8]

The mixed outcomes of aid and political conditionality

Whether aid and political conditionality are effective in promoting democratisation and human rights remains unclear. A 25-year lag shows that the span of Huntington's Third Wave of democratisation across Africa from the 1990s onwards has produced diverse outcomes (Cheeseman, 2015). After an initial enthusiasm that saw political miracles in the demise of one-party regimes

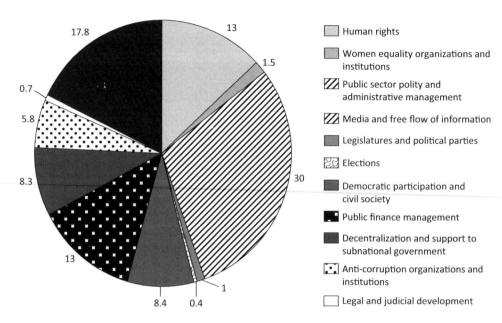

Figure 11.2 Percentage of EU development aid (gross disbursements) for good governance, as received by various sectors (2007–2016)
Source: OECD DAC, ODA – Creditor Reporting System data, via Zamfir (2018)

(Joseph, 1991) and highlighted the important gains of multiparty elections for democratic performance (Lindberg, 2006), more disenchanted assessments wondered if the democratic tide had faded out. In the face of authoritarian resilience, personalised rule and one-party dominance (Ndegwa, 2001) labels such as pseudo or hybrid democracies became mainstream in the portrayal of 'the reality across the sub-continent' (Lynch and Crawford, 2011: 281). The different meanings and definitions of democracy that exist (Diamond and Morlino, 2004) make the exercise of assessing the quality of democracy somewhat difficult. Still, most projects – despite using different definitions and estimation methods – depict Africa as the least democratic continent in the world.

Looking at Freedom House time-series data (Figure 11.3), it is possible to observe that after an initial boom in the early 1990s, the number of liberal (free) democracies froze and most countries remain stuck in the group of electoral democracies (partly free), meaning that they meet the minimum requirement of regular multiparty elections, or autocracies (not free), where substantive freedoms and political rights are absent.[9] In fact, from 2006 onwards, 'the expansion of freedom and democracy in the world came to a prolonged halt. … there has been no net expansion in the number of electoral democracies' (Diamond, 2015: 142).

The notion of human rights is also a subject for debate. According to Messer (1993: 222–223), four generations of human rights can be identified. The first generation – on political and civil rights and individuals' security – was strongly infused with Western political concepts and was emphasised in the United Nations Universal Declaration of Human Rights. The second generation placed welfare concepts – such as cultural, social and economic rights – at the centre. The third generation added important issues for Third World nations – especially in Africa – namely solidarity, development, rights to peace, a more equitable socio-economic order and a sustainable environment. The fourth generation sought to contest the universalism of Western human rights and underscored indigenous rights (Messer, 1993: 222–223).

Democracy and human rights promotion

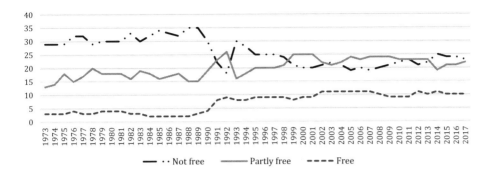

Figure 11.3 Freedom in Africa (1973–2017)
Note: The graph shows the number of countries in each category.
Source: Freedom House: https://freedomhouse.org/

Bearing this discussion in mind, in order to provide a longitudinal overview of human rights in Africa, we draw on three indices from the Cingranelli-Richards Human Rights Project, which are available for the 1981–2011 period. The Empowerment Rights Index is an additive index clustering indicators for foreign and domestic movement, freedom of speech, freedom of assembly and association, freedom of religion, workers' rights and electoral self-determination; it ranges from 0 (no government respect for these seven rights) to 14 (full government respect for these seven rights). The Physical Integrity Rights Index is an additive index constructed from the torture, extrajudicial killing, political imprisonment and disappearance indicators; it ranges from 0 (no government respect for these four rights) to 8 (full government respect for these four rights). Finally, the Women's Rights Index collapses the economic, political and social rights of women; it ranges between 0 (if none of these rights for women existed in the law and if systematic discrimination based on sex may have been built into the law) and 3 (if all or nearly all of women's social rights were guaranteed by law and the government fully and vigorously enforced these laws in practice).

As Figure 11.4 shows, there is a slight increase in terms of government respect for empowerment rights from 1990 onwards. This is no surprise, as many studies document that nearly all states in sub-Saharan Africa conducted important reforms between 1989 and 1994, entailing the changing of constitutions, introducing freedom of assembly and association, free political opposition, free media, inter alia (Bratton and van de Walle, 1997). Still, it is important to note that during this decade, the average government respect for empowerment rights was of 7 out of 14. This score then decreased in the new millennium, following the global democratic recession trends (Diamond, 2015). Governments' respect for physical integrity rights follows a downward trend in the years leading to 1990, but then it exhibits a small improvement over time. Notwithstanding, the average respect for physical integrity rights is 4 out 8. In terms of women's rights, advances are negligible. For most of the period observed, there is a situation in which women have some economic, political and social rights in law, but these rights are not effectively enforced. Countries that are consistently highly ranked in these three indices are: Mauritius, Cape Verde, São Tomé and Príncipe, Botswana and Namibia; these countries have been systematically rated as free democracies since political transition. At the opposite end, the most extreme cases of human rights violations include some of the most authoritarian regimes: Equatorial Guinea, Somalia, Democratic Republic of the Congo, Libya and Sudan.

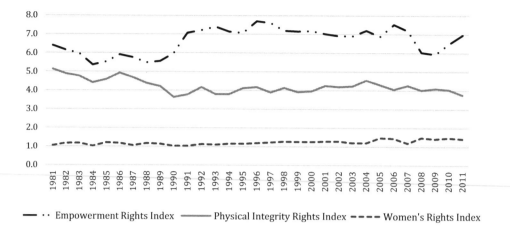

Figure 11.4 Overview of selected human rights in Africa (1981–2011)
Notes: Empowerment Rights Index (varies between 0 and14), Physical Integrity Index (varies between 0 and 8), Women's Rights Index (varies between 0 and 3).
Source: The Cingranelli-Richards Human Rights Data Project: www.humanrightsdata.com/

Several domestic and international factors can account for these developments, and one important question that has been debated is whether aid and conditionality actually promote democracy and what are the explanations for the mixed results observed (Hout, 2012; Brown, 2005; Crawford, 1997, 2005; Del Biondo, 2015, 2011; Olsen, 1998; Diamond, 1995). On the recipient side, it has been suggested that important structural impediments such as 'poverty and long-term economic crises, recent independence, a weak and often predatory state', 'few institutionalized democratic practices', clientelism and 'authoritarian legacies of administrative weakness' stalled democratic prospects (Brown, 2005: 183). On the donor side, it has been argued that conditionality often encourages a rapid transition to a formal electoral democracy that hinders democratisation in the long run, that it fuels rivalries and interethnic violence and that it does not prevent democratic reversals (Brown, 2005: 182). Moreover, although EU aid programs seek to conciliate democracy, good governance and development, the real practice falls short of that; in most sub-Saharan African countries, the democratic approach is limited (Del Biondo, 2011), the development models implemented are technocratic and apolitical, and development tends to prevail over democracy in cases of goal conflicts (Hout, 2012).

Taking a neorealist perspective, Olsen (1998: 346) argues that donors' actions are mainly 'determined by national interests' and that '"soft" issues such as human rights and democracy' are secondary when compared to 'hardcore issues like security and economic interests'. Using the example of South Africa, Olsen shows how the EU's main concern was with how the 'apartheid regime would threaten the stability and thereby the security of the whole South African region'; thus, support for democracy and human rights in South Africa was heavily motivated by EU security concerns (ibid.: 348–353). In fact, in several other studies, donors' strategic interests appear as an important factor for explaining aid allocation, selective application of political conditionality and sanctions (Alesina and Dollar, 2000; Reinsberg, 2015; Del Biondo, 2015; Warkotsch, 2008; Crawford, 1997). In addition to the aforementioned studies, Brown (2005) points to lack of commitment, lack of understanding of democratisation and how to assist it, failure to acknowledge domestic politics and competing economic, commercial and security priorities as the main problems on the donor side. The recipients' political performances also matter, as democratic countries or countries that have undergone a major political transition tend to receive more aid (Alesina and Dollar, 2000; Reinsberg, 2015). This follows an evolution from a more punitive kind of conditionality to aid selectivity, whereby recipients are required to meet certain political reforms first (Del Biondo, 2015: 75).

Regarding the application of sanctions, studies show that the EU is more likely to respond to non-compliance in more effective ways in neighbouring countries than in non-neighbouring ones and that member states tend to block strong measures against countries considered important to their national interests (Reinsberg, 2015; on the latter argument, see Crawford, 2005). Del Biondo's (2015) study also strengthens this idea. It demonstrates that sub-Saharan African countries that fall into the areas of interest of the donors or that present good developmental performance are shielded from sanctions, confirming that conditionality and sanctions are only applied in the absence of donor interests.

Reassessing the aid and democracy nexus

Research on democratisation has produced interesting findings on the global drivers of democracy (Norris, 2008; Teorell, 2010; Geddes, 2011). In Africa, three main lines of inquiry can be identified. A first stream argues about the relevance of structural factors – for example, colonialism, ethnicity and modernisation – for the likelihood of democracy. It claims that independence did not mean a complete rupture with colonialist power structures; instead, these structures often served as starting points for incumbents to continue implementing authoritarian rule and to craft personalised institutions (Clapham, 1993; Young, 2012). Ethnicity is far from being harmful to democracy (Kapstein and Converse, 2008) and is found to determine relatively little of how democracy will eventually play out (Beissinger, 2008: 89). In fact, high ethnic fractionalisation seems to be compatible with democracy, particularly where power-sharing institutions are at work (Linder and Bächtiger, 2005; Reilly, 2001; Norris, 2008). The evolutionary scheme brought to us by modernisation theorists (Lipset, 1959) appears to have little influence in Africa (Bratton and van de Walle, 1997) or elsewhere. In an already classical study, Przeworski and Limongi (1997: 177) demonstrate that 'the emergence of democracy is not a by-product of economic development' and that democracy 'can be initiated at any level of development' (for similar results, see Teorell, 2010).

A second stream focuses on the role of political institutions. While power-sharing institutions are positively linked to the quality of democracy, presidential powers and majoritarian political institutions seem to have the opposite effect (van Cranenburgh, 2011). Similarly, informal practices such as clientelism and patronage usually stand out in the literature as key mechanisms through which incumbents undermine effective bureaucracies, the rule of law and democratic representation (van de Walle, 2003). A third stream considers international determinants, particularly how the diffusion of democratic ideas, pressure from international financial institutions and membership in intergovernmental organisations (IGOs) affect democratisation (Geddes, 2011; Teorell, 2010: 89–90; Pevehouse, 2005; Finkel et al., 2007). However, only rarely have international factors been considered in large-N statistical analyses. A recent exception is Teorell's (2010) study on the determinants of democracy worldwide. It shows that whether a country is peripheral and heavily dependent on external aid, has a democratic or undemocratic neighbour and has membership in international organisations are important in explaining democratic outcomes.

Seeking to test the main arguments put forward by each literature stream, particularly the one focusing on the international dimensions of democracy, a set of ordinal panel regression analyses were performed. In all models, the dependent variable was the country's Freedom House score (1 = not free, 2 = partly free, 3 = free) between 1990 and 2016. The independent variables related to international influence included foreign aid, measured by ODA (as current US dollars and as a percentage of gross national income – GNI), and membership in IGOs, measured as the total number of organisations in which a state was a full member. Both were expected to act in favour of democracy. Aid exerts this influence through conditionality, while IGOs lead member states to commit to certain democratic principles and procedures through mechanisms of pressure, acquiescence and legitimation (Pevehouse, 2005).

In terms of political institutions, indices measuring judicial and legislative constraints on the executive level were included, as higher constraints on the executive level were also expected to benefit democracy (Kapstein and Converse, 2008: 57). Additionally, we expected the effects of international factors to interact with local political dynamics and institutions. In other words, the effect of development aid on democracy is likely to be more positive in countries where there are stronger institutional mechanisms for accountability than in countries where accountability mechanisms are weaker. These expectations were tested, controlling for important structural factors that compete to explain the likelihood of democracy: major episodes of political violence (sum of all societal and interstate conflicts), gross domestic product (GDP) (annual percentage growth), the Human Development Index (HDI) and ethnic fractionalisation (collapses levels of linguistic, ethnic and religious fractionalisation; varies between 0 = complete homogeneity and 1 = complete heterogeneity).[10]

The results presented in Table 11.3 support most of the theoretical expectations. Starting with Model 1, the higher the amount of ODA, as well as the levels of constraints on the executive branch, the higher the levels of democracy. Membership in IGOs is not a significant predictor, but it goes in the hypothesised direction, thereby confirming the extant literature on the topic (Finkel et al., 2007; Pevehouse, 2005; Teorell, 2010). Among the controls, only GDP is a systematic and significant predictor of democracy; all of the other structural variables have limited (major episodes of political violence and ethnic fractionalisation) or no significant effect on democracy (measured via the HDI). In Models 2 and 3, the aim was to confirm whether there was a joint and positive effect of aid and constraints on the executive branch. The results suggest that this is in fact the case; aid has a strong effect on democracy, particularly where there are higher judicial controls on the executive branch. The same happens when it comes to legislative constraints on the executive branch, though the effect is smaller.

Conclusion

Democracy and human rights are not exclusively driven by domestic forces. International dimensions such as aid flows also matter. Through mechanisms of pressure and conditionality, aid can serve as an engine for the improvement of democratic procedures, contents and outputs, including respect for basic human rights. In the preceding pages, we have seen that the 'lion's share' of aid goes to development issues and that conditionality (when it comes to applying sanctions) usually follows the donors' security or economic interests. Because of this, it may be the case that in some countries, aid actually hinders democratisation by fostering growth among authoritarian regimes (Teorell, 2010: 158). The empirical analysis conducted here highlights the relevance of aid, and most determinately it highlights the importance of domestic political institutions for democracy.

Table 11.3 Determinants of democracy

	Model 1		Model 2		Model 3	
	Coefficient	Standard error	Coefficient	Standard error	Coefficient	Standard error
International factors						
ODA (current USD)	0.00	(0.00)*	0.00	(0.00)*	0.00	(0.00)
Net ODA received (% of GNI)	0.01	(0.01)	0.01	(0.01)	0.01	(0.01)
IGO membership (total of IGOs)	0.01	(0.02)	0.02	(0.02)	0.02	(0.02)
Political institutions						
Judicial constraints on the executive branch index	8.36	(1.41)***	7.00	(1.48)***	8.32	(1.42)***
Legislative constraints on the executive branch index	7.20	(1.32)***	6.98	(1.33)***	6.80	(1.35)***
Interactions						
ODA (current US)#Judicial constraints on the executive branch index			0.00	(0.00)**		
ODA (current US)#Legislative constraints on the executive branch index					0.00	(0.00)+
Structural factors (controls)						
Major episodes of political violence	−0.20	(0.12)	−0.22	(0.13)+	−0.20	(0.13)
GDP (annual growth rate)	0.08	(0.03)**	0.08	(0.03)**	0.08	(0.03)**
HDI	1.85	(4.87)	2.12	(4.98)	1.27	(4.90)
Ethnic fractionalisation	−4.56	(3.30)	−6.70	(3.40)*	−5.42	(3.36)
Year dummies	yes		Yes		Yes	
Country dummies	yes		yes		yes	
/cut1	5.51	(3.21)+	4.14	(3.27)	4.44	(3.28)
/cut2	12.92	(3.35)***	11.56	(3.41)**	1.20	(3.41)***
/sigma2_u	0.00	(0.00)	0.00	(0.00)	0.00	(0.00)
Number of observations	965		965		965	
Number of groups	26		26		26	

Notes: order logistic regressions (xtologit); coefficients are significant at + $p<0.10$, * $p<0.05$, ** $p<0.01$, *** $p<0.001$.

Future studies should continue to explore the interaction between aid and recipient countries' political settings to see whether the direct effect of aid on democracy is mediated by the design of political institutions, the nature of competition for government and the levels of corruption. By the same token, it is important to see how the effects of aid vary according to different political and economic cycles. Additionally, there is still little evidence of the role of regional IGOs on the promotion of democracy and human rights, as well on how political parties and civil society organisations campaign on these issues. A focus on these topics would offer important contributions to the literature on the domestic and international driving forces of democracy and human rights in Africa. Finally, given the resilience of various forms of authoritarianism in Africa, it becomes increasingly important to reassess the effects of aid in authoritarian regimes.

Notes

1 In 2020, the ACP Group became the Organisation of African, Caribbean and Pacific States.
2 Molenaers et al. (2015) advance a new conceptualisation of PCs, departing from Stokes' definition of PCs as 'the use of pressure, by the donor government, in terms of threatening to terminate aid, or actually terminating or reducing it, if conditions are not met by the recipient' (1995: 12).
3 Donors included in the study were the governments of Sweden, the United Kingdom and the United States, as well as the EU.
4 European Parliament, Africa: www.europarl.europa.eu/RegData/etudes/fiches_techniques/2017/N54404/04A_FT(2017)N54404_EN.pdf; Cotonou Agreement: www.europarl.europa.eu/intcoop/acp/03_01/pdf/mn3012634_en.pdf
5 JAES: https://ec.europa.eu/europeaid/regions/africa/continental-cooperation/joint-africa-eu-strategy_en
6 Withdrawal Strategy Document: www.hrw.org/sites/default/files/supporting_resources/icc_withdrawal_strategy_jan._2017.pdf
7 Trust Fund Africa: https://ec.europa.eu/europeaid/regions/africa/eu-emergency-trust-fund-africa_en
8 List of EU electoral observation missions and election experts missions for 1993–2017: https://eeas.europa.eu/headquarters/headquarters-homepage/16679/list-eu-eom-and-eem-missions-1993-2017_en
9 According to Freedom House methodology, electoral democracies include countries that have met certain minimum standards for political rights and civil liberties. Most 'free' countries could be considered liberal democracies, while some 'partly free' countries might qualify as electoral, but not liberal, democracies. (https://freedomhouse.org/report/methodology-freedom-world-2018).
10 Sources: ODA (World Bank); membership in IGOs (Correlates of War – Intergovernmental Organizations data set); judicial constraints on the executive branch index and legislative constraints on the executive branch index (Varieties of Democracy); major episodes of political violence (Center for Systemic Peace); GDP (annual growth (%); World Bank); HDI (United Nations Development Programme); and ethnic fractionalisation (Alesina et al., 2003).

Bibliography

Alesina, A., Devleeschauwer, A., Easterly, W., Kurlat, S. and Wacziarg, R. (2003) Fractionalization. *Journal of Economic Growth*, 8, 155–194.
Alesina, A. and Dollar, D. (2000) Who gives foreign aid to whom and why? Journal of Economic Growth, 5 (1), 33–63.
Babarinde, O. and Wright, S. (2013) Africa-EU Partnership on Trade and Regional Integration. In J. Mangala (ed.) *Africa and the European Union: A Strategic Partnership*. New York: Palgrave Macmillan (pp. 93–122).
Bartelt, S. (2012) ACP-EU development cooperation at a crossroads? One year after the second revision of the Cotonou Agreement. *European Foreign Affairs Review*, 17 (1), 1–25.
Beissinger, M.R. (2008) A new look at ethnicity and democratization. *Journal of Democracy*, 19 (3), 85–97.
Börzel, T.A. and Risse, T. (2004) *One Size Fits All! EU Policies for the Promotion of Human Rights, Democracy and the Rule of Law*. Paper presented at the Workshop on Democracy Promotion. Stanford University, 4–5 October.

Bratton, M. and van de Walle, N. (1997) *Democratic Experiments in Africa: Regime Transitions in Comparative Perspective*. Cambridge: Cambridge University Press.

Brown, S. (2005) Foreign aid and democracy promotion: Lessons from Africa. *European Journal of Development Research*, 17 (2), 179–198.

Chabal, P. (1998) A few considerations on democracy in Africa. *International Affairs (Royal Institute of International Affairs)*, 74 (2), 289–303.

Cheeseman, N. (2015) *Democracy in Africa: Successes, Failures and the Struggle for Political Reform*. New York: Cambridge University Press.

Clapham, C. (1993) Democratisation in Africa: Obstacles and prospects. *Third World Quarterly*, 14 (3), 423–438.

Crawford, G. (1997) Foreign aid and political conditionality: Issues of effectiveness and consistency. *Democratization*, 4 (3), 69–108.

Crawford, G. (2002) Evaluating European Union promotion of human rights, democracy and good governance: Towards a participatory approach. *Journal of International Development*, 14 (6), 911–926.

Crawford, G. (2005) The European Union and democracy promotion in Africa: The case of Ghana. *European Journal of Development Research*, 17 (4), 571–600.

Del Biondo, K. (2011) Democracy promotion meets development cooperation: The EU as a promoter of democratic governance in sub-Saharan Africa. *European Foreign Affairs Review*, 16 (5), 659–672.

Del Biondo, K. (2015) Donor interests or developmental performance? Explaining sanctions in EU democracy promotion in sub-Saharan Africa. *World Development*, 75, 74–84.

Diamond, L. (1995) *Promoting Democracy in the 1990s: Actors and Instruments, Issues and Imperatives*. New York: Carnegie Corporation of New York.

Diamond, L. (2015) Facing up to the 'democratic deficit'. *Journal of Democracy*, 26 (1), 141–155.

Diamond, L. and Morlino, L. (2004) The quality of democracy. *Journal of Democracy*, 15 (4), 20–31.

Finkel, S.E., Pérez-Liñán, A. and Seligson, M.A. (2007) The effects of U.S. foreign assistance on democracy building, 1990–2003. *World Politics*, 59 (3), 404–438.

Flint, A. (2009) The end of a 'special relationship'? The new EU-ACP Economic Partnership Agreements. *Review of African Political Economy*, 36 (119), 79–92.

Geddes, B. (2011) What causes democratization. In R.E. Goodin (ed.), *The Oxford Handbook of Political Science*. Oxford: Oxford University Press (pp. 593–615).

Holland, M. (2002) *The European Union and the Third World*. Houndmills: Palgrave.

Hout, W. (2012) The anti-politics of development: Donor agencies and the political economy of governance. *Third World Quarterly*, 33 (3), 405–422.

Hurt, S.R. (2004) The European Union's external relations with Africa after the Cold War: Aspects of continuity and change. In I. Taylor and P. Williams (eds), *Africa in International Politics: External Involvement on the Continent*. London and New York: Routledge (pp. 155–173).

Joseph, R.A. (1991) Africa: The rebirth of political freedom. *Journal of Democracy*, 2 (4), 11–24.

Kapstein, E.B. and Converse, N. (2008) Why democracies fail. *Journal of Democracy*, 19 (4), 57–68.

Lindberg, S.I. (2006) *Democracy and Elections in Africa*. Baltimore, MD: Johns Hopkins University Press.

Linder, W. and Bächtiger, A. (2005) What drives democratisation in Asia and Africa? *European Journal of Political Research*, 44, 861–880.

Lipset, M.S. (1959) Some social requisites of democracy: Economic development and political legitimacy. *The American Political Science Review*, 53 (1), 69–105.

Lynch, G. and Crawford, G. (2011) Democratization in Africa 1990–2010: An assessment. Democratization, 18 (2), 275–310.

Mangala, J. (2013a) Africa-EU partnership on democratic governance and human rights. In J. Mangala (ed.), *Africa and the European Union: A Strategic Partnership*. New York: Palgrave Macmillan (pp. 69–92).

Mangala, J. (2013b) Africa-EU strategic partnership: Historical background, institutional architecture, and theoretical frameworks. In J. Mangala (ed.), *Africa and the European Union: A Strategic Partnership*. New York: Palgrave Macmillan (pp. 15–44).

Messer, E. (1993) Anthropology and human rights. *Annual Review of Anthropology*, 22, 221–249.

Molenaers, N. Dellepiane, S. and Faust, J. (2015) Political conditionality and foreign aid. *World Development*, 75, 2–12.

Ndegwa, S. (2001) A decade of democracy in Africa. Journal of Asian and African Studies, 36, 1–16.

Norris, P. (2008) *Driving Democracy: Do Power-Sharing Institutions Work?* New York: Cambridge University Press.

Olsen, G.R. (1998) Europe and the promotion of democracy in post Cold War Africa: How serious is Europe and for what reason? *African Affairs*, 97 (388), 343–367.

Panagariya, A. (2002) EU preferential trade policies and developing countries. *The World Economy*, 25 (10), 1415–1432.

Pevehouse, J.C. (2005) *Democracy from Above: Regional Organizations and Democratization*. Cambridge: Cambridge University Press.

Pirozzi, N. Sartori, N. and Venturi, B. (2017) *The Joint Africa-EU Strategy*. Brussels: European Parliament.

Przeworski, A. and Limongi, F. (1997) Modernization: Theories and facts. *World Politics*, 49 (2), 155–183.

Reilly, B. (2001) Democracy, ethnic fragmentation, and internal conflict: Confused theories, faulty data, and the 'crucial case' of Papua New Guinea. *International Security*, 25 (3), 162–185.

Reinsberg, B. (2015) Foreign aid responses to political liberalization. *World Development*, 75, 46–61.

Scheipers, S. and Sicurelli, D. (2008) Empowering Africa: Normative power in EU-Africa relations. *Journal of European Public Policy*, 15 (4), 607–623.

Sicurelli, D. (2010) *The European Union's Africa Policies: Norms, Interests and Impact*. New York: Ashgate Publishing Limited.

Stokke, O. (1995) *Aid and Political Conditionality*. London: Frank Cass.

Teorell, J. (2010) *Determinants of Democratization: Explaining Regime Change in the World, 1972–2006*. Cambridge, UK: Cambridge University Press.

van Cranenburgh, O. (2011) Democracy promotion in Africa: The institutional context. *Democratization*, 18 (2): 443–461.

van de Walle, N. (2003) Presidentialism and clientelism in Africa's emerging party systems. *The Journal of Modern African Studies*, 41 (2): 297–321.

Warkotsch, A. (2008) Non-compliance and instrumental variation in EU democracy promotion. *Journal of European Public Policy*, 15 (2), 227–245.

Wetzel, J. (ed.) (2011) *The EU as a 'Global Player' in Human Rights?* USA and Canada: Routledge.

Williams, A. (2004) *EU Human Rights Policy: A Study in Irony*. Oxford: Oxford University Press.

Young, C. (2012) *The Postcolonial State in Africa. Fifty Years of Independence 1960–2010*. Wisconsin: The University of Winsconsin Press.

Zamfir, I. (2018) *Democracy Support in EU External Policy*. European Parliament Briefing. Brussels: European Union.

12

Peace and security in the context of EU-Africa relations

Ueli Staeger and Tshepo T. Gwatiwa

Introduction

The EU's role in the context of Africa's peace and security is complex. Ahead of other actors, the EU has moved towards espousing a broader perspective of peace and security that goes beyond military security and armed conflict, to also include human, migration and environmental security. This broader definition of 'peace and security' posits that conflict ought to be approached in relation to the EU's broader policy goals. While describing the EU's approach to security through this broader perspective, this chapter uses two analytical lenses to explore the role of the EU in Africa's peace and security. First, An institutionalist lens sheds light on structural-institutional dynamics, including the EU's internal policy arrangements. A second lens uses the notions of African agency and postcoloniality. Both lenses make important analytical contributions, and this chapter espouses both perspectives.

In unpacking the peace and security dimension of EU-Africa relations, this chapter makes two main arguments. First, the EU advocates an admixture of security with development, which at best equips it with a long-term interest in institution-building that ought to ultimately benefit African citizens and political systems. At worst, however, this arrangement robs the EU of tactical and strategic finesse in intervening in armed conflict. Second, we argue that agency (the capacity for autonomous action without external predetermination) on both the EU and Africa, is a notion that ought to be problematised. A simple blaming of either side for the ails of African peace and security fails to apprehend of the complexity of the issue.

The first section sketches an overview of security and conflict in Africa. The second section introduces theoretical perspectives on peace and security of the EU, and the third summarises some of the key activities of the EU in Africa's peace and security and teases out a number of characteristics of the EU's policy. The fourth section turns to the institutionalisation of the EU's partnership on peace and security with the AU, with a focus on negotiation dynamics and contextual factors.

Security and conflict in Africa: An empirical overview

The face of peace and security in Africa differs from Europe's violent 20th century. While most African states today hold weaponry ranging from impressive to outdated, this arsenal is seldom used in interstate conflict. Violence at the local level, in urban settings or through insurgencies, dominate the face of African conflicts. Such lower-intensity conflicts transgress the state/non-state distinction, with coalitions that enable cooperation across different types of actors. This constellation of reciprocal interference through non-state factions has been called 'mutual intervention' (Cliffe, 1999). Moreover, the characteristics of African conflicts have shifted away from warfare centred on populations to resources and commercial networks. There is also a high fragmentation of state and non-state actors, as well as a high exposure of conflicts to external influence ingrained in the colonial roots of the African state and significant patronage networks (Reno, 2014: 22–24; Galtung, 1971).

In addition to lower-intensity conflict, Africa has sometimes also seen interstate armed conflict. Two conflicts in post-independence Africa stand out. First, the Eritrea-Ethiopia War from 1998 to 2000 was triggered by an escalated border dispute between the two states. Its financial and human cost was estimated at between 50,000 and 80,000 casualties and many more displaced persons. After the Algiers Agreement of 2000 failed to produce the desired progress, mediation efforts led by the United States and Rwanda largely sidelined the EU (Murphy, 2018; Plaut, 2016: 38). Only in July 2018 did intra-African and Gulf mediation efforts lead to the signature of a joint declaration officially ending hostilities. Second, the Great African War in the Democratic Republic of the Congo (1996–2008) involved around ten African states and numerous other factions and claimed several million victims (Turner, 2007; Reyntjens, 2009). Despite a peace agreement (2002), the war's humanitarian impact lasted well beyond formal peace. These conflicts inadvertently invite and shape the involvement of the EU and its member states, particularly through the International Conference on the Great Lakes Region.

European security intervention in Africa must be read against colonial and postcolonial ties between Africa and Europe. Practically all African states – except for Ethiopia and Liberia – gained independence from former European colonial powers, which often continue to enjoy privileged and problematic relationships. Many newly independent nations, especially former French colonies such as Togo and Gabon, concluded far-reaching secretive military cooperation agreements which continued Europe's military presence and intervention in Africa (Martin, 1995; Charbonneau, 2016; Walter, 2017). Against this backdrop of significant postcolonial ties, the EU has sought to promote regional integration. Discussions on colonies during the Rome Treaty negotiations in the 1950s revolved around trade, but security was also a key area (Garavini, 2012; Hansen and Jonsson, 2014). More recently, the EU's interest in peacebuilding through the Common Security and Defence Policy (CSDP) in Africa was possible after a constructive understanding between France and the United Kingdom as the member states with most significant historical interests and roles in Africa (Chafer and Cumming, 2010).

Theoretical perspectives on the EU, Africa and peace and security

Theorising the EU's foreign policy is a delicate balancing act between idiosyncratic theories about the EU specifically and the application of general theories of international relations. Peace and security is no exception. The policy area lies outside the EU's historical core policies concentrating on economic integration, and the EU studies literature only rarely theorises EU security policy (Bergmann and Niemann, 2013; Rodt et al., 2015). EU security interventions elsewhere, let alone the role of external actors on EU integration and policy, are yet to be theorised extensively.

The literature theorising the EU's peace and security policies in Africa can be divided into three broad families. First, the dominant approach is concomitant with EU (foreign policy) studies at large and builds on different variations of institutionalism. Contributions self-label as liberal institutionalist, new institutionalist and historical institutionalist, among others. This approach prioritises endogenous, institutional factors such as institutional design, operation and expertise in explaining outcomes of cooperation (March and Olsen, 1989; Powell and DiMaggio, 1991; Mahoney and Thelen, 2010; Haastrup, 2013a). This literature also proposes typologies of interregional relations, including 'pure', 'hybrid' and 'complex' interregionalism and designating different ways in which states and supranational secretariats may interact (Hänggi et al., 2006; Hardacre and Smith 2009). A particular branch in this approach focuses on 'structural power' to denote the deep-rooted structural changes that the EU's policies and practices cause in African peace and security (Holden, 2009). Scholars here focus on how the EU promotes regionalisation in Africa and in doing so diffuses its own model (Haastrup, 2013b; Lenz, 2013). Scholars also highlight how EU-driven institutionalisation and regionalisation often fail to produce effective alignment of African actors in practice (Dembinski and Schott, 2013; Gibert and Nivet, 2013).

A second strand of literature focuses less on EU institutions and policies, building instead on context-sensitive analyses of African conflicts. This literature ties into broader debates in security studies. The 'regime complex' literature helps understand how the EU deals with overlap and interaction with other security actors in the field (Brosig, 2011; Rodt and Okeke, 2013; Motsamai and Brosig, 2014). The literature on liberal peacebuilding, and particularly its vocal critics, provide a wealth of case studies on how liberal peacebuilding efforts, such as the EU's approach, often fail to appreciate context and politics in theatre (Pugh, 2004; Willett, 2005; Sabaratnam, 2011).

A third strand in the literature, although not fully developed, captures the link between postcoloniality and African agency. Postcoloniality is a condition that refers to a global phenomenon of 'interactions based on unequal power relations in an era that goes beyond the world of colonialism but that has been (and continues to be) decisively shaped by the logic of coloniality' (Hönke and Müller, 2012: 385; Mignolo, 2005: 69, 36). The postcolonial critique posits that because intervention is 'constituted through structural relations of colonial difference', it results in 'persistent drain on the human and financial resources to the state, even as it aims to supply them, a frequent switching of priorities depending on external trends and initiatives and a lack of flexibility in its forms of assistance' (Sabaratnam, 2017: 4, 132). More aptly, Africa has resorted to a radical use of common positions in international politics to push back against Western hegemony, which it deems 'pro-colonialism' (Zondi, 2013: 21). This resistance emanated from what is perceived as a negligence of the real causes of conflict in Africa, including, among other things, flawed decolonisation processes (Raeymaekers, 2014). For an Africa-EU partnership that was founded on equality and African ownership, a prevailing logic of coloniality raises questions about African agency in the security partnership with the EU.

EU policy in peace and security: Embedding security in the development agenda

Any student of EU foreign policy struggles with delineating the role of the EU from that of its member states. In peace and security, this problem is particularly acute, as 'security' is often considered a key aspect of national sovereignty. This section introduces the EU's unique blend of 'security-development nexus' policies and activities in peace and security, through which EU institutions seek to add value to member states' peace and security policies in Africa. After briefly introducing the EU's key policies, four key characteristics of the EU's policy are advanced.

Institutionalising the 'security-development nexus'

The security-development nexus has become a guiding concept in the EU's peace and security policy. Throughout its foreign policy development, the EU gradually attempted to act more holistically, as evinced by its 2013 Comprehensive Approach to External Conflict and Crises, the 2016 Global Strategy, and the 2017 New European Consensus on Development (European Commission, 2013; European Union, 2016, 2017). This holistic approach originates from United Nations (UN) policy circles and was promoted particularly by Western governments in the early 2000s (Chandler, 2007; Duffield, 2010; Hettne, 2010). The nexus describes and prescribes increasing interlinkages between security and development, and posits the two concepts as mutually beneficial (Hadfield, 2007; Bagoyoko and Gibert, 2009). At the policy level, the EU has introduced security in its agreements with African, Caribbean and Pacific countries particularly since the Cotonou Agreement. This transformation is co-determined by bureaucratic and national interests as well as changing African realities (Bagoyoko and Gibert, 2009). In line with an overarching commitment to holistic and comprehensive engagement, the EU has attempted to reconcile its security and development policy in Africa; thus, peace and security stands as one of eight priorities in the Joint Africa-EU Strategy.

In an effort to strengthen African ownership of peace and security policy, the AU and the EU agreed to open the African Peace Facility (APF) to contributions for military and defence purposes through European Development Fund (EDF) funding. The APF, – an instrument of the EU established in 2004 –, aims to enhance dialogue, operationalising the AU's African Peace and Security Architecture (APSA), and support peace support operations in Africa (European Commission, 2017). The EU has disbursed €2.7 billion through the APF since 2004 (European Commission, 2019). Both APSA and peace operations are African-owned initiatives, and the EU therefore lays a considerable deal of (formal) responsibility in the hands of the AU and some Regional Economic Communities (RECs).[1] However, the power of the EU's purse is vast because it shapes the strategic direction of these operations through its funding.

Intervention and expansionist policy experimentation

The EU shows willingness for policy innovation and experimentation in its security policy in Africa. Much of the institutional design and the practices of peace and security policy has first (or exclusively) been operationalised in African conflicts (Bueger, 2016). Haastrup (2013a) argues that incorporating security into EU-Africa relations as a novel policy area in turn also contributed to transforming existing relations. Security, as a newer policy aream makes for an interventionist and innovative EU. The European Commission has shown innovation particularly in designing regional programmes outside the EDF's budgetary envelope. The EU's Pan-African Programme as well as the Instrument for Stability, (formerly called the Rapid Reaction Mechanism), provide flexible policy instruments with which the European Commission can cooperate with regional African partners, also including states.

Policy experimentation is particularly strong in the EU's financial support to the AU, RECs and Regional Mechanisms. Positive evaluations of the APF have led to discussions on a more general funding instrument – the European Peace Facility – outside the EU's regular budget (ECDPM, 2018). Replicating the APF's off-budget structure allows for spending EU funds on military or defence purposes, which is not possible through the EU's regular budget. The European Peace Facility represents an important case of policy experimentation that is to be generalised to all EU partner countries and illustrates the EU's willingness to continue funding APSA.

A number of Trust Funds have sprung up in response to evolving developments in African security. The Trust Funds are led by the European Commission but open to EU member states, third states and other donors. Key trust funds are the EU Emergency Trust Fund for Africa (2015) and the New Partnership Framework (2016). Both initiatives indicate that the EU's policy innovation in the 2010s has been dominated by migration management and the readmission of rejected asylum seekers. Security has been interwoven with the goals of migration policy instruments. Policy innovation in security therefore tends to occur because of the EU's broader strategic priorities (see the section in Chapter 5 titled 'Foreign policy in defining an international role'). Consequently, the long-term perspective of development also influences the EU's peace and security programmes.

The enduring role of the EU in African security is attributable to the role of EU member states that formerly colonised Africa. France plays a large role within the Africa-EU security partnership. Of the several ongoing EU civilian and military missions, more than half are led by France in former French colonies. Due to increasingly diminishing pooled funding, the EU decided to let willing member states lead missions abroad as long as they were willing to fund the bulk of the mission. While some view this as a simple cost-cutting measure, Bagoyoko and Gibert (2009) demonstrate that former colonial powers Europeanised their Africa security policies through EU policy integration and then re-exported it through the partnership. France can lead these missions because it already has military bases in various African countries (Mays, 2002). This EU policy has, to an extent, enabled neocolonialism within contemporary and more formal channels. Expansionist policy experimentation therefore marks the EU's peace and security policy in Africa both by interaction with contemporary EU policy agendas and through member states' postcolonial interests.

A long-term approach to developing security

The EU's peace and security approach in Africa is marked by an insistence on the long term. This section reviews Security Sector Reform (SSR) as a telling example of this approach and insists on the trade-offs of such an approach. SSR has become a key area of EU engagement that operates particularly at the national level (European Commission, 2015). The concept denotes reforms of the governance, administration and military practices of police, military and other security services. The EU spent around €1 billion on SSR from 2001 to 2009, and it has steeply increased its spending since then (European Commission, 2016: 4). Within CSDP missions, the EU has engaged in SSR activities in almost all African missions. Appraisals and analyses suggest that while the EU aspires to long-term goals through SSR, interventions often failed to reflect context and local needs, and instead pursued unrealistic long-term goals (European Commission, 2011: 112; Rayroux and Wilén, 2014). Hence, the EU tends to fail to reconcile SSR programmes with local needs and concrete problems.

Insisting on long-term impact also risks running short on tactical, short-term security goals. The EU's development-focused security policy gradually came at the expense of the Responsibility to Protect, which featured prominently in the first half of the 2000s and then in NATO's interventions in Libya. Yet while the EU has significantly reduced its rhetoric in direct diplomacy and interventions, it continues to sponsor UN resolutions on Africa leading to peacekeeping missions (Sicurelli, 2010: 39–40). Overall, the EU arguably struggles with developing a security policy which is locally, tactically and longitudinally effective. That is why critical voices argue that African agency is better off with less EU 'experimentation' using security crises (Vines, 2010: 1107), thereby leaving room for better coordinated African-led interventions.

Specialisation in a dense policy field

The EU is not alone in supporting African peace and security. Across the conflict cycle, the peace and security field is highly networked. The global dimension of peace and security on the African continent cannot be understated. At the same time, regional and continental diplomacy among close-knit personal networks of African diplomats dominates crisis response and conflict mediation (Hardt, 2014). Yet beyond the African continent, significant material and historical ties mean that the course of peace and conflict is often shaped by external actors – bilateral and multilateral. Table 12.1 demonstrates this diversity through an overview of coinciding mission theatres of the EU, the AU and the UN in the same conflicts.

In practice, this significant overlap of actors causes considerable coordination cost between actors, and actors are often specialising in certain activities. Table 12.1 shows that temporally and geographically, the UN is by far the most comprehensive actor in peacekeeping, whereas the

Table 12.1 Overlap of EU, AU and UN peacekeeping missions in Africa, since 1990

Theatre	EU	UN	AU
Angola		1991–1995	
		1995–1997	
		1997–1999	
Burundi		2004–2007	2003–2004
Central African Republic	2006	1998–2000	2013–2014
		2014–	
Central African Republic & Chad	2014–2015	2007–2010	
Comoros			2004
			2006
			2007–2008
Côte d'Ivoire		2003–2004	
		2004–2017	
Democratic Republic of the Congo	2003	2010–	
	2005–2007		
	2008–2009		
	2005– (civilian)		
Ethiopia & Eritrea		2000–2008	
Guinea-Bissau	2008–2010 (civilian)		
Liberia		1993–1997	
		2003–	
Libya	2013–		
Mali	2013–	2013–	2012–2013
Mozambique		1992–1994	
Niger	2012–		
Rwanda		1993–1996	
Rwanda & Uganda		1993–1994	
Sierra Leone		1998–1999	
		1999–2005	
Somalia	2008–	1992–1993	2007–
		1993–1995	
South Sudan	2012–2014 (civilian)	2011–	
Sudan	2005–2006 (mixed)	2005–2011	2004–2007
		2011–	2008–

Note: The table does not give discrete mission dates but years of activity in theatre. It excludes AU-authorised missions carried out by AU members, electoral observation missions, border monitoring missions and missions by EU member states.

Sources: United Nations General Assembly (2016); European External Action Service, (2017a, 2017b); United Nations, 2017)

Table 12.2 Deployment of military, police and civilian personnel in peace and security in Africa (2018)

Organisation	Military		Police		Civilian		Total
EU	1,689	83%	78	4%	262	13%	2,029
UN	63,549	86%	6,597	9%	3,941	5%	74,087
AU mandated and authorised, and regional initiatives without UN mandate	42,875	94%	2,064	5%	605	1%	45,544

EU operates 'civilian' and 'military' missions. Due to limited resources, the AU takes a somewhat complementary role to the EU and the UN. Rather than the formal 'hatting' of missions, however, the EU's role in *financing* African peace and security initiatives is equally important. The EU has spent some €2.2 billion through the APF since 2004 (or €157 million/year on average) (European Commission, 2018: 10–11).

In the course of specialisation, the EU also prioritises civilian elements of peace and security more so than other actors in the policy field and 'military' peacekeeping missions (Rummel, 2011). Including civilian elements in peace and security policy is by no means exclusive, but the EU has, from the outset of its CSDP, sought to develop its civilian missions, despite internal resistance (Juncos, 2018). Even if the EU's absolute numbers of civilian personnel pale compared to the UN's, the EU deploys a considerably higher ratio of civilians in its missions than the UN and African actors do (Table 12.2). In its relationship with the AU (see 'Institutionalising the partnership'), the EU and its member states are leading supporters of the civilian components of APSA. The evidence above demonstrates both the above-mentioned aspiration for EU long-term impact and that the EU is required to specialise given a dense political field. Cooperation between the EU and the UN, but also with subregional and continental African security actors, has carved out complementary roles through functional specialisation. Cooperation is also achieved through 'handover missions' where the UN has taken over a mission from the EU in the Democratic Republic of Congo, Chad and Central African Republic (Charbonneau, 2009; Mérand and Rayroux, 2016). Here, the EU has moved from 'functional niches' to 'interlocking security' (Brosig, 2014). It may be a smaller actor in African security based on numbers of deployed personnel, but it is a major financial contributor.

Institutionalising the partnership: AU-EU relations in peace and security

When the Africa-EU partnership came into effect, there was fervency around the institutionalisation of the partnership. There were several reasons behind this passion. Primarily, there was mutual political will to effectuate the partnership. African negotiators successfully bargained for lessening 'Eurocentric perspective(s)' in the previous (Lomé) agreement (Organization of African Unity, 1999). As a result, African 'ownership' and 'leadership' were explicitly mentioned in the Africa-EU Strategic Partnership of 2007. The then Chairperson of the AU Commission, Alpha Konaré, also played a pivotal role by directly negotiating with his EU counterparts (Romano Prodi and José Manuel Durão Barroso). Many of the discussions between these high-level officials centred on peace and security issues. Thereafter, the onus was to institutionalise the partnership in such a way that it would accommodate African agency.

In the early years of the partnership, the AU Commission and the European Commission took a few steps towards institutionalisation. In October 2006, the EU launched a €55 million Support Programme to the African Union, under which senior members of the AU Commission could spend two to three years in a capacity building programme in Brussels (Schmidt, 2013: 31).

Moreover, the heads of the two commissions held annual meetings also comprising of various staff, technical experts and advisory boards in order to promote dialogue between the two organisations (Tywuschik and Sherriff, 2009).

The early phase of the institutionalisation of the partnership was characterised by mimicry of European security institutions. At the beginning of the partnership, the AU had few actual partners, especially in the area of peace and security. It became a primary sponsor of the idea of building a continental standing army which could effectively deal with conflict and intervene in cases of war crimes such as genocide, as per the AU's Constitutive Act. The EU's eagerness to support the idea of an African Standby Force was not surprising, because it resonated with an older Danish initiative for a multinational United Nations Standby Forces High Readiness Brigade (SHIBRIG). Although the idea of an African standby force dates back to the 1960s, the current African Standby Force starkly resembles the SHIBRIG in its nomenclature, force structure and command, deployment frameworks and rapid deployment capability (Sucharipa-Behrmann, 2001). For its part, the EU has been the largest conceptual and financial contributor in the initial design of the African Standby Force.

Change and continuity in EU Support to the AU

In comparison to other AU partnerships, this one is characterised by high-level engagement. Engagement takes place between the (AU) Peace and Security Council and the (EU) Political and Security Committee, both of which are made up of ambassadors. The AU Peace and Security Council is a comparably stronger and effective AU organ. It can effectively engage with its EU and UN (Security Council) counterparts because it has existed since the OAU era – then known as the Central Organ of the Mechanism for Conflict Prevention, Management and Resolution (or simply the Central Organ) (Bah et al., 2014). Its approach to conflict resolution in interregional contexts has gradually improved and proven effective. Since peace and security issues dominated the Africa-EU dialogue, the two organisations decided to transform this interaction.

The scope and frequency of high-level interaction between the two organisations has changed over the years. The heads of the two commissions decided to hold an informal annual meeting in order to reconcile differences. Prior to that, minor disagreements over preferences regarding institutional design, function and the funding disbursement mechanisms had emerged as a threat to the partnership. Holding more meetings provides greater latitude to address divergence as well as to pre-empt opportunities for forum shopping. As a result of this regular interaction, in 2014 the two organisations agreed to triangulate Africa-EU dialogue with UN meetings in New York in order to ensure that there is synergy in African peace and security projects (ibid.). This idea draws from the fact that both organisations uphold the legal and political primacy of the UN; as well as the fact that most AU peace operations (including those supported by the EU) tend to evolve into UN peace missions.

Contention, tensions and resistance in the partnership

The partnership's funding mechanism has created contentious politics of control and of latitude for the AU to exercise agency. The most contentious issue in the AU-EU financing mechanism is centred on accountability. In the 2010s, the EU decided to intertwine the flow of funding to the AU Commission and its RECs and Regional Mechanisms. During the first review of the partnership (which takes place every five years), the EU made it mandatory for the AU to coordinate with its RECs before it can disburse funding through the APF. It resulted in a lengthy and bureaucratic process which involves a thorough engagement between the RECs and their resident EU Delegations, the AU and its overseeing EU Delegations and the European Commission. On the one hand, Africans decry 'balkanisation' and mission stasis, while on the other, EU officials invoke issues of transparency and accountability to the European citizens. Under this arrangement, in 2015, the AU had to return two-thirds of the €40 million that had been allocated under the 10th EDF. Such issues are often viewed as a challenge to African agency and considered elements of postcoloniality. Contentious issues around funding in the EU-AU partnership also point to normative divergences between the two blocs that are caused by different positionalities in the historical relationship of the two continents (Staeger, 2016).

Forum shopping was a source of tension in the relationship before the parties agreed to triangulate their dialogue with their diplomatic counterparts in New York. A classic case of forum shopping between the EU, the UN and NATO occurred starkly in Libya in 2011. In the months leading up to the Western intervention in Libya in 2011, the United States asked the Arab League (which already had tensions with Libya) to sponsor a UN resolution to impose a no-fly zone in the country (Smith-Windsor, 2013). The UN Security Council mandated a NATO operation led by France and Italy (with major Norwegian input). The United States Africa Command paved the way for NATO's Operation Unified Protector by conducting Operation Odyssey Dawn 19 days prior (Gertler, 2011). The Africans unsuccessfully lobbied for an African solution in Libya but met resistance from the EU Delegation to the AU and Brussels, as well as the North Atlantic Council. The EU insisted that the AU would not use any of the funding from the EDF in Libya. This angered the Africans who considered this an affront to their agency in African security as well as deliberate use of forum shopping to protect Western interests.

Resisting coercion and projecting African agency

As illustrated in the preceding sections, the AU has limited bargaining power due to overdependence on external support. As a result, it relies a lot on agency slack to minimise the costs of dependency. This is illustrated in the case of the AU courting and engaging emerging powers, with China as a prominent example. The AU Commission (under Nkosazana Dlamini-Zuma) repeatedly lobbied China to play a more prominent role in African security. In October 2014, the Chairperson of the AU Commission and the Commissioner of Peace and Security, Smail Chergui, concluded a six-year strategic dialogue aimed at persuading China to play a greater role in African peace and security (African Union, 2014).[2] The idea was to receive support without conditionality, which would protect African preferences and agency within its security systems. China heeded the call and began making material contributions to African peace support operations, starting with the AU Mission in Somalia (AMISOM). However, the first disbursements were a flop, as there were complaints that some of the materials, such as apparel, vehicles and tactical equipment, did not fit the mission purpose and did not allow interoperability with existing equipment. Indeed, China's security footprint in Africa has been growing at a fast rate at both covert and overt levels. However, China has so far focused more on UN peace operations in Mali and Sudan, as it has economic interests within or adjacent to those territories.

Conclusion

This chapter showed that since colonisation, Europe's involvement in African peace and security has remained second to none. This postcolonial relationship has evolved significantly from colonial security cooperation to the EU becoming a key donor for African peace and security policy.

The EU's broader imperatives of policy coherence and its implementation of a development-driven version of the security-development nexus have not eluded its African peace and security policies, and the EU is therefore taking a long-term approach to security through and for development, as much as it increased its purely security-oriented activities on the continent.

As a regional organisation, the EU has been a steady, substantial partner of African security and its political integration. The AU's APSA lacks neither in ambition nor implementation difficulties, but arguably it has made significant contributions to institutionalising African peace and security institutions and creating strong collaborative links between RECs and the AU, as well as its external partners. The EU's funding of APSA has been criticised increasingly in past years, but until AU member states operationalise solid self-financing mechanisms (such as the Peace Fund, revitalised in 2018 but still not fully operational), European development funds will continue to play a vital role in APSA.

Since 2014, the AU has pursued the goal of 'silencing the guns' on the African continent by 2020 (African Union, 2014). Through its institutions and increasingly effective preventive diplomacy, the AU attempts to project African agency in peace and security; but this goal was not reached by 2020. As the EU's contributions are still direly needed to operate APSA, the AU has sought, in light of the EU's dominant role, to diversify its offer of external resources by developing partnerships with other actors, such as China. The EU and many of its bigger member states however have an appetite for long-term institutionalisation that does not sit well with calls for AU emancipation from European funds. We are faced with an uncomfortable embrace between the AU's short-term financial needs and the EU's long-term approach to security/development. The EU's prominent role in African peace and security is here to stay, at least for a little while.

Notes

1 This long-standing commitment is sometimes ruptured by episodes of disagreement; for example, in a complex dispute over troop stipends in Somalia, where the EU reduced its per troop reimbursement payments destined for AMISOM troop contributing countries after allegations of mismanagement by those countries (see Williams, 2018: 7).
2 African Union, Consolidated Briefing Note: Visit of Ambassador Smail Chergui, Commissioner for Peace and Security to China, 27–29 October 2014 (AU internal document).

Bibliography

African Union (2014) *Silencing the Guns: Pre-requisites for Realising a Conflict-free Africa by the Year 2020*. Arusha.

Bagoyoko, N. and Gibert, M.V. (2009) The linkage between security, governance and development: The European Union in Africa. *The Journal of Development Studies*, 45 (5), 789–814.

Bah, A.S., Choge-Nyangoro, E., Dersso, S.A., Mofya, B. and Murithi, T. (2014) *The African Peace and Security Architecture: A Handbook*. Addis Abiba: Friedrich-Ebert-Stiftung and the African Union.

Bergmann, J. and Niemann, A. (2013) Theories of European integration and their contribution to the study of European foreign policy. In *Proceedings of 8th Pan-European Conference on International Relations*. Warsaw: Academic Press.

Brosig, M. (2011) The emerging peace and security regime in Africa: The role of the EU. *European Foreign Affairs Review*, 16 (1), 107–122.

Brosig, M. (2014) EU peacekeeping in Africa: From functional niches to interlocking security. *International Peacekeeping*, 21 (1), 74–90.

Bueger, C. (2016) Doing Europe: Agency and the European Union in the Field of Counter-piracy Practice. *European Security*, 25 (4), 407–422.

Chafer, T. and Cumming, G. (2010) Beyond Fashoda: Anglo-French security cooperation in Africa since Saint-Malo. *International Affairs*, 86 (5), 1129–1147.

Chandler, D. (2007) The security–development nexus and the rise of 'anti-foreign policy'. *Journal of International Relations and Development*, 10 (4), 362–386.

Charbonneau, B. (2009) What is so special about the European Union? EU–UN Cooperation in crisis management in Africa. *International Peacekeeping*, 16 (4), 546–561.

Charbonneau, B. (2016) *France and the New Imperialism: Security Policy in Sub-Saharan Africa*. Abingdon: Routledge.

Cliffe, L. (1999) Regional dimensions of conflict in the Horn of Africa. *Third World Quarterly*, 20 (1), 89–111.

Dembinski, M. and Schott, B. (2013) Converging around global norms? Protection of civilians in African Union and European Union peacekeeping in Africa. *African Security*, 6 (3–4), 276–296.

Duffield, M. (2010) The liberal way of development and the development–security impasse: Exploring the global life-chance divide. *Security Dialogue*, 41 (1), 53–76.

ECDPM (2018) Evaluation of the implementation of the African Peace Facility 2014–2016 [online]. https://ecdpm.org/publications/evaluation-african-peace-facility/ (retrieved 11 May 2020).

European Commission (2011) *Thematic Evaluation of European Commission Support to Justice and Security System Reform*. Brussels: European Union.

European Commission (2013) The EU's Comprehensive Approach to External Conflict and Crises. JOIN(2013) 30 final. Brussels, 11 December.

European Commission (2015) Joint Communication. Capacity Building in Support of Security and Development – Enabling Partners to Prevent and Manage Crises. JOIN(2015) 17 final. Brussels, 28 April.

European Commission (2016) Joint Staff Working Document. Lessons Drawn from Past Interventions and Stakeholders' Views. Accompanying the Document Joint Communication to the European Parliament and the Council Elements for an EU-wide Strategic Framework to Support Security Sector Reform. SWD(2016) 221 final. Strasbourg, 5 July.

European Commission (2017) *African Peace Facility: Annual Report 2016*. Luxembourg: Publications Office of the European Union.

European Commission (2018) *African Peace Facility: Annual Report 2017*. Luxembourg: Publications Office of the European Union.

European Commission (2019) *African Peace Facility: Annual Report 2018*. Luxembourg: Publications Office of the European Union.

European External Action Service (2017a) Military and civilian missions and operations [online]. https://eeas.europa.eu/headquarters/headquarters-homepage_en/430/Military and civilian missions and operations (retrieved 3 January 2018).

European External Action Service (2017b) *Common Security and Defence Policy of the European Union: Missions and Operations Annual Report 2016*. Brussels: European Union.

European Union (2016) *Shared Vision, Common Action: A Stronger Europe. A Global Strategy for the European Union's Foreign And Security Policy*. Brussels: European Union.

European Union (2017) *The New European Consensus on Development 'Our World, Our Dignity, Our Future'*. Brussels: European Union.

Galtung, J. (1971) A structural theory of imperialism. *Journal of Peace Research*, 8 (2), 81–117.

Garavini, G. (2012) *After Empires: European Integration, Decolonization, and the Challenge from the Global South 1957–1986*. Oxford: Oxford University Press.

Gertler, J. (2011) *Operation Odyssey Dawn (Libya): Background and Issues for Congress* [online]. Congressional Research Service. https://fas.org/sgp/crs/natsec/R41725.pdf

Gibert, M.V. and Nivet, B. (2013) Dissonant paths to partnership and convergence: EU-Africa relations between experimentation and resistance. *African Security*, 6 (3–4), 191–210.

Haastrup, T. (2013a) *Charting Transformation through Security: Contemporary EU-Africa Relations*. New York: Palgrave Macmillan.

Haastrup, T. (2013b) EU as mentor? Promoting regionalism as external relations practice in EU–Africa relations. *Journal of European Integration*, 35 (7), 785–800.

Hadfield, A. (2007) Janus advances: An analysis of EC development policy and the 2005 Amended Cotonou Partnership Agreement. *European Foreign Affairs Review*, 12 (1), 39–66.

Hänggi, H., Roloff, R. and Rüland, J. (eds) (2006) *Interregionalism and International Relations*. London New York: Routledge.

Hansen, P. and Jonsson, S. (2014) *Eurafrica. The Untold History of European Integration and Colonialism*. London: Bloomsbury Publishing.

Hardacre, A. and Smith, M. (2009) The EU and the diplomacy of complex interregionalism. *The Hague Journal of Diplomacy*, 4 (2), 167–188.

Hardt, H. (2014) *Time to React: The Efficiency of International Organizations in Crisis Response*. New York: Oxford University Press.

Hettne, B. (2010) Development and security: Origins and future. *Security Dialogue*, 41 (1), 31–52.

Holden, P. (2009) *In Search of Structural Power: EU Aid Policy as a Global Political Instrument*. Farnham, UK, and Burlington, VT: Ashgate.

Hönke, J. and Müller, M. (2012) Governing (in)security in a postcolonial world: Transnational entanglements and the worldliness of 'local' practice. *Security Dialogue*, 43 (5), 383–401.

Juncos, A.E. (2018) Civilian CSDP missions: 'The good, the bad and the ugly'. In S. Blockmans and P. Koutrakos (eds), *Research Handbook on the EU's Common Foreign and Security Policy*. Cheltenham and Northampton, MA: Edward Elgar Publishing (pp. 89–110).

Lenz, T. (2013) EU normative power and regionalism: Ideational diffusion and its limits. *Cooperation and Conflict*, 48 (2), 211–228.

Mahoney, J. and Thelen, K.A. (eds) (2010) *Explaining Institutional Change: Ambiguity, Agency, and Power*. Cambridge and New York: Cambridge University Press.

March, J.G. and Olsen, J.P. (1989) *Rediscovering Institutions: The Organizational Basis of Politics*. New York: Free Press.

Martin, G. (1995) Continuity and change in Franco-African relations. *The Journal of Modern African Studies*, 33 (1), 1–20.

Mays, T. (2002) *Africa's First Peacekeeping Operation: The OAU in Chad, 1981–1982*. Westport, CT: Praeger.

Mérand, F. and Rayroux, A. (2016) The practice of burden sharing in European crisis management operations. *European Security*, 25 (4), 442–460.

Mignolo, W. (2000) *Local Histories/Global Designs: Coloniality, Subaltern Knowledges, and Border Thinking*. Princeton: Princeton University Press.

Motsamai, D. and Brosig, M. (2014) Modeling cooperative peacekeeping: Exchange theory and the African peace and security regime. *Journal of International Peacekeeping*, 18 (1–2), 45–68.

Murphy, S.D. (2018) The Eritrean-Ethiopian War. In T. Ryus, O. Corten and A. Hofer (eds), *Use of Force in International Law: A Case-based Approach*. Oxford: Oxford University Press.

Organization of African Unity (1999) *Key Issues in the Current ACP-EU Negotiations*. Technical Report No.1 Prepared for African Negotiators by OAU Advisory Panel of Experts on ACP-EU Negotiations. Addis Ababa: OAU.

Plaut, M. (2016) *Understanding Eritrea: Inside Africa's Most Repressive State*. London: Hurst & Company.

Powell, W.W. and DiMaggio, P. (eds) (1991) *The New Institutionalism in Organizational Analysis*. Chicago: University of Chicago Press.

Pugh, M. (2004) Peacekeeping and critical theory. *International Peacekeeping*, 11 (1), 39–58.

Raeymaekers, T. (2014) *Violent Capitalism and Hybrid Identity in the Eastern Congo: Power to the Margins*. New York: Cambridge University Press.

Rayroux, A. and Wilén, N. (2014) Resisting ownership: The paralysis of EU peacebuilding in the Congo. *African Security*, 7 (1), 24–44.

Reno, W. (2014) Conflict and war in Africa. In J.J. Hentz (ed.), *Routledge Handbook of African Security*. Abingdon and New York: Routledge (pp. 21–32).

Reyntjens, F. (2009) *The Great African War: Congo and Regional Geopolitics, 1996–2006*. Cambridge: Cambridge University Press.

Rodt, A.P. and Okeke, J.M. (2013) AU-EU 'Strategic Partnership': Strengthening policy convergence and regime efficacy in the African peace and security complex? *African Security*, 6 (3–4), 211–233.

Rodt, A.P., Whitman, R.G. and Wolff, S. (2015) The EU as an international security provider: The need for a mid-range theory. *Global Society*, 29 (2), 149–155.

Rummel, R. (2011) In search of a trademark: EU civilian operations in Africa. *Contemporary Security Policy*, 32 (3), 604–624.

Sabaratnam, M. (2011) The liberal peace? A brief intellectual history of international conflict management, 1990–2010. In S. Campbell, D. Chandler and M. Sabaratnam (eds), *A Liberal Peace? The Problems and Practices of Peacebuilding*. London: Zed Books (pp. 13–30).

Sabaratnam, M. (2017) *Decolonising Intervention: International Statebuilding in Mozambique*. London and New York: Rowman & Littlefield International.

Schmidt, E. (2013) *Foreign Intervention in Africa: From the Cold War to the War on Terror*. Cambridge: Cambridge University Press.

Sicurelli, D. (2010) *The European Union's Africa Policies: Norms, Interests, and Impact*. Farnham, UK, and Burlington, VT: Ashgate.

Smith-Windsor, B.A. (2013) NATO's Maritime Strategy and the Libya Crisis as Seen from the Sea. Research Paper, No 90. Rome: NATO Defense College, Research Division.

Staeger, U. (2016) Africa-EU relations and normative power Europe: A decolonial Pan-African critique. *JCMS: Journal of Common Market Studies*, 54 (4), 981–998.

Sucharipa-Behrmann, L. (2001) Peace-keeping operations of the United Nations. In F. Cede and L. Sucharipa-Behrmann (eds), *The United Nations: Law and Practice*. The Hague: Kluwever Law International (pp. 89–104).

Turner, T. (2007) *The Congo Wars: Conflict, Myth, and Reality*. London and New York: Zed Books.

Tywuschik, V. and Sherriff, A. (2009) *Beyond Structures? Reflections on the Implementation of the Joint Africa-EU Strategy*. Discussion Paper No. 87. Maastricht: ECDPM.

United Nations (2017) List of Peacekeeping Operations 1948–2017 [online]. https://peacekeeping.un.org/sites/default/files/unpeacekeeping-operationlist_1.pdf

United Nations General Assembly (2016) Report of the Joint African Union-United Nations Review of Available Mechanisms to Finance and Support African Union Peace Support Operations Authorized by the United Nations Security Council. A/71/410-S/2016/809.

Vines, A. (2010) Rhetoric from Brussels and reality on the ground: The EU and security in Africa. *International Affairs*, 86 (5), 1091–1108.

Walter, D. (2017) *Colonial Violence: European Empires and the use of Force*. London: Hurst & Company.

Willett, S. (2005) New barbarians at the gate: Losing the liberal peace in Africa. *Review of African Political Economy*, 32 (106), 569–594.

Williams, P.D. (2018) *Fighting for Peace in Somalia: A History and Analysis of the African Union Mission (AMISOM), 2007–2017*. Oxford: Oxford University Press.

Zondi, S. (2013) Common positions as African agency in international negotiations: an appraisal. In W. Brown and S. Harman (eds), *African Agency in International Politics*. London and New York: Routledge (pp. 19–33).

13
Regional integration

Giulia Piccolino

Introduction

When it comes to development aid, democracy promotion or trade, the European Union (EU) is only one among Africa's partners. The promotion of regional integration, however, constitutes a very specific feature of the EU's external policy and of EU-Africa's relations. Although other actors, such as the African Development Bank or the United Nations Economic Commission for Africa (UNECA), are involved in providing aid and technical support to regional organisations in Africa, the EU has the unique advantage of being both a donor and a prominent example of regional integration itself. The EU openly states that 'regional integration is an effective means of achieving prosperity, peace and security' (European Union, 2016) and assumes that other continents would benefit from strengthening regionalism. The EU promotes regional integration through incentives and sanctions, by providing or withdrawing aid and granting or denying access to trade. The EU also influences regionalism through a 'logic of appropriateness' (Börzel and Risse, 2009: 6) and presents itself as a model that other regions might want to follow. When it comes to Africa, the EU styles itself as an ideal partner for the African Union (AU) and the Regional Economic Communities (RECs).

The idea that regional integration is a positive phenomenon that can foster peace and development is popular in Africa, and the EU's ostensible commitment to export regional integration has been generally welcome on the continent, but with some reservations. African leaders see the EU as a source of inspiration for their regional projects. Although Africa has a long history of 'regionalism' in the broader sense of interconnection between the people of a same region, regional integration as a political project is a modern phenomenon which takes the nation state as the building block. As one of the first and most prominent examples of regional integration, the EU has held considerable attraction for Africa, with the AU and African subregional organisation choosing to emulate important features of the EU model.

However, when it comes to the EU's role as a partner that ostensibly aims to support regional integration in Africa, African perceptions are more mixed. African regional integration has been marked by a history of 'competing regionalisms' (Franke, 2009) going back to the post-independence period when the so-called Casablanca group called for immediate African unity, while the rival Brazzaville-Monrovia group favoured a looser form of cooperation that respected the sovereignty of individual states. The ideology of Pan-Africanism, which the 'radicals' embraced, has historically aimed to foster 'developmental cooperation', a form of regional integration rooted in dependency theory and 'based on the premise that Africa had been integrated into the world economy on profoundly disadvantageous terms' (Gibb, 2009: 706). From a Pan-Africanist perspective, the EU can be a positive example of how countries overcome divisions and create regional institutions, but it is also an organisation of Africa's former colonisers from which Africa needs to emancipate itself. African scholars and policymakers have suspected the European Economic Community (EEC)/EU at times to promote regional integration in Africa for its own interests and on its own terms, potentially undermining home-grown regional projects (Asante, 1986; Olofin, 1997).

These suspicions have been at least partially justified. During colonial times and in the immediate post-independence period, European powers created or promoted some African regional projects, yet they still continued to see Pan-Africanism as a threat to their interests. Although since the 1970s the EEC has provided aid for regional integration in Africa as part of its development policy, the EEC/EU has historically promoted a market integration approach to regional integration, 'based on the liberalisation of intra-regional trade designed to abolish discrimination between contracting parties' (Gibb, 2009: 705), and it has more recently emphasised 'open regionalism', which aims to 'promote integration in the world economy' (ibid.: 706). This view of regionalism created a wedge between the EEC and the Pan-African ideal.

With the end of the Cold War and the creation of the AU, the division between Pan-Africanists and 'moderates' has become less salient. The relaunch of continental integration and the launch of the African Peace and Security Architecture (APSA) have generated a strong demand for the support that the EU can give to foster regional integration. At the same time, the EEC has become the EU and has rethought its approach to promoting regional integration (European Union, 2006, 2008, 2012). It has committed to supporting African ownership and, in Toni Haastrup's (2013) words, to acting as a 'mentor' to the AU and African regional organisations. However, some episodes, such as the Economic Partnership Agreement (EPA) negotiations, have revived African fears that Europe is promoting regionalism on its own terms, rather than on African terms.

This chapter is organised as follows. The first section provides an overview of Europe's role in region-building in Africa since colonisation to the end of the Cold War. The second section looks at the EU's promotion of regional integration within the institutional and policy framework laid out by the 2000 Cotonou Agreement and by the 2007 Joint Africa-EU Strategy (JAES). It explores the way development aid, trade and political dialogue are used by the EU as tools for promoting regionalism. The third section looks at the indirect influence of the EU on Africa as a model and as an example of regional integration. I conclude by assessing the current appeal of the EU model of regional integration on Africa and highlighting some future challenges.

The historical origins of the promotion of regional integration

The EU's current promotion of regional integration should be situated in a history marked by many attempts at transferring foreign models of political and economic governance to Africa (Gibb, 2009), stretching back to the colonial time. Colonial powers initiated regional projects as a means to making their African empires easier to control. France, in particular, reorganised its colonies in two subregional federations, the Afrique Occidentale Française (AOF) and the Afrique Equatoriale Française (AEF). Although there was no comparable project in the more decentralised British empire, British colonialists at times also strived to integrate different territories. In Southern Africa in 1910, the British established what is now the oldest customs union in the world, the Southern African Customs Union (SACU). The East African High Commission, renamed in 1961 as the East African Common Services Organization (EACSO), brought together Kenya, Uganda and Tanganyika (currently Tanzania) in a regional union (Gladden, 1963).

Most colonial regional projects did not survive independence; this was because of the lack of consensus of African leaders in preserving them and the political U-turn of colonial powers. France in particular saw Pan-Africanism as an ideology potentially dangerous to European interest and favoured the maintenance of looser forms of regional cooperation. The AOF and AEF were dismantled in 1958 and the French colonies obtained independence as separate states. However, they continued to share the same currency, the franc CFA, which became the foundation of the current West African Economic and Monetary Union (WAEMU) in West Africa and the Communauté économique et monétaire de l'Afrique centrale in Central Africa. Among British colonies, SACU has survived up to now and the East African Community (EAC), which was founded in 1967 and revitalised in 2000 after a period of inactivity, builds on its colonial predecessor EACSO.

Until the accession of the United Kingdom to the common market, France's desire to maintain strong ties with its former colonies was the main driving force of the then EEC policy towards Africa. However, French interests blurred with the interests of the EEC Commission to become an actor in external relations. The first policymakers who discussed the relevance of the EEC model of regional integration for Africa were former French colonial officers working for the European Commission (Asante, 1986: 83). The second Yaoundé Convention, signed in 1969 with a group of mostly former French and Belgian colonies, opened up to the possibility to provide aid to groups of associate states (European Union, 1969). However, the EEC ignored the Organization of African Unity, founded in 1963 in Addis Ababa, and almost undermined the creation of the Economic Community of the West African States (ECOWAS) by supporting, under France's input, a rival organisation of former French colonies, the Communauté Economique de l'Afrique de l'Ouest (CEAO), the predecessor of WAEMU (Asante, 1986: 76).

From the mid-1970s, the United Kingdom's accession to the EEC in 1973 and the dynamism of some African policymakers in relaunching regional integration in their continent significantly modified the interregional landscape. In particular, Nigerian scholar and high-ranking civil servant Adebayo Adedeji played a major role in the launch of the 1980 OAU-sponsored Lagos Plan of Action for the Economic Development of Africa, which led to the establishment or revitalisation of a large number of new subregional agreements (Adebajo, 2014). With the 1991 Abuja Treaty, eight of these institutions – the RECs – received the official endorsement of the OAU as building blocks of African integration.

These internal and external developments set the scene for the adoption of the Lomé Convention with 46 African, Caribbean and Pacific (ACP) countries in 1975, which for the first time explicitly engaged the EEC to support 'the objectives of the ACP states in matters of regional and interregional cooperation' (European Union, 1975: Art. 47). Through the first and subsequent Lomé conventions, the EU channelled a part of the European Development Fund (EDF) aid to financing regional projects, particularly in the domains of transport, industry and rural development. Regional aid notably represented between 10% and 15% of total EDF aid between 1976 and 1990 (European Union, 1988).

In spite of the progress represented by the Lomé convention, there continued to be a series of limits and inconsistencies in the EU approach. Instead of establishing a partnership with the OAU, Lomé established an ad hoc group – the ACP Group[1] – built on European countries' postcolonial relationships, which included the Caribbean and Pacific region and excluded North

Africa. The EEC negotiated association agreements with North African countries, but there was no regional multilateral framework for the North African subregion. Moreover, some proponents of African regional integration saw the Lomé conventions as being at odds with the objective of Pan-Africanism to promote self-reliance (Olofin, 1977), because the Lomé framework focused on trade between developed and developing states rather than among developing countries.

Analysis of the actual use of regional aid under Lomé (Coste and Egg, 1998) has underscored two features: first, aid was unevenly disbursed to the African subregions, with West Africa – the region where the former French colonies were concentrated – keeping the lion's share; and, second, aid was disbursed in a manner that can be broadly described as low-profile and apolitical. Aid was not earmarked for strengthening regional institutions, and it seldom supported the future RECs. For instance, in the case of West Africa, ECOWAS, the main regional organisation, received only 6% of regional funding (ibid.). When the EU engaged in active region-building, it continued to give priority to supporting regional integration among former French colonies. In particular, the transformation of CEAO into WAEMU in 1996 benefited from the EU's generous technical cooperation and funding (Grimm, 1999).

The promotion of regional integration within the current policy framework

Support for regional integration has experienced a qualitative and quantitative leap in the first two decades following the end of the Cold War. Such change has been driven by both the demand for regional integration on the African side and the offer of support from the European side. The 1990s and the beginning of the new millennium were a crucial time for the transformation and relaunch of African regionalism, with the creation of the AU and the launch of the first regionally led peace operations. In parallel, in 1992, with the adoption of the Maastricht Treaty, the EEC became the EU. The Maastricht Treaty introduced the Common Foreign and Security Policy (CFSP) as a new 'pillar' of the European project. The political dimension of the EU was further strengthened by the 1997 Treaty of Amsterdam and the 2007 Treaty of Lisbon. At the global level, the push for the globalisation of exchanges and the establishment of the World Trade Organization clashed with the preferential trade regime established by Lomé.

These changes have led to a process of rethinking of the objectives and nature of the EU promotion of regional integration. First, since the 1990s, promoting regional integration has become a much more conscious and central objective of EU cooperation with developing countries than was the case before, as outlined by the 1995 and 2008 communications on regional integration (European Union, 1995, 2008) and the 2006 European Consensus on Development (European Union, 2006b). With respect to sub-Saharan Africa, the new approach has been operationalised in the current Cotonou Agreement with the ACP Group, which replaced Lomé in 2000, and in its mid-term renegotiations in 2005 and 2010 (European Union, 2012). The definition of regional integration has also been broadened. While the 1995 communication still focused on economic and trade-driven integration (European Union, 1995), the 2008 communication proposes a broader definition, characterising regional integration as 'the process of overcoming, by common accord, political, physical, economic and social barriers that divide countries from their neighbours, and of collaborating in the management of shared resources and regional commons' (European Union, 2008: 3). The toolbox that the EU uses to promote regional integration has also expanded. While development aid remains one of the main instruments, the EU has also expressed the intention to use others, such as trade cooperation and political dialogue.

In addition to the EU-ACP cooperation, the EU and the AU have also set up a broader institutional framework to promote regional integration. Since 2000, periodic summits have been held between the EU and Africa (since 2007 with the AU), and in 2007 the EU and the AU launched the JAES covering both North Africa and sub-Saharan Africa (African Union and European Union, 2007). It is important to notice however that the shift towards a continental approach is limited by the enduring importance of the ACP framework and the fact that the EU external policy continues to treat North Africa separately, through the 1995 Euro-Mediterranean Partnership and the 2008 Union for the Mediterranean.

In the following paragraphs, I discuss in more depth the role of regional integration in development aid and trade policy, through which the EU aims to promote regional integration following the logic of manipulation of utility calculation, and I look at how regional integration informs political dialogue, especially in the field of peace and security.

Aid and trade for regional integration

The Cotonou Agreement reaffirms that development cooperation shall contribute to regional integration and cooperation at both the continental and subregional levels (European Union, 2012: Art. 30). The disbursement of regional aid through the EDF is based on Regional Indicative Programmes, which are negotiated for each African subregion. Following Cotonou's adoption, there has been a marked quantitative increase in development aid for projects with a regional focus within the EDF programming (Table 13.1). Table 13.2 shows that the main areas currently supported are trade and economic integration, which also includes infrastructure development (1,620), peace, security and governance-related activities (453) and natural resource management (355). In addition to the Regional Indicative Programmes, the EU has also other financial instruments at its disposal that can be used for supporting regional integration. Within the EDF framework, the EU has committed to giving more importance to regional issues in the national envelopes and in the EDF all-ACP envelope (European Union, 2008).

In addition, specific instruments have been set up in order to support the priorities of the JAES. The most important one is the African Peace Facility (APF), which also draws from EDF founding but was established in 2004 at the request of the AU in order to support the AU and the RECs' peace and security agenda. The aim of the APF is to assist African regional institutions in the operationalisation of the APSA and provide funding to Africa-led Peace Support Operations. The APF has been endowed with an overall amount of more than €1.9 billion since 2004 (European Union, 2017). Funding for regional cooperation in the field of peacekeeping and crisis response is also provided through the Instrument contributing to Stability and Peace. Another programme set up within the framework of the JAES is the Pan-African Programme, which is funded through the Development Cooperation Instrument and aims at financing actions with a continental dimension.

Table 13.1 Financial allocations to regional programmes under the 8th, 9th, 10th and 11th EDF (€ million)

	8th EDF (1996–2001)	9th EDF (2002–2007)	10th EDF (2008–2013)	11th EDF (2014–2020)
West Africa	143	200	418	1,150
SADC	81	95	93	1,332
East Africa	154	203	548	
Central Africa	60	29	97	350
Total sub-Saharan Africa	438	527	1,156	2,832

Source: Compiled using European Union (2009) and data from the three Regional Indicative Programmes (2014–2020)

Table 13.2 Financial allocations to regional programmes under the 11th EDF (2014–2020) (€ million)

Regional Indicative Programme	Regional institutions involved	Peace and security	Economic and trade integration	Natural resource management	Other sectors	Total aid
West Africa	ECOWAS WAEMU	250	575	100	200 Resilience and food security 25 Institutional support	1,150
Central Africa	ECCAS	43	211	88	8	350
	Total	160	834	167	171	1332
	COMESA	0	85	0		
	EAC	14	45	20		
	IGAD	40	10	25		
	IOC	5	7	33		
Eastern Africa, Southern Africa and the Indian Ocean	SADC	15	47	9		
	Infrastructure envelope	0	600	0		
	Cross-regional envelope	85	40	80		
	Other				34 Institutional support 15 technical cooperation 122 performance reserve	
Total EDF aid		453 (16%)	1,620 (57%)	355 (13%)	404 (14%)	2,832 (100%)

Source: Compiled using data from the three Regional Indicative Programmes (2014–2020)

In the 1995 and 2008 communications, the European Commission insists that not only should more aid be given to regional integration but also support for regional integration must become smarter and consider the lessons from the past. The 1995 and 2008 communications and the Cotonou Agreement insists in particular on the importance of fostering ownership of regional integration processes (European Union, 1995: III) and ensuring that EU programmes are consistent with existing regional arrangements (European Union, 2012: Art. 28).

The implementation of the 9th and 10th EDF, however, has underlined several weaknesses in the regional aid framework. In 2009 the European Court of Auditors conducted an evaluation of aid for regional economic integration in East Africa and West Africa (European Union, 2009), two subregions where integration is relatively advanced. The conclusion of the Court was that 'EDF support for regional economic integration has so far been only partially effective' (ibid.: 7). The low institutional capacities and, in the case of East Africa, the incoherent membership of African regional institutions caused difficulties in absorbing and managing EU aid. Moreover, the Court pointed out that the European Commission had been unable to set a programming and monitoring strategy tailored to the specificity of regional cooperation. The Court expressed concern that the Commission had decided to double the financial allocation to regional programmes for the 10th EDF without considering past difficulties (ibid.: 28). Indeed, the problem of insufficient absorption capacities has continued to affect interregional cooperation and is likely to continue with the further increase of the regional envelope for the 11th EDF (Piccolino and Minou, 2017).

The EU seems to have adopted two strategies to respond to these challenges. The short-term strategy has been to divert funding to projects with a regional dimension but managed by national governments, international aid organisations and non-governmental organisations. While this has allowed the successful implementation of some projects, in practice it runs against one of the declared objectives of the EU regional integration promotion policy – strengthening regional governance and African ownership. The second strategy, which has found expression in the programming of the 11th EDF, has been to increasingly target aid at capacity building, through activities such as training and seminars. However, there are doubts about whether these activities can really tackle the problems that African regional organisations face (Piccolino and Minou, 2017).

'Regionalism' is also one of the four principles that, according to the Cotonou Agreement, should inspire the negotiations of the EPAs, the main framework of EU-Africa trade relationships. The EU negotiates the EPAs not with individual states but with five subregional blocks, labelled West Africa, Central Africa, Eastern and Southern Africa, East African Community and Southern African Development Community (SADC). The expectation of the EU is that the liberalisation of trade with the EU will be preceded or accompanied by the liberalisation of trade within the negotiating subregions, thus strengthening regional integration (European Union, 2008). Things have not gone as planned, however; and three main issues have complicated the EPA's fostering of regional integration.

First, the uneven level of regional integration of the five subregions and the overlapping memberships of some integration schemes has affected the objective of achieving coherent subregional agreements. Only two of the negotiating blocks – the EAC block and the West Africa block, corresponding to ECOWAS – clearly match an AU-recognised REC. The SADC EPA, in spite of the name, has been negotiated only with the members of SADC that have strong trade ties to South Africa.

Second, the principle of differentiation between countries at different levels of development, which is also part of the EPA negotiation framework, has clashed with the principle of regionalism. In particular, Least Developed Countries have benefitted since 2001 from the Everything but Arms initiative – under which all their imports to the EU, with the exception of armaments, are duty-free and quota-free – and they are thus under limited pressure to conclude an EPA. The EPA negotiations have had the effect of disrupting regional integration by creating a fragmented trade regime, with some countries in the same subregion benefitting from the Everything but Arms initiative, some concluding an interim individual EPA and some trading with the EU under the Generalised System of Preferences.

Finally, the overall framework of the EPAs has also been seriously questioned from the African side. Through the EPAs, the EU promotes a model of 'open regionalism' – integration within African subregions is seen as building blocks towards increased liberalisation and 'smooth integration into the global trading system' (European Union, 2008). In what looks to be the return of an old debate, it has been argued that this model is unlikely to stimulate regional trade and would, rather, fortify a pattern of unequal exchange between Africa and the EU (Sindzingre, 2016). The EU seems to have taken on board some of this criticism (European Union, 2008), without, however, backing down from its assertion that there is no contradiction between regional integration and openness to international trade.

Political dialogue and norm entrepreneurship

While development aid and trade negotiations follow a logic of utility calculation – African actors are given incentives, such as aid packages or access to European markets, if they implement policies seen by the EU as advancing regional integration – regionalism also informs dialogue and diplomatic engagement between the EU and its African counterparts. The EU sees dialogue as a tool that can promote regional norms through the mechanisms of persuasion and socialisation; African regional organisations consider it an occasion to put on the agenda regional issues that are important for them and to secure the EU support for their initiatives.

To some extent, the logic of dialogue has always been present in EU-Africa relations, with the European Commission Delegations and the ACP-EU joint institutions providing a regular point of contact between the EU and African governments. In the last two decades, however, with the creation of the CFSP, political dialogue has become increasingly institutionalised and has taken a broader focus, notably encompassing regional security cooperation. The 2010 revised text of the Cotonou Agreement specifically acknowledges the inclusion of regional organisations in the political dialogue (European Union, 2012: Art. 8.5). The first Africa-EU summit in 2000, the establishment of the AU and the launch of the JAES (African Union and European Union, 2007) have provided a new framework for the dialogue between the EU and its new continental partner. Although the political dialogue between the EU and African organisations has a broad focus, regional integration and regional cooperation on security matters are among the key cooperation areas identified by the JAES and have regularly figured in the agenda and in the final declarations of AU-EU summits (African Union and European Union, 2017: point 6; Bagoyoko and Gibert, 2009).

Dialogue might result into the establishment of new aid and development schemes – such as the case of the AFP or the Pan-African Programme. However, the expectation of constructivist theory is that dialogue will also have an impact per se on region-building through socialisation and persuasion. Through dialogue, the EU has notably attempted to influence the security and governance agenda of African regional organisations. On the one hand, it has insisted that Africans should cooperate more actively – a pattern that has been called 'the Africanisation of security' (Franke and Esmenjaud, 2008). On the other, it has tried to influence the normative underpinning of the AU and the RECs security policies, encouraging them to integrate notions of 'good governance' and 'human security' (Lopez Lucia, 2012) within regional cooperation.

It is important, however, not to overstate the EU contribution to the AU and the RECs' normative shift from non-interference to non-indifference. Norms on human security and democracy are universal in nature, and the EU is only one of many actors engaged in their promotion in Africa (Haastrup, 2013; Piccolino and Minou, 2017). More generally, the EU has not been in the driver's seat when it comes to African cooperation on matters of peace and security. The first regional peace operations and conflict management mechanisms have been launched in Africa in the 1990s as the response of African institutions to urgent security challenges. African regional organisations have displayed considerable agency and are themselves norm entrepreneurs when it comes to security (Aning and Edu-Afful, 2016). The EU has stepped in at their demand as a player at a later stage.

It is also important to consider that just as there are contradictions in the EU's cooperation and trade policies, there are also contradictions in the EU's stated commitment to empowering African regional organisations when it comes to security. When they perceive core interests to be at stake, European countries do not hesitate in intervening directly in Africa, often dragging the EU in the arena and, if necessary, sidestepping African institutions (Rye Olsen, 2015: 18), as seen in the launch of military operations in Libya and Mali.

The model-setting effect of the EU on Africa

Through instruments such as development, trade policy and political dialogue, the EU consciously aims at shaping or strengthening regional cooperation in Africa. Yet, the intensity of EU-Africa ties suggests that the influence of the EU has also been manifested indirectly and non-deliberately (Hartmann, 2016; Bach, 2015). At the time of the signing of the Rome Treaty, the EEC was perceived as a new type of regional organisation and inspired practitioners who wanted to following the EEC example. The EU got directly involved in the creation of some regional organisations, such as CEAO/WAEMU (Grimm, 1999). In other cases, the EU model was popularised by local norm entrepreneurs and epistemic communities, particularly UNECA, of which Adedeji was a long-time executive secretary. For instance, the example of the EEC was explicitly evoked during the talks that led to the establishment of ECOWAS (Asante, 1986: 55–56), and the organisation displayed a series of similarities with the EEC in its structure and objectives.

African officials have continued to engage with European regionalism as a source of inspiration for their own regional projects after the transformation of the EEC into the EU. The choice to name the OAU's successor the 'African Union' signalled a deliberate will by African officials to evoke the EU model. Public declarations of AU officials offer evidence that they explicitly look at the EU as a model from which they can draw useful lessons (Fioramonti, 2009: 9). Recent subregional organisations also display a similar engagement with the EU. For instance, officials from the EAC state that they look at the EU as a natural partner because it has gone through the same process the EAC aims to go through (Bachmann and Sidaway, 2010: 2).

The most visible affinities between the European and the African integration projects lie in the institutional set-up of the AU and of some subregional organisations. Similarities range 'from the establishment of commissions, councils and parliaments to the use of similar symbols' (Fioramonti and Mattheis, 2016: 675; Adebajo, 2012). The EU also inspires some of the underlying principles of African regionalism. Different from the loose forms of cooperation promoted by some Asian organisations, African regional integration projects have from the start tended to aim for political and economic integration (Bach, 2015).

The fact that African organisations have drawn so heavily from the EU raises a series of questions about the extent to which institutions and practices copied from the EU are transferable and how they work in a different context. The EU is characterised by advanced industrial economies and strong state institutions, while, in spite of recent economic growth, Africa remains the poorest continent and formal institutions in Africa are notoriously weak. It is not a surprise that there is a diffuse perception in the literature that African regionalism is an example of 'failed transfer' of the EU integration model. 'Grand ambitions', particularly in the domain of market integration, are said to contrast with 'little functional co-operation/integration' (Fioramonti and Mattheis, 2016: 685, Table 2; see also Adebajo, 2012).

Some scholars (Söderbaum, 2004; Gibb, 2009) have taken a cynical view, arguing that African elites, because of their subordinate position in the international system, see the formal adoption of EU-inspired institutions as a way to boost their international legitimacy and obtain foreign 'resources of extraversion', such as development aid and military cooperation. Indeed, few would dispute that institutional isomorphism can facilitate dialogue between organisations based in the global North and in the Global South and, subsequently, the provision of aid and technical support. Both Söderbaum and Gibb argue, however, that African leaders are not seriously interested in successfully appropriating the European model. 'Regime boosting regionalism' (Söderbaum, 2004) would reinforce neo-patrimonial regimes and not deliver any benefit to African citizens (Gibb, 2009: 716).

A related but more nuanced argument, drawn from organisational sociology, sees institutional organisations as systems that are created to conform to models that are considered successful. Their behaviour is driven by a concern for legitimacy rather than a preoccupation with efficiency (DiMaggio and Powell, 1983; Jetschke, 2009). Creating EU-inspired parliaments and commissions or invoking the creation of an EU-style economic and monetary union is a way for African institutions to claim legitimacy by associating themselves with the European model (Piccolino, 2020). Because of the heritage of colonialism, which has created a legacy of 'imported institutions', and the pressures on African bureaucracies to show that they are delivering 'good governance' and 'development', the mechanism of normative isomorphism is particularly powerful in the African context (ibid.).

An analysis of African regionalism that measures success in terms of ability to follow the European model risks falling into the trap of Eurocentrism and missing the mark. First, it is not clear if the EU model of integration through the creation of a common market would deliver the expected benefits to Africa in terms of stimulating development. The regional projects that have more clearly followed the European example, such as WAEMU, provide mixed evidence of its benefits (Piccolino, 2020). An excessive focus on the formal and superficial imitation of the EU model by African organisations and on their failure to achieve EU-inspired goals also risks downplaying the actual differences between European and African integration and the unique and original features of the African project of regional integration (Fioramonti and Mattheis, 2016; Haastrup, 2013).

A first important distinction between regionalism in Europe and Africa lies in the origin of the European and African integration project and their underlying ideal justification. The ideology of Pan-Africanism and the quest for liberation from colonialism and external interference that have underscored the foundation of African regional organisations have no equivalent in the EU case. It has been argued that Pan-Africanism 'provides a shared narrative of being African, which is not as apparent in Europe' (Haastrup, 2013: 790). Another notable difference is the territorially inclusive character of the AU and of the RECs, which contrasts with the EU's expansion from a core of committed states and the conditional nature of the EU's accession process. As a consequence, the AU 'incorporates a wide divergence in respect of both democratic ideals and economic performance' (Vines, 2013: 95). The AU and some of the RECs have reacted to this challenge by adopting provisions to sanction serious violations of democracy. It is significant that a similar provision – Article 7 – was introduced in the EU Treaty in 1997 partly as a response to the EU enlargement, which has meant that the EU has to deal with a broader and more diverse membership.

Finally, while some RECs are closer to the EU model because of their economic and trade focus, the development of the AU has been driven by high politics and the organisation has a strong security focus (Haastrup, 2013; Vines, 2013). The aspiration to continental peace is a core driver of both African and European regionalism, but there are differences in the threats to peace that African and European regional organisations have historically faced and in the solutions that they have adopted. The European project was born out of a devastating interstate conflict and the EEC/EU aimed to build peace by increasing interdependency between its member states. On the other hand, one of the core aims of the AU is to manage internal conflicts within its member states and to do this through direct peacekeeping and peace enforcement operations (Haastrup, 2013). African regional organisations have also acted as norm entrepreneurs in this domain, pioneering the Responsibility to Protect before its adoption by the UN (African Union, 2000: Art. 4h).

The turmoil that the EU has experienced in the last few years, with the crisis of the eurozone and the rise of nativist Eurosceptic movements in a number of countries, raise the question of whether the EU is still seen as a positive model of regional integration in the rest of the world. With regards to Africa, the EPA negotiations seem to have affected perception of the EU more than developments in Europe itself. Alice Sindzingre argues that 'the EU's explicit adherence since the 2000s to specific theoretical assumptions and policies has eroded the economic credibility of its model, and of the associated policies, as an optimal tool of growth and welfare' (2016: 82). It is worth observing that these assumptions, which 'include the affirmation of the benefits of competition, trade openness and fiscal adjustment as the only routes towards growth' (Sindzingre, 2016: 82), have been relatively recently embraced by the EU itself in its own regional integration project. However, the fact that they have informed the EPA trade negotiations is arguably one of the reasons why the EU has lost some of its appeal in Africa as a source of inspiration.

This is not necessarily a negative development for Africa, as there are signs that the crisis of the European project might stimulate a more critical way of thinking among African policymakers. During interviews conducted in 2013 in West Africa, possibly the subregion that has most closely followed the EU model, a number of high-ranking officials stressed the need for ECOWAS and WAEMU to distance themselves from the EU and be more innovative (Piccolino, 2020). It is however also possible that the crisis of the European integration project, the most important and ambitious experiment of regional integration, discourages the pursuit of regional integration in other parts of the world, including Africa.

Conclusion

Regional integration and its promotion have always played an important role in EU-African relations, and, at least potentially, this is the area where the EU can provide most 'added value', given its own experience of regional integration. African regional projects have been inspired by the European project in many ways. However, there have been historical inconsistencies both in the offer of regional integration by the EU and in its demand by African organisations. Current analysis of the EU's 'normative power', in particular, has neglected the role of historical factors such as colonialism and the neocolonial policies of EU member states in shaping the way Europe and Africa have engaged, including in the field of regional integration.

The new millennium and the creation of the AU seemed to have opened a new chapter in which the EU and Africa engage with each other on more equal terms when it comes to regional integration. However, a series of problems remain: the external support of the EU has tended to encourage isomorphic mimicry, where African regional organisations copy formal and institutional aspects of the EU model but are not always able to make these institutions work. Significantly, African regional organisations have made some of their major progresses in areas such as peace and security, where they have not taken inspiration from the EU. Moreover, episodes such as the EPA negotiations or European countries' disregard for African regional organisations when their own security interests are at stake have revived African fears that the EU promotes regional integration in Africa on its own terms and interests.

It is still unclear whether the crisis that the EU is currently experiencing with Brexit and the rise of Euroscepticism will have an impact on regional integration in Africa. The EU continues to be Africa's main donor and partner when it comes to external support for regional integration. However, the feeling that the EU is a positive model and that it has lessons to give to African regional organisations is slowly eroding. Whether this crisis helps African regionalism to emancipate itself from its European mentor and find locally rooted solutions to its problems, or whether it ultimately makes regional integration a less attractive option for Africa altogether, remains to be seen.

Note

1 The ACP Group is now known as the Organisation of African, Caribbean and Pacific States, having changed its name in 2020.

Bibliography

Adebajo, A. (2012) Paradise lost and found: The African Union and the European Union. In A. Adebajo and K. Whiteman (eds), *The EU and Africa: From Eurafrique to Afro-Europa*. Cape Town and London: Centre for Conflict Resolution and Hurst (pp. 45–82).

Adebajo, A. (2014) Two prophets of regional integration: Prebisch and Adedeji. In B. Currie-Alder, R. Kanbur, D.M. Malone and R. Medhora (eds), *International Development: Ideas, Experience, and Prospects*. Oxford: Oxford University Press (pp. 323–338).

African Union (2000) Constitutive Act of the African Union. Lomé, 11 July. www.africa-union.org/root/au/aboutau/constitutive_act_en.htm (retrieved 14 June 2013).

African Union and European Union (2007) The Africa-EU Strategic Partnership: A Joint Africa-EU Strategy [online]. www.africa-eu-partnership.org/sites/default/files/documents/eas2007_joint_strategy_en.pdf (retrieved 29 January 2018).

African Union and European Union (2017) Investing in Youth for Accelerated Inclusive Growth and Sustainable Development. AU-EU Summit, Abidjan, 29–30 November. https://eeas.europa.eu/headquarters/headquarters-homepage/37189/5th-au-eu-summit-joint-declaration-investing-youth-accelerated-inclusive-growth-and_en (retrieved 29 January 2018).

Aning, K. and Edu-Afful, F. (2016) African Agency in R2P: Interventions by African Union and ECOWAS in Mali, Côte d'Ivoire, and Libya. *International Studies Review*, 18 (1), 120–133.

Asante, S.K.B. (1986) *The Political Economy of Regionalism in Africa: A Decade of the Economic Community of West African States (ECOWAS)*. New York: Praeger.

Bach, D. (2015) *Regionalism in Africa: Genealogies, Institutions and Trans-State Networks*. Routledge Studies in African Politics and International Relations. Abingdon and New York: Routledge.

Bachmann, V. and Sidaway, J.D. (2010) African regional integration and European involvement: External agents in the East African Community. *South African Geographical Journal*, 92 (1), 1–6. https://doi.org/10.1080/03736245.2010.480841

Bagoyoko, N. and Gibert, M.V. (2009) The linkage between security, governance and development: The European Union in Africa. *The Journal of Development Studies*, 45 (5), 789–814. https://doi.org/10.1080/00220380802582312

Börzel, T.A. and Risse, T. (2009) *Diffusing (Inter-) Regionalism. The EU as a Model of Regional Integration*. Working Paper 7. The Transformative Power of Europe Series. Berlin: Free University of Berlin.

Coste, J. and Egg, J. (1998) L'appui de l'Union Européenne À L'intégration Régionale: Une (Double) Projection Trompeuse? Le Cas de l'Afrique de l'Ouest. In *La Convention de Lomé En Questions: Les Relations Entre Les Pays d'Afrique, Des Caraïbes et Du Pacifique (ACP) et l'Union Européenne Après L'an 2000*. Paris: Karthala (pp. 168–185).

DiMaggio, P. and Powell, W.W. (1983) The iron cage revisited: Collective rationality and institutional isomorphism in organizational fields. *American Sociological Review*, 48 (2), 147–160.

European Union (1969) Convention d'association entre la Communauté économique européenne et les États africains et malgache associés à cette Communauté. 70/540/CEE.

European Union (1975) Convention ACP-CEE de Lomé signée le 28 février 1975 et documents connexes. Secrétariat général du Conseil des Communautés européennes.

European Union (1988) Rapport spécial n° 4/88 sur la coopération régionale financée dans le cadre des conventions de Lomé, accompagné des réponses de la Commission. *Journal officiel*, no. C 188, July 18, 34–56. http://eur-lex.europa.eu/LexUriServ/LexUriServ.do?uri=CELEX:31988Y0718(03):FR:HTML (retrieved 31 December 2017).

European Union (1995) European Community Support for Regional Economic Integration Efforts among Developing Countries. Communication from the European Commission. COM (95) 219 final. 16 June. http://aei.pitt.edu/id/eprint/4328 (retrieved 14 June 2013).

European Union (2006a) Partnership Agreement Africa Caribbean and Pacific (ACP)-European Community (EC). Signed in Cotonou on 23 June 2000. Revised in Luxembourg on 25 June 2005. Consolidated version. Luxembourg: Office for Official Publications of the European Communities.

European Union (2006b) Joint Statement by the Council and the Representatives of the Governments of the Member States Meeting within the Council, the European Parliament and the Commission on European Union Development Policy: 'The European Consensus'. 2006/C 46/01. http://eur-lex.europa.eu/LexUriServ/LexUriServ.do?uri=OJ%3AC%3A2006%3A046%3A0001%3A0019%3AEN%3APDF (retrieved 28 January 2018).

European Union (2008) Regional Integration for Development in ACP Countries, Communication from the European Commission. COM(2008) 604 final/2. Brussels, 6 October.

European Union (2009) *EDF Support for Regional Economic Integration in East Africa and West Africa*. European Court of Auditors, Special Report 19. http://eca.europa.eu/portal/pls/portal/docs/1/8030724.PDF (retrieved 26 July 2013).

European Union (2012) The Cotonou Agreement. Signed in Cotonou on 23 June 2000. Revised in Luxembourg on 25 June 2005. Revised in Ouagadougou on 22 June 2010. Consolidated version. Luxembourg: Office for Official Publications of the European Communities.

European Union (2016) European Parliament Resolution of 16 April 2013 on Advancing Development through Trade. (2012/2224(INI)). 2016/C 045/02. http://eur-lex.europa.eu/legal-content/EN/TXT/?uri=CELEX%3A52013IP0119 (retrieved 28 January 2018).

European Union (2017) African Peace Facility [online]. International Cooperation and Development. https://ec.europa.eu/europeaid/regions/africa/continental-cooperation/african-peace-facility_en (retrieved 29 January 2018).

Fioramonti, L. (2009) *African Perceptions of the European Union: Assessing the Work of the EU in the Field of Democracy Promotion and Peacekeeping*. Stockholm: International Institute for Democracy and Electoral Assistance.

Fioramonti, L. and Mattheis, F. (2016) Is Africa really following Europe? An integrated framework for comparative regionalism. *JCMS: Journal of Common Market Studies*, 54 (3), 674–690. https://doi.org/10.1111/jcms.12307

Franke, B. (2007) Competing regionalisms in Africa and the continent's emerging security architecture. African Studies Quarterly, 9 (3), 31–64.

Franke, B. and Esmenjaud, R. (2008) Who owns African ownership? The Africanisation of security and its limits. *South African Journal of International Affairs*, 15 (2), 137–158. https://doi.org/10.1080/10220460802614486

Gibb, R. (2009) Regional integration and Africa's development trajectory: Meta-theories, expectations and reality. *Third World Quarterly*, 30 (4), 701–721. https://doi.org/10.1080/01436590902867136

Gladden, E.N. (1963) The East African Common Services Organization. *Parliamentary Affairs*, 16 (4), 428–439.

Grimm, S. (1999) Institutional change in the West African Economic and Monetary Union (WAEMU) since 1994: A fresh start after the devaluation shock? *Africa Spectrum*, 34 (1), 5–32.

Haastrup, T. (2013) EU as mentor? Promoting regionalism as external relations practice in EU–Africa relations. *Journal of European Integration*, 35 (7), 785–800. https://doi.org/10.1080/07036337.2012.744754

Hartmann, C. (2016) Sub-Saharan Africa. In T.A. Börzel and T. Risse (eds), *The Oxford Handbook of Comparative Regionalism*. Oxford: Oxford University Press (pp. 271–296).

Jetschke, A. (2009) Institutionalizing ASEAN: Celebrating Europe through network governance. *Cambridge Review of International Affairs*, 22 (3), 407–426.

Lopez Lucia, E. (2012) *A Tool for Security Governance: How Is the EU Fostering and Shaping ECOWAS Security and Defence Regionalization Process?* [online]. GR:EEN Working Paper No 17. www.greenfp7.eu/papers/workingpapers

Olofin, S. (1977) Ecowas and the Lomé Convention: An experiment in complementary or conflicting customs union arrangements? *JCMS: Journal of Common Market Studies*, 16 (1), 53–72.

Piccolino, G. (2020) Looking like a regional organization? The European model of regional integration and the West African Economic and Monetary Union (WAEMU). *Cambridge Review of International Affairs*, 33 (2), 179–203.

Piccolino, G. and Minou, S. (2017) The EU and regional integration in West Africa: What effects on conflict transformation? In N. Tocci and Diez, T. (eds), *The EU, Promoting Regional Integration, and Conflict Resolution*. Cham, Switzerland: Palgrave Macmillan (pp.109–130).

Olsen, G.R. (2015) *Providing Security in a Liberal World Order: The Only Tool Left for European Union in Africa?* Paper prepared for the EUSA Fourteenth Biennial Conference: Changing Agendas in EU-Africa Relations, Boston, 5–7 March.

Sindzingre, A.N. (2016) From an eroding model to questioned trade relationships: The European Union and sub-Saharan Africa. *Insight on Africa*, 8 (2), 81–95. https://doi.org/10.1177/0975087816646866

Söderbaum, F. (2004) Modes of regional governance in Africa: Neoliberalism, sovereignty boosting, and shadow networks. *Global Governance*, 10 (4), 419–436.

Vines, A. (2013) A decade of African Peace and Security Architecture. *International Affairs*, 89 (1), 89–109.

14
Interregionalism and bilateralism in the context of EU-Africa relations

Andrzej Polus

Introduction

This chapter aims at a critical presentation of interregionalism in the context of European Union (EU)-Africa relations with the special emphasis on the Visegrád (also known as V4) countries' role. It critically analyses these relations from global and Central European perspectives. Two general theoretical assumptions underpin this text. Firstly, relations between EU and Africa and the intra-EU relations are characterised by deep power disparities. Despite the emergence of the 'Africa rising' narrative in mainstream media and among consulting companies around 2011 (Kopinski et al., 2013: 14–37), Africa's place in the international division of labour has not changed since decolonisation (it might be argued that its position is actually waning due to the continent's deindustrialisation); and this situation is reflected in EU-Africa relations (Taylor, 2016). Despite the lip service paid to plans to transform EU-Africa relations into a 'partnership of equals', the Economic Partnership Agreement (EPA) negotiations – important from the perspective of Africa's future development – are giving almost no hope for change. This reflects and reinforces the unequal power relations between the EU and Africa. Power disparities also exist among EU member states. Migratory crisis forced coordinated actions between Central and Eastern European countries (CEECs), which are reflected among other initiatives in the Visegrád Group.

Secondly, a social constructivist ontological position is assumed, according to which phenomena in the international environment and their meanings are not fixed, but socially constructed. This approach draws attention to how knowledge 'production' in International Relations studies privileges certain research questions and the usage of intersubjective analytical categories which might have inbuilt assumptions about the ways international relations work. For example, the use of European integration processes as the main reference point for analysing regional integration in other parts of the globe is linked to the EU's policies towards other regional organisations. Assumptions about policy coherence are also implicated. This chapter shows, however, how the internal situation in CEECs states during the migration crisis renewed the Visegrad Group's interest in relations with African countries as well as the implications of this for how we think about interregionalism.

Within this context, the remainder of the chapter is organised as follows. The first section presents the global context for EU-Africa relations, focusing on the concept of interregionalism.

The second section critically discusses the major academic narratives on EU-Africa relations and reflects on the Visegrád Group's increased interest in relations with Africa. The next section briefly presents the V4 countries' initiatives in terms of their relations with African states and the internal situation in the EU. The last section concludes. One objection that can be raised concerning the text is linked to the fact that the narrative on EU-Africa relations is based mainly on sources produced in the Global North, which might serve to minimise the role of African regional organisations and African states in this discussion.

The global context for EU-Africa relations: Old wine in slightly refurbished bottles

At the beginning of the second decade of the 21st century, none of the leading analysts of international relations could have predicted Donald Trump in the White House, the annexation of Crimea by the Russian Federation, the impact of the migration crisis on the EU SARS Cov -2 pandemic, and the withdrawal of the United Kingdom from the EU (commonly known as Brexit). At the same time, the multilateral world order is in crisis. The United States government under the administration of Donald Trump is committed to defunding multilateral institutions and potentially withdrawing from some international schemes. It seems that multilateralism does not regulate hubris any more. In contrast, the EU, presented as a champion of multilateralism and a model of regional integration, must tackle the most serious confidence crisis in its history. The divisions between 'old' and 'new' Europe are becoming more and more evident, as is the rise of anti-EU sentiments in its member states, embodied in the rising support for a number of Eurosceptic political parties (Meijers, 2017). This situation is further reflected in the political idea of a 'two-speed Europe', (revived after the Brexit referendum in the United Kingdom) where the deeper integrated 'core' driven by France and Germany is opposed to the peripheries – mainly Central and Eastern Europe. This division is seen in the different priorities for EU foreign policy. While relations with Africa are deemed to be of more importance to the core EU countries, the Central and East European member states appear to demand higher priority for the Eastern Partnership, especially in terms of relations with Ukraine and Georgia.

There is further contestation within European institutions, with some advocating for more interest-orientated approaches, rather than values-orientated ones, which are also visible in EU-Africa relations. Arguably, in the mid and long-term, Brexit is the most important game changer, internally, when it comes to EU-Africa relations. In the short term, the migration crisis and the lack of political vision on how to tackle it will dominate political discussions.

At the same time, there are multiple emerging powers engaged in relations with Africa, even though, as is constantly stressed by the top EU officials, the EU remains Africa's major trade and investment partner (Tusk, 2017). Nevertheless, Europe's dominant position as Africa's oldest partner has ended, and there is a need for a new, well-defined format for the practice of mutual relations. As Taylor claims, Africa provides the EU with 'the greatest potential space to manoeuvre and overcome its failure to develop as a truly coherent global political actor' (2010: 112). China has been Africa's largest single trading partner since 2009. In 2015 China-Africa trade volume was estimated at USD 169 billion. Nevertheless, the combined value of EU trade with Africa was far higher, estimated by Eurostat at over €276 billion in 2015 (Copley, 2017). Thus, despite China's increased involvement in Africa, the gap between China's and the EU's trade volume with Africa exceeds €100 billion (Eurostat, 2019) however, the dynamics of world trade is slowing down in 2020 due to the Covid 19 pandemic..

Still, the dynamics of both Chinese trade and investment in Africa exceeds that of the EU, and, at least discursively, many African leaders perceive China to be an important partner.

Eastern African countries and Egypt see a lot of opportunities in the Chinese Belt and Road Initiatives, which plan to establish two regional hubs in Africa: in Kenya and Egypt. It is worth remembering, however, that Chinese trade relations with Africa are dominated by bilateral trade with just four African states: Angola, South Africa, the Democratic Republic of the Congo and Sudan. Many African politicians are aware that it will be extremely difficult to put industrialisation strategies into practice if Africa is to compete with China; and without industrialisation, the position of African countries in the international division of labour remains unchanged. Moreover, Africa's unchanging position in the international division of labour can be further enforced by the EU's EPAs (see Langan and Price in this volume). What is important to note is that in terms of relations with Africa, the dichotomy of China versus the West is false even though the implications of competition between China and the West are manifested in Africa.

In the context of the EU's and China's policies in Africa, cooperation is increasingly more visible than conflict, especially in the extractives sector. Chinese oil extraction corporations cooperate with their European peers when it comes to discussions on licencing and revenue collection systems in African states. Nevertheless, African collaboration with BRICS (Brazil, Russia, India, China and South Africa) or through the Forum on China-Africa Cooperation, or the promises to pump USD 60 billion into Africa in the coming years, slightly strengthen the position of African governments in their relations with the EU, including bilateral relations with member states. Additionally, in the second decade of the 21st century, the new axis of South-South cooperation has emerged. Brazil, Argentina, South Korea and Turkey are increasing their diplomatic and economic presences across the continent. According to United Nations Conference on Trade and Development estimates, in 2012, for the first time '[foreign direct investment] inflows from developing economies into Africa outstripped those from developed economies' (Kopinski et al., 2013: 45). In this context (along with the EU crisis) the V4 countries began planning to intensify relations with Africa, emphasising 'economisation of foreign policy', which was reflected in the Hungarian government's Southern Opening policy and the Polish Investment and Trade Agency's Go Africa programme, among other initiatives.

'Core' and 'peripheral' EU in EU-Africa relations

The history and development of EU-Africa interregional relations might be examined on several levels. Firstly, as argued by Farrell (2015), the evolution of economic relations – from Lomé Conventions through the Cotonou Agreements and the current negotiations of EPAs – reflects an interest-based approach on the part of the EU, rather than a value-based approach aimed at democracy and human rights promotion in the developing world. African regionalism based on free trade areas has often been presented in terms of a 'spaghetti bowl' metaphor, where the priorities of multiple regional organisations overlap. Despite such critical remarks on the efficiency of African regional organisations, the format of EPA negotiations leads to the assertion that the European Commission is actually attempting to put more noodles into the already existing spaghetti bowl, essentially weakening the negotiating position of African, Caribbean and Pacific states. It is quite ironic that the EU, which is trying to position itself as a model for regional integration, is actually further dividing Africa due to the composition of EPA negotiating blocks and the practice of EU European Neighbourhood Policy.

When it came to the EPA negotiations, the European Commission was very efficient in dividing the existing regional associations in Africa. Just one out of the five EPA negotiating blocks in sub-Saharan Africa is correlated with an already existing regional organisation – the East African Community (paradoxically this organisation had been dormant for over two decades and was revived only in 2000). For example, the 'region' of Eastern and Southern Africa, created for the sake of EPA negotiation, is made up of Djibouti, Eritrea, Ethiopia, Sudan, Malawi, Zambia, Zimbabwe, Comoros, Mauritius, Madagascar and Seychelles, and even the European Commission states that 'regional integration remains a challenge for this region' (2018). Moreover, looking at the economies of Eastern and Southern Africa states, it is hard to define the lowest common denominator that would allow these countries a deal via the EPA negotiations that is better than what they already enjoy under the Cotonou Agreement. In terms of interregionalism, the EU can definitely be referred to a 'region creator'; however, this name should be understood as the EU externally imposing creation of regions. Interestingly, the revitalisation of cooperation among the V4 countries was the result of the European Commission's policy towards Central and Eastern Europe. In this case, the initiative for regional cooperation came from the CEECs, but the impulse for this was the desire to strengthen the V4 countries' voice in the EU forum. We can, therefore, speak of imposed regionalism in terms of EU-Africa relations in which relatively weak states, not necessarily geographically close to each other, must adopt externally imposed 'regional' frameworks for cooperation with the EU; and we can also refer to inter-EU regionalism, as EU states with geographic proximity have created a block to strengthen their voice at the European level.

In the traditional understanding of multilateralism, various forms of transnational and international cooperation are efficient if there is a leading state (or group of states) which supports, finances and legitimises the very existence of multilateral forms of cooperation. That is the case of the V4 group, but the EU, despite its current crisis, remains, as a chief supporter of multilateralism, a major reference point in comparative studies and interregional relations. It is unsurprising then that comparisons with the EU lead to statements that 'regionalism on the African continent is seen as primitive, weak or simply a failure' (Soderbaum, 2013: 185). Soderbaum rightly argues that if we want to understand the dynamics of regionalism in Africa we should take off 'European lenses' and focus rather on questions based on functionalism and the international political economy (ibid.). For simple comparison, if we accept the possibility that the France-Germany alliance is an engine of European integration, then we can say that the same role has been played in the AU by Nigeria, South Africa and Libya. Cooperation between Nigeria and South Africa provided the basis for a major inter-African initiative in the post-Cold War era: the New Partnership for Africa's Development. However, cooperation for this partnership does not provide evidence of joint diplomatic activity within the AU or with regards to African relations with the EU.

Perhaps for this reason, the issue of the EU's potential to legitimise specific activities in the context of regional integration (or AU-EU relations) is rarely addressed in EU-Africa relations. This legitimisation was grounded in the 'success' of European integration, which has been challenged by Brexit.

Generally, research on the practices of so-called 'old' members of the EU has relied on the theory of intergovernmentalism. These studies usually focus on EU member states that have a clearly defined foreign policy line towards Africa, then examine their capacity/knowledge to translate their preferences to the EU level and make those preferences EU policy towards Africa. The implication is that certain countries feature much more in EU-Africa relations. For example, CEECs as a group has no enduring policies towards African states. Consequently, they are written out of accounts of the crafting of policies towards Africa within the EU institutions. Arguably, it also means these countries' priorities towards Africa, when filtered through the EU institutions, are non-existent. They are unable to influence directly or veto the European Development Fund (EDF) priorities due to their low levels of contribution, and, collectively, the Visegrád Group has just 38 votes, whereas the lowest number of votes needed to veto the EDF 11th edition was established at 280.

This, however, does not mean that EU institutions are not acting in the interest of member states; rather it means that since the CEECs do not have their own strategies towards Africa, they accept the priorities set by the EU institutions. These priorities, by necessity, are grounded in the negotiations between the European Commission and governments with prior relations with engaged with African states. CEECs whose policies towards African countries during the communist period were coordinated by Moscow[1] did not have specific goals and economic interests in Africa after 1989. Their main priority was integration with Euro-Atlantic structures, and after completion of this goal, their foreign policy objectives in terms of relations with Africa were demarcated by the EU. This situation is reflected in the position of the Polish Ministry of Foreign Affairs statement that 'since 2004, Poland's policy towards Africa has been increasingly incorporated into the overall EU activities aimed at peace, security and closer cooperation with this continent' (Ministry of Foreign Affairs, Republic of Poland, 2018).

Thus, since CEECs' relations with African states were in decline after the fall of communism – mainly due to the lack of political and ideological factors which had strengthened links between communist states and some African leaders during the Cold War – membership of the EU enforced adaptation of already established patterns of relations with Africa (Polus, 2016). This situation is reflected in the EU model of policymaking introduced by Andrew Moravcsik in the mid-1990s – liberal intergovernmentalism (Moravcsik, 1993). This approach focuses on a dual decision-making structure where the most powerful EU member states and EU institutions are involved in 'major bargains', the outcome of which becomes the policy towards Africa. This approach prioritises the economic interests of the most powerful EU member states. EU trade with the African continent is dominated by eight countries: France, Germany, the Netherlands, the United Kingdom, Belgium, Spain, Italy and Portugal. Eduard Marinov (2017: 170) estimates that these eight countries account for more than 90% of the EU trade with sub-Saharan Africa. It is not surprising then that CEECs are not actively involved in agenda-setting and implementation of EU policies towards Africa.

Yet, some minor initiatives exist to promote trade between African states and Central Europe, such as the Africa-Central Europe Economic Co-operation Forum, organised during the European Economic Congresses in Katowice (the Forum is unofficial and organised on an ad hoc basis) or the Budapest Africa Forum (which only had three editions). Despite the narrative of multiple mutual opportunities and widening potential for cooperation, the dynamics of trade between Central European states and Africa is far below its potential. The volume of trade between V4

Table 14.1 Selected EU Member States' embassies (with the exclusion of consulates) in Africa

Country	Number of embassies in Africa
France	47
Germany	42
Spain	29
Italy	24
Holland	24
United Kingdom	37
Poland	11
Czech Republic	11
Slovakia	5
Hungary	10

Source: Author's own elaboration on the basis of data provided by official web pages of the ministries of foreign affairs in France, Germany, Spain, Italy, Holland, the United Kingdom, Poland, Czech Republic, Slovakia and Hungary

countries and Africa reached €9.553 million in 2019 – even less than, say, Belgium's imports from Africa (Eurostat, 2020). Disparities in trade are mirrored in the number of diplomatic missions in Africa, which is correlated with political engagement in this part of the globe.

To a large extent then, interregional relations between the EU and Africa is shaped by Western European countries. The crisis of the EU might potentially create disruptions in terms of the Union's policy towards Africa. Since 2015, however, the topic of 'renewal' of CEECs' relations with Africa has been increasingly evident, particularly in academic discourse (Kurtagic, 2019; Chmiel, 2018; Cibian, 2017). Analysis of the V4 Group's renewal of relations with Africa in the context of EU political processes is presented below.

Drivers of V4 countries' renewed interest in Africa

Following the migration crisis of 2015 and the introduction of EU trade sanctions against the Russian Federation after the Crimea annexation, Central and East European states decided to cooperate more closely by adopting common positions within the EU, hence the revitalisation of the Visegrád Group (V4). The Visegrád Group, although unofficial, is one of the most important forums in terms of EU policy coordination for Poland, the Czech Republic, Hungary and Slovakia. Recently, the V4 countries have increasingly declared interest in trade with African countries. This was partly due to closure of the Russian market and the V4 position on the migratory crisis that instead of accepting migrants, it is necessary to help African and Middle East countries to develop their economies to pre-empt the reasons for migration to Europe. However, the V4 countries are relatively weak on development assistance; they did not live up to the promise of transferring 0.33% of gross domestic product (GDP) to official development assistance (ODA). On top of that, they refused to accept migrants within the framework of the mandatory relocation mechanism. According to the estimations of the Polish Institute of International Affairs in 2018, Poland, the Czech Republic and Hungary spent 0.14% of GDP on ODA, and Slovakia spent 0.13% (Jóźwiak, 2020). Despite performative actions – such as the creation of the position of Minister for Humanitarian Aid in Poland or the launch in Uganda of 'the largest foreign investment project' in Hungarian history, aimed at helping 'locals and refugees prosper in the country so that they do not need to migrate to Europe' (Hungary Today, 2019; see also Embassy of the Republic of Uganda Berlin-Germany 2019) – there has been no substantial increase in funds allocated to ODA. Despite pursuing this new kind of relationship, data from 2019 show that there is no visible increase in the trade between V4 countries and African states, and the COVID-19 pandemic will likely have a negative influence on trade volume in 2020. Arguably, establishing new trade contacts with African countries to open new market channels is all the more important (by opening an important market for agriculture products that has been lost in Russia).

The most commonly used rationalisation for the CEECs entering African markets is that the colonial legacy is absent and they maintained relatively good trade and political relations with African states during the Cold War. From the 1960s, tens of thousands of African students graduated from Central European universities. Some of these individuals are playing key roles in African politics. Alpha Oumar Konare, former Malian president and chairperson of the African Union Commission is one such notable graduate of the University of Warsaw. Politicians like this are presented as 'unused assets' in CEECs' relations with African states. Furthermore, products such as arms from Czechoslovakia (Muehlenbeck, 2016), Ikarus busses from Hungary and Polish machinery have a good reputation in Africa, which provides a basis for intensifying trade exchange. Some of the academic literature has also begun to pick up on this burgeoning relationship between CEECs and African states (Kurtagic, 2019; Chmiel, 2018; Cibian, 2017).

However, what is missing in these publications is a clear correlation between the 'turn towards Africa' and the internal political situation of the V4 countries (anti-migratory political rhetoric) and their desire to influence EU policy – especially turning attention and resources to the Eastern Partnership.

Entering the economic markets of African countries, however, will be reliant on renewed political presence in Africa. Poland and the Czech Republic decided to reduce diplomatic presence in sub-Saharan Africa after the financial crisis of 2008. Poland closed embassies in Tanzania, Zimbabwe, Senegal and the Democratic Republic of the Congo, while the Czech Republic closed its diplomatic missions in Angola, Kenya and the Democratic Republic of the Congo. However, there is an increasing reversal of this situation. Poland reopened embassies in Tanzania and Senegal, and the Czech Republic did the same in Kenya. Although the V4 presence in Africa is small, the process of reopening embassies was associated with investment projects. However, to date, none of the large investments in Africa planned by both state-owned and private entities from the V4 countries has taken place. One can actually build the argument that in the second decade of the 21st century, we can observe more Southern African capital penetrating the V4 countries than capital moving from V4 countries into Africa.

In addition to bilateral engagements, there has also been cooperation within the group related to the relationship with African countries. For example, in the context of relations with South Africa, V4 countries opened Visegrád House in Cape Town in 2010. Visegrád House provides consular services for V4 countries' citizens, and each of the states takes over the running of the House for one week per month. This is a cost-effective solution in terms of consular assistance for tourists. The 'new opening' of Central and Eastern Europe to Africa indicates that the V4 countries are moving towards adopting common positions in the context of EU-Africa relations, though the Eastern Partnership will remain their central priority.

Conclusion

The chapter presented various bilateral and interregional forms of interactions that exist in the context of EU-Africa relations, with special emphasis on the position of CEECs in these processes. The EU's political line towards Africa is being defined jointly by the EU institutions and the EU member states with the biggest trade interests in Africa. The migration crisis and Brexit have influenced the official narratives of the EU, which have become more explicitly interest-oriented. This phenomenon is visible not only in EU-Africa relations, but also in the idea of 'principled pragmatism' in the EU's new Global Strategy on Foreign and Security Policy. Despite the so-called equality, EU-Africa relations are characterised by asymmetry. This is most visible in the EPA process, where the EU was able to create new regions just for the sake of the negotiations. As a consequence, this will make it impossible for Africa to change its position in the international division of labour. In this context, EU engagement in Africa might be referred to as externally imposed regionalism. In intra-EU relations, a division is also visible between 'centre' and 'periphery'. This has resulted in revitalisation of cooperation within the Visegrád Group, which, during the migratory crisis, started to build policies aimed at not accepting migrants, strengthening Frontex (the European Border and Coast Guard Agency) and improving the situation in the migrants' countries of origin. Nevertheless, since their accession to the EU, the V4 countries have not participated in shaping EU policy towards Africa.

The collapse of the Soviet Union, the political and economic transformation of the 1990s and the lack of coordination of CEECs' foreign policies by Moscow weakened contacts between the CEECs and Africa. The V4, while joining the EU, did not have clearly defined priorities in terms of relations with Africa. The Visegrád Group believed that their priorities would be in line with

EU policies towards Africa, since most of its economic and political links with the African continent disappeared after the fall of the communism, a time when 'deep integration' with Euro-Atlantic structures was imperative. The migration crisis marks a turning point in the attitude of the Visegrád Group towards EU institutions. The revitalisation of cooperation under V4 took place due to opposition to the proposed forced relocation of migrants. It is obvious that the key foreign interests of the V4 states lie in the East, but Poland, the Czech Republic, Hungary and Slovakia needed engagement with Africa to justify its anti-migratory stances. The 'new opening' of Central and Eastern Europe to Africa was reflected both in the Central European media and in academic discourse. The political expression of the prioritising of relations with Africa was the reopening of embassies in this region of the world. Nevertheless, as of 2020 no major investment from V4 countries has taken place in Africa, and what is more, relations between Central and Eastern Europe and Africa are not institutionalised. The renewed interest in Africa among Central and Eastern European states was internally driven and should be perceived as an effect of 'new' member states' adaptation to/contestation of EU policies rather than a long-term involvement strategy. However, this process also indicates that the V4 countries will probably in the future adopt a common position in the context of EU-Africa relations, while the Eastern Partnership will remain their central priority.

Note

1   There are claims that CEECs tried to pursue an approach independent from USRR foreign policy in relation to Africa.

Bibliography

Chmiel, O. (2018) The Engagement of Visegrad Countries in EU-Africa Relations. Discussion Paper 24/2018. Bonn: Deutsches Institut für Entwicklungspolitik.

Cibian, S. (2017) *Central and Eastern Europe and Sub-Saharan Africa Prospects for Sustained Re-engagement.* London: Royal Institute of International Affairs, Chatham House. www.bosch-stiftung.de/sites/default/files/publications/pdf/2018-04/Research_Paper_CEE-Sub-Saharan-Africa_Cibian.pdf (retrieved 6 June 2020).

Copley, A. (2017) Figures of the week: Assessing Africa-EU trade relations [online]. Brookings, 2 March 2017. www.brookings.edu/blog/africa-in-focus/2017/03/02/figures-of-the-week-assessing-africa-eu-trade-relations/ (retrieved 8 March 2018).

Embassy of the Republic of Uganda Berlin-Germany (2019) Hungary grants 16 million euros to strengthen development cooperation with Uganda [online]. https://berlin.mofa.go.ug/data-dnews-148-HUNGARY-GRANTS-16-MILLION-EUROS-TO-STRENGTHEN-DEVELOPMENT-COOPERATION-WITH-UGANDA.html (retrieved 21 June 2020).

European Commission (2018) Economic partnerships [online]. http://ec.europa.eu/trade/policy/countries-and-regions/development/economic-partnerships/ (retrieved 8 March 2018).

Eurostat (2019) Africa-EU trade in goods: €1 billion surplus [online]. https://ec.europa.eu/eurostat/web/products-eurostat-news/-/DDN-20190923-1 (retrieved 24 June 2020).

Eurostat (2020) Africa-EU – international trade in goods statistics [online]. https://ec.europa.eu/eurostat/statistics-explained/index.php/Africa-EU_-_international_trade_in_goods_statistics (retrieved 24 June 2020).

Farrell, M. (2015) Europe-Africa relations over time: History, geopolitics and new political challenges. In K.E. Jorgensen A.K. Aarstad, E. Drieskens, K. Laatikainen and B. Tonra (eds), *The SAGE Handbook of European Foreign Policy*, Vol. 1. Los Angeles: Sage (pp. 779–794).

Hungary Today (2019) Szijjártó Discusses Major Investment Programme in Uganda [online]. https://hungarytoday.hu/szijjarto-discusses-major-investment-programme-in-uganda/ (retrieved 21 June 2020).

Jóźwiak, V. (2020) *Polityka rozwojowa państw Grupy Wyszehradzkiej na Bliskim Wschodzie i w Afryce.* Biuletyn, Polski Instytut Spraw Międzynarodowych, Nr 29 (1961), 21 February 2020.

Kopinski, D., Polus, A. and Tycholiz, W. (2013) *Africa-Europe on the Global Chessboard. The New Opening*. Warsaw: CEED Institute. http://ceedinstitute.org/report/1732 (retrieved 8 March 2018).

Kurtagic, D. (2019) *Central and Eastern Europe and Sub-Saharan Africa: The Potential of Investment Partnerships for Mutual Benefit*. London: Royal Institute of International Affairs, Chatham House. www.chathamhouse.org/sites/default/files/2019-10-31-Eastern-Europe-Africa-Investment.pdf (retrieved 6 June 2020).

Marinov, E. (2017) Bulgaria and Romania trade with sub-Saharan Africa: A Comparison. In I. Christova-Balkanska and E. Marinov (eds), *International Scientific Conference Proceedings 'Bulgaria and Romania: Country members of the EU, part of the global economy'*. Sofia: Bulgarian Academy of Science, Economic Research Institute (pp. 163–174).

Meijers, M.J. (2017) *Radical Right and Radical Left Euroscepticism: A Dynamic Phenomenon*. Jacques Delors Institute Policy Paper 191. Berlin: Jacques Delors Institut. www.delorsinstitut.de/2015/wp-content/uploads/2017/04/20170407_Euroscepticism-Meijers.pdf (retrieved 8 March 2018).

Ministry of Foreign Affairs, Republic of Poland (2018) Home page [online]. www.msz.gov.pl/pl/p/msz_pl/polityka_zagraniczna/inne_kontynenty/afryka/interesy_pl_w_afryce/?printMode=true (retrieved 8 March 2018).

Moravcsik, A. (1993) Preferences and power in the European Community: A liberal intergovernmentalist approach. *Journal of Common Market Studies*, 31 (4) 473–524.

Muehlenbeck, P. (2016) *Czechoslovakia in Africa, 1945–1968*. New York: Palgrave Macmillan.

Polus, A. (2016) Polish–Sub-Saharan African economic and political relations after 1989. *Politeja*, 3 (42), 93–110. www.akademicka.pl/ebooks/free/c3b7109ec2dbc4b3834ccd59bc1d59d3.pdf

Soderbaum, F. (2013) African regionalism and EU-African interregionalism. In M. Telo (ed.), *European Union and New Regionalism: Regional Actors and Global Governance in a Post-Hegemonic Era*. Aldershot: Ashgate (pp. 185–202).

Taylor, I. (2010) *The International Relations of Sub-Saharan Africa*. New York and London: Continuum.

Taylor, I. (2016) *Dependency redux: Why Africa is not rising*. Review of African Political Economy, 43 (147), 8–25.

Tusk, D. (2017), Opening remarks by President Donald Tusk opening the 5th African Union-European Union summit in Abidjan [online]. www.consilium.europa.eu/pl/press/press-releases/2017/11/29/remarks-by-president-donald-tusk-opening-the-5th-african-union-european-union-summit-in-abidjan/ (retrieved 8 March 2018).

15

Trade and the Economic Partnership Agreements in EU-Africa relations

Victor Adetula and Chike Osegbue

Introduction

Africa's trade relationship with the European Union (EU) is a long-standing one that dates back to the colonial era. However, it was only in the 1970s during the first decades of their independence that African countries formalised a relationship with the EU: a sizeable number of independent African states came together with other countries from the Caribbean and Pacific (ACP), formed the ACP Group[1] and negotiated a formal relationship with the European Economic Community. The EU later replaced the European Economic Community. The ACP Group is comprised of countries with common problems and development challenges. Besides the link with the EU, the group members have very little in common but poverty and commitment to modernisation and industrialisation. The original 46 ACP countries signed the Georgetown Agreement (ACP Secretariat, 1975), which formally established the ACP Group to consolidate, strengthen the existing solidarity, promote greater and closer trade and economic relations among themselves, encourage regional and interregional cooperation between the ACP states and work towards the realisation of the new international economic order.

The outcome of the negotiation between the EU and the ACP countries was the First European Community-Africa, Caribbean, and Pacific Convention (Lomé I), signed on 28 February 1975. Subsequently, the Lomé Convention was renewed three times: Lomé II (1980–1985), Lomé III (1985–1990) and Lomé IV (1990–2000). Between 1975 and 2000, the Lomé regime guided trade between the EU and Africa, guaranteeing access, including quotas, prices and duty-free access to African agricultural products. However, in mid-2000 the ACP-EU Partnership Agreement, commonly called the Cotonou Agreement, replaced the Lomé regime. It covers trade and development cooperation and contains a political dimension. Signed between 28 member states of the EU and the 79 ACP countries – 48 in Africa, 16 in the Caribbean and 15 in the Pacific – the agreement reflects the new realities in the global trading system and introduced changes with far-reaching consequences for EU-ACP trade. It introduced the principle of reciprocity and subsequently created trade arrangements titled Economic Partnership Agreements (EPAs) to promote and encourage a trade regime compatible with World Trade Organization (WTO) requirements.

The EU–Africa relationship is unequal, and trade is the most visible expression of the unequal partnership. The concept of 'Eurafrica' rationalises the EU–Africa trade. It conceals its nature of dependency by presenting 'the fate of Europe and Africa … as being naturally and inextricably linked at the political, economic, social and cultural levels' (Martin, 1982: 222). The ideology of Eurafrica assumes that Africa, because of its history and colonial connection, is joined by an umbilical cord to Europe. As such, the symbiotic relationship is mutually beneficial. Arguably, European elites have adopted Eurafrica as the ideological framework for the various contractual arrangements in place between Africa and Europe to date, for the latter to achieve its goals and to provide a few benefits for the African countries by default. Thus, from the days of the Yaoundé conventions through the EU-ACP conventions to the present Cotonou Agreement, which is being modified with the EPAs, Eurafrica has been used consistently to rationalise the neoclassical theory of international development and also to maintain the status quo in the international division of labour (Adetula, 2007, 2010a). In this chapter, we discuss the main highlights of the EU–Africa trade relationship under the Cotonou Agreement and the EPAs. The focus on trade is deliberate given the importance of trade as the most visible expression of the age-long partnership between Europe and Africa. In terms of geographical coverage, our focus is on sub-Saharan Africa.

The EU–Africa relationship presents mixed outcomes to careful observers. On the one hand, there have been some positive aspects of the relationship, mostly traceable to the days of the Lomé conventions. Between 1975 and 2000, the EU and Africa had a very engaged relationship within the context of the Lomé conventions, covering essential trade, aid, investments and industrial and financial cooperation. During this period, trade between the EU and ACP countries was governed by the Lomé preferences, which guaranteed access, including quotas, prices, duty-free access to African agricultural products like sugar, banana, beef, etc., subject of course to the implementation of the provisions of the Common Agricultural Policy. The principle of non-reciprocity was in place, and this granted trade preferences to the ACP countries. On the other hand, the EU-ACP framework, currently summed up in the Cotonou Agreement, is severely constrained, and its impact on African development has remained minimal. Under the Cotonou Agreement, preferential market access commitments are on a reciprocity basis, unlike in the Lomé regime. Thus, most African countries regard the EPA regime as a means of promoting unequal partnership between the EU and Africa. Nevertheless, trade relations between the EU and Africa remains an important area of cooperation. Africa is the fourth most important EU trading partner.

Cotonou Agreement and EPAs

By the end of the 1990s, global changes and developments significantly influenced the direction of multilateral trade relationships generally and North–South cooperation in particular. Since the end of the Cold War, the world has witnessed significant political and economic developments with far-reaching consequences for global order. For instance, the present neoliberal global order under the influence of the United States provides opportunities for the consolidation of neoliberalism, exemplified in increased support for democratisation, human rights protection, free trade and the predominance of market forces (see Adetula et al., 2010). The post-Cold War global order, based primarily on neoliberal principles and values, including the dominance of market forces, has generated significant pressures on North–South platforms like the EU-ACP framework. For example, the WTO became more defensive and protective of its rules and regulations to guarantee free trade and less responsive to the demands of countries in the Global South for better deals in the global trading system. Similarly, other initiatives emerged in North–South trade relations, such as the United States' African Growth and Opportunity Act, bearing strong allegiance to the ideals and logic of unrestricted free trade.

Developments in global trade regimes, strongly influenced by the prevalent neoliberal ideology, provided the setting for the framing and designing of a successor agreement to Lomé IV. As the neoliberal agenda gained prominence, countries in the Global South increasingly came under pressure to adapt and respond to the new realities of global trade relations, such as the total liberalisation of the international trading system. For example, the commitment of the United States to increased free trade with Africa came along with the key requirement of adherence to reciprocity. Thus, the negotiation and conclusion of the Cotonou Agreement took place in this context, reflecting the defining characteristics of the new neoliberal world order as well as the lessons learned from the previous agreements. For example, the European Commission launched a reflection in 1996, which resulted in the adoption of the Green Paper on Relations between the EU and the ACP Countries on the Eve of the 21st Century: Challenges and Options for a New Partnership. These interrelated processes produced the Cotonou Agreement (European Commission, 2000), signed on 23 June 2000.

Table 15.1 summarises the trade relations between the EU and Africa during the latter part of the 20th century and up to 2001.

Among other things, the Cotonou Agreement demonstrates the commitment of the EU to align trade relations under the EU-ACP framework with WTO rules. The conception of trade strictly in commercial terms sets the Cotonou Agreement apart from the previous agreements. EU-Africa trade is now more than ever in full agreement with the WTO-driven global free trade agenda. Thus, the Cotonou Agreement detaches trade and aid. Although labelled a 'partnership agreement' and dressed in beautiful and rosy language, the Cotonou Agreement is unable to challenge the power imbalance between Europe and Africa, which is in different forms and in different areas of 'partnership' and 'cooperation' – namely, trade, aid and investment.

The Cotonou Agreement introduces new fundamental principles for trade between EU and ACP countries. Article 34 of the Agreement stipulates that 'Economic and trade cooperation shall aim at fostering the smooth and gradual integration of the ACP states into the world economy'. This is to enable the ACP countries 'to play a full part in international trade', to 'manage the challenges of globalisation and to adapt progressively to new conditions of international trade, thereby facilitating their transition to the liberalised global economy'. Regional integration processes within the framework of the Cotonou Agreement will, among other things, support 'liberalisation of trade' (Article 29) as well as serving to 'foster the integration of the ACP countries with the world economy in terms of trade and private investment' (Article 1).

Article 36 of the Cotonou Agreement enjoins all parties to the Cotonou Agreement 'to ensure the conclusion of new WTO-compatible Economic Partnership Agreements', which are presented as 'development instruments, [aiming] to foster smooth and gradual integration of the ACP states into the world economy, especially by making full use of the potential of regional integration and South–South trade'. The Agreement provides for the replacement of the non-reciprocal, preferential regime with several new, reciprocal, WTO-compatible trade regimes between the EU and ACP countries. There are provisions for the terms and conditions of the reciprocal preferences to be negotiated between the EU and regional groupings within the ACP. However, the original time frame of 1 January 2008 for the conclusion of negotiation could not hold, and adjustments and changes were undertaken which allowed for a time extension. The expectation, especially on the side of the EU, was that the EPAs would come into force by 2008 and would liberalise around 90% of EU-ACP trade within 10–12 years.

Under the provisions of Articles 36 and 37 of the Cotonou Agreement, in 2002 the EU launched its negotiations with African regional groupings. These include the Economic

Table 15.1 Trends in EU–Africa trade (1980–2001)

	1980	1989	1990	1993	1994	1995	1996	1997	1998	1999	2000	2001
Imports (Mio ECU/€)	44,279	47,071	51,018	44,963	47,427	46,894	52,496	56,740	53,183	57,026	89,932	87,051
Share of imports (%)	16.0		11.6						7.4	7.3	8.1	8.4
Exports (Mio ECU/€)	40,258	46,326	46,514	46,344	47,522	51,580	53,712	52,060	58,659	56,598	65,746	69,584
Share of exports (%)	19.0		11.9						7.9	7.4	6.9	7.0
Balance of trade (Mio ECU/€)	−4,022	−745	−4,504	1,381	−5	4,587	1,216	−4,680	5,476	−428	−18,186	−17,468

Source: Compiled from European Communities (2002)

Community of West African States (ECOWAS) and Mauritania in West Africa; the Communauté Economique et Monétaire de l'Afrique Centrale and São Tomé and Príncipe in Central Africa; the eligible members of the Common Market for Eastern and Southern Africa (COMESA); and certain Southern African Development Community (SADC) members (Angola, Mozambique, Tanzania, Botswana, Lesotho, Namibia, Swaziland). During a long and tedious negotiation process, the EU declared its commitment to promoting multilateral trade liberalisation while it seeks free trade with Africa. Unfortunately, after a decade and half of intense negotiations, there has been only marginal success. Apart from the case of the EPA with the Southern African group, that entered into force on 10 October 2016, none of the other regional communities in Africa that were involved in negotiating the Agreement have signed and implemented it collectively. A number of EPAs exist and are subject to provisional application. These interim agreements with individual countries have been ratified by Mauritius, Zimbabwe, Seychelles and Madagascar (Eastern and Southern Africa); Cameroon (Central Africa); and Ghana and Ivory Coast (West Africa). In East Africa, although negotiations are ongoing at the regional level, the East African group seems not quite excited about a regional EPA.

A few EPAs are signed but not implemented, because they are pending further ratification by the respective national parliaments. In West Africa, for example, of the 16 countries that participated in the negotiation process, 13 signed the regional agreement. The EPA between the EU and West Africa may enter into force only if all ECOWAS member states sign and at least two-thirds ratify the agreement. Nigeria, the Gambia and Mauritania have not signed the EPA between the EU and ECOWAS plus Mauritania. Nigeria is the largest economy in the ACP Group and the group's biggest single trading partner with the EU, in terms of both exports and imports. Nigeria's role in the ACP Group is that of a leader, and it has helped in many respects to maintain the ACP countries as a unified group, especially because of global economic currents that are not favourable to the developing countries. Nigeria regards the EPA as a means of promoting unequal partnership between the EU and ECOWAS countries. Trade liberalisation components of the EU-ECOWAS EPA are not the same as those of the ECOWAS trade liberalisation regime in terms of goals, orientation and focus. Under the EPA, trade liberalisation is expected to move ECOWAS towards a WTO-compatible trade regime in its relationship with the EU. The establishment of a common external tariff, which is a key integration instrument, is antithetical to a WTO-compatible trade regime with an emphasis on reciprocity.

Benefits, risks and discontents

Both the Cotonou Agreement and the EPAs support unrestricted international free trade. Thus, the trade between Africa and the EU under the Cotonou Agreement framework is expected to result in economic growth in African countries. The assumption here is that trade liberalisation and market deregulation will build trade capacity and increased economies of scale for the African countries. This, in turn, will enhance their participation in trade with the EU based on the EPAs. The EU has declared that EPAs will change the EU-Africa relationship 'from one of dependency on EU tariff preferences' (2007) to a partnership that can guarantee sustainable development and promote trade and investment that, in turn, will help develop the national economy of African countries through job creation and income generation. These expectations are in agreement with classical liberal theory, which contends that trade is an engine of growth and free trade agreements are the catalyst towards achieving that growth. However, there is little or no evidence to suggest that the EU-Africa trade relationship has resulted in increased capacity for the African countries to become major players in the global trading system.

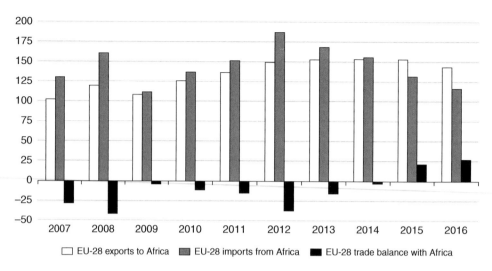

Figure 15.1 EU trade with Africa (2007–2016) (€ billion)

Source: © European Union, Eurostat, Africa-EU – key statistical indicators, 1995–2013: https://ec.europa.eu/eurostat/statistics-explained/index.php?title=Africa-EU_-_key_statistical_indicators (retrieved 30 August 2019)

Meanwhile, recent trade performance between the EU and Africa shows some familiar trends. The balance of trade between the EU and Africa recorded a surplus in 2015 and 2016 due to a continuous decrease of the value of EU imports from Africa since 2012, coupled with a more stable level of EU exports. In 2016, Africa's share of EU exports was 8%, and 7% for imports. Between 2007 and 2014, the EU consistently recorded a deficit in its trade in goods with Africa (see Figure 15.1). Since 2012, Africa has recorded a significant drop in its imports to the EU, due in part to a fall in mineral-fuel imports to the EU. In 2016, the imports from Africa stood at €116.7 billion, which was a significant drop of 38% compared to the peak of €186.7 billion in 2012. The fall in the value of crude oil and natural gas imports from Africa that was due in large part to the sharp drop in oil prices for these products accounted for this trend. In the evaluation of the performance of EU–Africa trade, one should go beyond a mere focus on trade balance concern to include consideration for such details as the components and structure of the trade (imports and exports) and in which items Africa has recorded increase or decrease (see Figure 15.2). For example, in 2016, Africa was second only to Russia as an EU source for energy products, particularly crude oil. Principal exports from Africa to the EU are mostly raw materials, primarily commodities that the EU would not usually like to restrict. On the other hand, the EU exports to Africa are more diversified.

A brief overview on the benefits of the EPAs to individual African countries that signed up to them is instructive with regard to the concerns about the structure of the trade between the EU and Africa and its potential as an agent of growth and development. In Madagascar, the textile producers have free access to the European market of 500 million consumers due to the EPA between the EU and the Eastern and Southern Africa region. Similarly, through the EPA, pineapple exporters in Ghana can invest more in processing and marketing their fruit. In Senegal, there is a prospect of a boom for mango production while in Côte d'Ivoire, cotton producers now have access to cheaper inputs such as fertilisers and machinery tools due to free-market access for their products in Europe. Also, in Swaziland, the EU's EPA with the SADC is putting

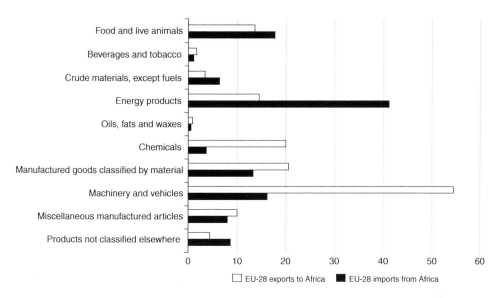

Figure 15.2 EU trade with Africa, by product group (Standard International Trade Classification section) (2016) (€ billion)

Source: © European Union, Eurostat, Africa-EU – key statistical indicators, 1995–2013: https://ec.europa.eu/eurostat/statistics-explained/index.php?title=Africa-EU_-_key_statistical_indicators (retrieved 30 August 2019)

the country's sugar exporters at an advantage, as they now enjoy permanently duty-free and quota-free access to the EU, just as those growing rooibos tea in South Africa enjoy protection for their products against possible discrimination and sanctions under the EU law (European Commission, 2013).

Based on relevant provisions in the Cotonou Agreement as well as the obligations under contracted EPAs, the EU has demanded from African regions 80% liberalisation of their import trade with the EU for a period of 15 years at most. In West Africa, in 2007, on account of the interim agreement, Côte d'Ivoire committed itself to liberalising 80.8% of its imports from Europe over a period of 15 years. Similarly, Ghana pledged to liberalise 80.1% of its imports over 15 years, including removing duties on 72.81% of its imports in the first 10 years. The SADC and Eastern and Southern Africa countries have committed to an opening up of 86% and 82%, respectively, over 15 years. As indicated above, the demands and preferences of the EU find easy accommodation within the ideology of Eurafrica, which acknowledges the 'complementarity' of Europe and Africa and justifies the need for African countries to open their markets to European products and also attract European investments in order to promote growth. The logic that the removal of tariffs on raw materials and finished products imported from Europe promotes competitiveness of businesses in Africa is faulty. The assumption that the environment and conditions for 'free and fair' competition with European products exist in the global trading system is not correct. North–South trade is determined by a variety of other conditions, structures and institutions that Africa does not have any control over. Besides, what exist presently in Africa are only close to free trade zones, most of which are undeveloped and therefore imperfect.

Arguably, the demand by the EU for 80% access to the markets of African countries through the regional EPAs is one-sided and self-interested, and it may not be in accordance with the WTO rules. Article XXIV of the General Agreement on Tariffs and Trade (GATT) is the legal basis of the operations of the regional trade agreements. The concepts of 'substantially all trade'[2] and 'reasonable period of time'[3] have generated much controversy, and still there is no consensus on how best to operationalise the two concepts. In this regard, the demand by the EU for 80% access to the markets of African countries is nothing but an imposition. It is only the West African region that has obtained a major concession from the EU, which offers 100% immediate tariff-free access to the EU market in return for a gradual liberalisation of 75% of the West African markets over a 20-year period.

The Cotonou Agreement's preferential market access operates on the principle of reciprocity. This has been criticised as being capable of promoting unequal exchange and as working against the trade liberalisation regimes in operation in some of the existing regional integration schemes in Africa. For example, ECOWAS, as a regional integration arrangement, aims to eliminate all tariff and non-tariff restriction on intra-ECOWAS trade, to establish a common external tariff and commercial policy against non-ECOWAS countries, to abolish all obstacles to the movement of all factors of production and to harmonise domestic policies across its member countries. In this regard, a comprehensive trade liberalisation programme is in place. It is largely a progressive reduction culminating in the elimination of all tariff and non-tariff barriers against intra-ECOWAS trade. In practical terms, the ECOWAS has not been able to increase intra-regional trade, which, according to the United Nations Conference on Trade and Development database, represents 8% to 11% of total ECOWAS trade. ECOWAS export and import trade with the EU is significantly higher in comparison. Europe accounts for about 28% of ECOWAS exports, with 23% for the EU.[4] The structure of trade links with the metropolitan countries has implications for the development of local industry in West Africa to produce manufactured goods as a component of intra-ECOWAS trade. Under the EPA, trade liberalisation is to move ECOWAS towards a WTO-compatible trade regime in its relationship with the EU. The EU has dismissed the fears and concerns of some Africans as unfounded and has promised to address the so-called 'supply side constraints' by providing funds to meet the 'adjustments costs' of EPAs.

By threatening and cajoling vulnerable African countries into signing interim agreements with the EU, the latter raises the risk level in the EU-Africa trade relationship. When countries that belong to a regional trade arrangement enter into an agreement outside their regional grouping to liberalise different baskets of products, they create new barriers to intra-regional trade. This sums up the logic behind the interim EPAs (Stevens et al., 2008: xiii), and it presents a big challenge for regional integration. The EU, through 'carrots and sticks', was able to get many African countries to sign interim agreements and insisted that that they implement them before 1 October 2014 or lose their access to the European market under preferential conditions. Through this, 'the EU created tensions within the African regions' (Dieye, 2017: 13). In regions where only a few countries have signed up to the interim agreements, it is not likely that other countries not currently signed up will reduce any of their tariffs towards the EU. Such will maximise the incompatibility between their trade regimes. For example, in West Africa, 'the non-conclusion of a regional EPA split the region into five different trade regimes with the EU' (ibid.). Both Ghana and Cote d'Ivoire have interim agreements, and their cases are used as illustration here. Their interim agreements have negative consequences for the ECOWAS Trade Liberalization Scheme. The interim agreements could become conduits for channelling goods originating from Europe to the West African markets under the guise of regional integration, which might affect the future of growing industries. There is already an overwhelming fear among the ECOWAS countries about the effects of unrestricted access into their markets for EU products. The fear is no doubt a genuine one, and it could be a threat to West African integration.

The trade liberalisation components of the EPAs are not the same as those of ECOWAS in terms of goals, orientation and focus. For example, while trade liberalisation is an important aspect of both, its aim differs under the two. Under the EPA trade, liberalisation is to move ECOWAS towards a WTO-compatible trade regime in its relationship with the EU. This has implications for the objectives of the ECOWAS Trade Liberalization Scheme, especially the rules of origin, which form the basis of the free movements of community-originating products. The establishment of a common external tariff, which is a key integration instrument, is antithetical to a WTO-compatible trade regime with emphasis on reciprocity. The removal of quantitative restrictions will create a situation whereby ECOWAS-originating products have to compete on national markets with imported good from EU countries. The fear is clearly not that of exposing the infant industries in ECOWAS countries to competition. Of course, all healthy and fair competitions have benefits. It is worrisome that under the EPA, community-originating products will be competing on national markets with heavily subsidised goods from the EU countries. It is possible to argue that competition will stimulate efficiency and improvement in industrial production. However, it makes sense to start with exposing the industries of ECOWAS countries to regional competition through effective operation of the ECOWAS liberalisation scheme and then later encouraging overall trade liberalisation such as that advocated by the EU and WTO. The liberalisation of trade in products that enjoy subsidies in industrialised countries, especially in Europe, will have adverse effects on trade development in Africa. Similar concerns are emerging about the consequences of the EPAs on the newly created African Free Trade Area (CFTA). Operating multiple trade liberalisation schemes within the same region/subregion is another major risk for regional integration.

Regional integration is a key principle of the EPAs. The justification for the quest for larger regional markets is that this will stimulate economic growth in the ACP and accelerate the integration of ACP countries into the world economy. The argument is simply that the abolition of trade restrictions and harmonisation of tariffs will promote regional integration and create larger markets. The European Commission argues that a customs union offers the best condition for entering into an EPA, followed by effectively implemented FTAs. Moreover, by negotiating EPAs on a regional basis, the ACP countries will have an opportunity to steer their regional integration process and create dynamic regional markets conducive to investment and development. However, the ACP countries seem not to be as optimistic about the prospect of a mutually reinforcing relationship between EPAs and regional integration. These was expressed in some civil society circles as the EPA negotiation process forced the ACP countries to affiliate themselves with one regional body to negotiate agreement with the EU, thus jeopardising autonomous regional integration initiatives.

The change from preferential to reciprocal trade relations implies many challenges for regional integration. The question is whether the regional approach that drove African countries to negotiate EPAs with the EU promotes or constrains regional integration in Africa. Theoretically, how is a North-South free trade area expected to help promote South-South integration? Indeed, there are concerns that the EPA agenda was too hasty. Also, rather than helping the African Union (AU) to bring together the various regional economic blocs like SADC, ECOWAS, or the East African Community, the EU is 'balkanising' Africa into four or five blocks for the purpose of EPA agreements. Also, the Everything but Arms initiative that provides non-reciprocal trade preferences to least developed countries is likely to create division and generate tensions between those countries and others in Africa.

Future of the trade relationship

The Cotonou Agreement expires in 2020. At the time of writing, there are ongoing preparations towards a successor ACP-EU framework. Within the EU, there is a strong preference for the status quo and indeed a commitment to build on the existing EU-ACP framework. Considering its interests, the EU is determined to negotiate with the ACP as one group, just as in previous negotiations. While the EU acknowledges Africa, the Caribbean and the Pacific as three separate regions, it seems unwilling to let go of the ACP concept and its most recent add-on – the EPAs. Thus, the Regional Economic Communities (RECs) may assume more responsibilities in the future EU-Africa relationship. The EU seems disposed towards framing the trade relationship between the EU and Africa as achieving a reasonable balance between EU interests and new global realities and challenges. Thus, future trade between the EU and Africa is most likely to follow the rules in the newly created EPAs. This means that the trade relationship between the EU and Africa will most likely align with the logics of the EPAs, espousing reciprocity.

The African countries wish to negotiate with the EU as one group, separate from the Caribbean and Pacific groups of countries. Within the ACP Group, there is an expressed concern about the position of the African group. However, the latter, represented by the AU, has gone ahead in adopting the African Common Position for Negotiations of a New Agreement of Cooperation with the European Union on the future of African Union/European Union relations Post 2020 (African Union Commission, 2018). Furthermore, an ad hoc working group was set up to ensure that the new agreement is based on 'a strong and sustainable continent-to-continent partnership', equality, equity, mutual respect and the shared responsibility of both continents. Also, the successor treaty to the Cotonou Agreement should reaffirm the interdependence between Africa and Europe and be based on African priority development pillars. Arguably, this position of the AU represents a desire for a post-Cotonou framework that supports equitable socio-economic transformation in ACP countries.

Continent-wide and regional arrangements like the AU, the New Partnership for Africa's Development (NEPAD), the CFTA and the RECs, such as ECOWAS, Economic Community of Central African States, EAC and SADC, are increasingly involved in the trade relations of African countries. There are, in addition, bilateral agreements between individual EU member states and various African states that have consequences for the EU-Africa trade relationship. The African countries in particular may revisit concern about the implications of the EU's separate arrangements with South Africa and some countries in North Africa. There are countries in North Africa that are members of the AU but not parties to the Cotonou Agreement. The AU complained that the Cotonou Agreement splits Africa into two parts. Already the position of the AU is that the existing bilateral agreements between the EU and African countries, such as the EU's agreements with North Africa and South Africa, be given adequate consideration. It is not likely that North Africa will be included in the new agreement, but there is a possibility that the North Africa countries will be encouraged to affiliate to the new agreement.

There are questions about Brexit and its implications for the trade relationship between Europe and Africa. The exit of the United Kingdom from the EU cannot be without consequence for EU-Africa trade. Britain is a valuable trading partner of most African countries. Until the end of the Brexit transition period in 2020, Great Britain is under obligation to respect the trade-related provisions of the existing EU-ACP framework. Similarly, the establishment of the CFTA has implications for EU Africa trade relationship. There is a concern in some circles that full implementation of the regional EPAs may create severe difficulties for CFTA. Besides, the current proliferation of mega-regional trade agreements, such as the (now suspended) Transatlantic Trade and Investment Partnership or the Trans-Pacific Partnership that has proceeded without the United States and with another name (the Comprehensive and Progressive Agreement for Trans-Pacific Partnership), may have their take on EU-Africa trade.

Even with many interim agreements in place in Africa, there are several uncertainties about the implementation of EPAs. There is no way to determine the extent of compliance with the rules and regulations of EPAs. The absence of explicit provisions on enforcement makes the situation even more complex. As pointed out by Christopher Stevens, 'the agreement is no more than the expression of good intentions. The EPAs contains only moderate enforcement provisions and some ambiguity over what needs to be done' (2013: 182).

Conclusion

The division of labour in the international system relegates Africa and other regions in the Global South to the periphery, with trade as one of the critical mechanisms for sustaining the status quo. The EU-Africa trade relationship to date has operated as an asymmetric partnership, which derives directly from the imbalance of power between Europe and Africa. This power relation is preserved by the structures and institutions of the international political system that generally favours the Global North to the disadvantage of the South. Worse still, depressed world commodity markets, discriminatory protection and debt crisis have persisted in the contemporary global economy. In this circumstance, the structural deficiencies that come through a bad free trade agreement will further aggravate the problems and challenges of Africa. Redressing the imbalance in power relations is unquestionably the challenge of a future relationship between the EU and Africa. Most visible expressions of the power imbalance between the EU and Africa are in the areas of trade, aid and investments. Of course, there are possibilities for addressing the power imbalance in EU-Africa trade, based on a well-thought-out African agenda for development. Thus, the African countries must identify the opportunities for change as well as the challenges that limit the possibility of change.

The world is changing rapidly and facing new challenges, and Africa is indeed reflecting these changes. For example, in September 2015, the UN Assembly, under the title of 'Transforming our World', adopted a new development agenda: the 2030 Agenda for Sustainable Development. It sets some goals to be met by 2030 – the Sustainable Development Goals (SDGs). The Economic Commission for Africa's (2015) *Regional Report on the Sustainable Development Goals* maintains that the main issue for a new development agenda for Africa is the need to reorient the impressive economic growth obtained in the continent in order to provide the basis for improved living conditions, reduced poverty and sustainable development. Unlike the Millennium Development Goals, which were written mainly for developing countries and presented the rich countries mostly as sponsors, the SDGs are universally applicable. This dominant paradigm must seek accommodation outside the present logic of the EU-ACP framework.

Africa's mounting development challenges abound. Civil war is a constant threat in many poor and badly governed countries in Africa. The continent presents some of the most daunting global security threats. Nevertheless, some progress has been made. For example, since the beginning of the millennium, Africa has recorded one of the highest economic growth rates in the world along with an improved business environment and investments climate and a rapidly expanding labour force. Moreover, there have been a number of initiatives towards increased regionalisation. This tendency is expressed at continental, regional and subregional levels. The initiatives include: the AU-New Partnership for Africa Development's African Union-NEPAD Capacity Development Strategic Framework; the AU's African Peer Review Mechanism; the AU's Agenda 2063; Paul Kagame's report on AU reform; Donald Kaberuka's plan to finance the AU (Securing Predictable and Sustainable Financing for Peace in Africa); and the recently established CFTA. How is the EU-Africa trade relationship influenced by these global currents and developments? These developments call for stakeholders to re-engage the discourse on North-South trade generally and, in particular, the current motives for EU-ACP trade partnership, which has been celebrated as a model of North-South dialogue.

The EPAs have generated a lot of controversy in Africa. Even so, the EU is committed to their implementation. In view of the unending debate about the benefits and risks of implementing the EPAs in Africa, it is important for both parties to take into consideration the changing regional and global contexts in which the EPAs and other similar North-South trade regimes operate. These include the expansion of the zone of liberal democracy beyond the West, the dominance of market forces and liberalisation of global trade, contemporary globalisation and transnationalism, growing interdependence among states and the emergence of new global economic powers (notably, the BRICS countries – Brazil, Russia, India, China and South Africa). In addition, what pressure will the exit of the United Kingdom from the EU put on EU-Africa trade relations?

Other major global changes have consequences for the EU-Africa trade relationship. For example, there is a trend of rising inequality across the world. Inequality among states has persisted as well as imbalance in the power distribution in the international system. The existing unequal power relations between the Global North and other regions are glaring. The decline of multilateralism as well as the continued fragmentation of the architecture of international regulations and global governance have not made things better for the less powerful states. However, the EU still appears committed to multilateralism, as is evident in its formulation the Comprehensive Strategy with Africa (European Commission, 2020), which makes Africa a testing ground for the practical demonstration of the EU's commitment to multilateralism. Another factor that has come into being since the Cotonou Agreement is the growing strength of the BRICS countries. The emergent global powers have demonstrated continued interest in Africa generally and its markets and natural resources in particular. These strong economies have projected themselves as being able to offer African countries alternatives to the EU trade agreement.

Notes

1 In 2020 the ACP Group became the Organisation of African, Caribbean and Pacific States.
2 Paragraphs 1(a) and (b) of GATT Article XXIV, respectively, provide that Customs Unions and Free Trade Areas shall cover substantially all trade to be considered as Regional Trade Agreements within the meaning of GATT/WTO.
3 Paragraph 5(c) of Article XXIV provides that any provisional agreement shall include a plan and programme for the establishment within a reasonable period of the customs union or free trade area.
4 ECOWAS home page: www.ecowas.int/doing-business-in-ecowas/import-and-export/ (accessed 10 September 2018).

Bibliography

ACP Secretariat (1975) *Georgetown Agreement*. Brussels: ACP Secretariat.
Adetula, V. (2007) Nigeria and the European Union: The Lomé Years and beyond. *Current Politics and Economics of Europe*, 18 (3/4), 413–437.
Adetula, V. (2010) NEPAD and Africa: EU Strategic Partnership Agreement. In O. Eze and A. Sesay (eds), *Europe and Africa in the 21st Century*. Lagos: Nigerian Institute of International Affairs (pp. 99–126).
Adetula, V. (2018) *The Future of EU-Africa Cooperation*. Policy Brief. Uppsala: Nordic Africa Institute.
Adetula, V., Kew, D. and Kwaja, C. (2010) *Assessing Democracy Assistance: Nigeria*. World Movement for Democracy/FRIDE project report. Madrid: FRIDE.
African Union Commission (2018) The African Union Executive Council Adopts the African Common Position for Negotiations of a New Cooperation Agreement with the European Union. Press Release. Addis Ababa.
Amin, S. (1977) *Imperialism and Unequal Development*. New York and London: Monthly Review Press.
Asante, S.K.B. (1981) The Lomé Convention: Towards perpetuation of dependence or promotion of interdependence? *Third World Quarterly*, 3 (4), 658–672.

Dieye, C.T. (2017) Europe and Africa: Can the misunderstanding be resolved? *Africa Agenda*, 20 (4), 11–13.

Economic Commission for Africa (2015) Regional Report on the Sustainable Development Goals. Addis Ababa: United Nations Economic Commission for Africa.

European Commission (2000) Green Paper on Relations between the European Union and the ACP Countries on the Eve of the 21st Century: Challenges and Options for a New Partnership. COM(96)570 final. Brussels, 20 November.

European Commission (2013) *The EU's Economic Partnership Agreements (EPAs) with countries in Africa, the Caribbean and the Pacific (ACP)* [online]. http://trade.ec.europa.eu/doclib/docs/2013/april/tradoc_151010.pdf. (retrieved 10 September 2018).

European Commission (2020) Joint Communication to the European Parliament and the Council: Towards a Comprehensive Strategy with Africa. JOIN(2020) 4 final. Brussels, 9 March. https://ec.europa.eu/international-partnerships/system/files/communication-eu-africa-strategy-join-2020-4-final_en.pdf

European Communities (2002) *External and Intra European Union Trade, Statistical Yearbook, Data 1958–2001*. Luxembourg: Office for the Official Publications of the European Communities.

European Union (2007) Position Paper: Sustainability Impact Assessment of EU-ACP Economic Partnership Agreements [online]. 16 November. http://trade.ec.europa.eu/doclib/docs/2007/november/tradoc_136958.pdf

Frank, A.G. (1981) *Crisis in the Third World*. New York: Holmes & Meier Publishers.

Hackenesch, C. and Keijzer, N. (2018) African-European Relations. In J. Abbink, V. Adetula, A. Mehler and H. Melber (eds), *Africa Yearbook. Volume 14: Politics, Economy and Society South of the Sahara in 2017*. Leiden: Brill Academic Publishers (pp. 21–36).

Homeku, T. (2017) Rethinking Africa-Europe relations after the Cotonou Partnership Agreement: Four lessons from 40 years of heartache. *African Agenda*, 20 (4), 5–10.

Kagame, P. (2017) *The Imperative to Strengthen our Union: Report on the Proposed Recommendations for the Institutional Reform of the African Union* [online].https://au.int/sites/default/files/pages/34915-file-report-20institutional20reform20of20the20au-2.pdf

Legum, C. (1962) *Pan-Africanism: A Short Political Guide*. New York: Frederick A. Praeger.

Mandez-Parra, M., te Velde, D.W. and Kennan, J. (2017) *Post-Brexit Trade Policy and Development Policy*. Policy Briefing. London: Overseas Development Institute.

Marcussen, H.S. and Torp, J.E. (1982) *The Internationalization of Capital: The Prospect for the Third World*. London: Zed Press.

Martin, G. (1982) Africa and the ideology of Eurafrica: Neo-colonialism or Pan-Africanism? *The Journal of Modern African Studies*, 20 (2), 221–238.

Mckinsey Global Institute (2010) *Lions on the Move: The Progress and Potential of African Economies*. Washington DC: McKinsey & Company.

Meltzer, J.P. (2016) Deepening the United States-Africa trade and investment relationship. Brookings, 28 January. www.brookings.edu/testimonies/deepening-the-united-states-africa-trade-and-investment-relationship/ (retrieved 10 September 2018).

Office for National Statistics (2016) The UK's Trade and Investment Relationship with Africa [online]. www.ons.gov.uk/economy/nationalaccounts/balanceofpayments/articles/theukstradeandinvestmentrelationshipwithafrica/2016 (retrieved 31 August 2019).

Onimode, B. (1988) *A Political Economy of the African Crisis*. London: Zed Books Ltd.

Onimode, B. (2006a) *Africa and the Globalised Economy of the 21st Century*. London: Zed Books Ltd.

Onimode, B. (2006b) *Imperialism and Underdevelopment in Nigeria*. London: Zed Books Ltd.

Sanu, O.E. (1978) *The Lomé Convention and the New International Economic Order*. Public Lecture No. 18. Lagos: Nigerian Institute of International Affairs.

Smith, B. (2006) Western concern at China's growing involvement in Africa [online]. www.asiantribune.com/show_article.php?id=3102 (retrieved 10 April 2007).

Stevens, C. (2013) Economic Partnership Agreements and Africa: Losing friends and failing to influence. In M. Carbone (ed.), *The European Union in Africa: Incoherent Polices, Asymmetrical Partnership, Declining Relevance?* Manchester: Manchester University Press (pp.165–188).

Stevens, C., Meyn, M., Kennan, J., Bilal, S., Braun-Munzinger, C., Jerosch, F., Makhan, D. and Rampa, F. (2008) *The New EPAs: Comparative Analysis of Their Content and the Challenges*. Final Report. London and Maastricht: ODI and ECDPM.

Wallerstein, I.M. (2004) *World-systems Analysis: An Introduction*. Durham and London: Duke University Press.

Zartman, W.I. (1993) *Europe and Africa: The New Phase*. Boulder, CO: Lynne Rienner Publishers.

16
Africa-Europe science, technology and innovation cooperation
Trends, challenges and opportunities

John Ouma-Mugabe and Petronella Chaminuka

Introduction

Africa and Europe are intensifying their cooperation in various areas of science and technological development and building capacity for expanding the knowledge base and fostering innovation. This is manifested in the growing number of collaborative science, technology and innovation (STI) initiatives that have been launched in the last decade. The African Union (AU) and the European Union (EU) have designed and adopted joint programmes and networks for STI, and some of Africa's Regional Economic Communities have entered into various STI collaborative agreements with the EU. Individual African countries are collaborating with the EU as a whole, or EU member states in various areas of STI.

The content of and changing trends in the Africa-EU STI collaborations, in response to common challenges for mutual benefits and equal partnership, is the focus on this chapter. Based on a synthesis of previous research and our ongoing participation in Africa-EU initiatives, we identify missing links, challenges and opportunities in the STI cooperation. The chapter discusses the evolution of STI cooperation between Africa and Europe within the Joint Africa-EU Strategy (JAES) and related policy instruments. It highlights the need to strengthen technology and innovation cooperation, moving beyond the established research and development (R&D) or science initiatives towards more equitable sustainable partnerships in product and process development. Greater private sector participation, including by small and medium-sized enterprises (SMEs), is recommended to spur more technology development and innovation. The rest of this chapter is organised as follows. After a brief overview of the evolution of STI cooperation between Africa and the EU, and the importance of the cooperation, there is a discussion of various African and EU policy instruments and institutional arrangements for promoting STI cooperation. The next section is about priorities, content and challenges for the bi-regional cooperation, and in the last section we discuss opportunities for strengthening the cooperation to focus more technology development and innovation on mutually agreed terms, as espoused by the Sustainable Development Goals (SDGs).

Evolution and importance of Africa-Europe STI cooperation: From Lisbon to Abidjan

Africa and Europe have a relatively long history of cooperation in various development and security areas, including STI. Dating back to the last century, countries from the two continents have been engaged in various forms of STI cooperation. At the bi-regional level, the AU and the EU have in the past two decades or so developed various STI collaborative initiatives. Several joint AU-EU policy networks and operational programmes for R&D were launched in the mid-2000s.

Africa-EU bi-regional STI cooperation is critical for at least four reasons. First, STI cooperation enables the two continents to contribute to resolution of global challenges and the attainment of SDGs. Many of the challenges, such as climate change and infectious diseases (e.g. HIV/AIDS, Ebola and the current COVID-19 pandemic), transcend national boundaries and require international STI cooperation to design and deploy scientific and technical solutions.

Second, as demonstrated by some studies (see Wagner, 2008; European Union, 2014; Carbonnier and Kontinen, 2014; Cherry and Du Toit, 2018), STI cooperation enables member states of the AU and EU, and the international community in general, to exploit economies of scale by sharing costs of R&D and technology development as well as technological innovation. Cherry and Du Toit posit that 'the sharing of resources, experience and expertise, especially to address shared challenges, or advance frontier science projects, has historically been regarded as a major driver for international cooperation in STI' (2018: 11–12). Infrastructure, including instrumentation or equipment for health research, is relatively expensive and not available (or accessible) to many researchers, particularly in poor or least developed countries. Through international research and innovation cooperation, researchers from different countries and regions are able to access and share scarce equipment that is necessary for the achievement of shared or common health research priorities.

Third, the Africa-EU STI cooperation helps to increase the productivity of both African and European researchers. It contributes to the expansion of the global pool of scientific knowledge. According to Lee and Bozeman (2005) there is a strong relationship between research cooperation and scientific productivity of researchers. As they emphasise,

> [r]esearch in many fields is more complex and requires more specialized knowledge, more than any single individual can expect to have. Collaboration permits individuals to play to their strong suits, contributing their strongest skills and deepest knowledge, relying on others to contribute other skills and knowledge.
>
> *(Lee and Bozeman, 2005: 677)*

STI cooperation thus helps to mobilise and use differentiated research capabilities of multiple countries, their institutions and scientists. In addition, through joint supervision of master's and doctoral students, partners in Europe are able to graduate more students and increase the geographic extent of their research focus, whilst African scholars are able to benefit from exposure and higher standards of education and research offered by some European universities. Cherry and Du Toit (2018) argue that for African partners, the main objective of the bi-regional partnership is support for human capacity development for Africa, whereas for most European countries, the investment in international researcher training and mobility aims at inculcating global perspectives and developing networks for future researchers.

Lastly, the Africa-EU STI cooperation can enable African countries to access existing scientific knowledge and technologies and European ones to have opportunities to work on global problems that are largely manifested in African contexts. In other words, Africa has access to existing knowledge and technologies, and Europe gets access to problem contexts or laboratories. Again, as Wagner states:

> Outbreaks of Ebola and Marburg viruses, for example, have been reported in Africa in Sudan, Zaire, Gabon and the two Congos: Republic of the Congo and Democratic Republic of the Congo. Research on such viruses conducted in Marburg, Germany, would most likely be applied to and aid people thousands of miles away.
>
> *(2008: 107)*

In agriculture, the different climatic zones between Africa and Europe, and the rich biodiversity of Africa present opportunities for researchers from both continents to explore sustainable solutions for global food and nutritional challenges. Mugabe et al. (2018) found that although beneficial to both African and European scholars, the contribution that African partners make in providing diversified research contexts and access to study populations is often undervalued and not quantified in monetary terms. Ralphs and Wagner (cited in Cherry et al., 2018: 134) put it more succinctly: 'money is not the only resource that fuels a partnership'.

Overarching policy frameworks for Africa-EU STI cooperation

It is in recognition of the mutual benefits of STI cooperation that Africa and the EU have adopted common policy frameworks and political declarations. The policy frameworks are the Lomé conventions to the Cotonou Agreement with the African, Caribbean and Pacific (ACP) Group[1], the European Community's Development Policy (2000) and the JAES. Of these, the JAES is the main framework for Africa-EU STI cooperation. It was adopted at the Second EU-Africa Summit in 2007 in Lisbon by 52 member states of the AU and 27 member states of the EU. The JAES has been implemented through five action plans, covering 2008–2018. Each of these plans has had priorities for STI cooperation.

There are two overarching policy frameworks for STI cooperation between Africa and Europe. These are the 2008 EU Strategic European Framework for International Science and Technology Cooperation and the 2014 AU Science, Technology and Innovation Strategy for Africa (STISA-2024). In 2008, the EU adopted A Strategic European Framework for International Science and Technology Cooperation (Commission of the European Communities, 2008). The strategy is premised on the basis that

> [g]lobalisation is accelerating, and this has an impact on the way we produce, share and use knowledge. Major global challenges such as climate change, poverty, infectious disease, threats to energy, food and water supply, security of the citizen, networks security and the digital divide highlight the need for effective global [science and technology] cooperation to promote sustainable development.
>
> *(ibid.: 1)*

It identifies bi-regional science and technology cooperation as being critical to efforts to address global challenges. The strategy notes that in the case of Africa, EU science and technology cooperation will focus on activities or actions aimed at achieving sustainable development with emphasis on food and nutrition security, health and well-being, and climate change adaptation and mitigation. These focus areas were reflected in funding priorities under societal challenges of the Horizon 2020 programme, and they align with some of the African continent's own priorities.

STISA-2024, adopted by the AU in 2014, is another important policy framework for the STI cooperation, although not specific to Africa-EU cooperation. It recognises the importance of international STI cooperation, as does Agenda 2063, the overall AU long-term plan for sustainable development. STISA-2024 is expected to promote African ownership, accountability and sustainability considerations in international cooperation. It is not clear how the strategy would help achieve these aspirations, since there are no specific policy and/or programmatic interventions for STI cooperation outlined in the document. The strategy does, however, identify priority action areas for research and innovation: (a) eradication of hunger and achieving food security; (b) prevention and control of diseases; (c) communication; (d) protection of space; (e) Living Together – Building the Society; and (f) wealth creation. Some of these priority areas are broad, but they can be aligned with JAES priorities and the SDGs.

From policy to practice: Trends in Africa-EU STI cooperation

Within the JAES framework, the EU has used a variety of financial mechanisms to support collaborative projects and networks. Both the EU (2014) and Cherry et al. (2018) examined various Framework Programmes (FPs) (FP6 and FP7) and trends in financing of joint Africa-EU projects. They show that under both FPs, there were significant budget allocations for joint initiatives, particularly in health and agricultural research and innovation. Initiatives such as the AU Research Grants Programme, financed by the EU and administered by the AU Commission, may have increased financial flows to Africa-based STI collaborative projects with the EU. The study by Cherry et al. (2018) provides a good detailed analysis of the various STI cooperation initiatives launched in the past decade or so within the JAES framework. It puts emphasis on Africa-EU operational programmatic initiatives in food and nutritional security, health and climate change and also profiles networks and policy processes for promoting the STI cooperation. According to most chapters in the study, in the context of the JAES, there is strengthened Africa-EU STI cooperation. When compared with existing bilateral initiatives in STI cooperation, coordinated bi-regional response under JAES could achieve greater resource efficiency and enhanced impact. There has been more structured AU-EU high-level policy dialogue that has helped to enhance Africa's participation in joint priority setting, building on the egalitarianism upon which the JAES is premised. The STI cooperation has also been strengthened through networks such as the Network for the Coordination and Advancement of Sub-Saharan Africa-EU Science and Technology Cooperation (CAAST-Net), the Platform for African European Partnership on Agricultural Research for Development, the European and Developing Countries Clinical Trials Partnership (EDCTP) and ERAfrica. According to Cherry and Du Toit (2018), however, some critics have questioned the influence of the AU in agenda setting, considering that the EU funds a majority of its programmes in bi-continental cooperation.

Several other studies on (and assessments of) Africa-EU STI cooperation initiatives show that there has been increased funding for food and nutritional security, climate change and health projects. For example, CAAST-Net Plus (2016) and Kraemer-Mbula et al. (2018) show that under FP7 (2007–2013) and Horizon 2020, the EU's allocation to international R&D cooperation with Africa increased. The EU contributed about €108 million to the ACP countries, and the EDCTP Phase 1 (2003–2015) received €378 million and funded 246 projects, and the second phase (2014–2024) received €700 million from the EU's Horizon 2020. This is in comparison to about €41 million allocated to Africa-EU health R&D under FP6. The fact that funding has increased between FP6 and FP7 should, however, not be taken as an indication of increased funding in the future. Despite the undisputed benefits of such cooperation, recent global challenges such as the migration problem and COVID-19 might result in a shift in some of the resources that could otherwise have been earmarked for science and technology cooperation.

The EU (2014) provided a synthesis and critical analysis of outcomes of various bi-regional research and innovation initiatives involving African countries and the EU over the period 2008–2012. It concludes that the bi-regional cooperation generated tangible outputs and had potential for economic and social impact. Between 2010 and 2016, CAAST-Net and Advancing Sub-Saharan Africa-EU Research and Innovation Cooperation for Global Challenges (CAAST-Net Plus) produced several studies to assess outcomes of Africa-EU research and innovation cooperation in food and nutritional security, health and climate change. The studies (e.g. CAAST-Net Plus, 2016) conclude that remarkable progress has been made in the cooperation, and outputs such as scientific publications, patents and graduates were produced by various joint programmes. The strengthening (and related outputs) of the Africa-EU STI cooperation have largely been associated with increasing financial resources to R&D, particularly from the EU, and enhanced political and policy focus on the role of STI for development in Africa. The scope of R&D expanded from an emphasis on agriculture to cover health and climate change. CAAST-Net Plus (2016) shows that in the area of health R&D, the number of bi-regional EU-Africa projects more than doubled between 2000 and 2013. Kraemer-Mbula et al. (2018), however, show that there are differences in the extent to which African partners participate under the different frameworks. In Horizon 2020 and FP7, South Africa had far higher numbers of participating organisations than other countries. The high level of participation in South Africa is attributed to concerted efforts by its Department of Science and Technology, through the European South African Science and Technology Advancement programme funded under FP7. The same authors also highlight the challenge of low participation by the African private sector and specifically SMEs.

Africa-Europe high-level summits around the JAES have provided platforms for leveraging political capital for the STI cooperation (Cherry et al., 2018). The High Level Policy Dialogue on STI established in 2014 has been instrumental in enlarging political support for the STI cooperation. On the part of Africa, the AU Summit in January 2007 seems to have steered some African political leaders' commitment to STI for development and helped locate an STI agenda within the AU Commission. On the part of the EU, the Lisbon Summit, also held in 2007, established the foundation for the STI cooperation. Since the 2007 Lisbon Summit, there have been other four Africa-EU summits of heads of state and government. In 2017, the fifth summit was held in Abidjan, Ivory Coast. The Abidjan Africa-EU Summit of Heads of State and Government was expected to renew commitment to STI cooperation between the two continents. The extent to which this was achieved is a subject of debate. No concrete new STI proposals were put forward; nor was there any indication of related new financial commitments from either the EU or the AU being considered at the Abidjan summit. According to some anonymous observers within AU circles, African political leadership for continental STI initiatives and bi-regional STI cooperation seems to have waned. While in 2007 the AU had an active African Ministerial Council on Science and Technology (AMCOST) steering an STI agenda through the Consolidated Plan of Action, in 2017 AMCOST had been collapsed into a technical committee broadened to cover education and training. African countries' failure to establish a continental financial mechanism for STI may also have weakened the continent's commitment to its own STI agenda and lessened domestic and international attention to STISA-2024.

Challenges to Africa-EU STI cooperation

There are a number of challenges to Africa-EU STI cooperation. Recent research (Mugabe et al., 2018; Cherry et al., 2018; European Union, 2014) highlights some of the challenges. These include weak African participation in agenda setting, governance and financing of Africa-EU STI cooperation, weak private sector participation, particularly by African SMEs, over-reliance on EU FPs and financing mechanisms, relatively low financing levels from African countries and some misalignment between African local priorities and those of the EU. The challenges are elaborated well in the studies. Ralphs and Wagner (2018) argue that existing stereotypes about African partners being weaker and in need of financial and technical support, while European partners are viewed as technically stronger and leaders in capacity development, often overcloud the many positive success stories of European and African STI cooperation. The EU (2014) also discusses the weak or low participation of African private companies in the Africa-EU STI cooperation and concludes that it undermines the translation of research into technology and innovation.

> New knowledge has yet to be fully translated into goods, services and technologies; new and adapted technologies have not gone to scale; and the effect of enhanced human and institutional capacity has not yet transformed the systems that those capacities serve.
>
> *(Ibid.: 16)*

There are several reasons why the African private sector, particularly SMEs, are not actively engaged in the STI cooperation. Two reasons are worth mention here. First is the absence of clear policy measures for private sector R&D and public-private STI partnerships in Africa. Most African countries do not have explicit policies and related institutional arrangements to encourage private companies to invest in R&D or even participate in public R&D initiatives, including those of foreign investors (Mugabe and Manyuchi, forthcoming). Legislation and institutions to safeguard intellectual property protection are relatively weak in most countries. Second, African SMEs have relatively low financial and technical capacities to invest in R&D or even to procure R&D inputs from universities and R&D institutes. Their financing models (including financial support by governments) are not configured well enough to enable them to invest in knowledge-intensive ventures. Recent calls for agricultural R&D funding (e.g. LEAP-Agri, AU Research Grants) require that EU and African partners responding to these calls should collaborate with private sector organisations in Africa. The private sector organisations are expected to bring in some funding or to at least pay their own way in the collaboration, as they cannot be in the consortium as beneficiaries from the funding. These kinds of conditions exclude partnering with the majority of small-scale African enterprises, which are usually more rooted in communities (and more impactful at local level), in favour of larger private sector companies, which are often multinational. This is in contrast to the more advanced private sector organisations in Europe, which are able to outsource R&D services and thereafter can protect the intellectual property and exploit it for profit purposes.

The challenge of low African financial contributions to the Africa-EU STI cooperation initiatives has been extensively discussed in various reports and in the High Level Policy Dialogue. The EU (2014) and Cherry et al. (2018) conclude that it is the main impediment to strengthening the cooperation as it undermines African ownership. Mugabe et al. (2018) argue that it is a barrier to improving the governance of Africa-EU partnerships for agricultural research and innovation. They found that challenge is further compounded by insufficient valuation of in-kind contributions in research projects. Attempts to establish an African continental mechanism, African Science and Innovation Fund or African Research Fund have so far not yielded much. This is despite the high-level discussions and consensus on the need for such mechanisms. As stated earlier, political leadership for the continental STI agenda, STISA-2024, seems to have weakened. The idea of an African fund for STI has not been properly normalised, nor public constituencies for it built within African countries. Legislatures and ministries of finance have not been adequately engaged in the discussions on the fund. A top-down approach, from AU summits of presidents, has not spurred broad-based public and political commitment to STISA-2024 and a funding mechanism for its implementation.

Opportunities and recommendations

Since the adoption of the JAES and STISA-2024, a number of important new policy agendas and processes have been set and new institutional arrangements established. In 2015, the international community adopted the United Nations (UN) Agenda 2030 and SDGs. Agenda 2030 and the SDGs provide renewed impetus for international STI cooperation. There are specific policy goals on STI cooperation in Agenda 2030 and the SDGs. In particular, SDG9 (infrastructure, industry and innovation) and SDG17 (partnerships) have explicit statements on the promotion of international cooperation on STI. SDG9.5 and SDG9.b promote international cooperation to enhance scientific research capacities of developing countries and foster innovation to achieve the goals. SDG17.6 is about enhancing North-South, South-South and triangular regional and international cooperation on and access to STI and the promotion of knowledge sharing on mutually agreed terms. A multi-stakeholder forum on STI for SDGs was established in 2016. It is comprised of governments, civil society, the private sector and UN agencies to promote international cooperation on STI. Agenda 2030 is a good framework for deepening and broadening Africa-EU STI cooperation in two respects: deepening the STI cooperation by enlarging private sector and civil society engagement; and broadening the scope of the cooperation beyond the current priority areas to include a focus on SDG9 and SDG17. The UN multi-stakeholders' forum on STI for SDGs invites both Africa and EU to engage in learning how best to improve their bi-regional STI cooperation.

Another opportunity for strengthening Africa-EU STI cooperation emerges from the renewed national efforts to design explicit STI policy instruments and establish national research and innovation funding mechanisms. In the past five years or so, several African countries (e.g. Botswana, Kenya, Ghana, Gambia and South Africa) have adopted new STI policy instruments or frameworks that have explicit measures for promoting international STI cooperation. Others, such as Namibia, Swaziland, Uganda and Zambia, are currently reviewing their STI policy frameworks and are likely to give emphasis to measures for promoting international STI cooperation. The entrenchment of provisions on international STI cooperation into African national policy frameworks is a good step, but it will need to be accompanied by specific concrete programmatic initiatives with local financial resources. For example, South Africa has dedicated budget lines for international STI cooperation, and several other countries are exploring ways of establishing such budgets. LEAP-Agri, an initiative focusing on food and nutrition security and sustainable agriculture, illustrates the commitment of some of the African countries to STI cooperation with European countries. The programme comprises 30 partners (funding agencies and ministries) from 18 countries in the two continents. The EU committed 33% of the funding for the programme. Twenty-seven projects, each with a minimum of two European and two African countries, were funded under the initiative, which will run for 36 months.

For African and EU partners interested in pursuing sustainable and mutually beneficial STI projects, several issues are important to consider. The EU identifies clear and joint definition of activities, outputs, outcomes and goals as being important. This is closely related to co-ownership and balance in terms of provision of financing and other resources, governance and project implementation. Ralphs and Wagner, (2018) note that there is growing body of literature on factors that influence partnership effectiveness at project and programme levels. Positive factors to be drawn from successful projects include joint agenda setting, strong mutual interests, joint publications and sharing of data, regular meetings, good interpersonal relations and high levels of commitment. In addition to factors controllable at institutional level, political support and a conducive policy environment, particularly on the African side, can determine the failure or success of STI projects.

Mugabe et al. (2018) concur with the EU (2014) on the importance of involving private sector partners, although in some cases it might be necessary for these partners to be supported through project funds. The EU (2014) further recommends the design of projects with diverse partners such as research and academic organisations, policy think tanks and local communities. Projects that build on existing networks and previous initiatives are also likely to have higher impact and sustainability.

There are two additional specific recommendations on strategic actions or measures that will help to strengthen Africa-EU STI cooperation. The first is about broadening the cooperation to include activities for building the policy design and policy learning capacities of African countries. As noted earlier, African countries need explicit government policies and related programmes for promoting STI cooperation. However, many governments of these countries do not possess the requisite capabilities to design and implement policies and related programmes for STI cooperation. It is largely because of weak policy capacities that many national policy frameworks and STISA-2024 lack concrete strategic provisions on international STI cooperation. The EU and the AU should develop a joint programme for STI policy capacity building. Such a programme would focus on strengthening policy design and STI diplomacy capacities of African governments.

The second strategic intervention is about widening participation in the STI cooperation to include more African private sector and government departments responsible for trade and industry. Currently, the cooperation is confined to research institutions and departments of science and technology, leaving out other institutional actors such as SMEs that are key players in innovation. To address this challenge, participation in the AU-EU High Level Policy Dialogue should be enlarged to include representatives of African SMEs or business associations and departments of industry. In addition, the AU Commission should design a comprehensive strategic plan for non-state actors (including private sector and civil society) engagement in the AU-EU STI cooperation.

Conclusion

This chapter has synthesised issues pertaining to Africa-EU STI cooperation. Drawing on recent studies, the chapter has identified trends in, as well as challenges to and opportunities for, the STI cooperation. The chapter also focused on the critical importance of strengthening African private sector participation in the bi-regional STI cooperation in order to ensure that knowledge outputs are translated into concrete technological solutions to address global challenges in Africa and Europe. The future of Africa-Europe STI cooperation is in building bi-regional partnerships for SDG9 – industry, infrastructure and innovation – in addition to the current focus on food and nutritional security (SDG2), health and well-being (SDG3) and climate change (SDG13). Yet for this to happen, African countries need to proactively bring the SDG9 agenda to the Africa–EU High Level Policy Dialogue, thus ensuring adequate support and sustainable partnerships in STI.

Note

1 The ACP Group changed its name in 2020 and is now known as the Organisation of African, Caribbean and Pacific States.

Bibliography

CAAST-Net Plus (2016) *Africa-EU Research Collaboration on Health: A Critical Analysis of the Scope, Outputs and Potential Outcomes*. Cape Town: Research Africa.

Carbonnier, G. and Kontinen, T. (2014) *North-South Research Partnership: Academia Meets Development*. EADI Policy Paper Series. Bonn: European Association of Development Research and Training Institutes.

Cherry, A. and Du Toit, D. (2018) The politics and drivers Underpinning Africa-Europe research and innovation cooperation. In A. Cherry, J.A. Haselip, G. Ralphs and I. Wagner (eds), *Africa-Europe Research and Innovation Cooperation: Global Challenges, Bi-regional Responses*. Cham: Springer (pp. 3–20).

Cherry, A., Haselip, J.A., Ralphs, G. and Wagner, I. (eds) (2018) *Africa-Europe Research and Innovation Cooperation: Global Challenges, Bi-regional Responses*. Cham: Springer.

Commission of the European Communities (2008) A Strategic European for International Science and Technology Cooperation. Communication from the Commission to the Council and European Parliament. COM(2008) 588 final. Brussels, 24 September.

European Union (2014) *Mapping Best Practice Regional and Multi-country Cooperative STI Initiatives between Africa and Europe*. Luxembourg: Publications Office of the European Union.

Kraemer-Mbula, E., Vaitsas, C. and Essegbey, G.O. (2018) The dynamics of EU-Africa research and innovation cooperation programmes. In A. Cherry, J.A. Haselip, G. Ralphs and I. Wagner (eds), *Africa-Europe Research and Innovation Cooperation: Global Challenges, Bi-regional Responses*. Cham: Springer (pp. 39–64).

Lee, S. and Bozeman, B. (2005) The impact of research collaboration on scientific productivity. *Social Studies of Science*, 35 (5), 673–702. www.jstor.org/stable/25046667

Mugabe, J.O. and Manyuchi, A. (forthcoming) Making foreign direct investment work for inclusive and sustainable industrialization in Africa. In *Handbook on African Development*. Springer Publishers.

Mugabe, J.O., Chaminuka, P. and Melo, A. (2018) Characterising partnership for research and Innovation in Sub-Saharan Africa: Lessons from the case of the Africa–EU ProIntensAfrica Initiative. *South African Journal of International Affairs*, 25 (4), 531–545.

Ralphs, G. and Wagner, I.E. (2018) Towards better joint work: Reflections on partnership effectiveness. In A. Cherry, J.A. Haselip, G. Ralphs and I. Wagner (eds), *Africa-Europe Research and Innovation Cooperation: Global Challenges, Bi-regional Responses*. Cham: Springer (pp. 123–140).

Wagner, C. (2008) *The New Invisible College: Science for Development*. Washington DC: Brookings Institution Press.

Part IV
External actors in Africa's international politics and the Africa-European Union relationship

Introduction to Part IV

Andrew Cottey

Introduction

Africa, of course, has long been a focus of external international actors, more so than African states or Africa collectively have been actors shaping global politics. With Africa constituting approximately 17% of the global population and African states about a quarter of the membership of the United Nations (UN), while Africa's collective gross domestic product (GDP) amounts to only 3–4% of global GDP, the underlying material circumstances underpinning this reality are unlikely to change soon. Any consideration of the Africa-European Union (EU) relationship, therefore, needs to incorporate the role of external actors other than the EU in Africa's international politics. This includes, most obviously, other states (especially major powers – in particular, the United States and China, but also others such as Russia, Brazil, Japan and India), but also international organisations (in particular, the UN, the World Bank and the International Monetary Fund (IMF)) and non-state actors (in particular, businesses and non-governmental organisations (NGOs)/civil society organisations (CSOs)). In the 1990s and 2000s, following the end of the Cold War, the international context for external engagement in Africa could be viewed in terms of the apparent consolidation of a liberal international order: the United States and other Western states were the dominant powers in the international system; multilateralism, democracy, human rights and market economics were the central international norms; and international institutions increasingly reflected this logic. The interaction between the Africa-EU relationship and other external actors in Africa followed similar lines: the Africa-EU relationship was underpinned by liberal principles (in particular, from the EU side); the United States and the EU could be viewed as following broadly similar policies in Africa; the policies of the main international organisations (the UN, the IMF and the World Bank) also reflected this liberal logic; and other external states were of secondary importance. From the mid-2000s and accelerating through the 2010s, the global context changed in important ways.

The rise of China made it the world's second superpower, and it developed a growing role in Africa. China, Russia and other authoritarian states began to challenge the liberal international order and the dominance of the West. The dramatic financial and economic crisis of 2008–2010 further undermined the material power of the West relative to that of rising powers and was also a major political shock to Western liberal self-confidence (or hubris, if one prefers). By the late 2010s and the beginning of the 2020s, the international context for external engagement in Africa was one of multipolarity rather than US or Western hegemony, in which hitherto dominant liberal norms were increasingly challenged (even perhaps in retreat) and international institutions were undergoing transitions reflecting these dynamics. Against this changing background, the chapters in this section examine the role of various external actors in Africa in the first decades of the 21st century and how this interacts with and impacts on the Africa-EU relationship.

In Chapter 17, Norman Sempijja examines the dynamics and problems of inter-organisational cooperation in Africa, focusing on the triangular relationship between the AU, the EU and the UN in the area of peacekeeping. Sempijja places his analysis in the context of a number of larger developments: the rise of multilateralism in general and of a plethora of international organisations with overlapping interests and mandates; the development since the end of the Cold War of cooperation in peacekeeping between the UN as 'the' global organisation and regional organisations as the UN's partners; and the problem of resource dependence, with international organisations very often lacking the resources (both material and non-material) to carry out their activities and consequently turning to other international organisations to address these resource problems. In terms of resources, the UN has legitimacy and financial resources (in the form of the UN peacekeeping budget), but lacks manpower for peacekeeping operations (with its peacekeeping mission already overstretched and member states often unwilling to contribute troops to UN operations). The AU – or more specifically its member states and often subregional organisations which are an important part of the overall configuration of the – can provide manpower and has legitimacy (although perhaps not as much as the UN), but lacks financial resources to fund peacekeeping operations. The EU does not have the same legitimacy as the UN or the AU in Africa, but it has greater financial resources and some advantages in terms of military deployability (albeit only for relatively small military operations). Sempijja also highlights that international organisations are to a significant degree the servants of their member states and that state interests thus constrain what they are able or willing to do. Against this background, Sempijja explores the three sides of the AU-EU-UN triangle. The EU-UN relationship in peacekeeping has been characterised by a general commitment to cooperation on the basis of shared principles, but in practice a reluctance on the part of EU member states to contribute forces to UN operations and a wariness, when EU operations have been established in Africa, to submit EU autonomy to large UN operations. The EU-AU relationship has been characterised by a rhetorical commitment to cooperation and partnership, but remains heavily shaped by the legacy of colonialism, and Sempijja suggests the relationship is to some extent a 'façade'. The EU has provided financial and logistical support for AU peacekeeping, but a more comprehensive partnership in this area has not yet emerged. The UN-AU relationship is the strongest side of the triangle, with the UN providing legitimacy, funds and equipment and the AU (and its member states) providing manpower, and this becoming an important part of the model for larger peacekeeping operations in Africa (as in the Democratic Republic of the Congo, Darfur, Somalia and Sudan). This has given some substance to the goal of African solutions to African problems. At the same time, however, Sempijja points out that African states and the AU have 'largely been shoved to the side' when external great powers decide to intervene in Africa militarily, as with the United States and its NATO allies in Libya in 2011 and France in Mali in 2013. The conclusion one draws from Sempijja's analysis is that the AU, the EU and the UN do share common interests in peacekeeping and to some extent cooperate on a triangular basis, but that the AU-UN relationship has become the strongest and most important leg of this triad and that the AU-EU and EU-UN relationships are relatively weak and less important.

In Chapter 18, Obert Hodzi examines the impact of China's increasing influence in Africa on the EU-Africa relationship. Hodzi argues that China has become an alternative partner for African states and the AU and consequently increased African leverage vis-à-vis the EU – a form of derivative power (a term originally coined by Michael Handel). Derivative power allows smaller/weaker actors to play major powers off against one another and thereby gain increased influence – something African states practiced in relation to the United States and the Soviet Union during the Cold War. Hodzi notes that China has become the largest contributor of troops for UN peacekeeping operations in Africa, a larger trade partner for Africa than any single EU state (although not the EU as whole) and an important source of investment and finance for many African states, as well as not having the colonial baggage that comes with Europe's relationship with Africa. Hodzi argues that the existence of China as an alternative to the EU as an external partner, perceptions of an EU-China competition for influence in Africa, and European concerns about loss of influence in Africa have allowed African states and the AU to make demands of the EU. This has resulted in a shift in European policy, involving in particular a reduced emphasis on conditionality and new willingness to treat Africa, at least in part, as a partner rather than simply a recipient of aid. Hodzi also explores African collective power: the hope that by acting collectively, in particular through the AU, Africa's influence on its own destiny and the wider world will be increased. Here, Hodzi suggests collective power has been something of a mirage: both the EU and China have sought to address Africa collectively, thereby reinforcing the sense of Africa (collectively) as the weaker side in hierarchical relationships with both Brussels and Beijing; at the same time, when their interests suit, the EU/European states and China turn instead to bilateral relationships with individual African states. Hodzi argues that although China's increased influence on the continent has given Africa a degree of increased leverage in relations with EU, it has not materially changed the fundamentals of an EU-Africa relationship that remains highly asymmetrical. He concludes that Africa's derivative power is 'only momentary'.

In Chapter 19, Carolina Pavese and Guilherme Ziebell de Oliviera explore Brazil's role in Africa, the EU-Brazil relationship and efforts to establish triangular EU-Brazil-Africa cooperation. While Brazil has had a long-standing role in Africa, by the 1990s the Brazil-Africa relationship was relatively quiescent. Pavese and Ziebell show that in the 2000s, under the administration of Brazilian President Luiz Inácio Lula da Silva (2003–2010), there was an important renaissance in Brazilian-African relations, including regular diplomatic contacts, the opening (or reopening) of embassies in African countries, support for Brazilian companies investing in Africa, Brazilian technical and financial assistance to African states and bilateral development cooperation projects. The context for this new relationship was Brazil's new status as an emerging power and Lula's efforts to diversify Brazil's foreign policy and diplomatic activity beyond existing relationships with Western states. Brazil's new engagement with Africa continued in the initial years of the administration of Dilma Rousseff (2011–2016), although with less enthusiasm than under Lula. Parallel to this, Pavese and Ziebell show that an EU-Brazil strategic partnership was established. In the 2000s, the EU's ambitions to establish itself as a global actor and Brazil's interest in recognition as an emerging power and diversifying its foreign policy ties created the context for this partnership. The EU-Brazil strategic partnership was formally established in 2007, regular summits where held from then on and a variety of institutional ties and sectoral dialogues were put in place. With Brazil and the EU now active players in Africa, the two partners also committed – at least rhetorically – to triangular cooperation on and with Africa. In examining the detail, however, Pavese and Ziebell conclude that 'in most of the cases, triangular cooperation was no more than lip service': some progress was made on electoral assistance to African states and biofuel projects were discussed but collapsed; however, beyond this, triangular

EU-Brazil-Africa cooperation has not progressed. As Pavese and Ziebell explore, more recent developments have made EU-Brazil-Africa cooperation even less likely: Brazil's status as an emerging power has been interrupted by an economic downturn and domestic political turbulence; the election of the populist Jair Bolsonaro in 2018 means that Brazil's interest in Africa and South-South cooperation will be further reduced, at least in the short term; and these developments have put the EU-Brazil strategic partnership in the deep freeze since 2014. Pavese and Ziebell's chapter highlights the extent to which countries foreign policies can be dependent on domestic politics and how this may impact external actors' engagement with Africa. Pavese and Ziebell's analysis, however, also suggests that even when external actors' interests and policies in Africa may be broadly similar and arguably synergistic – as was the case with Brazil and the EU in the 2000s and early 2010s – this does not easily or simply translate into triangular cooperation with Africa and African states.

Mark Langan and Sophia Price, in Chapter 20, examine the role of private non-state actors in Africa-EU relations. Langan and Price argue that there has been an important shift in the subfield of International Political Economy, away from a previous Westphalian focus on states as the central actors in international relations to an approach that recognises the importance of non-state actors (in particular, multinational corporations, business associations, trade unions and NGOs/CSOs) – which they describe as 'Westphalia plus'. This approach, they argue, is essential for properly understanding African international politics and the Africa-EU relationship. They explore how various non-state actors have sought to shape and interact with the African development agenda and how this impacts the Africa-EU relationship. Langan and Price argue that business associations and multinational corporations have influenced both the global development agenda (in particular the UN Sustainable Development Goals) and EU development policy (in particular Economic Partnership Agreements) and that this has resulted in an emphasis on 'aid blending' (the integration of state/EU development aid with private sector finance) and on the role of private-sector-led growth (often involving multinational corporations rather than local small and medium enterprises and arguably at the expense of other pro-poor models of development). Langan and Price also explore the role of NGOs/CSOs, noting how those in Africa have shaped African government and subregional organisation policies (e.g. by generating pressure against free trade agreements with the EU). They also show that both African and European NGOs/CSOs have successfully lobbied for their inclusion in processes of Africa-EU institution-building and dialogue, resulting in the establishment of the Africa-EU Civil Society Forum. Langan and Price argue that while this gives NGOs/CSOs a voice in shaping official policies, it also risks their co-option into the dominant neoliberal paradigm of economic development. Overall, Langan and Price make a convincing case that African international politics and economics cannot be understood without incorporating the significant role played by non-state actors and that thinking about how the Africa-EU relationship needs to include this dimension too.

Two other external actors not examined in the chapters in this section should also be noted: the United States (US) and Russia. As the world's leading power, albeit one in at least relative decline and facing an uncertain global future, the US is inevitably an important actor in Africa. Alongside the EU and China, the US remains one of the three big external economic actors in Africa in terms of trade, investment and aid. Nonetheless, in US foreign policy, Africa has long been a lower priority than Europe, Asia and the Middle East. US political and economic engagement with Africa, furthermore, has declined and also become more narrowly focused. In the wake of the September 2001 terrorist attacks, counterterrorism became a key focus of the George W. Bush administration's Africa policy, with a military-focused approach and the establishment in 2008 of the Africa Command as one of the US' regional military commands

(Africa had hitherto been part of the European Command's area of responsibility). Rhetorically at least, President Barack Obama sought to increase US engagement with Africa and to give it a broader focus (in particular on economic development issues). In practice, however, critics argued that Obama's presidency resulted in little change in US-Africa policy, with maintenance of a militarised approached to counterterrorism and a narrow focus on US economic interests in particular countries (Olsen, 2017; Van de Walle, 2015). Under President Donald Trump, this mix of focus on militarised counterterrorism, pursuit of economic interests in particular countries and disengagement from Africa's broader economic and political challenges continued (The Economist, 2020).

Following the end of Cold War and the break-up of the Soviet Union, Russia was relatively absent from Africa for three decades. In the 2010s, however, Russia made what many observers described as a remarkable comeback in Africa. In a number of countries across Africa, Russia was able to use combinations of economic investment, arms supplies, military/police training, military deployments and political advice to authoritarian regimes to establish a new political foothold in the regime. This prompted concern in the West about a possible return to Cold War-style geopolitical competition between Russia and the West in Africa (Faleg and Secrieru, 2020; Marten, 2019). Whether Russia would be able to develop or maintain a more extensive role in Africa, however, remained to be seen: in contrast to the EU, the US and China, Russia arguably lacks the economic basis to underpin an extended global impact, including in Africa.

The changing environment of external involvement in Africa raises important questions for policymakers and analysts in terms of how we should understand that environment and the challenges and choices it poses for Africa (both individual states and collectively via the African Union and the African subregional groupings), the EU and Africa-EU cooperation. One way of interpreting the situation in the 2010s and early 2020s is in terms of classical Westphalian 'balance of power' politics, with the major external actors (the US, China, the EU and perhaps Russia) competing for influence and economic opportunity. For African states and peoples, this once again raises the danger of them being the collateral damage of great power competition, but also the possibility that they may be able, to their own benefit, to play the great powers off against one another (although Obert Hodzi's chapter suggests that such opportunities are, in practice, of limited benefit to African states). There appear to be important elements of truth in this great power competition perspective, but it does not capture the entirety of a more complex picture. Notwithstanding elements of great power competition, there are also areas where the great powers cooperate vis-à-vis Africa: one of these is UN peacekeeping, where the five permanent members of the Security Council have remained able to agree mandates for UN peacekeeping operations in Africa over a 30–40 year period since the mid to late 1980s. Norman Sempijja's chapter also highlights the importance of the UN as an external actor in its own right in the field of peacekeeping, showing that states are not the only external actors playing important roles in Africa, that not all external actors are likely to frame their engagement in terms of competition for influence and that at least some external engagement in Africa is underpinned by a strong logic of partnership between African states/the AU and the external actor (in this case, the UN). An additional problem with the great power competition perspective is that it assumes or implies that such competition has a logic of its own which drives major powers to increasing engagement in regions such as Africa. As the US case over the last 20–30 years shows, however, one of the challenges can sometimes be great power disengagement or disinterest. While the US focus on counterterrorism and the militarisation of counterterrorism policy in Africa may be problematic, so too has the relative lack of US engagement on the challenges of peacekeeping, economic development and climate change in Africa.

Overall, therefore, the environment of external involvement in Africa in the 2010s and early 2020s may perhaps be better understood as one combining elements of great power competition, sometimes cooperation (between major powers, international institutions such as the UN, and African actors) and sometimes disengagement and disinterest from external actors. Escalating global tensions between the US and China, which some observers describe as a new Cold War, also raise questions about how far such dynamics will impact on and play out in Africa in future. More broadly, some observers suggest that the 21st century is likely to be increasingly shaped by competition between democratic and authoritarian great powers (primarily the US and its long-standing Western allies on the one side and China and Russia on the other) (Brands, 2018). Developing country democracies, including Africa's democracies, will likely seek to avoid polarised choices between democrats and authoritarians in international politics, and European states and the EU are also wary of being drawn into such dynamics. At minimum, however, the new great power politics are likely to create a complex and challenging environment for African states, the EU and future Africa-EU cooperation.

Bibliography

Brands, H. (2018) Democracy vs authoritarianism: How ideology shapes great-power conflict. *Survival*, 60 (5), 61–114.

Faleg, G. and Secrieru, S. (2020) *Russia's Forays into Sub-Saharan Africa*. Paris: European Union Institute for Security Studies (EUISS).

Marten, K. (2019) Russia's back in Africa: Is the cold war returning? *The Washington Quarterly*, 42 (4), 155–170.

Olsen, G.R. (2017) Obama and US policy towards Africa: A study in failure? *International Politics*, 54 (1), 73–88.

The Economist (2020) A strategy on autopilot. 22 February, 27–28.

Van de Walle, N. (2015) Obama and Africa: Lots of hope, not much change. *Foreign Affairs*, 94 (5), 54–61.

17

Inter-organisational cooperation in flux?

Impact of resources and state interests in the cooperation between the European Union, United Nations and African Union

Norman Sempijja

Introduction

The changing nature of global dynamics after the Cold War led to a rise in multilateralism and a desire by states to come together to resolve international issues ranging from economic, ecologic, security to health and social among others. Although international organisations had become global players since the turn of the 20th century, the post–World War II and post–Cold War eras saw increased prominence of institutions like the United Nations (UN), the European Union (EU) and the Organization of African Unity (later the African Union (AU)), to name but a few. Subsequently the post-Cold War dynamics which not only pitted states against each other but also resulted in non-state actors like terrorist groups led to a realisation that no single organisation can resolve international problems on its own. There was a need for multilateral approach to effectively resolve these issues. However, all organisations are not uniformly endowed, and there has been a need to depend on one another's resources to fulfil a given mandate. Yet this resource dependence is not without problems, especially as organisations are run by states and can only act as far as these states (which quite often are self-interested) are willing to let them.

The rise of multilateralism has permeated economic, social, security and political spheres of interstate relations. For instance, the post-Cold War intra-state conflicts led to a desire by the UN to engage more with regional organisations under Chapter VIII of its charter, to resolve conflicts. For instance former UN Secretary General Boutros Boutros-Ghali (1992) called for their use in preventive diplomacy, peacekeeping, peacemaking and post-conflict peacebuilding, because this decentralisation was going to lighten the UN burden and bring about a greater role in democratisation of international relations and, in the process, build consensus on problem-solving. Later on, the 2000 Brahimi report, which was compiled to bring about mechanisms of addressing organisational and political problems experienced by the UN during peacekeeping, made reference to a partnership between the UN and regional organisations in resolving conflicts (Tardy, 2004: 5).

The need for cooperation between the UN and regional organisations has further been enhanced by the lack of political will within the Security Council to intervene in conflicts or even to give missions strong mandates to carry out their duties. This has given credence to the view that international organisations like the UN are member-driven and can only be as effective as members are willing to allow (Szapiro, 2004: 356). States have specific interests as to why they support certain interventions and oppose others. Other UN members, according to Szapiro (ibid.: 356), have different views when it comes to the use of force in the international arena. Herrberg (2008) contends that the EU would favour a soft power approach to conflict resolution, as it was founded on principles of non-coerciveness.

Over the years, the UN and regional organisations have held biennial meetings (Wouters et al., 2006: 232). The first one was in 1994, and since then the list of participating organisations has increased: from 10 in 1994 to 20 in 2005. The meeting held under the guidance of Kofi Annan on 18 July 1998 called for the establishment of a framework of cooperation (Kronenberger and Wouters, 2004: 382–383). Other meetings held throughout the years have involved discussions on potential violence in respective regions of participating organisations, likely preventive measures and guidelines for coordinated regional effort; for example, setting up joint peacekeeping and peacebuilding units and assessing missions in the field (ibid.: 363).

These talks have resulted in the formation of an understanding between the UN and regional organisations. On a case-by-case basis, the UN has associated itself with different organisations in their respective areas. During the conflict in Sierra Leone, the UN supported the intervention in 1998 by the Economic Community of West African States (ECOWAS), without initial authorisation from the Security Council (Sarkin, 2009: 7). Indeed the UN has collaborated on peacekeeping with a number of regional bodies since the end of the Cold War. For instance, 'United Nations field missions have been deployed in conjunction with ECOWAS in Liberia and with CIS in Georgia. … there can be joint operations, such as the current human rights mission of the United Nations and the OAS in Haiti' (UN Secretary-General, 1999: 116). Also, the UN has worked with the AU in the Darfur region of Sudan (UN Security Council, 2017: 8). Nevertheless there is a need to have a holistic examination of the different strands of multilateralism in the international system. The chapter will discuss the theoretical framework, then delve into conceptualisation of multilateralism and effective multilateralism. The work will explore the nature of various relationships between the three organisations, beginning with EU-UN relations, then looking at EU-Africa relations and UN-Africa relations. The study will wrap up with an exploration of the impact of the UN on EU-Africa relations.

Why cooperate with regional bodies?

The post-World War II era witnessed the rise of international organisations as a conduit for states to interact and resolve conflicts. According to Biermman (2009: 7), intergovernmental organisations have grown four times since 1945. The UN, which replaced the League of Nations, has played a pivotal role in resolving international disputes and was crucial during the Soviet Union-United States stand-off during the Cold War. For example, Dag Hammarskjold came up with peacekeeping as a way of stopping the two superpowers from clashing in conflicts around the world. Yet in the post-Cold War era, the UN found itself stretched when faced with new intra-state conflicts for which it had neither the mandate nor the manpower to resolve. In the end it had to rely on regional powers, as stipulated in Chapter VIII of its charter. This lack of resources and the need to address it has situated this study in the resource dependence perspective.

Resource dependence

In exploring inter-organisational relations, Brosig (2015) and Sempijja (2016), among others, have delved into the theory of resource dependence and endeavoured to draw linkages with inter-organisation cooperation. Brosig and Motsamai (2014: 47) argue that resources are physical or non-physical materials transmitted from one organisation to another. For this chapter, physical resources will include military support in terms of troops and other military logistics. The non-physical materials will include the legitimising authority of the UN, UN mandates and EU and AU declarations.

Thus, to proponents of resource dependence, it is argued that due to the limited nature of resources, organisations' incentives are drawn from the need to exchange or depend on each other's resources to achieve objectives or to survive (Pfeffer and Salancik, 2003: 258). Organisations like the AU, the EU and the UN suffer insufficiencies in terms of exchangeable resources at one point. For example, post 1991, the UN faced mandate issues in regard to intervention in internal conflicts, as was the case in the former Yugoslavia, where the UN could not muster a rapid, muscular intervention force and had to rely on the North Atlantic Treaty Organization (NATO) to carry out robust intervention.

The exchange of resources included the military manpower of NATO and the legitimising authority of the UN. Therefore, in the international system, the UN provides legitimacy to other organisations like the AU and in turn benefits from their manpower and financial resources to achieve its mandate. Further still, the UN has continued to rely on organisations like the EU to robustly intervene in hot conflicts, as the case was in the Democratic Republic of the Congo in the 2000s; yet its missions have been mandated to operate under Chapter VII of its charter. The UN is still not properly equipped to deal with internal conflicts involving rebel groups, and it has had to rely on states like Malawi, South Africa and Tanzania (Force Intervention Brigade) in the Democratic Republic of the Congo.

Collaboration framework (neoliberal perspective)

Although as explored above, there have been challenges in terms of resources in the post-Cold War era, the triumph of liberalism, as discussed by Fukuyama, set the tone for inter-organisational engagements. The UN and EU are bodies led by a largely Global North group of states that subscribe to the neoliberal perspective both as an economic way of life but also as a way of building peace. Thus UN and EU engagements in post-conflict reconstruction have adhered to the main tenets of the neoliberal perspective, which has involved the opening up of markets of the state to foreign companies and the embracing of democracy. This is embodied in the definition by Harvey, who argues that

> Neo liberalism is in the first instance a theory of political economic practices that propose that human well-being can best be advanced by liberating individual entrepreneurial freedoms and skills within an institutional framework characterised by strong private rights, free markets and free trade. … Furthermore if markets do not exist … then they must be created by state action if necessary. But beyond these tasks the state must not venture
>
> *(2005: 2)*

The adherence to a neoliberal perspective has helped bring about collaboration between the EU and the UN, especially in peacebuilding through security sector reforms, rule of law, etc. Yet even without a similar approach by the AU (as will be explored later), the template of the neoliberal approach has helped these three organisations to collaborate on a wide range of issues, especially relating to peacebuilding.

From multilateralism to effective multilateralism and the transformation of EU relations with intergovernmental institutions

The term effective multilateralism was used by the EU in the European Security Strategy (ESS) document that was produced in 2003 in the aftermath of the fallout from the invasion of Iraq. The EU was deeply divided about whether Iraq was to be invaded without a second UN resolution. Major nations like France and Germany did not favour an invasion, while Britain and a few other nations sided with the United States, leading Donald Rumsfeld to coin the term 'old and new Europe'. The EU, at the instigation of its members on both sides of the debate, asked Javier Solana (former high representative of the union for foreign affairs and state security) to design a new strategy that was reiterated in the ESS.

However before delving into the concept of effective multilateralism, it is important to define the term 'multilateralism'. Koops notes that 'despite its long established salience in political rhetoric and practice, the general academic discourse on multilateralism itself seems rather fragmented, unsystemic and largely under-theorised' (2011: 66). Though there have been attempts at defining the concept, and among the renowned early experts are Ruggie and Keohane. Keohane defines multilateralism as 'institutionalized collective action by an inclusively determined set of independent states' (2006: 1), while Ruggie argues that multilateralism portrays a generic institutional form in international relations and goes further to define multilateralism as an

> institutional form which coordinates relations among three or more states on the basis of 'generalized' principles of conduct—that is, principles which specify appropriate conduct for a class of actions, without any regard for the particularistic interests of the parties or the strategic exigencies that may exist in any specific occurrence.
>
> *(1992: 570–571)*

Other definitions of multilateralism, which Koops (2011) puts in the traditional group, include that by Hemmer and Karzenstein who define it 'as a particularly demanding form of international cooperation which requires a strong sense of collective identity in addition to shared interests' (2002: 575–576). This definition, according to Koops, displays strong constructivist assumptions 'as it underlines the importance of norms, ideas, principles and even the existence and forging of collective identities' (2011: 72). He notes that multilateralism has gone through stages; for example, traditional multilateralism, which epitomised 'a clear emphasis on cooperation through international organisations and on multilateralism as a long-term organising principle for international order', lasted from the end of the Second World War to the late 1980s (ibid.: 72).

The post-Cold War period has witnessed a shift in theory and practice, especially after the failure of the UN to live up to the collective security and humanitarian intervention of the first decade after the Cold War, a situation that has been amplified since 9/11 by the US-led war on terror (Koops, 2011: 72). The post-Cold War period has seen what is known as new multilateralism. Koops notes the argument by Boyka Stefanova that the difference between classical/

traditional and new multilateralism is that the former, practiced under US hegemony, 'was an element of order', whereas '[n]ew multilateralism is a threat response' (ibid.: 73). Thus Koops (quoting Stefanova) postulates that

> due to the increase in unpredictable threats since the end of the Cold War, particularly those posed by international terrorism and rogue states, coupled with the alleged ineffectiveness of the UN systems, the tardiness of international institutions and the resurgence of the salience of military power in international relations, 'classical multilateralism' seems to have been refashioned into 'new multilateralism', which is a form of cooperation that 'displays a much more ends-means rationality rather than a structurally determined normative character'.
>
> *(Ibid.: 73)*

Other forms of multilateralism under the new multilateralism noted by Koops include genuine multilateralism and minilateralism, as advanced by Kahler. Genuine multilateralism is defined as 'incorporating a very large number of players', while minilateralism 'is limited great power collaboration within multilateral structures' (Koops, 2011: 74). The former was pursued in order to deal with impasses often encountered in large-number multilateralism.

Effective multilateralism

In the midst of the disagreement between the EU countries over the invasion of Iraq (discussed above), Biscop and Drieskens (2006) note that there was a realisation of the need for a strategic vision and a security strategy – and, more specifically, a definition of the overall policy objectives that could serve as a reference framework for everyday decision-making. The ESS document, which was designed by a team headed by Janvier Solana (Biscop and Drieskens, 2006), coined the term 'effective multilateralism', arguing that

> In a world of global threats, global markets and global media, our security and prosperity increasingly depend on an effective multilateral system. The development of a stronger international society, well-functioning international institutions and a rule-based international order is our objective.
>
> *(Council of the European Union, 2003: 11)*

In light of the above, it is very tempting to see effective multilateralism in the context of the EU. Indeed Koops notes that 'Sven Biscop argues the best way of summarizing the ESS is by effective multilateralism' (2011: 79). Koops goes further to argue that the

> overall consensus is that effective multilateralism represents the EU's own distinctive approach to international affairs, which seeks to integrate the norms and rules and institutions of traditional multilateralism ... with a more pragmatic, actively interventionist and even more military-geared culture akin to some form of output oriented new multilateralism.
>
> *(Ibid.: 80)*

This conclusion is drawn from the perception that the ESS brings about an interpretation of effective multilateralism that aspires to combine military intervention in the form of early response with the development of international law and support for the UN (ibid.: 80).

Furthermore, effective multilateralism can be viewed in the context of strengthening the EU's role in international politics. For instance the ESS document states that

> the increasing convergence of European interests and the strengthening of mutual solidarity of the EU makes us a more credible and effective actor. Europe should be ready to share in the responsibility for global security and in building a better world.
>
> *(Council of the European Union, 2003: 9)*

The EU views multilateralism as a vehicle to making it a credible and more integrated actor in the international arena. The ESS emphasises cooperation between the EU and UN, thereby integrating international institutions into the definition and attributes of multilateralism. Most authors who have attempted to define it have viewed multilateralism as mainly involving states. With the ESS there is emphasis on institutions. Indeed Koops argues that the ESS, which he views as the EU's foreign policy philosophy, 'represents a rather novel development, as it seems to promote multilateralism between international organisations instead of a multilateralism hitherto centred on states' (Koops, 2011: 78). Although effective multilateralism has mainly been used in the context of the EU, it can be applied on a wider scale for other organisations like the AU and NATO. The UN stays at the centre as the legitimising power, leaving other organisations to coordinate with it in creating a secure world. Further still, the definition of multilateralism has been enlarged to incorporate international organisations. Coupled with this is the fact that when examined from the background of traditional and new multilateralism, effective multilateralism has shown an ability to combine aspects of the two types to suit the needs of the contemporary world.

The rise of EU-UN collaboration

Since the end of the Cold War, the EU has shown a willingness to cooperate with the UN. The main reason for this stems from the inherent favourable predisposition of the EU towards multilateralism and the recognition that the UN is the main actor as far as maintenance of international peace and security is concerned. Throughout its formation and metamorphosis, as witnessed in the various treaties, the EU has maintained adherence to multilateralism and recognised the leadership of the UN in maintaining peace and security in the international system. According to Wouters, in 1995, when the UN was celebrating its 50th anniversary, 'the EU strongly reaffirmed its attachment to the UN Charter and pledged to support the UN in a Declaration adopted at the Cannes European Council in June 1995' (2004).

In Helsinki (December 1999), the European Council unequivocally declared: 'The Union will contribute to international peace and security in accordance with the principles of the UN Charter. The Union recognises the primary responsibility of the UN Security Council for the maintenance of international peace and security' (European Union, 1999).

Furthermore, in the latter part of 2000, according to Tardy (2005: 54), the European Security and Defence Council (ESDP) report to the Nice European Council was released, highlighting the value of cooperation between the EU and UN during a time when the EU was developing its crisis management and conflict prevention capabilities. The report acknowledges that the efforts to foster the cooperation would help the EU to respond more efficiently to requests from organisations like the UN. The willingness of the EU to cooperate with the UN took a new turn in 2003 in Bosnia, where the UN's International Police Task Force mission was replaced by the EU Police Mission. The EU also led Operation Artemis in the Democratic Republic of the Congo to relieve UN forces that were trapped in Ituri in 2003. The success of these missions showed the desire of the EU to partner with the UN in peacekeeping, therefore presenting itself as a viable option among regional organisations.

Moreover, the willingness of the EU to work with the UN is attributed to the interest of its member states in key regions of conflict. It has played a key role in rebuilding successor states in the former Yugoslavia because the region is in its own backyard. This could explain why the EU played a crucial role in the diplomatic manoeuvres as the conflict raged on in the 1990s. Further still, as with the launch of the EU Police Mission in Bosnia, the EU was deployed to take over from the UN in some states. An example is Operation Althea as a successor to the NATO-led stabilisation force in 2004. However, Operation Althea was authorised by the Security Council (Knauer, 2011). Apart from intervening in its backyard, the EU has further intervened in areas outside its geographical setting, as seen in the Democratic Republic of the Congo with the launch of Operation Artemis. States like France and Belgium had key national interests in the area and subsequently had the EU on board when launching Artemis in 2003.

Nature of EU-UN collaboration

When examining the nature of the EU-UN partnership, Tardy (2005) does not paint a glamorous picture. First of all, Tardy views EU member states' policies towards the UN as being ambivalent. He argues that 'on the one hand, the EU and its member states are strong supporters of the UN, in accordance with the European Security Strategy and the concept of effective multilateralism' (ibid.: 51). This is because they are connected to the centrality and legitimising power of the UN Security Council, have achieved political influence within UN bodies beyond the responsibility held by the Commission in economic and development affairs and have supported the UN by making large contributions to the regular and peacekeeping budgets, to the tune of 37.75% and 39%, respectively (ibid.: 51). On the other hand, Tardy stresses that

> the strong emphasis that the EU places on its political autonomy leads it to somehow distance itself from the UN. For example, obtaining UN mandates for ESDP operations does not appear to be a requirement as long as these operations are deployed in Europe, with the consent of the host state, and are of a non-coercive or civilian nature.
>
> *(Ibid.: 51)*

Furthermore, although the EU member states make big troop contributions to UN mandated peace operations, they are anonymous when it comes to contributing to UN-led operations. By early spring 2005, the EU accounted for only 6.25% of UN troops. When it came to Africa, the EU contributed a mere 2.24% of the whole UN troops contingents to Africa (Tardy, 2005: 52). The likelihood of using EU military capabilities in UN-led operations is very low and comes with very specific conditions. For Tardy,

> the general reticence of the European states to place troops under UN command, in addition to their skepticism about the reliability of the UN structure in general, are concerns that are echoed within the EU itself and its politico-military structure, and that both negatively impact on the EU-UN relationship.
>
> *(Ibid.: 52)*

Novosseloff (2004: 11) argues that the use of elaborated principles and prerequisites has been in response to UN expectations and demands. Apart from the Political Security Council retaining the political control and strategic direction of any of its operations, the EU further follows the principle of cooperation with the UN on a case-by-case basis. 'There would be no automatic involvement; the EU does not constitute a pool of forces but can only intervene by conducting specific missions or operations, and there would be no earmarked forces to any stand-by arrangements' (ibid.: 11). Major (2008: 13) wades in by hypothesising that the EU–UN relationship is influenced by the pursuit of EU interests, as opposed to what the UN may require. This is mainly because the EU has pursued an autonomous policy in that it determines where and how to intervene by considering a multitude of external and internal factors. The overlap between what the UN desires and what the EU is willing to provide has come to define the limits of the cooperation between the two. The situation is complicated further by the fact that the EU is an intergovernmental organisation and not a unitary actor; therefore, much depends on the member states' political will. For instance, factors like foreign policy goals, economic situation and unanimous decision-making have to be taken into consideration.

The EU reluctance to re-hat its assets and to make them available to the UN after Operation Artemis, which endangered the integrity of the UN Organization Stabilization Mission in the Democratic Republic of the Congo, also highlights the ambivalence of the EU towards the UN.[1]

> In the context of EU–UN relations, the European stance revealed the limits of cooperation; it showed what the EU and its member states were ready to do (offer support through a separate operation), but also what they would not do (offer support within the UN operation).
>
> (Tardy, 2005: 55–57)

Nevertheless, the collaboration resulted in institutionalisation of EU–UN cooperation with their 2003 joint declaration (European Union–United Nations, 2003), which led to joint training exercises in spite of what was seen as the EU's self-interested peacekeeping policy. Besides, 'the EU–UN relationship has developed further and faster than the relationship between the UN and any other regional organisation. Moreover, this relationship may be seen as a model to be replicated, between the UN and African organisations for example' (Tardy, 2005: 58). Thus in 2003, the EU and the UN established 'a joint consultative mechanism at the working level. This was to examine ways and means to enhance mutual co-ordination and compatibility' (European Union–United Nations, 2003: 2). The areas to be covered by mutual coordination and compatibility included planning, training, communication and best practices (ibid.: 2).

The 2007 EU–UN declaration, according to Major (2008), was a reiteration of the 2003 declaration, yet in essence it was designed to restate the issues that had not been addressed since 2003. This involved sharing confidential information (ibid.: 13). The UN does not have a procedure to handle sensitive information, which is a major hindrance to operational cooperation. According to the report submitted on behalf of the Defence Committee by Ine Aasted-Madsen and René Rouquet (2009: 9–10), information sharing on the operational level is still a contentious issue that has proved to be politically and technically hard to solve as there is no agreed framework, and it continues to be dealt with on a case-by-case basis. On institutionalising the EU–UN relations, significant advances have been made in communication and liaison, though 'a notable lack of guidelines and common definitions continues to inhibit the relationship in the field and prevent efficient cooperation' (ibid., 2009: 9–10). Koops (2011: 78) notes that some of the statements made by the EU in the ESS were opportunistic in nature. For instance, EU insistence on strengthening the UN was interpreted as an opportunistic approach to multilateralism in that 'the EU was portrayed as the "rescuer of the United Nations Systems", and thus with a distinct principle for enhancing the EU's own international actorness and profile' (ibid.: 78).

EU-Africa (incorporating economic and security cooperation)

The EU and African states had built up a postcolonial relationship over the years through the Lomé Convention of 1975 and the Cotonou Agreement of 2000, which was to be revised every five years. But the March 2010 EU-Africa negotiations saw Africa addressing more of its challenges with the cooperation in an attempt to even the scales of the agreement and, therefore, benefit more from it. The challenges were to do with trade strategies, especially aid for trade, and their dissatisfaction with the preference erosion. Peacebuilding and prevention of conflict for a better secured development environment and climate change were other key issues discussed in the second revision.

Thus, cooperation between the EU and Africa has been going on for centuries, and although the African communities and, later, states have lacked agency, the post-2007 meeting in Lisbon elected to change that. There has been a move from Euro-Afrique (or Eurafrique) to Afro-Europa (Adebajo and Whiteman, 2012). Euro-Afrique, which the EU has dispensed with, originated from the colonial period, an era during which Europe and Africa were interconnected politically, socially, economically and culturally (ibid.: 1). Nevertheless, the desire to give African states agency has not escaped the interests of individual states within the EU. Hence the Afro-Europa rhetoric has come across as a façade for the EU to strengthen its role in Africa and ward off interest from China in particular. Therefore, Adebajo et al. argue that 'Africa and Europe still appear not to have fully escaped the burdens of history' (ibid.: 19).

UN-AU cooperation

The UN-AU relationship is normally envisaged in the context of Chapter VIII of the UN Charter, as shown earlier. The UN is required to utilise regional arrangements to maintain peace and security. Yet as with the EU, the relationship between the UN and the AU has evolved post-Cold War period. It should be noted that, hitherto, due to the geopolitical interest of some African countries in matters related to neighbours going through conflict, the UN was initially hesitant to rely on the AU as a partner. For instance the UN ignored a call for regional continental force in the Democratic Republic of the Congo in 2003 at the height of the fighting between the Hema and Lendu (British Broadcasting Corporation, 2003). Instead the UN elected to go with the EU. However, with the AU being transformed from the Organization of African Unity the new organisation has come up with a more robust mandate in regard to maintenance of peace and security on the African continent. This robust approach has been facilitated by intolerance to coup d'états, especially as the organisation was previously viewed as a cosy club for dictators.

Secondly, the AU is backed up by vocal and assertive subregional organisations like the Economic Community of West African States (ECOWAS), the South African Development Community (SADC) and the East African Community (EAC), among others. Both the ECOWAS and the SADC have in their ranks emerging regional hegemons like Nigeria and South Africa, respectively, which have been at the forefront of supporting AU efforts in dealing with/helping member states in turmoil. For example Nigeria was at the forefront of the Economic Community of West Africa Monitoring Group in the 1990s, that helped quell the civil war in Sierra Leone and Liberia (Adebajo, 2002; Yoroms, 1993). South Africa under President Mbeki, through quiet diplomacy (Adelmann, 2004), resisted attempts by the United Kingdom and the United States to get rid of former President Mugabe through force. The situation in Zimbabwe has since been resolved internally.

Recently, South Africa under President Zuma (Esmenjaud, 2014) came up with the African Capacity for Immediate Response to Crises as a rapid-response force to aid those countries that are facing gross human rights violation. This mechanism developed within the AU structures shows the renewed involvement of regional hegemonies and subregional bodies in aiding the AU to become a more apt body for dealing with crises on the continent. This indeed bodes well, especially with a stretched UN that, at times, is not able to deal with conflicts quickly enough. Apart from subregional developments, the AU has developed a mechanism referred to as the Peace and Security Architecture, which includes a number of bodies like the African Standby Force, The Peacebuilding Unit, the Panel of the Wise and the Continental Early Warning Mechanism (Vines, 2013). These instruments are aimed at equipping the organisation to handle continental security problems adequately.

In terms of collaboration with the UN, the AU has largely relied on the financial support and legitimising power of the UN, as shown by the African Mission in Sudan (AMIS 1 and 2) and African Mission in Somalia (AMISOM), among others. Plus more recently there has been an emergency of what has come to be seen as a hybrid mission (the UN mission in Darfur (UNAMID)). This has combined the AU and UN into a single mission (Murithi, 2008) with one command and control structure (Kreps, 2007). This has given the AU more agency working within UN structures, and it is seen as a learning curve as the organisation develops more capabilities in resolving conflicts on the African continent. Quite different from UNAMID, the AMISOM mission is made up different states (Uganda, Kenya, Ethiopia, Djibouti and Burundi), with a decentralised command and control structure, although Uganda plays the leading role and intervening states make up the military operations coordinating committee to ensure cohesion in the force (Freear and De Coning, 2013). With the support of the UN and its partners, AMISOM has gained access to a small number of outsourced helicopters to help with medical evacuation and transport for troops that are scattered over a wide geographical area (ibid.). This was necessary due to the lack of specialist equipment and satisfactory military facilities within AMISOM (ibid.). Funding has been dependent on bilateral relations with the EU African Peace Facility:

> In 2009 the United Nations stepped in with an unprecedented solution to reinforce the existing revenue streams. Security Council Resolution 1872 created a combined structure of UN assessed contributions and voluntary funding for the Mission, with a logistical support mission in the form of the United Nations Support Office to AMISOM (UNSOA).
> *(Ibid.)*

Nevertheless, the lack of funding from the UN has led to attempts to withdraw by Uganda, Burundi and Kenya (British Broadcasting Corporation, 2016; Nimubona, 2016). Yet it is not only financial woes plaguing AMISOM; competing national interests of different countries hamper it too. For example, Burundi has used threats to withdraw from AMISOM when facing criticism of election rigging or dictatorial tendencies (Buchanan, 2017). In the same vein, Rwanda, on being criticised in the UN report for its role in pillaging the Democratic Republic of the Congo, threatened to withdraw from UNAMID (British Broadcasting Corporation, 2010). Thus, such problems make it difficult for the AU to develop a more coherent mechanism which can be utilised by the UN to maintain security in Africa. Moreover, as most of the funding comes from outside the AU, the organisation has quite often not been able to stamp its authority on proceedings when resolving conflicts. For example, the AU had to look on as international forces intervened in Libya under the 'responsibility to protect' norm. The UN and the EU did not utilise Chapter VII of the UN Charter in that instance. The same applied in Mali in 2013 when France intervened to stem attacks from Islamist rebels who had acquired weapons from

Libya after the fall of Gaddafi. The Secretary-General of the UN, Ban Ki-moon welcomed the intervention, which came to be known as Operation Serval, though the UN Security Council had just passed Resolution 2085 calling for an African regional force to be deployed (British Broadcasting Corporation, 2013).

The AU member states have increasingly partnered with the UN; for example, the Force Intervention Brigade made up of Tanzania, South Africa and Malawi has played a key role in helping the UN mission in the Democratic Republic of the Congo (MONUSCO) in dealing with rebel movements in eastern Congo. Resource sharing between the AU and the UN has been epitomised by the latter providing legitimising power and funds plus equipment while the former has provided the manpower. Although this has created resource dependence between the two organisations, the AU has gained more agency by taking more responsibility in conflict resolution through working within UN structures (UNAMID) and on its own (AMISOM). This has also provided organisational learning for the AU in the long run. The UN on the other hand has had to trust the AU more as it grappled with continent-wide security issues. Plus, as the EU has continued to play a less robust role on the African continent, it has been a matter of urgency for the UN to bring the AU on board help develop its capabilities to take on more security-related responsibilities on the continent.

Impact of the UN on EU-Africa relations

The relationship between the EU, the AU and the UN has been rooted in complementarity and comparative advantage (Center for International Peace Operations and Institute for Peace and Security Studies, 2015: 3), mainly in relation to the supply of resources that each organisation needs. With regard to the AU, the relationship has further evolved from capacity building to partnership with the other two organisations (ibid.). Yet, in what Rein (2015) refers to as interregionalism, the AU continues to face challenges relating to finances and credibility among its own member states, like Nigeria, South Africa, Egypt and Algeria, to name but a few. This makes it difficult for the EU to build partnership with the AU; hence the need for the UN to bridge the credibility gap and make the AU a viable partner (ibid.).

Furthermore, Rein (2015: 2) notes that the joint Africa-EU strategy (JAES), set up to foster continent-to-continent partnership between the EU and Africa, most of the time addresses issues related to the UN. Moreover, quite often the UN has asked the EU to take leadership on JAES issues. By encouraging the EU to take on more responsibilities, this has created further engagement between the EU and the AU. For example, as per the report by the Centre for International Peace Operations and Institute for Peace and Security Studies (2015), the EU has played a crucial role in aiding the AU in Somalia, Mali and the Central African Republic.

The enhancement of the collaboration between the EU and the AU has reduced the tendencies of unilateral actions by EU member states, as was the case by France in Mali (Boeke and Schuurman, 2015). Instead, the EU and the AU are working together in a complementary fashion, with the AU taking more responsibility by launching missions like AMISOM while the EU provides the finances and training missions, such as those in Somalia and Mali (ibid.). To foster this collaboration, the EU and the AU get legitimacy from the UN Security Council. The pursuit of neoliberal peacebuilding strategies by the UN and the EU has helped the former influence the relationship between the AU and the latter through organisational learning. Aside from receiving financial support from the EU, the AU has continued to learn peacebuilding practices espoused by the EU under the guidance of the UN. The EU acknowledges that the UN is the organisation tasked with maintenance of international peace and security and, therefore, acknowledges its legitimising power and at the same time commits to support its efforts to this end. For instance, the EU Global Strategy reiterates that

> Without global norms and the means to enforce them, peace and security, prosperity and democracy – our vital interests – are at risk. Guided by the values on which it is founded, the EU is committed to a global order based on international law, including the principles of the UN Charter, which ensure peace, human rights, sustainable development and lasting access to the global commons. This commitment translates into an aspiration to transform rather than simply preserve the existing system. The EU will strive for a strong UN as the bedrock of the multilateral rules-based order, and develop globally coordinated responses with international and regional organisations, states and non-state actors.
>
> (2016: 39)

Therefore, the UN has had a positive impact on the EU–Africa relations in the long run, especially as there is an understanding that the interests of the three organisations are aligned, particularly on the maintenance of international peace and security. That is why they have been engaged in continuous efforts to draw lessons and find better ways of collaborating with each other.

Conclusion

In conclusion, the redefining of the EU–Africa relationship has to some extent reduced the interventionist approach of the EU; for example, since Operation Artemis, EUFOR RD Congo and EUFOR Chad/CAR, there has been a reduction of EU military operations in Africa. This was reinforced by the refusal of the EU to intervene in the Democratic Republic of the Congo in 2008 when General Nkunda was attacking the country from the east. Instead the EU sought a diplomatic solution which also saw the involvement of Rwandese forces in defeating the rebels. However it should be noted that although the EU seemed to be playing a hands-off role in Africa and allowing African states to find solutions to their problems, it was blighted by divisions – especially with former colonial masters like Belgium, interested in an interventionist approach while small Eastern European states were more concerned about the threat from a resurgent Russia. In the end, the UN has co-opted more African states, and this has produced a wide range of mission scenarios. For instance, operations like AMID have incorporated both AU and UN contingents; AMISOM, though made up of African states, is financed by both the EU and the UN; and the Force Intervention Brigade is providing robust support to MONUSCO in the Democratic Republic of the Congo. Such opportunities for African states to play a role in peacekeeping would not have been developed so fast had the EU remained as proactive in intervention as it had been at the turn of the century.

The resource dependence between international organisations still persists, with the UN primarily providing legitimacy for the EU and the AU under Chapter VIII of its Charter. The EU continues to provide finances and technical support to the AU as it builds capacity to take over missions more independently in the future. The rhetoric, however, has changed from capacity building to partnership; and there has been a concerted effort to give African states agency, as shown by the refocusing of the EU-African relations to Africa-EU partnership. Moreover, the UN has also helped foster cooperation between the EU and African states, especially on security matters. Yet state interests still play a role in the way these resources are shared. The UN-EU relationship has been driven more by what the latter is willing to give than what the former actually needs. For the AU, the mantra of an African solution to African problems has seen it take a more robust approach to intervention (as shown in Somalia and the Democratic Republic of the

Congo); but it has largely been shoved to the side when the interests of the big states like France and the United States have come into play (as was the case in Libya and Mali).

Note

1 The re-hatting of forces was implemented in East Timor in 1999, where Australia, which acted as the lead nation in the UN-mandated Operation INTERFET, agreed to keep some of its troops in the UN-led operation (UNTAET), thus guaranteeing its credibility. The 'East Timor model' has often been praised by UN representatives, who see in it the opportunity for the UN to benefit from Western states' key military assets, but who are also anxious to 'narrow the commitment gap' between the developing and the developed world' (Tardy, 2005: 56–57).

Bibliography

Aasted-Madsen, I. and Rouquet, R. (2009) European Union Support for UN Peacekeeping Operations. Reply to the Annual Report of the Council. Submitted on Behalf of the Defence Committee to the European Security and Defence Assembly. Western European Union Document A/2049 2/12/09.

Adebajo, A. (2002) *Liberia's Civil War: Nigeria, ECOMOG, and Regional Security in West Africa*. Boulder, CO, and London: Lynne Rienner.

Adebajo, A. and Whiteman, K. (eds) (2012) *The EU and Africa: From Eurafrique to Afro-Europa*. New York: Columbia University Press.

Adelmann, M. (2004) Quiet diplomacy: The reasons behind Mbeki's Zimbabwe policy. *Africa Spectrum*, 39 (2), 249–276.

Biermann, R. (2009) Inter-organizationalism in theory and practice. *Studia Diplomatica*, LXII (3), 7–12.

Biscop, S. (2004) The European Security Strategy and the Neighbourhood Policy: A new starting point for a Euro-Mediterranean security partnership? In F. Attinà and R. Rossi (eds), *European Neighbourhood Policy: Political, Economic and Social Issues*. Catania: University of Catania (pp. 25–36).

Biscop, S. and Drieskens, E. (2006) Effective multilateralism and collective security: Empowering the UN. In K. Verlin Laatikainen and K.E. Smith (eds), *The European Union at the United Nations*. Palgrave Macmillan, London (pp. 115–132).

Boeke, S. and Schuurman, B. (2015) Operation 'Serval': A strategic analysis of the French intervention in Mali, 2013–2014. *Journal of Strategic Studies*, 38 (6), 801–825.

British Broadcasting Corporation (2003) Q&A: DR Congo's ethnic flashpoint. 13 May. http://news.bbc.co.uk/1/hi/world/africa/3025031.stm (retrieved 12 September 2020).

British Broadcasting Corporation (2010) Ban urges Rwanda not to withdraw UN peacekeepers. 8 September. www.bbc.co.uk/news/world-africa-11229201 (retrieved 29 January 2018).

British Broadcasting Corporation (2013) Mali conflict: UN backs France's military intervention. 15 January. www.bbc.co.uk/news/world-africa-21021132 (retrieved 23 January 2018).

British Broadcasting Corporation (2016) Uganda threatens to withdraw troops from Somalia's AMISOM force. 23 June www.bbc.co.uk/news/world-africa-36606194 (retrieved 1 January 2018).

Brosig, M. (2015) *Cooperative Peacekeeping in Africa: Exploring Regime Complexity*. Abingdon: Routledge.

Brosig, M. and Motsamai, D. (2014) Modeling cooperative peacekeeping: Exchange theory and the African peace and security regime. *Journal of International Peacekeeping*, 18 (1–2), 45–68.

Buchanan, E. (2017) Burundi: Will President Nkurunziza really withdraw his troops from AMISOM in Somalia? *International Business Times*, 2 February. www.ibtimes.co.uk/burundi-will-president-nkurunziza-really-withdraw-his-troops-amisom-mission-somalia-1601767 (retrieved 30 January 2018).

Center for International Peace Operations and Institute for Peace and Security Studies (2015) *Report of the Roundtable on Trilateral Cooperation in Peace Operations in Africa*. Addis Ababa, 7–8 October. www.zif-berlin.org/fileadmin/uploads/analyse/dokumente/veroeffentlichungen/ZIF_Conference_Report_Trilateral_Cooporation_Addis_022016.pdf

Council of the European Union (2003) *European Security Strategy: A Secure Europe in a Better World*. Brussels: European Communities. https://europa.eu/globalstrategy/en/european-security-strategy-secure-europe-better-world (retrieved 22 January 2018).

Esmenjaud, R. (2014) The African capacity for immediate response to crisis: Conceptual breakthrough or anti-imperialist phantom? *African Security Review*, 23 (2), 172–177.

European Union (1999) Helsinki European Council Conclusions of the Presidency. 10–11 December. www.europarl.europa.eu/summits/hel1_en.htm (retrieved 12 January 2018).

European Union (2016) Shared Vision, Common Action: A Stronger Europe, A Global Strategy for the European Union's Foreign and Security Policy. Luxembourg: Publications Office of the European Union. https://eeas.europa.eu/archives/docs/top_stories/pdf/eugs_review_web.pdf (retrieved 19 December 2019).

European Union-United Nations (2003) Joint Declaration on UN-EU Co-operation in Crisis Management. 24 September. www.eu-un.europa.eu/articles/en/article_2768_en.htm (retrieved 31 January 2018).

Freear, M. and De Coning, C. (2013) Lessons from the African Union Mission for Somalia (AMISOM) for peace operations in Mali [online]. *Stability: International Journal of Security and Development*, 2 (2). DOI: http://dx.doi.org/10.5334/sta.bj.

Ghali, B. (1992) An Agenda for Peace. Preventive Diplomacy, Peacemaking and Peace-keeping. Report of the Secretary-General A/47/277–S/24111. www.un.org/Docs/SG/agpeace.html (retrieved 11 November 2017).

Harvey D. (2005) *A Brief History of Neoliberalism*. Oxford: Oxford University Press.

Hemmer, C. and Karzenstein, P.J. (2002) Why is there no NATO in Asia? Collective identity, regionalism, and the origins of multilateralism. *International Organization*, 56 (3), 575–607.

Herrberg, A. (2008) Mediation as an instrument for conflict prevention and crisis response: An opportunity to maximise the impact of the EU's soft power. In *From Early Warning to Early Action: The Debate on the Enhancement of the EU's Crisis Response Capability Continues*. Luxembourg: Office for Official Publications of the European Communities (pp. 209–211).

Keohane, R. (2006) *The Contingent Legitimacy of Multilateralism*. GARNET Working Paper No 09/06.

Knauer, J.B. (2011) *EUFOR Althea: Appraisal and Future Perspectives of the EU's Former Flagship Operation in Bosnia and Herzegovina*. Bruges: College of Europe.

Koops, J. (2011) *The European Union as an Integrative Power? Assessing the EU's Effective Multilateralism towards NATO and the United Nations*. Brussels: VUB Press.

Kreps, S.E. (2007) The United Nations-African Union Mission in Darfur: Implications and prospects for success: Essays. *African Security Review*, 16 (4), 66–79.

Kronenberger, V. and Wouters. J. (eds) (2004) *The EU and Conflict Prevention Policy and Legal Aspect*. The Hague: TMC Asser Press.

Major, C. (2008) *EU-UN Cooperation in Crisis Management: The Experience of EUFOR RD Congo in 2006*. Occasional Paper No. 72. Paris: European Union Institute for Security Studies.

Murithi, T. (2008) The African Union's evolving role in peace operations: The African Union Mission in Burundi, the African Union Mission in Sudan and the African Union Mission in Somalia. *African Security Studies*, 17 (1), 69–82.

Nimubona, D. (2016) Burundi threatens to withdraw Somalia troops over non-payment. Bloomberg, 30 December. www.bloomberg.com/news/articles/2016-12-30/burundi-threatens-to-withdraw-somalia-troops-over-non-payment (accessed 1/1/2018).

Novosseloff, A. (2004) *EU-UN Partnership in Crisis Management: Developments and Projects*. New York: International Peace Academy.

Pfeffer, J. and Salancik, G.R. (2003) *The External Control of Organizations: A Resource Dependence Perspective*. Stanford: Stanford University Press.

Rein, C. (2015) EU-AU inter-regional relations and the role of the UN. *Ifriqiya*, 1 (4).

Ruggie, J. (1992) Multilateralism: The anatomy of an institution. *International Organization*, 46 (3), 561–598.

Sarkin, J. (2009) The role of the United Nations, the African Union and Africa's sub-regional organizations in dealing with Africa's human rights problems: Connecting humanitarian intervention and the responsibility to protect. *Journal of African Law*, 53 (1), 1–33.

Sempijja, N. (2016) Does dependence lead to cooperation? The case of resource exchange between the European Union and the United Nations in DR Congo. *African Security*, 9 (4), 259–277.

Szapiro, M. (2004) International organisations and cooperation in field of conflict prevention. In V. Kronenberger and J. Wouters (eds), *The EU and Conflict Prevention Policy and Legal Aspect*. The Hague: TMC Asser Press (pp. 347–368).

Tardy, T. (2004) *The Brahimi Report Four Years On*. Proceedings of a Workshop held at the Geneva Centre for Security Policy. ww.civcap.info/fileadmin/user_upload/Research_Reports/Tardy_Report.pdf (retrieved 14 January 2018).

Tardy, T. (2005) EU-UN cooperation in peacekeeping: A promising relationship in a constrained environment. In S. Biscop, F. Francioni, K. Graham with T. Felício, J. Laurenti and T. Tardy (eds), *The European*

Union and United Nations: Partners in Effective Multilateralism. Challiot Paper 78. Paris: EU Institute for Security Studies (pp. 49–68).

United Nations Security Council (2017) Report of the Secretary-General on Strengthening the Partnership between the United Nations and the African Union on Issues of Peace and Security in Africa, including on the Work of the United Nations Office to the African Union. S/2017/744. http://undocs.org/en/S/2017/744 (retrieved 12 September 2020).

United Nations Secretary-General (1999) *Report of the Secretary-General on the Work of the Organization*. New York: United Nations.

Vines, A. (2013) A decade of African Peace and Security Architecture. *International Affairs*, 89 (1), 89–109.

Wouters, J. (2004) *The United Nations, the EU and Conflict Prevention: Interconnecting the Global and Regional Levels*. Institute for International Law Working Paper No 60. K.U. Leuven: Institute for International Law. www.law.kuleuven.be/iir/nl/onderzoek/wp/WP60e.pdf (retrieved 6 January 2018).

Wouters, J., Hoffmeister, F. and Ruys, T. (eds) (2006) *The United Nations and the European Union: An Ever Stronger Partnership*. The Hague: TMC Asser Press.

Yoroms, G.J. (1993) ECOMOG and West African regional security: A Nigerian perspective. *African Issues*, 21 (1–2), 84–91.

18

The China effect

African agency, derivative power and renegotiation of EU-Africa relations

Obert Hodzi

Introduction

Africa and the European Union (EU) are mapping a post-Cotonou era in a changing geopolitical context in which 'the global order is contested, and fundamental principles are being challenged' (Tusk, 2017). The rise of populism in Europe, mass illegal migration from Africa to Europe and persisting notions in Africa of a condescending Europe also make the context. This, against China's increasing geopolitical and geo-economic influence in Africa, makes future Africa-EU relations complex. In addition, Europe's pre-eminence as Africa's biggest trading partner, investor and provider of humanitarian aid are increasingly being challenged. China is now the biggest provider of United Nations (UN) peacekeeping troops in Africa, and it is now Africa's biggest trading partner (compared to EU member states as single entities), thus emphasising trade rather than aid. Also, unlike European powers, China does not have colonial baggage in Africa. But then, with the diversity of African countries, varying economic and political interests as well as different degrees of bilateral engagements with China and EU member states, it is puzzling how Africa as a collective can articulate and sustain a common position regarding its relations with the EU.

Further complicating Africa's position is that in terms of material capabilities, Africa does not matter. With a collective gross domestic product (GDP) of USD 1.5 trillion, sub-Saharan Africa is less than half the size of Germany; indeed, according to the World Bank (2019), it is the region with the least GDP. Even in terms of military spending, for a continent riddled with conflict and violence, Africa spent USD 19.2 billion compared to Germany's USD 41.1 billion. In terms of humanitarian assistance and foreign aid, Africa is the EU's biggest beneficiary. And in 2014, China published figures indicating that 54% of its aid went to sub-Saharan Africa. This, and the fragility of most African states, widespread poverty, perceptions of corruption and ineffective governments further reduce Africa's potency. Africa is therefore a continent 'permanently under the yoke of external actors' as Jean-François Bayart (2009: 36) puts it. While that might seem an overstatement, Africa's inability to deal with illegal migration push factors and to underwrite its own development, peace and security perpetuate perceptions of a continent at the mercy of foreign powers. In sum, Africa appears to have no power base of its own to bargain with or leverage the EU.

Africa is, however, pushing back. It is seeking to redefine present and future relations with the EU. From anti-Western leaders like Robert Mugabe, Zimbabwe's former president, to President Paul Kagame of Rwanda and Ghana's President Nana Addo Dankwa Akufo-Addo, there is a re-emergence of patriotism, Afro-nationalism and Pan-Africanism in the 21st century Africa. The essence of these leaders' actions and message, which build on Thabo Mbeki's African Renaissance, is that Africa is not small and that it can determine its future. What is the source of this emerging sense of African power and leverage? Is Africa's power collective or derivative? This chapter explores the sources of Africa's bargaining power with the EU in the context of a rising China. Using the concept of derivative power, the chapter examines how Africa as a continent and its constituent members is using bourgeoning relations with China to increase its power and demand equality. It further examines the exploitation of perceptions of competition and rivalry between China and the EU over Africa by African countries to increase their bargaining leverage in negotiations with the EU. This will lead to an assessment of whether this derivative power is enough to guarantee policy outcomes that reflect Africa's independence and ensure symmetrical relations with the EU. In exploring the derivative nature of Africa's bargaining power, this chapter redirects attention to Africa's agency and exploitation of foreign powers to redefine its relations with the EU.

Africa's collective power

African countries, as single entities, have little or no influence in global politics. Apart from lacking material capabilities, they also lack structural power, defined by Susan Strange as the power 'to decide how things shall be done, the power to shape frameworks within which states relate to each other, relate to people, or relate to corporate enterprises' (1988: 25). And in an international system where 'beyond the formal pretense of sovereign equality …, informal dynamics of hierarchy prevail at the multilateral table' (Pouliot, 2016: 9), African countries are at the bottom of the hierarchy of states and exercise no significant influence in setting the global agenda. Nonetheless, to increase their global influence, they have, through the African Union (AU), advanced the notion of strength in numbers – collective power in multilateral processes. Acting as a continental block in the UN General Assembly and other multilateral forums is often cited as a reflection of Africa's collective diplomatic power, making it possible for the continent to influence international politics. In simplistic terms, the rationale is that individual African states have no clout on their own unless they coalesce with each other. That coalescing with other African states epitomised by the AU is the 'fundamental base of [their] collective power' (Long, 2017: 198), leading to an assumption that African countries have substantial impact on multilateral processes when they act as a continental block.

That assumption is, however, misleading because it assumes influence in multilateral processes is only determined by numbers. Irrespective of the numbers, the AU's relationship with the EU, as it is with China, is hierarchical and reflective of the proverbial 'he who pays the piper calls the tune'. For instance, the EU, including its member states, provides more than 80% of the AU Commission's budget (European Commission, 2016). Even in cases where the AU and regional groupings (such as the Economic Community of West African States (ECOWAS)) have insisted on 'African solutions to Africa's problems', they still turn to the EU for funding and technical support. For example, Article 4(2) of the ECOWAS decision mandating the ECOWAS Standby Force to uphold the results of the presidential election in the Republic of the Gambia stated, 'Where necessary, the President of the ECOWAS Commission shall seek financial and logistics support from the United Nations, European Union' (ECOWAS Commission, 2016), and so on. Likewise, Mali requested the French military for assistance in its battle against insurgents in

Northern Mali. France and Britain (and by extension the EU) due to their colonial ties with the continent, end up assuming much of the responsibility – such as for stemming illegal migration to Europe through Libya – not only out of their own volition but because African countries expect and demand that they act. Accordingly, regardless of the 'African solutions to African problems' mantra, options available to African countries 'are structured by their long-term economic and political dependency on great powers' (Long, 2017: 189). Africa's collective power is therefore marauded by its inability to achieve self-sufficiency and underwrite its programmes.

It follows that without financial independence, the multilateralism resulting from the AU's relations with the EU and emerging powers is based on a fallible ideal of equality. Elissa Jobson (2017), an adviser on AU relations at the International Crisis Group, argues that 'equality should, of course, remain an aspiration. But the two unions [the AU and the EU] are not the same'. In the same way, a Finnish diplomat argued that the AU will never be equal to the EU, nor will it set the agenda at EU-Africa summits, for as long as it cannot contribute to funding requirements. This will likely continue for as long as sub-Saharan Africa is 'for the most part *still* poor, weak, underdeveloped, peripheralized in global institutions, and lack[s] the material power (defined through wealth or the means of violence) to bring about systemwide change in their own interests' (Persaud, 2003: 57). Thus, due to a combined lack of material and structural power, Africa's collective power is limited to negotiating how the EU and emerging powers such as China must assist Africa. The kind of multilateralism emerging between the AU, the EU and China is therefore asymmetrical and re-emphasises the hierarchical nature of their relationship rather than the collective power of the AU.

Further perpetuating hierarchical relations between the AU and the EU as well as China is that fact that it is these external actors that are pre-eminent in regarding Africa as a collective. Through geographical instruments aimed at fostering regional integration and facilitating better accountability of funds, the EU and China have largely promoted the AU as a representative of the African continent. Understandably, this is aimed at avoiding duplication of efforts and resources. The EU finds it expedient to regard Africa as one for purposes of addressing common political and economic problems on the continent. However, the 'collectivisation' of the continent borders on treating Africa as a homogenous single country. Furthermore, the EU and emerging powers, including Turkey, India, Brazil and China, have over the past two decades advanced notions of a united Africa through 'Africa summits' – the Turkey-Africa Forum, the India-Africa Forum Summit, the Brazil-Africa Forum and the Forum on China-Africa Cooperation (FOCAC). Yet, even within this emerging multilateralism, it is hardly the case that Africa converts its numbers into bargaining power and into influence on trade and economic policies. As put by Elissa Jobson (2017), 'discussions tend to be asymmetrical, heavily focused on crises in African countries and dominated by what the EU will and will not pay'. The same is true for discussions between Africa and China or any other emerging power at their respective Africa summits. Like the EU, emerging powers combine African countries for convenience, enabling them to declare their policies and strategies to all African countries at one go. Yet, the notion of Africa's collective power is a myth with an imagined resonance.

The EU has assisted in creating that imagined resonance. The Joint Africa-EU Strategy states that in addressing issues of common concern such as peace and security, migration and development, 'both sides will treat Africa as one and upgrade the Africa-EU political dialogue to enable strong and sustainable continent-to-continent partnership' (European Union and African Union, 2009). The downside is that the externally induced African unity is not backed by consensus among African countries, the majority of which still prefer bilateralism due to their distinct differences in development and national interests. For instance, contrary to EU assumptions that there is consensus in Africa on the issue of irregular migration, the AU's lack of coherent response to the migration crisis is indicative. In the end, the EU abandoned the collective approach and made bilateral deals with Libya, Tunisia, Niger and Chad to stem the flow of illegal migrants across the Mediterranean. What is emerging is that external actors swing between multilateralism and bilateralism in dealing with African countries, depending on what best suits their objectives. Paul Collier argues that when it comes to trade,

> Europe has negotiated with individual countries, and that has been destructive for the African regional trade bloc. … What Europe should be exporting to Africa – in terms of ideas – is Europe's own trade integration. And instead we've been trying to coerce individual African countries into opening the doors to European imports.
>
> *(Collier, cited in Becker, 2016)*

This is because Africa's integration is issue-specific and often funded and promoted by China and the EU; thus, where integration works against their interests, they simply revert to bilateralism, which deals a blow to Africa's collective power.

What are the characteristics of derivative power?

Due to limitations in Africa's collective power, African countries often increase their bargaining leverage with third parties by associating with global powers like the United States, Russia and China. Tom Long describes the power gained through association with such great powers as derivative power, which among other things can 'offer small states a much greater amount of power over a third party, and perhaps at a lower cost' (2017: 197). In obtaining and manipulating 'the power of other, more powerful states in their own interests' (Handel, 2006: 190), African countries are able to explore prospects for independence and influence despite their lack of material and structural power. It means African states adopt proactive policies and strategies that manipulate geopolitical rivalries and shifting global power patterns to obtain benefits and achieve national interests that they would otherwise be incapable of obtaining. For example, in the Cold War era, African countries often aligned with the United States or the Soviet Union, or they claimed to be non-aligned; but in turn, they used that alignment or non-alignment to achieve their objectives by threatening to shift allegiance. They therefore mastered the art of playing superpowers off each other such that they are 'not always as powerless in the face of the superpowers as a crude comparison of relative capabilities would suggest' (Clapham, 1996: 135).

In the bipolar and unipolar global order, Africa's manoeuvrability was limited – there were at most two superpowers to play off each other and derive bargaining leverage from. The emergence of China and other emerging powers within a multipolar global order has expanded Africa's options and enhanced its 'strategic position vis-à-vis the superpowers … [and renewed its] potential to leverage their position' (Corkin, 2013: 17). Emmerson Mnangagwa, the new president of Zimbabwe, told the *Financial Times* that Zimbabwe 'will continue to impress [the EU] and continue to interact and deepen our economic cooperation with them but there is now *a broader spectrum where we can go fishing*' (cited in Russell, 2018, emphasis added). The same is echoed by political elites across Africa who regard the presence of China in Africa as presenting them with an alternative to the EU and, hence, increasing their leverage and bargaining power with the EU and other traditional partners. The basis of Africa's bargaining power is therefore simply derived from China being an alternative source of financing, trade and development assistance. Thus, just by having China as an alternative, African countries feel emboldened to demand and expect more from the EU, which they would not be able to do based on their collective power or material capabilities.

Africa's portrayal of China as an alternative to the EU is aimed at forcing a reframing of Africa-EU relations. African countries are demanding a paradigm shift to their donor-recipient relationship with the EU, which they claim is underpinned by European paternalism in Africa. And they frame their demand in China-EU comparative terms. Yoweri Museveni, the president of Uganda claimed that

> Western ruling groups are conceited, full of themselves, ignorant of our conditions, and they make other people's business their business. Whereas the Chinese just deal with you, you represent your country, they represent their own interests, and you do business.
>
> *(Museveni, cited in Akaki, 2008)*

Similarly, in 2014, Jacob Zuma, the former president of South Africa, argued that

> the countries that have been dealing with us before, particularly old economies, they've dealt with us as former subjects, as former colonial subjects. ... The Chinese don't deal with us from that point of view. They deal with us as people that you must do business (with), at an equal level so to speak.
>
> *(Zuma, cited in Fin24, 2014)*

The strategy of these African leaders is to use their relations with China as a model that the EU should follow, thereby 'shaming' the EU into reconsidering how it engages Africa; while at the same time subtly warning that the EU risks losing its influence in Africa to China if it does not treat Africa with 'respect', as China does. Paul Kagame said that 'the Chinese bring what Africa needs: investment and money for governments and companies. I would prefer the Western world to invest in Africa rather than hand out development aid' (cited in Clayton, 2009). The strategy seems to be working, because Germany's Federal Ministry of Economic Cooperation and Development (BMZ) suggested in a document referred to as the Marshall Plan for Africa that 'African ownership must be strengthened and the days of "aid" and of "donors and recipients" put behind us' (BMZ, 2017: 4). This shift in the EU's attitude toward the continent is largely attributable to African leaders' ability to use the presence of China in Africa to bargain for a more equal EU-Africa relationship.

Reframing external perceptions of Africa constitutes one of the main objectives of the pan-African agenda to have relations with external actors based on equality. The AU's Agenda 2063 seeks to harness Africa's collective power to frame Africa as a 'strong, united and influential partner on the global stage. ... In short, a different and better Africa' (African Union, 2015: 2). But then, Africa's 'united voices' have been drowned by persistent narratives, particularly in Europe, of armed conflict, corruption, irregular migration and poverty, which project Africa as a source of, rather than a solution to, global challenges. The African solutions to African problems that China has rhetorically adhered to by not prescribing solutions to Africa's challenges epitomises the ideal of an Africa able to resolve its problems and one that is an equal partner on the global stage. Thus, to maintain representations of a confident and strong Africa, the AU and its member states are emboldened by China's development trajectory and insistence on states' sovereign right to determine their own development path and set their development priority areas without EU interference. It is within this context that Emmanuel Macron announced in Burkina Faso that 'I am of the generation that doesn't come to tell Africans what to do' (cited in Irish, 2017).

Emmanuel Macron's statement is largely a response to the presence of China in Africa, which neither imposes political conditions nor outrightly 'tell[s] Africans what to do'. In addition, it is a response to pressure from African countries for the EU and its member states to reduce their emphasis on good governance, human rights and transparency as preconditions for getting EU development assistance, mainly because China does not impose such conditions. A joint communique issued after the ninth EU-China Summit in September 2006 in Helsinki states:

> The EU reaffirmed its attachment to the principles of good governance and human rights as embodied in its Africa Strategy. The Chinese side emphasised the upholding of the five principles of peaceful coexistence, in particular the principle of non-interference into others [internal affairs].
>
> *(Council of the European Union, 2006)*

In making demands for the EU to abandon its claim for human rights and good governance, African countries are only taking advantage of existing EU-China differences on the issue of conditionality in their respective Africa strategies. Accordingly, 'China has become a factor in accelerating a process of reorientation of EU-Africa partnership as its no-strings-attached business-like approach provides African countries with alternatives to the post-Cold War development model' (Wissenbach, 2016: 257).

The result is a growing consensus in Europe that if the EU is to retain influence in Africa, it must refrain from imposing conditions and solutions on Africa. A few days before the EU-Africa Summit in Cote d'Ivoire, Emmanuel Macron said: 'the president of France shouldn't explain to an African country how it should organise its constitution, how it should organise its elections or the freedom of opposition. Incidentally, I wouldn't expect this from an African president on European affairs' (cited in Washington Post, 2017). Similarly, Paul Collier warned European countries against telling African countries what to do and prescribing solutions to African problems. Although some European powers such as Germany insist that the EU should deepen 'developmental cooperation with those partners who implement reforms aimed at good governance, protection of human rights and economic development' (BMZ, 2017: 6), if Macron's statement is suggestive of the 'feeling' within the EU, then there is bound to be paradigmatic shift in Africa-EU relations and the EU's normative influence on the continent. Interestingly, a declaration issued by the AU and the EU at the end of their 2017 summit held in Abidjan states that

> We are committed to mutually respectful, constructive and equal political dialogue on equal footing aimed at enhancing democracy, good governance and human rights in line with the provisions of the UN Charter, the AU Constitutive Act and related AU Governance frameworks and the EU Lisbon Treaty.
>
> *(African Union and European Union, 2017)*

The use of terms such as 'mutually respectful' and 'equal footing' mirror terms such as 'mutually beneficial on an equal basis' (which China uses to describe its relations with Africa), reflecting signs of an EU capitulating to Africa's demands for a 'China-like' relationship with the EU.

African countries have also individually and, in a few circumstances, collectively manipulated perceptions of geopolitical competition between China and the EU to demand rebalancing of power dynamics within EU-Africa relations. In their engagement with China, African leaders have sought to portray the EU as a mutual enemy. For instance, at the 2015 FOCAC Summit in Johannesburg, Omar al-Bashir said: '*Our detractors* have sought to portray our relationship to purely commercial ties, driven by China's desire to extract our mineral resources, (but) our relations go much deeper' (cited in Straits Times, 2015, emphasis added). In a seeming response, Donald Tusk (2017) stated in his opening speech at the AU-EU Summit in 2017 that we 'cannot accept the narrative that pits Africa and Europe against each other'. African countries are also using their relations with China to demand more development assistance from the EU. In a speech at the 2015 FOCAC Summit in Johannesburg, Robert Mugabe, then Chair of the AU, taunted the EU saying that Xi Jinping 'is doing to us what we expected those who colonised us yesterday to do. Let them, if they have ears to hear, let them hear'.

The same sentiment was echoed by the head of the African Affairs department in the Chinese Ministry of Foreign Affairs, who queried: 'What have Western countries done for Africa in the 50 years since independence? Nothing. All they have done is criticise China and that is unfair' (Ng'wanakilala and Obulutsa, 2013). The notion that the EU has not done enough to develop Africa is pervasive, although trade and development assistance statistics suggest otherwise. That perception is, however, evidence that what Europe has been doing in postcolonial Africa has not been effective in achieving the intended objectives. Even so, African countries have used it to coax more development assistance and concessions from the EU and, at the very least, change the EU's focus from development and humanitarian assistance to trade and cooperation. The German government is already urging the EU to 'move away from the donor-recipient mentality that has predominated for many decades and shift towards an economic partnership based on initiative and ownership' (BMZ, 2017: 5). This call for a change of EU approach toward Africa is arguably 'a reflex that is triggered by China's strong presence in the region' (Tull, 2008: 7). Alex Vines (2014) concurs that 'with multiple suitors competing for access to Africa's natural resources and markets, European countries can no longer assume advantage of access as a neo-colonial legacy'.

Without the backing of a global power, Africa's demands for reform of the international system have largely fallen on deaf ears. They lack both the continental consensus and ability to back their demands for more say in global governance because they have largely depended on the West for funding and development. The emergence of China has shifted those power dynamics and renewed confidence among some African countries that with the backing of China in the UN Security Council and in other multilateral forums, their demands will be met and that their requests for fair trade practices will be seriously considered by the EU. Mugabe argued at the 2015 FOCAC Summit that

> the rise of China and Africa as two significant players will have positive and far reaching impact in international relations to ensure the democratisation of the international system of governance. The perpetuation of the historic injustices of the current system be it in the UN Security Council or the Bretton Woods institutions is unhealthy and undesirable and now together with China we shall fight for real democracy at the UN. We continue to count on China's support and solidarity in addressing this situation.

Mugabe's assertions are based on the understanding that 'the most important condition for the security of weaker states is their ability to appeal to other states for help and support'. It is therefore not surprising that the 2017 AU-EU Summit declared that the two agreed to

> pursue constructive cooperation and dialogue in the ongoing comprehensive institutional reforms of multilateral institutions, in particular the three strands of UN reform launched by the UN Secretary General, as well as the revitalisation of the United Nations General Assembly and the reform of the United Nations Security Council.
>
> *(African Union and European Union, 2017)*

Conclusion

The emergence of multipolarity has provided African countries with more room 'to manoeuvre in the international system, to choose allies, to take advantage of the conflicts and tensions between the powers' (Handel, 2006: 190). Africa has more alternatives and can play China against the EU to derive more benefits and achieve its objectives. China has also indirectly empowered African countries to overcome vulnerabilities consistent with states that lack structural and relational power in international relations. While the EU is in theory toning down its demands for democracy, human rights and good governance, it still retains extensive influence on the continent's politics and economics, because it still is Africa's biggest investor, trading partner and provider of humanitarian and development assistance as well as the major contributor to Africa's integration, peace and security. Without economic independence as well as China principally focused on trade and infrastructure development with no significant development aid and humanitarian assistance, Africa's derivative power is limited in how much it can do for the continent. Furthermore, as China's economy transitions beyond low-level manufacturing and moves from being commodity driven, Africa will likely lose its strategic position in China's foreign policy, thus reducing its bargaining leverage.

Africa's agency based on derivative power and collective power – playing the numbers game – in Africa-EU relations and in other multilateral forums is unsustainable due to the continent's structural deficiencies. Lacking in material capabilities to underwrite its own development, peace and security programmes, Africa often must go with what the EU or China is willing to fund. African countries are unable to 'draw up their own development policies and co-ordinate them at regional and continental level to better negotiate with their traditional and emerging partners' (African Development Bank et al., 2011: 93). Because the AU is predominantly funded by external actors, which is also the case with Regional Economic Communities (RECs) and individual African countries, there seemingly is competition for funding due to different regional and national priorities in their engagement with the EU and China. Furthermore, by only using its collective power on issues specific to Africa – mostly humanitarian and development assistance – or those that have a bearing on Africa, African countries have often failed to engage with strategic international matters. The result is that there is usually no consensus, which is essential to 'unifying African voices' on the global stage. Africa's collective and derivative power is therefore in a state of malfunction because of the lack of economic freedom and material power.

As further observed by the Brookings Institute, the several reform initiatives and attempts to 'unify voices' have 'foundered because of lack of implementation' (Leke, 2017), mostly attributable to competing national interests and regional geopolitical rivalries. The idea of using RECs to enhance continental integration through regional integration has led to regional fragmentation. Of the existing RECs, ECOWAS, the Southern African Development Community and the East African Community have been more successful in strengthening regional economic integration, enhancing regional trade and free movement of goods and people, whereas the AU remains ad hoc in its operations, is issue based – focusing more on peace and security – and is often slow in responding to crises. More importantly, due to the diversity of its membership, the AU is weighed down by member states' preference for bilateralism, especially in dealing with external powers such as the EU. A survey conducted by Afrobarometer in 2015 reported that in the 36 African countries surveyed, former colonial powers have the greatest influence (Lekorwe et al., 2016). The result is that there is little consensus at regional and continental levels on fundamental foreign policy principles and underlying consensual objectives in relating with external actors.

Although Africa has been able to compel the EU to reconsider its attitude toward the continent and reframe the Africa-EU relations in equality terms rather than the traditional donor-recipient relationship, it has not been successful in materially changing the fundamentals of the relationship in that Africa remains unable to solve its own problems without EU technical and financial support. Even with China's trade and investment, Africa has 'not transformed the structure and patterns of production nor created a new international division of labour' (Melber, 2013: 13), so as China recalibrates its economy and engagement with Africa, the derivative power that Africa relied on is slowly diminishing. The reorientation of EU's policy towards Africa is of course attributable to China's presence on the continent, but it is not entirely the case that Africa has gained enough power to have a symmetrical relationship with the EU. The reorientation is largely because the EU does not want to lose geopolitical and geo-economic influence in Africa to China. Europe, as the closest continent to Africa, will still need to maintain strong influence to contain terrorism, irregular migration and other non-traditional security threats emanating from Africa. Africa's derivative power is therefore only momentary and unable to influence policy outcomes.

Bibliography

African Development Bank, Organisation for Economic Co-operation and Development, United Nations Development Programme, United Nations Economic Commission for Africa (2011) African Economic Outlook 2011. [online]. www.africaneconomicoutlook.org/sites/default/files/content-pdf/AEO2011_EN.pdf (retrieved 16 January 2018).

African Union (2015) *Agenda 20163: The Africa We Want*. Addis Ababa: Africa Union Commission. www.un.org/en/africa/osaa/pdf/au/agenda2063.pdf (retrieved 16 January 2018).

African Union and European Union (2017) Investing in Youth for Accelerated Inclusive Growth and Sustainable Development. Declaration of the AU-EU Summit. AU-EU/Decl.1(V). Abidjan, 29–30 November. www.consilium.europa.eu/media/31991/33454-pr-final_declaration_au_eu_summit.pdf (retrieved 3 January 2018).

Akaki, S. (2008) Is Africa a Cold War battleground? [online]. Global Research, 23 July. www.globalresearch.ca/is-africa-a-cold-war-battleground/9648 (retrieved 19 January 2018).

Bayart, J.F. (2009) *The State in Africa: The Politics of the Belly*, 2nd edition. London: Longman.

Becker, A. (2016) Paul Collier: 'Let's stop preaching to Africa' [online]. Deutsche Welle, 28 December. www.dw.com/en/paul-collier-lets-stop-preaching-to-africa/a-36929683 (retrieved 16 January 2018).

Clapham, C. (1996) *Africa and the International System: The Politics of Survival*. Cambridge: Cambridge University Press.

Clayton, J. (2009) China tightens grip on Africa with $4.4bn lifeline for Guinea junta. *The Times*, 13 October. www.thetimes.co.uk/article/china-tightens-grip-on-africa-with-dollar44bn-lifeline-for-guinea-junta-blbsnm3psnj (retrieved 16 November 2017).

Corkin, K. (2013) *Uncovering African Agency: Angola's Management of China's Credit Lines*. London: Routledge.

Council of the European Union (2006) Ninth EU-China Summit. Helsinki 9 September 2006 Joint Statement [online]. Press Release, 11 September. http://europa.eu/rapid/press-release_PRES-06-249_en.htm (retrieved 17 October 2017).

ECOWAS Commission (2016) Mandating the ECOWAS Standby Force to Uphold the Results of the Presidential Election in the Republic of the Gambia. Decision A/DEC, 2/12/17. Abuja, 17 December.

European Commission (2016) African Union Commission and European Commission Meet to Address Shared EU-Africa Challenges. Press Release, 5 April. http://europa.eu/rapid/press-release_IP-16-1226_en.htm (retrieved 13 February 2018).

European Union and African Union (2009) The Africa-EU Strategic Partnership: A Joint Africa-EU Strategy [online]. www.africa-eu-partnership.org/sites/default/files/documents/eas2007_joint_strategy_en.pdf (retrieved 3 December 2017).

Federal Ministry of Economic Cooperation and Development (BMZ) (2017) *Africa and Europe – A New Partnership for Development, Peace and a Better Future: Cornerstones of a Marshall Plan with Africa*.

Bonn: Federal Ministry of Economic Cooperation and Development. www.bmz.de/en/publications/type_of_publication/information_flyer/information_brochures/Materialie270_africa_marshallplan.pdf (retrieved 16 November 2017).

Fin24 (2014) Zuma: China treats SA as equal, not a subject [online]. 28 February. www.fin24.com/Economy/Zuma-China-treats-SA-as-equal-not-a-subject-20140227 (retrieved 24 January 2018).

Handel, M. (2006) Weak states in the international system. In C. Ingebritsen, I. Neumann and S. Gsthl (eds), *Small States in International Relations*. Seattle: University of Washington Press (pp.149–192).

Irish, J. (2017) France will no longer dictate to Africans, Macron says. *Reuters*, 28 November. https://uk.reuters.com/article/uk-africa-france-macron-speech/france-will-no-longer-dictate-to-africans-macron-says-idUKKBN1DS1B1?il=0 (retrieved 28 November 2017).

Jobson, E. (2017) EU's desire to contain migration is Africa's opportunity. *Politico*, 29 November. www.politico.eu/article/europe-migration-africa-migration-african-union-eu-desire-to-contain-migration-is-opportunity/

Leke, A. (2017) Reforming the African Union: The vital challenge of implementation [online]. Brookings Institute. www.brookings.edu/blog/africa-in-focus/2017/05/03/reforming-the-african-union-the-vital-challenge-of-implementation/ (retrieved 24 January 2018).

Lekorwe, M., Chingwete, A., Okuru, M. and Samson, R. (2016) *China's Growing Presence in Africa Wins Largely Positive Popular Reviews*. Afrobarometer Dispatch No 122, 24 October. http://afrobarometer.org/sites/default/files/publications/Dispatches/ab_r6_dispatchno122_perceptions_of_china_in_africa1.pdf (retrieved 9 December 2017).

Long, T. (2017) Small states, great powers? Gaining influence through intrinsic, derivative, and collective power. *International Studies Review*, 19, 185–205.

Melber, H. (2013) *Europe and China in Africa: Common Interests and/or different Approaches?* Stockholm: Institute for Security and Development. http://isdp.eu/content/uploads/publications/2013-melber-europe-and-china-in-africa.pdf (retrieved 2 December 2017).

Ng'wanakilala, F. and Obulutsa, G. (2013) China's Xi tells Africa he seeks relationship of equals. Reuters, 25 March. www.reuters.com/article/us-china-africa/chinas-xi-tells-africa-he-seeks-relationship-of-equals-idUSBRE92O0W320130325 (retrieved 19 October 2017).

Persaud, R.B. (2003) Reconceptualizing the Global South's perspective: The end of the Bandung spirit. In J.A. Braveboy-Wagner (ed.) *The Foreign Policies of the Global South: Rethinking Conceptual Frameworks*. Boulder, CO: Lynne Rienner (pp. 49–64).

Pouliot, V. (2016) Hierarchy in practice: Multilateral diplomacy and the governance of international security. *European Journal of International Security*, 1 (1), 5–26.

Russell, A. (2018) Transcript of FT interview with Emmerson Mnangagwa. Financial Times, 19 January. www.ft.com/content/b5bcf4b2-fd13-11e7-9b32-d7d59aace167 (retrieved 19 January 2018).

Straits Times (2015) China's Xi pledges US$60 billion for development in Africa [online]. 4 December. www.straitstimes.com/asia/east-asia/chinas-xi-pledges-us60-billion-for-development-in-africa (retrieved 19 October 2017).

Strange, S. (1988) *States and Markets*. London: Pinter Publishers.

Tull, D.M. (2008) *China in Africa: European Perceptions to the Chinese Challenge*. SAIS Working Papers in African Studies 02-08. Washington DC: School of Advanced International Studies. www.swp-berlin.org/fileadmin/contents/products/fachpublikationen/Tull_China_Africa_SAIS_WP.ks.pdf (retrieved 7 October 2017).

Tusk, D. (2017) Opening remarks by President Donald Tusk opening the 5th African Union-European Union summit in Abidjan [online]. www.consilium.europa.eu/en/press/press-releases/2017/11/29/remarks-by-president-donald-tusk-opening-the-5th-african-union-european-union-summit-in-abidjan/ (retrieved 21 January 2018).

Vines, A. (2014) EU-Africa Summit: Time to end preconceptions? [online]. EU Observer, 1 April. https://euobserver.com/opinion/123694 (retrieved 28 November 2017).

Washington Post (2017) Macron: France will no longer dictate to African countries. *Washington Post*, 28 November. Available at: www.washingtonpost.com/video/world/macron-france-will-no-longer-dictate-to-african-countries/2017/11/28/37c4144a-d456-11e7-9ad9-ca0619edfa05_video.html?utm_term=.0292a810e7b6 (retrieved 28 November 2017).

Wissenbach, U. (2016) The EU's response to China's Africa safari: Can triangular cooperation match needs? In S. Henson and O.F. Yap (eds), *The Power of the Chinese Dragon: Implications for African Development and Economic Growth*. Basingstoke: Palgrave Macmillan (pp. 250–267).

World Bank (2019) Gross domestic product 2019 [online]. http://databank.worldbank.org/data/download/GDP.pdf (retrieved 24 January 2020).

19
EU-Brazil-Africa triangular cooperation in the 21st century
Unfinished business

Carolina Pavese and Guilherme Ziebell de Oliveira

Introduction

'Today, Africa is an unquestionable priority for Brazil' (President Lula, 2007). When the Brazilian president delivered these words at a meeting with the African Ambassadors in Brazil on 25 May 2007, he actually meant it. In the first decade of the new millennium, the ascent of Brazil as an 'emerging power' injected the enthusiasm the country needed to expand her international presence. As a result, Brazil's engagement with Africa increased exponentially and on several fronts, under the so-called South-South diplomacy. The revamping of relations with the continent was a multipurpose strategy, since it would legitimise the country's role as an interlocutor of the Global South in international affairs while also serving the economic interests of domestic stakeholders. Meanwhile, for Africa, that represented an opportunity to develop a partnership on 'equal levels', mostly driven by shared interests promoted through collective action.

Arguably, this rapprochement contributed to an ongoing change in the international architecture of power that was already requiring the EU to reconsider its foreign policy towards Africa. Against this background, the EU and Brazil could compete for influence in the region; or, alternatively, they could join efforts on issues of shared interest in a 'win-win' arrangement that would mutually reinforce their presence in Africa. They opted for the latter. In 2007 the EU and Brazil launched a Strategic Partnership, aspiring to enhance the level of their long-standing relationship in terms of agenda and scope. From the EU's perspective, forging alliances with 'key global players' to promote 'effective multilateralism' was at the heart of the European Security Strategy (2003). Similarly, for Brazil, this was an opportunity to reinforce her image as an 'emerging power' in global affairs. Thus, setting the promotion of EU-Brazil-Africa cooperation as one the purposes of the Strategic Partnership was certainly a novelty but not entirely a surprise, as it matched the interests of both partners.

More than a decade later, the Strategic Partnership seems to have lost momentum. Successful engagement is recorded in particular cases, but triangular cooperation with Africa, our specific concern, never took off as planned. From the 2010s, the Brazilian economy entered a slowdown, a situation aggravated by the political crisis that led to the questionable impeachment of former president Dilma Rousseff in 2016. As a result, Brazil's global presence began to wane, and the same applies to her relations with Africa and the EU. Nevertheless, the early 2000s were undoubtfully fruitful and innovative years for Brazil's ties with the African continent, ultimately contributing to a new context for EU-Africa relations, also reflected in the partnership between the EU and Brazil.

Scrutinising these intertwining relationships, this chapter first provides an account of Brazil's approach towards Africa in the 21st century. The second part of the analysis discusses EU-Brazil relations, with emphasis on the 2007 Strategic Partnership, and then explores Brazil-EU-Africa trilateral cooperation as established throughout the 2000s. The chapter concludes by examining major outcomes of these endeavours and offering insights on the prospects of Brazil-EU-Africa relations.

Brazil-Africa relations in the 21st century

Brazil and Africa share long historical links that dates back to the 16th century. Yet, their relationship never followed a linear path and has alternated from stagnation to greater rapprochement. After a decline in the 1990s, the initial years of the 21st century were marked by the beginning of a fruitful phase, with Brazil's renewed interest in the continent. Under Lula's administration (2003–2010), the country prioritised the diversification of partnerships, combining the strengthening of traditional ties (such as the United States and Europe) with the forging of alternative alliances, mainly with strategic countries and regions from the developing world. Equally important, the new foreign policy employed significant efforts to increase participation in multilateral fora and other arenas, including those scarcely occupied over the previous decades (Suyama et al., 2016; Silva, 2010; Vigevani and Cepaluni, 2007). Under this new approach, the relationship with Africa became a key element of Brazil's South-South diplomacy.

The strengthening of partnership 'between equals' was understood as an opportunity to jointly address mutual social and economic difficulties (Saraiva, 2012). At the same time, Brazil made clear that greater engagement with the continent would contribute to raising her international profile in global affairs and also guarantee further market access to domestic actors (Brazil, 2011a). As a result, the country significantly expanded her presence in Africa between 2003 and 2010. The number of Brazilian diplomatic representations in the continent doubled in this period, with the opening or reopening of more than 18 embassies. Likewise, African countries inaugurated 13 new embassies in Brazil, reaching a total of 29 diplomatic representations by 2010. Reflecting a 'presidential diplomacy', during his two terms Lula went to Africa on 13 occasions, visiting 28 countries – some more than once. In reciprocity, representatives from 27 African states travelled to Brazil on a total of 47 occasions. This intensifying of formal meetings could be verified also at ministerial level. While the Brazilian Foreign Minister Celso Amorim made 66 trips to 25 countries in the continent, chancellors from 32 African states visited Brazil on 62 occasions (Brazil, 2011a, 2011d; Leite and Cavalcante, 2016).

Frequently, these diplomatic missions to Africa attended to both public and private strategic interests and were accompanied by national entrepreneurs. Envisaging the promotion of economic and trade interests, Brazilian agencies and companies came into play. The Brazilian National Bank for Economic and Social Development (BNDES) exercised a pivotal role in the internationalisation process of national companies, providing loans to those operating in strategic sectors in Africa (Pinho, 2013; Meana, 2016). During the period 2003–2010, the BNDES granted just over USD 2.6 billion in financial support to Brazilian companies operating in Africa (BNDES, 2018). The sponsorship allowed the expansion of activities in several countries, especially in the services and infrastructure sectors (Miyamoto, 2011; Vilas-Bôas, 2011) Some of the largest beneficiaries include Odebrecht, Camargo Correa, Andrade Gutierrez and Queiroz

Galvão, all private companies. Major state-owned business also profited from these incentives, namely, Petrobras, the Brazilian National Oil Company, and companies operating in the defence industry, like Embraer and Emgepron (Brazil, 2011b; Miyamoto, 2011).

Development cooperation was another key area of Brazil-Africa relations. For Africa, this opportunity allowed engagement in an agenda that was more in touch with the reality shared by developing countries, addressing issues like the fight against poverty and epidemics (Oliveira, 2015). Several countries expressed an interest in adopting initiatives akin to the successful social programmes implemented in Brazil under Lula's administration. From 2005, Brazil began providing technical support to African governments – Ethiopia, Mozambique and Senegal, among others – interested in the implementation of an income transfer programme. In addition to the missions carried out by the Brazilian Ministry of Social Development and the Fight Against Hunger to Africa, representatives from more than 20 African countries, including Zambia, Ivory Coast, Sudan and Lesotho, visited Brazil to discuss the implementation and management of such programs (Stolte, 2012).

Beyond diplomatic dialogue, numerous concrete actions to improve cooperation on development-related issues were taken. The Brazilian Agricultural Research Corporation (Embrapa) opened an office in Ghana and established a model farm for the production of cotton in Mali. Also, the Brazilian National Service of Industrial Training (SENAI), in partnership with the governments of Guinea-Bissau and Cape Verde, installed professional training centres in those countries. Addressing the bioenergy sector, a strategic one for Brazil, the Program to Support the Renovation and Implantation of Sugar Cane Fields (Pró-Renova) was created in 2009, coordinated by the Division of New and Renewable Energy of the Ministry of Foreign Affairs. Aimed at the promotion of the production and use of biofuels, the programme led to the signing of several memoranda of understanding for bilateral technical cooperation (Schlesinger, 2012; Moraes and Mattos, 2012).

Besides, bilateral agreements with African governments were concluded to facilitate the creation of air routes between the two regions and to promote bilateral flows of goods and people (Brazil, 2011a). Another measure of impact was the support of the pacification and reconstruction processes occurring in Africa, with Brazil granting assistance and credit to the African countries in various areas and forgiving the external debt of some countries, such as Mozambique, Cape Verde, Gabon and Nigeria (Oliveira, 2015). Additionally, 53 bilateral acts with 22 countries were celebrated, establishing cooperation programmes in health and education areas, including projects to help combat malaria and HIV/AIDS and diagnose sickle cell anemia (Brazil, 2011c).

Linked to the Ministry of Foreign Affairs, The Brazilian Cooperation Agency (ABC) remains the primary organisation responsible for coordinating international projects developed by Brazilian agencies with third parties (Abdenur, 2018). From 2003 to 2010 activities were intense, with the ABC promoting 481 cooperation projects with African countries (ABC, 2018). Africa was becoming more of a priority for development cooperation. Brazilian investments in this line of projects were valued at approximately USD 500,000 in 2003, sharply rising to USD 19.8 million by 2010, a growth of more than 3,800% (ABC, 2018). In 2009, half of ABC's expenditures was destined for Africa, a number that increased to nearly 60% of the total budget by 2010 (World Bank and IPEA, 2011).

Security issues were another core element of the Brazil-Africa relations promoted in this period. Brazil signed and ratified cooperation agreements in the defence area with several African countries. New initiatives included, for example, the creation of a Security Forces Formation Centre in Guinea-Bissau, collaborating with the reform of the country's defence sector, and the provision of instructors for a Centre for Enhancement of Demining and Clean-up Actions in Benin (Brazil, 2011b). Additionally, old instruments were also revitalised, namely the South

EU-Brazil-Africa triangular cooperation

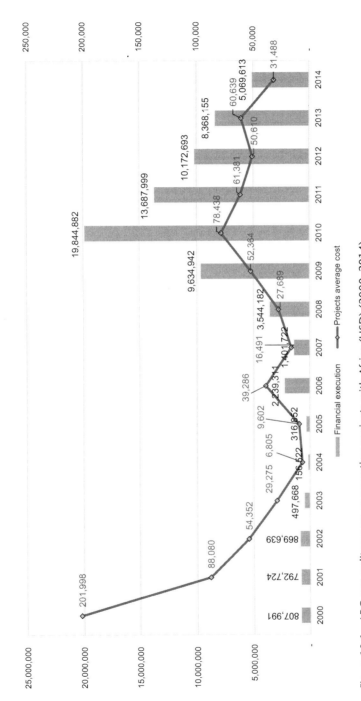

Figure 19.1 ABC expenditures on cooperation projects with Africa (USD) (2000–2014)
Source: Data from ABC (2018)

Atlantic Peace and Cooperation Zone (ZOPACAS). Established in 1986 (Resolution 41/11 UNGA), the activities of the organisation were interrupted by the end of the 1990s. But the concern to protect new oil reserves in the Brazilian coasts renewed interest in the alliance. Thus, in 2007, in a meeting held in Luanda by an Angolan initiative with Brazilian support, ZOPACAS resumed the High-level Summits (Ribeiro-Hoffmann and Marcodes, 2017).

In another move to promote permanent alliances, Brazil sponsored the creation of the Africa-South America (ASA) summits. Originally perceived as an extension of the Brazil-Africa Forum (Mattheis, 2015), the ASA summits are a permanent mechanism for cooperation, gathering representatives from 65 countries of the two regions (Brazil, 2011a). So far, three High-Level Summits have been held: in 2006, 2009 and 2012. Despite diplomatic dialogue, the partnership failed to produce more than political solidarity, as the parties are still agreeing on the mechanisms to implement cooperation and achieve concreate deliverables (African Union, 2019). By the end of President's Lula second term, Brazil-Africa relations were at new and improved levels. Dilma Rousseff assumed the Brazilian presidency in 2011, naming Antônio Patriota as the Minister of Foreign Affairs. In their inauguration speeches, both committed to preserving the principles and ideals that oriented the previous government, indicating a continuation of agenda and priorities (Meana, 2016). The Brazilian foreign policy, therefore, maintained a revisionist stance, characterised by the interest in reinforcing international institutions as well as a willingness to take active action in multilateral fora, while keeping the aspiration to be a leader of the Global South (Saraiva, 2014). The African continent, thus, would remain central for the international insertion of Brazil.

The first year of the new administration was a fruitful one for Africa-Brazil relations. While attending the 5th India-Brazil-South Africa Forum in Pretoria in 2011, Rousseff also guaranteed that her predecessor would be engaged with her government; for instance, naming former President Lula as Brazil's official representative at the 17th African Union Summit (World Bank and IPEA, 2011). Expanding the framework for cooperation, the Africa Group was created in 2011, engaging representatives from different ministries as well as experts and executives from the private sector. The objective was to associate Brazilian investments and sales to African development programmes as a means of providing greater mutual gains. At the same time, the Africa Group served as an arena for Brazil to coordinate the activities of national companies in the continent (Cabral, 2011). Influenced by these endeavours, 81 new cooperation projects were established with African countries, mainly in the security sector (ABC, 2018). Concrete results from cooperation at the multilateral level were also delivered in 2011. A clear case was the election of José Graziano, a former minister in the Lula administration, as Director-General of the UN Food and Agriculture Organization (FAO), largely due to the support of African allies (Saraiva, 2012).

The enthusiasm for and engagement with Africa continued throughout the following two years. In 2012, 37 cooperation projects were established with African countries. These included new military training projects and technical support for the presidential elections in Guinea-Bissau (ABC, 2018) and a cooperation agreement with Mozambique to implement Luz para Todos (Light for All), a Brazilian programme aiming to provide access to electricity in rural areas (Pinho, 2013). In total, over that year, the BNDES provided USD 642 million in financing to Brazilian companies operating in the continent – an increase of 46% on the previous year (Marull, 2013). In 2013, Rousseff resumed the agenda of visits to the African continent, attending the 3rd ASA Summit, in Malabo, the 5th Summit of Heads of State and Government of the BRICS, in Durban, and the 50th anniversary celebrations of the Organization of Africa Unity/AU. Furthermore, the 37th Brazilian embassy was opened, education cooperation programmes were strengthened, and new military training and cooperation projects with Angola,

Mozambique, São Tomé and Principe and Senegal were adopted. In a very important move, the president announced the forgiveness and restructuring of USD 900 million in debt across 12 African countries[1] (Marull, 2013; Vilella, 2013). Finally, in that same year, the BNDES opened an office in South Africa, seeking to improve relations with regional and local institutions and promote business between Brazil and the continent, further reaffirming the priority given by the Brazilian government to relations with Africa (BNDES, 2013).

In 2014 new military training projects were established as well as a cooperation project with Côte d'Ivoire for the sustainable development of the fishing industry and aquaculture in the country and a triangular cooperation project with Angola and the FAO (ABC, 2018). However, there was no official presidential visit to the continent, and slowly the enthusiasm began to change. While cooperation projects and investments continued, the official position adopted at the beginning of Rousseff's administration, the effective impact and importance of Africa for Brazilian foreign policy was called into question. Besides a notable weakness in the use of presidential diplomacy, expressed by the significantly smaller number of visits of the president to the continent in relation to Lula, cooperation with Africa through the ABC also weakened (only 125 new projects were established), and a drastic and steady reduction of the budget occurred (ibid.). Yet, throughout Rousseff's first term, Brazil's trade with Africa maintained high levels; this was USD 26 billion in 2014 – a lower figure than in the previous year, when it reached its highest historical mark of USD 28 billion, but still a significant increase from the previous decade (ITC, 2018) (see Figure 19.2).

In spite of the questioning of the importance of Africa for Brazil, there seems to be no evidence pointing to a rupture in the foreign policy model for Africa that had been adopted since the Lula administration, but rather a reduction in the intensity with which policy objectives were pursued (Meana, 2016; Oliveira, 2015). This can be explained by the different conjunctures – both national and international – experienced in the governments of the two presidents. Internally, President Rousseff faced a more complex context than her predecessor. Based on the expansion of consumption in the domestic market and the income redistribution that was occurring, the economic growth model adopted at the beginning of Rousseff's administration started to show signs of unsustainability in the long run. Brazil's economic performance was significantly

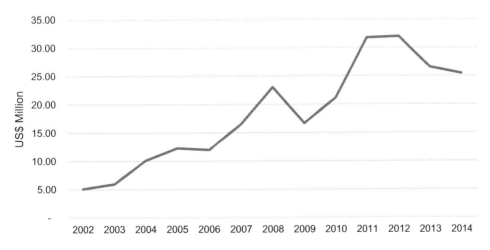

Figure 19.2 Brazil-Africa bilateral trade (USD million) (2002–2014)
Source: Data from ITC (2018)

affected, and the gross domestic product growth rate declined exponentially from 2010 (World Bank, 2018). With the maintenance of high interest rates and exchange rate appreciation, the situation demanded increasing attention and efforts from the federal government (Teixeira and Pinto, 2012). Additionally, the renewal of the national infrastructure for the 2014 World Cup and for the 2016 Olympic Games proved to be a major challenge not only economically, but also politically, leading to popular surges across the country that served to increase the political turbulence already being felt (Meana, 2016; Oliveira, 2015).

Besides the shifts in the domestic context, Dilma Rousseff also faced a more hostile external environment (Pereira, 2012) with the effects of the 2008 global economic crisis reaching the country more sharply in her government. The global economic slowdown had a negative impact on the price of commodities exported by Brazil, which further hampered the Brazilian economic and political situation (Abdenur, 2018). Furthermore, the Rousseff administration faced the consequences of the Arab Spring on the African continent. The increase in volatility and instability has created an environment of difficulty and uncertainty for the maintenance of foreign policy and investments in the region, especially due to the difficulty of identifying partnerships with growth potential (Meana, 2016).

With a relative depletion of the Brazilian 'diplomatic activism' of the previous government and in a context of crisis in the multilateral negotiations (WTO and UN) in the period, Rousseff's administration turned attention to domestic politics (Abdenur, 2018; Oliveira, 2015). As Silva (2018) claims, this pulling back of Brazilian foreign policy occurred in spite of the pursuit of continuity with the previous government. Central elements that guided Brazilian foreign policy between 2003 and 2010 remained present in the Rousseff government, despite its more discreet profile. Nevertheless, the effects of the political, economic and institutional crisis in Brazil, as well as the changes that have taken place on the international scene, have seriously compromised the international insertion model by weakening and limiting its results (Silva, 2018). As a result, relations with Africa inevitably waned.

EU-Brazil relations: Forging a strategic partnership

Brazil was the first Latin American country to establish diplomatic ties with the European Communities (EC), in 1960. Engagement between the two actors has waxed and waned across the decades, but has increased overall in terms of agenda and degree of institutionalisation. Back in the 1960s, Latin America and the Caribbean were under the strong influence of the United States, and Africa was a priority region for the EC. Thus, initially, the EC opted to engage with Latin American countries mainly through an interregional framework, progressively increasing its presence in the region in the 1970s and 1980s. Permanent instruments for interregional cooperation were established, and bilateral relations were boosted with the adoption of the EC-Brazil bilateral agreements in the 1980s, essentially covering trade and investment.

The end of the Cold War, the accession of Portugal and Spain to the EU, and the suppression of military rule in Brazil were important factors that prompted EC/EU-Brazil relations to a new level. The 1992 Framework Cooperation Agreement was the first to address the entire gamut of bilateral issues, providing a legal basis for this relationship (Wisniewski and Dahab, 2017; Gratius, 2018). The agreement also includes the possibility to extend actions to 'cooperation in the field of regional integration and cooperation', making explicit that the clause regards 'agreements with countries in the same region'. Regionally, engagement with Brazil was further institutionalised with the 1995 EU-Mercosur Framework Cooperation Agreement. Interestingly, though, none of the agreements adopted mention cooperation at the multilateral level or with other regions, suggesting that Brazil was considered by the EU as a regional player at most.

By the turn of the millennium, the enthusiasm for this new phase of EU-Brazil relations had faded away. The EU was taken by its own issues, preparing for an unprecedented enlargement process and implementing a series of new EU treaties. Moreover, Europe was still struggling to come to terms with the end of Cold War and Germany's reunification – there was just too much on the EU's plate. Meanwhile, Mercosur was making slow progress in delivering regional integration, which inevitably delayed the negotiations of an EU-Mercosur trade agreement (Ferreira-Perreira, 2015; Gratius, 2018). As Brazil emerged as a relevant economic and political power on the international scene, it was about time to reboot and redesign the relationship with the EU; and the interest was reciprocated. From the EU's perspective, a *rapprochement* with Brazil was in line with the 2003 European Security Strategy. A landmark in the development of the EU's approach to security issues, addressing global issues and promoting 'effective multilateralism', the European Security Strategy identifies the 'need to pursue our objectives both through multilateral cooperation in international organisations and through partnerships with key actors' (Pavese, 2014, 2018).

In a Communication to the Council and the European Parliament entitled 'Towards an EU-Brazil Strategic Partnership', adopted in 30 May 2007, the European Commission highlighted the main reasons to forge an alliance with Brazil. The document stresses shared core values and interests, namely respect for the rule of law and human rights, tackling climate change and promoting sustainable development and social justice. The Commission emphasises the country's importance as the mayor destination for European trade and investment in Latin America, naming Brazil a 'vital ally for the EU' in addressing global issues and an undeniable regional power. Central to our analysis is the fact that the 2007 Communication is the first official document in which EU-Brazil-Africa triangular cooperation is mentioned. The Commission draws attention to the increasing South-South approach of Brazilian foreign policy. It also stresses that Brazil is known for promoting innovative multilateral and trilateral schemes, sharing the EU's approach to development cooperation as a means to promote peace and security. As it concludes, 'the Commission is ready to intensify cooperation with Brazil in the field of development assistance, notably in relation to triangular co-operation with the [Community of Portuguese speaking countries] on development co-operation activities' (European Commission, 2007: 6). In addition, not mentioned in the Communication, the EU was concerned with the growing presence of China and the United States in Brazil; a partnership would reduce this loss (Meissner, 2017).

From the Brazilian perspective, a partnership with the EU was in line with the country's foreign policy universalist approach, oriented towards autonomy and diversification. Moreover, the revisiting of relations with Brussels would entail an opportunity to break up the hierarchical 'donor-recipient' structure and establish a partnership between actors of 'equal levels', recognising Brazil as a global player. Gains were also envisaged from increasing trade and investment relations as well as further cooperation in old and new areas, including multilateral issues (Pavese, 2014, 2018). Converging interests led to the EU-Brazil Strategic Partnership, launched at the occasion of the 1st EU-Brazil High Level Summit in Lisbon on 4 July 2007. As a rather ambitious and broad agreement, the overall objective of the partnership is to enhance cooperation at different levels and across a myriad of issues. The two joint action plans (JAPs), adopted in 2008 and 2011, and the joint declarations of the seven High Level Summits held between 2007 and 2014 provide details of the agenda and measures for its implementation (Council of the European Union, 2007, 2008, 2009, 2010, 2011, 2013, 2014).

A remarkable departure from the conventional agenda of what the partners considered as bilateral issues, JAP I places significant emphasis on cooperation in the multilateral arena – an approach not witnessed before the Strategic Partnership. Another important novelty is the adoption of triangular cooperation, with emphasis on partners from the developing world, as one the main objectives of the new instrument. Covering the period of 2008 to 2011, implementation of the JAP was revisited during the EU-Brazil High Level Summits held in 2009 and 2010. Adopted during the 5th EU-Brazil High Level Summit in 2011, JAP II essentially reiterates the commitments to triangular cooperation already established in JAP I. As protocol, the ongoing practices of the Strategic Partnership were reported at the next High Level Summit, in 2013. With a lifespan of three years, JAP II was expected to be revisited in 2014, but that never happened. The 7th EU-Brazil Summit did take place as planned, but it pushed the launch of what would have been the third JAP to 2015. The problem is that, despite the release of a joint statement to mark the tenth anniversary of the Strategic Partnership in July 2017, there has not been another EU-Brazil High Level Summit since 2014, let alone a new JAP (Gomes Saraiva, 2017; Ayuso and Gratius, 2018).

As Gomes Saraiva (2017) argues, since the first term of Rousseff's administration (2011–2014) it became clear that relations with the EU were not approached with the same enthusiasm as during Lula's years. At least two factors account for that. Firstly, already in 2011 the euphoria with Brazil's economic growth was replaced by economic difficulties, later accentuated with institutional and political crisis. Additionally, the external environment was less welcoming of Brazil's aspiration to take a leadership role.

According to Saraiva (2017) and Ayuso and Gratius (2018), following the impeachment of Rousseff on 31 August 2016, the emphasis on South-South cooperation and the principles of autonomy and diversification were revisited under the Temer administration (2016–2018). Brazil was back to prioritising Western alignment and liberal values and agenda within a discourse of 'commercial diplomacy'. However, foreign policy remained an issue of secondary importance in national politics, largely influenced by the president's unpopularity and the country's economic situation. Regarding the Strategic Partnership, relationships at the highest political level was at a new low. Now, the future of EU-Brazil relations depends largely on the new government.

Overall, during the first ten years of the Strategic Partnership (2007–2017), cooperation made limited progress. Between 2008 and 2016, the EU and Brazil jointly promoted and co-sponsored 228 sector dialogues, focusing on either technical issues or the exchange of best practice in specific matters. Dialogue also increased on multilateral issues, leading to occasional cooperation on particular issues and specific contexts. Meanwhile, difficulties in concluding the EU-Mercosur free trade agreement challenged the impact of the Strategic Partnership at the regional level. Regarding triangular cooperation, the Strategic Partnership paved the way to a rather promising EU-Brazil alliance with third parties. The next section assesses whether or not that cooperation was delivered as promised.

EU-Brazil-Africa cooperation: Expectations not delivered

> I am convinced that through triangular cooperation we can multiply successful initiatives.
> (President Lula, 2010)

Cooperation with third parties beyond the Latin American and Caribbean region became one of the pillars of EU-Brazil relations with the establishment of the Strategic Partnership. General statements providing a road map in triangular cooperation first figured in the instruments of the Strategic Partnership from JAP I. From 2008, this was a permanent component of the agenda of the High-Level Summits held until 2014, restated as a priority area in the 2nd JAP.

As Table 19.1 demonstrates, from the adoption of JAP I in 2008, bioenergy has been a priority area for EU-Brazil collaborative actions with developing countries, an interest also reflected in the agenda of bilateral cooperation between the two partners. Brazil already had cooperative

Table 19.1 EU-Brazil Strategic Partnership and triangular cooperation with Africa

Event/document	Place and date	Content
I EU-Brazil High Level Summit – Joint Declaration	Lisbon 4 July 2007	No mention
II EU-Brazil High Level Summit – Joint Action Plan; Joint Declaration	Rio de Janeiro 22 December 2008	• Cooperate on human rights issues, for instance by using the EC Agreement with the CPLP • Cooperate on peacebuilding and post-conflict assistance in lusophone developing countries • Explore opportunities for triangular cooperation in the field of agriculture with African countries • Cooperate to bring sustainable development to interested developing countries in sectors such as health, energy, agriculture and education, in light of the MDGs
III EU-Brazil High Level Summit – Joint Declaration	Stockholm 6 October 2009	• Commitment to implement triangular cooperation with interested developing countries, such as the PALOP and Timor Leste as well as Haiti in the sectors of health, energy, agriculture, education and other appropriate areas • Welcoming of the progress made towards the identification of common principles, including those set out in the Accra Agenda for Action, working modalities and potential pilot projects • Set up a joint work programme on triangular cooperation • Work together on a joint initiative for the sustainable development of bioenergy in Africa, focusing on biofuels and bio-electricity. Additionally, cooperate in this field together with the African Union Commission
IV EU-Brazil High Level Summit – Joint Declaration	Brazil 14 July 2010	• Adoption of the Joint Work Programme on triangular cooperation that establishes the foundations for Brazil and the EU to promote the development of the PALOP, Timor Leste and Haiti • Launch of a cooperation on the sustainable development of bioenergy in interested African countries • Welcoming of the Partnership for the Sustainable Development of Bioenergy agreed with Mozambique
V EU-Brazil High Level Summit – Joint Action Plan; Joint Declaration	Brussels 4 October, 2011	• Promote joint initiatives for trilateral cooperation with developing countries on the sustainable development of bioenergy
VI EU-Brazil High Level Summit – Joint Declaration	Brazil 24 January 2013	• Promote trilateral cooperation to support electoral processes in the PALOP and East Timor
VII EU-Brazil High Level Summit – Joint Declaration	Brussels 24 February 2014	• General recognition of the achievements of the trilateral initiatives on development cooperation between EU members and Brazil in benefit of developing countries

Source: Authors' elaboration

schemes on this issue with certain African countries and other long-standing partners from the developed world. According to the European Commission (2010), efforts to plan and deliver actions on energy cooperation were articulated at the occasion of a seminar jointly promoted by the EC Delegation, the ABC and the German Cooperation Ministry, in May 2009 in Brazil. Attended by other EU embassies, the parties discussed triangular cooperation with the African, Caribbean and Pacific countries. A few months later, as stated in the declaration of the third EU-Brazil High Level Summit (Council of the European Union, 2009), the two partners agreed to promote trilateral cooperation for the production of bioenergy and ethanol in the African continent.

According to Afionis et al. (2016), these cooperative endeavours were set to begin with two partners: Kenya and Mozambique. Dividing tasks, the EU was in charge of leading the activities conducted with the first, whereas Brazil was in charge of projects with the latter. In both cases, cooperation failed to deliver the expected results. Already in the first meetings back in 2010, divergence regarding the policy outcomes of triangular cooperation on bioenergy and ethanol with Kenya set the two strategic partners apart. The EU was also rather uncomfortable with Brazil's drive for market opportunity. Identifying other priorities, Brussels kept delaying the authorisation for the EU Delegation in Kenya to agree on a trilateral project in the country and start implementing it. The sustainability dimension of biofuels under scrutiny by the international community contributed to bringing negotiations to a halt (ibid.).

In parallel, the EU and Brazil were also trying to put into practice cooperation with Mozambique. The Brazil-EU-Mozambique Joint Declaration on the Partnership for the Sustainable Development of Bioenergy was launched at the fourth EU-Brazil High Level Summit in 2010. The agreement involved setting up a technical working group to study the modalities for the implementation of the strategy, envisaging two main lines of action: the elaboration of a country study to assess the prospects for the development of bioenergy in Mozambique in a sustainable manner; and the promotion of bioenergy projects along the lines of sustainability, funded by private and public actors (InfoRel, 2010). For Brazil, this was another investment opportunity that expanded the country's already established presence in that market via bilateral agreements and trilateral arrangements with other partners like the United States (Flexor and Kato, 2017). Moreover, investing in sub-Saharan Africa could also serve the purpose of getting Brazilian companies cheaper market access to Europe, benefiting from tariff concessions granted by the EU to Africa. The EU also had an interest in this deal, as it would increase its biofuel supplies (Leopold and Dietz, 2012). The announcement soon sparked criticism from civil society, calling attention to the social and environmental impacts for Mozambique – a country fighting famine – of increasing land use for growing biofuels for export purposes (All Africa, 2010). In addition to facing certain opposition, like in the case of Kenya, by overlooking the implementation aspects of these projects before launching the initiatives, the EU and Brazil ended up missing another opportunity to actually promote trilateral cooperation. As Cabral (2014) asserts, the EU was also sceptical of the capacity of the Mozambic government to operationalise projects (that were eventually launched). And there were also concerns about the role played by Brazilian private stakeholders in the country's approach to cooperation. As a result, the Brazil-EU-Mozambique Partnership never went further than concluding of the feasibility (Cabral, 2014).

Another arena in which the two players aspire to engage is among lusophone countries, namely the Community of Portuguese Language Countries (CPLP) and the Portuguese-speaking African Countries (PALOP). Dating back to 1996, the CPLP aims to promote cooperation among nine states that have Portuguese as their official language, including the PALOP (Rizzi, 2014). Established in 2007, the EU-CPLP partnership provided a permanent framework for Brazil and the EU to cooperate directly with the PALOP. Interested in exploring this fertile terrain in the instruments of the Strategic Partnership, the two parties committed to exploring engagement with Africa on joint actions addressing issues from health to education, security to energy, and agriculture to electoral processes (see Table 19.1). Yet, over the past decade, triangular cooperation with CPLP/PALOP at the diplomatic level has been very shallow and produced little concrete results. A case of relative success was cooperation on support for electoral processes in the PALOP and Timor Leste. Under the framework of the Strategic Partnership, the Supreme Electoral Court of Brazil and the European Commission agreed a letter of intent on cooperation in the field of elections, on 14 July 2010. In parallel, both Brazil and the EU were establishing their own bilateral agreements with CPLP/PALOP-TL to cooperate on this matter. Later in 2011, Brazil signed a memorandum of understating with the United Nations Development Programme (UNDP) to jointly implement the project Support to Electoral Cycles in Portuguese Speaking African Countries and Timor Leste (Pro PALOP-TL). The project was fully funded by the EU under the 10th European Development Fund, with a budget of €6.1 million covering the period of 2010 to 2013, to be managed by the UNDP (Brazilian Supreme Electoral Court, 2011). The resources applied to activities for electoral assistance in six countries: Angola, Cape Verde, Guinea-Bissau, Mozambique, São Tomé and Principe, and Timor Leste. There was a division of labour in this task: while the EU granted financial support, Brazil lent technical support and capacity building for monitoring, evaluation and implementation of the electoral processes in the recipient countries (UNDP, 2013).

Preparatory works for the establishment of the EU-Brazil Sector Dialogues Support Facility began in 2006. Two years later, the initiative was officially launched, as part of JAP I. The new instrument consisted of a financial mechanism to promote a broad portfolio of sector dialogues. Promoting Triangular Cooperation is one those dialogues, created under the 'global challenges' thematic area. The first project sponsored for this agenda was the Triangular Cooperation Seminar – New directions for development, held on 20 and 21 May 2009 in Brazil. The objective of the meeting was 'to bring concepts together and build consensus on the principles, objectives, methods and practices of such cooperation'. Ten years later, this is the only project funded for that portfolio (Sector Dialogues, 2019).

Under the framework of the EU-Brazil Scientific and Technological Cooperation Agreement, in force since 2007, the partners agreed with South Africa the Belem Statement on Atlantic Research and Innovation Cooperation in 2017 (European Commission, 2019). Integrating marine research as part of the sector dialogue agenda, actions adopted so far have resulted in two meetings of academics from 15 countries that share the Atlantic shore, both of which took place in 2018 (Sector Dialogues, 2019).

Conclusion

This chapter addressed the development of EU–Brazil–Africa triangular cooperation in the new millennium and the complex web of relationships it entails. Considering that the many aspects of EU-Africa relations are discussed in depth in the other chapters of this book, particular attention was devoted to explaining Brazil-Africa relations. The African continent undeniably occupied a prominent place in Brazilian foreign policy throughout the first decade of the 21st century. The closer ties brought mutual benefits in all spheres. Yet by the second decade of this century, this situation had begun to change. The difficulties imposed by the changes in the environment – international and especially national – were determinants for the drawing back of the Brazilian international performance as a whole, as well as impacting on the relationship with the African continent. Although Africa still held the same conceptual space in Brazilian foreign policy formulation, the government, constrained by the crisis, concentrated its efforts on completing projects that were already under way, creating few new fronts for cooperation.

EU-Brazil relations followed a similar path. Since its inception, the EU and Brazil engagement was exercised fundamentally at bilateral and regional levels. From the 21st century, the relationship was promoted to new standards, and the 2007 EU-Brazil Strategic Partnership was looking like a very promising initiative. Yet, as far as triangular cooperation is concerned, the deliverables were few. Looking beyond political diplomacy, the EU and Brazil lost an opportunity to promote concrete triangular cooperation. In the case of bioenergy, an area of strategic interest for both the EU and Brazil, cooperation failed to take off, largely due to a lack of agreement on the specific terms and modalities to implement joint action. As biofuels evolve as a controversial issue, the current context is no longer as favourable for triangular cooperation as before; at least not under the terms discussed. Regarding the support to electoral processes in the CPLP/PALOP-TL triangular cooperation included a fourth and very important party, the UNDP. The EU contributed with financial support, replicating a common role for developed economies in this sort of agenda. Thus, the success of this collaborative endeavour needs to be considered with this caveat in mind.

Given the current void in the EU-Brazil summit diplomacy since 2014, the sector dialogues have provided the most active platform for discussion and actual implementation of joint actions. Yet the agenda of these dialogues is restricted to specific issues, normally with practical implication and technical dimension. There is no replacement for high-level political engagement. Moreover, even with limited scope, triangular cooperation is not a priority area for sector dialogues, and the lack of projects developed under this portfolio is evidence of this claim. To conclude, under the Strategic Partnership framework, the EU and Brazil embraced a rather ample and ambitious agenda for triangular cooperation; but they failed to deliver it. Political enthusiasm seemed to have dampened the perception of the importance and the complexity of reaching an agreement on the specific terms and provisions of the projects for their successful implementation. In most of the cases, no more than lip service was given to triangular cooperation.

Overall, this chapter demonstrated that the strengthening of Brazil's relations with both Africa and the EU was, to certain degree, defined by two factors: first, the pursuit of an engaging foreign policy approach and, second, a favourable international scenario that allowed the rise of Brazil as an emerging power. This is no longer the case, as domestic and international factors have led to a retreat of Brazil from the international scene. Expectations for triangular cooperation to finally be delivered are conditional on the revitalising of Brazil's bilateral relations with Africa and the EU, which, at the moment, are at a new low.

Note

1 The countries were the Democratic Republic of the Congo, Tanzania, Ivory Coast, Gabon, Republic of Congo, Guinea, Mauritania, São Tomé and Principe, Zambia, Senegal, Sudan and Guinea-Bissau.

Bibliography

ABC – Agência Brasileira de Cooperação (2018) Projetos – Cooperação Sul-Sul [online]. www.abc.gov.br/projetos (retrieved 10 December 2018).

Abdenur, A. (2018) Brazil-Africa relations: From boom to bust? In D. Nagar and C. Mussa (eds), *Africa and the World: Bilateral and Multilateral International Diplomacy*. Gewerbestrasse: Palgrave MacMillan (pp. 189–208).

Afionis, S., Stringer, L., Favreto, N., Tomei, J. and Buckerige, M. (2016) Unpacking Brazil's leadership in the global biofuels arena: Brazilian ethanol diplomacy in Africa. *Global Environmental Politics*, 16 (3), 127–150.

African Union (2019) Africa South-America. The Africa-South America Summit (ASA) [online]. https://au.int/en/partnerships/africa_southamerica (retrieved 10 January 2019).

All Africa (2010) Critics slam EU-Africa biofuel plan [online]. 26 July. www.africanagriculture.co.zw/2010/07/critics-slam-eu-brazil-african-biofuel.html (retrieved 9 January 2019).

Ayuso, A. and Gratius, S. (2018) *The Economic Agenda between Brazil and the EU: Prospects for a Bilateral and Global Upgrading*. IAI Papers 18(8). Rome: Istituto Affari Internazionali.

Banco Nacional de Desenvolvimento Econômico e Social (BNDES) (2018) Transparência – Dados sobre operações em financiamento [online]. www.bndes.gov.br/wps/portal/site/home/transparencia (retrieved 2 November 2018).

BNDES – Banco Nacional de Desenvolvimento Econômico e Social (2013) BNDES inaugura escritório de representação na África [online]. www.bndes.gov.br/SiteBNDES/bndes/bndes_pt/Institucional/Sala_de_Imprensa/Noticias/2013/Todas/20131206_africa.html (retrieved 4 March 2015).

Brazil, Ministério das Relações Exteriores (2011a) *Balanço de Política Externa 2003–2010 – Resumo Executivo*. Brasília: MRE.

Brazil, Ministério das Relações Exteriores (2011b) *Balanço de Política Externa 2003–2010 – África – Defesa*. Brasília: MRE.

Brazil, Ministério das Relações Exteriores (2011c) *Balanço de Política Externa 2003–2010 – África – Saúde*. Brasília: MRE.

Brazil, Ministério das Relações Exteriores (2011d) *Visitas internacionais do Presidente Lula e visitas ao Brazil de Chefes de Estado e de Chefes de Governo: 2003- 2010*. Brasília: MRE.

Brazilian Supreme Electoral Court (2011) Memorandum of Understanding between Supreme Electoral Court of the Federative Republic of Brazil (SEC) and United Nations Development Programme (UNDP) on cooperation between the Brazilian Electoral Justice, through the Supreme Electoral Court (SEC) of the Federative Republic of Brazil and the United Nations Development Programme (UNDP), here represented by its Resident Representative in the Republic of Guinea Bissau Office, in implementing the project 'Support to Electoral Cycles in Portuguese Speaking African Countries and East Timor (Pro PALOP – TL)', funded by the European Union. http://english.tse.jus.br/arquivos/memorandum-of-understanding-between-supreme-electoral-court-and-united-nations-development-programme (retrieved 10 November 2018).

Cabral, L. (2014) *The EU-Brazil Partnership on Development: A Lukewarm Affair*. ESPO Policy Brief 10. Madrid: FRIDE.

Cabral, L. (2011) *Cooperação Brazil-África para o desenvolvimento: Caracterização, tendências e desafios*. Textos Cindes, N°26. Rio de Janeiro: Centro de Estudos de Integração e Desenvolvimento (CINDES).

Council of the European Union (2007) EU-Brazil Summit Joint Statement. 11531/07 Presse 162. Brussels, 4 July.

Council of the European Union (2008) Brazil-European Union Strategic Partnership. Joint Action Plan. 2nd Brazil- European Union Summit. Rio De Janeiro, 22 December.

Council of the European Union (2009) Third European Union-Brazil Summit. Joint Statement. 14137/09, Presse 285. Stockholm, 6 October.

Council of the European Union (2010) 4th EU-Brazil Summit. Joint Statement. 12302/10, Presse 209. Brazil, 14 July.

Council of the European Union (2011) 5th EU-Brazil Summit. 15084/11, Presse 348. Brussels, 4 October.

Council of the European Union (2013) 6th EU- Brazil Summit. Joint Statement. 5715/13, Presse 29. Brazil, 24 January.

Council of the European Union (2014) 7th EU-Brazil Summit. 6930/14, Presse 96. Brussels, 24 February.

European Commission (2007) Communication from the Commission to the Council and the European Parliament: Towards an EU-Brazil Strategic Partnership. COM(2007) 281 final. Brussels, 30 May.

European Commission (2010) *Country Strategy Paper/National Indicative Programme 2007–2013. Mid Term Review and National Indicative Programme 2011–2013*. Brussels: Commission of the European Communities.

European Commission (2019) Roadmap for EU-Brazil STI cooperation [online]. https://ec.europa.eu/research/iscp/pdf/policy/br_roadmap_2018.pdf (retrieved 12 January 2019).

Ferreira-Pereira, L. (2015) The European Union's partnership policy towards Brazil: More than meets the eye. *Cambridge Review of International Affairs*, 29 (10), 55–77.

Flexor, G. and Kato, K. (2017) Biofuels and inclusive development: the Brazilian experience. *Development in Practice*, 27 (2), 157–167.

Gomes Saraiva, M. (2017) The Brazil-European Union Strategic Partnership, from Lula to Dilma Rousseff: A shift of focus. *Revista Brasileira de Política Internacional*, 60 (1), 1–17.

Gratius, S. (2018) Brazil and the European Union: From liberal inter-regionalism to realist bilateralism. *Revista Brasileira de Política internacional*, 6 (1), 1–21.

InfoRel (2010) Brazil-EU-Mozambique Joint Declaration on the Partnership for the Sustainable Development of Bioenergy [online]. www.inforel.org/noticias/noticia_Ingles.php?not_id=3943 (retrieved 9 January 2019).

ITC – International Trade Centre (2018) World Trade Map [online]. www.trademap.org/Index.aspx (retrieved 10 December 2018).

Leite, A. and Cavalcante, T. (2016) A Cooperação Brasileira para a África: da diplomacia presidencial de Lula da Silva à diplomacia comercial de Dilma Rousseff. *Brazilian Journal of International Relations*, 5 (2), 342–370.

Leopold, A. and Dietz, K. (2012) *Transnational Contradiction's and Effects of Europe's Bioenergy Policy. Evidence from Sub-Saharan Africa*. Fair Fuels Working Paper 4. Berlin: Fair Fuels.

Marull, Y. (2013) Brazil confirma prioridade da África em sua política externa ao perdoar dívidas. *Yahoo Notícias*. www.br.noticias.yahoo.com/brasil-confirma-prioridade-áfrica-política-externa-aoperdoar-194047683.html (retrieved 12 July 2014).

Mattheis, F. (2015) *Regionalism and Interregionalism: The Case of Latin America and Sub-Saharan Africa*. Scientific Paper No 23. Atlantic Future Project.

Meana, A. (2016) *A política africana do Brazil nos governos de Lula (2003–10) e no primeiro mandato de Dilma Rousseff (2011–14)*. MA thesis, Instituto Superior de Ciências Sociais e Políticas da Universidade de Lisboa.

Meissner, K. (2017) Resorting to Bilateralism: The EU, MERCOSUR, and the Strategic Partnership with Brazil. *Journal of European Integration*, 40 (1), 51–66.

Miyamoto, S. (2011) A política externa brasileira para a África no início do novo século: interesses e motivações. *XI Congresso Luso Afro Brasileiro de Ciências Sociais*. Salvador.

Moraes, I. and Mattos, B. (2012) Cooperação Brazil-África em biocombustíveis durante o governo Lula: uma parceria para o desenvolvimento. *Conjuntura Austral*, 3 (13), 54–71.

Oliveira, G. (2015) Política Africana do Brazil: mudança entre Lula e Dilma? *Conjuntura Austral*, 6 (29), 33–47.

Pavese, C. (2014) *Level-linkage in European Union–Brazil Relations: An Analysis of Cooperation on Climate Change, Trade, and Human Rights*. PhD thesis, The London School of Economics and Political Science (LSE).

Pavese, C. (2018) *The European Union and Brazil in the Quest for Global Climate Governance: Potentials and Perils of a Partnership*. IAI Paper Series, 18 (11).

Pereira, A. (2012) Continuity is not lack of change. *Critical Sociology*, 38 (6), 777–787.

Pinho, C. (2013) Cooperación Sur-Sur para el Desarrollo: Las Relaciones Brazil África en la Promoción de las Políticas Públicas (2003–2012). *América Latina Hoy*, 63, 91–112.

President Lula (2007) *Discurso do Presidente da República, Luiz Inácio Lula da Silva, por ocasião da audiência com embaixadores africanos*. Brasilia, Palácio do Planalto, 25 May.

Ribeiro-Hoffmann, A. and Marcondes, D. (2017) Maritime regions and the South Atlantic. *Contexto Internacional*, 39 (2), 229–236.

Rizzi, K. (2014) *O grande Brazil e os pequenos PALOP: a política externa brasileira para Cabo Verde, Guiné-Bissau e São Tomé e Príncipe (1974–2010)*. Porto Alegre: Leitura XXI.

Saraiva, M. (2014) Balanço da política externa de Dilma Rousseff: perspectivas futuras? *Relações Internacionais*, 44, 25–35.

Saraiva, F. (2012) *África parceria do Brazil atlântico: Relações Internacionais do Brazil e da África no início do século XXI*. Belo Horizonte: Fino Traço.

Schlesinger, S. (2012) *Cooperação e investimentos internacionais do brasil: A internacionalização do etanol e do biodiesel*. São Paulo: FASE.

Silva, A. (2010) As transformações matriciais da Política Externa Brasileira recente (2000–2010). *Meridiano 47*, 11 (120), 18–24.

Silva, A. (2018) *A política externa do governo Dilma Rousseff: identificando interesses e condicionantes*. 4º Seminário de Relações Internacionais da ABRI. Foz do Iguaçu: ABRI.

Stolte, C. (2012) *Brazil in Africa: Just Another BRICS Country Seeking Resources?* Chantham House Briefing Paper, No 1. London: Chantham House.

Suyama, B., Waisbich, L. and Leite, I. (2016) Brazil as a development partner under Lula and Rousseff: Shifts and continuities. In J. Gu, A. Shankland and A. Chenoy (eds), *The BRICS in International Development*. London: Palgrave MacMillan (pp. 25–62).

Teixeira, R. and Pinto, E. (2012) *A economia política dos governos FHC, Lula e Dilma: dominância financeira, bloco no poder e desenvolvimento econômico*. UFRJ – Textos para Discussão, No 006. Rio de Janeiro: UFRJ.

UNDP (2013) *Project in Support of 2010–2012 Electoral Cycles in the Portuguese-speaking African Countries and Timor-Leste (ProPALOP/TL)*. Final Report. UNDP.

Vigevani, T. and Cepaluni, G. (2007) A política externa de Lula da Silva: a estratégia da autonomia pela diversificação. *Contexto internacional*, 29 (2), 273–335.

Vilas-Bôas, J. (2011) Os investimentos brasileiros na África no governo Lula: um mapa. *Meridiano 47*, 12 (128), 3–9.

Vilella, F. (2013) Feira de defesa e segurança vai trazer bons acordos para o Brazil, diz Amorim. *Agência Brazil*. www.ebc.com.br/noticias/brasil/2013/04/feira-de-defesa-e-seguranca-vai-trazer-bons-acordos-para-o-brasil-diz-amorim. (retrieved 22 September 2014).

Wisniewski, B. and Dahad, S. (2017) The European Union Strategic Partnership Agreement with Brazil: Ten years of action in place and future perspectives. *Studia Europejskie*, 4, 55–71.

World Bank and IPEA – Instituto de Pesquisas Econômicas Aplicadas (2011) *Ponte sobre o Atlântico: Brazil e África Subsaariana, parceria Sul-Sul para o crescimento*. Brasília: IPEA.

World Bank (2018) DataBank [online]. http://databank.worldbank.org (retrieved 15 November 2018).

20

Toward a post-Westphalian turn in Africa-EU studies?

Non-state actors and sustainable development

Mark Langan and Sophia Price

Introduction

Private non-state actors have increasingly emerged as the focus of scholarly work within the field of International Political Economy (IPE) and Development Studies. Moving beyond strictly Realist and/or Westphalian paradigms, IPE as an emergent discipline has sought to fully recognise the potential clout of non-state agents in shaping the contours of economic globalisation – and therein of interstate power relations and sovereignties. In particular, much work has been paid to the role of business associations within global value chains (see, for example, Bair, 2002), the role of trade unions in shaping core labour standards and decent work prerogatives (see, for example, Vosko, 2002), the role of individual corporations in pushing forward private sector development (PSD) in the Global South (see, for example, Madeley, 1999) and the role of non-governmental organisations (NGOs) and civil society in pushing forward new global agendas, such as on trade justice and migration (see, for example, Hughes et al., 2008). In this vein, scholars have adopted a post-Westphalian outlook – or what might more accurately be termed a 'Westphalia Plus' perspective – within IPE which recognises the importance of nation states and of state sovereignties, yet moves beyond the strict state-centrism of orthodox International Relations (IR).

This shift, via IPE, towards a 'Westphalia Plus' perspective is an essential component of any contemporary study of Africa-EU relations. Of course, nation states do continue to play a crucial role in shaping both the economic and political relationship between the two blocs. It is nation states that form the constituent members of both the African Union (AU), the African, Caribbean and Pacific (ACP) Group[1] and the European Union (EU) – the three most vital institutional interlocutors in terms of pushing forward Africa-EU affairs. It is imperative, however, to temper any analysis of AU/ACP and EU ties with proportionate focus on the agency of trade unions, corporations, civil society and other private non-state actors. Only by understanding the agency and potential clout of such bodies in (re)shaping agendas and implementing 'development' policies, can the contours of Africa-EU affairs be realised. Omitting consideration of private non-state actors within a myopic focus on Westphalian nation states and supranational agencies would surely lead to lopsided analysis on a number of policy fronts – whether trade, environment, gender justice or aid delivery. It would also surely miss how these private non-state actors can either support or undermine developing country sovereignties within Africa-EU affairs.

This chapter, accordingly, examines the role of non-state actors with regards to sustainable development, sovereignty and neo-colonialism in Africa, both north and south of the Sahara. It examines (i) business associations and corporate actors with regards to PSD and economic development and (ii) NGOs and civil society with regards to trade justice. In so doing, the chapter explores the influence of non-state private actors in shaping African states' sovereign space (or lack thereof) for pro-poor development. For instance, the chapter explores the role of Unilever in pushing forward PSD strategies as part of the United Nations (UN) Global Compact, which in turn has had a marked influence on the 'pro-poor' growth policies of the European Commission. Moreover, the chapter illustrates how individual corporate actors such as Tullow Oil often work in tandem within official state bodies (such as the United Kingdom's Department for International Development [DFID]) to influence European policy, often with dubious consequences for empirical sovereignty within African countries. In addition, the chapter details how business associations – such as the National Association of Nigerian Traders – may play a progressive role in relation to African state sovereignties for pro-poor economic development. For example, it explores warnings about the likely impact of premature trade liberalisation and neo-colonialism under EU-sponsored free trade agreements (FTAs) in both sub-Saharan Africa and the Maghreb.

In a similar vein, the chapter illustrates how NGOs and civil society groups have played an active role in shaping policy space for sustainable development with regard to FTAs. In so doing it illustrates how NGOs and civil society bodies may represent a voice for greater social justice and African state sovereignties within bi-continental affairs. However, the chapter demonstrates that in some instances civil society can do more to reinforce neo-colonial economic relations than to meaningfully restructure Africa-EU ties towards greater emphasis on genuine sustainable development. As a foreground to these discussions, meanwhile, the chapter first reflects on existing works within Africa-EU studies that have drawn attention to the importance of analysing private non-state actors' agency. This underscores how scholars of Africa-EU ties have increasingly embraced a Westphalia Plus perspective to better grasp issues surrounding trade and economic relations. It also serves as a necessary reminder of the complexities of the Africa-EU relationship and as a springboard for the chapter's interrogation of the significance of private non-state actors in shaping African state sovereignties for sustainable development.

A Post-Westphalian turn within Africa-EU Studies?

Historically there has been a strong Westphalian and/or Realist leaning within studies of the Africa-EU relationship, defined in terms of EU ties with the Maghreb and with the ACP grouping (of which sub-Saharan African nations form the majority). Notably, in the negotiations leading up to- and during the lifetime of- the ACP-EU Lomé Conventions (1975–2000), the majority of authors adopted state-centric perspectives in alignment with preponderant debates within IR. Seminal contributions from Zartman (1971) and Ravenhill (1985), for instance, examined nation states' negotiation capacities in terms of North-South power relationships. Zartman (1971: 1–4) argues that developing countries could utilise their 'weak' status to morally cajole 'strong' developed nations in Europe into making significant concessions on terms of trade, as well as aid allocations. This chimes with the 'spirit of Lomé' in which ACP countries did manage to secure significant concessions from the then European Economic Community (EEC), particularly in terms of the promise of non-reciprocal trade (which did *not* expect ACP countries to reduce tariffs in return for advantageous access to Europe). Ravenhill (1985), meanwhile, in a landmark monograph on 'collective clientelism' interrogated how former colonies could band together to secure significant concessions from the European metropole even within relations of dependency. This cautiously optimistic outlook, in terms of African states' capacity to achieve concessions in North-South ties, was echoed within a number of additional studies; for instance, Gruhn (1976) argues that ACP countries and the EEC were slowly inching towards interdependence (as opposed to dependency relations).

State-centric/Westphalian perspectives were also widely adopted in terms of the more radical or 'critical' contributions within studies of Africa-EU ties during this time the Lomé conventions. Galtung, for instance, explored theories of imperialism in his influential text *The European Economic Community: A Superpower in the Making* (1973). In his discussion, he identifies how the EEC politically manipulated North African and sub-Saharan African nations and perpetuated relations of economic dependency through skewed trade and aid linkages. His broad thesis was supported by numerous other authors, including Robert (1980), who critiqued unequal development and dependency in terms of the EEC and the Maghreb (North Africa) and the Mashreq (Arabia), and Martin (1982), who critiqued European officials' embrace of Eurafrican discourse in order to perpetuate domination over territories in sub-Saharan Africa under consecutive ACP-EU agreements. While departing from the more optimistic findings of Zartman, Ravenhill and Gruhn, the critical scholars nevertheless maintained a preponderant focus on the behaviour of states within the international system – as in keeping with the zeitgeist of IR prior to the emergence of IPE.

However, with impactful contributions, such as by Strange (1986), Rosenau (1988) and Hocking and Smith (1997), helping to construct and cement IPE as a separate (sub)discipline within the study of economic globalisation, the literature on Africa-EU affairs increasingly turned towards a post-Westphalian focus. Usefully here, the work of Price and Nunn (2016) creates a typology of rival critical interpretations of the Africa-EU relationships, highlighting how in addition to the Realist tradition, there have emerged alternative accounts that share materialist foundations, broadly understood as Gramscian or uneven and combined development approaches, as well as non-materialist social constructivist accounts. Within the variety of these critical approaches, there has been a concerted attempt to balance consideration of state strategies with the simultaneous examination of the role of private non-state actors, including the business community, trade unions and civil society groups. In 1999, for instance, Bretherton and Vogler (1999) offered an ambitious critique of the EU as a global actor with focus on both North and sub-Saharan Africa. In so doing they sought to locate the EU within a complex web of international agents, including transnational corporations and civil society. Gibb (2000), meanwhile, provides a detailed account of the role of Chiquita, the multinational fruit company, in sparking the 'banana wars' between the EU and the United States, hence precipitating the demise of the ACP-EU Lomé Conventions and their preferential trade scheme. In more recent times, this Westphalia Plus perspective has been augmented by a number of studies, such as by Langan (2011), who focused on business stakeholder perspectives within vulnerable ACP sectors; Teivainen and Trommer (2017), who examined civil society campaigns in West Africa with regards to the controversial Economic Partnership Agreements (EPAs); Hurt (2016), who has assessed trade union influence in EPA negotiations; and Orbie et al. (2016), who have considered the role played by civil society groups in Africa-EU trade reforms.

Within these varied readings there has been a discernible movement from the sole focus on Westphalian nation states and supranational EU institutions to consideration of private non-state actors. They have not denied the importance of state actors' decision-making. On the contrary, they have sought to contextualise how African countries' sovereign policy space is shaped and conditioned by the behaviour of corporations, trade unions and civil society (in addition to the actions of the EU and its member states). Following their example, the chapter now examines the agency of private non-state actors and NGO/civil society groups in shaping African state sovereignties for the achievement of sustainable development. In so doing, it provides critical discussion of neo-colonialism and how non-state actors may at times enhance – and at other times diminish – African countries' empirical sovereignty in relation to 'development' cooperation with the EU.

Business and the private sector: Whither African sovereignty for sustainable development?

It is imperative for contemporary studies of Africa-EU relations to interrogate the role of business sector associations and multinational corporations in relation to African countries' sovereign space for sustainable economic growth. This section explores examples of a variety of such interventions within the ACP-EU relationship, particularly in relation to the promotion of PSD strategies, the development of public-private financing mechanisms and attempts to both influence and oppose European policy.

Blended aid finance mechanisms

Business interests have increasingly worked in tandem with the EU to provide and support development finance. In particular, the European Commission (2016) has increasingly advocated the need for 'aid blending' – that is, marrying public aid monies with private investment from major European corporations into perceived investment opportunities in Africa. This will apparently mobilise sufficient capital for job creation and economic expansion, thereby leading in turn to poverty reduction through trickle-down growth. In one notable articulation of this PSD rationale, the European Commission confidently asserts that:

> The development landscape is expanding … the private sector is increasingly a key partner in fostering more sustainable models of development. Combining public and private resources to leverage more investments is allowing to step up engagement, also in challenging environments. A realignment of global resources and investments is needed to achieve sustainable development.
>
> *(European Commission, cited in Langan, 2018: 180)*

In such narratives, private sector actors are welcomed as a 'missing link' within development policies and as vital partners for national (and supranational) institutions, including the both the Commission and the European Investment Bank (EIB). The EU's preference for aid blending rests on the ways in which public and private finance combine to attract additional financing. 'It is estimated that since 2007, EUR 2 Billion worth of EU grants have leveraged approximately EUR 20 billions of loans by European finance institutions and regional development banks' (European Commission and the High Representative of the Union for Foreign Affairs and Security Policy, 2016: 111). Trust funds are a key blending mechanism developed within the current European Development Fund, which introduced two types: the Emergency and Post Emergency Trust Funds (designed to address crises) and the Thematic Trust Funds (aimed at addressing global challenges). Examples include the EU-Africa Infrastructure Trust Fund (2007), the Caribbean Investment Facility (2012), the Investment Facility for the Pacific (2012) and the Africa Investment Facility (2015) (ibid.).

Nevertheless, there is considerable evidence that the EU's emphasis on public-private partnerships is not necessarily a progressive step forward for genuine sustainable development in Africa. Experience – both north and south of the Sahara – indicates that the behaviour of European corporate actors, and that of the EU's own institutions, often transgresses ostensible norms relating to poverty reduction and equitable growth. Perhaps most infamously, the EIB was heavily censured by the European Parliament for its financial involvement with Glencore Plc. and (therein) mining operations within conflict-affected states including the Democratic Republic of the Congo (Counter Balance, 2011). The EIB in this instance was criticised for leveraging funds to Glencore's portfolio investments despite concerns about environmental hazards, workers' rights and the siphoning of profits via tax havens (depriving the host nation of otherwise lucrative taxation revenues) (ibid.). Importantly, a coalition of NGOs – including Eurodad, Oxfam and ActionAid – maintain that the European Commission has not yet learnt the lessons of episodes such as that of the EIB-Glencore affair (Eurodad, 2014). They state that the EU continues to favour aid blending in the interests of European corporations, rather than channelling funds to small and medium-sized enterprises within African countries, that might genuinely provide the engine of growth. In stark language these NGOs claim that it is 'questionable whether EU companies should be supported through development policy given the need for additional development resources and the risk of increasing aid tied to the delivery of European goods and services' (ibid.).

Private sector development and the UN Global Compact

In the timeframe of the UN Sustainable Development Goals (SDGs) and the European Commission's championing of Goal 8 on PSD and equitable economic growth, it becomes immediately apparent that corporate actors have played a significant role in shaping 'development' interventions in Africa. Most notably, major corporate actors, including Unilever, grouped together within the UN Global Compact and voiced their relative dissatisfaction with the human needs focus of the preceding Millennium Development Goals (MDGs) (Langan, 2018: 179–180). The business community – via UN organs – expressed the need for a more hard-headed approach to development, focused on the stimulation of the private sector and on trickle-down free market growth. Subsequently, the contemporary SDGs – in contrast to the MDGs – now explicitly reinforce the role of the private sector within development. This is further evidenced in, for example, Unilever's Sustainable Living Plan. The plan proposes a conceptualisation of sustainability based on a virtuous circle of growth that revolves around Unilever brands, people and operations, which generate profitable volume growth, cost efficiencies and innovation with marketing investment. This business-orientated approach to sustainability is reinforced and legitimised through the partnerships with NGOs, such as Unilever's relation with Oxfam, which sits on its Sustainable Sourcing Advisory Board.

Mawdsley (2015) convincingly argues that the post-2015 SDG agenda has cemented the ideational and institutional focus on PSD, paving the way for increased reliance on so-called 'public-private partnerships' for sustainable development. For Price and Nunn (2016), this amounts to legitimisation processes for the expansion of the world market. This private sector focus within the UN SDGs has had a marked impact on the language and policy outlook of the European Commission with regard to its interventions in Africa. EU officials have enthusiastically welcomed the PSD discourse emanating from the UN and have emphasised that EU action for sustainable development will likewise prioritise the business community as part of public-private initiatives.

Leveraging policy influence

While the partnership between the private sector and policymakers is often celebrated and encouraged, there have been concerns raised about the uncomfortable alliances between official governance institutions (such as the European Commission) and corporate actors at the level of the EU member states themselves. Attention has been focused on the manner in which individual corporate actors can work in tandem within official state bodies in order to influence European policy, often with dubious consequences for empirical sovereignty within African countries. In the case of the United Kingdom, for instance, there has been much concern about the relationship between DFID and the Anglo-Irish corporation Tullow Oil. In the case of Tullow investments in Ghana's oil discoveries, for instance, there are claims from local campaigners that DFID funding towards the Ghana Oil and Gas for Inclusive Growth programme helped to pressure the Ghanaian Parliament into passing the controversial Oil Exploration and Production (E&P) bill (Lungu, 2016a). Specifically, there were concerns that DFID monies had filtered down to co-opted think tanks who in turn lobbied local politicians to support the legislation, despite the fact that it would enable the energy minister to overturn the results of competitive tendering. Moreover, the E&P bill, now passed by the Ghanaian legislature, was condemned for failing to secure sufficient oil proceeds from Tullow Oil and other foreign investors (ibid.).

Opposing EU policy

It is important to note though that there are progressive instances of private sector actors and business associations doing more to support African state sovereignties for genuine sustainable development, rather than perpetuating neo-colonial economic extraction as with the case above. Notably, business associations north and south of the Sahara have raised local objections to the European Commission's pursuit of premature trade liberalisation via FTAs. In West Africa, for instance, the National Association of Nigerian Traders has played a leading role in mobilising Nigerian politicians in resistance to the imposition of an EPA (European Parliament, 2014: 20). In turn, through Nigeria's hardening position on the EPAs, the European Commission has been frustrated in its realisation of a region-wide EPA with the Economic Community of West African States (ECOWAS). The National Association of Nigerian Traders, through their media campaigns and convincing critique of the impact of tariff dismantling for nascent industry and agro-processing within Nigeria and West Africa, has thereby helped to stall implementation of detrimental trade deals. In similar fashion, North African business leaders have raised alarms about the potential implications of the EU's pursuit of Deep and Comprehensive Free Trade Agreements with nations such as Tunisia and Morocco (ATTAC/CADTM Morocco, 2015). For instance, a European Commission (2015) engagement with Tunisian stakeholders, including businesspeople, indicated a number of core concerns about the impact of premature liberalisation, as well as export barriers into the EU common market. In Morocco, meanwhile, the General Confederation of Morocco Enterprises successfully lobbied its government to enact studies of the likely implications of the proposed Deep and Comprehensive Free Trade Agreements for core economic sectors. Through such actions, business representatives north and south of the Sahara have signalled their deep concerns with EU trade agendas, stimulating wider public and political awareness of the potential dangers of liberalisation both at home and in the political corridors of the EU (ATTAC/CADTM Morocco, 2015: 9).

Civil society organisations and other NGO engagement in the EU-Africa partnership

The public and political concerns about the programmes of trade liberalisation between Africa and the EU have been particularly evident in the EU-ACP relationship since the signing of the Cotonou Agreement in 2000 and the EPA negotiations that it spawned. In particular, civil society groups have argued that the pursuit of free trade through the EPA process will undermine the sustainable development of the EU's partners across the Global South. As such, the opposition mounted to the EU's trade liberalisation agenda by certain sections of the private sector has been matched by trade unions and other civil society actors and organisations.

In South Africa, for example, debate has been ongoing in relation to the country's free trade negotiations with the EU. The Congress of South African Trade Unions (COSATU) has been a long-standing critic of EU-South Africa free trade relations, both under the Trade and Development Cooperation Agreement signed in 1999 and the EPA between the EU and the South Africa Development Cooperation (SADC) (Hurt, 2016). COSATU argued that tariff reductions would result in job losses, particularly in the textile sector, and that the costs of adjusting to trade liberalisation would be disproportionately carried by South Africa rather than the EU. COSATU viewed FTAs as opportunities for the EU to open up markets in Africa for the benefit of European capital, incorporating those areas of trade that proved difficult to deal with at a global level through World Trade Organization agreements (known as the Singapore issues). They argued that EPAs would undermine regional integration and sustainable development, supporting the position of those states that refused to sign or ratify the agreements and interim agreements. A particular critique made by COSATU was that the negotiations included a relatively narrow range of actors with a lack of engagement with trade unions and civil society organisations (ibid.).

In West Africa, meanwhile, these core debates were replicated by other civil society organisations (CSOs) in reaction to the EU-West Africa proposals for trade liberalisation. A network of West African global justice NGOs, local NGOs and trade unions emerged and coalesced around the West Africa EPA negotiations (Teivainen and Trommer, 2017). This regional civil society network, called Plateforme des Acteurs de la Societe Civile Ouest Africane sure L'Accor do Cotonoue (the Platform), included 15 development, anti-poverty and global social justice organisations, social movements and trade unions from 11 countries. It emerged in the late 1990s as a group of actors concerned with EU-Africa development and trade cooperation and opposed to the liberalisation of West African economies, both in relation to its tradeties relations with the EU and the wider global economy. The Platform sought to highlight societal concerns with trade policies based on free trade and to develop alternative development frameworks, which included a preference for greater regional cooperation and civil society engagement.

Attempts by the Platform to gain a voice in the EU-West Africa negotiations were initially met with resistance by ECOWAS officials, who felt that they were challenging their role as they had been mandated to negotiate free trade deals. Teivainen and Trommer (2017: 25–26) outline three core tactics employed by the Platform in order to gain a position in the ECOWAS negotiating team. First, it questioned the conceptualisation of trade as a neutral realm, arguing instead that is a contested developmental issue that needs civil society inclusion. Second, it provided legal and economic expertise to balance the negotiating capacity between the two sides. Third, it worked on building the solidarity between West African civil society and trade officials. Over time, West African public officials accepted the inclusion of the Platform, as it added technical capacity and was able to wield influence towards EU public officials. The Platform gained a position on the ECOWAS negotiating team, with its representatives having access to the policy-making process and being able to speak at ECOWAS meetings. Teivainen and Trommer argue that as such their access amounted to a 'rare level of political inclusion in international trade negotiations' (ibid.: 25). In this way, this disparate network of civil society actors was able to shape state sovereignty in order to achieve a particular conceptualisation of sustainable development.

Other proposed trade liberalisation agreements have, however, not been met with such organised and widespread opposition. For example, while there has been mobilisation against the

EU-Morocco Deep and Comprehensive Free Trade Agreement, this is described by ATTAC/CADTM Morocco (2015: 9) as 'paltry' in relation to the scale of change the deal proposes. The alliance has sought to publicise the threat posed to the Moroccan economy and people through trade liberalisation with the EU, arguing there are a number of key issues in relation to this agreement. They argue that there is a need for greater democracy, transparency and public debate surrounding trade negotiations, and they highlight the threat to Moroccan sovereignty from what they regard as the EU's colonialist agenda, based on the economic imbalance between the 'partners'. The alliance raises a similar range of concerns to that of CSOs in other parts of Africa in relation to the economic impact of trade liberalisation with the EU, arguing that this will worsen inequalities between regions and bring commodification and dismantling of public services.

While these examples of anti-free trade campaigns from North, West and Southern Africa have drawn on the activism of CSOs and trade unions at a regional level, their concerns have an obvious internationalist dimension, particularly in relation to the implications for European labour and the competitive position of interregional and global trade liberalisation agendas. However, there have been difficulties in building coalitions of opposition between labour movements in both the EU and Africa. For example, COSATU sought to build transnational labour solidarity with organised labour in Europe through cooperation with both The European Trade Union Confederation and the International Confederation of Free Trade Unions. The positions of these organisations, however, differed to that taken by COSATU, as they neither challenged the underlying ethos of free trade nor questioned the impact on partners. Instead these organisations focused on 'reformist' positions; for example, with proposals to lengthen transition periods and to include a social clause to balance the impact of free trade (Hurt, 2016: 547–548). However, recently, within the EU there has been growing social organisation and trade union activism against trade liberalisation; for example, by the Trade Justice Movement, which is a United Kingdom-based coalition of nearly 70 CSOs. Such organisations however have been most active in countering the EU's trade negotiations with both the United States, in relation to the Transatlantic Trade and Investment Partnership, and Canada, in relation to the EU-Canada Comprehensive Economic Trade Agreement, rather than those with Africa. While such campaigns tend to have a global perspective in pursing trade rules that have a poverty reduction and sustainable development focus, they have been particularly successful in garnering public support and mobilisation in relation to the issue of domestic public sector marketisation in the Global North as an integral part of the trade liberalisation agenda.

The public and political concern, both in Africa and the EU, about free trade and its consequences for labour and the environment have driven the inclusion of a sustainable development chapter in the EU trade agreements, which creates institutionalised mechanisms for civil society participation. For example, in relation to the EU-SADC EPA, the SADC-EU Outreach South Africa Initiative and the SADC-EU EPA High Level Civil Society Forum have been created as vehicles for civil society engagement. The inclusion of these mechanisms into the EPA negotiations across the EU's ACP partners is designed to address core issues such as labour rights, environmental principles and economic development. This ongoing commitment to the inclusion of civil society actors in the EU-ACP relationship has been matched by a similar approach in the broader Africa-EU partnership. This includes a commitment to 'facilitate and promote a broad-based and wide-ranging people-centred partnership by ensuring the effective participation of civil society and the private sector and by delivering direct benefits for African and European citizens' (Africa-EU Partnership, n.d.). The Joint Africa-EU Strategy (JAES) which underpins the partnership contains a firm commitment to the creation of a permanent platform for information, participation and mobilisation of a broad spectrum of civil society actors in the EU and Africa and beyond.

As part of this commitment in the JAES, the Africa–EU Civil Society Forum brings together representatives of African and European CSOs. The forum prioritises sustainable development and has outlined a range of core concerns, which include: (i) the decent work agenda and the inclusion of core labour standards into trade agreements; (ii) the involvement of civil society in the implementation and monitoring of the EU External Investment Plan; (iii) public-private partnerships that support national development priorities; and (iv) the use of official development aid to support poverty reduction and not to let it become a subsidy for businesses (Africa-EU Civil Society Forum, 2017: 1–5). The explicit commitment within the JAES to the inclusion of civil society actors into the Africa-EU relationship has been problematised in a variety of ways. The Africa-EU Civil Society Forum itself has highlighted how, despite the formal recognition of the valuable role that civil society actors can play in the Africa-EU partnership, the space for such organisations has shrunk and they occupy a relatively weak position in the strategic framework. This prompted the forum to call on EU and African institutions and leaders to deliver a series of reforms: (i) increased support for the involvement of CSOs; (ii) the improvement of the flow of information and entry points for such organisations; (iii) increased financial support and the delivery of the political commitments to create a truly enabling environment for civil society participation; and (iv) to ensure the inclusion of the full range of society as part of a multi-stakeholder policy process (ibid.).

Such demands for an increased space and role for civil society actors, however, raise broader issues of representation and legitimacy as well as questioning the extent to which organisations should be permitted to exert influence over governance practices and agreements. For example, in relation to the West Africa-EU EPA negotiations, public officials raised questions about the role played by the Platform and about the legitimacy of their knowledge and position. Criticisms were levelled against the Platform that, instead of representing regional civil society, they were promoting their own sectional interests (Teivainen and Trommer, 2017: 25–26). The Platform contested this position, drawing on human and civil rights discourses to legitimate their position not as representatives but as participants. More broadly, another core concern is the risk of CSO co-optation into neoliberal paradigms that both legitimise and lock in inequality. Through participatory frameworks, NGOs and CSOs can, therefore, play a regressive rather than a progressive role in Africa-EU relations. The risks of co-optation are particularly dangerous for NGOs focused on environmental, human and labour rights.

Specifically, through CSO participation in trade liberalisation negotiations these bodies could become (or could be seen to become) legitimising forces for the neoliberal orientation of the EU's trade agreements. Cooke and Kothari (2001) refer to this as the tyranny of participatory development, which can lead to the unjust and illegitimate exercise of power. This exercise of power is not only through the practice of participatory development but also through its discourse. They argue that the emergence of participatory approaches, in opposition to the imposition of 'top-down' approaches, was aimed at co-opting those most affected by development decisions into decision-making procedures. Those most marginalised people therefore are provided with decision-making authority over their own lives. However, through their integration into neoliberal development policy and practice (seen here as trade liberalisation), the core agenda is ideologically legitimised. Kothari (2005) argues that this co-optation of 'alternative' approaches to mainstream neoliberal agendas, in turn, results in the ongoing professionalisation and technicalisation of the 'development industry'. The conscription of critical voices and contesting discourses into neoliberal frameworks and practices thus limits the effectiveness of their opposition.

In relation to the EU-ACP relationship, the potential critique of participatory development models has been recognised by Orbie et al. (2016). The authors argue that civil society actors are aware of the risks of co-optation and are able to successfully navigate them. However, they also concede that power asymmetries between non-profit and business actors risk reinforcing existing power relations. At times, however, preferences of the private sector and NGO/CSOs can coincide. In relation to EU-West Africa liberalisation, the opposition of the Platform to the proposed EPA coincided with an organised West African business and private sector, and both shared a focus on mobilising Nigerian politicians to resist the imposition of FTAs, ultimately stalling their implementation. However, the underlying rationales differed: for the Platform, the concern was that West Africa economic policy choices had not benefited West African populations, but rather represented vested interests; while business and private sector actors sought to protect themselves from competition from the EU.

Conclusion

As this chapter has shown, there has been both an increasing focus on the inclusion of non-state actors in the frameworks that govern Africa-EU relations and a need to develop the analytical and conceptual tools that help to understand those processes. In exploring these, attention needs to be placed on the role of private sector actors and CSOs and the manner in which these play an important role in shaping not only EU policies towards Africa, but also the possibilities for the exercise of empirical sovereignty within African polities themselves. Major corporate actors have played a significant role in shaping preferences at the national, regional and interregional levels, pursuing positions that have at times converged with civil society activists and organisations. It is evident therefore that non-state actors can either play a progressive or a regressive role in terms of equalising relations between ACP developing countries and the EU member states, particularly in terms of the co-optation of CSOs into neoliberal paradigms that lock in inequality. This prompts us to look beyond traditional Westphalian approaches, with their rigid focus on nation states and supranational institutions, to analyses that focus on the ways in which private non-state actors may support or close down, avenues for progressive African agency vis-à-vis the EU metropole.

Note

1 The ACP Group became the Organisation of African, Caribbean and Pacific States in 2020.

Bibliography

Africa-EU Civil Society Forum (2017) Declaration. Tunis, 12 July. www.africa-eu-partnership.org/sites/default/files/userfiles/africa-eu_civil_society_forum_-_declaration_en_final.pdf (retrieved 1 April 2018).

Africa-EU Partnership (n.d.) What is the Partnership? [online]. www.africa-eu-partnership.org/en/about-us/what-partnership (retrieved 1 April 2018).

ATTAC/CADTM Morocco (2015) *Free Trade Agreements: Colonial Agreements Against the People.* www.rosalux.eu/fileadmin/user_upload/Publications/free-trade-agreement-book-web.pdf (retrieved 1 April 2018).

Bair, J. (2002) Beyond the Maquila Model? NAFTA and the Mexican apparel industry. *Industry and Innovation*, 9 (3), 203–225.

Bretherton, C. and Vogler, J. (1999) *The European Union as Global Actor.* London: Routledge.

Cooke, B. and Kothari, U. (2001) *Participation and the New Tyranny?* London: Zed Books.

Counter Balance (2011) *The Mopani and Glencore Case: An Overview.* Brussels: Counter Balance. www.counter-balance.org/the-mopani-and-glencore-case-an-overview/ (retrieved 1 April 2018).

Eurodad (2014) *Policy Brief on the Role of the Private Sector in Europe's Development Co-operation.* Brussels: Eurodad. http://eurodad.org/files/pdf/548870976e1f9.pdf (retrieved 1 April 2018).

European Commission (2015) *Results of the Stakeholder Consultation.* Brussels: European Commission. http://trade.ec.europa.eu/doclib/docs/2017/april/tradoc_155469.pdf (retrieved 1 April 2018).

European Commission (2016) *Sustainable Development: EU Sets Out Its Priorities.* Brussels: European Commission.

European Commission and the High Representative of the Union for Foreign Affairs and Security Policy (2016) Joint Staff Working Document Executive Summary of the Impact Assessment. SWD(2016)250final. Strasbourg, 15 July 2016.

European Parliament (2014) *African, Caribbean and Pacific (ACP) Countries' Position on the Economic Partnership Agreements (EPAs).* Brussels: European Parliament.

Galtung, J. (1973) *The European Community: A Superpower in the Making.* London: Allen & Unwin.

Gibb, R. (2000) Post-Lome: The European Union and the South. *Third World Quarterly*, 21 (3), 457–481.

Gruhn, I. (1976) The Lomé Convention: Inching towards interdependence. *International Organization*, 30 (2), 241–262.

Hocking, B. and Smith, M. (1997) *Beyond Foreign Economic Policy: The United States, the Single European Market and the Changing World Economy.* London: Pinter.

Hughes, A., Wrigley, N. and Buttle, M. (2008) Global production networks, ethical campaigning and the embeddedness of responsible governance. *Journal of Economic Geography*, 8 (3), 345–367.

Hurt, S. (2016) The EUs Economic Partnership Agreements with Africa: 'Decent work' and the challenge of trade union solidarity. *Third World Thematics*, 1 (4), 547–562.

Kothari, U. (2005) Authority and expertise: The professionalisation of international development and the ordering of dissent. *Antipode*, 37 (3), 425–446.

Langan, M. (2011) Uganda's flower farms and private sector development. *Development and Change*, 42 (5), 1207–1240.

Langan, M. (2017) *Neo-colonialism and the Poverty of 'Development' in Africa.* New York: Palgrave.

Lungu, N. (2016a) This Mahama-Dagadu-Buah 2016 E&P Bill is a vulture bill for oil companies. *The Voiceless.*

Lungu, N. (2016b) Mahama loses $6 billion of Ghana's oil money and still claims 'remarkable economic achievements'. Ghana Web, 13 August.

Madeley, J. (1999) *Big Business, Poor Peoples: How Transnational Corporations Damage the World's Poor.* London: Zed Books.

Martin, G. (1982) Africa and the ideology of Eurafrica: Neo-colonialism or Pan-Africanism? *Journal of Modern African Studies*, 20 (2), 221–238.

Mawdsley, E. (2015) DFID, the private sector and the re-centring of an economic growth agenda in international development. *Global Society*, 29 (3), 1–20.

Orbie, H., Martens, D., Oehri, M. and Van den Putte, L. (2016) Promoting sustainable development or legitimising free trade? Civil society mechanisms in EU trade agreements. *Third World Thematics*, 1 (4), 526–546.

Price, S. and Nunn, A. (2016) Managing neo-liberalisation through the Sustainable Development Agenda: The EU-ACP trade relationship and world market expansion. *Third World Thematics*, 1 (4), 454–469.

Ravenhill, J. (1985) *Collective Clientelism: The Lomé Convention and North South Relations.* New York: Columbia University Press.

Robert, A. (1980) The EEC and the Maghreb and Mashreq countries. In D. Seers and C. Vaitsos (eds), *Integration and Unequal Development: The Experience of the EEC.* London: MacMillan. (pp. 261–278).

Rosenau, J. (1988) The state in an era of cascading politics: Wavering concept, widening competence, withering colossus or weathering change. *Comparative Political Studies*, 21 (1), 13–44.

Strange, S. (1986) Casino Capitalism. Oxford: Blackwell.

Teivainen, T. and Trommer, S. (2017) Representation beyond the state: Towards transnational democratic non-state politics. *Globalizations*, 14 (1), 17–31.

Vosko, L. (2002) The shifting role of the ILO and the struggle for global social justice. *Global Social Policy*, 2 (1), 19–46.

Zartman, I.W. (1971) *The Politics of Trade Negotiations between Africa and the European Economic Community: The Weak Confront the Strong.* New York: Princeton University Press.

Part V
Opportunities to cooperate on new global challenges

Introduction to Part V

Asteris Huliaras and Sophia Kalantzakos

Every year, on 9 May, the European Union (EU) celebrates 'Europe Day'. On that day in 1950, the French Foreign Minister Robert Schumann presented his plan for political cooperation in Europe. The so-called Schumann Declaration is considered to be the founding text of European integration. Schumann, like all of Europe's founding fathers – which include Jean Monnet, Guy Mollet, Paul-Henri Spaak, Konrad Adenauer and Alcide de Gaspari – was convinced that Europe's best hope of becoming an independent power in a bipolar world was to increase its land mass, population and material wealth. Reflecting this thinking, Europe's founding fathers were passionate advocates of the idea of 'Eurafrica'. The Schumann Declaration made explicit reference to the development of Africa as one of the main objectives of the nascent European Community. However, this aspect of the Schumann Plan 'is often squeamishly excised from the text' (Hansen and Jonsson, 2016: 123). Indeed, it was the colonial era and the colonialist ideology that were lurking beneath the surface of the Eurafrica concept.

Europeans and Africans, however, both wanted to leave this past legacy behind. The journey which began in Rome in 1957 as a primarily colonial and paternalistic donor–recipient relationship, half a century later in Lisbon had become a professed 'partnership of equals'. The EU has made further significant strides in this direction over the last decades. Although increasingly challenged by China, the EU continues to be Africa's principal trading partner. Moreover, it is by far Africa's main source of foreign investment and its largest provider of development aid. The scope of the Euro-Africa relationship has been broadened beyond the traditional instruments of trade and aid to include new or redefined areas of cooperation, such as good governance, peace and security, migration and combatting terrorism. The United Nations Sustainable Development Goals (SDGs) have also become a point of reference that include, but are not limited to, poverty and hunger eradication, the reduction of inequality, security, environmental protection and climate change. In an interview just before the German election of 2019, Chancellor Angela Merkel proudly argued that the EU's 'policies on Africa now follow a common strategy, which a few years ago would have been unthinkable' (Guardian, 2019).

This new thinking was reflected in the EU Strategy for Africa adopted in 2005 and in the launch of the Africa-EU Strategic Partnership of 2007, which is implemented through periodic action plans. The EU has also negotiated a series of Economic Partnership Agreements (EPAs) with the 48 countries of sub-Saharan Africa. These agreements aim to liberalise trade in compliance with World Trade Organization rules and to create a shared trade and development partnership backed by development aid support. The European Development Fund (EDF) finances development programmes and initiatives in Africa with a budget of around €30 billion for the period 2017–2020. The EDF also provides funding for an African Peace Facility to finance the African Union's (AU) military operations on the continent. The EU Commission and the AU Commission now meet regularly, in the context of a 'continent-to-continent partnership'. Africa-EU summits are held regularly: in Cairo in 2000, Lisbon in 2007, Tripoli in 2010, Brussels in 2014 and Abidjan in 2017. Finally, the EU has deployed a number of military and civilian missions in Africa to promote peace and security.

EU-Africa relations have become more comprehensive and complex in response to a diverse array of new challenges and opportunities. Yet they also reflect geopolitical realignments that are currently under way. The writers in Part 5 of this volume examine important issues that inform the EU-Africa agenda, such as migration, environment and climate change, agriculture and land reform, and technology and innovation. They also question not only the gendered nature of the ongoing cooperation, but additionally the definition and role of civil society in EU-Africa engagement. As the EU-Africa partnership becomes more comprehensive, however, recurring questions of policy incoherence threaten to undermine efforts to reimagine the relationship. Relevant literature has examined different types of incoherence, including: horizontal incoherence, which reflects problems created by the interaction of various policy areas; vertical incoherence, which refers to policy coordination between the member states and the Commission; internal incoherence, which relates to consistency among the EU's different decision-making bodies and departments; external incoherence, which reflects donor-recipient relations; multilateral incoherence, which has to do with the relationships among international organisations; and finally narrative incoherence, which refers to the difference between what the EU does and what claims it is doing (Carbone, 2013).

One salient example of EU policy incoherence is migration. For many EU members, Africa figures as a continent on the move, its final destination the EU. Stemming off migration flows has become the central priority and increasingly the lens through which Africa policies are viewed in order to be acceptable to those EU members without a colonial past and for which there is no burning national interest for deeper engagement there. Perceived security interests, therefore, increasingly drive relations, with spillover effects in all areas of cooperation. The EU's approach to tackling migration has been to work with African countries in order to strengthen borders and crack down on smuggling networks. This has been accompanied by economic incentives in the form of new programmes, processes, partnerships and 'compacts'. In June 2016, the European Council agreed to deepen cooperation with key African countries of origin and transit. The EU has put into place and implemented this framework, starting with a number of priority countries – Mali, Nigeria, Niger, Senegal and Ethiopia. The so-called 'compacts' with these countries were designed to deliver clear targets and joint commitments combining different policy elements like development aid, trade, mobility, energy, security and digital policy in order to regulate migration.

However, the EU strategy to curb migration has undermined the EU's objective to promote democracy, the rule of law, respect for human rights and fundamental freedoms, bringing internationally isolated authoritarian leaders in from the cold. These African leaders are now seen by European policymakers as 'partners in migration management' (Hirt, 2018).

Another example of policy incoherence in relation to migration is evident in the EU's attempt to use development policy for pressuring African countries in an effort to control migration. A problem that arose from this strategy was that development aid actually enables migration by providing individuals with resources that facilitate movement across borders. After all, most migrants to Europe come from Senegal, which is richer than Mali, or from the more developed southern than the less developed northern region of Nigeria. Thus, it appears that the more the EU supports African development, the more increasing migration raises red flags vis-à-vis EU policy coherence. Still, a recent study based on data from 101 developing countries spanning 25 years has shown that governance aid does in fact reduce emigration rates from developing countries, in contrast to social and economic aid that seems to have no impact (Gamso and Yuldashev, 2018).

Development cooperation has, in fact, become subordinated to the EU's Common Foreign and Security Policy and linked to external security priorities. This has led to increasing tensions between the Directorate-General (DG) for External Relations in the European Commission and DG for International Cooperation and Development (DG DEVCO): the first criticises the second for not being focused enough on the wider foreign policy goals of the EU – and especially on security. Although on paper the Commissioner for Development has the portfolio for all developing countries, in practice DG DEVCO has become an 'empty shell' (Hurt, 2010: 166). Accordingly, the securitisation of the migration issue, as pointed out by Ana Paula Moreira Rodriguez Leite, Daniele Dionisio and Thauan Santos (Chapter 21), points to new areas of consideration such as a better understanding of the push and pull factors driving migration flows, but also how the Mediterranean as a space creates a maritime bridge to the coast of EU member states. A re-evaluation of governance structures and security mechanisms employed to stem off maritime migration in combination with new development strategies may help to offset irregular migration flows to Europe.

Another example of policy incoherence can be seen with respect to EU Common Agricultural Policy (CAP). For years, the CAP has been criticised for having a deleterious impact upon many African countries, thus undermining EU development aid priorities. EU subsidies have often led to overproduction, with excess production being 'dumped' on developing countries. Apart from this, the ever more stringent sanitary and environmental standards imposed by the EU represent an additional obstacle for African agricultural exports. As a result, the EU's CAP has been considered, with much justification, as impairing the EU's development policy that focuses on poverty reduction. Some analysts have argued that changes in EU policies in the last decade, however, have brought important benefits to African farmers through reductions in the anti-competitive subsidies paid to European producers and preferential access to European markets through the Everything But Arms initiative and the subsequent EPAs. Moreover, the EU and each EPA region in Africa have agreed on a list of sensitive agricultural products that are exempted from tariff liberalisation. In this area, therefore, it can be argued that there has been much progress towards greater policy coherence. Other analysts, however, disagree. For them the liberalisation of African agricultural markets under EPAs may provide further advantages to EU farm exports, leading to the decline of African agriculture incomes (e.g. Akokpari, 2017: 61).

In Chapter 24, Edward Lahiff presents an overview of how land, agriculture and natural resources have historically been at the heart of EU–Africa relations. He traces the evolution of the relationship in the interrelated areas of agriculture land, and food. He argues that only in recent years have policymakers and donors turned their attention to African smallholder farming as an important component of the domestic economy. In the past, both treaties and local land policies had favoured a small minority of larger-scale and commercially oriented farmers and companies. These had pushed for the production of commodities for export to Europe and had favoured the EU consumer. According to Lahiff, the AU has been central in this important policy shift, which also reflects current thinking about the impacts of the climate crisis and the drive to fulfil the SDGs. Areas of mutual concern for the EU and Africa now include addressing rising food insecurity, land tenure reform and job creation to offset migration.

Climate change and the environment as interlinked issues have been a focal point in EU-Africa relations, as pointed out by Simon Lightfoot in Chapter 22. EU policies across the board have sought to incorporate, address and fulfil SDGs. Moreover, in the past few years, the green economy, transnational water management and wildlife conservation have been prioritised by the EU's African partners. The African continent is particularly vulnerable to the impacts of the climate crisis. Although the framing of climate change and environmental issues may not necessarily align exactly with EU framings, Africans have become more vocal and assertive in ranking the issues that they prioritise locally. In this instance, African priorities with environmental and climate implications include the building of infrastructure, energy, land, food security and industrialisation efforts. The interplay between climate change and the environment is evident in the 2007 Joint Africa-EU Strategy (Council of the European Union, 2007: 2). Because the relationship continues to be asymmetrical, however, Africans are weary of an EU that designs climate and environmental policies that, in the end, seem to champion its own interests. As a result, there has been a push back and a demand for policies to better reflect the African context.

With the fourth industrial revolution already underway, Europe and Africa are hard pressed to deepen their cooperation in science, technology and innovation (STI). John Ouma-Mugabe and Petronella Chaminuka have pointed to the need to strengthen existing cooperation beyond established research and development as well as to promote science initiatives. They argue for the need to prioritise greater participation of the private sector and particularly small and medium-sized enterprises in order to spur technological development and innovation. They also stress the need to address new challenges and fulfil the SDGs. This project should be, in their opinion, a leading priority for EU-AU cooperation that can lead to capacity building. Keeping in line with local priorities, the authors emphasise the importance of STI in health research, food and nutrition, security and climate change.

In her contribution (Chapter 23), Uzoamaka Madu analyses the role and increasing centrality that civil society is playing in the evolution of the EU-Africa relationship. From the outset, Uzoamaka Madu argues not only that civil society as a concept is fluid, but that definitions of civil society are diverse, with differences rooted in alternative social and political philosophies. Its role, therefore, is heavily dependent on the socio-economic, political and cultural context within which it operates. Moreover, it is a European construct that might have limited application in EU-Africa relations. The chapter maps out the role of civil society over the last six decades of institutional relations between the EU and Africa and how it has been operationalised to serve as a watchdog that holds institutions to account; an advocate that raises societal awareness to promote change; a service provider responding to urgent societal needs, leading to its de facto NGOisation; and a source of expertise whose unique knowledge and experience helps shape policies and solutions. However, although the Cotonou Agreement marked the introduction of civil society into the institutional architecture of relations between the EU and the African, Caribbean and Pacific Group (which became the Organisation of African, Caribbean and Pacific States in 2020), forming the base for its 'embeddedness' in the Euro-African relationship, in the subsequent EPA agreements the provisions for civil society engagement were 'weak or lacking entirely'. Nevertheless, civil society organisations in both Europe and Africa were quite active in pressuring EU and African governments to rethink the EPAs (Del Felice, 2014).

In Chapter 24, Laura Davis raises the challenging question of how cooperation between the EU and the AU is gendered. To build her argument, she first examines the gendered nature of the EU as a foreign policy actor. She analyses the EU Global Strategy in order to assess the foreign policy content of EU-AU relations, which, she argues, cannot be assumed to be neutral or beneficial to gender equality. In the second part of her contribution, Davis considers how the Women, Peace and Security agenda and gender equality are addressed in different Africa-EU cooperation instruments. She seeks to demonstrate how EU-Africa cooperation needs to be understood within the context of an EU foreign policy that is highly gendered, patriarchal and Othering.

The authors in this section have pointed to new challenges and opportunities that will drive and inform EU-Africa relations in the future. Certainly, the world order is going through a period of major geopolitical realignment as China's Belt and Road Initiative seeks to unite Eurasia and Africa in a seamless web of connectivity through trade, infrastructure and the decarbonisation and digitalisation of the economy. Moreover, the growing climate crisis has already begun to trigger mass population movement and has impacted food and security in Africa. Disruptions, fatalities and economic downturns will now be more frequent, as COVID-19 has already indicated. Global challenges will need to be addressed in conditions of growing renationalisation narratives that threaten inter-state cooperation and the success of multilateral solutions. Therefore, the EU-Africa relationship should become an even greater priority for both continents, as their interdependence cannot be denied. A colonial Eurafrica is a legacy that neither side would like to resurrect. With growing African agency, however, a true partnership may emerge; one in which the asymmetry of power is progressively rectified.

Bibliography

Akokpari, J. (2017) The EU and Africa: The political economy of an asymmetrical partnership. In A. Montoute and K. Virk (eds), *The ACP Group and the EU Development Partnership*. London: Palgrave Macmillan (pp. 55–77).

Carbone, M. (ed.) (2013) *The European Union in Africa: Incoherent Policies, Asymmetrical Partnership, Declining Relevance?* Manchester: Manchester University Press.

Council of the European Union (2007) *The Africa-EU Strategic Partnership: A Joint Africa-EU Strategy*. Brussels: European Union.

Del Felice, C. (2014) Power in discursive practices: The case of the STOP EPAs campaign. *European Journal of International Relations*, 20 (1), 145–167.

Gamso, J. and Yuldashev, F. (2018) Targeted foreign aid and international migration: Is development-promotion an effective immigration policy? *International Studies Quarterly*, 62 (4), 809–820.

Guardian (2019) Merkel: Europe must unite to stand up to China, Russia and US. May 15. www.theguardian.com/world/2019/may/15/angela-merkel-interview-europe-eu-unite-challenge-us-russia-china

Hansen, P. and Jonsson, S. (2016) *Eurafrica: The Untold History of European Integration and Colonialism*. London: Bloomsbury.

Hirt, N. (2018) European missteps on African migration. *Current History*, 117 (799), 175–180.

Hurt, S.R. (2010) Understanding EU development policy: History, global context and self-interest? *Third World Quarterly*, 31 (1), 159–168.

21
Migration and the Mediterranean Sea
A maritime bridge between the EU and Africa

Ana Paula Moreira Rodriguez Leite, Thauan Santos and Daniele Dionísio da Silva

Introduction

Given the relations between redefined spaces and borders, it is not appropriate to define an exact concept and/or typologies for classifying migrants, especially because the migratory phenomenon is a constant in the history of human beings and their relationship with time and space. When considering the motivations for mobility, voluntary and forced migrations stand out. In the first case, it is necessary to identify the economic motivations that act as factors of repulsion for people who migrate looking for better living conditions, which, until the 20th century, were understood in terms of wage and employability. However, this concept has currently become more fluid and linked to the structural conditions of welfare states, especially when considering the South-North migratory axis. On the other hand, in forced migrations, the drivers are external and lead to the impossibility of survival or permanence (due to conflict or persecution in the basis of ethnic/religious origin). This can generate a flow of internally displaced persons (who do not cross the borders of the country itself) or refugees (who do cross national borders). Recently, a new modality has also been discussed: forced migration in the face of natural or environmental catastrophes. In this case, in the absence of international legislation that gives individuals adequate status, it is up to each recipient state to adapt its legal system for reception (Pereira, 2019).

The United Nations (UN) (1998) defines migration as a change of country and political-administrative structure, change of residence and establishing ties of integration, which may vary between a permanent or temporary duration. Besides, within the scope of the 2030 Agenda for Sustainable Development, migrants represent a priority attention group, since structural problems in countries generate global inequalities, which drive mobility due to extreme poverty, conflicts and poor living and working conditions. In this chapter, we examine migratory relations between the European Union (EU) and Africa from the perspective of the Mediterranean Sea, understood as a maritime bridge. Migration historically has been based around paths built through the maritime environment, although these are unregulated, and little mapped, and rarely studied in the theoretical-conceptual currents applied to migration. This lack of critical analysis may come from the lack of internationalist or borderline studies on the maritime environment.

Since 1960, we see an increase of the strategic relevance of the sea for states, mainly due to the development of new marine technologies. Furthermore, the sea, which was only a pathway, or an area of expansion of the terrestrial environment, also becomes a wider source of resources (more than just fishing resources). In this way, strategic documents and national and international legislation for the management of the sea emerged. Then, the process of securitising these areas arose to delimit threats such as human trafficking and smuggling, arms and drugs trafficking, piracy and armed robbery, or even terrorist acts such as the Mumbai bombings in 2008. Even today, the possibility of applying laws and practices from the terrestrial environment in sea areas and the delimitation of ownership over maritime areas (the idea of territorialisation) is not uncommon; however, many limitations of this extrapolation can be seen. In addition, in general, analyses that bring together migration and securitisation processes have their basis also in border debates and practices on land. As Dickson (2019) highlights, there has been little attention dedicated to how the sea is a living geography in its own right. Based on the processes of migration and securitisation taking place at sea, we discuss the particularities of migration through the maritime environment. We consider the Mediterranean Sea as a semi-closed sea with a unique historical, strategic and economic importance between Africa and Europe.

To this end, this chapter is structured as follows: initially, migration relations between the EU and Africa, as well as the forms adopted by the EU to regulate flows, are discussed from a strategic and a humanitarian perspective. Then, the analysis related to the case study of the three Mediterranean routes is presented. The data come from the databases of the European Border and Coast Guard Agency (Frontex) and the United Nations High Commissioner for Refugees, covering the period from 2015 to 2019. Because some data are not fully consolidated and/or updated, some analyses take 2018 as the base year. Finally, the maritime migration peculiarities are covered and we consider the case of boat people on the Mediterranean Sea. We try to show gaps in international maritime law, and offer some conclusions.

Migration relations in the EU-Africa-Mediterranean as a laboratory of dialogues

The European continent has historically received African migrants on its Mediterranean borders, which is why we suggest the Mediterranean Sea as a maritime bridge between the EU and Africa. Since the 1990s, however, the flow of migrants has increased in the South-North direction around the world, and the Global North, at the end of the Cold War, sought new hegemonic reorganisations. In parallel, the classification of 'new threats' has defined elements that could affect the security of states (among which is illegal immigration), presenting to an alternative to the humanitarian perspective traditionally applied to migrations. There are two nomenclatures to designate the situation of an immigrant: irregular and illegal. From a humanitarian perspective, an individual who migrates without meeting the host country's requirements is considered irregular, also referred to as undocumented; there is no illegality in the act of migrating even when the individual has no documents (and, therefore, the possibility to regularise their situation). However, from the state strategic perspective, this is considered illegal, since the individual has not fulfilled the requirements requested.

In fact, states are sovereign to create migratory policies according to their own conceptions, even in a more restrictive or selective way, taking into account national security objectives or humanitarian perspectives. In the EU, a communitarianisation of migratory policies has been managed according to the precepts of sharing competences, where states assumed the

Migration and the Mediterranean Sea

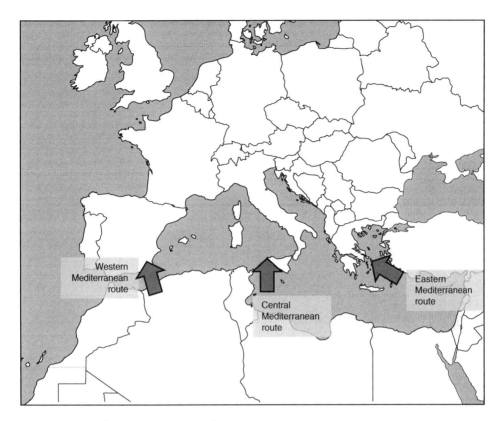

Figure 21.1 Mediterranean routes to the EU

commitment to follow supranational guidelines (Leite, 2016). According to Falzon (2012), 'the influx of immigrants has been very consequential indeed; on a popular level and in the public sphere, migration has become a "hot" topic'. As states change their migratory policies based on the production of (media, state or social) discourses from a 'fortress Europe' that closed itself off to an 'external enemy', the image of the migrant is criminalised, justifying increasing migratory controls.

Ergo, what would be the best way to reduce irregular migratory flow in a secure way, reconciling it to humanitarian action with the Mediterranean Sea as a bridge? For Zapata-Barrero (2019), human mobility has generated a singularity in the Mediterranean Sea, so that today it is a laboratory of dialogues. The solution envisaged by the EU would be external action by the Community aimed at reducing the factors of repulsion in nearby regions, thus discouraging the undertaking of migration. The region that would benefit from this agreement is the strategic environment comprising Africa, Asia and the Middle East. In the Mediterranean Sea, we highlight some cooperation projects, such as the European Neighbourhood Policy (ENP), created in 2003 in the form of a common policy with the aim of strengthening relations with the Union's neighbouring states to ensure that governments of the closest countries have the same security, cooperation and development goals, to achieve peace. Attention is focused on the Mediterranean Sea, extending the role of security policy beyond the Union's external borders. According to Lannon (2012), the ENP sought to reconcile unilateral, bilateral and multilateral initiatives, guided by strategy documents and action plans and using cooperation tools based

Table 21.1 Irregular arrivals by sea, by route (2015–2019) and by main origins, main destinations and sex (2018)

Sea irregular arrivals	2015	2016	2017	2018	2019	2018 Main origins	Main destinations	Men*	Women*
Western Mediterranean route***	7,004	9,990	23,063	57,034	23,733	Unknown, Morocco, Guinea	Spain, Canary Islands	48,000	4,638
Central Mediterranean route	153,946	181,376	118,962	23,485	13,760	Tunisia, Eritrea, Sudan	Italy, Malta	16,600	2,035
Eastern Mediterranean route***	885,386	182,277	42,319	56,561	82,564	Syria, Afghanistan, Iraq	Greece	25,400	12,902
Total	**1,046,336**	**373,643**	**184,344**	**137,080**	**120,057**	**Unknown, Syria, Morocco**	**Spain, Italy**	**90,000**	**19,575**

Notes: * Approximated values; ** In the remaining 4% of reported cases, the sex of the children was not available; *** Caution is needed when it comes to these two routes, as they are often considered both sea and land border types.

Source: Own elaboration based on Frontex and United Nations High Commissioner for Refugees (2019)

on soft law, rather than legal norms that create obligations for EU member states. In line with this, the Barcelona Process (1995) established as a priority the support for economic transition through the creation of a free trade zone that would serve as a foundation for development and socio-economic balance and, above all, as an environment of peace and stability.

For Leite (2016), the Euro-Mediterranean Regional Strategy and Indicative Programme (2007–2013) is based on the ENP and the Barcelona Process and defines objectives and priorities for regional cooperation seeking to act beyond bilateral relations. The strategy established three priorities: political cooperation, justice, security and migration; sustainable economic development; and social development and cultural exchange. In this document, cooperation for migration establishes measures of trust and civil protection for peace and analysis of migration, security and justice policies. Until the signing of these cooperation agreements, the migratory pattern between the regions was entirely different from the current one. With the Arab Spring in North Africa (from the end of 2010 on), there has been a massive escape of people, culminating in the biggest refugee crisis since World War II. According to Zanker (2019), the topic started to receive renewed attention at the Valletta Summit (2015) at a meeting with more than 60 heads of state and governments from Africa and the EU to establish strategies and partnerships between the two continents. This action plan is based on the cooperation mechanisms already established in the Rabat Process (2006), the Khartoum Process (2014) and the Joint Africa-EU Strategy (2007). Nonetheless, it is noteworthy that although these cooperation mechanisms have the objective of taking development to more vulnerable regions, we observe that there is a common security element, the main objective of the Community's migration policy and aimed at the neighbourhood.

In the same conjuncture mentioned before, if we direct these dialogues to Community migration policy and actions to the Mediterranean Sea area, we observe an increase of patrolling community actions through the operations of navies, coastguards and other government agencies. From October 2013 to the end of 2014, Operation Mare Nostrum (an Italian patrol system supported by the European Commission) charted vessels not following the registration rules for maritime safety and security, crossing the Mediterranean Sea in an illegal way. To this, there was added Operation Triton, restricted to European waters and executed by Frontex. Initially, Triton had fewer vessels and personnel than Mare Nostrum, and it focused on protecting borders rather than assistance, search and rescue.

According to Dickson (2019), since 2018 the Council of the European Union has established four Community operations in the Mediterranean Sea, focused specifically on securing European borders, disrupting smuggling networks and rescuing individuals in conditions of risk (European Council, 2018). Three of these operations were within Frontex jurisdiction: Indalo, Themis (which replaced Triton) and Poseidon. The fourth, Operation Sophia, started in 2015 and was framed as a European Mediterranean naval force, with naval and air assets and surveillance systems. Somehow, despite the securitisation process of maritime migration, European operations started to include steps of assistance, rescue and salvage at Sea (Bevilacqua, 2017).

Mediterranean migration data

In aggregate, detected illegal border-crossings at the EU's external borders in 2018 totalled 150,114 (−28,7% compared to 2017). 'This reversal continues to be the most significant development at the EU's external borders since the implementation of the EU-Turkey statement' (European Parliament, 2019: 8). Since 91.3% come via three Mediterranean routes (Western, Central or Eastern Mediterranean) (Figure 21.1), this chapter analyses the share of migrants according to these sea routes.

Table 21.1 shows irregular arrivals by sea routes only, between 2015 and 2019, according to main (African) origins, main (EU) destinations and the sex of migrants. There was drop in total sea irregular arrivals in the 2015–2018 period (−87.0%), although the volume through the Western Mediterranean route increased in the same period (+70.3%). Even if that figure exceeded 1 million migrants in 2015, this only corresponded to 0.21% of the total EU population (509.7 million, according to World Bank data), falling to 0.03% in 2018. In this period, the flow through the Western Mediterranean route begins to grow in June 2018 and reached its peak in October, followed by a sustained fall from January 2019. Regarding the flow from the Central Mediterranean route, it grew in May and August 2015, reaching its peak in October 2016, followed by a sustained drop from July 2017. Finally, the flow from the Eastern Mediterranean route started to grow from February 2015 and reached its peak in October, followed by a decline and then stability from April 2016.

In 2018, the share of the total flow of irregular arrivals by sea via the Eastern Mediterranean route was 41.7%, via the Western Mediterranean route, 41.0%, and via the Central Mediterranean route, 17.3%. In the same year, it is noteworthy that the main origins of migrants taking the Western Mediterranean route were unknown, Morocco and Guinea; for the Central Mediterranean route, the main origins were Tunisia, Eritrea and Sudan; and for the Eastern Mediterranean route, Syria, Afghanistan and Iraq. The presence of adult males stands out, with 65.7% of migrants in this category compared to 14.3% being female and 20.1% children; there was a high share of boys on the Western Mediterranean route (89%) and the Eastern Mediterranean route (56%). Regarding sea routes in 2018, it is worth mentioning the following:

- *Western Mediterranean route:* Morocco was the main departure point for irregular migrants (more than doubling in this year), and its main migratory pressure was linked to sub-Saharan countries.
- *Central Mediterranean route:* Tunisia was the main country of departure for irregular migrants (September, October and December), replacing Libya (−87%) and Algeria (−50%, almost). Together with Eritreans, they accounted for more than 33% of all detected migrants.
- *Eastern Mediterranean route:* Syria was the main country of departure for irregular migrants, followed by Afghanistan and Iraq. Due to preventions of departure from Turkey, the number of detections in the Eastern Aegean Sea was roughly unchanged.

For the three Mediterranean Sea routes, the top three nationalities in 2018 were Syrian (14,378, 10.5%), Moroccan (13,269, 9.7%) and Afghan (12,666, 9.2%), highlighting the importance of Eastern and Western Mediterranean routes in this year. Still in 2018, it is worth stressing flows related to other routes from Africa to the EU, such as the Western African route (1,531), the Circular route from Albania to Greece (4,550), the Western Balkan route (5,869) and the Eastern Borders route (1,084). In general, the total refusals of entry per sea reached 4,481 (−41,3% compared to 2017), corresponding to only 2.3% of the total refusals. 'Italian seaports reported much of the decrease with refusals being issued to passengers coming from Albania' (Frontex, 2019: 19).

For the 2015–2018 period, the Missing Migrants Project has documented almost 30,900 deaths, mainly via the Mediterranean Sea route (64%). In 2018, the Mediterranean Sea still had the highest number of deaths during migration, with an increasing share on the Western Mediterranean route.

A total of 813 deaths were recorded on this sea crossing from the coast of Northern Africa to Spain in 2018, compared with 272 in 2017. Nearly 570 deaths during migration were recorded in North Africa in 2018, mostly due to the harsh natural environment, violence and abuse, dangerous transportation conditions, and sickness and starvation. Despite the ongoing war and humanitarian crisis in Yemen, in 2018 the migration route to the country from the Horn of Africa across the Red Sea and the Gulf of Aden continued to be in high use.

(International Organization for Migration, 2019: 32)

In addition, we note that the routes start from the interior of Africa, where Niger is a key country, being a major hub for smuggling many West and Central African migrants. In line with this situation, Libya has recently become an important hub for smuggling as well as the main departure point when it comes to the Central Mediterranean route (İçduygu, 2018). It is worth mentioning that these people face serious human rights violations on these routes, which are sometimes also used as trafficking routes.

The peculiarities of maritime migration and the case of boat people on the Mediterranean Sea

Considering the historical perspective of migration in the Mediterranean Sea as well as recent data (see the previous section), it could be considered a 'membrane' between the colonial and the metropolis worlds in the 19th and 20th centuries. Nowadays, it could be considered a 'plasma membrane', a much more complex and selective passageway than previously, as its own structure ends up interfering in the migratory displacement processes. In line with the increasing number of migrants in recent years (which has been falling), the number of organisations that participate in these migratory displacement processes and influence the flows is also growing. As an example, we can observe policing systems of several European countries competing in the task of finding mobile individuals migrating via the Mediterranean Sea; these are working in the same areas and at the same time as vessels from European NGOs and with the same task of finding migrants. We can highlight that through this plasma membrane flow state and non-state actors, military and civilian actors, subnational, national and supranational actors; they move either of their own free will or by imposition, often without a passport, identity or even nationality.

As Dickson states, 'during the Greek thalassocracy, the sea was treated as a central vantage point facilitating a multidirectional connectivity that was realised through micro-seafaring practices' (2019: 1). Indeed, in this 21st century, micro and macro seafaring practices are taking place at the same time in an area much larger than the Greek Mediterranean, establishing a dense diffuse network of connectivity. This network ends up being delineated by environmental sea conditions and oceanographic issues, which reflect directly on the sea migration routes. Thus, following Dickson, we 'take the sea as a central point of analysis in migration control, opening up this space for consideration not simply as a border, but rather as a productive and dense political space demonstrating iterations of a modern thalassocracy' (ibid.: 2). It would be important to look inside the Mediterranean Sea and observe its structural characteristics, something that has only recently begun due to the European mobility control agenda. The structural characteristics include the authorities on sea, the rights of policing and interdiction of areas and vessels and the responsibility to combat crimes on the sea or to carry out assistance, rescue and salvage actions on the sea.

The input of Hugo Grotius and the idea of 'the free seas', or *mare liberum*, proposed in the 17th century represent the opposite of delimitation of the Mediterranean Sea in 'national portions'. At the end of the 20th century, sovereignty (an extrapolation of terrestrial laws) was applied on a maritime area of 12 nautical miles from the coastline to the coastal state, and from there the sea would be heritage to everyone (an area called the high seas), where only the rules of international law could be applied. This maritime area was referred to as territorial sea and delimited by the United Nations Convention on the Law of the Sea (UNCLOS) (United Nations, 1982), specific international law for the maritime environment. UNCLOS supports the logic of the free seas, but it also provides for progressive territorialisation (sovereignty and sovereignty rights) in maritime areas, with the territorial sea being an area with wide and unrestricted application of coastal state rules. Another delimitation under UNCLOS is the exclusive economic zone (from 12 to 200 nautical miles); in this area, the coastal State has sovereign rights only for the exploration and exploitation of resources and the conservation and management of resources.

These UNCLOS sovereign rights can be viewed in different ways; for example, with the sea being a source of strategic resources of the waters superjacent to the seabed and of the seabed and its subsoil, or the sea as a means of displacement (a pathway for people and goods). In this second approach, we can frame the displacement of boat people[1] (the focus of this section), individuals that move through the maritime environment without requirements for international regulation of maritime flows. Furthermore, the migration of the boat people and the control actions refer to the water column and/or the air space above the sea.

In the 2000s, sea migrants already existed, but they migrated in few flows from Yugoslavia through the Adriatic Sea, or from the Maghreb to Spain. In 2011, just after the Arab Spring, a new, slightly more intense flow was established with migrants from Libya or Tunisia to Italy. As a consequence of recent conflicts in the Middle East and North Africa, the increase in numbers and multiple flows has made the displacement of boat people much more visible, politicised and even securitised, bringing forth multiple responses from states and civil entities.

The legal status of the sea migrant is difficult to define, and different future classifications can be suggested, such as asylum seeker, humanitarian refugee, stowaway, trafficked person. From other perspectives, they can be classified as social, environmental or economic migrants, and the application of rights such as non-refoulement, reception[2] or provision of health care and food can be questioned. The process of politicising this issue can be extended to include the boat people as criminals or shipwrecked. However, while they are still in the maritime environment, they are only maritime migrants in the Mediterranean Sea. And considering them as shipwrecked, we cannot ignore the long tradition of state authorities giving help at sea, something linked to the bilateral and multinational cooperative agreements signed by European countries.

The shipwrecked perception stems from the fact that the crossing of the Mediterranean Sea is done in boats or in overcrowded vessels without the minimum requirements of maritime safety. At the end of the second decade of the 21st century, the perception of boat people changes from shipwrecked to criminal, and vice versa, and this is reflected in the common European security policy through the actions of European navies and coastguards. These policies, instead of providing for simple assistance, rescue and salvage actions on the sea, linked to actions carried out on land, ended up influencing a redesign of the routes of maritime migration.

As an example, the highest number of deaths of boat people was recorded in 2016 when the smallest and least dangerous route from Turkey to Greece was closed after an agreement between the EU and the Eurasian country (EU-Turkey Statement, 2016).[3] After that, this migrant route was redirected to the Balkan route, so the countries in this region tried to close their borders as Turkey did. We should point out that in viewing the Mediterranean Sea as a plasma membrane, we overlap the maritime jurisdictions of the Mediterranean states, the multiple migration routes and the multiple actors that act in the policing or the humanitarian assistance, rescue and salvage of the boat people.[4]

In order to understand the peculiarities of this type of migration according to the states' jurisdiction over maritime areas, a brief analysis of UNCLOS as a legal framework for the sea would help us. The first point to consider is that the convention is based on geographical delimitation, so the divisions are the territorial sea, the contiguous zone, the exclusive economic zone and the high seas. Thus, the principles of free seas or areas and resources submitted to the authority of the state emerges. Given that the Mediterranean Sea is a semi-closed sea with archipelagic or strait regions, in order to avoid overlapping state jurisdictions, the sovereign rights up to 200 nautical miles are limited and adjusted on a case-by-case basis. Therefore, we find different variables to be observed according to whether boat people are on the European Exclusive Economic Zones (EEZs), the African EEZs, the Middle East EEZs or in the high seas areas. This complexity can be seen in the delimitation of maritime jurisdictions presented in Figure 21.2.

Some parts, sections or articles of UNCLOS can contribute to analysis of the boat people and can let us point to gaps in international maritime law. It is important to stress that UNCLOS was developed in the early 1980s when there was not such intense maritime migration and no association of this migration with human trafficking; for this reason, we observe fewer articles in the convention on this topic compared to piracy.

First, we can look at the issue of sovereignty and sovereignty rights in each area. For example, Article 2 sets out that the sovereignty of the coastal state extends beyond its territory and its inland waters to an adjacent sea area called the territorial sea (12 nautical miles from the coast), including the air space overlying the territorial sea, as well as the seabed and subsoil. Thus, in fact, rescue or policing actions to hold boat people in the territorial sea would have similarities to the legal standards outlined on land borders – with some caveats of course. On the other hand, similar actions in the EEZ should be limited by other legal standards, and any flow management (or policing) action in the EEZ is open to question if compared to actions carried out in the territorial sea (Article 56).

Second, innocent and in-transit passage of ships that carry maritime migrants into the territorial sea is allowed, as ships of any state have these rights (Article 17) if the passage is continuous and fast. However, this passage must not harm the peace, the good order or the security of the coastal state. This passage can be considered outside this prerogative if it violates immigration laws and regulations (Article 19). The coastal state may temporarily suspend the right of innocent passage in certain areas if it is essential to protect its security (Article 25). Thus, the right of in-transit or innocent passage can be suspended in cases where those ships with boat people can be considered an element that undermines the peace, good order or security of the coastal state.

Third, the boat people can be classified as criminals or irregular migrants. The UNCLOS mentions that the coastal state will not exercise criminal or civil jurisdictions on board a foreign ship, except in the case of the infraction having consequences for the coastal state or disturbing peace and order, or even in order to suppress illicit trafficking in narcotic drugs or psychotropic substances (Article 27). However, in this article, unregulated migration is not included. Therefore, if the ship is found to be part of a human trafficking network, the criminal dimension may be based on additional international law documents, such as the United Nations Convention against Transnational Organized Crime and its two supplementary protocols.

A fourth point concerns the rights and duties of states on the high sea, an area where no limitation is applied to freedom of navigation for ships that comply with the rules of international law (Article 87). Every state shall issue documents to ships granted the right to fly its flag (Article 91), but this does not happen with the vessels of the boat people. It should be added that every state should control administrative, technical and social issues over ships flying its flag. So the vessels of the boat people usually do not have a state flag or, due to their small size, they have special prerogatives. On the other hand, based on Article 94, where the vessels of the boat

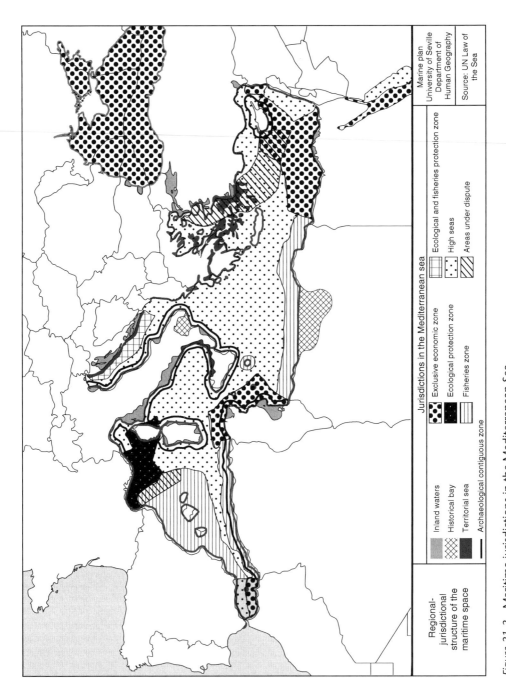

Figure 21.2 Maritime jurisdictions in the Mediterranean Sea
Source: Reproduced with permission; Vivero & Mateos (2007)

people do not comply with the necessary measures to ensure safety at sea, they could be framed as a threat to maritime safety and subject to inspection and policing actions on the high seas.

A fifth point relates to the perspective of boat people as shipwrecked, emphasising that every ship has a duty to render assistance to any person found at sea in danger of being lost (Article 98). From the perspective of the coastal state, it must promote search and rescue service to guarantee safety and cooperate with neighbouring states through regional adjustments. Thus, for these two actors, in a way, there is a legal prerogative of assistance, rescue and salvage of boat people.

A sixth point concerns the relationship between the boat people and the transport of slaves, since every state shall take effective measures to prevent and punish this transport in ships authorised to fly its flag, and any slave taking refuge on board any ship shall ipso facto be free (Article 99). Considering this theme, Article 110 highlights the right to visit and points out that a warship on the high seas will only have the right to visit if there is a suspicion, among other things, that the ship is dedicated to trafficking of slaves; or if the ship has no nationality. These two elements could legitimise policing actions against boat people by European countries. There is also the possibility of persecution if there are reasons to believe that the ship has violated laws and regulations, and this can only be done by warships or military aircraft, or by other ships or aircraft that have clear and identifiable signs of being in the service of a government and duly authorised (Article 111). However, these points were designed for ships that are regularly inserted in the maritime merchant flow, and not for the vessels of the boat people.

A seventh interesting point is the exercise of powers of enforcement, a term that appears only in Part XII referring to 'protection and preservation of the marine environment'. In order to do this, only officially qualified employees as well as warships or military or other aircraft ships or aircraft in the service of a government and are duly authorised may exercise powers of enforcement over foreign ships (Article 224).

Another international document that contributes to the analysis of boat people, considering the perspective of navigation safety, is the International Convention for the Safety of Human Life at Sea (1974) outlined in the sphere of the International Maritime Organization (2005). It should be added that this is a more technical document that states, in Article II, that SOLAS will apply to ships authorised to fly the flag of states whose governments are contracting governments and also to shipwrecked persons or someone inside the ship who is outside international standards. In Chapter V, the presents elements of navigation safety and quotes the search and rescue service, emphasising that all contracting governments have to ensure necessary measures to coordinate assistance in their area.

Conclusion

Regarding the aspects discussed so far, there is no doubt that the conflicts in North Africa and the Middle East originated several processes that came together to configure a crisis of transnational dimensions. Given the humanitarian tragedy on its borders, the EU is going through a moment of re-evaluation and remodelling of policies that once were in line with the migratory issue. These conflicts resulted in changes in the political life of the EU, given the migratory processes towards it without any security.

From the data analysed, we can conclude that although there are mechanisms for cooperation or adoption of restrictive measures at land or sea borders, these are not sufficient to achieve the objectives of EU migration policies to reduce irregular flows of migrants. Thus, as these security mechanisms become more intense, the consequence is the redirection of flows and their ways of acting (which is evidenced by the evolution of flows in the three Mediterranean routes in recent years).

Another important point of this chapter is that the sea should be considered central in any analysis of the control of maritime migration. In addition, migration control practices in general do not happen in a linear way in the Mediterranean Sea, as is reflected in overlaps of policies and practices, of state and non-state actors, and of civilians and military organisations operating in different ways and in different geographies. Due to the increase of migratory flows, the North Atlantic Treaty Organization becomes an extra-regional actor participating in these patrolling actions, on the Aegean Sea through Operation Sea Guardian and, more recently, on the Central Mediterranean Sea, providing extra logistical support for EU agencies.

The analysis of UNCLOS showed that these maritime areas have different jurisdictions, which may create disputes or cooperation for the governance of maritime migration. Besides, the peculiarities of migration by the sea show the gaps in maritime law applied to vessels carrying the boat people. In this context, boat people can be understood as individuals who move through the maritime environment without requirements for international regulation of maritime flows, sometimes without a passport, identity or even nationality; and inside crowded vessels without requirements for international maritime safety or security. The designation 'boat people' started to be used for these maritime migrants in the Mediterranean Sea, as it allows individuals to become visible, politicised and even securitised.

From the analysis of the Mediterranean routes, the relationship between migratory flows and the vulnerabilities of non-European neighbours is clear, through problems ranging from conflicts to structural issues that lead to low development. Over time, the EU has been adapting its migratory policies in order to contain irregular flows, but what we see is a discourse that is detached from practice. As advocated, migration is a human right recognised by the UN Charter; however, sovereign states still have the power to regulate entry through their borders, making this right limited and often not respected. For the future, it is expected that the commitments adopted by states under the 2030 Agenda will move towards adoption of policies that promote development in the most vulnerable regions. It is expected that the right of mobility is effectively recognised among those countries that are the biggest recipients, so that human dignity is respected above all.

Notes

1. Other authors (e.g. Ellebrecht (2020) call these individuals 'the Refugee Boat'.
2. Considering the reception, the governments of Italy and Greece have tried to block access to their ports for vessels transporting boat people rescued in international waters, especially if they are vessels of European NGOs, such as the French SOS Méditerranée and Médecins Sans Frontières, the German Lifeline, and the Spanish Open Arms Fund. These NGOs claim to have made a 'reception on European soil' during the rescue, considering the legal prerogatives associated with the flag of a ship. On the other hand, European governments argue that the activities of European NGOs provide incentives for migrants to try to cross the Mediterranean Sea.
3. The agreement between the EU and Turkey sets out that all irregular migrants who arrive in Greece from Turkey after 20 March 2016 will be returned to Turkey. For every Syrian sent back to Turkey from the Greek Islands, another Syrian will be resettled in the EU, giving priority to migrants who have not entered irregularly. The main objective of the agreement is 'to break the business model of the smugglers and to offer migrants an alternative to putting their lives at risk'.
4. In general, assistance, rescue and salvage and maritime safety were set up by other international documents, such as the International Convention for the Safety of Life at Sea (1974).

Bibliography

Bevilacqua, G. (2017) Exploring the ambiguity of Operation Sophia between military and search and rescue activities. In G. Andreone (ed.), *The Future of the Law of the Sea*. Cham: Springer, (pp. 165–189).

Dickson, A.J. (2019) *Modern Mobilities and Ancient Thalassocracies: Re-imagining Power and Order in the Mediterranean*. Paper presented at 6th European Workshop International Studies, Krakow.

Ellebrecht, S. (2020) *Mediated Bordering Eurosur, the Refugee Boat, and the Construction of an External EU Border*. Verlag.

EUR-Lex.europa.eu (2007) *Estratégia e programa indicativo regional euro-mediterrânico 2007–2013*. https://eur-lex.europa.eu/ legal-content/PT/TXT/HTML/?uri=LEGISSUM:r15011&from=EN (retrieved 9 April 2020).

European Council (2018) European Council Conclusions. EUCO 13/18. Brussels, 18 October. www.consilium.europa.eu/media/36775/18-euco-final-conclusions-en.pdf (retrieved 14 September 2020).

European Parliament (2019) *Consolidated Annual Activity Report 2018*. Reg. No. 5865 [online]. www.europarl.europa.eu/cmsdata/185405/CAAR%202018.pdf (retrieved 6 April 2020).

Falzon, M. (2012) Immigration, rituals and transitoriness in the Mediterranean island of Malta. *Journal of Ethnic and Migration Studies*, 38 (10), 1661–1680.

Frontex (2019) *Risk Analysis for 2019*. Warsaw: Frontex. https://migrationdataportal.org/themes/migration-data-sources (retrieved 6 April 2020).

Içduygu, A. (2018) Middle East. In A. Triandafyllidou and M. McAuliffe (eds), *Migrant Smuggling Data and Research: A Global Review of the Emerging Evidence Base*, Vol. 2. Geneva: IOM (pp. 19–44).

International Maritime Organization (2005) *International Convention for the Safety of Life at Sea* [online]. www.mar.ist.utl.pt/mventura/Projecto-Navios-I/IMO-Conventions%20(copies)/SOLAS.pdf (retrieved 11 April 2020).

International Organization for Migration (2019) *World Migration Report 2020*. Geneva: International Organization for Migration. https://publications.iom.int/system/files/pdf/wmr_2020.pdf (retrieved 5 April 2020).

Lannon, E. (2012) Instruments, principes et méthodologie de la Politique européenne de voisinage. In E. Lannon (ed.), *Les défis de la politique européenne de voisinage*. Bruxelles: P.I.E. Peter Lang.

Leite, A.P.M.R. (2016) *O Complexo de Segurança na União Europeia: um estudo das implicações de segurança e defesa a partir da análise da crise de refugiados*. PhD thesis, PPGHC/UFRJ.

Pereira, G. (2019) *Direitos Humanos e Migrações Forçadas*. Porto Alegre: EDIPUCRS.

United Nations (1982) United Nations Conventions on the Law of the Sea [online]. www.un.org/depts/los/convention_agreements/texts/unclos/unclos_e.pdf (retrieved 11 April 2020).

United Nations (1998) *Recommendations on Statistics of International Migration*. Statistical Papers, Series M, No 58, Rev. 1. http://unstats.un.org/unsd/ publication/SeriesM/seriesm_58rev1e.pdf (retrieved 6 April 2020).

United Nations High Commissioner for Refugees (2019) *Routes Towards the Mediterranean* [online]. www.unhcr.org/ 5d1327ab7.pdf (retrieved 6 April 2020).

Vivero, J.L.S. and Mateos, J.C.R. (2007) *Atlas of the European Seas and Oceans Marine Jurisdictions, Sea Uses and Governance*. Barcelona: Ediciones del Serbal http://hurricane.us.es/ATLAS_ EUROPA.pdf (retrieved 10 April 2020).

Zanker, F. (2019) Managing or restricting movement? Diverging approaches of African and European migration governance [online]. *Comparative Migration Studies*, 7 (1): 17. https://link.springer.com/article/10.1186/s40878-019-0115-9 (retrieved 15 March 2020).

Zapata-Barrero, R. (2019) Mediterranean Cities as Laboratories for Rethinking Human Mobility and Governance of Diversity: Looking at a New Geopolitics of Mediterranean Migration. Paper presented at IMISCOE Annual Conference: Mediterranean Cities and Migration Studies. Malmö, 26–28 June.

22
Environment and climate change in the context of EU-Africa relations[1]

Simon Lightfoot

Introduction

The environment and climate have become increasingly central to European Union (EU)-African relations. This was especially the case in the negotiations of the United Nations Framework Convention on Climate Change (UNFCCC), where African countries were important allies for the EU in its bid to secure a legally binding global agreement. While once concerns about the environment were seen mainly as an EU concern, in the last decade debates on the Green Economy, climate change and transnational water management and wildlife conservation (see European Commission, 2015) have risen up the agenda of African governments and forums. Authors such as Death (2016) argue that environmental issues have long been central to African states but have been framed in locally appropriate ways that may not coincide with northern/EU framings (e.g. as land use and access to resources, etc.). We examine the rise of Africa as an increasingly vocal green actor by identifying which environmental and/or climate change policies form the priorities of the African Union (AU) and comparing them to those promoted by the EU, especially via the Joint Africa-EU Strategy (JAES). We critically examine how the current approaches reflect a broader power imbalance within African-EU relations by highlighting how the rules that frame the relationship reflect those of the EU. In particular, we highlight the crucial roles played by both the EU member states and the relevant Directorate-Generals (DGs) within the Commission and contrast them to key actors within the AU and its member states. We conclude by examining the opportunities offered by new actors in Africa and the impact this will have on the EU.

The global context

The issues of environment and climate change are interconnected. The Earth Summit in 1992 and the creation of the UNFCCC signalled a major step forward in global efforts to tackle climate change. The global context is the broad concept of 'who pays?' It is well documented that as a continent Africa is the most vulnerable to the effects of climate change, that it lacks the resources to effectively mitigate these effects and that it produces 4% of global carbon dioxide (Toulmin, 2009). In contrast, the EU emits around 13%, with EU states some of the largest historic polluters, especially per capita. The basic disagreement within global climate change negotiations is the extent to which historic polluters must foot the bill for climate change or the extent to which it is a shared problem (see Gupta, 2015). This is 'common but differentiated responsibilities' as promoted in the Kyoto Protocol. 'Common but differentiated responsibilities' argues that 'industrialized countries are not only responsible for historic emissions that have caused climate change to date and, thus, should reduce their emissions, but they have the capacity to do so. In contrast, developing countries are not culpable and thus should not be required to reduce emissions.' In addition, the concept extends to developed countries actively assisting developing countries to reduce emissions or adapt to climate change (Brunnée and Streck, 2013). These debates also link into broader ones about climate justice (Page, 2013). This principle is not without controversy, as a growing number of developed countries argue that the largest emitters now are developing countries. Developed states also want to future-proof agreements because it is clear that as African states industrialise and urbanise, their carbon emissions are likely to rise. As a result, we can see global climate diplomacy shifting in focus from being a 'northern issue' to a truly global issue.

The broadening of the debate reflects the increased number of actors involved. The focus on the EU and in recent years China has tended to overlook Africa in international relations. This is changing, and as Brown and Harman (2013) say, rather than asking how external actors determine African realities, we need to ask how far, and in what ways, are African political actors impacting on, and operating within, the international system. African countries have little hard power in the negotiations: they cannot offer major emission reductions or financial support to other countries. Traditionally their position has been typecast as passive recipients of climate diplomacy rather than active participants (Chin-Yee, 2016). This is clear in the field of the environment, which was often seen as a developed world concern. Some authors (see Death, 2016) argue that environmental issues have long been central to African states but have been framed in locally appropriate ways that may not coincide with Northern/EU framings. The framing of the debate has led to criticism. Despite the strong emphasis on the unequal impact of climate change on developing countries, there is very little evidence of framing that recognises the capacity within developing countries to cope with climate change (Roeck et al., 2016). Roeck et al. (2016) argue that the EU uses a growth framework, with documents noting that climate change could 'hamper economic development' of developing countries. In this sense, adaptation in development becomes a matter of ensuring that the pursuit of economic growth can continue unabated. Implicitly, a geopolitical reality of the 'developed' Global North and the 'underdeveloped' Global South is installed, in which Northern donors are responsible for the 'resilience' of the passive Southern aid recipients by installing technologies like centralised risk management schemes and scientific monitoring systems. The rise in agency of African states within discussions that materially affect them is where this chapter goes next.

The complex framework of Africa-EU relations

The interplay between climate change and environment is clear in one of the main documents that governs EU-Africa relations – the 2007 JAES (Africa-EU Partnership, 2007: 2). The JAES aims to offer a 'continent-to-continent partnership' through which to address issues of 'common concern' as a 'partnership of equals' (Barainde, 2019). Obviously EU-African relations are complex with overlapping memberships of international organisations on the part of some African states (Tavares and Tang, 2011). The main division relevant for EU-African relations is between the AU and the African, Caribbean and Pacific (ACP) Group.[2] The ACP Group comprises 48 sub-Saharan African states while the AU comprises 55 African states (the 48 African ACP states plus 5 European Neighbourhood Policy (ENP) North African states). All North African countries are part of the ENP and benefit from its financial instrument, whereas relations with countries in sub-Saharan Africa take place under the Cotonou Agreement, which covers both political dialogue and financial cooperation, predominantly via the European Development Fund (EDF). The African ACP states also are part of regional groupings, including the Economic Community of West African States (ECOWAS), the East and Southern Africa and the Indian Ocean, Central Africa and the South African Development Community (SADC). Tension between the ACP and the AU is clear in the current discussions around the post-2020 Cotonou Agreement, but has been an issue for a number of years (Carbone, 2018). Environmental issues have also been integrated into EU Development Policy and the various consensuses on development (Adelle et al., 2018: 82–83). Environment and climate change feature in agreements between the EU and both the AU and the ACP. This section explores the relationship via the lens of the JAES.

The JAES and climate change diplomacy

A key element of the initial JAES was environmental sustainability and climate change (see Lightfoot, 2013). Climate change was chosen as one of eight 'Africa-EU Partnerships' through which political dialogue in the JAES was pursued in the period 2008–2010 (Sherriff and Kotsopoulos, 2013). An overarching objective of the Partnership on Climate Change was to build a common agenda on climate change policies and cooperation. More specifically, the partnership aimed to help the two continents work together to push forward an ambitious post-2012 climate agreement. The EU has historically been seen as a leader in climate change negotiations (see Karlsson et al., 2011). Some of the claims made for the EU in this field are telling. Eckersley (2004: 251) argues that the EU is the best hope for an evolving green transnational state. She also goes on to show that to avoid green imperialism charges, green states would spread by emulation not imposition – they would be copied by means of respectful persuasion or example (ibid.: 211). This links to the EU's own self-image in this policy sphere – that of a normative power. From Kyoto onwards, the EU has seen itself as leading the field and shaping global environmental norms. To do that, it needs to build alliances. However, the EU can be seen to be a contradictory actor pursuing both norms and interests in climate negotiations (Van Schaik and Schunz, 2011). This tension will be a core theme of this section.

Africa-EU declarations in the field of climate change were seen to be 'proof of convergence between the two continents', and indeed the declaration agreed on an interregional position for the UNFCCC negotiations, including specific targets of 2°C reductions (Sicurelli, 2013). The issue of money created problems from the start, given that the declaration was signed one year before the start of the Euro crisis. Due to lack of agreement between the EU and African countries, the much-vaunted call for joint action in the key global forum of the UNFCCC (Sherriff and Ferreira, 2010) never occurred. Part of the disagreement stemmed from the fact that the EU was seen as a 'paternalistic actor'. African partners often perceive Europe as having double standards, following realpolitik when it comes to security and economic concerns and professing values (human rights, democracy and good governance) when its critical interests are not at stake (Tondel et al., 2015: 21). Davis Cross (2018) argues that often the core pre-requisite of a narrative resonating with other states was missing from negotiations and, therefore, 'mutual recognition was absent'. As a result, while there may have been shared issues between Africa and Europe, there were not 'necessarily shared interests' (Sherriff and Ferreira, 2010: 19). The EU saw the AU's lack of preparation and political will as key issues. However, it felt that the EU negotiators took the support of African, especially ACP states, for granted during the negotiations.

What the EU had failed to appreciate was that the African Group of Negotiators (AGN) over the period under study have become a prominent group in the UNFCCC and an influential environmental voice on the continent (Roger and Belliethathan, 2016). Evidence for this is seen in the development of a common position for the UNFCCC in Algiers in 2008 and cemented in Nairobi in 2009 (Death, 2016). Interestingly, the position draws on broad positions of G77 + China and the least developed countries (LDCs), which creates further overlapping groupings (see Makina, 2013; Spies 2019).³ Makina's (2013) argument that an 'African position can be described as one that articulates Africa's unique interests in the negotiations' might seem obvious, but the skill in managing 55 states to support a common African position, especially in the face of competing interests and overlapping group memberships, cannot be overstated. The main position for the AGN revolves around:

1. financial compensation, which they argued should represent 1.5% global gross domestic product;
2. common but differentiated responsibility; and
3. commitment to a twin-track approach: annex 1 – binding commitments; and annex 2 – climate adaptation.

The AGN and LDC groups shared the view that a transparent, rules-based, legally binding multilateral regime is the best way to tackle climate change. As such, they kept the pressure on developed countries to reduce greenhouse gas emissions by 40% below 1990 levels by 2020, with the vital aim of keeping global temperature rises below 1.5°C. Although the AGN has notable weaknesses in its starting position for global negotiations, its unity can be its strength (Makina, 2013). For example, the AGN walked out of negotiations in Barcelona in 2009 (a preparatory summit) because developed countries were holding back on specific targets, although its stance did lead to tensions with the G77 + China (Death, 2016: 223). Vickers (2013) highlights that this agency is negative as a veto player rather than positive as an agenda setter. Maintaining unity is crucial in agenda setting and the fact that the unity of the AGN 'fractured' at Copenhagen in 2011 weakens the collective power. Support from smaller African states was crucial in buttressing the EU's demand for clearer and more committed action from all signatories, including annex 2 states such as China and India (Death, 2016: 224). These states tended to view the financial and economic benefits of the ACP relationship as stronger than any AU unity.

We also witnessed the key African regional powers break ranks and act in their own interest. In part, that was due to differential vulnerabilities to climate change (see Lioubimtseva, 2013), but it was mainly down to differential interests and the power of different states. There is also the fact that different states have different relationships with the EU; as the Economic Partnership Agreement (EPA) negotiations show, some states are more reliant on the EU for aid and for market access than others (see European Commission, 2019, for the current state of play). In these negotiations, the Sudanese chair of G77 accused South Africa of 'capitulat[ing] to EU pressure' (Death, 2016: 223). South Africa in particular has grown in prominence in this field (see Adelle and Kotsopoulos, 2017), but as a result, other states felt it undermined the AGN by acting on its own (Death, 2016: 222–223). Nelson argues that African regional powers do not share the same interests as the rest of the continent. Not only do they differ based on energy production (Nigeria) and consumption (South Africa), but also in terms of their general vulnerabilities and readiness to face climate change. Even where they share interests, they often view these negotiation processes as serving goals other than solving the problems of climate change (Nelson, 2016). It also weakens the position that all developing states be treated the same (Vickers, 2013). The rise of these states also creates issues for the EU as its role in global negotiations has had to evolve (Keukeleire and Hooijmaaijers, 2014). Overall, the Copenhagen outcome and the rise of Africa was matched by 'backsliding' on commitments to both financial and binding mechanisms – the lack of a firm target of 1.5°C and the fact that on finance commitments not much has changed (Chin-Yee, 2016).

We can see the tensions between the EU and the AU start to play out even before Copenhagen, with the AU refusing to sign a second declaration in 2010 (Sicurelli, 2013). Instead, climate change became one of the 'issues' within the global and emerging issues in the Roadmap 2014–2017 adopted at the 4th EU-Africa Summit in Brussels (European Commission, 2014a, 2014b). As a report for the European Parliament notes,

> contrary to the JAES Action Plan 2011–13, which assigned Climate change and Environment to a specific Partnership …, quite surprisingly the new Roadmap downgrades the importance of this issue, which is now included in the area of the more general Global Challenges Priority.
>
> *(Pirozzi et al., 2017: 27)*

This trend continued at the 5th AU-EU Summit in 2017.

Although it proved to be impossible to maintain a unified continental position at Copenhagen, it was clear that the ideal of continental solidarity was a meaningful aspiration both within Africa and in relation to how the African negotiators were seen by other actors – whether there was in fact one continent, one voice (Death, 2016). Vickers argues that 'the era of relative passivity for many African countries in international relations is over' (2013: 691). It is clear that EU-supported projects have improved African agency in this area, in particular the ClimDev-Africa programme, which aims to provide African actors with climatic information to support climate policymaking (ClimDev Africa, 2013). The programme has facilitated Africa's contribution to the negotiation process on the post-2012 climate agreement through analytical studies, consultative workshops and support for the development of a common African position on climate issues (Africa-EU Partnership, 2016). The support of the ClimDev-Africa programme therefore played a constructive role in helping African actors develop a common position on climate issues and in strengthening the AGN so that they could play an influential role in the UNFCCC negotiations. This section highlights clearly how the interplay of domestic and international factors shape EU-Africa relations in this policy field.

Interestingly, post Copenhagen there has been a convergence in the positions of the AU and the EU. In part, this is due to a change in EU negotiating style, with a greater focus on informal negotiations and alliance building on the margins of the UNFCCC negotiations (Davis Cross, 2018). The fact is, the EU's own image took a hit during the Copenhagen climate negotiations when it was sidelined by other actors (see Groen and Niemann, 2013). This reflected a shift in the global balance of power, with China flexing its muscles in this policy arena. As a result, the image of the EU in climate change has shifted from that of a normative power shaping global norms to perhaps a more subtle role of bridge builder mediating between the developed and the developing world – a 'leadiator' (Bäckstrand and Elgström, (2013). According to Vogler (2016), the failure to deliver a new climate settlement at Copenhagen in 2009 and the relative exclusion of the Union from the negotiation of the 'Accord' were seen as an adjustment to new and changed international realities. The Copenhagen Conference of the Parties was seen by the EU as a 'wake-up call' to change its approach to global climate change leadership (Adelle et al., 2018). Davis Cross argues that the Paris Summit 'showcased what is possible when the EU mobilizes its full diplomatic capacity to pave the way towards agreement' (2018: 586). Although we saw the 'political exercise of linguistic gymnastics: how to craft 'creative language' that mentions 1.5

degrees without making it the official operational goal' the outcome of the summit reflected EU and AU objectives (Dimitrov, 2016:4). This was quite a feat in the face of opposition from the United States, and this highlights that the AU can be an effective international actor and that the EU's new negotiating stance appears to be paying dividends.

Beyond climate change: Environmental policy on the ground?

Interestingly, post Paris, we saw a 'change in direction' in EU-ACP relations in the environment field (Carbone, 2019). The focus on ACP countries appeared to reflect a move in EU thinking, from seeing the AU as a strategic partner to the AU being another regional partner. After negotiations, the slightly messy compromise was to have a separate compact on the EU-Africa partnership set within a renewed EU-ACP agreement, with the AU more actively involved than in the past (Carbone, 2019). The fact that the post-Cotonou negotiations were in full swing perhaps explains why the ACP was forefront in the minds of the African member states. However, the second Action Plan of the JAES had already broadened the scope of the partnership (and renamed it the Partnership on Climate Change and Environment) to include capacity building initiatives relating to deforestation and biodiversity conservation.

These mid-level, more technical environmental diplomacy initiatives and the EU's support for regional environmental institutions in Africa that build the capacity of African actors to engage on environmental governance on the continent have consistently proved to be more successful for the EU than higher-level diplomacy (see Adelle and Lightfoot, 2018). As argued before, this may mean that the AU Commission may not be the best interlocutor for the EU with regard to the environment; other organisations, such as the African Ministerial Conference on the Environment (AMCEN), may be better placed. In this regard, regular interactions between DG Environment and AMCEN are already under way. The focus on specific environmental issues also allows the EU to overcome the claims of Eurocentrism by focusing on issues that are relevant to African states (see Beringer, 2019). This section focuses on a selection of these initiatives.

Water and access to water is clearly a major challenge in many African states and links directly to food security, sanitation and health. The goal of the EU Water Initiative is to contribute to the achievement of specific targets on access to water and sanitation by increasing the efficiency of water development aid through better coordination and harmonisation of donor activities (see Fritsch et al., 2017). The water initiative highlights some of the issues already discussed in this chapter. Some authors have seen it as EU dominated, and it has suffered from a lack of coordination with other EU initiatives (Fritsch et al., 2017: 431). The water example also highlights the changing nature of the EU as an actor, as the policy evolved over time to better reflect the African context, although problems remain, particularly around financial commitments (Fritsch et al., 2017).

Deforestation is another cross-cutting issue linked to agriculture, food security, land degradation, income generation and energy. A specific African initiative that has attracted EU capacity building support under the Partnership on Climate Change is the Great Green Wall of the Sahara and the Sahel Initiative (GGWSSI) (GGWI, n.d.). According to Sicurelli (2013), African governments endorsed the original proposal for a Partnership on Climate Change only under the condition that a separate priority action on land degradation and desertification was included in the partnership. The GGWSSI brings together 20 African countries, many of which are on the border of the Sahara, to focus on dry land ecosystems and the reduction of local communities' vulnerability to climate change, land degradation and drought (Africa-EU Partnership, 2016). The initiative originally aimed at establishing a 15-kilometre-wide strip of vegetation across the continent, from Senegal to Dijibouti, but over time its objectives have broadened to encompass poverty reduction and food security regionally as well as supporting local communities to adapt to climate change (Tondel et al., 2015; GGWI, 2013). The fact that the GGWSSI eventually evolved into a regional sustainable landscape programme that contextualised climate change actions within long-standing African priorities of food security and poverty reduction helps explain its success (Tondel et al., 2015). Connected is the Forest Law Enforcement, Governance and Trade Voluntary Partnerships Agreements and REDD+, which aims to reduce illegal logging and deforestation. The EU also attempts to promote the integration of biodiversity frameworks in national development planning (Overdevest and Zeitlin, 2018).

Biodiversity has therefore become an area of common interest between the partners. To some extent this has been opportunistic on the part of the EU. According to Sicurelli (2013), the EU was able to establish itself as the preferred partner for developing countries in the Nagoya Conference of the Parties of the Convention on Biological Diversity in October 2010 (in contrast to the failure of the Copenhagen Conference of the Parties of the UNFCCC). LaRocco argues that biodiversity has less of a political and public profile than climate change, but offers the EU a 'low-stakes high-profile environmental cause' (2019: 62). The Biodivesity for Life initiative focuses on the overlap between biodiversity loss and LDCs. Whilst this still reflects the dominance of resilience thinking in EU discourse (something continued in both the EU Global Strategy and the updated European Consensus for Development) (Roeck et al., 2016), the coincidence of interests between African states and the EU is telling, especially as while the concept of biodiversity might be abstract, the reality can produce visible changes.

The policy field that connects many of the above is energy. Only about one-third of Africa's population have access to electricity, and this is unreliable. This impacts on economic growth. The electricity that is produced relies on fossil fuels, which contribute to climate change. Household energy tends to rely on traditional fuels, which contribute to deforestation and have a negative gender dimension. As part of the JAES, the Africa-EU Energy Partnership (AEEP) was created to improve access to secure, affordable and sustainable energy for both continents, with a special focus on increasing investment in energy infrastructure in Africa. In particular, the AEEP focuses on harnessing the potential for renewable energy in many parts of Africa. However, energy policy (as a core EU shared competence) has a focus on liberalising markets and competition via their inclusion in the EPA negotiations (Kuzemko and Hadfield, 2016), which can add to the tension within the partnership, as the EU can be perceived to be pursuing different agendas at the same time. Despite DG Development playing a greater role in energy, the fundamental tension remains between the EU's focus on exporting its liberal energy model and its focus on poverty alleviation, because 'it implies a fundamental clash between considering energy as a social service or as a marketable commodity' (Keating 2012).

Conclusion

The chapter demonstrates that the relationship between the EU and Africa is still profoundly asymmetrical, notwithstanding the rhetoric to the contrary, particularly in global fora (see Babarinde, 2019). However, some large regional African partners have been able to push back against the EU's power, and the EU has modified its positions to better reflect the African context. Building up trust and African capacity have aided this change on the part of the EU, but the perceived inconsistency between what the EU says and what it does (especially around trade, EPAs and finance) remains. The structures also do not help (see Kotsopoulos and Mattheis, 2018). As Carbone (2018) highlights, some additional tensions are created via the overlap of ACP and AU memberships. The rise of other actors such as China and India also change the dynamic in favour of some African states (Grimm and Hackenesch, 2016).

The EU's pursuit of its external environmental objectives through capacity building appears to have been relatively more successful, especially when in line with African initiatives and priorities. Climate finance, especially for the African priority of climate adaption (e.g. through the Global Climate Change Alliance), has also played an important part in the EU's support for capacity building. In addition, this fund has provided incentives for African countries to become part of the UNFCCC process as well as helping improve the EU's position in the debate in the eyes of African actors. More coercive tactics, such as attempting to insert environmental chapters in the EPAs, have been resisted by African partners, and tensions persist around the EU's use of the sustainable development agenda (Price and Nunn, 2016).

Issues of distrust and perceived asymmetries between the partners discussed in this chapter point towards caution in the EU pursuing its own ideals and aspirations on the continent too zealously, unless they closely align with those of African actors. More fundamentally, it might be worth the EU considering how it frames 'the environment' in its relations with Africa. The environment (as framed by the EU in terms of pollution, climate change, biodiversity, etc.) is somewhat abstract for African political agendas, and interest in this is still low, including within civil society (see Death, 2016). The EU is finding more success reformulating its environmental objectives so that they better fit a wider set of 'African' priorities, such as infrastructure, energy, land, food security and industrialisation.

Notes

1 I would like to thank Camilla Adelle for introducing me to Carl Death's Green State work and for allowing me to develop ideas from our joint chapter. I would also like to thank the editors for their advice and patience.
2 In 2020 the ACP Group changed its name to the Organisation of African, Caribbean and Pacific States.
3 African countries negotiate through the Group of 77 + China (G77) and through the Africa Group. There are also smaller powerful coalitions such as Brazil, South Africa, India and China (BASIC), least developing countries (LDC), Alliance of Small Island States (AOSIS) and Organization of the Petroleum Exporting Countries (OPEC) (see Makina, 2013).

Bibliography

Adelle, C. and Kotsopoulos, J. (2017) The EU–South Africa Strategic Partnership and global environmental governance: Towards effective multilateralism after Copenhagen? *South African Journal of International Affairs*, 24 (2), 229–248.

Adelle, C. and Lightfoot, S. (2018) Africa: Searching for shared issues and overcoming asymmetries. In C. Adelle, K. Biedenkopf and D. Torney (eds), *European Union External Environmental Policy: Rules, Regulation and Governance Beyond Borders*. Cham: Palgrave Macmillan (pp. 258–273).

Adelle, C., Delputte, S., de Roeck, F. and Nicholson, S. (2018) Environmental instruments in development cooperation: Promoting better development and environmental outcomes? In C. Adelle, K. Biedenkopf and D. Torney (eds), *European Union External Environmental Policy. Rules, Regulation and Governance Beyond Borders*. Cham: Palgrave Macmillan (pp. 81–101).

Africa-EU Partnership (2007) *The Africa-EU Strategic Partnership: A Joint Africa-EU Strategy* [online]. www.africa-eu-partnership.org/sites/default/files/documents/eas2007_joint_strategy_en.pdf (retrieved 9 December 2016).

Africa-EU Partnership (2016) Achievements and milestones [online]. www.africa-eu-partnership.org/en/areas-cooperation/global-and-emerging-issues/climate-change-and-environment/achievements-and 28

Bäckstrand, K. and Elgström, O. (2013) The EU's role in climate change negotiations: From leader to 'leadiator'. *Journal of European Public Policy*, 20 (10), 1369–1386.

Babarinde, O. (2019) New directions in EU-Africa development initiatives: Between norms and geopolitics in EU development policies. In M. Thiel, S. Maier and S.L. Beringer (eds), *EU Development Policies: Between Norms and Geopolitics*. New York: Palgrave Macmillan (pp. 111–134).

Beringer, S. (2019) Energy, climate change and EU development policy. In M. Thiel, S. Maier and S.L. Beringer (eds), *EU Development Policies: Between Norms and Geopolitics*. New York: Palgrave Macmillan (pp. 17–34).

Brown, W. and Harman, S. (eds) (2013) *African Agency and International Relations*. Abingdon: Routledge.

Brunnée, J. and Streck, C. (2013) The UNFCCC as a negotiation forum: Towards common but more differentiated responsibilities. *Climate Policy*, 13 (5), 589–607.

Carbone, M. (2018) Caught between the ACP and the AU: Africa's relations with the European Union in a post-Cotonou Agreement context. *South African Journal of International Affairs*, 25 (4), 481–496.

Carbone, M. (2019) Purposefully triggering unintended consequences: The European Commission and the uncertain future of the EU-ACP partnership. *The International Spectator*, 54 (1), 45–59.

Chin-Yee, S. (2016) Briefing: Africa and the Paris climate change agreement. *African Affairs*, 115, 359–368.

ClimDev (2013) The Africa Climate Change Conference [online]. www.climdev-africa.org/acc2013 (retrieved 23 August 2019).

Davis Cross, M.K. (2018) Partners at Paris? Climate negotiations and transatlantic relations. *Journal of European Integration*, 40 (5), 571–586.

de Roeck, F., Delputte, S. and Orbie, J. (2016) Framing the climate-development nexus in the European Union. *Third World Thematics: A TWQ Journal*, 1 (4), 437–453.

Death, C. (2016) *The Green State in Africa*. New Haven, CT: Yale University Press.

Dimitrov, R.S. (2016) The Paris agreement on climate change: Behind closed doors. *Global Environmental Politics*, 16 (3), 1–11.

Eckersley, R. (2004) *The Green State*. Cambridge, MA: MIT.

European Commission (2014a) *EU-Africa Ministerial Statement on Climate Change*. Brussels, 2 April. Brussels: European Commission.

European Commission (2014b) *Pan-African Programme 2014–2020: Indicative Multi-annual Programme 2014–2017*. Brussels: European Commission.

European Commission (2015) *Larger than Elephants: Inputs for an EU Strategic Approach to Wildlife Conservation in Africa. Synthesis*. Brussels: European Commission.

European Commission (2019) Overview of Economic Partnership Agreements [online]. https://trade.ec.europa.eu/doclib/docs/2009/september/tradoc_144912.pdf (retrieved 23 August 2019).

Fritsch, O., Adelle, C. and Benson, D. (2017) The EU Water Initiative at 15: Origins, processes and assessment. *Water International*, 42 (4), 425–442.

Great Green Wall Initiative (n.d.) The Great Green Wall for the Sahara and the Sahel [online]. www.greatgreenwallinitiative.org/sites/default/files/publications/Great%20Green%20Wall%20Brochure.pdf (retrieved 28 April 2016).

Great Green Wall Initiative (2013) About [online]. www.greatgreenwallinitiative.org (retrieved 28 April 2016).

Grimm, S. and Hackenesch, H. (2016) China in Africa: What challenges for a reforming European Union development policy? Illustrations from country cases. *Development Policy Review*, October, 1–18.

Groen, L. and Niemann, A. (2013) The European Union at the Copenhagen Climate Negotiations: A case of contested EU actorness and effectiveness. *International Relations*, 27 (3), 308–324.

Gupta, J. (2015) The North-South divide. In K. Bäckstrand and E. Lövbrand (eds), *Research Handbook on Climate Governance*. Cheltenham: Edward Elgar (pp. 142–152).

Helly, D., Bekele, E. and Fassi, S. (2014) *The Implementation of the Joint Africa Europe Strategy: Rebuilding Confidence and Commitments*. EXPO/B/AFET/2013/42. Brussels: European Parliament.

Karlsson, C., Parker, C., Hjerpe, M. and Linnér, B.-O. (2011) Looking for leaders: Perceptions of climate change leadership among climate change negotiation participants. *Global Environmental Politics*, 11 (1), 89–107.

Keating, M.F. (2012) Re-thinking EU energy security: The utility of global best practices for successful transnational energy governance. In C. Kuzemko, A.V. Belyi, A. Goldthau and M.F. Keating (eds), *Dynamics of Energy Governance in Europe and Russia*. International Political Economy Series. London: Palgrave Macmillan (pp. 86–105).

Keukeleire, S. and Hooijmaaijers, B. (2014) The BRICS and other emerging power alliances and multilateral organizations in the Asia-Pacific and the Global South: Challenges for the European Union and its view on multilateralism. *Journal of Common Market Studies*, 52 (3), 582–599.

Kotsopoulos, J. and Mattheis, F. (2018) A contextualisation of EU–Africa relations: Trends and drivers from a reciprocal perspective. *South African Journal of International Affairs*, 25 (4), 445–460.

Kuzemko, C. and Hadfield, A. (2016) Defining and projecting EU energy policy. In J.M. Godzimirski (ed.), *EU Leadership in Energy and Environmental* Governance. London: Palgrave (pp. 21–50).

LaRocco, A.A. (2019) The Biodiversity for Life (B4L) flagship initiative: The EU, Africa, and biodiversity conservation. In M. Thiel, S. Maier and S.L. Beringer (eds), *EU Development Policies: Between Norms and Geopolitics*. New York: Palgrave Macmillan (pp. 55–77).

Lightfoot, S. (2013) Climate change and the EU-Africa Strategy: Coherence, leadership, and the 'greening' of development. In M. Carbone (ed.), *The European Union in Africa: Incoherent Policies, Asymmetrical Partnership, Declining Relevance?* Manchester: Manchester University Press (pp. 238–257).

Lioubimtseva, E. (2013) Africa and global climate change: Impacts, vulnerabilities and adaptation challenges. In T. Murithi (ed.), *Handbook of Africa's International Relations*. London: Routledge (pp. 219–230).

Makina, A. (2013) Managing climate change: The Africa Group in multilateral environmental negotiations. *Journal of International Organizations Studies*, 4, 36–48.

Nelson, M.B. (2016) Africa's regional powers and climate change negotiations. *Global Environmental Politics*, 16 (2), 110–129.

Overdevest, C. and Zeitlin, J. (2018) Experimentalism in transnational forest governance: Implementing European Union Forest Law Enforcement, Governance and Trade (FLEGT) Voluntary Partnership Agreements in Indonesia and Ghana. *Regulation & Governance*, 12, 64–87.

Page, E. (2013) Climate change justice. In R. Falkner (ed.), *The Handbook of Global Climate Change and Environmental Policy*. Hoboken, NJ: Wiley-Blackwell (pp. 231–247).

Pirozzi, N., Sartori, N. and Venturi, B. (2017) *The Joint Africa-EU Strategy*. Policy Department, European Parliament Directorate-General for External Policies.

Price, S. and Nunn, A. (2016) Managing neo-liberalisation through the Sustainable Development Agenda: The EU-ACP trade relationship and world market expansion. *Third World Thematics: A TWQ Journal*, 1 (4), 454–469.

Roger, C. and Belliethathan, S. (2016) Africa in the global climate change negotiations. *International Environmental Agreements*, 16, 91–108.

Sherriff, A. and Kotsopoulos, J. (2013) Africa and the European Union: An assessment of the EU-Africa Joint Strategy. In T. Murithi (ed.), *Handbook of Africa's International Relations*. London: Routledge (pp. 305–315).

Sherriff, A. and Magalhães Ferreira, P. (2010) Between the summits. In *Beyond Development Aid: EU Africa Political Dialogue on Global Issues of Common Concern*. Lisbon: Europe Africa Research Network (pp. 7–30).

Sicurelli, D. (2013) Africa-EU Partnership on Climate Change and the Environment. In J. Mangala (ed.), *Africa and the European Union: A Strategic Partnership*. New York: Palgrave Macmillan (pp. 149–169).

Spies, Y.K. (2019) *Global South Perspectives on Diplomacy*. London: Palgrave Macmillan.

Tavares, R. and Tang, V. (2011) Regional economic integration in Africa: Impediments to progress? South African Journal of International Affairs, 18 (2), 217–233.

Tondel, F., Knaepen, H. and van Wyk, L.-A. (2015) *Africa and Europe Combatting Climate Change: Towards a Common Agenda in 2015*. ECDPM Discussion Paper 177. Maastricht: ECDPM.

Toulmin, C. (2009) *Climate Change in Africa*. London: Zed Books.

Van Schaik, L. and Schunz, S. (2011) Explaining EU activism and impact in global climate politics: Is the Union a norm- or interest-driven actor? *Journal of Common Market Studies*, 50 (1), 169–186.

Vickers, B. (2013) Africa and the rising powers: Bargaining for the 'marginalized many'. *International Affairs*, 89 (3), 673–693.

Vogler, J. (2016) *Climate Change in World Politics*. Palgrave Macmillan: Basingstoke.

23
The role of civil society in EU-Africa relations

Uzoamaka Madu

Introduction

This chapter aims to investigate the role of civil society in European Union (EU)-Africa relations. This requires, first, an investigation into the conceptual relevance of the term civil society in the transnational context that is the EU-Africa relationship, which exists as a complex, multilevel interaction process and has its roots in a European political philosophy; and, second, to elaborate on the functional development of civil society in EU-Africa fora over the duration of the relationship. In this chapter we begin by conceptualising civil society, taking an analytical exploration of the concept – specifically, considering its European origins and how common descriptive parameters for understanding the concept of civil society in the EU-Africa context can be discerned by understanding and appreciating the concept by applying the African gaze. The chapter then offers a historical overview of how civil society emerged and developed from the start of the EU-Africa institutional relationship, before measuring the expanding and shrinking space that civil society currently occupies and examining to what extent current modalities and approaches to the role of civil society could act as a blueprint for the future.

Defining civil society in EU-Africa relations

> Although the term civil society is widely used in academic and policy circles, it has yet to acquire a commonly accepted meaning. Definitions of civil society are bewilderingly diverse and the differences between them are often rooted in alternative social and political philosophies.
>
> *(Orji, 2009: 76–77)*

Civil society is one of the most enduring and confusing concepts in social science; therefore, an analytical exploration of the concept and its origins makes for a suitable starting point to assess its role within the multilevel context of EU-Africa relations. This multilevel context adds a specifically unique complexity to the concept. This is, first, because the concept of civil society has restrained meaning outside its European origins; rather, it is rooted in an external political reality for the African constituent of this relationship. Second, civil society in this context is transnational – thus diffusing and extending the social, political and economic processes between and beyond the sovereign jurisdictional boundaries of nation states and consequently shifting the unit of analysis from individual states to a global system.

The concept of civil society finds its origins in both the Liberal and Marxist traditions of European political thought in the late 18th century, when the state became strong enough to maintain law and order, but not too strong to become oppressive, a balance which Brown (2000) argues is a prerequisite for the existence of civil society. Following the symbolic collapse of communism during the fall of the Berlin Wall in 1989 and the much wider democratic openings that followed – namely in Eastern Europe – the idea of civil society returned to the centre of intellectual and political debate. Civil society thus continued to gain in prominence throughout the 1990s (Edwards, 2013), and a strong civil society became one of the cornerstones of democracy, good governance, pluralism and the achievement of important social and economic goals. Michael Walzer's often quoted definition contributes common descriptive parameters for understanding the concept of civil society: 'Uncoerced human association between the individual and the state, in which people undertake collective action for normative and substantive purposes, relatively independent of government and the market' (1998: 123–124).

The common conceptual pillars of understanding what civil society is identifies it first as operating outside the state and the market and, second, as undertaking collective action for change concerning the government and the market. Walzer's take on civil society reflects commonalities in the concept which can be identified across a range of academic works of literature. Antonio Gramsci, for example, emphasises the role of civil society in challenging state power (Bratton, 1994), while Jürgen Habermas' theory of the 'public sphere' draws attention to the processes of citizen participation which seeks to shape political and market-based outcomes (Cohen and Arato, 1992). With such strong European roots, any attempt to shape an understanding of civil society in the EU-Africa context must consider African realities.

'Civil society is a concept made to order for the political reality of Western society' which has 'limited explanatory power' for the complexities of African associational life (Maina, 1998: 137).

Civil society theories are highly context-specific and presuppose a modern secular industrialised society (Brown, 2000), whereas most African societies have economies that are yet to be industrialised and are also largely traditional and religious, or spiritual, and as such, there is a tension (Ellis and Ter Haar, 2004). It follows that this civil society definition cannot be directly transposed to a vastly different political reality and, therefore, has major limitations in the EU-Africa context. According to Kurfi (2013), the postcolonial African state does not facilitate political participation, because it lacks autonomy, and this can be since in many cases there is an over-reliance on foreign aid or government sponsorship. Yet, African societies have created their diverse methods for managing confrontations, debates, tensions and conflicts, which may be deemed to be outside the Eurocentric concept of civil society. Africans, far from passively accepting the political systems [of Europe], have chosen different forms of civil society, altered them and developed entirely new ones. According to Makumbe, civil society in Africa is a 'composite of counter-hegemony, a pressure on the state from without, and a social base for pressure on state institutions' (1988: 305). Bratton (1994) goes further in stating that civil society is a society in confrontation with the state, existing only insofar as its 'self-consciousness' of its opposition to the state. This reflects the conceptual commonalities identified in the European context, namely influencing the state or market forces, albeit in a more adversarial way. Orji's (2009) conception of African civil society is less adversarial; according to him, they create room for debate on the direction of social development and make it possible for people to influence and control both the state and market. Lewis (2001) argues there is an adaptive view of civil society – a middle way between crudely imposing the concept from outside or simply abandoning it altogether as being inappropriate. Therefore, there is a case for accepting hybridity of the concept based on the two major commonalities in both assessments of civil society viewed in Europe and Africa: (i) civil society influences the state and the market; and (ii) civil society exists outside the market and the state.

The birth of the economic and social committee

The Treaty of Rome, signed in 1957, established the European Economic Community (EEC) – the precursor to the modern-day EU. In parallel, this legal constitution marked the beginning of formal institutional relations between Africa and the EEC. In a bid to secure a loosening grip on its African colonies, countries in the EEC incorporated African countries into the legal framework of the Treaty of Rome – establishing a customs union, dismantling tariff barriers and creating a community of the same size and scale as their colonial empires, extending beyond 20 African countries and territories. The treaty provisions were agreed unilaterally by the EEC member states, pointing to an aggressive power imbalance in this colonial relationship; this power imbalance is heavily reproduced in civil society relations too. Under the Treaty of Rome, the Economic and Social Committee (ESC) was formed, which would consist of representatives from various categories of economic and social activity – from producers to farmers, craftsmen and representatives of the general public – and its role was to be a consultative body for the EEC. Consultation of the ESC was mandatory in certain areas: agriculture, social policy and freedom of movement of workers and where EU law, namely directives, would involve amending legislation in one or more member state. The treaty also makes provision for the optional consultation of the ESC where it is considered appropriate. Consequently, the ESC has been regarded as an emerging parliamentary-legislative assembly whilst also an institution whose role is rather ill-defined.

Up until the 1970s, the ESC was given the role of consultative body (with the right to be consulted by the European Commission and Council of Ministers and to transmit its opinions to them for consideration). Yet, representatives from African countries and territories were not included in the machinery of the ESC at this time, meaning the EU-Africa civil society space did not provide room for all ideas and values to be heard, promoted, or given legitimacy (Benessaieh, 2011). In the years that followed, the ESC would put in effort to establish itself and to become the meeting place of the economic and social forces and a permanent centre for economic and social dialogue, including on EU-Africa issues.

Developing civil society dialogue in EU-Africa relations

In 1964, 18 newly independent Associated African States and Madagascar (AASM), minus Guinea, requested for their association with the EEC to continue on terms compatible with their independent status under the Yaoundé Convention (1964–1969). The ESC was now playing a more active and agenda-setting role in delivering opinions and calling the EEC to act on external relations issues at this time. In 1964, for example, the ESC called on the Commission to quickly find a solution to the problem posed for the French departments overseas, as a result of the EEC establishing a common market for sugar. However, it was during the lifecycle of the second Yaoundé Convention (1971–1975) that the ESC acquired the right to deliver opinions on its initiative and have its opinions published in the Official Journal, marking a breakthrough in its increasing influence. The following year saw the European Commission seek the ESC's views on the future relations between the EEC, the present AASM as well as the newly formed the Africa, Caribbean and Pacific (ACP) Group of States,[1] and in that year it was foreseen that the ESC would carry out its future work on the renewal of the Yaoundé Convention. The ESC had now matured into the role of influencing and shaping issues and policy, albeit limited by the upon-request nature of its inclusion into the process by the other organs of the EEC. In the lead-up to the adoption of the next phase of the EU-Africa relationship, the Lomé Convention, the ESC issued its Own-Initiative Opinion on the principal aspects of the negotiations in 1974, a year before the agreement was adopted, recommending that a dialogue and contacts be established between representatives of trade unions and business and other interest groups in the EEC and the signatory states of the future association agreement. The fact-finding visit made to West Africa (Niger, Senegal and Côte d'Ivoire) by a committee delegation in March 1974 was regarded as the first step along this road. This was further strengthened upon issuance of the final report on the future of the EU in 1975, in which the ESC had managed to not only determine its own rules of procedure, and be less restricted by the processes laid down by the EEC, but moreover to act as 'A forum for the representatives of all the economic and social groupings in the Community to increase the contact both among themselves and with their counterparts in the associated countries'.

The Lomé Convention (1975) itself did provide provisions to set up an advisory body representing economic and social interest groups, and the ESC leveraged this to further its influence in the decision-making process of future Lomé agreements in 1981, 1986 and 1989. Following the adoption of the 1975 Lomé Convention, the ESC adopted its Opinion on the convention, which resulted in the creation of what we know now to be the ACP-EU Joint Parliamentary Assembly (known then as the Joint Committee ACP-EEC Consultative Assembly), which started to meet from June 1976. However, the funding to ensure civil society engagement within this institutional architecture was only apportioned under the EU's 10th European Development Fund (2008–2013), when €5 million was provided to facilitate the participation of ACP civil society organisations (CSOs) in Joint Parliamentary Assembly meetings. Yet this mechanism still only offered limited opportunities for civil society participation. The participation of civil society under the Lomé framework overall was principally functional in nature and was primarily to ensure the successful completion of projects, as an extension or implementing arm of the EU. The focus was therefore not on the empowerment of civil society as an outsider of market and state, but rather as a civil servant implementing already agreed policy.

Civil society as agents of Normative Power Europe

In 1991, the Council passed a resolution on Human Rights, Democracy and Development which remains one of the most decisive EU decisions on civil society participation in development policy to date. The resolution afforded a distinct priority in development policies to 'promoting the role of NGOs and other bodies in civil society' to support human rights and democratisation in development. This shift in role suggests the EU using its normative power, as an 'ideational' actor characterised by common principles and acting to diffuse norms through contagion, informational diffusion, procedural diffusion, transference, overt diffusion and the cultural filter (Manners, 2006) within international relations. This is closely linked to the NGOisation of civil society – where NGOs are 'invested with a preponderant role in organizing economic redistribution, setting political objectives, and determining the moral economy' (Szántó, 2016: 134). 'The "NGOisation" of civil society denotes a reality in which NGOs are the primary component of civil society and act primarily as service providers to governments, international organisations and corporations' (Obadare, 2014: 476). The EU's approach to democratisation in the African (Caribbean and Pacific) region has always been a combination of bottom-up support for civil society and top-down influence over political elites; and in this resolution, it was explicitly articulated (Bossuyt et al., 2016). Then 1995 signalled an enhancement to European plans of promoting civil society actors within the development cooperation space, with the introduction of the Lomé IV Convention. The ESC soon became a fully fledged consultative body in its own right – serving not only the Council and the Commission but in 1997, under the Treaty of Amsterdam, the European Parliament.

The existence of a transnational language among NGOs is examined in greater detail in the research of Tvedt (1998) on the interactions between Northern European aid agencies and primarily African-based NGOs, and of Mawdsley et al. (2002) and Mawdsley et al. (2005) on the relationships between European donors and women's groups in Ghana. All these observers point to the dominant role of donors in promoting a vocabulary that is used by Southern NGOs to make their concerns fit into the frameworks of their Northern-based interlocutors. In this literature, the translation by Southern NGOs of their concerns into the words preferred by Northern supporters is seen not as mere wordplay but as reflecting the resource predominance of Northern-based participants in the 'global development industry'. From a critical study of NGOs and global civil society, Batliwala (2002) and Chandhoke (2005) show the extent to which global civil society is based in the North and characterised by the discursive predominance of the norms and values of Western liberal societies in identifying priorities. Consequently, this calls into question the extent to which those civil society groups from the weaker side of the bargaining table – African civil society groups – can play a strategically meaningful role in the EU-Africa relations architecture.

The promise of more civil society

The Cotonou Agreement, signed on 23 June 2000, enshrined civil society as a development actor in the text of the agreement. This was its key innovation, since the previous Lomé conventions had closed this gap quite securely despite the rhetoric. Provisions were specifically mapped out under the Cotonou Agreement for civil society to play a role in capacity building; the design, implementation and evaluation of strategies and programmes; political dialogue; peacebuilding, as well as conflict prevention and resolution. Beyond this, the Council of Ministers, representing EU member states and the Joint ACP-EU Parliamentary Assembly, were encouraged to conduct an ongoing dialogue with civil society actors. The Cotonou Agreement also made financial commitments to the actorness of civil society by including funding opportunities for ACP civil society representatives to participate in consultation meetings. According to Carbone (2003), many CSOs at this time had moved from a 'supply-side' approach, which concentrated only on development projects, to also a 'demand-side' approach, which seeks to help communities articulate their preferences and concerns in order to become more active participants in the development process. The Cotonou Agreement, in his view, acknowledges this change because for the first time in the history of the relationship between the EU and the ACP, CSOs are to be involved in the planning, implementation and evaluation stages of the cooperation programmes while, at the same time, they have greater access to funds and capacity building support. There remains, however, a strong, defined role for them as an implementer and almost an agent of the EU institutions, being the means by which the EU actions its normative power in international relations.

Shortly after the Cotonou Agreement came into effect, the ACP Civil Society Forum was established, and during its first meeting in Brussels in July 2001, involving over 120 ACP civil society actors, representatives of European NGOs, ACP states, the European Commission and the ACP Secretariat, a declaration and plan of action was adopted. ACP CSOs made it clear they wanted to participate in the programming exercise – shaping how development aid would be distributed. However, what followed was that focal points of the Forum were merely mandated to continue facilitating the establishment of national platforms, building capacities in their regions and further structuring the Forum as the global platform to promote participation in the Cotonou process in general.

European Commission services produced a preliminary assessment of the involvement and consultation of CSOs in the EU-ACP programming process between 2002 and 2006 and found that in several countries the strategy is geared at enhancing civil society participation in all sectors of EU cooperation and mainstreaming. Second, civil society involvement is mainly foreseen in the focal sectors. Third, support to civil society in non-focal sectors is provided either as a means for targeting poor population groups or as a contribution to good governance and conflict prevention. As a response, Eurostep, a network of European CSOs, encouraged civil society actors across ACP countries to make their assessment of civil society participation in their national process and found that while the basis for engaging civil society is being built, it is fragmented. In too many instances participation is equated with consultation, which is not the same. These consultations were inadequately prepared and had little consistency, and participation often seemed to be based on an arbitrary selection of civil society representation. Yet, according to Frans Polman, CONCORD President in 2003, Dialogue on ACP-EU cooperation is carried out also at a broader level, such as in the ACP-EU Joint Parliamentary Assembly and the ACP-EU Joint Council of Ministers. In these forums he argues that EU civil society is just as involved as ACP civil society. Whilst, Gahamanyi (2003) concludes that ACP civil society is active and involved in implementing the Cotonou Agreement, its level of participation is still minimal. Despite efforts of CSOs and positive initiatives on the part of institutions and certain ACP and EU countries, a low level of involvement in programming and preparing trade negotiations persisted. At this stage, CSOs realised they needed to take a proactive attitude if their participation was to be guaranteed.

The Cotonou Agreement, up until the present day, encourages the integration of civil society expertise in this broad and inclusive partnership, seemingly unlocking new institutionally recognised spaces for civil society to implement and monitor economic, social and development policies, programmes and projects as service providers. This is as well as taking part in formulating policy as experts in their consultative roles within the Council of Ministers and the EU-ACP Joint Parliamentary Assembly, both key decision-making entities within the EU-ACP framework. This service provider role to governments, however, reflects a growing and intentional tendency for the NGOisation of civil society (Obadare, 2011). Despite the institutional introduction of civil society into the EU-ACP infrastructure, civil society from the EU and from ACP countries has been rather hesitant to contribute to Cotonou procedures and institutions.

A 2013 study shows a mixed picture when it comes to civil society's performance within the ACP Civil Society Forum (Koekebakker, 2013). According to the study, the role of the forum is 'an invaluable source of expertise and experience' (ibid: 28), yet the data shows that in the African context their most impactful work is in holding the state accountable, setting good governance standards for the sector and meeting societal needs (service delivery). Member organisations of the Forum also highlighted the fact that meetings were not taking place as prescribed, which turned out to be a major challenge. Three meetings took place, in 2001, 2006 and 2009, after which the forum ceased activities. Moreover, the lack of a clear mandate and funding were also underlined as major challenges, and an obstacle in the first years was that many representatives were directly appointed by governments and therefore did not represent genuine civil society in the early stages of the forum, but rather functioned as an extension of the state.

African civil society finding its voice in EU-Africa relations

The Cotonou Agreement also laid out a framework for a new trade and development relationship – the infamous Economic Partnership Agreements (EPAs) between the EU and ACP countries. Negotiations on the EPAs began in September 2002 and were supposed to be completed by 31 December 2007. However, on this issue civil society, labour unions and business groups in the ACP countries studied the implications and found their voice, coming out with vigorous campaigns which eventually had a role to play in the lack of progress on the EPAs.

In 2012, when the pressure to sign the EPAs was at its height, a coalition of organisations known as the Economic Justice Network (EJN) delivered a caution to politicians which presented the EPAs as a threat to African economic integration. Participants of the EJN were unanimous in their calls to African governments not to sign the EPAs. Their input provided the impetus for African policymakers to rethink its development paradigm, and at the time of writing only one regional EU-African EPA. with the Southern African Development Community (SADC), out of the proposed five EPAs has been implemented, largely due to the increasing pressure of CSOs. The African Union of Civil Society Organisations took part in a pre-summit meeting in Accra in July 2007, and this ended with a call for member countries to resist signing the EPAs, but also to carry forward the will of AU member states on the EPAs. Under the Nairobi Declaration on EPAs, issued in April 2006, the AU insists that EPAs should constitute tools for the economic development of Africa and expresses its profound disappointment with the EU position. Ministers urge that the review 'be inclusive and consultative with all stakeholders, including civil society and parliamentarians and conducted at national, regional and continental and ACP levels'. Civil society's pressure on state institutions to rethink the EPAs with the EU shows them to be holding institutions to account and promoting transparency and accountability, particularly when it comes to the economy, trade and regional integration. The role of African civil society in this respect has been reflected in its activities and engagements on ACP issues. The 2013 report on the Africa-EU Civil Society Forum showed that their most impactful work was when they were taking up their role as a watchdog (Koekebakker, 2013). The Africa-EU Civil Society Forum in 2013 also sought to push for development-friendly EPAs, those that align the geographical scope of these agreements with the Regional Economic Communities (RECs).

West African civil society and national organisations in Benin, Burkina Faso, Côte-d'Ivoire, Gambia, Ghana, Guinea, Guinea Bissau, Mali, Niger, Nigeria, Senegal and Togo issued their declaration against signing the EPAs following a gathering in Dakar, Senegal, in February 2014. In the declaration, civil society is proposing itself as a service delivery organisation. In the declaration, civil society representatives seek to 'inform and train stakeholders in West Africa, including parliamentarians, members of the Economic and Social Council, the private sector, trade unions and the press, among others, on the content, issues and challenges of the EPA'. The civil society representatives in this sense are working in a more collaborative capacity with the state but against or outside the RECs and the EU who would be a party to the EPAs.

Yet, in the text of the African EPAs, the provisions for civil society engagement is weak or lacking completely. Within the EU-SADC EPA, there is no space for civil society – it fails to refer to it; and in the case of EPAs concerning the Economic Community of West African States and the East African Community, there is an absence of formal domestic civil society meetings envisaged in the text. However, in these two instances there is a rendezvous clause which provides an entry point for discussions on sustainable development, though nothing beyond this.

The Joint Africa-EU Partnership: Wide ambitions but a shrinking space

Under the Cotonou Agreement, the first Africa-Europe Summit between heads of state took place in Cairo on 3–4 April 2000, the same year the agreement was introduced. Civil society's role within the declaration that resulted from the summit was as a driving force for guaranteeing the promotion and protection of human rights, democratic principles and institutions, good governance and the rule of law – again, positioning civil society almost as a watchdog of values and norms (Manners, 2006) within the agreement. The declaration also seeks greater inclusion of civil society in the 'decision-making [process] concerning the management and allocation of resources'. However, the Cairo Declaration of 2000 ended up being declaratory rather than pragmatic, merely recognising CSOs as important but nothing more substantive. Going beyond the rhetoric of civil society inclusion and moving towards creating recognised frameworks for its participation in the decision-making landscape came several years later, following the second EU-Africa Summit, which took place in Lisbon on 9 December 2007, with the first-ever Joint Africa-EU Strategy (JAES) (Africa-EU Parnership, 2010) and Action Plan 2008–2010 designed as a 'people-centred partnership', focused on peace and security, democratic governance and human rights, trade and regional integration. This institutionalised civil society within the Africa-EU architecture, inter alia, by establishing mechanisms for closer cooperation and dialogue between the AU Economic, Social and Cultural Council (ECOSOCC) and the European Economic and Social Committee (EESC); mapping existing European and African civil-society networks; facilitating consultations with CSOs ahead of key policy decisions; inviting representatives from civil society in Europe and Africa to express themselves ahead of the ministerial troika meetings; and establishing joint expert groups on all priority actions identified in the Action Plan in which CSOs can participate.

However, this major shift was not without its shortcomings. The ability of the Joint Expert Groups (JEGs) to bring in CSOs and generate new ideas were severely constrained: the JEGs, for example, are not entitled to take new policy decisions, contrary to what was initially expected. Yet between 2007 and 2009, CSOs in Europe and Africa organised themselves to respond to the aspirations of the JAES. From the European side, the EU Civil Society Steering Group was launched. From the African side, the JAES spurred on the reactivation of a dormant civil society steering group, and following a consultation meeting on African civil society involvement in Bamako, Mali, in March 2008, the AU ECOSOCC re-emerged as an official advisory body to the AU and could shape the implementation and monitor the development of the JAES within the AU structures from a civil society perspective. However, within this institutionalised mandate given by the protagonists of the EU-Africa relationship, it was evident that civil society was still struggling to define its role and would continue to do so for many years to come.

After over 53 years of EU-Africa institutional relations, the first civil society dialogue forum was organised. It took place in 2010 in Cairo, Egypt, and civil society actors participating in the forum included trade union movements, academia, youth, persons with disabilities, women, NGOs and the media. The central aim of the forum was to tap in to the huge resource potential and technical expertise available from civil society and receive feedback when implementing the second JAES (2011–2013). The forum delivered on providing input into shaping the second JAES, and participants also noted that civil society should organise around partnerships between Europe and Africa to work on the different thematic partnerships of the next JAES. This seemed to be a reaction to the EU-centricity that was noted in the consultation process, specifically on topics like energy, trade, infrastructure, regional integration, democratic governance and human rights. Furthermore, the main criticism raised was the need to enhance and strengthen the role of civil society, particularly African civil society. This phase of civil society involvement was very much centred on enhancing the role of African CSOs within the JAES.

An agreement on the second JAES Action Plan (2011–2013) was reached at the third Africa-EU Summit in Tripoli, 29–30 November 2011, and civil society spoke to the practical challenges faced when considering how to integrate civil society into the political landscape, insofar as the 'lack of practical commitment of resources [financial, material and human resources] to fully carry out the defined JAES Action Plan'. This indicated that the first JAES Action Plan may have been paying lip service to increasing the involvement of civil society. Therefore, civil society was now requesting a partnership role in all processes of the JAES to maintain and broaden their involvement in policy processes and ensure that resources were committed to their involvement.

Therefore, the second JAES Action Plan set out to further embed civil society into the political architecture of the JAES and expand their role by, inter alia, creating an Africa-EU Joint Task Force (JTF) to allow civil society to contribute more actively to the implementation of the JAES. Additional areas of responsibility for civil society also included the promotion of natural resources governance, increasing revenue transparency and applying appropriate fiscal regimes; participation in developing African agriculture; contributing to progress and holding government and development partners to account on the Partnership on Water Affairs and Sanitation; and overcoming the lack of necessary climate information, analysis and options required by policy and decision makers at all levels. Yet, the plan fell short of committing he requisite political and operational resources to the JAES for civil society.

The second Africa-EU Civil Society Forum in 2013 gathered representatives from 32 African and 36 European organisations to develop ideas for reforming the JAES. The forum recommended precise modes and frameworks for its participation, including

> the integration of civil society through the establishment of thematic working groups with a consultative and monitoring role … the establishment of a secretariat of the Partnership, which would facilitate civil society involvement and information sharing about the partnership and its progress. This requires dedicated resources for civil society participation.

Yet the third JAES action plan (2014–2017) did not take heed of these requests. Instead, it streamlined the priorities of the partnership from eight down to five. And in this spirit of cutting back, civil society's space was also subject to institutional efficiency, as references to civil society in the third JAES Action Plan is scarce.

By the 2017 Africa-EU Civil Society Forum it was evident that the space for CSOs had reduced, and their visibility remains weak within the strategic framework. This almost falling out between the institutional class and the representatives of citizenry was evident in the lead-up to the 2017 EU-Africa Summit in Abidjan, Cote d'Ivoire. Civil society groups made their frustrations clear when referring back to a Joint Annual Forum that was never convened in Brussels, which in turn meant the main mechanism for civil society participation disappeared and key previous action points from the resolution in the previous Civil Society Forum were not followed through. Furthermore, the 2017 Africa-EU Civil Society Forum Declaration adopted in July, ahead of the EU-Africa Summit, explicitly noted that 'the space for CSOs has shrunk' and that previous action points relating to civil society involvement in the JAES have not been followed through. The forum requested to have the political, financial and logistical support for the involvement of all CSOs across all areas of the partnership and, more pointedly, a meaningful space during the summit to present their recommendations. Yet, the fifth EU-Africa Summit in 2017 was the pinching point of this increasingly shrinking space, as having been placed on the agenda, civil society (EU and African) and youth were prevented from speaking. Despite the lack of formal justification for this decision being taken, the development of the JAES itself reflects an increasing unwillingness to afford civil society the roles and responsibilities afforded to it from the outset.

Since the 2017 summit, however, the focus on cooperation between Africa and EU civil society for the inclusion and empowerment of young people in Africa has become razor sharp. In 2018, the AU-EU Youth Cooperation Hub was launched; this actively involves young people in proposing new ideas for the Africa-EU Partnership. The call for proposals contributes to implementing the priorities identified at the fifth AU-EU Summit and in the Abidjan Declaration, covering seven thematic clusters (education and skills; business, job creation and entrepreneurship; peace and security; environmental preservation and climate change; culture, arts and sports; governance, political and democratic inclusion and activism; remittances). Whilst this project goes beyond previous youth summit outcomes, it is not necessarily a sign of a change in tide since the theme for the 2017 summit was the youth. Furthermore the 2017 summit declaration, whilst taking note of the pre-summit events organised by civil society, only made one additional mention of civil society – that is, to recognise that civil society, as well as media and democratic institutions have an important role to play in governance.

Conclusion

The role of civil society in EU-Africa relations is a complex issue, not least because it is difficult to define in this transnational space. Despite it being of European origin it is forced into making sense in an African context. Somehow, in applying it to this context, we find ourselves settling for a compromised conceptual understanding somewhere in between. The difficulty in conceptualising and defining civil society adds to the complexity of being able to understand and assess its role, not least because it means a variety of different things to different actors in this political game. Beyond the conceptualisation of civil society, its role in EU-Africa relations has been largely shaped by, and subject to, the behest of EU institutions, since it is the partner who pays; by being the financier of the relationship, it is able to use this hard power to drive the political direction of the relationship, which includes the role of civil society.

From the very start of the institutional relationship, the EU has been working within its own rules and institutions to create a role in civil society within the EU-Africa context. The emergence and burgeoning power of the EESC is a case in point. It was a European construct set up to advise and guide the policymaking process of the EU institutions, but soon bolstered an increasingly active role in the EU's external relations and carved out a brokerage role on EU-ACP relations, representing civil society from both sides of the relationship. Later on, civil society began to emerge as a distinct stakeholder in of itself and outside the strict EU remit of the EESC, when the European Commission published its decisive 1991 paper on civil society in development policy. The role of civil society soon became the purveyor of normative Europe: upholding and expanding the normative values of Europe in the development context, with a focus on the African continent as one of the leading recipients of EU development funding. To some extent, we see the reconceptualisation of civil society by the EU so that it can exert its normative power beyond its own borders.

Yet with the introduction of the Cotonou Agreement, there was a realisation that both sides of the relationship needed to have a space and role in directing, shaping and implementing the agreement for it to be delivered and politically acceptable. This is when the advent of truly bilateral institutions and processes were set up to encourage and guide the participation of civil society as a stakeholder with a vested interest in the relationship, but also from the institutional side as a stakeholder who really mattered. However, the processes fell short of budgetary commitments and practical arrangements to make them work efficiently and effectively. This is where the shrinking space of civil society began to become evident, culminating in a slow but comprehensive chipping away at the roles and responsibilities placed on it, until we arrive at the current situation where the last EU-Africa Summit declaration makes a mere passing reference to the important role civil society has to play in governance. Until the role of both sides are more balanced and Africa speaks with one united voice, there can be very little talk of a civil society space in EU-Africa relations – rather civil society is employed to put pressure on African governments not living up to the normative values placed upon them by Europe within the legal framework of the Cotonou Agreement.

Note

1 The ACP Group is now known as the Organisation of African, Caribbean and Pacific States, following a change of name in 2020.

Bibliography

Africa-EU Partnership (2010) First Africa-EU Intercontinental Civil Society Forum Communiqué [online]. https://africa-eu-partnership.org/en/stay-informed/news/first-africa-eu-intercontinental-civil-society-forum-communique

Batliwala, S. (2002) Grassroots movements as transnational Actors: Implications for global civil society. *International Journal of Voluntary and Non-profit Organizations*, 13 (4), 393–410.

Benessaieh, A. (2011) Global civil society: Speaking in northern tongues? *Latin America Perspectives*, 38 (6), 69–90.

Bossuyt, J., Keijzer, N., Medinilla, A. and De Tollenaere, M. (2016) *The Future of ACP-EU Relations: A Political Economy Analysis*. ECDPM Policy Management Report 21. Maastricht: ECDPM.

Bratton, M. (1994) Civil society and political transition in Africa. *IDR Reports*, 11 (6), 1–21.

Brown, C. (2000) Cosmopolitanism, world citizenship and civil society. *Critical Review of International Social and Political Philosophy*, 3 (1), 7–26.

Carbone, M. (2003) The role of non-state actors in development policy: Perceptions and changing practices. *The Courier: The Magazine of ACP-EU Development Corporation* (199), July–August, 14–19.

Chandhoke, N. (2005) How global is civil society? *Journal of World Systems Research*, 11 (2), 355–371.

Cohen, J.L. and Arato, A. (1992) *Civil Society and Political Theory*. Cambridge, MA: MIT Press.

Edwards, M. (2013) *Civil Society*. New York: Wiley.

Ellis, S. and Ter Haar, G. (2004) *Worlds of Power: Religious Thought and Political Practice in Africa*. New York: Oxford University Press.

Gahamanyi, B.M. (2003) Civil society participation and the Cotonou process in West Africa. *The Courier: The Magazine of ACP-EU Development Corporation* 199, July–August, 24–26.

Koekebakker, W.E. (2013) *The ACP Civil Society Forum Study: Final Report*. European Union.

Kurfi, H.M. (2013) Beautifully imperfect: Applying the Western civil society model to Africa. *Journal of Studies in Social Sciences*, 5 (1), 146–159.

Lewis, D. (2001) *Civil Society in Non-Western Contexts: Reflections on the 'Usefulness' of a Concept of Civil Society*. Working Paper 13. Centre for Civil Society. London: London School of Economics and Political Science.

Maina, W. (1998) Kenya: The state, donors and the politics of democratization. In A. Van Rooy (ed.), *Civil Society and the Aid Industry*. London: Earthscan (pp. 134–163).

Makumbe, J.M. (1998) Is there civil society in Africa? *International Affairs*, 74 (2), 305–317.

Manners, I. (2006) Normative power Europe reconsidered: Beyond the crossroads. *Journal of European Public Policy*, 13 (2), 182–199.

Mawdsley, E., Townsend, J., Porter, G. and Oakley, P. (2002) *Knowledge, Power and Development Agendas: NGOs North and South*. Oxford: INTRAC.

Mawdsley, E., Townsend, J. and Porter, G. (2005) Trust, accountability, and face-to-face interaction in North–South NGO relations. *Development in Practice*, 15 (1), 77–82.

Obadare, E. (2014) *The Handbook of Civil Society in Africa*. New York: Springer.

Orji, N. (2009) Civil society, democracy and good governance in Africa. *CEU Political Science Journal*, 4 (2), 76–101.

Szántó, D. (2016) The NGOization of civil society in Sierra Leone: A thin dividing line between empowerment and disempowerment. In M. Mustapha and J.J. Bangura (eds), *Democratization and Human Security in Post-war Sierra Leone*. New York: Palgrave Macmillan (pp. 133–162).

Tvedt, J. (1998) *Angels of Mercy or Development Diplomats: NGOs & Foreign Aid*. Oxford: James Currey and Africa World Press.

Walzer, M. (1998) The idea of civil society: A path to social reconstruction. In E.J. Dionne (ed.), *Community Works: The Revival of Civil Society in America*. Washington, DC: Brookings Institution Press (pp. 293–304).

24
Agriculture and land in EU-Africa relations

Edward Lahiff

Introduction

Land, agriculture and natural resources have been at the heart of relations between Europe and Africa since ancient times. In the 19th century, European colonialism created an elaborate system of resource extraction, based on widespread dispossession and exploitation of the African population, the influence of which endures to the present day. Decolonisation in the latter half of the 20th century saw the rise of technical assistance to newly independent states from the former colonial powers, although this largely focused on the continued production of primary commodities for export to Europe, supported by multilateral treaties such as the Lomé Convention (Organisation of African, Caribbean and Pacific States, 2019) and the Cotonou Agreement (European Council, 2019). Smallholder and subsistence farmers – the vast majority of producers on the continent – remained relatively marginalised, characterised by basic technology, low productivity and continuing poverty. Domestic land policies, largely based on state control of land, tended to favour a small minority of larger-scale, commercially oriented famers and companies and to disregard the majority who lived with insecure and ill-defined tenure on land under various forms of communal or state tenure.

Only in the early years of the 21st century did policymakers and donors turn their attention to African smallholder farming as an important component of the domestic economy, against a background of sluggish economic growth rates, widespread unemployment, particularly in rural areas, and rising anxieties about food security and climate change (see, for example, Byerlee et al., 2008; and the collections edited by Adebajo and Whiteman, 2012, and Carbone, 2015b).

This chapter provides an overview of the evolution of the relationship between the European Union (EU) and African states in the interrelated areas of agriculture, land and food.

Trade in agricultural commodities

The Treaty of Rome created the European Development Fund (EDF), launched in 1959, as the European Economic Community's (EEC's) main instrument for providing development aid to African, Caribbean and Pacific (ACP) countries and to overseas countries and territories. The first formal association of the EEC and developing countries was under the Yaoundé I agreement

(1963–1969). The foundation of a comprehensive relationship on agriculture between Europe and Africa was further developed in the context of the Lomé Convention, which set out the principles and objectives of European cooperation with the wider ACP countries. Among the provisions of the first Lomé agreement were non-reciprocal preferences for most exports from ACP countries to the EEC and a price stabilisation mechanism to compensate ACP countries for the shortfall in export earnings due to fluctuation in the prices of commodities (Carbone, 2015a: 5). It provided for most ACP agricultural and mineral exports to enter the EEC free of duty. Separate trading protocols granted preferential access to European markets based on a quota system for bananas, sugar and beef. ACP countries, especially in the Caribbean, came to depend heavily on preferential trade into the European market. Moreover, the EEC committed significant funding for aid and investment in the ACP countries. Lomé II (signed in 1979) and Lomé III (1984) gradually shifted attention towards self-reliant development based on self-sufficiency and food security (Spero and Hart, 2010). Lomé IV (1990) extended the financial provision to partner countries but also marked a new emphasis on the promotion of human rights, democracy and good governance; strengthening of the position of women; protection of the environment; decentralised cooperation; diversification of ACP economies; promotion of the private sector; and increasing regional cooperation (Organisation of African, Caribbean and Pacific States, 2019). Funding for aid and development also increased steadily over the lifetime of the convention, reaching ECU 12 billion under Lomé IV. The importance and reach of the convention also grew over time: some 70 ACP countries were party to Lomé IV, compared to the 46 signatories of Lomé I. The preferential trading arrangements agreed under Lomé eventually succumbed to the pressures of the EU single market and opposition from the United States in the 1990s.

The Cotonou Agreement entered into force in 2003 and was subsequently revised in 2005 and 2010; it is set to expire in 2020. The agreement includes amongst its aims the reduction and eventual eradication of poverty while contributing to sustainable development and to the gradual integration of ACP countries into the world economy. The principles of the agreement include equality of partners, global participation by state and non-state actors, dialogue and regionalisation. The first round of the agreement (2000–2007) was designed to establish a comprehensive partnership with three distinct pillars: development cooperation; political cooperation; and economic and trade cooperation. The revised Cotonou Agreement (from 2010) added additional dimensions, such as food security, regional integration, state fragility and aid effectiveness (Hurt, 2003). Carbone (2015a: 4) sees the transition from Lomé to Cotonou as part of the 'normalisation' of relations between the EU and the countries of the Global South; as trade preferences gave way to principles of free trade, aid became more conditional and security moved up the political agenda. Elsewhere, Carbone (2015b: 121) argues that while Cotonou brought more aid from the EU to the ACP region, it also brought greater emphasis on conditionality, aid targeting for poverty reduction, and aid effectiveness; accompanied by greater coordination of aid activities amongst EU members and an increasingly important role for the European Commission, greatly influenced by the Paris Declaration on Aid Effectiveness, led by the OECD, in 2005.

From Africa-EU partnership to Africa-Europe alliance

With the new millennium came a closer engagement between Africa and the EU that went beyond traditional concerns with trade and aid, heralding a new level of political engagement, greatly boosted by the formation of the African Union (AU) and the New Partnership for African Development in 2001. Globally, the development climate was also being influenced at this time by the adoption of the United Nations (UN) Millennium Development Goals (MDGs) in 2000 and the Doha Development Round of the World Trade Organization in 2001 (Carbone, 2015a: 6). This brought a renewed emphasis on the importance of agriculture, and trade in agricultural commodities, to the relationship between the EU and Africa. A major milestone was the first Africa-EU Summit, held in Cairo in 2000, hosted jointly by the Organization of African Unity, as it still was, and the UN – the first meeting of its kind between European and African leaders. The Cairo Declaration committed the partners to a new strategic partnership between Africa and Europe, in a spirit of equality, respect, alliance and cooperation (African Union, 2019a). It also marked the beginning of what would become the Africa-EU Strategic Partnership (also the Africa-EU Partnership), designed to become the formal political channel through which the EU and the AU would dialogue and organise their cooperative relations. Ultimately, the Africa-EU partnership would come to support a range of projects across security, governance, higher education and economic integration.

The Cairo Declaration contained important commitments in the area of agriculture and the wider agri-food sector. Section 10 highlighted the developmental aspects of the expanding trade relationship, agreeing to 'co-operate so as to ensure that in the framework of multilateral trade negotiations special attention is paid to products, including processed agricultural products, which are of export interest to developing countries' (Organization of African Unity and European Union, 2000).

Food Security was given particular emphasis in Section 97: 'We recognise that economic performance and poverty eradication are strongly linked to food security in Africa, which includes issues such as agricultural development, fisheries, livestock, and forestry development'. Both the developmental and the food security dimensions were further captured in Section 99 of the agreement, which recognised the need to ensure that agricultural production is not excessively centred on traditional export commodities as well as the need 'to support overall food security and nutrition strategies adopted by Africa and to enhance co-operation in these areas'.

In the wake of the Cairo Summit, the EU adopted a Strategy for Africa in 2005, combining elements of development and peace and security. The purpose of the strategy, according to the European Commission (2005), is 'to give the EU a comprehensive, integrated and long-term framework for its relations with the African continent'. According to Carbone (2015a: 7), this did little more than reiterate existing commitments. It did, however, mark an important step towards the more elaborate Joint Africa-EU Strategy (JAES) that would follow. In what was a very substantial statement, the EU acknowledged that it was the biggest export market for African products, highlighting that approximately 85% of Africa's exports of cotton, fruit and vegetables are imported by the EU (European Commission, 2005: 13). The Commission acknowledged the dependence of many African economies on a narrow range of exports, and their vulnerability to long-term price decline and fluctuations in the world prices of such commodities: long-term decline in prices of sugar, cocoa coffee and cotton are cited. Unlocking growth, it argued, would require measures such as increases of crop yields and diversification into non-traditional agricultural exports such as horticulture. Specific attention is thus given to boosting the role of agriculture and fisheries as drivers of economic growth and to the scope for enhanced regional integration.

Europe and Africa, it noted, are also bound by substantial and predictable aid flows: in 2003 the EU's development aid to Africa totalled €15 billion, compared to €5 billion in 1985, accounting for 60% of the total official development assistance going to Africa. In addition, in the context of the Euro-Mediterranean Partnership and the European Neighbourhood Policy, the EU and its North African partner countries committed themselves to further liberalisation of trade in agriculture, processed agricultural and fisheries products and the liberalisation of trade in services, with the aim of concluding negotiations by the end of 2006. The emerging Africa-EU partnership was further enhanced with the second EU-Africa Summit in Lisbon in 2007, which adopted the JAES, committing both partners to a closer relationship across economic, social and political dimensions, with a strong emphasis on human rights, peace and development. According to the joint statement: 'There is now a need for a new phase in the Africa-EU relationship, a new strategic partnership and a Joint Africa-EU Strategy as a political vision and roadmap for the future cooperation between the two continents in existing and new areas and arenas' (Africa-EU Partnership, 2007). Carbone (2015a: 7) argues that the JAES marked an important advance on previous agreements, addressing both developmental issues on the African continent along with global issues of human rights, peace and security, and good governance. This was accompanied by a detailed action plan and eventually by eight Africa-EU Partnerships; none of these specifically addressed agriculture, but agriculture was referenced under the agreement on Trade and Regional Integration (see Babarinde and Wright, 2013).

The JAES, as signed at the Lisbon Summit in 2007, makes specific commitments in the area of agriculture and food security (Articles 72–74), covering agricultural development, institutional reform and fisheries (Africa-EU Partnership, 2007). The third Africa-EU Summit held in Tripoli in November 2010 recommitted the partners to seize together new opportunities for broader and mutually beneficial initiatives and particularly the determinacy to progress in the identified priority areas of cooperation and towards reaching the MDGs in Africa (see Africa-EU Partnership, 2010). Despite this close level of engagement and cooperation, throughout this period (2005–2010) African states complained vociferously that the EU was continuing to use trade agreements in a selective manner that maximised benefits to the EU and continued to impose unacceptable levels of political conditionality on governance, security and human rights. Matthews (2015: 203) argues that changes to EU policy in the first decade of the new century brought important benefits to African farmers, through reductions in the anti-competitive subsidies paid to European producers and preferential access to European markets through the Everything But Arms agreement in 2001 and the subsequent signing of Economic Partnership Agreements. Set against this, however, is the continued competition on local markets from European producers of cereals and dairy products, in particular. The demise of commodity protocols, notably sugar, Matthews (ibid.: 204) argues, can be seen as a form of development assistance, but brought with it the unintended consequence of supporting unsustainably high production costs among African producers, leaving them vulnerable in the more market-oriented environment of the new century. While trade prospects are generally positive, Matthews warns about risks to food security as African producers chase more remunerative export markets for high-value committees while continuing to rely heavily on imports of cereals and other foodstuffs. This will, Matthews argues, require continued commitment by African governments to meeting – and extending – its commitments to agricultural development under the CAADP, with ongoing support from the EU under the JAES and other special measures such as the EU Food Facility (ibid.: 205).

By the occasion of the 4th EU-Africa in Brussels in 2014, food and agriculture were the subject of closer engagement, despite the rapidly expanding range of political, security and development issues vying for attention. In the summit declaration, leaders highlighted the close nature of EU-Africa relations and the shared values of democracy, respect for human rights, the rule of law and good governance as well as the right to development. Agriculture was mentioned in the final declaration (briefly, in respect of economic development and climate change), which specifically committed the partners to work for the development of African agriculture through the CAADP and noted the importance of reform of the CAP for 'achieving progress as regards coherence with the objectives of agricultural development in Africa' (European Council, 2014, paragraph 31).

More importantly, perhaps, at the request of the EU-Africa Summit of 2014, an EU-Africa Expert Group was tasked, under the guidance of the HLPD (High Level Policy Dialogue on Science, Technology and Innovation) to draft a roadmap towards an EU-Africa Research and Innovation Partnership on Food and Nutrition Security and Sustainable Agriculture (FNSSA). This roadmap, adopted at the HLPD Senior Officials Meeting in Addis Ababa in April 2016, is structured around four main pillars: sustainable intensification; agriculture and food systems for nutrition; expansion and improvement of agricultural markets and trade; and cross-cutting issues.

In addition, research funding of approximately €150 million was earmarked for the period 2016–2020 to support the implementation of the partnership Funding was through a mix of Horizon 2020 projects, created in response to targeted calls to Africa focusing on FNSSA, and allowing for synergies with emphasis on local multi-stakeholder action; and AU Research Grants, supported by the EU Pan-African Programme and managed directly by the AU Commission with a view to building a system of competitive research grants at pan-African level. In a follow-up to the Brussels summit, the AU-EU Contact Group on Agriculture, Food Security and Food Safety met in Brussels in April 2015 and issued a detailed set of recommendations for joint actions across the fields of agriculture, food, forestry and fisheries (see Africa-EU Partnership, 2015). The Malabo Declaration (Malabo Declaration on Accelerated Agricultural Growth and Transformation for Shared Prosperity and Improved Livelihoods) was adopted by AU Heads of State and Government in June 2014. It commits leaders to a set of actions intended to accelerate agricultural growth and transformation across the continent. The declaration was a recommitment to the principles and values of the Comprehensive Africa Agriculture Development Programme (CAADP) adopted by the AU Assembly of Heads of State and Government through the Maputo Declaration in 2003 and designed to improve food security and nutrition and increase incomes in Africa's largely agriculture-based economies.

From 2016, the work of the AU-EU summits has been carried forward in the form of meetings of senior officials and minsters of agriculture. Under the EU Presidency of the Netherlands, a conference was held between the EU and the AU, in Noordwijk, The Netherlands, in July 2016, which focused on advancing the cooperation between both continents in the field of agriculture. The conference concluded with a High-Level Agriculture Ministerial meeting from African and European Member States and both Commissioners, which built on the commitment of African leaders as expressed at the 2014 AU Summit in Malabo (Africa-EU Partnership, 2016). The meeting put particularly emphasis on the role of agricultural policy cooperation in food security and nutrition improvement.

A year later, in July 2017, ministers met again at the AU-EU Agriculture Ministerial Conference (Making Sustainable Agriculture a future for youth in Africa) in Rome and, clearly influenced by the ongoing migration crisis, agreed on a common vision on 'to generate sustainable and inclusive growth, supporting job creation in the agri-food sector and the rural economy for African youth, and ensuring a sustainable management of natural resources' (European Commission, 2017a). Commissioner Phil Hogan told the conference of the need to foster responsible investment in African agriculture, to create an enabling environment for the private sector.

The fifth AU-EU Summit was held in Abidjan, Côte d'Ivoire, in November 2017, under the theme of 'Investing in Youth for Accelerated Inclusive Growth and Sustainable Development', echoing the ongoing concerns with employment and, increasingly, climate change (African Union, 2017). Agriculture was mentioned only briefly in the context of economic development, with reference to job creation and sustainable development (para. 61) and with reference to support for CAADP (para. 67), particularly support for agribusiness and agri-value chains; promoting market access for smallholders; strengthen AU-EU agriculture business relations through the AU-EU Agribusiness platform; and support for training and education in sustainable agriculture and agri-food entrepreneurial activities.

Ahead of the 2017 summit, a study on the JAES was released by the Commission (European Union, 2016). Here, agriculture is largely dealt with under Section 2.4.2 (Agriculture, food security and food safety), just a single paragraph in a 54-page document. This references the recently agreed EU-Africa Research & Innovation Partnership on Food and Nutrition Security and Sustainable Agriculture (FNSSA) (signed in Addis Ababa in 2016) and the Pan-African Programme of the EU's Directorate-General for International Cooperation and Cooperation (DG DEVCO) (see European Commission, 2019d; European Union and African Union, 2018).

The LIVE2Africa programme is intended to make a significant contribution to the objectives of the 2025 Africa Accelerated Agricultural Growth and Transformation agenda adopted by the Heads of State and Government of the AU in Malabo in 2014. LIVE2Africa aims at 'supporting the transformation of the African livestock sector for enhanced contribution to environmentally sustainable, climate resilient, socioeconomic development and equitable growth'. Its specific objective is to strengthen the systemic capacity of continental, regional and national livestock sector stakeholders for the economically, environmentally and socially sustainable transformation of the sector. It was implemented with a total budget of €20 million, of which €19 million came from the European Commission (African Union, 2019b; European Commission, 2016). In his State of the Union Address on 12 September 2018, then President of the European Commission Jean-Claude Juncker proposed to deepen the EU's economic and trade relationship with Africa through investment and job creation, in the form of a new Africa-Europe Alliance for Sustainable Investment and Jobs (European Commission, 2018a). The alliance would build on the commitments taken during the 2017 AU–UN Summit in Abidjan in November, when the parties agreed to strengthen their partnership.

Of the six proposed actions, none directly address agriculture, but it features indirectly within the broad areas of economic development and trade. In December, only three months after the launch of the Africa–Europe Alliance, High-Level Forum Africa-Europe was held in Vienna, jointly hosted by the EU and AU, chief executive officers of global companies, innovators, start-ups and various stakeholders. President Juncker reiterated Europe's ambition for a true and fair partnership among equals between Africa and Europe and presented the first results of the Africa–Europe Alliance for Sustainable Investment and Jobs (Africa-EU Partnership, 2018). As a direct outcome of the alliance, Task Force Rural Africa was established under the agriculture heading, with the specific objective of examining and providing advice on how to strengthen the partnership with Africa in food and farming. The Task Force was led jointly by DG Agriculture and Rural Development and DG DEVCO. It reported in March 2019, making four major recommendations: a territorial approach for income and job creation; sustainable land and natural resources management and climate action; sustainable transformation of African agriculture; and the development of the African food industry and food markets (European Commission, 2019b).

Following the Task Force's report, it was reported that the EU would commit to three specific actions: twinning and exchange programmes between African and European agricultural bodies; an AU-EU Agribusiness platform to link European and African businesses to help identify challenges and opportunities for private investment and trade; and innovation hubs to support 'agripreneurs' and the African agri-food sector to facilitate digitalisation and skills development. According to Josefa Leonel Correia Sacko, AU Commissioner for Rural Economy and Agriculture, 'The Task Force report recognises the new reality of Africa and Europe as global partners on an equal footing. It demonstrates that farmers and the food industry should work hand in hand to take on new opportunities' (European Commission, 2019a).

Edward Lahiff

EU–AU foreign ministers met again in Brussels in January 2019. Chaired by the EU High Representative for Foreign Affairs and Security Policy Federica Mogherini and Minister of Foreign Affairs of Rwanda Richard Sezibera, the meeting brought together participants from the 28 EU member states and from the 55 members of the AU. While trade, investment and economic integration of the African continent featured prominently, little specific attention was given to agriculture, land or agri-food issues (Africa–EU Partnership, 2019).

Agriculture and food in EU development policy

The above account traces the recent history of food and agriculture within high-level Africa–EU relations, particularly in the areas of cooperation and trade. Some further, specific activities are, however, contained within the EU's development policy and related actions. Since 2011, EU development policy has been under DG DEVCO (or EuropeAid; DG DEVCO was formed in 2011 following the merger of the EuropeAid Cooperation Office with the DG for Development and Relations with ACP States). DG DEVCO has overall responsibility for the programming and implementation of the European Commission's external aid instruments financed by the UN budget and the EDF. DEVCO/EuropeAid was reformed in 2015, when the DG for International Cooperation and Development became a department of the European Commission, operating under the authority of the European Commissioner for International Cooperation and Development. The EU is the world's largest aid donor. Its development aid is financed directly by the EU budget (70%) and by the EDF (30%), made up of voluntary contributions by EU member states. The EU is currently implementing its 11th EDF for the period 2014–2020, with an aid budget of €30.5 billion.

In 2006 the EU launched its European Consensus on Development, revised as the New European Consensus on Development in 2017 (European Commission, 2017b). Carbone (2015b: 12) argues that the European Consensus on Development was accompanied by significant increases in aid volumes.

> The novelty of the Consensus was that it committed the EU member states not only as participants in the supranational development policy but also as bilateral donors. In particular, the Consensus reiterated that the primary objective of EU development policy is poverty reduction and reaffirmed the commitments made by all member states to delivering more and better aid.
>
> *(Carbone, 2015b: 131)*

In 2007, the Committee of Development of the European Parliament published its *Report on Advancing African Agriculture* (Committee on Development, 2007), describing the main current challenges facing agricultural production in Africa. Seven areas of cooperation were proposed, spanning agricultural development, trade, research, governance, natural resources, livestock disease and risk management. This was followed by the 2010 EU Policy Framework to Assist Developing Countries in Addressing Food Security Challenges (European Parliament, 2010; Concord, 2015).

In 2016, the European Parliament broadly supported the New Alliance for Food Security and Nutrition in Africa (NAFSN), launched in May 2012 under the auspices of the G8, which aimed to create the conditions that will allow the African countries involved – Burkina Faso, Benin, Côte d'Ivoire, Ethiopia, Ghana, Malawi, Mozambique, Nigeria, Senegal and Tanzania – to improve agricultural productivity and develop their agri-food sectors by attracting more private investment in agriculture. Criticisms were levelled, however, at the lack of clear commitment to shift to sustainable modes of agricultural production and to support farmers' seed systems; on the dangers associated with the emergence of a market for land rights, or on the regulation of contract farming; and on the weak recognition of women's rights and gender empowerment (European Parliament, 2016). The NAFSN has also been criticised by civil society voices for promoting the interests of transnational corporations rather than those of African small-scale food producers and local small and medium-sized enterprises. The non-governmental organisation (NGO) Concord highlighted the increased emphasis on private-sector-led approaches to development within EU development policy:

> The New Alliance is an alarming example of the new wave of PPPs. Launched at the 2012 G8 Summit the New Alliance now covers 10 African countries and brings well over 180 companies to the table as investors, in addition to the G8 governments and the European Union as donors. This initiative 'aims to accelerate responsible investment in African agriculture and lift 50 million out of poverty by 2022' through a partnership that 'includes specific commitments from African leaders, private sector companies, donor partners'.
>
> *(Concord, 2015: 4)*

In 2017, EU External Action announced it was scaling up its response to famine- and drought-affected countries in the Horn of Africa with an additional €165 million. This was in addition to over €400 million that the EU allocated in 2016 to address the humanitarian crises in the region and €200 million which the EU also approved in 2017 to support the new Government of Somalia to continue transitioning out of fragility and building a resilience society (European Union External Action, 2017). In 2018, DG DEVCO reported that UN-funded interventions completed between 2013 and 2017 contributed to the introduction of sustainable land management practices on over three million hectares of agricultural and pastoral ecosystems, and nearly four million people received rural advisory services and nearly a million people have secure tenure of land (European Commission, 2018b).

The reform of the CAP from 2011 clearly set out the tensions between the desire of the EU to remain a major global producer of food and the desire to support small farmers and agricultural enterprises in developing countries. The EU food and agriculture policies have been widely criticised by many in the NGO community, particularly for their negative impact on developing economies (or the inherent contradictions with EU development policy). For example, Concord (2009: 18) has highlighted the EU's emphasis on competitiveness and 'non-interventionism', which, even without subsidies or special treatment, promotes agri-food exports from the EU and puts developing country producers at a disadvantage. This in turns calls for vast imports of agri-food raw materials, such as soy beans and biofuels, the demand for which has negative impacts on small farmers, food markets and land availability in developing countries. The export of the EU's milk surplus to African countries is frequently cited as an example of a serious disruption of efforts to develop the local economy for this high-value agri-food product. Concord (2015: 7) sums up its criticism of the EU approach to policy coherence for development in the following terms: 'The EU's commitment to [policy coherence for development] and the right to food is jeopardised by its investment frameworks and by current trends in its development cooperation'.

Africa-EU land policies

During the latter decades of the 20th century, land and land reform were highly politicised issues in the context of unresolved issues of dispossession, conflict and dualism dating from the colonial era. British involvement with land reform in Zimbabwe from 1980 was seen as problematic, and

World Bank and other donor support for market-based land reform in South Africa from 1994 brought little progress. The sensitive matter of land tended, therefore, to be avoided by donors and external agencies. With the new millennium, greater democracy in Africa brought with it a renewed pragmatism around land, leading to a modest degree of involvement by donors and development partners, amongst them the EU. Highlights in this regard were the establishment of the EU Task Force on Land Tenure in 2002, the adoption of the 2004 EU Land Policy Guidelines and the adoption of the Voluntary Guidelines of 2012.

The EU Task Force on Land Tenure (2002) was intended to form the basis for a common reference framework to support land policy and land reform processes, thereby contributing to greater co-ordination among EU donors and with bilateral and multilateral donors, to support interventions in land policy and administration in developing countries. In 2004, the European Council and Parliament endorsed the 2004 EU Land Policy Guidelines (Guidelines for Support to Land Policy Design and Land Policy Reform Processes in Developing Countries), based on growing international concern around so-called land-grabbing in Africa and elsewhere (see Commission of the European Communities, 2004; Access to Land, 2019).

The communication from the European Commission identifies rural land as an asset 'of the greatest importance' in both developed and developing countries (Commission of the European Communities 2004: 2), citing its relevance to income, employment and export earnings in developing countries and its centrality to the fight against poverty. Attention to land issues, the communication argues, flows from the overall objective of EU development policy on poverty reduction, arguing that sustainable land policies are 'an essential element of rural development and food security' (ibid.: 2). The policy guidelines are also justified in terms of requests from developing countries for support to land policy reforms. The communication outlines the various elements of an EU approach to support land policy implementation. A set of eight 'key principles' are set out (ibid.: 8), including locally specific solutions; firm political support from the state and wider civil society; in-depth dialogue with the state; long-term commitment; gender-aware legislation and policy; promotion of public information and awareness; policy-relevant research; and specific attention to prevention of further marginalisation of women, poor people, ethnic minorities or indigenous people. The communication also calls for enhanced engagement and coordination among member states and the EU (ibid.: 8–9), recommending a number of specific measures that include initiation of a common approach; integration of land policy reforms into wider national development processes; collaboration with UN agencies such as the Food and Agriculture Organization of the UN (FAO), the International Fund for Agriculture Development and the UN Development Programme; and initiatives around applied research and development on the linkages between land reform and poverty, environment and wider processes of socio-economic development.

The JAES (Africa-EU Partnership, 2007) contains nothing on land reform and only passing mentions of land management and land degradation in the context of climate change (Article 65). The Action Plan 2011–2013 – following the summit theme of 'Investment, economic growth and job creation' – mentions (under MDG Partnerships) land policy and sustainable agriculture (Article 15), the need to further align initiatives of EU and AU member states behind the CAADP processes for food security and agriculture and the need 'to foster the cooperation on accelerating the implementation of the African Land Policy Guidelines' (Article 16). One specific example of a land-related project is EuropeAid's support for land governance worldwide. This project, at a total cost of €240 million, runs from January 2012 to December 2021 and is jointly implemented with NGOs, national governments, UN agencies and others. A leading role is played by the FAO, working with 18 African countries, with a specific budget of €60 million (European Commission, 2019c). A common framework for implementation is provided by the

Voluntary Guidelines on the Responsible Governance of Tenure of land, Fisheries and Forests in the Context of National Food Security (FAO, 2012), the AU Declaration on Land Issues and Challenges in Africa (African Union, 2009) and the Framework and Guidelines for Land Policy in Africa (African Union, African Development Bank and Economic Commission for Africa, 2010).

In a commentary on the 2004 Guidelines, the non-governmental network Concord (2015: 3) highlights the need to consider the traditional and informal land rights of villages, families and individuals; respect the specific local social and institutional context; and institute participatory processes involving the competent public authorities and civil society actors. Furthermore, it criticises what it describes as the regressive role taken by countries such as Belgium and Germany in actively opposing legislation in Congo that protected local smallholders from dispossession by European investors – including threatening to withhold development funding unless the legislation was revised (ibid.: 5).

Potentially the most far-reaching initiative in the area of land are the Voluntary Guidelines on Responsible Governance of Tenure of Land, Forestry and Fishery, launched in 2012 (Windfuhr, 2017). According to the FAO, the purpose of these guidelines is

> to serve as a reference and to provide guidance to improve the governance of tenure of land, fisheries and forests with the overarching goal of achieving food security for all and to support the progressive realization of the right to adequate food in the context of national food security.
>
> *(2012: iv)*

The EU is cooperating with other donors to promote the global debate and actions about responsible land governance, particularly through the Global Donor Working Group on Land, created in 2013. It is also working with the Committee of World Food Security, the AU and various G7/G8 initiatives, and it contributed to the discussion and endorsement of the Voluntary Guidelines (European Commission, 2019c). The programme currently supports around 40 governments for the reform of legislation or the improvement of land administrators' skills for guiding the registration of local land rights.

Conclusion

Agriculture, along with food and land, has been a recurring theme in African-EU relations over the past half-century, although the precise focus has changed considerably. In earlier decades, the emphasis was on production of food and fibre commodities for export and the conditions that facilitated this trade. African agriculture suffered at this time due to the perception of the sector, at home and abroad, as being of secondary importance in terms of economic growth and development when compared to industrial and services sectors. Over time, however, agriculture, including small-sale farming, has come to be seen as essential to broad-based and sustainable growth, poverty alleviation and food security on the continent. Central to this shift has been the establishment of the AU and its various development programmes, which have brought renewed energy to the challenges of agricultural development, including the greater inclusion of smallholders, a shift from production of primary commodities in favour of higher-value and more processed agri-food products, market deregulation and a greater emphasis on domestic and cross-border trade. The new millennium has also witnessed the rise of major new issues of mutual concern that intersect with agricultural policies, including peace and security, food security, land tenure, job creation – particularly in the context of the migration crisis – and, perhaps above all, climate change.

The evolution of EU trade policy bas broadly favoured African producers, but has been criticised by civil society organisations and some African governments as conferring even greater benefits on European consumers, continuing to protect key aspects of the European farm economy and leading to unfair competition on African domestic markets, notably for dairy and grain products. Apart from trade, the EU engages with the agriculture and related sectors in Africa under a range of headings, including bilateral and multilateral programmes of support to agriculture, development aid, food security, land tenure reform and poverty reduction – as shown in this paper. While the EU itself provides voluminous documentation on funding, programme objectives and the like, there is rather less on programme outcomes. There is also very little independent scholarship, at country or continent level, critically evaluating the impact of this multifaceted engagement. It is, therefore, difficult to make a definitive assessment of the impact of African-EU partnership in this important area. What we can say with confidence is that food and agriculture remain of critical importance to the African continent and to the livelihoods of millions of the poorest, mainly rural, people on the continent. Progressive trade policies and aid programmes can be of great assistance, but it is likely to be the policies developed by African governments themselves, individually and collectively, that make the greatest difference. In the era of multiple global challenges, from poverty to climate change, Africa and the EU will continue to depend on each other in order to meet their common objectives.

Bibliography

Access to Land (2019) EU policy [online]. https://www.accesstoland.eu/-International-Policy (retrieved 27 May 2019).

Adebajo, A. and Whiteman, K. (eds) (2012) *The EU and Africa: from Eurafrique to Afro-Europa*. London: Hurst & Co.

Africa-EU Partnership (2007) *The Africa-EU Strategic Partnership: A Joint Africa-EU Strategy*. www.africa-eu-partnership.org/sites/default/files/documents/eas2007_joint_strategy_en.pdf (retrieved 27 May 2019).

Africa-EU Partnership (2010) 3rd Africa-EU Summit [online]. www.africa-eu-partnership.org/en/our-events/3rd-africa-eu-summit (retrieved 27 May 2019).

Africa-EU Partnership (2015) Report of the Contact Group on Agriculture, Food Security and Food Safety. Brussels, 20 April. www.africa-eu-partnership.org/sites/default/files/report_from_the_agri_contact_group_for_2015_c2c_0.pdf (retrieved 11 August 2019).

Africa-EU Partnership (2016) EU–AU Ministerial to advance cooperation in agriculture [online]. 25 July. www.africa-eu-partnership.org/en/stay-informed/news/eu-au-ministerial-advance-cooperation-agriculture (retrieved 11 August 2019).

African-EU Partnership (2018) Africa-Europe Alliance: First projects kicked off [online]. 18 December. www.africa-eu-partnership.org/en/stay-informed/news/africa-europe-alliance-first-projects-kicked

Africa-EU Partnership (2019) European Union and African Union Foreign Ministers take stock of their strong partnership [online]. 23 January. www.africa-eu-partnership.org/en/stay-informed/news/european-union-and-african-union-foreign-ministers-take-stock-their-strong

African Union (2009) *Declaration on Land Issues and Challenges in Africa*. Assembly/AU/Decl.1(XIII) Rev.1. www.uneca.org/sites/default/files/PublicationFiles/au_declaration_on_land_issues_eng.pdf (retrieved 27 May 2019).

African Union (2017) Final Declaration: Investing in youth for accelerated inclusive growth and sustainable development [online]. 7 December. hts://au.int/en/pressreleases/20171207/final-declaration-investing-youth-accelerated-inclusive-growth-and

African Union (2019a) The Africa-EU Partnership [online]. www.africa-eu-partnership.org/en/our-priorities/projects (retrieved 27 May 2019).

African Union (2019b) Projects: LIVE2Africa [online]. www.africa-eu-partnership.org/en/projects/live2africa-pan-african-support-au-ibar-sustainable-development-livestock-livelihoods (retrieved 27 May 2019).

African Union, African Development Bank and Economic Commission for Africa (2010) *Framework and Guidelines on Land Policy in Africa*. Addis Ababa: AUC-ECA-AfDB Consortium.

Babarinde, O. and Wright, S. (2013) Africa-EU Partnership on Trade and Regional Integration. In Jack Mangala (ed.), *Africa and the European Union: A Strategic Partnership*. New York: Palgrave Macmillan (pp. 93–122).

Byerlee, D., De Janvry, A., Sadoulet, E., Townsend, R. and Klytchnikova, I. (2008) *World Development Report 2008: Agriculture for Development*. Washington, DC: World Bank Group. http://documents.worldbank.org/curated/en/587251468175472382/World-development-report-2008-agriculture-for-development

Carbone, M. (2015a) EU-Africa relations in the twentieth-century: Evolution and explanations. In M. Carbone (ed.), *The European Union in Africa*. Manchester: Manchester University Press (pp. 3–24).

Carbone, M. (2015b) Foreign aid, donor coordination and recipient ownership in EU-Africa relations. In M. Carbone (ed.), *The European Union in Africa*. Manchester: Manchester University Press (pp. 121–141).

Commission of the European Communities (2004) EU Guidelines to Support Land Policy Design and Reform Processes in Developing Countries. Communication from the Commission to the Council and the European Parliament. COM (2004) 686 final.

Committee on Development (2007) *Report on Advancing African Agriculture – Proposal for Agricultural Development and Food Security in Africa*. European Parliament. www.europarl.europa.eu/sides/getDoc.do?pubRef=-//EP//NONSGML+REPORT+A6-2007-0432+0+DOC+PDF+V0//EN (retrieved 18 August 2019).

Concord (2009) *Spotlight on Policy Coherence: Report 2009*. Brussels: European NGO Confederation for Relief and Development. https://concordeurope.org/wp-content/uploads/2012/09/DEEEP-REPORT-2014–045.pdf (retrieved 27 May 2019).

Concord (2015) *Investing for Development? Examining the Impacts of the EU's Investment Regime on Food Security, the Right to Food and Land Governance*. Brussels: European NGO Confederation for Relief and Development. https://library.concordeurope.org/record/1633/files/DEEEP-REPORT-2016-007.pdf (retrieved 27 May 2019).

European Commission (2005) EU Strategy for Africa: Towards a Euro-African Pact to Accelerate Africa's Development. Communication from the Commission to the Council, the European Parliament and the European Economic and Social Committee. COM(2005) 489 final. Brussels, 12 October. https://ec.europa.eu/europeaid/sites/devco/files/communication-eu-strategy-for-africa-com2005489-20051012_en.pdf

European Commission (2016) *LIVE2Africa: Pan-African Support to the AU-IBAR for a Sustainable Development of Livestock for Livelihoods in Africa* [online]. https://www.africa-eu-partnership.org/sites/default/files/live2africa_factsheet.pdf (retrieved 27 May 2019).

European Commission (2017a) Focus on sustainability and youth gives new impetus to EU-Africa partnership in agriculture [online]. NEWS, 5 July https://ec.europa.eu/info/news/focus-sustainability-and-youth-gives-new-impetus-eu-africa-partnership-agriculture-2017-jul-05_en

European Commission (2017b) *The New European Consensus on Development: 'Our World, Our Dignity, Our Future'. Official Journal of the European Union*, 60, 30 June 2017. Luxembourg: European Union. https://eur-lex.europa.eu/legal-content/EN/TXT/PDF/?uri=OJ:C:2017:210:FULL&from=EN (retrieved 18 August 2019).

European Commission (2018a) *Strengthening the EU's Partnership with Africa: A New Africa-Europe Alliance for Sustainable Investment and Jobs. State of the Union 2018*. Brussels: European Commission. https://ec.europa.eu/commission/sites/beta-political/files/soteu2018-factsheet-africa-europe_en.pdf (retrieved 27 May 2019).

European Commission (2018b) *An Introduction to the European Union's International Cooperation and Development Policy*. Brussels: Directorate-General for International Cooperation and Development. https://publications.europa.eu/en/publication-detail/-/publication/54e701cf-9aba-11e8-a408-01aa75ed71a1/language-en/format-PDF/source-82684854 (retrieved 27 May 2019).

European Commission (2019a) Africa-Europe Alliance: European Commission committed to a sustainable African agri-food sector. Press Release. Brussels, 7 March. https://ec.europa.eu/commission/presscorner/detail/en/IP_19_1569

European Commission (2019b) *An Africa-Europe Agenda for Rural Transformation: Report by the Task Force Rural Africa*. Brussels: European Commission: Agriculture and Rural Development. https://ec.europa.eu/info/sites/info/files/food-farming-fisheries/farming/documents/report-tfra_mar2019_en.pdf (retrieved 27 May 2019).

European Commission (2019c) *EU Support to Land Governance for Improving Food Security, Poverty Reduction and Inclusive Development*. Brussels: European Commission, International Cooperation and Development. https://ec.europa.eu/europeaid/case-studies/eu-support-land-governance-improving-food-security-poverty-reduction-and-inclusive_en (retrieved 27 May 2019).

European Commission (2019d) Pan-African Programme [online]. https://ec.europa.eu/europeaid/regions/africa/continental-cooperation/pan-african-programme_en (retrieved 18 August 2019).

European Council (2014) Fourth EU-Africa Summit, 2–3 April 2014. Brussels Declaration [online]. www.consilium.europa.eu/media/23894/142096.pdf (retrieved 27 May 2019).

European Council (2019) Cotonou Agreement [online]. www.consilium.europa.eu/en/policies/cotonou-agreement/ (retrieved 27 May 2019).

European Parliament (2010) Assisting Developing Countries in Addressing Food Security Challenges. European Parliament Resolution of 27 September 2011 on an EU Policy Framework to Assist Developing Countries in Addressing Food Security Challenges. 2010/2100(INI). www.europarl.europa.eu/meetdocs/2009_2014/documents/deve/dv/peresolution_/peresolution_en.pdf (retrieved 18 August 2019).

European Parliament (2016) The New Alliance for Food Security and Nutrition. European Parliament Resolution of 7 June 2016 on the New Alliance for Food Security and Nutrition. 2015/2277(INI). www.europarl.europa.eu/doceo/document/TA-8-2016-0247_EN.pdf (retrieved 27 May 2019).

European Union (2016) The Joint Africa-EU Strategy. Brussels: Directorate-General for External Policies of the European Union. https://publications.europa.eu/en/publication-detail/-/publication/487e148b-cb4a-11e7-a5d5-01aa75ed71a1/language-en (retrieved 27 May 2019).

European Union and African Union (2018) *EU-Africa Research and Innovation Partnership on Food and Nutrition Security and Sustainable Agriculture* [online]. https://ec.europa.eu/research/iscp/pdf/policy/eu-africa_research_innovation_cooperation_on_fnssa_en.pdf (retrieved 11 August 2019).

European Union External Action (2017) *EU Scales-up its Response to Famine and Drought Affected Countries in Horn of Africa with an Additional €165 Million*. Brussels, 19 March 2017. https://eeas.europa.eu/headquarters/headquarters-homepage/23001/eu-scales-its-response-famine-and-drought-affected-countries-horn-africa-additional-eu165_en (retrieved 27 May 2019).

FAO (2012) *Voluntary Guidelines on the Responsible Governance of Tenure of Land, Fisheries and Forests in the Context of National Food Security*. Rome: Food and Agriculture Organization of the United Nations. www.fao.org/3/i2801e/i2801e.pdf

Hurt, S.R. (2003) Co-operation and coercion? The Cotonou Agreement between the European Union and ACP states and the end of the Lomé Convention. *Third World Quarterly*, 24 (1), 161–176.

Matthews, A. (2015) Unfulfilled expectations? The EU's agricultural and fisheries policies and Africa. In M. Carbone (ed.), *The European Union in Africa*. Manchester: Manchester University Press (pp. 189–208).

Organization of African Unity and European Union (2000) Cairo Declaration [online]. http://europa.eu/rapid/press-release_PRES-00-901_en.pdf (retrieved 27 May 2019).

Organisation of African, Caribbean and Pacific States (2019) The Lomé Convention [online]. www.acp.int/content/lome-convention (retrieved 27 May 2019).

Spero, J.E. and Hart, J.A. (2010) *The Politics of International Economic Relations*. Boston MA: Wandsworth Cengage.

Windfuhr, M. (2017) FAO: Voluntary guidelines on responsible governance of tenure of land, forests and fisheries: Relevance, reception and first experiences in implementation. In H. Ginzky, I. Heuser, T. Qin, O. Ruppel and P. Wegerdt (eds), *International Yearbook of Soil Law and Policy 2016*. Cham: Springer. (pp. 203–218). https://link.springer.com/chapter/10.1007/978-3-319-42508-5_15

25
Gendering cooperation

Laura Davis

Introduction

> Gender equality is a principle that flows through the engagements of all EU Institutions in all their internal and external activities and it is mainstreamed throughout the different stages of EU policies, strategies, action plans and projects on development, humanitarian aid, education, migration, etc.
>
> *(Council of the European Union, 2018: 6)*

This chapter considers how cooperation between the European Union (EU) and the African Union (AU) is gendered. To do so, it first examines the gendered nature of the EU as a foreign policy actor through analysis of the EU Global Strategy (EUGS) (European External Action Service, 2016) to assess the foreign policy context of EU/AU relations, as we cannot assume these to be neutral, let alone beneficial, in relation to gender equality. It then reflects on policy areas particularly pertinent to EU-AU relations, specifically the Joint Communication for a renewed impetus of the Africa-EU Partnership (European Commission and High Representative of the Union for Foreign Affairs and Security Policy, 2017) and the Communication on supporting the prevention of radicalisation leading to violent extremism (European Commission, 2016). This latter policy is not limited to, or even explicitly focused on, the AU or its member states, but it is included here given the prominence in the EUGS of preventing and countering violent extremism, particularly from the EU's Southern Neighbourhood, which includes North Africa. The second section then considers how the Women, Peace and Security (WPS) agenda[1] and gender equality are addressed in different Africa-EU cooperation instruments.

Feminist theory provides the tools to analyse how 'gender' is constructed in key EU foreign policy documents, all of which sit within the European External Action Service (EEAS). Gender constructs in policy matter because they influence interventions in third countries (Muehlenhoff, 2017; Kronsell, 2016), in this case, relations with the AU. Feminist analysis of EU policy examines how gendered power hierarchies are realised in institutions, in policy and in practice (Kronsell, 2016). This analysis is necessary because 'if masculine power is embedded in European integration and not carefully examined, it is simply reproduced' (Kronsell, 2016: 104). Power is central to understanding 'gendered cooperation', the subject of this chapter. Scholarship on how 'gender' has translated into policy at the United Nations (UN) has demonstrated that it has been 'defanged' (Charlesworth, 2005: 16), reduced to be synonymous with *women* and limited to a patriarchal, heteronormative and monolithic understanding of Woman, from which all power, critical or political potential has been stripped (Charlesworth, 2005; Peto and Manners, 2006; Kouvo, 2014); and scholarship of different EU external policy areas has come to similar conclusions (Guerrina and Wright, 2016; Kronsell, 2016; Haastrup, 2018).

If gender constructs in policy matter, then arguably intersectional gender constructs in policy matter even more. There is a growing concern of the dangers of Eurocentrism in scholarship concerning EU external action in general (Fisher Onar and Nicolaïdes, 2013) and of EU conflict prevention in particular (Davis, 2015). This reflects the far longer-standing feminist concerns with the assumptions of many first wave feminists that White, Western, heterosexual, middle-class experience of womanhood was universal in opposition to masculine hegemonic power. Challenges for feminism to include and address differences of race, class, sexuality, age and (dis) ability (Crenshaw, 1989; Haraway, 1991; Mohanty, 1991) led to more inclusive, or intersectional, understandings of gender.

As European and Other women (and men) experience EU external action differently, intersectional feminism may help us if not avoid then at least limit misrepresentation by acknowledging Eurocentrism both in EU analysis and in feminist analysis. This means that it matters how 'Other' women are presented, as victim subject politics deny women's agency and feed conservative and protectionist rather than liberating responses (Kapur, 2002). Intersectionality can be understood as the different ways in which social divisions, such as class, race and ethnicity, gender and sexuality, ability and age combine to create differential access to economic, political and cultural resources. Intersectionality also acts as a reminder that not all difference is equal, and not all differences have the same or universal application. We cannot, therefore, assume the same constellation or effect in each case as each will be dependent on specific social, economic and political processes. Understanding how power flows through intersectional gendered relations is therefore central to understanding access to power and resources (Yuval-Davis, 2006).

To this we add the power between the EU as an external actor and the Other recipient/beneficiary. Nancy Fraser problematises this as 'newly visible meta-injustice ... *misframing*', which happens when 'the state-territorial frame is imposed on transnational sources of injustice' (2010: 114). For our purposes, the concept of misframing is useful for identifying risks that initiatives to promote gender equality within the foreign policy apparatus of the EU will create divisions between European and Other women (and men), the supposed beneficiaries of EU external action in the context of EU/AU relations, and so replicate injustice. This will help us guard against the assumption that more gender equality for some people (especially, in this case, European women) in some areas of policy will also benefit other people (particularly, in this case, Other, African women).

Gender in EU foreign policy

Article 2 of the Treaty on European Union states that 'equality between women and men' is a founding value of the EU (European Union, 2012b: Art. 2). This is an explicitly binary representation of gender, and of women and men. It excludes people with non-binary gender identities, and the positioning of women and men suggests and reinforces heterosexual hegemony. Other gender identities are excluded, even if the Charter of Fundamental Rights of the European Union (2012a) prohibits discrimination on grounds of sexual orientation (Art. 21). This section analyses the gender constructs in the EUGS (European External Action Service, 2016) and the Joint Communication for a renewed impetus of the Africa-EU Partnership (European

Commission and High Representative of the Union for Foreign Affairs and Security Policy, 2017), key policies that frame cooperation between the EU and AU and therefore provide insight into the gendered nature of that cooperation.

EU Global Strategy

Maria Stern analysed the gender and colonial tropes of the European Security Strategy (ESS), titled *A Secure Europe in a Better World* (Council of the European Union, 2009), concluding that the EU acts as a 'civilising patriarch' that aims 'to civilise barbaric Others through, at best, example, and at worst, force' (Stern, 2011: 50). In 2016, the EU launched the EUGS, titled *Shared Vision, Common Action: A Stronger Europe*, to replace the ESS, dropping the ESS's ambition of a 'better world' for that of a 'stronger Europe'. Following Stern, the analysis of the document reveals a more exclusive, patriarchal and Othering foreign policy than that envisaged in 2003. The EUGS focuses on hard security to protect (explicitly) EU citizens, particularly from terrorism within the Union and from dangers emanating from Europe's (Southern) Neighbourhood, particularly North Africa, and to support the EU 'defence community'. The primary and intertwined priorities of EU foreign policy are now preventing or countering violent extremism and counter-terrorism and stemming migration into the EU.

In its final version, the EUGS includes several brief references to both 'gender' and 'women'.[2] It acknowledges the 'multiple dimensions [of conflicts] – from security to gender, from governance to the economy' (European External Action Service, 2016: 28). There is no elaboration on what a 'gender dimension' to conflict might be as an isolated subject of analysis, but by separating gender from security, governance and the economy, some of the most important ways in which people organise and are organised, the gendered power relations inherent within and across each of these are therefore dismissed.

The few references to 'women' in the EUGS are also revealing: 'thousands of men and women serving under the European flag for peace and security' (European External Action Service, 2016: 4) in civilian and military Common Security and Defence Policy missions around the world; 10 out of the 16 of these missions are in/with AU member states (European External Action Service, 2019). European women in this citation are active, if subordinated to male colleagues, in masculine hard-security roles. The EUGS also states that the participation of (European) women in foreign policy making will be strengthened (European External Action Service, 2016: 48).

The EUGS states the EU's ambition to develop more 'creative approaches to diplomacy', including 'promoting the role of women in peace efforts – from implementing the UNSC Resolution [sic] on Women, Peace and Security to improving the EU's internal gender balance' (European External Action Service, 2016: 31). Framing increasing women's participation in peace efforts in the context of developing its diplomacy, the EUGS implies that it is European women – professional, middle-class, predominantly White European women – whose roles in peace efforts are to be promoted; the participation of Other women in peace processes, whether they are stakeholders in the conflict and its resolution or experts from other parts of the world, is overlooked and excluded.

The EUGS seeks to empower European women in peacemaking efforts, but not Other women. Not only does this deny Other women the opportunities extended to European women but it risks essentialising European women's participation. This may then be taken to represent the universal Woman and used as cover to deny Other women's participation and agency. Other women in the EUGS are passive recipients of aid, often lumped together with youth – 'decent work opportunities, notably for women and youth' (European External Action

Service, 2016: 26) – and with children – 'We will significantly step up our humanitarian efforts ... focusing on education, women and children' (ibid.: 27). While the (potential) agency of European women is partially recognised within a masculinised security apparatus, Other women are infantilised, vulnerable, weak and passive recipients of European largesse. Other young men and young women, boys and girls are ungendered and passive recipients. Men are not mentioned; their agency is taken for granted throughout.

The Joint Communication for a renewed impetus of the Africa-EU Partnership (2017)

Within the joint communication's priority to 'prevent conflict, address crises and peacebuilding' (European Commission and and High Representative of the Union for Foreign Affairs and Security Policy, 2017: 7), the emphasis is firmly placed on protecting EU security interests, over those of the African populations. The response that follows is driven by a hard-security approach that concentrates on building up state capacities for hard security, suggesting that the security of the regime may be more important than the safety of the population. The priority 'Strengthening governance systems' identifies strong, democratic institutions as a measure of resilience. '[T]he involvement of youth and women in formal political processes will increase trust in state institutions' (p. 9). This reference infantilises and instrumentalises women: Women's (and youth) 'involvement' is to increase public trust in state institutions rather than to reform state institutions so that they deliver women's and young people's (diverse) interests. The implication is that men's power, including through the institutions, is assumed. Women and youth need to feel involved so that they deliver public trust – acquiesce to the system rather than the system change to meet their various needs. The proposed remedy is '[d]eepening the empowerment of women, youth as well as vulnerable people, through targeted programmes fostering their participation in decision making processes' (p. 11). 'Vulnerable people' are not defined, but they, along with women and youth, are, collectively, weak bodies held back by their lack of empowerment. The onus is on these weak bodies to empower themselves, with the EU's assistance, to ensure their own inclusion, to assert their agency and so end their own exclusion. There is no suggestion that the institutions reform exclusive policies and practices.

The same section also includes support for broadening civic space. As the civic space available to women and sexual and gender minorities tends to shrink more quickly than elite male civic space, this is important. Yet the section on governance is subordinated to security and security concerns – often connected to migration, the third priority – which are frequently used as cover for reducing civic space. The section on migration and mobility makes no reference to the highly gendered opportunities for mobility and patterns of migration, an oversight that underscores how limited the integration of any gender analysis, however superficial, has been.

Countering terror and violent extremism

Counterterrorism and preventing and countering violent extremism are increasingly dominant policy areas within and beyond the EU, including, as we have seen, with EU relations with Africa. The Counter Terrorism Strategy (Council of the European Union, 2005) is completely gender blind: women, men and gender are simply not mentioned.

Gender is not mentioned in the more recent European Commission Communication on supporting the prevention of radicalisation leading to violent extremism, but this does refer to (Other) women twice. In the first instance, Other women are instrumental – the European Commission should help 'empower' women as a way to reduce radicalisation, rather than as an end in itself. There is latent potential for Other women's agency – they may prevent radicalisation, if empowered to do so by the European Commission. The second reference places women and very young children as passive victims of radical ideology, suggesting that women and the very young share inherent characteristics that differentiate them from men. Once again, there is latent potential agency, although in this case as a threat (to European security). Other women and (presumably) their children may become radicalised and so move from passivity to agency. In both cases, agency requires an external, masculinised actor, either for good (European Commission) or ill (radical ideologue).

Gendered foreign policy

This section has demonstrated that EU foreign policy in general and towards Africa specifically is highly gendered and has become increasingly Othering. The overriding concern is on protecting Europeans within Europe from security threats from barbaric Others, particularly from the Southern Neighbourhood. Other women are understood as weak, vulnerable, infantilised and passive recipients of aid, with little agency, although with masculine intervention, they may be instrumentalised to prevent or further violent extremism. European women are encouraged to participate in projecting Europe's force. The agency of European and Other men and boys is assumed – invisible and omnipotent. Sexual and gender minorities are invisible and excluded. This is the political climate in which EU-AU cooperation must be understood.

Gender equality and the Women, Peace and Security agenda in Africa-EU cooperation

The WPS agenda is based on a set of United Nations Security Council Resolutions (UNSCRs), starting with UNSCR 1325 in 2000,[3] and has high visibility in both Africa and the EU. These UNSCRs on WPS have focused on the need for women's participation, in different forms, in some aspects of peace and security (O'Rourke, 2014). The UNSCRs on WPS and the national action plans (NAPs) that result from them have also provided a much-needed platform for women and women's organisations to voice their opinions and space for activism far from New York (Otto, 2010), even if there are serious limitations to the 'participation' envisaged by the WPS agenda (O'Rourke, 2014) and gender mainstreaming remains a challenge (Charlesworth, 2005).

The WPS agenda has its origins at the UN and has had considerable traction in Africa, particularly south of the Sahara. (Tunisia is the only North African state to have adopted a NAP.) West Africa has a high concentration of the NAPs and the Economic Community of West African States (ECOWAS) has adopted a regional action plan. The regional organisations in West Africa (ECOWAS), Southern Africa and Eastern Africa (the Intergovernmental Authority on Development and the East African Community) have also adopted regional gender equality policies, which tend to be disconnected from WPS policy provisions (Desmidt and Davis, 2019: 22), a challenge African regional organisations share with the EU (see below). The EU adopted its Comprehensive approach to the EU implementation of the UNSCRs 1325 and 1820 on women, peace and security (henceforth: CA 1325) in 2008 (Council of the European Union, 2008), which was updated in 2018, and the EU Strategic Approach to WPS was adopted in December 2018 (Council of the European Union, 2018). Unlike its African equivalents, the EU's strategy and action plan focus on external action, beyond the EU and the wider European continent. They thus form part of the EU's external action architecture – although their place in the hierarchy is problematic (discussed below).

The Strategic Approach was adopted in late 2018 after a consultative process that included input from EU member states and European civil society actors, although not from civil society outside Europe even though the document is conceived primarily as a foreign policy tool, relative to EU external action rather than inward-looking. Its EU-internal provisions are mainly concerned with recruiting European women to the EU's peace and security – that is, outward-facing – institutions. Both these policy documents are long and detailed, but neither includes gender and sexual minorities, despite the adoption in 2013 of the EU's Guidelines to promote and protect the enjoyment of all human rights by lesbian, gay, transgender and intersex (LGBTI) persons (Council of the European Union, 2013).

At the time of writing, it is too early to consider the implementation of the EU Strategic Approach, or of its Action Plan, adopted in July 2019 (European External Action Service, 2019). However, implementation of the previous action plans were a challenge and mainly focused on recruiting European women to the EU peace and security architecture, rather than considering whether and to what extent EU external action in the outside world promoted gender equality. EEAS senior management has not adequately prioritised the WPS agenda across EU external action (Davis, 2018).

The other instrument that the EU has at its disposal regarding gender equality in external action is the EU Gender Action Plan, currently in its second iteration and known as GAP II (European Commission, 2015). As a Commission tool, this sits institutionally separate from the EEAS WPS Action Plans, and reporting in the past has been uncoordinated, although this has improved since 2017 (Desmidt and Davis, 2019) and is expected to be better with GAP III.

Gender equality and/or WPS in EU cooperation with Africa[4]

The Joint Africa-EU Strategy 2007 (JAES) (Council of the European Union, 2007) and the Cotonou Agreement between the EU and the African, Caribbean and Pacific Group of States and the European Community and its Member States (2010) provide the framework for EU cooperation with Africa. Both Cotonou and the JAES refer to the importance of gender equality, but neither refer to the WPS agenda or the UNSCRs on which this is based. The European Development Fund (EDF) is the main instrument for implementing the Cotonou Agreement, while the JAES is implemented through the appropriate geographic and thematic EU funding instruments, including the EDF, the Development Cooperation Instrument (DCI), the European Neighbourhood Instrument, the Instrument contributing to Stability and Peace (IcSP) and the European Instrument for Democracy and Human Rights (EIDHR).

At the time of writing, there was no information available for how much the EU spent on gender equality and/or the WPS agenda in Africa, reinforcing the more global problem of quantifying EU spending on gender equality and/or the WPS agenda worldwide (Davis, 2018). Recent research suggests that the EDF and the IcSP are the most commonly used funding instruments to promote and support the WPS agenda in Africa (Desmidt and Davis, 2019).

A review of the whether and how the main financing instruments address WPS and/or gender equality concerns reveals inconsistencies and missed opportunities. For instance, the EDF is administered through national indicative programmes and regional indicative programmes, which are agreed between the relevant government/regional organisation and the EU member states; the regional indicative programme for West Africa places emphasis on promoting women's participation in conflict prevention and the development of gender expertise through ECOWAS, but has no implementation strategy. Of the national indicative programmes, it would appear that only the one for Liberia includes specific reference to the WPS agenda.

The Pan-African Programme, financed through the DCI, was established in 2014 in order to give the JAES a dedicated financial instrument. Projects implemented through this programme have not made direct references to the implementation of the WPS agenda, although some projects have addressed women's empowerment. In general, however, this programme was a missed opportunity for advancing the WPS agenda/gender equality through the Africa-EU partnership. The IcSP is a thematic financing tool for EU external action, mainly focussing on short-term response to crises. 'Gender equality and the empowerment of women' falls into its remit as a cross-cutting issue for programming it supports (Council of the European Union, 2014). In 2017, however, an evaluation of this programme found that gender had not been adequately mainstreamed and that only 11% of programmes addressed gender equality and the empowerment of women directly.

Like the IcSP, the EIDHR is a thematic instrument, focused primarily on short-term projects. Its main recipients are civil society organisations. Its objectives include support to the WPS agenda, and the CA 1325 implementation report of 2017 cites it as an important tool for furthering the WPS agenda (Council of the European Union, 2017), but it is not possible to ascertain how much support for WPS-related work has been allocated in Africa. This brief review demonstrates that despite the high visibility of the WPS agenda and of gender equality in key policy and programming documents that underpin Africa-EU relations, there is little and inconsistent follow-up. WPS and gender equality are simply not the priorities that the policy documents cited boldly claim, for apparently these provisions can be taken or left at will. Even the EIDHR and IcSP, which as thematic instruments are far smaller in scope and budget than the EDF and DCI, seem to miss the opportunity to support African initiatives for the WPS agenda and gender equality.

Even where there are references to the WPS agenda and/or gender equality, very few projects or programmes took WPS as their starting point. The EU is not an important supporter of WPS NAPs in Africa, even though support to NAPs is an indicator for CA 1325; UN Women and UN regional offices are far more active than the EU in this field. Within projects that have supported the WPS agenda, 'activities and projects have focused on protection rather than prevention, participation or relief and recovery' (Desmidt and Davis, 2019: 2) even if participation, especially in political decision-making and peace mediation, is gaining attention (Desmidt and Davis, 2019).

This focus on protection to the detriment of other WPS pillars is problematic. We have seen how passive Other women are portrayed in the key policy documents analysed in previous sections. Review of the EU's CA 1325 and GAP II reports show there are frequent references to sexual violence, which identify women and girls as the primary – or only – victims of sexual and gender-based violence, which then becomes the dominant 'women's issue'. Male victims are ignored. The overwhelmingly male perpetrators are invisible, which diminishes their culpability (Davis, 2018). Without detracting from the harm victims and survivors – women, men, boys and girls – suffer, framing policies around female victimhood in this way perpetuates racist and colonial images of the weak, constrained and vulnerable – and, in this case, sexualised – Other women. This kind of victim subject politics denies women's agency and feeds conservative and protectionist rather than liberating responses (Kapur, 2002). The positioning of Other women and girls as primarily victims of sexual violence exacerbates this risk, especially in the context of emphasising protection over prevention or participation.

Conclusion

This chapter has demonstrated that EU-Africa cooperation has to be understood within the context of EU foreign policy that is highly gendered, patriarchal and Othering. Other – in this case, African – women are weak, vulnerable, infantilised and instrumentalised recipients of

European aid. They are instrumentalised: 'empowerment' is a means to achieve EU-security objectives rather than contribute to gender equality. Sexual and gender minorities are invisible and excluded. Heterosexual men are invisible and their agency assumed throughout. The WPS Agenda has high visibility in both Africa and Europe, but closer examination of whether and how the EU integrates WPS and/or gender equality provisions into its cooperation with Africa does not suggest that action lives up to rhetoric. The EU mobilises significant funds through the EDF and DCI, yet with little provision to support the WPS agenda and/or gender equality. The EU is not a primary supporter of NAPs in Africa, even though this is an indicator for the EU's CA 1325; nor can precise figures for WPS and/or gender equality expenditure be found. Even through the thematic IcSP and EIDHR – far smaller programmes than the EDF or DCI – it seems that these programmes underperform on support to WPS and/or gender equality. Our analysis has also shown how EU cooperation in these fields prioritises protection over participation and prevention, again reinforcing a gendered, patriarchal and Othering power relationship between the EU and Africa. Africa-EU cooperation has, therefore, been a missed opportunity for supporting African initiatives to further gender equality and the WPS agenda.

Notes

1 This draws in large part on (Davis, 2018).
2 Earlier versions reportedly did not include any references to either.
3 They are: UN Security Council Resolutions 1325 (2000); 1820 (2009); 1888 (2009); 1889 (2010); 1960 (2011); 2106 (2013); 2122 (2013) and 2242 (2015).
4 This section draws on Desmidt and Davis (2019: 27–33).

Bibliography

African, Caribbean and Pacific Group of States and the European Community and its Member States (2010) Agreement Amending for the Second time the Partnership Agreement between the Members of the African, Caribbean and Pacific Group of States and the European Community and its Member States. 'Cotonou Agreement'. 4 November.

Charlesworth, H. (2005) Not waving but drowning: Gender mainstreaming and human rights in the United Nations. *Harvard Human Rights Journal*, 18, 1–18.

Council of the European Union (2005) The European Union Counter-Terrorism Strategy. 14469/4/05. Brussels, 30 November.

Council of the European Union (2007) The Africa-EU Strategic Partnership: A Joint Africa-EU Strategy. 16344/07 (Presse 291). Lisbon, 9 December.

Council of the European Union (2008) Comprehensive Approach to the EU Implementation of the UN Security Council Resolutions 1325 & 1820 on Women, Peace and Security. 15671/1/08. Brussels, 1 December.

Council of the European Union (2009) *European Security Strategy: A Secure Europe in a Better World*. Brussels: Publication Office of the European Union.

Council of the European Union (2013) Guidelines to Promote and Protect the Enjoyment of all Human Rights by Lesbian, Gay, Transgender and Intersex (LGBTI) Persons. 11153/13. Brussels, 24 June.

Council of the European Union (2014) Second Report on the EU-indicators for the Comprehensive Approach to the EU Implementation of the UN Security Council Resolutions 1325 & 1820 on Women, Peace and Security. 6219/14. Brussels, 6 February.

Council of the European Union (2017) Third Report on the EU Indicators for the Comprehensive Approach to the EU Implementation of the UN Security Council Resolutions 1325 and 1820 on Women, Peace and Security. 14692/17. Brussels, 22 November.

Council of the European Union (2018) Women, Peace and Security – Council Conclusions (10 December 2018). 15086/18. Brussels, 10 September.

Crenshaw, K. (1989) Demarginalizing the intersection of race and sex: A black feminist critique of antidiscrimination doctrine, feminist theory and antiracist politics. *University of Chicago Legal Forum*, 1989, Article 8, 138–167. http://chicagounbound.uchicago.edu/uclf/vol1989/iss1/8

Davis, L. (2015) Reform or business as usual? EU security provision in complex contexts: Mali. *Global Society*, 29 (2), 260–279.

Davis, L. (2018) *Kissing the Frog: Gender Equality in EU Conflict Prevention and Other Fairy Tales*. EU CIVCAP, 16 July. https://eucivcap.files.wordpress.com/2018/05/eu-civcap_deliverable_3-4_web.pdf (retrieved 13 September 2019).

Desmidt, S. and Davis, L. (2019) Rhetoric and Real Progress *on the Women, Peace and Security Agenda in Africa*. ECPDM Discussion Paper 245. European Centre for Development Policy Management.

European Commission (2015) Joint Staff Working Document: Gender Equality and Women's Empowerment: Transforming the Lives of Girls and Women through EU External Relations 2016–2020. SWD(2015) 182 final. Brussels, 21 September.

European Commission (2016) Communication on Supporting the Prevention of Radicalisation Leading to Violent Extremism. COM(2016) 379 final. Brussels, 14 June.

European Commission and High Representative of the Union for Foreign Affairs and Security Policy (2017) Joint Communication to the European Parliament and the Council for a Renewed Impetus of the Africa-Partnership. (SWD(2017) 150 final. Brussels, 4 May.

European External Action Service (2016) *Shared Vision, Common Action: A Stronger Europe. A Global Strategy for the European Union's Foreign and Security Policy*. Brussels: EEAS.

European External Action Service (2019) EU Action Plan on Women, Peace and Security (WPS) 2019–2024. EEAS(2019) 747.

European Union (2012a) Charter of Fundamental Rights of the European Union. *Official Journal of the European Union*, C326/391.

European Union (2012b) Consolidated version of the Treaty on European Union. Official Journal of the European Union, 55, C326/17.

Fisher Onar, N. and Nicolaïdes, K. (2013) The decentring agenda: Europe as a post-colonial power. *Cooperation and Conflict*, 48 (2), 283–303.

Fraser, N. (2010) *Scales of Justice: Reimagining Political Space in a Globalizing World*. New York: Columbia University Press.

Guerrina, R. and Wright, K.A. (2016) Gendering Normative Power Europe: Lessons of the Women, Peace and Security agenda. *International Affairs*, 92 (2), 293–312.

Haastrup, T. (2018) Creating Cinderella? The unintended consequences of the Women Peace and Security agenda for EU's mediation architecture. *International Negotiation*, 23 (2), 218–237.

Haraway, D.J. (1991) *Simians, Cyborgs, and Women. The Reinvention of Nature*. New York: Routledge.

Kapur, R. (2002) The tragedy of victimization rhetoric: Resurrecting the 'native' subject in international/post-colonial feminist legal politics. *Harvard Human Rights Journal*, 15 (1), 1–37.

Kouvo, S. (2014) *Making Just Rights? Mainstreaming Women's Human Rights and a Gender Perspective*. Uppsala: Iustus Forslag.

Kronsell, A. (2016) The power of EU masculinities: A feminist contribution to European integration theory. *Journal of Common Market Studies*, 54 (1), 104–120.

Mohanty, C.T. (1991) *Third World Women and the Politics of Feminism*. Bloomington: University of Indiana Press.

Muehlenhoff, H.L. (2017) Victims, soldiers, peacemakers and caretakers: The neoliberal constitution of women in the EU's security policy. *International Feminist Journal of Politics*, 19 (2), 153–167.

O'Rourke, C. (2014) Walk[ing] the halls of power: Understanding women's participation in international peace and security. *Melbourne Journal of International Law*, 15, 128–154.

Otto, D. (2010) Power and danger: Feminist engagement with international law through the UN Security Council. *The Australian Feminist Law Journal*, 32, 97–121.

Peto, A. and Manners, I. (2006) The European Union and the value of gender equality. In S. Lucarelli and I. Manners (eds), *Values and Principles in European Union Foreign Policy*. Abingdon: Routledge (pp. 97–113).

Stern, M. (2011) Gender and race in the European Security Strategy: Europe as a 'force for good'? *Journal of International Relations and Development*, 14, 28–59.

Yuval-Davis, N. (2006) Intersectionality and feminist politics. *European Journal of Women's Studies*, 13 (3), 193–209.

Conclusion

Luís Mah, Toni Haastrup and Niall Duggan

This handbook explores changing dynamics and uncertainties of the relationship between Africa and the European Union (EU). At its core, the handbook acknowledges the role of a rising agency of African actors and how it has been playing to reframe and transform the unequal rules of the game between the two blocs. The authors in this handbook have attempted to analyse the institutions, rules, norms, narratives and practices that have moulded the behaviour of African actors vis-à-vis their EU counterparts and to assess new opportunities for cooperation between them to tackle global challenges.

What Africa is, and how it is located within the global political economy in recent years, oscillates between, on the one hand, a very particular strand of Afro-pessimism which narrates the continent as a challenging environment and, on the other hand, the narrative of 'Africa rising'. Whereas, the former focuses on the impacts of anti-Black racism, colonialism and the ill effects of globalisation on the continent, the latter positions Africa as an attractive continent on the global frontier of the 21st century, focusing on the levels of growth, industrialisation and the extent to which capital is present. The juxtaposition of Africa the hopeless versus Africa rising has become a key topic of debate within multilateral organisations, leading think tanks, consultancy firms and the media. Early in January 2020, before COVID-19 became a pandemic, the African Economic Outlook 2020 (African Development Bank, 2020) stated that the continent's economic prospects were improving and for the first time in a decade, investment represented more than 50% of the continent's growth. The continent has been home to some of the fastest-growing economies in the world throughout the first two decades of this century. A series of factors explain its recent economic trajectory, from increasing domestic demand helped by a fast- growing population, rising remittances and foreign capital flows and favourable commodity prices to enhanced export volumes. However, the African Economic Outlook also makes it clear that this economic growth has been far from inclusive, with high degrees of inequality within the region (ibid.). Despite improvements since the Millennium Development Goals agenda in the 2000s, the continent overall continues to deliver the lowest human development indicators in the world (United Nations, 2019), and issues related to peace and security continue to negatively affect stability and population safety. The UN lists as least developed countries a big majority of sub-Sahara African countries (United Nations Conference on Trade and Development, 2020).

Conclusion

The rapidly changing economic and social dynamics in Africa have developed alongside new patterns of global engagement between the continent and the rest of the world – most notably China, as pointed out by several authors in this handbook. Within this new context, African leaders are now emerging as more self-confident and sufficiently comfortable in voicing their opinions in terms of policy choices. This new posture impacts the relational patterns of the continent with its most important investment, trading, humanitarian and development aid partner, the EU (see Kell and Vines, this volume). As several of the authors stress in this handbook, Africa-EU relations tend to be regarded as asymmetrical in favour of Europe. But the negotiations, practices and outcomes related to the Economic Partnership Agreements (EPAs), an institutionalised dimension of Africa-EU relations, challenge these assumptions to an extent. Adetula and Osegbue, in their contribution show that the negotiations have been fraught. While many African leaders see EPAs as strengthening the continent's dependence on the EU, they have also pushed back on what they see as the EU's attempt to sow divisions among African countries. Thus, despite strong EU pressure to have African countries signing on to the EPAs by 2007, only few countries have done so, and its uptake is very fragmented. In this sense, African leaders have shown that they can exercise agency and challenge the EU. For Hodzi (this volume), growing and stronger relations with China offers more power and bargaining leverage to African leaders in their negotiations with the EU. Whether or not this recently gained so-called *derivative* and *collective* power is enough to guarantee more African agency, policy space and outcomes that reflect the continent's independence and more symmetrical relations with the EU remains to be seen. This new context only makes more relevant Weldeab Sebhatu's argument that a postcolonial approach is crucial to understanding and articulating African agency within Africa-EU relations, thus overcoming Eurocentric-shaped perspectives.

Since 2015, the AU has increasingly asserted its role as representing pan-African interests in the global arena, though still with major capacity fragilities as exposed by Akokpari and Bimha in this volume. Yet, the AU continues working to build greater coherence, cooperation and African-led solutions to African and global challenges. This is attested by the launching of Agenda 2063 in 2013, the AU's strategic master plan to transform the continent into a global force in 50 years, the establishment of the African Union Development Agency in 2018, responsible for the implementation of the Agenda and, more recently, the agreement establishing the African Continental Free Trade Area (AfCFTA). The creation of the AfCFTA comes with the expectation of lower tariffs across the continent, an increase in the regional production power of Africa and trade to help build and boost regional value chains. Above all, this new integration initiative provides an opportunity for the continent to reclaim and lead its own development agenda (Signé and Gurib-Fakim, 2019).

These moves by the AU have been paralleled by the EU's pivot to Africa by the new 'geopolitical' European Commission led by Ursula von der Leyen. In a presentation to the new Commission in September 2019, the President-elect said of Africa's importance to the EU:

> I would like Europe to have a **comprehensive strategy on Africa,** our close neighbour and our most natural partner.
>
> It is a continent full of opportunity and potential for cooperation and for business. It will become home to the youngest, fastest growing middle class in the world, with private consumption expected to reach €2 trillion a year by 2025. We must make the most of the political, economic and investment opportunities that these changes will bring.
>
> *(von der Leyen, 2019a: 18, emphasis in original)*

This statement shows how von der Leyen has embraced the 'Africa rising' narrative, recognising the potential of the continent for Europe. This is also evident of her mission letters to Jutta Urpilainen and Phil Hogan, the new Commissioners for International Partnerships and Trade, respectively.

The relabelling of former Commissioner for International Cooperation and Development into the Commissioner for International Partnerships seems to show von der Leyen's willingness to push for a more political and strategic cooperation with regions that traditionally benefited from EU development cooperation (Teevan and Sheriff, 2019). In the mission letter to Urpilainen, the president asks her to guarantee a strategic and effective 'European model of development' that creates 'value for money' to 'contribute to our [EU's] wider political priorities' (von der Leyen, 2019b: 4). The overarching goal of poverty reduction, the cornerstone of the EU's international development policy as set out in Article 208 of the 2009 Treaty of Lisbon, seems to have been forgotten in the mission letter. Instead, the 2017 European External Investment Plan is prioritised as a tool to promote private sector investment ostensibly leading to economic growth, trade opportunities and better migration management. This seems to be the continuation of a policy that reinforces what Langan and Price call 'aid blending'. Aid blending promotes public-private partnerships as the means to achieving sustainable development. Additionally, in the mission letter to new Trade Commissioner Hogan, von der Leyen asserted:

> I want you to prioritise our trade and investment partnership with **Africa**. The implementation of the African Continental Free Trade Agreement should be seen as a step towards our long-term objective of a continent-to-continent free trade area between Africa and the EU.
> *(von der Leyen, 2019c: 5, emphasis in original)*

A few days after starting her mandate in December 2019, von der Leyen visited the AU in Addis Ababa, her first official visit outside the EU. Arguably, this signalled a new recognition of the AU as the main regional interlocutor. Soon after, in early February 2020, EU Council President Charles Michel attended the annual AU leaders' summit as a precursor to the commission-to-commission meeting. This was followed by another visit, on behalf of the EU, by Josep Borell, the High Representative of the Union for Foreign Affairs and Security Policy. Borell presented the EU's new Africa strategy, focusing on five partnerships: green transition and energy access; digital transformation; sustainable growth and jobs; peace, security and governance; and migration and mobility (European Commission, 2020). As Kell and Vines point out in this volume, while the strategy is 'less paternalistic' in its tone, it does not offer the 'precise instruments and financing mechanisms' to help its implementation. Moreover, it is worth noting that the same critique can be levied against this strategy as was done of the similar 2005 strategy – that is, it presents a European vision of Africa rather than one informed by African actors. Since the launch of the strategy, however, Commissioner Urpilainen has indicated a consultative process including civil society and African interlocutors will follow the strategy to derive more precision.

How to use its external financial instruments in more efficient and strategic ways is on the forefront of EU considerations and planning, and this has implications for the EU's relationship with African countries and institutions. In September of 2018, the European Commission began pushing with a communication submitted to the European Parliament, the European Council, the Council and the European Investment Bank for the need to set 'a more efficient financial architecture for investment outside the European Union' to respond to the EU strategic interests (European Commission, 2018). This was followed by the establishment by the

Council of the European Union in April 2019 of a High-Level Group of Wise Persons on the European Financial Architecture for Development. This group was given the task of reflecting on the 'challenges to and opportunities for rationalising the European financial architecture for development' and offering 'scenarios' for its evolution (Council of the European Union, 2019).

Eight months later, in October 2019, the High-Level Group released its report, entitled *Europe in the World: The Future of the European Financial Architecture for Development* (Wieser et al., 2019). The High-Level Group recognised that the current EU financial architecture for development is a complex and fragmented system with '**overlaps, gaps and inefficiencies, sectoral and geographical**, especially in terms of presence and experience in Africa' (ibid.: 3, emphasis in original). Consequently, it argued for

> **consolidation and streamlining of development finance and climate activities outside the EU into a single entity, a European Climate and Sustainable Development Bank,** in order to avoid overlaps, and strengthen the EU's presence, role and long-term capacity to deliver on EU development priorities.
> *(Wieser et al., 2019: 3, emphasis in original)*

The European Commission's proposal to bring all the existing EU international development programmes and budget lines under a single platform, the Neighbourhood, Development and International Cooperation Instrument, within the 2021–2027 Multiannual Financial Framework is regarded by the High-Level Group as a potential 'catalyst for improvement' of the European financial architecture for development. Whether this new budget will be approved exactly as proposed by the European Commission within the new COVID-19 pandemic context remains to be seen. But the current situation points to a potential delay the implementation of the new EU strategy for Africa.

But while the new geopolitical Commission has placed Africa at the core of its external policy, it has been hard to see if the same level or degree of importance could be found on the African side. Uzo Madu notes an absence of excitement on the part of the AU especially for Africa-EU relations. This, she notes, is because the 'AU is undergoing a major internal reform to ensure it can create the right environment to position itself and act as a global player rather than at its margins' (Madu, 2020). As South African president and chair of the AU, Cyril Ramaphosa noted in February 2020 that the AU's reform process is centred on revitalising and actioning the rhetoric of African solutions to African problems. Ramaphosa also offered an Africa-centric vision on trade, stressing that 'the era of colonialism and imperialism, under which Africa is a pit-stop in the global assembly, line has passed' (African Union, 2020: 5). It is too early to assess how the emergence of the pandemic and its economic and social impacts in the continent might weaken these attempts to strengthen African agency and build its own possibilities and avenues. This possibility is worth considering given that most regions all over the world seem to have halted large-scale global governance initiatives in 2020, and those within Africa-EU relations have been no different. What is clear is that Africa continues to strengthen its position and articulate its agency vis-à-vis the EU. Moreover, while the EU seeks a boost in its relationship with the African continent, it is only one actor among many vying for attention in Africa. And this is the leverage that Africa has. To effectively utilise it, however, may require deeper moves towards integration and greater competencies for institutions like the AU to act on behalf of states and people. The contributions in this handbook show that the the futures of Africa and Europe will remain entwined for many years to come, and while it is uncertain what this relationship may look like, it is no longer business as usual.

Bibliography

African Development Bank (2020) *African Economic Outlook 2020: Developing Africa's Workforce for the Future*. Adis Ababa: ADB. https://au.int/sites/default/files/documents/38116-doc-african_economic_outlook_2020_.pdf (retrieved 27 June 2020).

African Union (2020) *Acceptance Statement by South African President Cyril Ramaphosa on Assuming the Chair of the African Union for 2020*. Adis Ababa: African Union. https://au.int/sites/default/files/speeches/38086-sp-au_acceptance_statement-english.pdf (retrieved 01 April 2020).

Council of the European Union (2019) Council Decision on the Establishment of a High-level Group of Wise Persons on the European Financial Architecture for Development. 6559/1/19. Brussels, 2 April. https://data.consilium.europa.eu/doc/document/ST-6559-2019-REV-1/en/pdf (retrieved 21 June 2020).

European Commission (2018) Towards a More Efficient Financial Architecture for Investment Outside the European Union. Communication from the Commission to the European Parliament, the European Council, the Council and the European Investment Bank. COM (2018) 644 final. Brussels, 12 September. https://ec.europa.eu/commission/sites/beta-political/files/soteu2018-investment-outside-eu-communication-644_en_0.pdf (retrieved 28 June 2020).

European Commission (2020) Towards a Comprehensive Strategy with Africa. Joint Communication to the European Parliament and the Council. Join (2020) 4 final https://ec.europa.eu/international-partnerships/system/files/communication-eu-africa-strategy-join-2020-4-final_en.pdf (retrieved 22 June 2020).

Madu, U. (2020) What does Africa want from the EU? International Politics and Society, 20 March. www.ips-journal.eu/regions/africa/article/show/what-does-africa-want-from-the-eu-4176/ (retrieved 28 April 2020).

Signé, L. and Gurib-Fakim, A. (2019) The high growth promise of an integrated Africa. Brookings, 2 August. www.brookings.edu/opinions/the-high-growth-promise-of-an-integrated-africa/ (retrieved 25 June 2020).

Teevan, C. and Sherriff, A. (2019) *Mission Possible? The Geopolitical Commission and the Partnership for Africa*. ECDMP Briefing Note No 113. Maastricht: ECDPM. https://ecdpm.org/publications/mission-possible-geopolitical-commission-partnership-africa/ (retrieved 22 June 2020).

United Nations (2019) *The Sustainable Development Goals Report 2019*. New York: United Nations. https://unstats.un.org/sdgs/report/2019/The-Sustainable-Development-Goals-Report-2019.pdf (retrieved 25 June 2020).

United Nations Conference on Trade and Development (2020) UN list of least developed countries [online]. https://unctad.org/en/Pages/ALDC/Least%20Developed%20Countries/UN-list-of-Least-Developed-Countries.aspx (retrieved 25 June 2020).

von der Leyen, U. (2019a) *A Union that Strives for More: My Agenda for Europe*. Political Guidelines for the Next European Commission, 2019–2024. Luxembourg: Publications Office of the European Union. https://op.europa.eu/en/publication-detail/-/publication/43a17056-ebf1-11e9-9c4e-01aa75ed71a1 (retrieved 28 June 2002).

von der Leyen, U. (2019b) Mission Letter to Jutta Urpilainen, Commissioner-Designate for International Partnerships. Brussels, 10 September. European Commission. https://ec.europa.eu/commission/sites/beta-political/files/mission-letter-jutta-urpilainen_en.pdf (retrieved 28 June 2020)

von der Leyen, U. (2019c) Mission Letter to Phil Hogan, Commissioner-Designate for Trade. Brussels, 10 September. European Commission. https://ec.europa.eu/commission/sites/beta-political/files/mission-letter-phil-hogan-2019_en.pdf

Wieser, T., Alonseo, J.A., Barbut, M., Berglof, E., Dominik, J., Kleiterp, N., Kloppenburg, N., Passacantando, F. and Ulbaek, S. (2019) *Europe in the World. The Future of the European Financial Architecture for Development*. Brussels: Council of the European Union. www.consilium.europa.eu/media/40967/efad-report_final.pdf (retrieved 21 June 2020).

Index

Note: Page numbers in *italics* indicate figures and in **bold** indicate tables on the corresponding pages.

Abidjan Summit, 2017 112–114
Adebajo, A. 249
Afionis, S. 276
African, Caribbean and Pacific (ACP) group 1, 10–11, 13, 16; Cotonou Partnership Agreement and 65–67; Economic Partnership Agreements (EPAs) and 211–212; expansion of interregionalism and 34–35; fluid regional delineations and 30–31; interregionalism and asymmetry and 31; interregionalism and institutionalisation and 32–33; regional cohesion and 32; regional integration and 190–195, **192–193**; regionalism-interregionalism nexus and 33–34; trade policies and 336–337
African Continental Free Trade Area (AfCFTA) 2, 11, 28
African Mission in Somalia (AMISOM) 250
African Peace and Security Architecture (APSA) 189
African Peace Facility (APF) 178
African Union (AU) 128; Constitutive Act of 126; cooperation with the UN 249–251; democracy and human rights promotion under 162; EU-Africa relations in historical perspective and 122–123; International Criminal Court (ICC) and 126; introduction to 121–122; LGBT rights and 127; limited interlocutory role of 123–127; weakened capacity to lead exhibited by 127–128
Afro-nationalism 257
agency, African 11–12
agriculture and land: from Africa-EU partnership to Africa-Europe alliance 337–342; conclusions on focus on 345–346; in EU development policy 342–343; introduction to 336; recent Africa-EU policies on 343–345; trade policies and 336–337
Ake, C. E. 16
Akufo-Addo, N. A. D. 257
Al Bashir, O. 126

Algeria, European Neighbourhood Policy (ENP) in 95–101
anarchist movements 15, 18
Arab Spring 90, 305
Associated African and Malagasy States (AAMS) 61, 326–327
asymmetry and interregionalism 31
Ayuso, A. 274

Baert, F. 139
Bagoyoko, N. 179
Bah, A. B. 11
Barcelona Process 305
Barroso, J. M. 75
Batliwala, S. 328
Bayart, J.-F. 256
Bemba, J.-P. 126
Biermman, R. 242
bilateralism 139–140; *see also* interregionalism
Biscop, S. 245
blended aid finance mechanisms 285–286
Borell, J. 360
Bouteflika, A. A. 74
Boutros-Ghali, B. 241
Brazil-Africa relations: in the 21st century 267–272, *269*, *271*; conclusions on 277–278; in cooperation with the EU 274–277, **275**; EU-Brazil relations and 272–274; introduction to 266–267; *see also* BRICS (Brazil, Russia, India, China and South Africa)
Bretherton, C. 10, 284
Brexit 21, 198, 203, 220
BRICS (Brazil, Russia, India, China and South Africa) 204, 222; *see also* Brazil-Africa relations
Brosig, M. 243
Brown, C. 325
Brown, G. 107
Brown, W. 12, 14, 315
Brussels Summit and Roadmap, 2014-2017 110–111

363

Index

CAAST-Net Plus 227
Cabral, L. 276
Callghy, T. M. 122
Carbone, M. 320–321, 328, 337, 339, 342
Carlsnaes, W. 70
Cebeci, M. 91
Chafetz, G. 71
Chandhoke 328
Chandra, U. 40
China effect 203–204; Africa's collective power and 257–259; characteristics of derivative power and 259–262; conclusions on 263–264; introduction to 256–257
Chissano, J. 74
Chutel, L. 127
civil society: African, voice of 330; as agents of normative power Europe 327–328; birth of economic and social committee and 326; conclusions on role of 333–334; defining 324–326; dialogue development for 326–327; introduction to 324; Joint Africa-EU Strategy (JAES) and 289–290, 331–333; promise of more 328–329
Civil Society Neighbourhood Facility 94
civil society organisations (CSOs) 46, 284–285, 287–291
climate change: complex framework of Africa-EU relations and 315–319; conclusions on EU and Africa relations and 320–321; and environmental policy on the ground 319–320; global context of 314–315; introduction to 314
cohesion, regional 32
Cold War, the 189, 207, 241
collective clientelism 283–284
collective power, African 257–259
Collier, P. 259
coloniality 40
Common Foreign and Security Policy (CFSP) 70, 90
Concord 343
Congress of South African Trade Unions (COSATU) 288
constructivism 19–21
contractual associationism 61–62
Cooke, B. 290
coordination imperative, EU: conclusions on effectiveness of 154–155; critical perspectives on 150–154; different explanations for 147–150; excessive focus on EU level 152–154; introduction to 144–145; meaning of *145*, 145–147; overly technocratic approach in 150–152
Cotonou Partnership Agreement of 2000 1, 16, 30, 44, 54–55, 65–67, 106, 108; civil society and 328–329; democracy and human rights promotion under 161–162; Economic Partnership Agreements (EPAs) and 123–124,

212–215, **214**; impact on foreign policy 73; negotiations after expiration of 114–116; regional integration and 192–193; trade policies and 337; *see also* Joint Africa-EU Strategy (JAES)
counterterrorism 352–353
COVID-19 pandemic 1, 4, 228
Crawford, G. 161
Crawford, R. M. A. 14
Cross, M. K. D. 73

Davis Cross, M. K. 316, 318
Death, C. 314
decentring of Europe 42–43
Del Biondo, K. 169
Del Felice, C. 46
democracy and human rights promotion 76, 77, 135–137, 170–172, **171**; historical perspective on EU 159–165, **163–164**, *165*; introduction to 159; mixed outcomes of aid and political conditionality in 165–169, *166–168*; reassessing the nexus between aid and 169–170
dependency theory 28
derivative power, characteristics of 259–262
de Roeck, F. 315
Development Cooperation Agreement (DCI) 108–109
Development Studies 282
Dickson, A. J. 302, 305, 307
Drieskens, E. 245
Dunn, K. C. 14
Du Toit, D. 227

East African Common Services Organization (EACSO) 190
East African Community (EAC) 28, 190
Economic Community of West African States (ECOWAS) 17, 19, 21, 288; African Union (AU) and 124; European External Action Service (EEAS) and 83–84; regional integration and 190; *see also* Economic Partnership Agreements (EPAs)
Economic Partnership Agreements (EPAs) 38, 46–47, 65, 122–124, 189; benefits, risks, and discontents with 215–219, *216–217*; civil society and 330; conclusions on challenges for 221–222; Cotonou Agreement and 123–124, 212–215, **214**; future of trade relationships and 219–221; introduction to 211–212
effective multilateralism 244–248
Englebert, P. 14
EU-Africa relations: bilateralism and interregionalism in 139–140; conclusions on 358–361; development cooperation and trade policy between coordination and coherence in 137–139; external international actors in 235–240; governance of (*see* governance); historical overview of issues in 134–135;

364

historical perspective on 122–123; International Relations (IR) theory and 14–22; new global challenges and 295–299; organizations involved in 1–4; political conditionality in 135–137; postcolonial approaches to 12, 38–47; post-Westphalian turn within 283–285; regionalism and interregionalism in 26–35; setting the agenda for the future of 140–142; theorising 9–13; Women, Peace and Security agenda in 353–355

EU-Africa Strategy 2, 73–74, 295

EU Emergency Trust Fund for Africa 178

Eurafrica 12

Eurocentrism 26–27; African regionalism and 27–28; postcolonial theory and 40–41

Euro-Mediterranean Partnership (EUROMED) 91

European Commission 93, 95, 285

European Development Fund (EDF) 60, 62, 178, 205, 295–296

European Economic Community: A Superpower in the Making, The 284

European External Action Service (EEAS) 55–56, 88; coordination imperative and 148; in EU's external relations 81–83; inter-institutional contestation and division of labour in 85–88; introduction to 80–81; role in EU-Africa relations 83–85

European Investment Bank (EIB) 94

European Neighbourhood Policy (ENP) 56–57, 303; in Algeria and Tunisia 95–101; consistency and change in, 2004-2015 93–95; democracy and human rights promotion under 162; development of 91–93; introduction to 90–91; recommendations for better results from 101–102; relative financial contributions under 97–98

European Union (EU): blended aid finance mechanisms 285–286; bureaucratic procedures of 151–152; commitment to multilateralism 139, 151; coordination imperative of (*see* coordination imperative, EU); 'core' and 'peripheral' 204–207, **206**; Europe Day in 295; gender in foreign policy of 350–353; model-setting effects of 196–198; as normative power 134–137, 327–328; relations with Brazil 272–274

Europe in the World: The Future of the European Financial Architecture for Development 361

Euroscepticism 198

Eyinla, B. M. 17

Falzon, M. 303

Farrell, M. 204

feminist theory *see* gendered cooperation

foreign policy 55, 77–78; in defining international roles 70–71; diverging principles and practice in 73–75; European External Action Service (EEAS) and 55–56, 80–88; finding common ground in multilateralism and 75–77; gendered 353; introduction to 70; from normative Europe to principled pragmatism 71–73

Fraser, N. 350

Freedom House 166, 167

Galtung, J. 284

gendered cooperation: conclusions on Othering and 355–356; gender equality and the Women, Peace and Security agenda in Africa-EU 353–355; gender in EU foreign policy and 350–353; introduction to 349–350

General Agreement on Tariffs and Trade (GATT) 60, 64

Gilbert, M.V. 179

Gomes Saraiva, M. 274

Govantes, B. 97

governance 53–58; conclusions on evolution of 67–68; Cotonou Partnership Agreement of 2000 1, 16, 30, 44, 54–55, 65–67; foreign policy and 55, 70–78; Lomé Convention 43–44, 62–65; Treaty of Rome 42, 54, 59–61; Yaoundé Convention of Association 61–62

Gratius, S. 274

Graziano, J. 270

Great Green Wall of the Sahara and the Sahel Initiative (GGWSSI) 319–320

Grotius, H. 307

Gruhn, I. 18, 284

Haastrup, T. 10, 21, 47, 189

Hammarskjold, D. 242

Hansen, P. 12

Harman, S. 12, 14, 315

Harvey, D. 243

Hay, C. 11

Hemmer, C. 244

Hill, C. 15, 71

historical amnesia 42–43

Hocking, B. 284

Hogan, P. 360

Holy Grail of development *see* coordination imperative, EU

human rights *see* democracy and human rights promotion

Hurt, S. R. 47, 284

imperialism, global 15–16

institutionalisation and interregionalism 32–33

International Criminal Court (ICC) 66, 77, 126

International Political Economy (IPE) 282

International Relations (IR) theory 282; constructivist perspective in 19–21; liberalism and EU-Africa interregional dependence and 17–19; realism and international anarchy in 15–17; structural pattern and 14–15

Index

inter-organisational cooperation *see* multilateralism
interregionalism: asymmetry and 31; conclusions on 208–209; 'core' and 'peripheral' EU and 204–207, **206**; drivers of V4 countries' renewed interest in Africa and 207–208; expansion into interregionalisms 34–35; fluid regional delineations in 30–31; global context for 203–204; institutionalisation and 32–33; introduction to 202–203; peace and security and 177; quasi- 139–140; -regionalism nexus 33–34; role with Europe 28–30; *see also* regionalism
intervention and expansionist policy experimentation 178–179

Jobson, E. 258
Joint Africa-EU Strategy (JAES) 1, 57–58, 74–75, 116–117; Abidjan Summit, 2017, and 112–114; Africa's collective power and 258–259; agriculture and land policies 339, 344–345; background to 105–106; Brussels Summit and Roadmap, 2014-2017, and 110–111; civil society organisations and 289–290, 331–333; climate change and 316–319, 320; democracy and human rights promotion under 162; early implementation of, 2007-2013 106–108; economic partnership and instruments of 108–109; institutional change under 112; introduction to 105; migration and 305; peace and security with 109–110; post-Cotonou negotiations and future of 114–116; science, technology and innovation (STI) cooperation and 226–228
Jonsson, S. 12
Junker, J. C. 2

Kaberuka, D. 221
Kagame, P. 221, 257, 260
Karzenstein, P. J. 244
Kell, F. 360
Kenyatta, K. 126
Keohane, R. 17–18, 244
Khadiagala, G. 74
Khartoum Process 305
Koops, J. 244–246
Kothari, U. 290
Kotsopoulos, J. 38, 46
Kraemer-Mbula, E. 227, 228
Kurfi, H. M. 325
Kyoto Protocol 315

Langan, M. 284, 360
Lannon, E. 303
Latin America 27–28
Leite, A. P. M. R. 305
Lewis 325
LGBT (lesbian, gay, bisexual, and transgender) persons 76, 77; African Union (AU) and 127

liberalism 17–19
Limongi, F. 169
Lisbon Treaty 2, 106, 146, 148; European External Action Service (EEAS) and 81, 83; Joint Africa-EU Strategy (JAES) and 107
Lomé Convention 43–44, 62–65, 327; democracy and human rights promotion under 160; impact on foreign policy 73; regional integration and 190–191; trade policies and 337
Long, T. 259
Lula, President 267, 270, 274

Maastricht Treaty 145
Mackie, J. 75
Macron, E. 261
Major, C. 248
Mälksoo, M. 71
maritime migration 307–311, *310*
market liberalisation 45–46
Martin, G. 284
Mattheis, F. 38, 46
Matthews, A. 339
Mawdsley, E. 286, 328
Mbeki, T. 74
Mediterranean Sea *see* migration, Mediterranean Sea
Messer, E. 166
Meyn, M. 41–42
Michel, C. 360
migration, Mediterranean Sea: conclusions on 311–312; data on 305–307; dialogues on 302–305, *303*, **304**; introduction to 301–302; peculiarities of maritime migration and case of boat people in 307–311, *310*; routes of 302–303, *303*
Mnangagwa, E. 259
model-setting effect of the EU on Africa 196–198
Moravcsik, A. 18
Morocco 97, 106
Motsamai, D. 243
Mugabe, J. O. 231
Mugabe, R. 106–107, 257, 262
multilateralism 75–77, 139, 151, 252–253; Africa's collective power and 257–259; cooperation between EU and Africa in post-colonial 249; effective 244–248; impact of the UN on EU-Africa relations and 251–252; introduction to 241–242; nature of EU-UN collaboration and 247–248; neoliberalism and 243–244; reasons for 242–244; resource dependence and 243; rise of EU-UN collaboration and 246–247; UN-AU cooperation in 249–251
Murray-Evans, P. 11
Museveni, Y. 260

Neack, L. 71
negotiated associationism 61–62

neoliberalism 243–244
neo-patrimonial order 18–19
New Alliance for Food Security and Nutrition in Africa (NAFSN) 342–343
Newman, E. 72
New Partnership Framework 178
New Regionalism Approach 30
Nigeria 109
normative power, EU as 135, 327–328
norms entrepreneurship 195
Novosseloff, A. 247
Nunn, A. 284, 286

Obasanjo, O. 74
Olsen, G. R. 168
Orbie, H. 284, 290
Organization of African Unity (OAU) 28, 29, 47, 121; *see also* African Union (AU)
Orji, N. 324, 325
Othering 45, 355–356

Pan-Africanism 29–30, 189, 257
Paris Declaration 150
paternalism 43–45
Patriota, A. 270
peace and security: AU-EU relations in 181–183; conclusions on progress in 183–184; embedded in development agenda 177–181, **180–181**; institutionalising 'security-development' nexus and 177–178; intervention and expansionist policy for 178–179; introduction to 175; Joint Africa-EU Strategy (JAES) and 109–110; long-term approach to 179; overview of African 175–176; specialisation in dense policy field of 179–181, **180–181**; theoretical perspectives on EU and African 176–177
Pirozzi, N. 318
postcolonial theory and approaches 12, 38–40; colonial legacy, historical amnesia and decentring Europe in 42–43; components of 40–42; market liberalisation and changing world order in global economy and 45–46; paternalism and the ontological Other in 43–45; politicisation and regional actorness in 46–47; and regionalism in Africa 28–30
post-Westphalian turn 283–285
power: Africa's collective 257–259; characteristics of derivative 259–262
Prebisch, R. 27–28
Price, S. 284, 286, 360
principled pragmatism 136–137
private non-state actors: business sector associations and 285–287; civil society organisations and other NGO 287–291; introduction to 282–283; post-Westphalian turn with Africa-EU studies and 283–285

Przeworski, A. 169
public-private partnerships 286

quasi-interregionalism 139–140

Rabat Process 305
Ralphs, G. 231
Ramaphosa, C. 361
Ravenhill, J. 283–284
realism 15–17
refugee crisis 20
regional integration: conclusions on 198; historical origins of promotion of 189–191; introduction to 188–189; model-setting effect of the EU on Africa and 196–198; promoted within current policy framework 191–195, **192–193**
regionalism: beyond Eurocentrist reading of African 27–28; cohesion in 32; EU-Africa relations through lens of 30–35; from European to regional integration in 26–27; fluid regional delineations in 30–31; -interregionalism nexus 33–34; postcolonial 28–30; *see also* interregionalism
Rein, C. 251
resource dependence 243
Reus-Smit, C. 19
Robert, A. 284
Rodney, W. 15
Romaniuk, S. N. 71
Rosenau, J. 284
Rosenberg, J. 20
Rousseff, D. 266–267, 270–272, 274
Ruggie, J. 244

Sabaratnam, M. 40, 46
Saraiva, M. 274
Schumann, R. 295
science, technology and innovation (STI) cooperation: conclusions on 231–232; evolution and importance of Africa-Europe 225–226; introduction to 224; opportunities and recommendations for 230–231; overarching policy frameworks for 226–227; trends in 227–228
Sebhatu, W. 12
security *see* peace and security
Security Sector Reform (SSR) 179
Sempijja, N. 243
Shared Vision, Common Action: A Stronger Europe 351
Sicurelli, D. 319
Smith, M. 284
Sócrates, J. 106
Söderbaum, F. 10
Solana, J. 245
South Africa 108–109; LGBT rights in 127
Southern African Customs Union (SACU) 190
STABEX 63, 65

Index

Stålgren, P. 10
Stefanova, B. 244–245
Stern, M. 351
Stevens, C. 221
Strange, S. 284
supranationalism 27
SYSMIN 65

Tardy, T. 246, 247, 248
Teivainen, T. 284, 288
Teorell, J. 169
terror and violent extremism 352–353
theorising Africa-EU relations 9–13; African agency in 11–12; contextualising 10–11; International Relations (IR) theory in 14–22; peace and security and 176–177; postcolonial theory in 12, 38–48; regionalism and interregionalism in 26–35
Tieku, T. K. 12
Trade, Development and Co-operation Agreement (TDCA) 108–109
trade relationships *see* Economic Partnership Agreements (EPAs)
Treaty of Rome 42, 54, 59–61, 326; democracy and human rights promotion under 160
Trommer, S. 284, 288
Trump, D. 203
Tunisia, European Neighbourhood Policy (ENP) in 95–101
Tusk, D. 262
Tvedt, J. 328

unilateral associationism 59–61
Union for the Mediterranean (UfM) 91
United Nations: AU cooperation with 249–251; Convention on the Law of the Sea (UNCLOS) 308–309; Framework Convention on Climate Change (UNFCCC) 314, 317–318; Global Compact 286–287; impact of EU-Africa relations 251–252; increased multilateralism and 241–242; on migration 301; Millennium Development Goals 66, 106, 286; nature of EU collaboration with 247–248; rise of EU collaboration with 246–247; Standby Forces High Readiness Brigade (SHIBRIG) 182; Sustainable Development Goals 147, 221, 224, 286
Urpilainen, J. 360

Vallette Summit 305
Vickers, B. 317, 318
Vines, A. 360
Visegrád Group (V4) countries 207–208
Vogler, J. 10, 284, 318
von der Leyen, U. 3, 360

Wagner, C. 226
Wagner, I. E. 231
Wallace, W. 70
Wendt, A. 19–20
West African Monetary and Economic Union (WAEMU) 17, 21, 190
Wieser, T. 361
Williams, A. 160
women *see* gendered cooperation
World Trade Organization (WTO) 39, 41, 65; Economic Partnership Agreements (EPAs) and 212–215, *214*
Wouters, J. 246

Xi Jinping 262

Yaoundé Convention of Association 61–62, 326–327; democracy and human rights promotion under 160; impact on foreign policy 73

Zanker, F. 305
Zapata-Barrero, R. 303
Zartman, I. W. 283
Zenawi, M. 74
Zuma, J. 260